Guide to Parallel Operating Systems with Windows 7 and Linux

Second Edition

Ron Carswell

Shen Jiang

Terrill Freese

COURSE TECHNOLOGY
CENGAGE Learning™

Australia • Brazil • Japan • Korea • Mexico • Singapore • Spain • United Kingdom • United States

COURSE TECHNOLOGY
CENGAGE Learning™

Guide to Parallel Operating Systems with Windows 7 and Linux, Second Edition

Ron Carswell, Shen Jiang, Terrill Freese

Vice President, Editorial: Dave Garza

Director of Learning Solutions: Matthew Kane

Executive Editor: Stephen Helba

Acquisitions Editor: Nick Lombardi

Managing Editor: Marah Bellegarde

Product Manager: Natalie Pashoukos

Developmental Editor: Dan Seiter

Editorial Assistant: Sarah Pickering

Vice President, Marketing: Jennifer Ann Baker

Marketing Director: Deborah Yarnell

Senior Marketing Manager: Erin Coffin

Associate Marketing Manager: Erica Ropitzky

Senior Production Director: Wendy A. Troeger

Production Manager: Andrew Crouth

Content Project Manager: Brooke Greenhouse

Senior Art Director: Jack Pendleton

For product information and technology assistance, contact us at **Cengage Learning Customer & Sales Support, 1-800-354-9706**.

For permission to use material from this text or product, submit all requests online at **www.cengage.com/permissions**. Further permissions questions can be e-mailed to **permissionrequest@cengage.com**.

Library of Congress Control Number: 2011927995

ISBN-13: 978-1-111-54370-9

ISBN-10: 1-111-54370-4

Course Technology
20 Channel Center Street
Boston, MA 02210
USA

Cengage Learning is a leading provider of customized learning solutions with office locations around the globe, including Singapore, the United Kingdom, Australia, Mexico, Brazil, and Japan. Locate your local office at: **international.cengage.com/region**

Cengage Learning products are represented in Canada by Nelson Education, Ltd.

For your lifelong learning solutions, visit **www.cengage.com/coursetechnology**

Purchase any of our products at your local college store or at our preferred online store **www.cengagebrain.com**

Visit our corporate website at **cengage.com**.

Some of the product names and company names used in this book have been used for identification purposes only and may be trademarks or registered trademarks of their respective manufacturers and sellers.

Microsoft and the Office logo are either registered trademarks or trademarks of Microsoft Corporation in the United States and/or other countries. Course Technology, a part of Cengage Learning, is an independent entity from the Microsoft Corporation, and not affiliated with Microsoft in any manner.

Any fictional data related to persons or companies or URLs used throughout this book is intended for instructional purposes only. At the time this book was printed, any such data was fictional and not belonging to any real persons or companies.

Course Technology, a part of Cengage Learning, reserves the right to revise this publication and make changes from time to time in its content without notice.

The programs in this book are for instructional purposes only. They have been tested with care, but are not guaranteed for any particular intent beyond educational purposes. The author and the publisher do not offer any warranties or representations, nor do they accept any liabilities with respect to the programs.

Printed in the United States of America
1 2 3 4 5 6 7 15 14 13 12 11

Brief Contents

Table of Contents

Introduction

Welcome to *Guide to Parallel Operating Systems with Windows 7 and Linux*, Second Edition. This book offers real-world examples and more than 100 hands-on activities that reinforce key concepts and help you prepare for a career in the information technology (IT) field.

This book offers in-depth study of the functions and features of two important operating systems: Microsoft Windows 7 and Fedora 13. The book emphasizes how the two operating systems are used by computer programmers, database administrators, and network administrators. The book assumes that students have previously used a personal computer with either Windows or Linux.

Guide to Parallel Operating Systems with Windows 7 and Linux uses a unique approach to explain operating systems. After a brief introduction to each concept, the book demonstrates Oracle VirtualBox, which allows students to switch instantly between the two operating systems and complete the numerous hands-on activities. Such activities reinforce the similarities and differences of the two operating systems.

The appendices provide setup instructions to use three popular virtualization software applications. Although the text uses Oracle VirtualBox, the appendices also provide setup instructions for Microsoft Virtual PC and VMware workstation. ***You must follow the setup instructions in Appendix B, C, or D before performing the activities in the text.***

Because numerous colleges are integrating Windows and Linux into their curricula, this text provides a vehicle to learn about both operating systems in one course. This text is also designed to meet the needs of a wide range of disciplines, including programming, networking, and database administration. To succeed in class work and the workplace, students need to be competent in both Windows and Linux.

Throughout the book, detailed activities provide firsthand experience with Windows 7 and Fedora 13. Review questions reinforce the concepts introduced in each chapter, and case projects prepare you to manage real-world situations in an IT environment.

Intended Audience

Guide to Parallel Operating Systems with Windows 7 and Linux is intended both for students who are getting started in IT and for users with experience in Windows 7 or Fedora 13 in a school or corporate environment. To best understand the material in this book, you should have a working knowledge of one of these operating systems.

Chapter Descriptions

This book has 11 chapters and four appendices, as follows:

Chapter 1, "Hardware Components," introduces virtual machine technology—the vehicle that permits Microsoft Windows 7 and Fedora 13 to operate in parallel. Chapter 1 also provides an overview of the components that make up a PC system, and concludes with useful information for PC care.

Chapter 2, "Software Components," covers the functions and characteristics of the two operating systems.

Chapter 3, "Using the Graphical User Interface," explains how to interact with a PC by manipulating visual elements such as icons and windows.

Chapter 4, "Installing and Configuring Applications," covers the use of applications in each operating system.

Chapter 5, "File Systems," describes the use of file systems supported by the two operating systems.

Chapter 6, "Directory Commands," introduces various commands and techniques for working with directories.

Chapter 7, "Files and File Attributes," covers the files used by various applications and search techniques used to locate files.

Chapter 8, "Text Editors," covers three text editors that are used by the two operating systems.

Chapter 9, "The Command Line," explains how to use the command-line interface in the two operating systems.

Chapter 10, "Operating System Management," explains how to manage processes executed on a PC, how to measure factors that indicate PC performance, and how to manage system reliability.

Chapter 11, "Networking," explains networking terminology, viewing TCP/IP settings, accessing network resources, and viewing folder and file sharing permissions.

Appendix A, "Numbering Systems and Data Representation," explains how to convert numbers from one base to another, how data is represented by ASCII characters, and the representative storage of data in memory.

Appendix B, "Working with Virtual PC 2007," provides the setup instructions to use Windows 7 and Fedora 13 virtual machines with Microsoft Virtual PC. The data files and scripts for students are available on the Cengage Learning Web site at *www.cengage.com.* Read through the setup instructions in Appendix B to download the files.

Appendix C, "Working with VirtualBox," provides the setup instructions to use Windows 7 and Fedora 13 virtual machines with Oracle VirtualBox. The data files and scripts for students are available on the Cengage Learning Web site at *www.cengage.com.* Read through the setup instructions in Appendix C to download the files.

Appendix D, "Working with VMware," provides the setup instructions to use Windows 7 and Fedora 13 virtual machines with VMware Workstation. The data files and scripts for students are available on the Cengage Learning Web site at *www.cengage.com.* Read through the setup instructions in Appendix D to download the files.

You must follow the setup instructions in Appendix B, C, or D before performing the activities in the text.

Features and Approach

Guide to Parallel Operating Systems with Windows 7 and Linux differs from other OS books in its unique integration of Windows 7, Oracle VirtualBox, and Fedora 13. To help you understand how to use both operating systems, the book covers them in parallel. In the interest of brevity, some references are missing from command descriptions throughout the text.

- **Chapter Objectives**—Each chapter begins with a detailed list of the concepts to be mastered. This list provides a quick reference to the chapter's contents and can be a useful study aid.

- **Activities**—Activities are incorporated throughout the text to give you a strong foundation for carrying out tasks in the real world. Because the activities tend to build on each other, you should complete the activities in each chapter before moving to the end-of-chapter materials and subsequent chapters.

- **Chapter Summaries**—Each chapter's text is followed by a summary of concepts introduced in the chapter. These summaries provide a helpful way to recap and revisit the chapter's ideas.

- **Key Terms**—All of the terms that are introduced in boldface text in a chapter are listed together after the chapter summary. This list lets you check your understanding of the terms.

- **Review Questions**—The end-of-chapter assessment begins with a set of questions that reinforce the ideas introduced in the chapter. Answering these questions helps ensure that you have mastered important concepts.

- **Case Projects**—Each chapter closes with a section that asks you to evaluate real-world situations and decide on a course of action. This valuable tool helps you sharpen your decision-making and troubleshooting skills, which are important in IT.

Fedora 13 DVD

The DVD that accompanies this textbook contains a 32-bit copy of the Fedora 13 operating system. You can use this DVD to install the Linux operating system on your PC so that you can complete the exercises in each chapter. Follow the instructions in Appendix B, Appendix C, or Appendix D to set up your host computer to install Fedora 13 on a virtual machine.

Text and Graphic Conventions

Additional information and exercises have been added to this book to help you better understand the chapter discussions. Icons throughout the text alert you to these additional materials:

Notes present additional helpful material for the subject being discussed.

The Caution icon identifies important information about potential mistakes or hazards.

Activity icons precede each activity in this book.

Case Project icons mark the end-of-chapter case projects. These scenario-based assignments ask you to independently apply what you learned in the chapter.

Instructor's Resources

A wide array of instructor's materials is provided with this book. The following materials are provided on the book's Instructor Resources CD (ISBN 1-111-54371-2).

Instructor Resources CD

Electronic Instructor's Manual. The Instructor's Manual that accompanies this book includes additional material to assist in class preparation, including suggestions for classroom activities, discussion topics, and additional projects.

Solutions are provided for review questions and case projects.

ExamView®. This book is accompanied by ExamView, a powerful testing software package that allows instructors to create and administer printed, computer-based, and Internet exams. ExamView includes hundreds of questions that correspond to the topics covered in this text, enabling students to generate detailed study guides that include page references for further review. The computer-based and Internet testing components allow students to take exams at their computers and save time by grading each exam automatically.

PowerPoint presentations. This book comes with Microsoft PowerPoint slides for each chapter. These slides can be used as a teaching aid for classroom presentation, made available to students on a network for chapter review, or printed for classroom distribution. Instructors can also add their own slides to cover additional topics they introduce to the class.

Figure files. All of the figures and tables in the book are reproduced on the Instructor's Resource CD in bitmap format. Like the PowerPoint presentations, these files can be used as a teaching aid in class, made available to students for review, or printed for classroom distribution.

Student files. All of the scripts and data files are available from the Cengage Learning Web site. Download instructions are presented in Appendix B, C, or D for each virtualization application.

CourseMate

Guide to Parallel Operating Systems with Windows 7 and Linux includes CourseMate, a complement to your textbook. CourseMate includes the following resources, which you can access at *login.cengage.com*:

- An interactive eBook with highlighting, note taking, and search capabilities
- Interactive learning tools, including quizzes, flash cards, PowerPoint slides, and glossary
- Engagement Tracker, a first-of-its-kind tool that monitors student engagement in the course

The CourseMate materials have the following ISBNs:

- Printed access code (ISBN 1-1115-4372-0)
- Instant access code (ISBN 1-1115-4373-9)

Minimum Lab Requirements

To install the three software components, you must have the following minimum hardware configuration:

Component	Requirement
CPU	Intel or AMD 2 Core 1.6 GHz (4 Core 2.0 GHz or higher is recommended) 64-bit processor
BIOS	Intel VT or AMD-V Virtualization available
Memory	At least 2 GB of RAM (4 GB recommended)
Disk space	At least 32 GB of free space (48 GB recommended)
Drive	DVD-ROM
Networking	Network interface card

Setting up the Virtual Machines

To complete the lab activities in this text, you must first set up the virtual machines to run Oracle VirtualBox, Microsoft Virtual PC, or VMware Workstation, as described in Appendices B, C, and D. The following figure provides an overview of the required environment. Windows 7 Professional or later is recommended for the host operating system. Windows 7 Professional or later and Fedora 13 are required for the two virtual machines.

Choose one of the three virtualization applications to perform the chapter activities. Although the text illustrations picture Oracle VirtualBox, the lab activities have been tested with Microsoft Virtual PC and VMware Workstation as well.

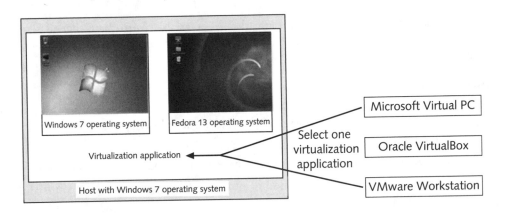

Acknowledgments

Ron Carswell

This text is a product of many talented people. First, I want to give a well-deserved pat on the back to my coauthors, Shen and Terrill. Next, I want to thank the staff at Course Technology, especially my product manager, Natalie Pashoukos, for her patience and help.

And, of course, thanks to our development editor, Dan Seiter, for providing the inspiration to mold our thoughts clearly and concisely.

I also thank my wife, Coleen, for patience and support during many nights of writing and editing.

Shen Jiang

Thanks to Ron for the patience he showed, especially when I was overseas at the beginning of the project, and to Terrill for signing on to this project. Thanks to John Baker for providing insightful feedback. The team at Course Technology was very supportive and helped us persevere. Special thanks go to Natalie Pashoukos for keeping us on track and to Dan Seiter for showing us how we could make the text even better and more consistent. Thanks to my husband for being understanding, patient, and supportive.

Terrill Freese

Thanks to Shen and Ron for their patience with my schedule and to Nick Lombardi, Natalie Pashoukos, and Dan Seiter for their excellent efforts to keep everything consistent and on track. I am honored to be included in this project. Thanks to my father for convincing me that I could be anything I wanted to be, and to my mother for enduring the resulting journey.

About the Authors

Ron Carswell has more than 20 years of computer experience with both small and large organizations. Ron holds a bachelor's degree in business administration from the University of Texas and a master's degree in business administration from Baylor University. He has received A+, N+, CTT+, MCSA, MCSE, and MCDST certifications. He is currently an assistant professor at San Antonio College, where he teaches A+, N+, MCSA, and MCDST certification courses. Ron has written numerous lab manuals and texts for Course Technology. In addition, Ron coauthored the *Guide to Microsoft Virtual PC 2007 and Virtual Server 2005*.

Shen Jiang has nine years of experience with large organizations. She holds a master's degree in Computer Information Systems from South Dakota State University and a master's degree in linguistics from Jilin University. She is currently an assistant professor at San Antonio College, where she instructs in all levels of database courses, program logic and design, basic programming, and fundamentals of networking. She has earned both Oracle9i and Oracle10g certifications.

Terrill Freese has more than 15 years of computer experience in the telecommunications, software support, and financial industries. She holds a bachelor's degree in applied computer science from Illinois State University and a master's degree in the Technology in Training and Education curriculum from Nova Southeastern University. She has earned both CCNA and CCAI certifications. She is currently an instructor at San Antonio College, where she teaches various networking, operating system, and computer literacy courses.

chapter 1

Hardware Components

After reading this chapter and completing the exercises, you will be able to:

- Explain the use of virtual machine technology to run multiple operating systems concurrently
- Describe the hardware components of a personal computer system
- Describe the peripheral components that may be attached to a personal computer system
- Describe the preventive maintenance for a computer system
- Connect and test a personal computer system

This text covers the use of Windows and Linux—two prevalent operating systems (OSs) for the personal computer (PC). Using virtual machine technology, these two seemingly incompatible operating systems can work in parallel.

You will undoubtedly purchase numerous PCs in your lifetime. Some will be for your job, and others will be for personal use. The goal of this chapter is to provide an overview of the components that make up a PC system. Some of these components are within the PC, and some are attached to it. Whether you purchase a major brand or decide to "build your own," knowing these components will help you understand the day-to-day workings of your OS.

When using a PC, proper maintenance is important. This chapter provides information to help you care for your PC, and offers guidance on the proper way to dispose of it when the time comes.

Virtual Machine Technology

Virtualized systems—systems that appear to be real but are actually simulations—are used in many environments. Airline pilots use flight simulators for flight practice and testing, whereas computer games like Sim City let the player create a virtual city in a game environment that feels real but actually exists in the hardware and software of the game.

In the Information Technology (IT) world, **virtualization** refers to the use of virtualization software that allows the physical hardware of a single PC to run multiple operating systems simultaneously in **virtual machines (VMs)**. The virtualization software simulates enough hardware to create an environment that allows an unmodified **guest operating system** (the one running inside a VM) to be run in isolation on a **host operating system** (the one running on the physical computer system).

This text uses examples of virtual machine technology, which allows multiple operating systems to run concurrently on a single PC. With virtual machine technology, you can run various Windows operating systems as well as Linux within Windows 7. In this text, you will do both. Figure 1-1 shows Windows 7 and Linux images on the Windows 7 desktop within Oracle VirtualBox virtualization software. This text uses the Fedora 13 distribution of Linux.

Virtualization means that you can concurrently operate seemingly incompatible operating systems in one hardware environment, as shown in Figure 1-2. Consider the following:

- The host computer—in this case a laptop—is running Windows 7 with one hard drive, 4 GB of memory, and a network adapter, keyboard, touch pad, and liquid crystal display (LCD) screen.
- The first virtual machine is running Windows 7 with three hard drives, 1 GB of memory, and a network adapter, keyboard, mouse, and monitor. (All hardware is virtualized.)
- The other virtual machine is running Fedora 13 with three hard drives, 1 GB of memory, and a network adapter, keyboard, mouse, and monitor. (Again, all hardware is virtualized.)
- The virtualization software provides the hardware environment for the two virtual machines for a total of six hard drives, 2 GB of memory, two network adapters, two keyboards, two mice, and two monitors.

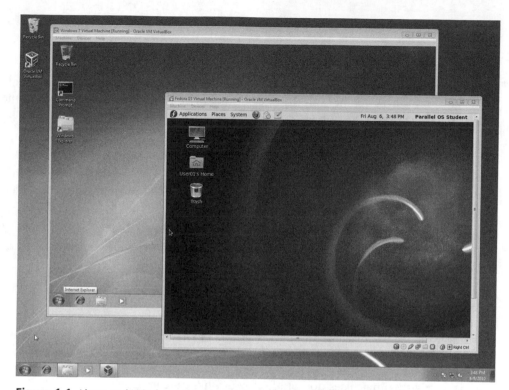

Figure 1-1 Linux and Windows virtual machines on desktop

Source: Course Technology/Cengage Learning

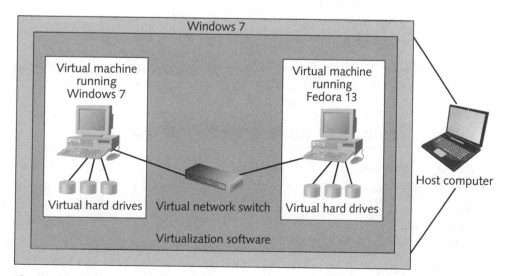

Figure 1-2 Virtual machine technology

Source: Course Technology/Cengage Learning

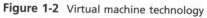

How does the virtualization software do this?

- The six hard drives are six files on the laptop; these files appear to the virtual machines as real hard drives.
- The two network adapters appear as virtualized network adapters to the virtual machines. These adapters are connected to the virtual network switch. Within the host, software exists to provide network connections from the virtual network switch to the laptop's network.
- The 2 GB of memory comes from the 4 GB of physical memory on the laptop.
- The keyboards, mice, and monitors are switched between the two virtual machines by clicking the window of the desired virtual machine. You can only interact with one virtual machine at a time.

Of course, given enough memory and processor cycles, virtualization software will scale to run more than two virtual machines. It is not unreasonable for a powerful server to run 100 or more virtual machines.

To summarize, you can install multiple guest operating systems in virtual machines, which look like any other applications you would use on your physical computer. Virtualization software mimics physical PCs so closely that the operating systems installed in them do not distinguish the virtual machine from a physical computer. Instead of installing operating systems on multiple costly computers or creating unwieldy multiboot installations, you can install the operating systems in multiple inexpensive virtual machines. Another benefit is that changes you make in virtual machines do not affect your physical computer.

Oracle VirtualBox is not the only virtualization software on the market. This text is written to allow you to select from three different virtualization products:

- Microsoft Virtual PC 2007
- Oracle VirtualBox
- VMware Workstation

The text of the main book uses Oracle VirtualBox, but you can consult the appendices to see how to use the other virtualization products.

Activity 1-1: Starting Virtual Machines

Time Required: 10 minutes

Objective: Use the virtualization console to start the two virtual machines.

Description: In this activity, you will open the virtualization console installed on the computers that you will use in your class, and then you will start the two virtual machines. Recall that you will use one of the three virtualization applications.

1. If necessary, log on to your host PC with **User01** and a password of **Secret1**.

If you are not sure which virtualization software you are using, ask your instructor.

2. Start your virtualization software by selecting one of the following choices:
   - To start the Microsoft Virtual PC console, click **Start**, point to **All Programs**, and then double-click **Microsoft Virtual PC**.
   - To start the Oracle VM VirtualBox console, double-click the **Oracle VM VirtualBox** on the desktop.
   - To start the VMware console, click **Start**, point to **All Programs**, and then double-click the **VMware Workstation**.

3. To start the Fedora 13 virtual machine, double-click the **Fedora 13 Virtual Machine** icon.

4. To start the Windows 7 virtual machine, double-click the **Windows 7 Virtual Machine** icon.

5. To log on to the Windows 7 virtual machine, click the **User01** icon within the Windows 7 virtual machine window, type **Secret1**, and then press **Enter.**

6. To switch to the Fedora 13 virtual machine, click within the Fedora 13 virtual machine window.

7. To log on to the Fedora 13 virtual machine, click the **Parallel OS Student** icon within the Fedora 13 virtual machine window, type **Secret1**, and then press **Enter.**

8. Leave the virtual machines logged on for future activities.

Hardware Components of a PC System

A desktop computer is a PC that is designed to fit conveniently on or under a typical office desk. The desktop computer typically contains several devices that are assembled in a computer case:

- Power supply—Provides the necessary voltages
- Cooling system—Removes the heat generated by the PC
- Motherboard—The main circuit board for the PC
- Microprocessor—The central processing unit (CPU) for the PC
- Memory—The electronic holding area for programs and data
- Firmware—Computer programming instructions in read-only memory, used to test and start the PC
- Ports—Used to connect external devices to the PC
- Adapters—Cards that provide capabilities to the PC

These components are explained in more detail in the following sections.

Cases

In a PC, the case houses and protects the main electronic components. You may purchase a PC in various sizes and shapes. The **form factor** is the size, configuration, or physical arrangement of a computer case or one of its internal components, such as a **system board** (which contains basic electronic circuitry and components).

The IBM XT PC set an early, de facto standard for case configuration. The desktop computer has since evolved through the AT (advanced technology) model, the mini AT, and the

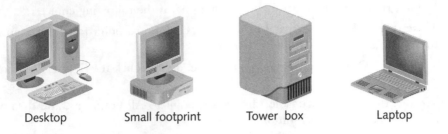

Desktop   Small footprint   Tower box   Laptop

Figure 1-3 Form factors

Source: Course Technology/Cengage Learning

small-footprint PC. A later development was the vertical or tower chassis configuration, which was designed to be placed under a desk. Recent developments reduced the size of the PC for laptop or notebook computers. Figure 1-3 illustrates various form factors.

The style of PC case that you purchase determines a number of factors. For example, what motherboard will be supported by the case?

A portable computer is a PC designed to be easily transported and relocated. The earliest portable computers were simply called portables. As the size and weight of most portables decreased, they became known as laptop computers and later as notebook computers.

A laptop computer is a battery- or AC-powered PC, generally smaller than a briefcase, that can be used on airplanes, in libraries, in temporary offices, at meetings, and so on. A laptop typically weighs less than five pounds.

Netbooks are a smaller, lightweight, inexpensive version of notebook computers suited for both general PC and Web-based applications. Typically, Netbooks have smaller displays, less memory, and less powerful processors.

Laptops usually come with displays that use LCD-screen technology. Laptops use several approaches for integrating a mouse into the keyboard, including the touch pad and the trackball. Your laptop computer may not possess the same ports as a desktop computer; for example, laptops may be restricted to using video and USB ports. However, many laptops have built-in network adapters and wireless access. CD-ROM and DVD disc drives may be built in or attachable. This is explained in the following sections.

Power Supplies

Your computer's power supply, as shown in Figure 1-4, is a sealed metal box that contains power conversion hardware. The power supply converts the 110-volt alternating current (AC) in your office or household to the various direct current (DC) levels required by your PC. The power supply provides clean power feeds to the components in your computer: the system board, disk drives, cooling fans, and so on. Power supplies have standardized plugs that work with all kinds of components; if you use a plug that fits the device, you are sure to get a correct voltage. However, you must pay attention to the orientation of the plugs.

Do not open the power supply! The internal components are not user-serviceable.

Figure 1-4 Power supply

Source: Course Technology/Cengage Learning

Most older computer power supplies are not very efficient. 80 PLUS is an initiative to promote more electrical energy-efficient computer power supplies; it certifies products that have more than 80% energy efficiency at rated loads. That is, units that waste 20% or less electric energy as heat at the specified load reduce electricity use.

Cooling Systems

Computers generate heat—lots of it. A PC's microprocessor produces 75 to 100 watts of heat, which is as much as a regular household lightbulb. Other internal computer components generate more heat; in sum, your desktop PC could generate more than 300 watts. Poor heat dissipation can cause many problems ranging from mysterious system crashes to major hardware damage. Overheating increases the risk that your computer's components will fail prematurely.

Air is circulated within the case to dissipate the heat generated by the computer's electronic components. Air enters the case and is pulled out with one or more fans in the front or back of the case. Although most PCs rely on the circulated air to remove the generated heat, some faster PCs resort to liquid cooling for the microprocessor.

The microprocessor in your PC has a **heat sink** attached to dissipate the generated heat. Generally, your microprocessor's temperature should not run in excess of 120 to 130 degrees Fahrenheit (hot even for south Texas) while under a full load. The heat sink is attached to the microprocessor chip, is usually made of aluminum, and has extended fins. An active heat sink is one that comes with a fan; it is sometimes called a heat sink/fan combo (HSF).

Motherboards

The **motherboard**, or system board, is the main circuit board inside a PC case. It contains the processor socket, memory slots, hard drive connectors, expansion slots, and other components. Additional boards, called daughter boards, can be plugged into the motherboard (see Figure 1-5).

In our politically correct world, it has been suggested that we use the term *systemboard* rather than the gender-indicative term *motherboard*. However, a quick search of the Internet indicates that the more common term is *motherboard*.

NOTE

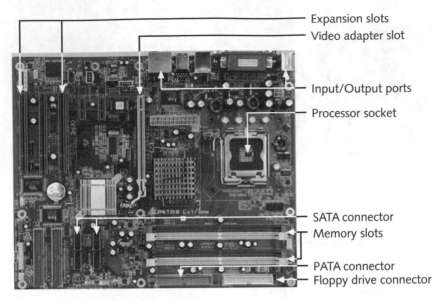

Expansion slots
Video adapter slot
Input/Output ports
Processor socket
SATA connector
Memory slots
PATA connector
Floppy drive connector

Figure 1-5 Motherboard

Source: Course Technology/Cengage Learning

The following sections explain the numerous components of a motherboard.

Microprocessor The heart of the PC system is the **microprocessor** (see Figure 1-6). It contains the logic circuitry that performs the instructions of a computer's programs. Microprocessors were once known as central processing units (CPUs); today, a microprocessor is a CPU on a single chip. This "electronic engine" is activated when you turn on your computer. The microprocessor contains a set of instructions designed to perform such tasks as arithmetic (adding, subtracting), logic operations (comparing two numbers), and transferring numbers from one register to another. A **register** is a small amount of high-speed memory.

Buses The **bus** is a set of circuits on the motherboard through which data is transferred from one part of a computer to another. You can picture the metaphor of data hopping

Figure 1-6 AMD microprocessor

Source: Course Technology/Cengage Learning

Figure 1-7 Memory module

Source: Course Technology/Cengage Learning

aboard a bus to travel within a computer. The term *bus* usually refers to an internal bus that connects all the internal computer components to the microprocessor and main memory. In addition, an expansion bus permits adapter boards to access the microprocessor and memory.

All buses consist of two parts: a data bus and an address bus. The data bus transfers actual data, whereas the address bus transfers information about where the data should go.

The size of a bus—known as its width—is important because it determines how much data can be transmitted at one time. For example, a 32-bit bus can transmit 32 bits (4 bytes) of data, whereas a 64-bit bus can transmit 64 bits (8 bytes) of data.

Memory Memory is an electronic holding area for your programs and data. Memory usually contains the main parts of the OS and some or all of the applications and related data that are being used. Memory is often used as a shorter synonym for random access memory (RAM). This kind of memory, as shown in Figure 1-7, is located in the memory slots on the motherboard. You can think of RAM as an array of boxes, each of which can hold a single byte of information. A computer that has 4 GB of memory can hold about 4,096 million bytes (or characters) of information.

Several types of memory can be used in your PC:

- **RAM** (random access memory)—The term *RAM* refers to read-and-write memory, meaning that you can write data into RAM and read data from it. Most RAM is volatile—it requires a steady flow of electricity to maintain its contents. When power is turned off on the PC, any data that was in RAM is lost.

- **ROM** (read-only memory)—A PC almost always contains a small amount of ROM that holds instructions for starting the PC. Unlike RAM, you cannot write to ROM.

- **PROM** (programmable read-only memory)—A PROM is a memory chip on which you can store a program. Once the PROM has been used, you cannot erase it and store something else on it. Like ROMs, PROMs are nonvolatile.

- **EPROM** (erasable programmable read-only memory)—An EPROM is a special type of PROM that you can erase by exposure to ultraviolet light.

- **EEPROM** (electrically erasable programmable read-only memory)—An EEPROM is a special type of EPROM that you can erase by applying an electrical charge.

Firmware ROMs, PROMs, EPROMs, and EEPROMs that contain recorded programs are called firmware. **Firmware** is a combination of software and hardware.

The **BIOS** (basic input/output system) is firmware that supports the PC during start-up. In addition, the BIOS contains the program code required to control the keyboard,

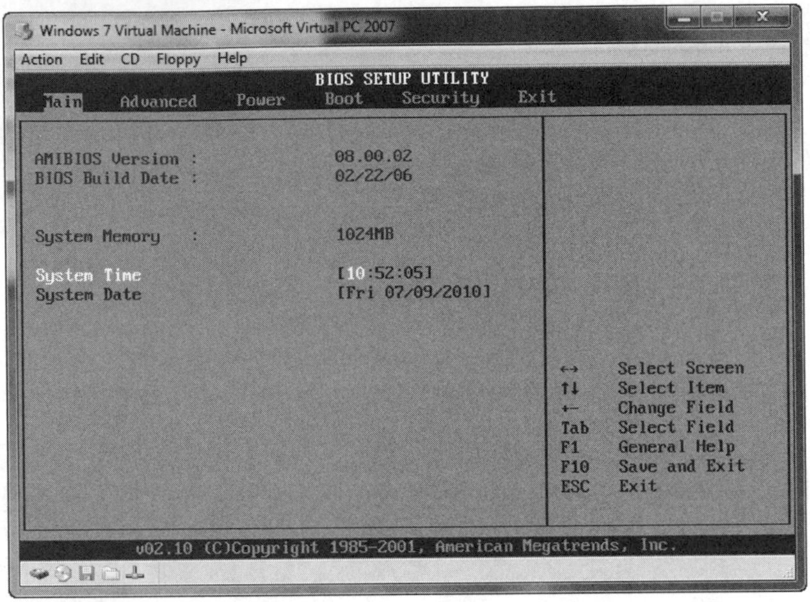

Figure 1-8 BIOS setup screen in Virtual PC 2007

Source: Course Technology/Cengage Learning

display text on the screen, read from disk drives, and perform a number of miscellaneous functions.

The BIOS is typically placed in a firmware chip that comes with the computer; it is often called a ROM BIOS. This placement ensures that the BIOS will always be available and will not be damaged by disk failures; it also enables a computer to start itself. PCs have a flash BIOS, which means that the BIOS has been recorded on a flash memory chip (normally an EEPROM) that can be updated if necessary.

You can see which hardware is controlled by the BIOS by entering the setup program when your PC starts. Figure 1-8 shows the BIOS setup screen for the Microsoft Virtual PC virtualization software. From this screen, you configure the virtual environment for Virtual PC. Check the screen to see which key you should press to enter the setup program. For example, pressing the Delete key starts many setup programs.

Input/Output Ports

A PC typically comes with standard input-output ports, as shown in Figure 1-9. These ports are often called I/O (pronounced *eye-oh*) ports. Serial ports are used for modems, digitizer tablets, and other devices, while parallel ports are used for printers. Serial and parallel ports have fallen into legacy status and may not be installed on new PCs. Almost every peripheral that is connected via serial or parallel ports is now available as a USB device. Extra USB ports are often present on the front of the case, as are FireWire ports.

Connectors are identified by gender. When copper pins are exposed in the connector, its gender is male. In Figure 1-9, the serial connector is a male connector. The parallel connector is female because holes are present.

These I/O ports are discussed in the following sections.

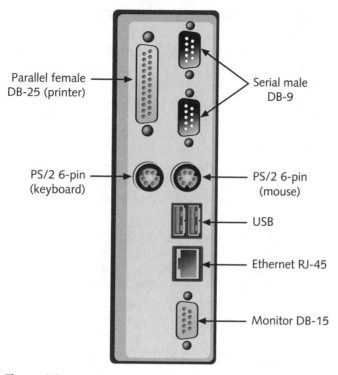

Parallel female
DB-25 (printer)

Serial male
DB-9

PS/2 6-pin
(keyboard)

PS/2 6-pin
(mouse)

USB

Ethernet RJ-45

Monitor DB-15

Figure 1-9 Back of computer showing I/O ports

Source: Course Technology/Cengage Learning

Serial Ports A serial port transfers data in or out one bit at a time. Throughout most of the history of PCs, this transfer was accomplished using **RS-232** (short for *recommended standard-232*), a standard interface approved by the Electronic Industries Alliance (EIA) for transferring data over simple cables that connect the computer to a device such as a modem. You can connect mice, keyboards, and other devices to a serial port. Serial ports are legacy hardware.

You can identify the serial ports on the back of a PC by checking for male connectors. If you check your BIOS settings, you may see that your PC has allocated the first four serial ports as COM1, COM2, COM3, and COM4.

Parallel Ports While a serial port transfers data in or out one bit at a time, a **parallel port** transfers multiple bits in parallel. Parallel ports are frequently used to connect legacy printers. You can identify the parallel ports on the back of a PC by checking for female connectors. Traditionally, the PC can support up to three parallel ports—LPT1, LPT2, and LPT3.

Universal Serial Bus (USB) The **Universal Serial Bus** (USB) was developed to simplify the connection of peripheral devices to the PC. Almost every peripheral that once could be connected via a serial or parallel port is now available with a USB connector. The major goals of USB were to make it inexpensive to add peripherals to a PC and as easy to connect as a telephone to a wall jack. USB originally featured a minimum bandwidth of 1.5 Mbps (megabits per second) for low-speed devices such as mice and keyboards, and a maximum bandwidth of 12 Mbps for higher-speed devices such as Web cameras, printers, scanners, and external CD-RW drives. You can connect up to 127 USB peripherals with five levels of hubs to a single USB host controller.

In a quest for additional speed, USB 2.0 was introduced. The maximum speed of the connection jumped from 12 Mbps on USB 1.1 to 480 Mbps. USB 2.0 is both forward and backward compatible with USB 1.1. The USB connectors and cables are identical, which means that you can use the older USB 1.1 devices by plugging them into the newer USB 2.0 ports. You can even plug a high-speed USB 2.0 device into a legacy USB 1.1 port and simply operate at reduced throughput. Both Hi-Speed USB 2.0 and original USB 1.1 peripherals can operate on a PC at the same time. The new USB 2.0 expansion-hub design manages the transition of data rates between the high-speed host and lower-speed USB peripherals while maintaining full bandwidth utilization. If you have a digital camera, you can take advantage of this increased speed to transfer larger pictures with higher densities.

At the time this text was written, USB 3.0 devices were beginning to appear on the market. A new major feature is the "SuperSpeed" bus, which provides a fourth transfer mode at 5.0 Gbps. The raw throughput is 4 Gbps, and the specification considers it reasonable to achieve 3.2 Gbps (0.4 Gbps or 400 MBps) or more after protocol overhead. To accommodate the additional pins for SuperSpeed mode, the physical form factors for USB 3.0 plugs and receptacles have been modified from those used in previous versions.

FireWire Sometimes called IEEE 1394, **FireWire** is a very fast digital input/output system that provides transfer rates of up to 400 Mbps. The IEEE 1394 FireWire manages the digitization, compression, and audio synchronization processes while you shoot video with your camcorder. This system puts broadcast-quality video footage directly into your computer or DV (digital video) editing system. With IEEE 1394, you can even connect external hard drives and optical drives. At the time this text was written, FireWire in consumer products was expected to reach 3200 MBps or 3.2 GBps.

Expansion Cards

An **expansion card** is a printed circuit board that you can insert into a motherboard to add functionality to a PC. One edge of the expansion card holds the contacts that fit into the expansion slot on the motherboard, establishing contact between the card's electronics (mostly integrated circuits) and the motherboard.

An expansion card could add more USB ports to a desktop computer. Laptop designs do not allow for expansion cards because of the compact placement of internal components.

You might refer to an expansion card as an adapter card that allows one system component to connect to and work with another. An adapter is often a simple circuit that converts one set of signals to another; however, the term often refers to devices that are more accurately called controllers. For example, display adapters (video cards) and SCSI (small computer system interface) adapters perform extensive processing, but they are still called adapters.

Video Adapters You would plug a **video adapter** board, as shown in Figure 1-10, into a PC to give it display capabilities. These capabilities, however, depend on both the logical circuitry and the display monitor. Each adapter offers several video resolutions (pixel densities).

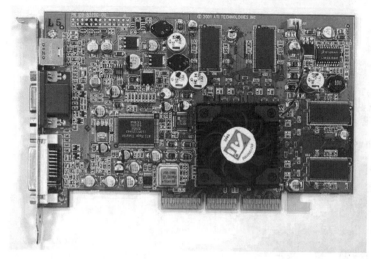

Figure 1-10 Video adapter

Source: Course Technology/Cengage Learning

Modern video adapters contain memory so that the computer's RAM is not used for storing displays. With larger amounts of memory, you can display greater resolutions with a larger number of colors. To save money, the manufacturer of your PC may use the system memory for text and graphics. While using part of the main system memory may save costs, it may also result in poor performance.

In addition, most adapters have their own graphics coprocessor for performing graphics calculations. These adapters are often called graphics accelerators. Your computer will render graphics faster if it uses a graphics accelerator.

Sound Adapters A **sound adapter**, which is also called a sound board or audio adapter, is an adapter card that records and plays back sound, as shown in Figure 1-11. Sound adapters support both digital audio and Musical Instrument Digital Interface (MIDI) formats. Sound cards provide an input port for a microphone or other sound source and output ports for speakers and amplifiers.

As an alternative to a sound adapter, your PC may have integrated sound circuits provided by a chipset on the motherboard. If you need to install a separate sound card, the integrated sound circuits can be disabled. An example of integrated audio is AC' 97, which was introduced in 1996 by Intel. AC' 97 provides audio with six channels, which is comparable to the sound on a home theater system.

Disk Drive Controllers

A disk drive controller manages the transfer of data from a motherboard to a disk drive and vice versa. In PCs, the controllers are often single chips. When you purchase a computer, it comes with all the necessary controllers for standard components, such as disk drives. However, if you add disk drives, you may need to insert new controllers that come on expansion boards.

Controllers must be designed to communicate with a computer's expansion bus. There are three standard controller architectures for PCs—the ATA, SATA, and SCSI. Therefore, when

Figure 1-11 Sound adapter

Source: Course Technology/Cengage Learning

you purchase a disk drive, you must ensure that it conforms to your computer's controller architecture.

ATA Controllers (Parallel) ATA, or Advanced Technology Attachment, is a disk drive implementation that integrates the controller on the disk drive itself. An enhanced version of the ATA interface transfers data at rates up to 100 MB/sec; these enhancements are called ATA/100.

ATA is also called **PATA**, or Parallel ATA. Parallel controllers transfer data bits over multiple data lines in parallel. (Contrast Parallel ATA with Serial ATA in the next section.) In PATA, which is also known as Integrated Drive Electronics or IDE, each motherboard controller supports one or two devices, which could be hard drives or CD-ROM drives. Your computer system most likely has two IDE controllers—a primary and secondary controller. Each controller supports two drives—a master and a slave. Using ATA technology, you can attach up to four drives.

SATA Controllers (Serial) SATA, or Serial Advanced Technology Attachment, is an evolution of the Parallel ATA physical storage interface. Serial ATA is a serial link—a single cable with a minimum of four wires that creates a single connection between the controller and the drive. Transfer rates for Serial ATA range from 1.5 to 3.0 Gbps; the latter rate is faster than PATA. An even faster SATA that offers 6.0 Gbps is on the drawing boards. Besides faster transfer rates, the SATA interface has several advantages over the PATA interface. For example, SATA drives each have their own independent bus, so there is no competition for bandwidth, as there is with Parallel ATA. SATA cables are more flexible, thinner, and less massive than the ribbon cables required for conventional PATA hard drives, resulting in less air-flow restrictions.

Serial ATA is a better, more efficient interface than the dated PATA standard. If you want to buy a computer that will support fast hard drives for years to come, make sure that it comes with a SATA interface.

SCSI Controllers SCSI (pronounced *skuzzy*), or small computer system interface, is a parallel interface standard used for attaching peripheral devices to PCs. If your PC does not have a SCSI controller, you can add a SCSI adapter card and attach disk drives. The speeds for SCSI adapters meet and may exceed the speeds of SATA controllers. Although you are limited in the number of devices you can attach to a PATA or SATA controller, SCSI allows you to connect up to 15 peripheral devices to a single SCSI controller. Note, however, that the lack of a single SCSI standard means that some devices may not work with some SCSI boards. Although SCSI is a standard of the American National Standards Institute (ANSI), it has many variations, so two SCSI interfaces may be incompatible. For example, SCSI supports several types of connectors.

Storage Devices

Storage devices refer to various devices for storing large amounts of data. Modern mass storage devices include all types of disk drives and tape drives. Mass storage is distinct from RAM memory, which refers to temporary storage areas within the computer. Unlike RAM memory, mass storage devices retain data even when the computer is turned off.

The main types of storage devices are:

- Hard drives—These disks are very fast and have large capacities. Some hard drive systems are portable (with removable cartridges), but most are not.

- Optical drives—Unlike floppy and hard drives, which use electromagnetism to encode data, optical disc systems use a laser to read and write data. Optical drives have very large storage capacity, but they are not as fast as hard drives.

- Tape drives—These drives are relatively inexpensive and often have very large storage capacities, but they do not permit random access of data.

- USB drives—These small, portable drives use flash memory or external hard drives to store data for backup or transfer between PCs.

Hard Drives A **hard drive** uses rigid rotating platters to read and write on magnetic media. A typical hard drive design, as shown in Figure 1-12, consists of a spindle on which the platters spin at a constant speed. Moving along and between the platters on a common armature are the read/write heads, with one head for each platter face. The armature moves the heads radially across the platters as they spin, allowing each head access to the entirety of the platter.

Hard drives are cabled to a disk drive controller. Depending on the configuration of the PC you purchase, these hard drives might be connected to PATA, SATA, or SCSI hard drive controllers. It is also possible to connect external hard drives to USB ports.

Optical Drives Figure 1-13 shows an **optical drive** storage device that uses light produced by lasers instead of magnetism to store data on optical discs. These discs include CDs and DVDs, which are made up of millions of small bumps and dips. Lasers read these bumps and dips as ones and zeroes, which the computer can understand.

Common types of optical drives include CD-ROM, CD-RW, DVD-ROM, and DVD-RW drives. CD and DVD writers, such as CD-R and DVD-R drives, use lasers to both read and

Figure 1-12 Hard drive

Source: Course Technology/Cengage Learning

Figure 1-13 Optical drive

Source: Course Technology/Cengage Learning

write data on the discs. The laser used for writing data is much more powerful than the other laser because it must "burn" the bumps and dips into the disc. Although optical drives can spin discs at very high speeds, they are still significantly slower than hard drives, which store data magnetically. However, because optical media are inexpensive and removable, they are the most common format used for distributing computer software.

Tape Drives A **tape drive** is a device that stores computer data on magnetic tape, especially for backups (see Figure 1-14). Like an ordinary tape recorder, a tape drive records data on a loop of flexible celluloid-like material that can be read and erased. Tapes have a

Figure 1-14 Tape drive

Source: Course Technology/Cengage Learning

large capacity for storing data and are less expensive than hard drive storage. A disadvantage is that tape drives store data sequentially rather than randomly (as hard drives do), and the user can only access specific data by starting at the beginning and rolling through the tape until the desired data is located.

USB Drives A USB drive is a small, portable flash memory device (see Figure 1-15) that plugs into any computer with a USB port and functions as a portable drive with up to 256 GB of storage capacity. USB flash drives are easy to use and can be carried in a pocket. USB flash drives are also called jump drives, pen drives, key drives, or simply USB drives. These drives have less storage capacity than an external hard drive, but they are smaller and more durable because they have no internal moving parts.

Figure 1-15 USB drive

Source: Course Technology/Cengage Learning

A USB drive may also refer to a portable hard drive, CD drive, or DVD drive that plugs into a computer's USB port. A portable hard drive is a disk drive that is plugged into an external port on a computer, such as a USB or FireWire port. Typically used for backup, but also as secondary storage, such units rival internal drives in capacity.

Communications Devices

Communications devices support transmission of data from one PC to another, or from one device to another. For example, modems, network interface cards, and wireless adapters are all communications devices.

Modems   Modem is short for *modulator-demodulator*. A phone modem, as shown on the left in Figure 1-16, is a device that enables a PC's digitally stored information to be transmitted over telephone lines in the form of sound waves. A phone modem converts between these two forms.

With the proliferation of cable TV, broadband communications became readily available for the transmission of digital data. A **cable modem**, as shown on the right in Figure 1-16, is designed to operate over cable TV lines. Because the coaxial cable used by cable TV provides much greater bandwidth than telephone lines, your cable modem enables extremely fast access to the World Wide Web.

Network Interface Cards   A **network interface card** (NIC), as shown in Figure 1-17, is an expansion board that you insert into a computer so that it can be connected to a local area network (LAN). A network card can be either an expansion card that plugs into a computer's bus or an interface on the motherboard.

Wireless Adapters   A **wireless adapter**, as shown in Figure 1-18, permits a mobile user to connect to a LAN through a wireless (radio) connection. Access is similar to NIC access, but a wireless adapter allows more freedom of movement. Many newer laptop computers have wireless adapters built into the motherboard. If your laptop computer does not have a wireless adapter, you can purchase a wireless PC card or USB wireless adapter.

Phone modem

Cable modem

Figure 1-16 Phone and cable modems

Source: Course Technology/Cengage Learning

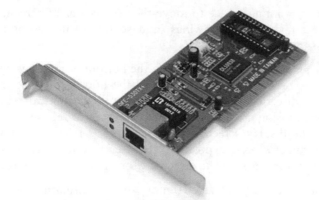

Figure 1-17 Network interface card

Source: Course Technology/Cengage Learning

Figure 1-18 Wireless adapter

Source: Course Technology/Cengage Learning

Peripheral Devices

Peripheral devices are external to the PC. For example, keyboards, pointing devices, printers, and external disk drives are common peripheral devices that are not part of the PC but are used in conjunction with it.

In the sections that follow, you will learn about input and output devices.

Input Devices

Input devices feed data into the PC. Examples include keyboards, pointing devices, biometric devices, and digital/video cameras. Although storage devices can provide input, this section is restricted to devices that you use to enter data yourself.

Keyboards Computer keyboards are similar to electric-typewriter keyboards, but they contain additional keys. Keyboards are designed for text entry and to control the operation of the computer. The standard U.S. keyboard has 105 keys. In addition to the 26 letters and 10 digits, special character keys extend the character set. Additional keys are used to control the computer.

Pointing Devices You use a pointing device to move the pointer on the screen, choose commands, click buttons, select text, create drawings, and so on. Examples of pointing devices include mice, trackballs, and touch pads.

A **mouse** consists of a metal or plastic housing, a sensor on the bottom of the housing that is rolled on a flat surface, and one or more buttons on top of the housing. As the mouse is moved over the surface in any direction, the sensor (which could be optical or a laser) sends impulses to the computer, causing a mouse-responsive program to reposition a visible indicator (called a cursor) on the display screen. The positioning is relative to a variable starting place. By viewing the cursor's present position, the user readjusts the position by moving the mouse. The mouse buttons are used to select text or options on the screen.

Essentially, a **trackball** is a mouse lying on its back. To move the pointer, you rotate the ball with your thumb, your fingers, or the palm of your hand. A trackball usually has one to three buttons next to the ball; you use them just like mouse buttons. You may prefer a trackball to a mouse because the trackball is stationary and does not require much space to use.

A **touch pad** is a small, touch-sensitive pad used as a pointing device on some laptop computers. By moving your finger along the pad, you can move the pointer on the display screen. You click by tapping the pad or pressing the button below the touch pad.

Biometric Devices Biometrics is the science and technology of measuring and statistically analyzing biological data. In information technology, biometrics usually refers to technologies for measuring and analyzing human body characteristics—such as fingerprints—for authentication purposes.

A **fingerprint scanner** (see Figure 1-19) has two basic jobs—recording an image of your finger and determining whether the pattern of ridges and valleys in the image matches the pattern in a previously scanned image. When the image matches, you are permitted to access the PC. Fingerprint scanners are included with a number of high-end laptop computers.

In addition to scanning fingerprints, biometric devices control access by measuring the retina and iris of the eye, voice patterns, and facial characteristics.

Digital/Video Cameras A **digital camera** stores images digitally rather than recording them on film. Typically, the image is stored on a flash card. After a picture is taken, it can be downloaded to a PC and then manipulated with a graphics program and printed. Unlike

Figure 1-19 Fingerprint scanner

Source: Course Technology/Cengage Learning

photographs on film, which have extremely high resolution, digital photos are limited by the amount of memory in the camera.

A **digital video camera** stores frames on digital tape or a digital card. After you shoot a video movie, you can download it to a PC and then manipulate it with a video-editing program.

Output Devices

Output devices such as CRT monitors, LCD panels, and printers provide output from a PC. Although storage devices can also provide output, this section is restricted to devices that you use to view information yourself.

CRT Monitors CRT is an abbreviation for *cathode-ray tube*, the technology used in older televisions and computer display screens. The most important aspect of a monitor is its screen size. Like televisions, monitor screen sizes are measured in diagonal inches—the distance from one corner to the opposite corner diagonally. Typical sizes run from 15 to 17 inches. The resolution of a monitor indicates how densely packed the pixels are. In general, more pixels produce a sharper image. Most modern monitors can display 1024 by 768 pixels, the SVGA standard. Some high-end models can display 1280 by 1024 pixels, or even 1600 by 1200.

LCD Panels LCD is short for *liquid crystal display*, a type of display used on laptop computers. LCD displays use two sheets of polarizing material with a liquid crystal solution between them. An electric current passed through the liquid causes the crystals to align so that light cannot pass through them. Each crystal, therefore, is like a shutter, either allowing light to pass through or blocking the light.

Although laptops have used LCDs almost exclusively as their flat-panel technology, LCD panels are also the most popular choice for flat-panel desktop monitors.

Consider an LCD panel for your desktop; it offers excellent viewability in a convenient package.

Printers A printer is a device that prints text or illustrations on paper. Many different types of printers are available. In terms of the technology used, printers fall into the following categories:

- Dot matrix—Creates characters by striking pins against an ink ribbon. Each pin makes a dot, and combinations of dots form characters and illustrations.
- Ink-jet—Sprays ink at a sheet of paper. Ink-jet printers produce high-quality text and graphics.
- Laser—Uses the same technology as copy machines. Laser printers produce high-quality text and graphics.

An ink-jet printer may be your best choice when color printing is required. You should consider a laser printer when you need high volumes of black-and-white output.

Activity 1-2: Reviewing System Information for Windows 7

Time Required: 10 minutes

Objective: Use the System Information program to review which components are available on the Windows 7 virtual machine.

Description: In this activity, you open the System Information window and review the available components on your PC.

1. If necessary, start your virtual machines using the appropriate instructions in Activity 1-1.

2. To open the System Information window, click **Start**, type **msinfo32** over "Search programs and files" in the search text box, and then click **msinfo32** under Programs.

3. To review component information, expand the **Components** folder.

4. To review the input components, expand the **Input** folder.

5. To review information about the pointing device, click **Pointing Device**.

6. To review information about the network adapter, expand **Network** and then click **Adapter**.

7. To review information about drives, expand **Storage** and then click **Drives**.

8. To review information about disks, click **Disks**.

9. Close the System Information window.

10. Leave the virtual machine logged on for future activities.

Activity 1-3: Reviewing System Information for Fedora 13

Time Required: 10 minutes

Objective: Use the System Information program to review which components are available on the Fedora 13 virtual machine.

Description: In this activity, you open the System Information window and review the available components on your Fedora 13 virtual machine.

1. If necessary, start your virtual machines using the appropriate instructions in Activity 1-1.

2. To open the terminal console, point to **Applications**, point to **System Tools**, and then click **Terminal**.

3. To open the System Information window, type **hardinfo** and press Enter.

If you see a "Command not found" message, contact your instructor.

4. To review component information, click **Summary**.

5. To review operating system information, click **Operating System**.

6. To review processor information, click **Processor**.

7. To review the input components, click **Input Devices**.

8. To review storage information, click **Storage**.

9. Close the System Information window.

10. Leave the virtual machine logged on for future activities.

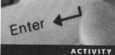

Activity 1-4: Reviewing the Devices on your Windows 7 Virtual Machine

Time Required: 10 minutes

Objective: Use the Device Manager program to review which devices are available on your Windows 7 virtual machine.

Description: In this activity, you open the Device Manager and review the available devices on your PC.

1. If necessary, start your virtual machines using the appropriate instructions in Activity 1-1.

2. To open the System applet, click **Start, right-click Computer,** and then click **Properties.**

3. To open the Device Manager, click the **Device Manager** link in the left pane.

4. If a Device Manager warning appears, read it and then click **OK**.

5. To review information on the disk drive, expand the **Disk drives** folder.

6. Repeat Step 5 for the remaining folders.

7. Close the Device Manager and System windows.

8. Leave the virtual machine logged on for the next activity.

Activity 1-5: Closing the Virtual Machines

Time Required: 3 minutes

Objective: Properly close the virtual machines.

Description: In this activity, you will log off and shut down the two virtual machines. The virtual machines must be properly shut down; otherwise, damage may occur to the virtual hard disks that support the virtual machines.

1. If the screen saver was activated on the Windows 7 virtual machine, log on to the Windows 7 virtual machine, type **Secret1, and then press Enter.**

2. To shut down the Windows 7 virtual machine, click **Start,** and then click **Shut Down.**

3. If the screen saver was activated on the Fedora 13 virtual machine, type a password of **Secret1 and then click Unlock.**

4. To shut down the Fedora 13 virtual machine, click **System,** click **Shut Down,** and then click **Shut Down** again.

5. Leave the computer logged on for the next student.

Preventive Maintenance

When you own or use a PC, you may be responsible for its maintenance. For example, you might need to regularly clean the unit, which can extend its life. You also need to know that a number of potential hazards, including static electricity, can damage the PC. And what will you do with your PC when you no longer need it? This section addresses all of these topics.

Cleaning

Your PC's mortal enemy is excessive heat, which accelerates the deterioration of its delicate circuits. The most common causes of overheating are dust and dirt: Clogged vents and CPU cooling fans can keep heat-dissipating air from moving through the case, and even a thin coating of dust or dirt can raise the temperature of PC components.

In most locations, such as dusty offices, your system may need a cleaning every few months. Most cleaning requires only a can of compressed air, lint-free wipes, cotton swabs, and a few drops of a mild cleaning solution in a bowl of water.

Always turn off and unplug the system before you clean any of its components. Never apply liquid directly to a component. Spray or pour the liquid on a lint-free cloth, and wipe the PC with the cloth.

Cleaning the Outside   Start by cleaning the outside of the case and attached peripherals. Wipe the case with a mild cleaning solution. Clear the ventilation openings of any obstructions. Use compressed air, but do not blow dust into the PC or its optical and floppy drives.

When the on-screen pointer moves erratically, it is time to clean your mouse. If your mouse contains a ball, unlatch the ring on the bottom of the unit and remove the ball. Locate the two rollers that are set 90 degrees apart inside the ball's housing. Use a moist cotton swab to clean the residue off the rollers.

Turn the keyboard upside down and shake it to clear any crumbs from between the keys. If that does not suffice, blast it briefly with compressed air.

Wipe the monitor case and clear its vents of obstructions without pushing dust into the unit. Clean the screen with a standard glass cleaner and a lint-free cloth. If your monitor has a degauss button (look for a small magnet icon), push it to clear magnetic interference.

Be careful when cleaning LCD panels. These surfaces should only be cleaned with a nonabrasive, lint-free cloth and water. Avoid using glass cleaner and any cleaning solution that contains ammonia, as it will damage the plastic surface of the screen.

Dirty optical discs should be cleaned carefully using a soft, dry, lint-free cloth. Hold the disc by its outer edges or center hole, and then gently wipe outward from the center hub toward the outside edge. Stubborn fingerprints or stains can be removed using a soft, dry, lint-free cloth lightly moistened with water. Never wipe a disc in a circular motion.

Cleaning the Inside Continue your cleaning with the inside of the case. Before cleaning the components in the case, take precautions to ground the static electricity before you touch any of the internal components. You should ground the static electricity by touching the internal metal frame of the computer's case while the computer is plugged into an electrical socket. The static electricity will be discharged and grounded because the electrical circuit is grounded via the AC outlet. Be sure to unplug the power cord before you clean the inside of the case.

Use antistatic wipes to remove dust from inside the case. Avoid touching any circuit-board surfaces. Pay close attention to the various fans. Spray these components with a blast of compressed air to loosen dust. To remove the dust rather than rearrange it, you should use a small vacuum.

If your PC is more than four years old, or if the expansion cards plugged into its motherboard are exceptionally dirty, remove each card, clean its contacts with isopropyl alcohol, and reseat it. If your system is less than two years old, just make sure each card is firmly seated by pressing gently downward on its top edge without touching its face. Likewise, check your power connectors and other internal cables for a snug fit.

Electrostatic Discharge

Electrostatic discharge (ESD) is the rapid discharge of static electricity from one conductor to another conductor of a different potential. An electrostatic discharge can damage integrated circuits in the PC. Whenever the PC case is opened and its internal workings are exposed (for example, to add an adapter card), you could damage the computer with the buildup of static electricity that your body holds.

The internal workings of a computer, and especially the hard drive, are extremely susceptible to static electricity. Human beings are not able to perceive static electricity until it has reached about 1,500 volts. (Walking across a rug can produce up to 12,000 volts of static electricity.) Although it is not life threatening to people, even a very low voltage of static electricity can seriously damage a hard drive or motherboard.

To avoid zapping internal computer components, be sure to ground the static electricity before you touch them, as described in the previous section.

To be on the safe side, always handle electronic circuitry on its insulated areas; avoid touching the circuits themselves. This advice applies to handling the motherboard, video card, modem, sound card, and hard drive, as well as any other internal components.

Hazards

While electrical problems can damage your PC, many hazards can injure you, including high-voltage shocks. You need to be aware of these hazards and know how to prevent them.

High Voltages in Capacitors
The interiors of PC power supplies, monitors, and laser printers contain capacitors that may retain a charge long after power is removed from a circuit; this charge can cause damage to connected equipment and shocks (even electrocution). You should not attempt to service equipment that contains large or high-voltage capacitors.

Power Supplies Whenever you repair or perform maintenance on your PC, you must unplug it after discharging any static electricity. Modern PC motherboards have a small voltage running when the PC is plugged in.

You should not attempt to repair a power supply. The safest choice is to replace it.

CRT Monitors The voltages inside a CRT monitor can kill you! Recall that capacitors can retain a charge long after power is removed from a circuit; this charge can cause shocks and even electrocution. Another dangerous part of the monitor is the **flyback transformer,** which generates up to 20,000 volts.

Fires You may never have a PC fire, but an electrical fire can strike your office or home. The smoke can harm you as well as your PC. You should use a type C or type ABC fire extinguisher on an electrical fire. Never spray or throw water on an electrical fire; the electrical current could travel up the water stream into you!

Disposal

Many PC components contain harmful ingredients and toxins, including lead, mercury, arsenic, cadmium, selenium, and hexavalent chromium. About 70 percent of the heavy metals (mercury and cadmium) in landfills come from electronic waste. These toxins can cause allergic reactions, brain damage, and cancer.

You must make prudent decisions when disposing of PCs and peripherals.

- Batteries contain toxic chemicals (lithium, mercury, nickel cadmium) and should not be thrown in the trash. You can take batteries to a recycling depot. In some cases, you can send the batteries back to the manufacturer.

- CRTs contain lead. If you toss them in the trash, the lead will end up in a landfill. For this reason, CRTs must be recycled or turned over to a hazardous waste program.

- Significant amounts of gold, silver, copper, steel, aluminum, wire, cable, and other resources can be extracted from computers. Many of these materials are recyclable.

You can drop off used computer equipment at participating Goodwill donation centers. It is free, and you will be given a receipt for tax purposes. At the same time, you will help protect the environment and benefit your community.

Connecting Components and Testing a PC

You should know how to "cable up" a PC. In this section, you will learn to identify and plug in the cables and connectors of a typical desktop or laptop system.

USB Cables

You can use USB cables to connect many devices to your computer, including flash memory devices, portable media players, and digital cameras. You can also connect accessories such as

USB A/B cable   USB A/Mini-B cable   USB A/Micro-B cable

Figure 1-20 USB cables with common connectors

Source: Course Technology/Cengage Learning

VGA cable   DVI cable   HDMI cable   DVI/HDMI cable

Figure 1-21 Video cables

Source: Course Technology/Cengage Learning

mice, keyboards, portable hard drives, DVD-CD drives, and microphones. Web cameras, printers, scanners, and speakers can also be connected to the computer through the USB ports.

The Standard USB connector, called a USB-A, is a rectangular connector found on every USB cable; it connects to your computer. The other end of the USB cable may have a variety of connectors, including the USB-B, a square connector used with printers, portable drives, and larger devices. Smaller connectors such as the Mini-USB and Micro-USB are commonly used with smaller portable devices, including media players and cameras. Figure 1-20 shows a variety of USB cables with their connectors.

Video Cables

One of the most common video connectors for computer monitors is the 15-pin VGA cable. For example, you can use this cable to connect a PC to a projector. Figure 1-21 shows some common video cables.

If you recently purchased a PC, you may have a Digital Visual Interface (DVI). Newer, thinner laptops use smaller versions of the DVI such as the Mini-DVI and Micro-DVI. A DVI cable has 29 pins, although some connectors may have fewer pins. DVI's signal is compatible with HDMI; cables can convert between the two formats.

Sound Cables

The most common sound cable is the standard headphone jack. While it is available in several sizes, the 1/8-in. mini-audio cable (shown in Figure 1-22) is used with computers.

Figure 1-22 Sound cable

Source: Course Technology/Cengage Learning

FireWire 6-pin/4-pin cable   eSATA cable

Figure 1-23 Data cables

Source: Course Technology/Cengage Learning

Phone cable   Ethernet cable

Figure 1-24 Networking cables

Source: Course Technology/Cengage Learning

Data Cables

Figure 1-23 shows the most common data cables: FireWire and eSATA. FireWire, also known as IEEE 1394, is commonly used for connecting digital camcorders and portable drives. FireWire cables typically have 6 pins, although a 4-pin variety is common as well.

While SATA cables are used internally to connect SATA drives to disk controllers, eSATA cables are designed for portable hard drives. The eSATA connector is larger than the internal SATA cable and has more shielding.

Networking Cables

The phone cable, known as the RJ-11, is still used to connect modems to phone jacks for Internet connectivity. The connector has 4 pins and a retaining clip (see Figure 1-24).

Ethernet is the standard for wired networking. The Ethernet connector, otherwise known as the RJ-45, is attached to an 8-wire twisted pair cable. It looks like a phone plug but is thicker and wider. It has a retaining clip to maintain a tight connector.

Cabling Up and Testing the PC

Start by arranging the components for your PC in the general area where you will use them: Put the keyboard in front of the monitor, the mouse to the right or left of the keyboard, and so on. Slowly move the PC case until you can view the connectors.

 Do not turn on the power to any components before connecting them.

You should connect the various cords in sequence. For example, if you are working with a tower case, start with the bottom connection and proceed to the top connector. For a tower case, you would most likely complete the connections in the following order:

1. Locate the monitor cable and attach it to the blue DB-15 female connector. (This connector has three rows of five holes.)

2. If you have a LAN cable, place it in the RJ-45 black connector. (It looks like a phone connector but has a provision for eight wires.)

3. Locate the audio line to the speakers (the one with the lime green mini-phone plug) and place it in the lime green mini-phone connector.

4. Locate the keyboard cable with a USB connector and place it in a USB port.

5. Locate the mouse cable with a USB connector and place it in a USB port.

6. Connect the power cord to the power connector.

7. Review your connections. If they appear to be correct, turn on your monitor and PC.

You should delay the connection of remaining USB devices—except for the keyboard or mouse—until the PC has completed start-up and you have logged on to the OS. USB devices are initialized by the OS and can be configured as they are plugged into the USB ports.

You should test each component to determine if it is working. For example, the CRT monitor or LCD panel should display an image, the mouse should move the cursor, and so on. If you have problems, check the connection of the device to the PC. Verify that each external device has power and that the device is powered on.

If necessary, turn off all components and correct the problem. For example, a USB connector for a printer might have been connected before the PC was started.

Connecting to a laptop is similar to the preceding steps, but there are fewer connectors: perhaps only a single VGA connector and two or three USB ports.

Chapter Summary

- Virtual machine technology allows multiple operating systems to run concurrently on a single PC. With virtual machine technology, you can run various Windows operating systems as well as Linux within Windows 7.

- Many hardware components make up a PC. The case houses and protects the main electronic components. The power supply is a sealed metal box that contains power conversion hardware. The motherboard, or main circuit board, contains the microprocessor, bus, memory, and expansion slots. The BIOS is firmware that supports the PC during start-up. VGA and USB ports permit the connection of devices. Video and sound expansion cards permit graphical and audio communication with the user. Disk drive controllers (such as PATA, SATA, and SCSI) allow the connection of hard drives and optical drives. Communication with other devices is permitted by modems, network interface cards, and wireless adapters.

- Peripherals include input devices such as keyboards, mice, trackballs, touch pads, fingerprint scanners, and digital cameras, which permit input and communication from the user. Output devices include CRT monitors, LCD panels, and printers.

- Preventive maintenance is the responsibility of the PC's owner. To avoid heat damage, keep the PC clean. Clean the inside and outside of the case and the attached peripherals.

- Many hazards can injure a PC user or damage the PC. For example, electrostatic discharge can damage a PC's internal components. Capacitors in power supplies and CRT monitors retain high voltages. Use a type ABC or type C fire extinguisher on electrical fires.

- Some PC components are not internal but are connected to the PC. Common connectors such as USB simplify the connection of these components. Connect components starting with the connector that is farthest from the power supply connector.

Key Terms

ATA   An acronym for *Advanced Technology Attachment*; the disk drive standard commonly known as Integrated Drive Electronics (IDE).

biometrics   The science and technology of authenticating a person's identity by measuring physiological features.

BIOS   An acronym for *basic input/output system*; the set of essential software routines that test a PC at start-up and start the OS.

bus   The set of hardware lines used to transfer data among the components of a PC.

cable modem   A device that sends and receives data through coaxial cables.

CRT   An acronym for *cathode-ray tube*; the basis for the standard PC display screen.

digital camera   A type of camera that stores photographic images electronically rather than on film.

digital video camera   A camera that captures and stores images on a digital medium. Also known as a camcorder.

EEPROM   An acronym for *electrically erasable programmable read-only memory*; a type of EPROM that can be erased with an electrical signal.

electrostatic discharge (ESD)   The discharge of static electricity from an outside source—such as human hands—into an integrated circuit, often damaging the circuit.

EPROM   An acronym for *erasable programmable read-only memory*; a type of memory chip that can be reprogrammed after manufacture.

expansion card   A circuit card that is plugged into a PC's bus to add extra functions.

fingerprint scanner   A scanner that reads human fingerprints for comparison to a database of stored fingerprint images.

FireWire   A PC and digital video serial bus interface standard offering high-speed communications. FireWire is also known as IEEE 1394.

firmware   Software routines stored in read-only memory (ROM).

flyback transformer   A transformer in a CRT monitor that generates up to 20,000 volts.

form factor   The physical size and shape of a device. The term is often used to describe the size of PC cases.

guest operating system   The operating system running within a virtual machine.

hard drive   A device that reads data from and writes data to one or more inflexible platters.

heat sink   A device that absorbs and dissipates heat created by an electronic device, such as a microprocessor.

host operating system   An operating system running on a physical machine that executes virtualization software.

LCD   An acronym for *liquid crystal display*; a type of display that uses a liquid compound with a polar molecular structure sandwiched between two transparent electrodes.

memory   An area where data can be stored and retrieved.

microprocessor   A central processing unit (CPU) on a single chip.

modem   Short for *modulator/demodulator*; a communications device that enables a PC to transmit data over a standard telephone line.

motherboard   The main circuit board containing the primary components of a PC.

mouse   A common pointing device.

network interface card (NIC)   An expansion card used to connect a computer to a local area network.

optical drive   A disk drive that reads and may write data to optical (compact) discs.

parallel port   An input/output connector for a parallel interface device.

PATA   An acronym for *Parallel Advanced Technology Attachment*. PATA is the same as ATA, which was renamed when SATA was introduced.

PROM   An acronym for *programmable read-only memory*.

RAM   An acronym for *random access memory*; semiconductor memory that can be read or written by the microprocessor or other devices.

register   A small amount of high-speed memory.

ROM   An acronym for *read-only memory*; a semiconductor circuit in which data is permanently installed by the manufacturer.

RS-232   An industry-accepted standard for serial communications.

SATA An acronym for *Serial Advanced Technology Attachment*, which transfers data serially to and from the hard drive.

SCSI An acronym for *small computer system interface*. It is used to connect SCSI devices to PCs.

sound adapter An expansion card that supports the recording and playback of sound.

system board *See* motherboard.

tape drive A device for reading and writing data on magnetic tapes.

touch pad A pointing device that responds to movement of a finger on a surface.

trackball A pointing device with a stationary housing that contains a ball you roll with your hand.

Universal Serial Bus (USB) A serial bus that connects devices to a PC. USB supports hot plugging.

USB drive A small, portable flash memory card that plugs into a PC's USB port and functions as a portable hard drive with up to 2 GB of storage capacity.

video adapter Electronic components that generate the video signal sent to a video display.

virtual machine A software implementation of a machine (i.e., a computer) that executes programs like a physical machine.

virtualization A technology that permits one or more guest operating systems to run on an operating system.

virtualized systems Systems that appear to be real but are actually simulations.

wireless adapter A device that supports a wireless connection through a radio connection to a wireless LAN.

Review Questions

1. With virtual machine technology, you move from one OS to another by _____.

   a. restarting the system

   b. pressing the F2 key

   c. clicking the other OS window

   d. logging off the system

2. Which of the following operating systems can be used with virtual machine technology? (Choose all that apply.)

   a. Windows 7

   b. Linux

   c. Macintosh

   d. physical

   e. logical

   f. emulated

   g. free

3. Oracle VirtualBox mimics physical PCs so closely that the applications you install in them don't distinguish the virtual machine from a(n) _____ computer.

   a. supported

   b. emulated

   c. guest

   d. physical

4. The _____ is the size, configuration, or physical arrangement of the PC hardware.

   a. system board

   b. motherboard

   c. form factor

   d. none of the above

5. A power supply _____. (Choose all that apply.)

   a. provides clean power feeds to PC components

   b. is a sealed metal box

   c. has standardized plugs that work with all kinds of components

   d. is user-serviceable

6. The _____ is the main circuit board inside a PC. (Choose all that apply.)

   a. system board

   b. motherboard

   c. form factor

   d. none of the above

7. _____ is the electronic holding place for programs and data.

   a. EPROM

   b. RAM

   c. EEPROM

   d. ROM

8. Which of the following memory types could be used to hold the BIOS firmware? (Choose all that apply.)

   a. EPROM

   b. RAM

   c. EEPROM

   d. ROM

9. Which of the following are considered I/O ports? (Choose all that apply.)

   a. serial

   b. parallel

    c. USB

    d. FireWire

10. Which BIOS settings could be allocated for serial ports? (Choose all that apply.)

    a. COM1

    b. COM2

    c. LPT1

    d. LPT2

11. The _____ was developed to simplify the connection of peripheral devices.

    a. serial port

    b. parallel port

    c. universal serial bus

    d. none of the above

12. Which of the following could be used as hard drive controllers? (Choose all that apply.)

    a. ATA

    b. PATA

    c. SATA

    d. SCSI

13. The main types of data storage are _____. (Choose all that apply.)

    a. hard drives

    b. optical discs

    c. tape

    d. USB Jump drives

14. Which of the following are small and portable with flash memory? (Choose all that apply.)

    a. jump drives

    b. pen drives

    c. key drives

    d. USB drives

15. Which of the following are communications devices? (Choose all that apply.)

    a. modem

    b. network interface card

    c. wireless adapter

    d. graphics adapter

16. Which of the following are input devices? (Choose all that apply.)
    a.   keyboard
    b.   mouse
    c.   trackball
    d.   fingerprint scanner
    e.   touch pad

17. _____ is the mortal enemy of a PC.
    a.   Dirt
    b.   Dust
    c.   Heat
    d.   Grime

18. Wipe the case with a(n) _____ solution.
    a.   alcohol
    b.   arsenic
    c.   mild cleaning
    d.   selenium

19. A person cannot perceive static electricity until it has reached _____ volts.
    a.   110
    b.   1,500
    c.   12,000
    d.   25,000

20. Computers contain which of the following toxic ingredients? (Choose all that apply.)
    a.   lead
    b.   mercury
    c.   arsenic
    d.   cadmium

Case Projects

Case 1-1: Using Virtual Machine Technology

Your boss has been reading about virtual machine technology. He has received a request for 10 new PCs to run a Linux application for the Engineering Department. The engineers have one-year-old PCs that run Windows 7 with 4 GB of memory, 250-GB hard drives, and the fastest processors available. Your boss knows that you are using virtualization technology in your operating systems course at a local community college. He wants you to write a one-page report on the possibility of using Oracle VirtualBox on the existing Windows 7 OS to run Linux and the Linux application. He expects your report to explain the potential cost savings of using virtualization technology. Because the engineers are technically savvy, your report must provide the technical reasons for your recommendation.

Case 1-2: Configuring a PC

You have a budget of $1,000. Using the Web site of a major PC manufacturer, configure a PC and printer. Provide a report indicating the configuration and component costs.

Case 1-3: Keeping the PC Clean

Your boss has asked you to develop a procedure to keep the PCs in your work area clean and working. Provide detailed information about the use of various cleaning agents. Include precautions regarding inappropriate actions that could damage components.

Software Components

After reading this chapter and completing the exercises, you will be able to:

- Describe historical milestones for three popular operating systems
- Describe the architecture of common PC operating systems
- Describe the functions of an operating system
- Describe the interaction between an operating system and its components
- Describe utilities that are available for Windows 7 and Fedora 13
- Describe applications that are available for Windows 7 and Fedora 13

A PC is made up of hardware and software. You learned about hardware in Chapter 1, and you will learn about software in this chapter. The traditional definition of hardware is "something you can touch"; the traditional definition of software is "the instructions that make the PC work."

The **software components** that enable a PC to accomplish tasks are the operating system, **utilities** (programs that perform system-related tasks and maintenance on the operating system), and **applications** (programs that perform user-related tasks). To use the software on a PC effectively, you need to know the characteristics of all three types of components. In addition to describing these components, this chapter provides a brief history of operating system milestones, explains the functions of an operating system, and explains the interaction between an operating system and applications.

To be able to choose an operating system for your PC, you need to know the characteristics of the two prevalent operating systems—Windows and Fedora 13.

Common Operating Systems

Many different operating systems run on PCs. You may not have even heard of operating systems such as MINIX, Mach, XNU, MorphOS, EROS, Chorus, and Amoeba. Many of the more popular operating systems grew out of research at major universities, including Mac OS X, Fedora 13, and Microsoft Windows. In this text, you will use the command-line interface within Microsoft Windows 7 and Fedora 13.

Disk Operating System (DOS)

DOS can refer to any OS, but it is most often used as shorthand for MS-DOS (Microsoft disk operating system). Originally developed by Microsoft for IBM, MS-DOS was once the standard OS for the PC.

DOS is one of the most basic operating systems in use today. The first version of DOS was primitive, but after a few changes, it provided all the functions an OS needed. DOS is a single-tasking operating system, which means that it can run only one program at a time.

As with other operating systems, DOS began with the efforts of a single person: Tim Patterson of Seattle Computer Products. Patterson created QDOS, the "Quick and Dirty Operating System," which was purchased by Microsoft and became the seed of MS-DOS.

Microsoft released many versions of DOS, culminating with the last version in 1994:

- August 1981—PC-DOS 1.0 appears on the IBM-announced PC.
- May 1982—MS-DOS 1.1 supports 320-KB double-sided floppy disk drives.
- March 1983—MS-DOS 2.0 is written from scratch. It supports 10-MB hard drives, a tree-structured file system, and 360-KB floppy disks.
- August 1984—MS-DOS 3.0 adds support for 1.2-MB floppy disks and hard drives of more than 10 MB.
- November 1984—MS-DOS 3.1 adds support for Microsoft networks.
- November 1988—MS-DOS 4.01 includes a graphical interface and support for hard drive partitions of more than 32 MB.

- June 1991—MS-DOS 5.0 adds a full-screen editor, undelete and unformat utilities, and task swapping.

- March 1993—The MS-DOS 6.0 upgrade includes DoubleSpace disk compression.

- June 1994—MS-DOS 6.22 introduces DoubleSpace disk compression under the name DriveSpace. (Some people consider this the last version of MS-DOS.)

You might be wondering why you should learn DOS, but there are several reasons. For example, the command line is useful for accomplishing such tasks as copying a large number of files between hard drives or changing file attributes. If you are studying to become an administrator, you need to perform your tasks as efficiently as possible. Using the command line is efficient once you learn the commands; on a Microsoft Windows server, the command-line interface is sometimes the proper tool.

Later in this chapter and throughout the book, you will enter commands in the Activity exercises.

Windows 7 Operating System

Microsoft Windows is a range of environments and operating systems for PCs that was introduced in 1985 to counter Apple's new system, the Macintosh, which used a graphical user interface. Both Apple and Microsoft followed in the footsteps of the OS developed at Xerox PARC (Palo Alto Research Center). Xerox PARC is best known for essentially creating the modern PC graphical user interface. Microsoft continued Windows with the development of Windows NT (New Technology); the company hired Dave Cutler, a chief architect of Virtual Memory System (VMS) at Digital Equipment Corporation (DEC), to develop NT into a more capable operating system. Cutler had been developing a follow-up to VMS at DEC, called Mica; when DEC dropped the project, he brought his expertise and some engineers with him to Microsoft.

Microsoft has cornered more than 80 percent of the desktop OS market. Windows is proprietary closed-source software, meaning that Microsoft owns the software's copyright and controls its distribution.

Microsoft has released many versions of Windows; the first versions were DOS-based and culminated with Windows Me. The Windows NT thread started with Windows NT 3.1 and continues today with Windows 7 and Windows Server 2008 R2. The time lines for these two versions of Windows sometimes overlap.

The Windows time line appears in the following list:

- November 1985—Windows 1.0 implements a graphical interface. The selection of applications is sparse, however, and Windows sales are modest.

- October 1987—Windows 2.0 adds icons and overlapping windows. Windows/386 provides the capability to run multiple DOS applications simultaneously in extended memory.

- May 1990—Windows 3.0 is a complete overhaul of the Windows environment. It can address memory beyond 640K and has a much more powerful user interface.

- July 1993—Windows NT 3.1 is intended for use in network servers, workstations, and software development machines. It is based on an entirely new OS kernel.

- December 1993—Windows for Workgroups 3.11 (code name Janus) is the first integrated Windows and networking package offered by Microsoft. It provides peer-to-peer file and printer-sharing capabilities that are highly integrated into the Windows environment.

- September 1994—Windows NT 3.5 (code name Daytona) provides improved performance and reduced memory requirements.

- August 1995—Windows 95 (code name Chicago) is a 32-bit system providing full preemptive multitasking, advanced file systems, threading, and networking.

- July 1996—Windows NT 4.0 (code name Cairo) contains advanced security features, advanced network support, a full 32-bit operating system, advanced multitasking, and user administration.

- June 1998—Windows 98 (code name Memphis) gives the desktop a browser-like interface. New hardware supports the latest technology, such as DVD, FireWire, and USB.

- February 2000—Windows 2000 (NT 5.0) provides an impressive platform of Internet, intranet, extranet, and management applications that integrate tightly with Active Directory.

- September 2000—Windows Me (code name Millennium, short for Millennium Edition) is aimed at the home user. It is basically an upgrade to the DOS-based code on previous Windows 98 versions.

- October 2001—Windows XP (code name Whistler, NT 5.1) contains the 32-bit kernel and driver set from Windows NT and Windows 2000.

- April 2003—Windows Server 2003 (code name Whistler Server, NT 5.2) is a multi-purpose OS capable of handling a diverse set of server roles. It provides security, reliability, availability, and scalability.

- April 2005—Windows XP 64-bit is designed to use the expanded 64-bit memory address space provided by the x86-64 architecture.

- January 2007—Windows Vista (code name Longhorn) includes an updated graphical user interface and visual style dubbed Aero. Vista aims to increase the level of communication between machines on a home network, using peer-to-peer technology to simplify sharing files and media between computers and devices.

- February 2008—Windows Server 2008 (code name Longhorn Server) is built from the same code base as Windows Vista; therefore, it shares much of the same architecture and functionality.

- October 2009—Windows 7 (code name 7) includes a number of new features, such as advances in touch and handwriting recognition, support for virtual hard disks, improved performance on multi-core processors, and improved boot performance.

- October 2009—Windows Server 2008 R2 (code name Windows Server 7) includes new virtualization capabilities and supports up to 64 physical processors or up to 256 cores per system.

Fedora Operating Systems

Linux refers to the family of UNIX-like computer operating systems that use the Linux **kernel** (the essential center of a computer operating system). It is the result of the free and open source software collaboration from the Linux community around the world. Typically, all the underlying source code in open source software can be used, freely modified, and redistributed, both commercially and noncommercially.

Fedora 13 owes its parentage to UNIX, which was created by Ken Thompson and Dennis Richie. Interestingly, the acronym UNIX does not actually stand for anything. The original OS was called UNiplexed Information and Computing System (Unics)—a pun for the larger Multics OS—and the name was later changed to UNIX.

Prior to the creation of Linux, a number of significant UNIX releases occurred, as shown in Table 2-1. The first edition included more than 60 commands, many of which are still in use today.

Linus Torvalds developed the Linux kernel while he was a student at the University of Helsinki in Finland. He began his work on the kernel in 1991 and released version 1.0 in 1994.

Richard Stallman began working on the GNU project while working at the Massachusetts Institute of Technology (MIT) artificial intelligence lab. Today, this project includes assemblers, command processors, compilers, debuggers, interpreters, shells, text editors, and many other utilities needed to support development. GNU is short for "GNU's Not UNIX."

Linux uses the X window system for graphical displays. The X (or X11) system was developed at MIT in 1984 by Jim Gettys and Bob Scheifler. It was originally designed as a platform-independent graphics system so that students could use computers from many different vendors.

Linux is usually packaged in a format known as a Linux distribution for desktop and server use. A Linux distribution is built on top of the Linux kernel. According to the Web site DistroWatch, Fedora was the second most popular Linux-based operating system as of July 2010.

Date	UNIX release
November 1971	First edition
December 1972	Second edition
February 1973	Third edition
November 1973	Fourth edition
June 1974	Fifth edition
May 1975	Sixth edition
January 1979	Seventh edition
February 1985	Eighth edition
September 1986	Ninth edition
October 1989	Tenth edition

Table 2-1 UNIX software releases

The Fedora Project was created in late 2003. Fedora 13, code-named Goddard, was released in May 2010. It is a general-purpose OS released under the **GNU General Public License**, which guarantees your freedom to share and modify free software. As part of Linux, Fedora 13 is open source software. The basic idea behind open source is simple: When programmers can read, redistribute, and modify the source code for a piece of software, the software evolves. People improve it, adapt it, and fix bugs in it, often at astonishing speeds compared with the slow pace of conventional software development.

Today, many desktops are available for Fedora 13. A desktop is the main workspace in a graphical user interface. The electronic desktop is a metaphor for the top of an actual desk, where one finds files, folders, and writing instruments. The GNOME desktop—created by Miguel de Icaza and some of his friends from universities in Mexico—is the default desktop for Red Hat's distribution of Fedora 13. KDE began in Germany in 1996; it is now the default desktop for the SUSE distribution of Linux. In this text, you will use the GNOME desktop.

Common Operating System Architectures

For an operating system to be a useful and convenient interface between the user and the hardware, it must provide certain basic services, such as the ability to read and write files, allocate and manage memory, and make access control decisions. These services are provided by a number of routines that collectively make up the operating system. Applications invoke these routines through the use of specific system calls. This underlying structure and its design are called the system architecture.

You will learn about three operating system architectures—DOS, Windows 7, and Fedora 13—in the following sections.

DOS Architecture

DOS is a real-mode operating system, which means all program modules share the same address space. The DOS user interface is a **command-line interface (CLI),** meaning you must type text-based commands and view responses when interacting with the OS. Windows 7 provides a CLI for interacting with the OS. Figure 2-1 shows the flow of DOS commands through the operating system.

MS-DOS uses the following basic steps to process a command:

1. You type a command at the command prompt in the CLI.

2. When you press the Enter key, Command.com interprets your command, and then processes your request with a resident, internal command or loads an external command.

3. The command makes a logical input/output (I/O) request, which is passed to MSDOS.SYS.

4. MSDOS.SYS accepts the command and prepares a physical I/O request with the assistance of a device driver. Device drivers take two general forms: Character mode drivers, which work with devices such as keyboards, and block mode drivers, which work with 512-byte blocks for devices such as disk drives.

5. MSDOS.SYS passes the physical I/O request to IO.SYS.

6. IO.SYS, which controls physical devices, interacts with the peripheral device.

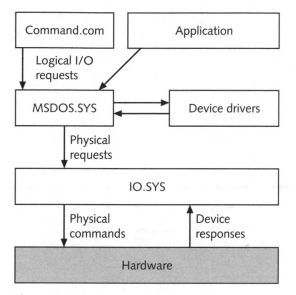

Figure 2-1 Simplified DOS architecture

Source: Course Technology/Cengage Learning

Command.com can load and turn over control of the PC to an application such as a word processor. Suppose that the word processor needs to display a character string on the display. The process progresses as before:

1. The word processor makes a logical I/O request, which is passed to MSDOS.SYS.

2. MSDOS.SYS accepts the I/O request and prepares a physical I/O request with the assistance of a display device driver.

3. MSDOS.SYS passes the physical I/O request to IO.SYS.

4. IO.SYS, which controls the display and interacts with it, queries the display status and sends the character string to the display. If an error occurs, the display sends an error response to IO.SYS, which passes the error response back through the chain.

In Chapter 1, you learned about video adapters and display monitors. In reality, the I/O process is more complicated. However, the basic flow through the operating system is correct as presented in the preceding steps.

Windows 7 Architecture

A simplified view of the Windows 7 architecture is shown in Figure 2-2. Notice the horizontal line that divides the user mode and kernel mode. The kernel mode modules shown below the line share a common address space—the system space. All four basic types of user mode processes execute in protected-mode address spaces and thus reside in their own private address space.

The basic types of user mode processes are:

- System support processes—Processes such as logons (Winlogon) and the session manager that are not service processes

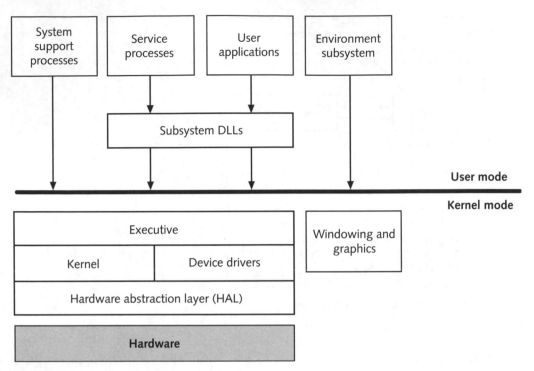

Figure 2-2 Simplified Windows 7 architecture

Source: Course Technology/Cengage Learning

- Service processes—Host services such as the Task Scheduler and print spooler services; these processes are started by the service control manager
- User applications—DOS, Win32, and Win64 applications
- Environment subsystem—Exposes native OS system services to user applications

Notice the Subsystem DLLs box in Figure 2-2. User applications do not call the native Windows 7 OS services directly. The calls are passed through one or more dynamic link libraries. A **dynamic link library** (**DLL**) is a library of executable functions or data that can be used by a Windows application. Typically, a DLL provides one or more particular functions, and a program accesses the functions by creating a link to the DLL. However, a DLL can also just contain data; in this case, the DLL translates the documented function into the appropriate internal function in the Windows 7 kernel mode, thus insulating the kernel mode from the user applications.

The kernel mode components of Windows 7 include:

- Executive—Provides basic OS services, such as memory management, process and thread management, and security
- Kernel—Provides low-level OS functions, such as thread scheduling
- Device drivers—Translates user I/O requests into specific hardware I/O requests; in Windows 7, only the kernel mode can communicate directly with hardware through the hardware abstraction layer
- Hardware abstraction layer (HAL)—Insulates the kernel and device drivers from the intricacies of hardware; only the HAL interfaces with the Hardware layer

- Windowing and graphics—Implements the windowing interface or graphical user interface (GUI)

For additional information related to these components, see the "Functions of an Operating System" section later in this chapter.

Fedora 13 Architecture

A simplified view of the Fedora 13 architecture is shown in Figure 2-3.

Notice the horizontal line separating the user mode and kernel mode. As a user, you associate with the OS by way of the user space; its processes do not access the kernel directly. Processes interact by way of system calls that reside at the outermost layer of the modules defined by the kernel. For example, hardware management takes place within the kernel space. Within the kernel, modules call on other modules to gain additional granularity.

The subset of modules that are not visible to the user mode is made up in part by device drivers and kernel subsystem functions. The Fedora 13 kernel is composed of five main subsystems:

- Process scheduler (SCHED)—The SCHED controls process access to the processor. The scheduler enforces a policy that ensures processes will have fair access to the processor, while ensuring that necessary hardware actions are performed by the kernel on time.

- Memory manager (MM)—The MM permits multiple processes to securely share the machine's main memory system. In addition, the memory manager supports virtual memory that allows Fedora 13 to support processes that use more memory than is available in the system. Unused memory is swapped out to persistent storage using the file system and then swapped back in when needed.

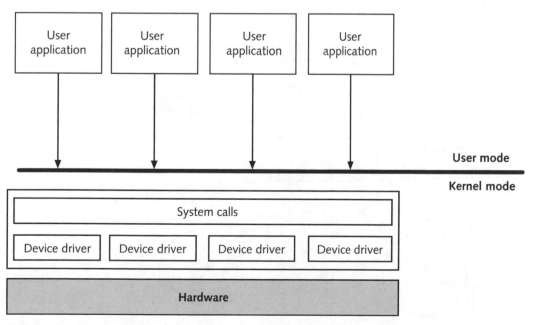

Figure 2-3 Simplified Fedora 13 architecture

Source: Course Technology/Cengage Learning

- Virtual file system (VFS)—The VFS abstracts the details of the various hardware devices by presenting a common file interface to all devices. In addition, the VFS supports several file system formats that are compatible with other operating systems.
- Network interface (NET)—The NET provides access to several networking standards and a variety of network hardware.
- Interprocess communication (IPC)—The IPC supports several mechanisms for process-to-process communication on a single Fedora 13 system.

Fedora 13 provides dynamically loadable device drivers that permit the inclusion of system code without having to compile the kernel code to include a device driver. This allows device drivers to be loaded and unloaded in real time without having to restart the OS.

Related information about these components is included in the next section.

Functions of an Operating System

The operating system's job is to manage all available resources on the PC. In fact, the OS should maximize the use of available resources, as shown in Figure 2-4.

These functions are described in the following sections.

Processor Management

The Microsoft disk operating system was a single-user, single-tasking OS that used a command-line interface. A single-tasking OS allows only one program to run at a time. In other words, if you are working in a spreadsheet and you want to write a report, you must

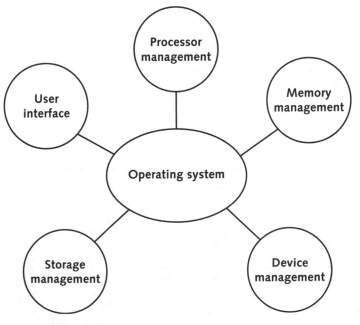

Figure 2-4 Functions of an operating system

Source: Course Technology/Cengage Learning

shut down the spreadsheet application before you start the word processor. This is unproductive, especially if you need to quote some data from the spreadsheet in your report.

Newer operating systems like Windows 7 and Fedora 13 were designed to allow multiple programs to run at the same time, a process called **multitasking**. In this process, programs take turns using the processor. Multitasking allows a single user to have a spreadsheet and word processor open at the same time.

You may be tempted to think of a process as an application, but this would paint an incomplete picture of how processes relate to the operating system. The application you see is certainly a process, but the application may cause one or more threads to begin for such tasks as spell checking or printing.

Also, numerous processes run without ever giving direct evidence that they exist. For example, Windows 7 and Fedora 13 can have dozens of background processes running to handle memory management and disk management.

The OS creates a process for the purpose of running a program, and every process has at least one thread. A **thread** is short for a "thread of execution," or a sequence of instructions. In this context, the term is analogous to the way that threads are interwoven to make a piece of fabric. With **multithreading** (multiple threads executed in parallel), a program splits into two or more tasks that run simultaneously. A common use of threads is to have one pay attention to the graphical user interface while others do a long calculation in the background. As a result, the application more readily responds to a user's interaction. All modern operating systems support multithreading and multitasking.

Because the threads spawned by a process share the same address space, one thread can modify data used by another thread. This is both good and bad; it facilitates easy communication between threads, but a poorly written program may cause one thread to inadvertently overwrite data used by another thread. Sharing a single address space is one reason that multithreaded programming is usually considered more difficult and error prone than single-threaded programming.

The heart of managing the processor comes down to ensuring that each process and application receives enough of the processor's time to function properly. The key to allocating processor cycles is the scheduling of processes or threads.

Multitasking allows the OS to schedule multiple tasks, seemingly at the same time. However, task execution is switched very rapidly among each program, giving the impression of simultaneous execution. This process is also known as task switching. On single-processor machines, multitasking is implemented by letting a process own the processor for a while (a time slice), and then replacing the process with another, which then owns the processor.

The two most common methods for sharing CPU time are:

- **Cooperative multitasking**—Running applications must work together to share system resources, which requires that tasks voluntarily cede control to other tasks at programmer-defined points.

- **Preemptive multitasking**—The OS executes an application for a specific period of time, according to its assigned priority. When the time expires, the task is preempted, and another task is given access to the processor for its time slice. Preemptive multitasking prevents a single thread from monopolizing a processor.

To illustrate the differences between cooperative and preemptive multitasking, consider a young mother with two small children: Jerry is six and Carol is eight. Carol is by far the more talkative of the siblings. When asked how school was that day, Carol takes the floor and begins to talk. When Carol winds down, several minutes later, Jerry is permitted to talk. This is an example of cooperative multitasking; the program must reach a stopping point for Mom—the operating system—to gain control.

Now consider the same mother and two children in a preemptive multitasking system. Mom asks the two children about their day at school. As before, Carol goes first. After a preset interval, Mom interrupts Carol and allows Jerry to talk for his interval. Mom then cycles between the two children, allowing each a time slice. When Jerry has finished his say, Carol could get consecutive time slices, if need be. In this situation, Mom—the operating system—remains in control of the schedule.

On PCs with multiple processors, multiprocessing is implemented. **Multiprocessing** is traditionally known as the use of multiple concurrent threads in a system, as opposed to a single process, at any one instant. Like multitasking, which allows multiple processes to share a single CPU, multiple CPUs may be used to execute multiple threads within a single process. In **symmetric multiprocessing (SMP)** systems, several CPUs execute programs and distribute the computing load over a small number of identical processors. For multiprocessing, Windows 7 supports two processors; Fedora 13 supports two or more processors.

Processors were originally developed with only one core. The **core** is the part of the processor that actually reads and executes instructions. Single-core processors can only process one instruction at a time.

A multi-core processor is a system composed of two or more independent cores. One can describe it as an integrated circuit to which two or more individual processors (called cores in this sense) have been integrated. A dual-core processor contains two cores, a quad-core processor contains four cores, and a hexa-core processor contains six cores.

Multiuser operating systems allow multiple users to share a computer and run programs at the same time. Windows 7 supports multiple users and PC sharing through **Fast User Switching**. With this feature, if you need to use the PC, the previous user does not have to close applications first.

Fedora 13 is designed to support more than one independent user at a time on the same PC, permitting multiple users to interact with the OS. This means that you can log on using multiple user accounts and that each account can have a separate console.

Memory Management

Memory management is the act of handling computer memory. In its simpler forms, this management provides ways to allocate portions of memory to programs at their request and to allocate free memory back to the system for reuse when it is no longer needed.

Memory management is one of the most important parts of Windows 7 and Fedora 13. With the size of applications today, systems sometimes need more memory than what exists physically in a PC. Virtual memory makes the PC appear to have more memory than it actually does by storing unneeded data and instructions on the hard drive. When the data or instructions are needed, the OS fetches them from the hard drive.

In virtual memory, all addresses are **virtual addresses,** which are memory locations that intervening hardware and software map to physical memory. These addresses should not be confused with **physical addresses,** which are numbers that identify an actual storage (memory) location in the physical memory on a computer. The amount of memory that can be addressed by the processor is called physical memory. The virtual addresses that a process uses do not represent the actual physical location of an object in memory. Instead, the OS maintains a page map for each process; this internal data structure is used to translate virtual addresses into corresponding physical addresses. Each time a thread references an address, the OS translates the virtual address to a physical address.

To maximize its flexibility in managing memory, the OS can move pages of physical memory to and from a paging file onto a disk. When a page is moved into physical memory, the OS updates the page maps of the affected processes. When the OS needs space in physical memory, it moves the least recently used pages of physical memory to the paging file. Manipulation of physical memory by the OS is completely transparent to applications, which operate only in their virtual address spaces.

In Windows 7, you can control the size and location of the paging file. To locate this information, click Start, right-click Computer, click Properties, click the Advanced System Settings link, click the Settings button under Performance, click the Advanced tab, and then click the Change button. The virtual memory settings are displayed, as shown in Figure 2-5. The default settings permit Windows 7 to automatically manage the size of the paging files. If you receive warnings that your virtual memory is low, increase the size of the paging file. Windows 7 sets the initial minimum size of the paging file to the amount of random access memory (RAM) installed on your computer plus 300 MB. The maximum size is set by

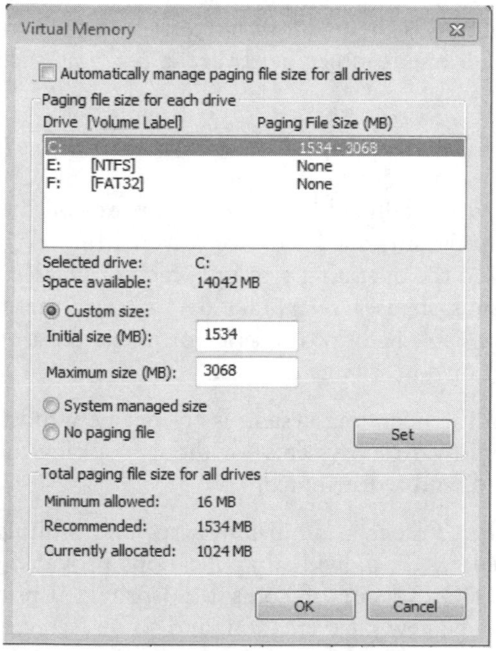

Figure 2-5 Virtual memory in Windows 7

Source: Course Technology/Cengage Learning

default to three times the amount of installed RAM. If you receive warning messages, increase the minimum and maximum sizes.

From the Advanced tab on the Performance Options dialog box, you can change the way memory is used between data caching and instruction storage. The default option, Programs, permits your PC to run faster than when memory is set aside to optimize data caching.

If you use multiple physical hard drives in Windows 7, you can increase performance by moving the paging file to a hard drive other than the one that contains the Windows 7 OS.

Memory management is quite complicated in any operating system, and Fedora 13 is no exception. Several differences exist between memory management in Windows 7 and Fedora 13; for example, you can make more detailed decisions in Fedora 13 about how memory is managed. You should only make modifications after carefully considering what you have to work with and what you want to accomplish. Other differences are that with Fedora 13, you can look at the source code and know exactly how memory is being managed, you can know exactly which algorithms are being used, and you can use the source code to expand your knowledge of memory management.

In Fedora 13, it is possible to use a whole partition of the hard drive for virtual memory. Though you can use a file for swapping, you should use a separate partition because it eliminates fragmentation, which reduces performance when swapping.

Modern operating systems like Windows 7 and Fedora 13 are available in 32-bit and 64-bit versions. The difference between 32-bit and 64-bit computers lies with the processor and how it manages information. A 64-bit processor can handle 64 bits of data at one time, while a 32-bit processor can only handle 32 bits. You can install a 32-bit operating system on a system with a 64-bit processor. However, if you have a 32-bit processor, only a 32-bit operating system can be installed. Another consideration is the memory limitation of 4 GB for 32-bit operating systems (actually closer to 3.2 GB due to other hardware allocations such as graphics card memory).

Device Management

The path between the operating system and virtually all hardware that is not on the computer's motherboard goes through a special program called a device driver. Much of a driver's function is to translate data streams between the operating system (which originated with the application programs) and the hardware subsystems. Drivers take data streams that the operating system has defined as a file and translate them into a series of pixels on a display or into streams of bits placed in specific locations on storage devices.

One reason that drivers are separate from the operating system is so that new functions can be added to the driver—and thus to the hardware subsystems—without requiring the operating system itself to be modified, recompiled, and redistributed.

One way to view device management is to consider a familiar task such as printing. Before operating systems like Windows 7 and Fedora 13, individual applications provided software that controlled printers. For example, the DOS version of Lotus 1-2-3 provided printer software and drivers that controlled printer fonts, new page creation, and so on (see Figure 2-6). Lotus had to provide a driver for each printer on the market; these drivers were hard to write, and Lotus, like most developers, was struggling to keep up with new printers as they came to market. In short, it was an untenable approach.

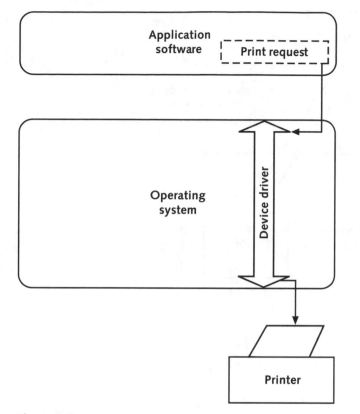

Figure 2-6 Application support for printing

Source: Course Technology/Cengage Learning

In the Windows 7 approach, the OS provides a device driver for the printer. These device drivers meant that applications like Lotus no longer had to deal with printer drivers themselves, but only had to provide an interface to a Windows component called the **graphical device interface (GDI)**. Within the OS, a device driver connects the GDI to a printer (shown in Figure 2-7). The application speaks Windows language to the GDI, which talks to the printer driver, which in turn controls the printer. The GDI possesses additional capabilities—for example, it allows applications to talk to all display devices, including graphics cards. In this scheme, the printer drivers are the responsibility of the printer manufacturer, although Microsoft wrote some of these drivers for the manufacturers.

In Fedora 13, the flow for the print model is essentially the same. The application produces **PostScript**—a page description language developed and marketed by Adobe Systems—which goes to **Ghostscript**, a suite of free software based on an interpreter of the Adobe PostScript and Portable Document Format (PDF) page description languages. In turn, the flow is passed to the device driver. Ghostscript converts the PostScript to the printer formatting commands required by the printer. The OS provides the printer driver for every printer that it supports.

The basis of a printing system in a modern OS is the spooler, as shown in Figure 2-8. *Spool* is an acronym for simultaneous peripheral operations online. The spooler manages queues of print jobs. A queue is usually associated with a single printer, and jobs submitted by users are processed on a first-come, first-served basis. For Windows 7, the application generates output that is passed

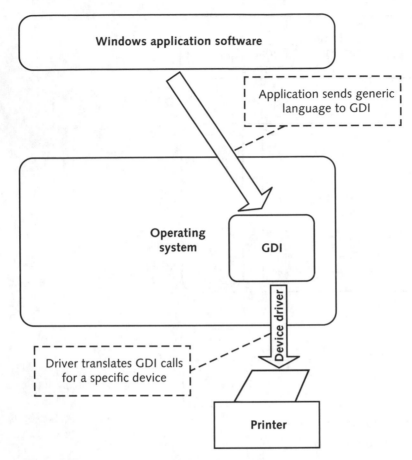

Figure 2-7 Operating system support for printing

Source: Course Technology/Cengage Learning

to a module, such as the GDI. The module then calls the printer driver to render the output. The output is then passed to the print monitor, which controls the transfer to the printer. The printing is done in the background while the user interacts with other applications in the foreground.

Storage Management

In DOS, you use the `fdisk` command to create a partition and the `format` command to prepare the partition for use. The `format` command creates a new root directory and file allocation table for the disk. It can also check for bad areas on the disk and can delete all data on the disk. In order for DOS to be able to use a new disk, you must first use the `format` command to format the disk.

 Do not experiment with `fdisk`. If you accidentally delete a drive or partition, you will lose data from your hard drive and possibly your operating system.

A modern OS provides the tools to manage the storage areas on the PC's hard drives. In Windows 7, Disk Management is a system utility for managing hard drives and the partitions

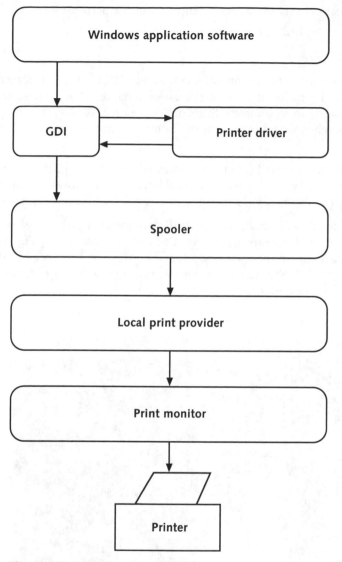

Figure 2-8 Printing system

Source: Course Technology/Cengage Learning

they contain. With Disk Management, you can initialize disks, create partitions, and format volumes with the FAT, FAT32, or NTFS file systems. Disk Management enables you to perform most disk-related tasks without restarting the system or interrupting users; most configuration changes take effect immediately.

In Fedora 13, you use the `fdisk` command to add a partition to a hard drive. After the partition is created, you use the `mke2fs` command to create the ext2, ext3, ext4, and vfat32 file systems.

In addition to the previous tasks, the OS performs a number of other tasks as you use your PC:

- File maintenance—Provides functions to delete, copy, move, rename, and view files, and to manage directories or folders

- Security—Controls access to sensitive files by supporting file permissions
- Quotas—Limits overuse of disk space by individual users

User Interface

In DOS, you enter commands using the command-line interface (CLI). A CLI is a method of interacting with a computer by giving it lines of textual commands (that is, a sequence of characters) from the keyboard. In its simplest form, the computer displays a prompt, you type a command with the keyboard and then press the Enter key, and the computer executes the command.

The latest interface incarnation is the GUI (usually pronounced *GOO-ee*), which is a graphical interface for using a computer rather than a purely textual interface. Windows 7 is an example of a GUI interface, as shown in Figure 2-9. From the GUI interface, you can still use a CLI.

Likewise, Fedora 13 provides a GUI interface. **GNOME** (pronounced *guh-nome*) is part of the GNU project and part of the free software, or open source, movement (see Figure 2-10). Open source software is available for anyone to modify. GNOME is a Windows-like desktop system that works on Fedora 13. GNOME's main objective is to provide a user-friendly suite of applications and an easy-to-use desktop.

Figure 2-9 Windows desktop

Source: Course Technology/Cengage Learning

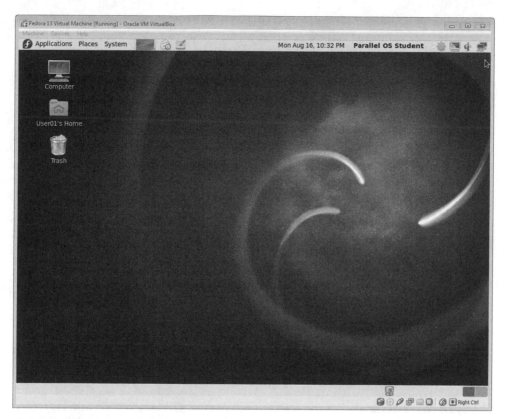

Figure 2-10 Fedora 13 GNOME desktop

Source: Course Technology/Cengage Learning

By default, Fedora 13 configures six different types of consoles for use. You may not even realize that these consoles are available. Typically, a system administrator is logged on to a PC on several different consoles (maybe with several different user IDs) at the same time. You can easily switch between consoles by simultaneously pressing the Alt and F keys of the console in use. This allows you to work efficiently on several tasks at the same time.

OS Interaction

An OS is designed to interact with the major components of a PC—hardware and applications. You need to know how the OS controls the hardware and what valuable services it provides to applications used on the PC. This section covers both types of interaction.

Interaction with Hardware

Windows 7 and Fedora 13 take different views on the interaction with hardware in a PC. All versions of Microsoft Windows after Windows 95 have implemented the **Windows Driver Model (WDM).** WDM is a technology developed by Microsoft to create drivers that are source-code compatible for a number of Windows operating systems, including Windows 7. WDM works by channeling some of the work of the device driver into portions of the code that are integrated into the operating system. The WDM device driver becomes more stream-lined with less code and works at greater efficiency. Fedora 13 divides devices into three major categories: character devices, block devices, and network devices. Each approach has merit.

The Windows View of Hardware   There are three kinds of WDM drivers:

- **Bus drivers**—Drive an I/O bus and provide per-slot functionality that is device-independent. In the context of WDM, a bus is any device to which other physical, logical, or virtual devices are attached. Windows 7 contains WDM support for the following buses: PCI, dynamic Plug and Play serial I/O buses (including USB and IEEE 1394), SCSI, NDIS, and Remote NDIS (RNDIS).

- **Function drivers**—Drive an individual device; Windows 7 contains WDM support for USB device classes, such as the Human Interface Device (HID) class, cameras/scanners, video capture over IEEE 1394, audio, and USB and IEEE 1394 storage devices.

- **Filter drivers**—Filter I/O requests for a device, a class of devices, or a bus; for example, a file system filter driver intercepts requests targeted at a file system. By intercepting the request before it reaches its intended target, the filter driver can extend the functionality provided by the original target of the request. An antivirus agent uses a filter driver to intercept files that contain viruses.

The Fedora 13 View of Hardware   Fedora 13 divides hardware devices into three major categories:

- **Character devices**—Can be accessed as streams of characters; examples include the **standard input device** (the keyboard) and the **standard output device** (the screen, or monitor). Other examples of character devices are serial ports and PCMCIA memory cards.

- **Block devices**—Handle input/output operations one or more blocks at a time; a block is normally 512 bytes, but it can be any larger power of two. Examples of block devices are disk drives, CD drives, and loop devices.

- **Networking devices**—Handled differently by the kernel than character devices or block devices; with character and block devices, the kernel uses read and write calls to deal with input and output. With networking devices, the kernel must deal with **packets** (units of information transferred over a network, or network data).

Interaction with Applications

Operating systems provide a software platform on top of which other programs, called application programs, can run. These application programs require support from the operating system. The following sections explain important OS interactions with applications:

- Installing applications
- Running applications
- Managing disks and files
- Connecting to a network
- Printing documents

Installing Applications When you obtain a software application, you must install it before you can use it. Most applications today are installed from a CD-ROM. When requested, the OS installs the application, copying the program files to the hard drive, creating an entry on a start menu or application menu, and configuring the application for your use. If software is not installed from a CD-ROM, the software is downloaded from a Web site and installed.

The **Microsoft Windows Installer** is an installation and configuration service that ships as part of the Microsoft Windows 7 operating system. Using the Windows Installer, administrators keep software up to date by efficiently installing and configuring products and applications.

Fedora 13 uses **YUM** (Yellowdog Updater, Modified), which is the most common utility for installing and configuring software on Red Hat Linux systems such as Fedora 13. YUM is an automatic updater and package installer/remover for RPM packages. The name **RPM (Red Hat Package Manager)** refers to the software packaged in this format. It automatically determines how to safely install, remove, and update RPM packages. YUM efficiently and easily retrieves information on any package installed or available in a repository.

Running Applications What happens when you type a command or click a program icon? The OS performs a series of steps:

- When you logged on to your PC, your privileges and group membership(s) were determined by the OS. These group memberships are used to control access to the resources on the PC. Whenever a thread or process interacts with a file or tries to perform a system task that requires privileges, the OS checks to determine your level of authorization.

- The OS provides an address space (a range of available memory addresses) for the program. The address space has a specific range of values; the limits of this range restrict the amount of memory available to the executing process.

- The OS loads the program into the address space and schedules the process or thread for execution.

- The OS monitors the execution of the thread or process.

- The OS shares the processor resources by multitasking—that is, concurrently running all active processes and threads on the system.

- When the executing program requests it, input/output operations are queued for execution. The OS opens the requested device and reads the requested data or writes data to the indicated device.

- When the program requests termination, connections to the devices are closed and the address space is released.

Managing Disks and Files The OS provides an organized storage system to aid in the location of files. Data files are arranged in a hierarchy according to standards that vary by operating system. You need to understand this arrangement to efficiently store the data you generate with various applications.

Windows 7 implements a folder structure to store and organize files, just as you use manila folders to organize information in a filing cabinet. Fedora 13 organizes files in a hierarchical structure similar to Windows 7, but uses the term *directories* instead of folders.

In Windows 7, you view the folder structure and file attributes with Windows Explorer. Fedora 13 provides a number of tools to view the directory structure and filenames. For example, you will learn to use the ls and tree commands in Chapter 6.

You also need to be aware of the concept of a **home directory**, which the OS provides for a user to store data. In Fedora 13, you use the /home directory. In Windows 7, the "home" folder is named after the user's logon. Each user has a set of personal folders, as shown in Figure 2-11. The home folder has a number of subfolders to store files by file types.

In either case, the OS creates the home directory when the user account is created. When you log on to the PC, the OS points to the home directory, where you can access your data files.

Windows 7 also supports the use of **libraries** to help you manage your documents, music, pictures, and other files. In some ways, a library is like a folder. For example, when you open a library, you will see one or more files. However, unlike a folder, a library gathers files that are stored in multiple locations, as shown in Figure 2-12. This is a subtle yet important difference: libraries don't actually store files. Windows 7 monitors folders that contain your files, and lets you access and arrange the files in different ways. For example, you could have your music files stored on both the internal disk drive and a USB external drive and access your files at once from the music library.

Connecting to a Network Your applications can use files that are shared and stored in a central repository, such as a file server. The OS provides the necessary support for file

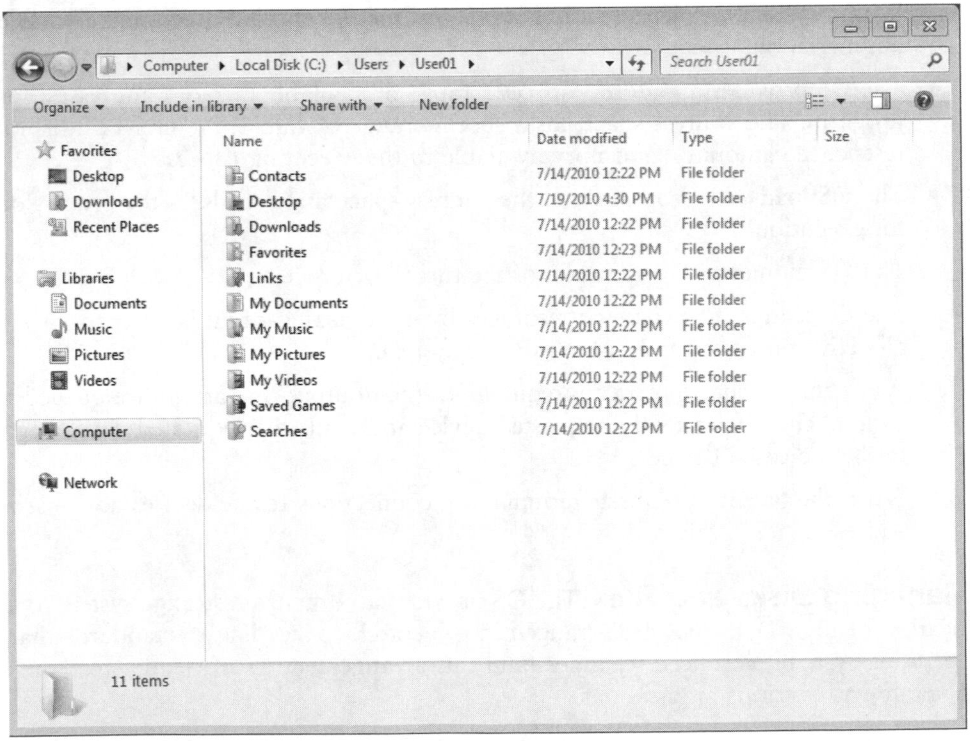

Figure 2-11 User's folders

Source: Course Technology/Cengage Learning

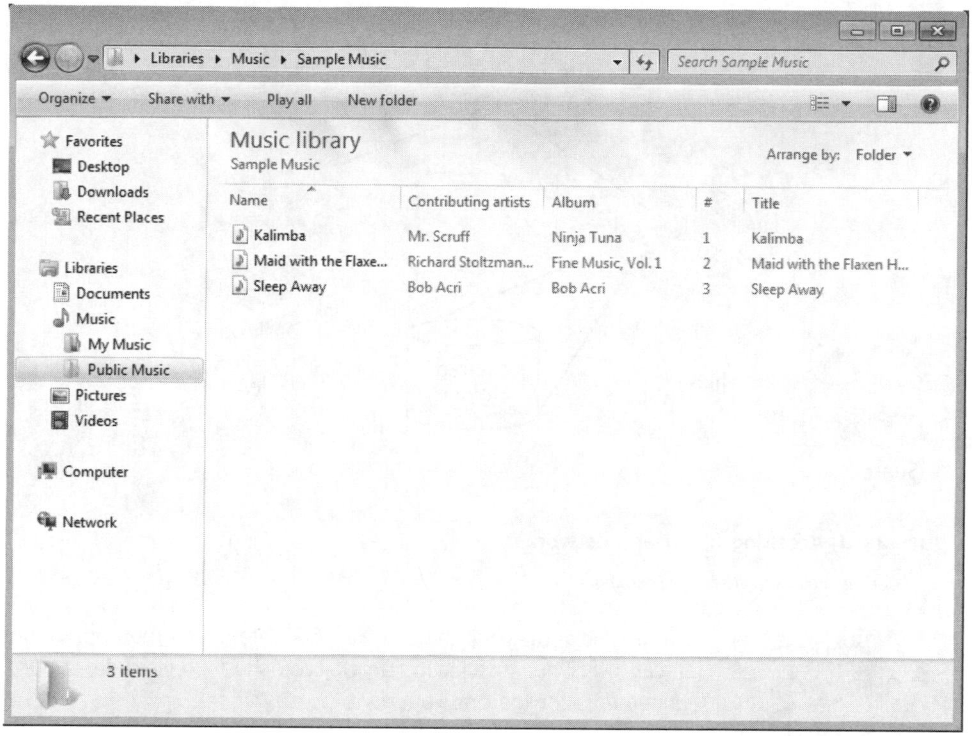

Figure 2-12 Music library

Source: Course Technology/Cengage Learning

sharing. You need to understand file sharing because it provides access to files, data, and information from multiple computers.

You can set up your PC to share the directories or folders on your hard drive with other PCs on a network, as shown in Figure 2-13. You can grant access to desired users and keep other users out. This sharing of resources is not limited to files. To save costs, for example, you could share a laser printer with several others on your network.

Windows-based operating systems support file-sharing traffic across a network by using the **Server Message Block (SMB)** communications protocol. Fedora 13 provides equivalent access capabilities using **Samba**.

Windows 7 provides the **Network folder** in Windows Explorer to locate and connect to shared folders on networked computers. With Fedora 13, you connect to the remote share by using the Network command within File Browser.

You will continue to learn more about network connections in Chapter 11.

Printing Documents The primary output for most documents is the printed page. The OS provides access to local and network printers. Windows 7 provides the **Add Printer Wizard** to make a printer available for your applications. In Fedora 13, you use the **Add Printer** program to set up your printer. Once the printer is installed and configured, you use it as indicated by your application.

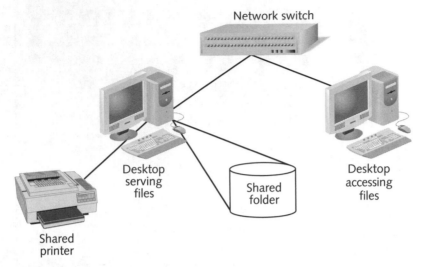

Figure 2-13 Accessing files over a network

Source: Course Technology/Cengage Learning

To a great extent, your choice of an OS determines the applications you can use. Prior to selecting an OS, you should review the support requirements for the one you want to use.

System Utilities

You use system utilities to perform various tasks on your PC. Key utilities include text editors, configuration editors, and system information monitors, as explained in the following sections.

Text Editors

A **text editor** allows you to enter, modify, and delete data in a text file. Text files are used for many purposes; for example, you can write source code for a program in a text editor. In fact, most source code is stored in text files. As a network administrator, you may write many scripts, most of which will be stored in text files. You will learn to use three text editors in Chapter 8.

Most system utilities only know how to deal with text files. In DOS, the `type` command lists the contents of a text file within the command prompt window, as shown in Figure 2-14. For example, you can use the `type` command to show the contents of the hosts TCP/IP configuration file.

In Fedora 13, the `cat` command performs the same function as the `type` command. For example, you can use the command to display the contents of the hosts file on the standard output device (the computer monitor). See Figure 2-15.

Files in other formats normally require specific programs to handle them.

Operating System Configuration

As an administrator, you may need to update many PC configuration entries. Within Windows, you may need to make entries to the **Registry,** a hierarchical database that contains

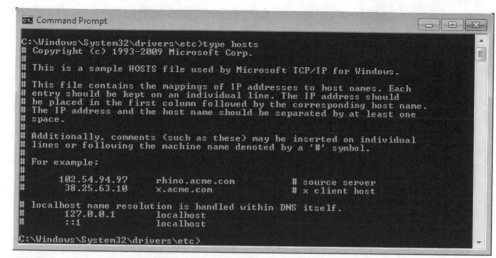

Figure 2-14 Text file listed with DOS type command

Source: Course Technology/Cengage Learning

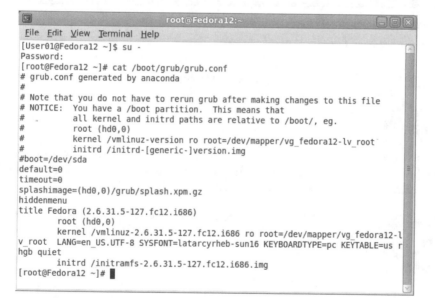

Figure 2-15 Text file listed with `cat` command

Source: Course Technology/Cengage Learning

configuration entries. Most of the configuration files in Fedora 13 that control a computer system are stored as text files.

Windows 7 Configuration Regedit is a special utility that allows a system administrator to edit Registry entries (see Figure 2-16). Microsoft uses the Registry in Windows to hold a tremendous amount of information that is critical to the normal operation of your PC. You need to be exposed to the Registry, but do not attempt to edit it in any manner.

Figure 2-16 showing the Registry Editor window with the navigation tree on the left (Computer, HKEY_CLASSES_ROOT, HKEY_CURRENT_USER, HKEY_LOCAL_MACHINE, etc.) and the registry entries table on the right:

Name	Type	Data
(Default)	REG_SZ	(value not set)
BootArchitecture	REG_DWORD	0x00000003 (3)
Capabilities	REG_DWORD	0x00000541 (1345)
Component Inf...	REG_BINARY	00 00 00 00 00 00 00 00 00 00 00 00 00 00 00 00
Configuration D...	REG_FULL_RESOU...	ff ff ff ff ff ff ff ff 00 00 00 00 02 00 00 00 05 00 00 00 24 00 00 00 00 ...
Identifier	REG_SZ	AT/AT COMPATIBLE
PreferredProfile	REG_DWORD	0x00000000 (0)
SystemBiosDate	REG_SZ	06/23/99
SystemBiosVersi...	REG_MULTI_SZ	VBOX - 1
VideoBiosVersion	REG_MULTI_SZ	Sun VirtualBox Version 3.2.6 VGA BIOS Sun VirtualBox Version 3.2....

Computer\HKEY_LOCAL_MACHINE\HARDWARE\DESCRIPTION\System

Figure 2-16 Registry entries displayed with Regedit

Source: Course Technology/Cengage Learning

Editing the Registry is an advanced skill that most normal users should not attempt. One small mistake in editing the Registry can be fatal to your PC.

Rather than using a Registry like Windows 7, Fedora 13 maintains most configuration settings in text files within the /etc directory. If necessary, these text files can be edited with the VIM text editor. You will learn about this editor in Chapter 8.

You must take great care when editing the text files in the /etc directory. If you make errors during editing, you could disable your computer.

visudo in Fedora 13 In Fedora 13, one configuration file—sudoers in the /etc directory—requires the use of a **configuration editor**. As an administrator, you normally have permissions to execute any command. Users are typically divided into groups based on function. Each group often has a group administrator who has permission to execute system commands needed to manage the group. The /etc/sudoers file holds the configuration that allows group administrators to execute privileged instructions and do their jobs. You must edit this file with the **visudo command** (see Figure 2-17).

You should not edit the sudoers file with a text editor. One small mistake in editing this file can be fatal to your PC.

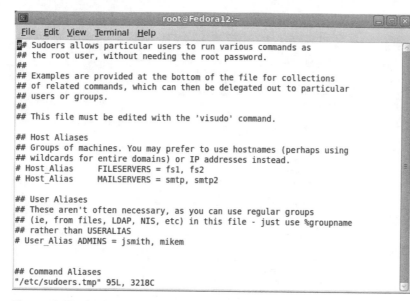

Figure 2-17 Editing with `visudo` command

Source: Course Technology/Cengage Learning

System Information

You can view information about your PC by using the information tools provided by the OS. In Windows 7, you can use the Help and Support tool for information about your system. In Fedora 13, you can use the System Profiler.

Windows 7 System Information The System Information tool provides summary information and configuration information about the computer. To access and use this tool, see Activity 2-1. Figure 2-18 shows the System Summary of the System Information tool.

Activity 2-1: Reviewing Processor Information

Time Required: 10 minutes

Objective: Use Windows Help and Support to review information about your PC's processor.

Description: In this activity, you start the Windows 7 virtual machine and review its system information. This activity is useful if you want to obtain system information.

1. Start your virtual machines using the appropriate instructions in Activity 1-1. Click **Start**, click **Help and Support**, type **system information** over "Search Help," and then press **Enter**.

2. Click the **What is System Information** link, and then click the **Click to open System Information** link.

3. Review the system information in the right pane.

4. Close the System Information and Help and Support Center windows.

5. Leave the virtual machine logged on for future activities.

System Information		
File Edit View Help		

System Summary
  ⊞ Hardware Resources
  ⊞ Components
  ⊞ Software Environment

Item	Value
OS Name	Microsoft Windows 7 Enterprise
Version	6.1.7600 Build 7600
Other OS Description	Not Available
OS Manufacturer	Microsoft Corporation
System Name	WINDOWS7
System Manufacturer	innotek GmbH
System Model	VirtualBox
System Type	X86-based PC
Processor	Intel(R) Core(TM)2 Duo CPU E6750 @ 2.66GHz, 2569 Mhz, 1 C
BIOS Version/Date	innotek GmbH VirtualBox, 12/1/2006
SMBIOS Version	2.5
Windows Directory	C:\Windows
System Directory	C:\Windows\system32
Boot Device	\Device\HarddiskVolume1
Locale	United States
Hardware Abstraction Layer	Version = "6.1.7600.16385"
User Name	Windows7\User01
Time Zone	Central Daylight Time
Installed Physical Memory (RAM)	Not Available
Total Physical Memory	1.00 GB
Available Physical Memory	717 MB
Total Virtual Memory	2.00 GB

Find what: [   ]   [Find]   [Close Find]

☐ Search selected category only   ☐ Search category names only

Figure 2-18 System Information tool

Source: Course Technology/Cengage Learning

Fedora 13 System Profiler To see what type of CPU your computer uses, click Applications, point to System Tools, and click System Profiler and Benchmark. To review the system summary, click Summary. The summary is shown in Figure 2-19.

Activity 2-2: Using the Fedora 13 System Profiler

Time Required: 15 minutes

Objective: Use the Fedora 13 System Profiler to review summary information about the system. Note that you cannot perform this activity until you install the hardinfo program, as described in Appendix C.

Description: In this activity, you start the Fedora 13 virtual machine and then review system information. This activity is useful if you want to review processes and the performance of your virtual machine.

1. If necessary, start your virtual machines using the appropriate instructions in Activity 1-1.

2. To open the System Profiler, click **Applications**, point to **System Tools**, and then click **System Profiler and Benchmark**.

3. Click **Summary** and review the system information.

4. Close the window.

5. Leave the virtual machine logged on for future activities.

System Monitors

To help you identify problem areas and obtain the best service possible, it is important that you know exactly what is happening in your PC. As a system administrator, you use many

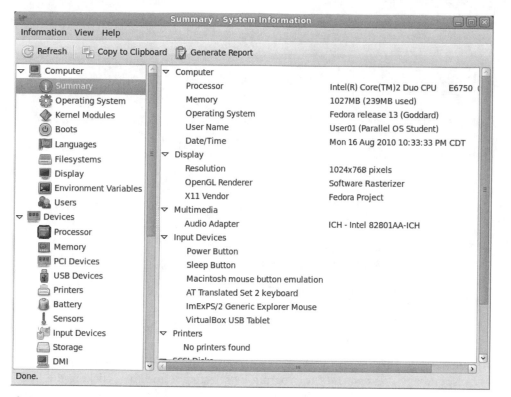

Figure 2-19 Summary in System Profiler

Source: Course Technology/Cengage Learning

tools to perform daily tasks. In Windows 7, you can use the **Task Manager** to see useful information about system performance; in Fedora 13, you use **System Monitor**.

To a system administrator, the most important question is "What do I need to do?" Once you answer this question, using the Task Manager or System Monitor is easy.

Windows Task Manager You use Task Manager to monitor applications and processes that are running on your computer. For example, when using Task Manager, you can selectively stop a hung application or process to get out of a jam. You can start Task Manager in one of three ways:

- Press Ctrl+Alt+Delete.
- Press Ctrl+Shift+Esc.
- Right-click an empty area of the taskbar and click Task Manager from the menu.

You can use the tabs shown in Figure 2-20 to control applications and processes as well as view system and network performance. The following sections discuss many of these tabs.

A sixth tab, Users, is available if your computer system is in a Windows workgroup or is a stand-alone system with no networking capabilities installed. This tab is not available to computer systems in a domain network.

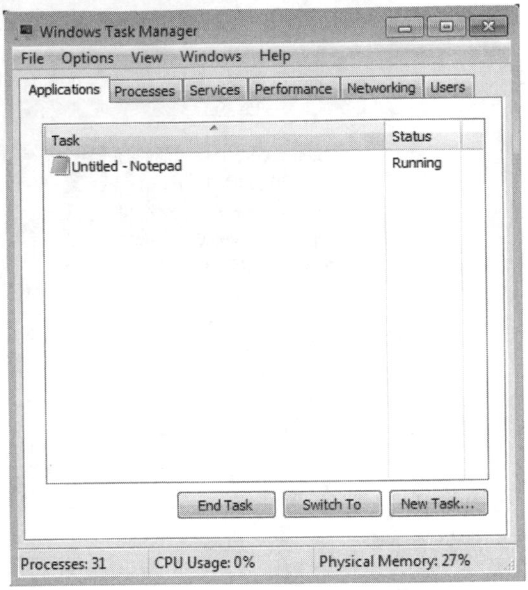

Figure 2-20 Windows Task Manager

Source: Course Technology/Cengage Learning

Applications Tab From the Applications tab, you can determine if a program is hung or not responding. You can end the program by selecting it and then clicking the End Task button. You can use the other two buttons to switch to a listed program or start a new program.

Processes Tab You can use the Processes tab (see Figure 2-21) to view the names of processes running on the computer and to display processor (CPU) and memory usage. You can

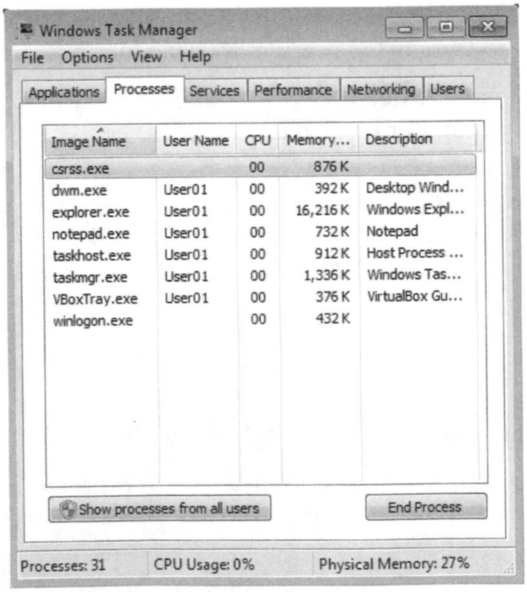

Figure 2-21 Processes tab of Windows Task Manager

Source: Course Technology/Cengage Learning

then use this information to troubleshoot problems by determining which programs are using the most processing or memory. A program with an abnormally high CPU value could be hung. A program with an extremely large amount of memory usage might have a memory leak—memory usage of a process grows without bounds. To stop a process, select the program and click the End Process button. On this tab, you can sort any column of data by clicking the column name.

 By ending a process, you could render your computer unstable or lose valuable data in memory! Be careful.

Performance Tab From the Performance tab (see Figure 2-22), you can quickly review your computer's CPU usage and memory usage. You can also see a variety of counts for other items on your computer, which are of lesser value for troubleshooting. A high CPU usage (consistently over 90 percent) indicates that the processor speed is inadequate. A high rate of page file activity indicates that the computer needs additional RAM memory. To access more detailed information, click the Resource Monitor button.

Networking Tab You can use the Networking tab, as shown in Figure 2-23, to view a graph of network activity related to the computer's network card. This tab is only displayed when a network card is present.

Windows Resource Monitor You can click the Resource Monitor button on the Performance tab to monitor the usage of four critical resources: CPU, hard disk, network, and memory. Resource Monitor automatically opens to the Overview tab. Figure 2-24

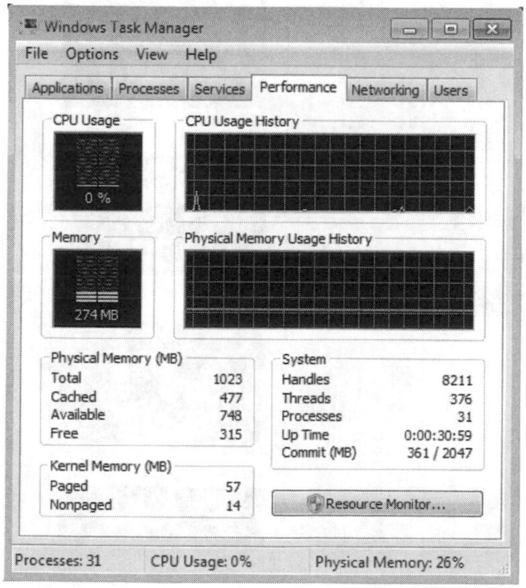

Figure 2-22 Performance tab of Windows Task Manager

Source: Course Technology/Cengage Learning

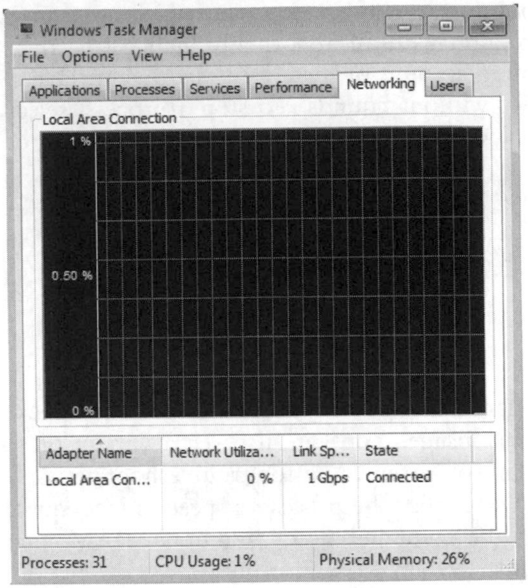

Figure 2-23 Networking tab of Windows Task Manager

Source: Course Technology/Cengage Learning

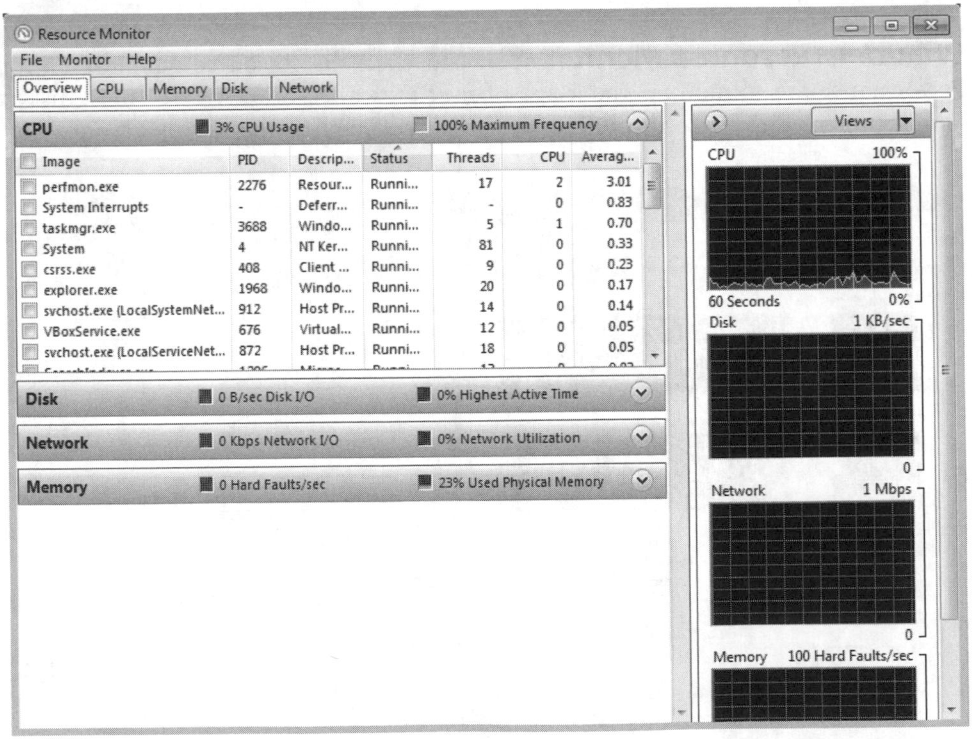

Figure 2-24 Resource Monitor showing CPU details

Source: Course Technology/Cengage Learning

shows an overview of resource usage. In addition, four graphs appear along the right side. Click one of the four chevrons to reveal more detailed information. Click the CPU, Memory, Disk, or Network tab for additional information and statistics for each of these components.

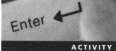

Activity 2-3: Using the Windows 7 Task Manager

Time Required: 15 minutes

Objective: Use the Windows 7 Task Manager to see how the PC is performing.

Description: In this activity, you open the Applications tab of the Task Manager and review information about which applications are running. Open the Processes tab to review the processes running on the PC in Windows. To quickly review CPU performance on the PC, click the Performance tab. Below the performance chart, you can review a number of key counters to determine the number of active objects (handles), threads with all processes, and processes. Next, you review the total memory in use in the Commit (MB) field. Finally, you will explore the Resource Monitor for additional information. This activity is useful if you want to review tasks and the performance of your PC.

1. If necessary, start your virtual machines using the appropriate instructions in Activity 1-1.

2. To start the Task Manager, right-click the **taskbar** and then click **Start Task Manager**.

3. To determine which applications are running, click the **Applications** tab, if necessary.

4. Review the applications listed.

5. To determine which processes are running and review them, click the **Processes** tab.

To sort information by a particular column in the Processes tab, click the column heading. For example, to locate the process that is using the most CPU resources, click the CPU heading.

6. To review performance for CPU usage, click the **Performance** tab.

7. To determine the number of active objects, threads with all processes, and processes, review the data in the Totals section.

8. To determine the amount of memory in use, review the **Commit (MB)** field.

9. To obtain more detailed information, click the **Resource Monitor** button.

10. Review the process in the CPU pane and then click the **CPU** chevron.

11. To review the disk usage, click the **Disk** chevron. After reviewing the disk usage, click the **Disk** chevron again.

12. To review network usage, click the **Network** chevron. After reviewing the network usage, click the **Network** chevron again.

13. To review memory usage, click the **Memory** chevron. After reviewing the memory usage, click the **Memory** chevron again.

14. Close all the windows within the Windows 7 virtual machine.

15. Leave the virtual machine logged on for future activities.

Fedora 13 System Monitor You can use System Monitor to review process activity in real time. The utility displays a list of the most CPU-intensive tasks on the PC. Figure 2-25 shows the process activity sorted by percentage of CPU usage. To sort by the % CPU column, click its column heading. By default, the display is updated every five seconds.

System Monitor contains more tabs than just the Processes tab. As shown in Figure 2-26, the System tab displays a summary of the operating system and processor.

From the Resources tab (see Figure 2-27), you can review real-time information about the following performance measures:

- CPU History—The graphic shows CPU usage and current percentage of CPU usage.
- Memory and swap usage—The graphic shows memory and swap space usage.
- Network activity—The graphic shows network activity in terms of bytes received and sent.

Figure 2-28 shows the File Systems tab in System Monitor, which displays the total space, free space, and available space for each allocated partition.

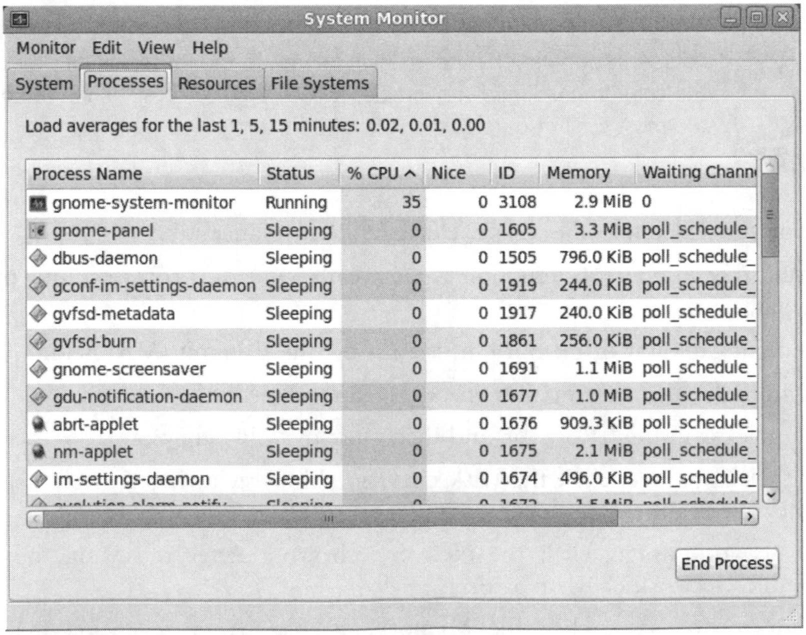

Figure 2-25 Process activity shown in Fedora 13 System Monitor

Source: Course Technology/Cengage Learning

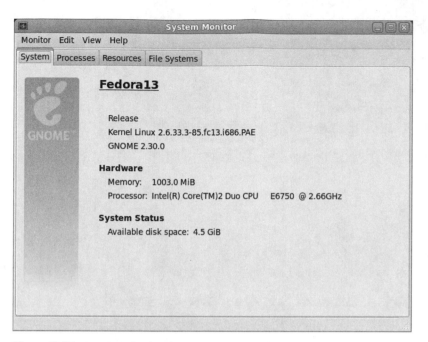

Figure 2-26 System tab of Fedora 13 System Monitor

Source: Course Technology/Cengage Learning

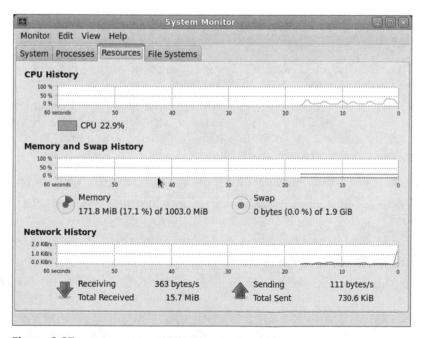

Figure 2-27 Resources tab of Fedora 13 System Monitor

Source: Course Technology/Cengage Learning

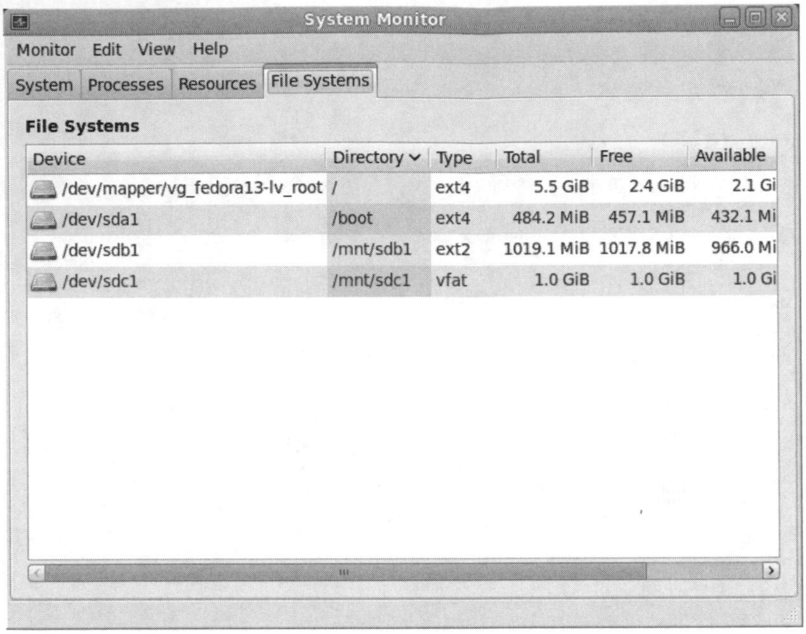

	System Monitor	□◻☒
Monitor Edit View Help		

System | Processes | Resources | **File Systems**

File Systems

Device	Directory ∨	Type	Total	Free	Available
/dev/mapper/vg_fedora13-lv_root	/	ext4	5.5 GiB	2.4 GiB	2.1 Gi
/dev/sda1	/boot	ext4	484.2 MiB	457.1 MiB	432.1 Mi
/dev/sdb1	/mnt/sdb1	ext2	1019.1 MiB	1017.8 MiB	966.0 Mi
/dev/sdc1	/mnt/sdc1	vfat	1.0 GiB	1.0 GiB	1.0 Gi

Figure 2-28 File Systems tab of Fedora 13 System Monitor

Source: Course Technology/Cengage Learning

Activity 2-4: Using the Fedora 13 System Monitor

Time Required: 15 minutes

Objective: Use the Fedora 13 System Monitor to review the performance of the virtual machine.

Description: In this activity, you open System Monitor in Fedora 13. From the Processes tab, you sort by percentage of CPU usage to locate the active processes. Use the other tabs to view important information about your system. This activity is useful if you want to review processes and the performance of your virtual machine.

1. If necessary, start your virtual machines using the appropriate instructions in Activity 1-1.
2. To open System Monitor, click **Applications**, point to **System Tools,** and then click **System Monitor**.
3. To review the OS and hardware summary, click the **System** tab.
4. To review the processes, click the **Processes** tab.
5. To determine the most active processes, click the **% CPU** button until the chevron points up.
6. To see the graphs for system resources, click the **Resources** tab.
7. To determine the amount of free disk space, click the **File Systems** tab.
8. Close the System Monitor window.
9. Leave the virtual machine logged on for future activities.

Applications

You use many applications on your PC, including word processors, spreadsheets, presentation software, a Web browser, an e-mail client, games, and graphics software. It is not unusual for an application to be made up of many smaller programs that work together. Applications are the reason that people use computers.

Microsoft Office is a suite of programs developed for the Windows OS. Its components include:

- Microsoft Word—A word processor that is considered the main program in Office 2010; it possesses a dominant share of the word-processor market. Its proprietary DOC format is considered a de facto standard, although its most recent version also supports an XML-based format.

- Microsoft Excel—A spreadsheet program; like Microsoft Word, it possesses a dominant market share. It was originally a competitor to Lotus 1-2-3, but it eventually became the de facto standard.

- Microsoft PowerPoint—A popular presentation program; it is used to create slide shows composed of text, graphics, movies, and other objects. The slides can be displayed on screen or printed on transparencies or slides.

OpenOffice.org is a collection of applications that work closely together to provide the features expected from a modern office suite. Many of the components are designed to mirror those in Microsoft Office. In addition to running on Fedora 13, OpenOffice runs on Windows versions after Windows 95, on Solaris and FreeBSD, and on Mac OS X. Its components include:

- Writer—A word processor that has a similar look and feel to Microsoft Word and offers a widely overlapping range of functions and tools; Writer allows you to create Portable Document Format (PDF) files with no additional software.

- Calc—A spreadsheet that is similar to Microsoft Excel and has a similar range of features; Calc also provides features that are not present in Excel, including a system that automatically defines series for graphing, based on the layout of the user's data. Calc can also write spreadsheets directly as PDF files.

- Impress—A presentation program that is similar to Microsoft PowerPoint; Impress can export presentations to Macromedia Flash (SWF) files, allowing them to be played on any computer that has the Flash player installed. You also can create PDF files with Impress.

NOTE If you are running the Fedora 13 OS, OpenOffice is an excellent choice. For Windows 7 users, OpenOffice is an inexpensive choice—it's free. However, if you are a student who shares documents with users running Microsoft Office, the Office Home and Student Edition would be a better choice for Windows 7.

The number of business applications supported by Fedora 13 continues to grow. Table 2-2 lists various categories of applications and the offerings for Windows 7 and Fedora 13 in each category.

Freeware for Windows 7

Freeware is software that is available free of charge for personal use. Freeware is frequently distributed on the Web. Although it is available at no cost, the author retains the copyright,

Category	Windows 7	Fedora 13
Web browser	Microsoft Internet Explorer	Firefox, Netscape, Opera, Google Chrome
E-mail client	Outlook Express	Evolution, Thunderbird
Project management	Microsoft Project	Planner
Diagramming	Microsoft Visio	Dia
Image editing	Adobe Photoshop	GIMP
PDF reader	Adobe Acrobat	Adobe Acrobat
Database	Microsoft Access	Rekall RAD DBMS
FTP client	GlobalSCAPE CuteFTP	gFTP

Table 2-2 **Business applications**

Category	Freeware product	Web site for downloading
Web browser	Firefox	*www.mozilla.org/products/firefox/*
Antivirus software	AVG	*http://free.grisoft.com/*
Firewall	Zone Alarm	*www.zonelabs.com/store/content/company/products/znalm/freeDownload.jsp*
Office suite	OpenOffice	*www.openoffice.org/*
Text editor	Metapad	*www.liquidninja.com/metapad/*

Table 2-3 **Freeware for Windows 7**

which means that it cannot be altered or sold. See Table 2-3 for examples of freeware that is available for Windows 7.

Activity 2-5: Using the Windows WordPad Application

Time Required: 15 minutes

Objective: Use the WordPad application to write a short note.

Description: In this activity, you use the WordPad application to write a short paragraph detailing your experiences with Windows 7 and Fedora 13. (WordPad is an example of a Windows application that is installed by default.) This activity is useful if you want to type a short note while working on your PC.

1. If necessary, start your virtual machines using the appropriate instructions in Activity 1-1.

2. To start WordPad, click **Start**, point to **All Programs**, click **Accessories**, and click **WordPad**.

3. Type a short note about your experiences with Windows 7 and Fedora 13.

4. Click the **WordPad chevron** (located in the upper-left corner of the WordPad ribbon), click **Save As**, type **Note***fml* (where *fml* represents your initials), and then click **Save**.

5. Close all the windows within the Windows 7 virtual machine.

6. To shut down the virtual machine, click **Start,** and then click the **Shut Down** button.

7. Wait a moment for the Windows 7 virtual machine to completely shut down.

8. Leave the PC logged on for the next activity.

Activity 2-6: Using the Fedora 13 OpenOffice Application

Time Required: 15 minutes

Objective: Use the OpenOffice application to write a short note.

Description: This activity is similar to Activity 2-5, but this time you use a Fedora 13 application—OpenOffice.org Writer—to write a short paragraph detailing your experiences with Windows 7 and Fedora 13. (OpenOffice.org Writer is an example of a Fedora 13 application that is installed by default.) This activity is useful if you want to type a short note with a Fedora 13 application.

1. If necessary, start your virtual machines using the appropriate instructions in Activity 1-1.

2. To start OpenOffice Writer, click **Applications,** point to **Office,** and then click **OpenOffice.org Writer.**

3. Based on your reading so far in this text, type a short note about whether you might prefer to use Windows 7 or Fedora 13.

4. Click the **File** menu, click **Save As,** type **Note**_fml_ (where _fml_ represents your initials), and then click **Save.**

5. Close the OpenOffice.org Writer window.

6. To shut down the virtual machine, click **System,** click **Shut Down,** and then click the **Shut Down** button.

7. Wait a moment for the Fedora 13 virtual machine to completely shut down.

8. Close any remaining open windows, log off, and shut down your PC.

Chapter Summary

- The software components of a PC are used to perform a variety of tasks. All components work together, many without a user's knowledge. Each component plays a specific role in the PC's overall performance, and no component is less important than another. PC resources are managed by many programs working within the operating system.

- The first OS for the PC was DOS. The core of a PC's operating system is the kernel, which is where the hardware is secured and each application is serviced.

- The OS manages resources by controlling the processor, memory, devices, storage, and the user interface. Modern operating systems support preemptive multitasking, multithreading, and virtual memory.

- The OS interacts with both hardware and applications. For example, the OS interacts with applications by installing and running them. The OS provides disk and network access as well as printing.

- Many operating systems exist for PCs. The most common are DOS, Windows, and Fedora 13. Each has evolved from its inception to allow users to work with editors, graphical user interfaces, and peripheral devices such as printers, keyboards, monitors, and disk drives. The best operating systems are stable, secure, and scalable products.

- The operating system works with different system utilities to perform various tasks on your PC. Operating systems use different terminology and utilities to perform these tasks. For example, to update a configuration file, you need a configuration editor. When using Windows 7, you use Regedit to update a Registry file; with Fedora 13, you use the visudo command to edit the /etc/sudoers file. When you need to monitor your system, you use Task Manager in Windows 7 and System Monitor in Fedora 13. Different types of editors are used depending on whether the Registry or configuration file refers to the operating system, utilities, or applications.

- You use many applications on your PC, including word processors, spreadsheets, and a Web browser.

Key Terms

Add Printer   A utility used in Fedora 13 to make a printer available for your applications.

Add Printer Wizard   A wizard used in Windows 7 to make a printer available for your applications.

application   A program that helps users perform tasks on a PC, such as creating a spreadsheet.

block device   A device that moves information in blocks or groups of bytes instead of characters. An example is a disk drive.

bus driver   A WDM driver for an I/O bus. It provides per-slot functionality that is device driven.

character device   A device that transmits or receives information as streams of characters, one character at a time. An example is a keyboard.

command-line interface (CLI)   A program you use to give commands to an operating system.

configuration editor   A special program that helps you create or edit files that contain specific operating instructions for a PC.

cooperative multitasking   A form of multitasking in which each process controls the length of time it maintains exclusive control over the CPU.

core   The part of the processor that actually reads and executes instructions.

DOS   A generic term for any operating system that is loaded from disk devices when the system is started or restarted.

dynamic link library (DLL)   A library of executable functions or data that can be used by a Windows 7 application.

Fast User Switching   A feature in Windows 7 that allows users to switch between user accounts on a single PC without quitting applications and logging out.

filter driver   A WDM driver that filters the I/O requests for a device, a class of devices, or a bus.

freeware   Software that is available free of charge for personal use. Freeware is frequently distributed on the Web.

function driver   A WDM driver that drives an individual device.

GDI (graphical device interface)   The display language interface for Microsoft Windows systems.

Ghostscript   A suite of free software based on an interpreter of the Adobe PostScript and Portable Document Format (PDF) page description languages.

GNOME   The default desktop for Red Hat's distribution of Fedora 13.

GNU General Public License   A set of programs written by the Free Software Foundation to provide a free UNIX framework. (GNU stands for "GNU's Not UNIX.")

home directory   A directory associated with a user account under Fedora 13.

kernel   The core of an operating system. The kernel manages memory, files, and peripheral devices, as well as starting applications and allocating system resources.

libraries   File structures that help you manage your documents, music, pictures, and other files.

Linux   Refers to the family of UNIX-like computer operating systems that use the Linux kernel.

Microsoft Windows Installer   An installation and configuration service that ships as part of the Windows 7 operating system.

multiprocessing   The simultaneous execution of instructions by multiple processors within a single computer.

multitasking   Concurrently running all active processes and threads on the PC.

multithreading   Running several processes in rapid sequence (multitasking) within a single program.

Network folder   A folder used to locate and connect to shared folders on networked computers.

networking device   A category used by Fedora 13 for network devices. The Fedora 13 kernel uses packets with these devices.

packet   A unit of information transferred as a whole from one device to another on a network.

physical address   A number that identifies an actual storage (memory) location in the physical memory on a computer.

PostScript   A page description language developed and marketed by Adobe Systems.

preemptive multitasking   A multitasking process in which the OS ensures that all active threads have the opportunity to execute. Preemptive multitasking prevents a single thread from monopolizing a processor.

Regedit   An application that allows the user to edit the entries in the Registry.

Registry   A central hierarchical database used by Windows 7 to store information that is needed to configure the system for one or more users, applications, and hardware devices.

RPM (Red Hat Package Manager)   The Fedora 13 manager that provides installation services for applications.

Samba   A communications protocol used by Fedora 13 to support resource sharing across a network.

Server Message Block (SMB)   A communications protocol used by Windows-based operating systems to support resource sharing across a network.

software components   A collection of applications that make up and relate to the operating system.

standard input device   A computer device used for data input, such as a keyboard.

standard output device   Another term for a computer monitor.

symmetric multiprocessing (SMP)   A system that distributes tasks among CPUs using a load-sharing method.

System Monitor   A utility in Fedora 13 that lets you review process activity in real time.

Task Manager   An application used to track the progress of and provide necessary resources for separate tasks running on a Windows computer.

text editor   A program that allows a user to create or edit text files.

thread   The basic unit of program execution. A process can have several threads running concurrently, each performing a different job.

utility   A program that performs system-related tasks and maintenance on the operating system.

virtual address   A memory location that intervening hardware and software map to physical memory.

visudo command   The command in Fedora 13 used to edit the /etc/sudoers file.

Windows Driver Model (WDM)   A 32-bit architecture for creating Windows device drivers.

YUM   An installation and configuration service that ships as part of Fedora 13.

Review Questions

1. Which of the following are considered an operating system kernel's job? (Choose all that apply.)

   a.   making certain that the application is serviced properly

   b.   managing all the resources in a computer system

   c.   installing all hardware for a computer system

   d.   securing the hardware

2. Which of the following management tasks are functions of an operating system? (Choose all that apply.)

   a.   processing

   b.   memory

   c.   devices

   d.   storage

   e.   applications

3. The type and cat commands are used to _____.

   a.   enter text into text files

   b.   display the contents of a text file

   c.   modify text files

   d.   modify scripts

4. To edit the Windows Registry file, you need to use _____.

   a.   Windows Regedit

   b.   the Fedora 13 visudo command

   c.   a regular text editor

   d.   Microsoft Word

5. To execute the privileged instructions in the /etc/sudoers file, a Fedora 13 system administrator would use _____ to edit the file.

    a. Notepad

    b. the vim editor

    c. the `cat` command

    d. the `visudo` command

6. To view detailed system usage information in Windows 7, you would use _____.

    a. System Profiler

    b. Windows Task Manager

    c. Windows Regedit

    d. the `visudo` command

7. Which of the following are considered applications? (Choose all that apply.)

    a. spreadsheet

    b. Web browser

    c. Internet

    d. word processor

    e. graphics software

8. The reason most people use computers is to _____.

    a. learn about operating systems

    b. repair them

    c. build additional computers at home

    d. use application software

9. How many consoles are installed with Fedora 13?

    a. 2

    b. 1

    c. 4

    d. 6

10. Which of the following tabs are displayed by the Task Manager? (Choose all that apply.)

    a. Applications

    b. Programs

    c. Performance

    d. Networking

11. Which of the following are categories of drivers for Windows? (Choose all that apply.)

    a. bus drivers

    b. block drivers

    c. function drivers

    d. filter drivers

    e. network drivers

12. Which of the following are categories of devices for Fedora 13? (Choose all that apply.)

    a. function devices

    b. network devices

    c. bus devices

    d. character devices

    e. block devices

13. A _____ is an example of a Fedora 13 character device.

    a. keyboard

    b. CD drive

    c. packet

    d. disk drive

14. A _____ is an example of a Fedora 13 block device.

    a. serial port

    b. disk drive

    c. packet

    d. keyboard

15. Which of the following are examples of Windows devices that are controlled by a bus driver? (Choose all that apply.)

    a. PCI

    b. USB

    c. SCSI

    d. keyboard

16. Microsoft Windows Installer _____.

    a. needs to be purchased separately

    b. needs to be installed by the user

    c. does not exist as of the printing of this text

    d. ships as part of the Microsoft Windows 7 operating system

17. The protocol used for file sharing in Windows 7 is _____.
  a. Samba
  b. Add Network Places
  c. the `mount` command
  d. SMB

18. To share files in Fedora 13, you need to use _____.
  a. the `mount` command
  b. Add Network Places
  c. SMB
  d. Samba

19. The disk operating system (DOS) was first used with _____.
  a. Fedora 13
  b. IBM PCs
  c. Windows 7
  d. MorphOS

20. Which of the following are applications of OpenOffice? (Choose all that apply.)
  a. Word
  b. Calc
  c. Excel
  d. PowerPoint
  e. Impress

Case Projects

CASE PROJECTS

Case 2-1: Viewing the Performance of a PC

Your boss is concerned that several Windows 7 and Fedora 13 computers are running near capacity. What tools could help you gain additional insight into this problem? Create a short report for your boss that details how to obtain and interpret this information.

Case 2-2: Comparing Word-Processing Applications

You see an opportunity to save your company money by adopting the OpenOffice suite for the new PCs in the Engineering Department. Your boss is interested in your suggestion, but wants to see a list of pros and cons for using the Microsoft Office system versus using the OpenOffice suite. Prepare the list.

Case 2-3: Discussing the Functions of an Operating System

You have been selected to present a short talk on the functions of an operating system for the weekly tech meeting. To support your talk, you must prepare a handout for the attendees. The handout should include a summary outline of the information that you have learned about this topic.

Case 2-4: Discussing How Applications Interact
with Operating Systems

You have been asked to prepare a short lecture for users in the Accounting Department. They have expressed interest in learning more about how the operating system supports the applications they use. Your boss would like to review your lecture notes prior to the class, so you need to save them to a document. Your notes should provide details of your lecture.

Using the Graphical User Interface

After reading this chapter and completing the exercises, you will be able to:

- Use the Start menu and Applications menu
- Tailor the desktop
- Access data on your computer

A graphical user interface (or GUI, sometimes pronounced "gooey") is a method of interacting with a PC by manipulating visual elements such as icons and windows. Xerox developed the first GUI as the primary interface for its Alto computer in 1973, and most modern GUIs are derived from it. Besides icons and windows, a GUI consists of such graphical elements as menus, radio buttons, and check boxes, and employs a pointing device such as a mouse or a trackball to manipulate these elements. Microsoft used many of these ideas in its first version of Windows.

One benefit of using GUIs is that they standardize how you use computer programs. In other words, once you become proficient with a GUI, you can pick up other GUI programs more quickly and reduce your learning curve.

In this chapter, you will learn about the Windows Start menu and the Applications menu in Fedora 13. You will also learn how to tailor the desktop and how to access local and network data resources. Access to local resources is easy when you use a GUI.

Using the Start Menu and Applications Menu

The Windows **Start menu** and the **Applications menu** in Fedora 13 are launching pads for applications because both contain pointers to programs stored on the hard drive. These pointers are called **shortcuts**. In the following sections, you will learn to use and tailor these menus.

Using the Windows 7 Start Menu and Taskbar

You can access the most useful programs and documents on your Windows 7 computer by clicking the Start menu in the lower-left corner of the screen. You can also control which items appear on the Start menu by right-clicking it and opening the Properties dialog box. The default installation of Windows 7 includes icons for Recent Documents, Pictures, Music, and Computer in the Start menu.

Use the taskbar to switch rapidly between open programs. The taskbar contains a button for each open window and highlights the active window. Click a different button on the taskbar to switch to another window.

This section explains how to customize and use the Start menu and the taskbar.

Start Menu Views The default Start menu, shown in Figure 3-1, appears when you start Windows 7 for the first time.

 Illustrations of the Start menu in this chapter may show items that are not included in the default Start menu. These small discrepancies occur because the items were added in previous chapters to facilitate examples in the text.

If you used a version of Windows before Windows 7, you may have used the classic Start menu, which is no longer installed. However, several programs on the Internet provide an alternative classic menu that you can download.

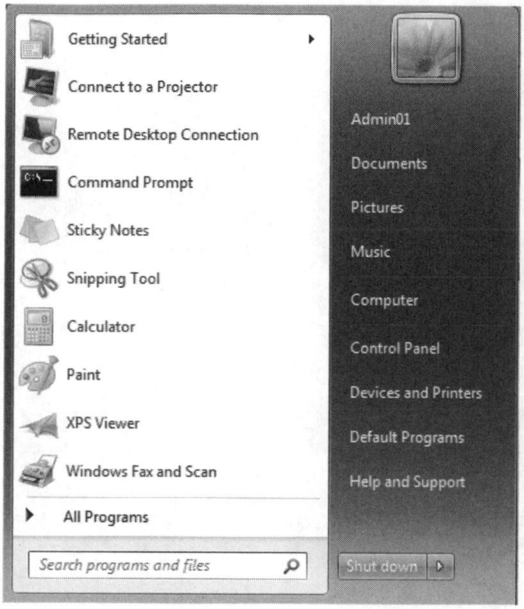

Figure 3-1 Default Start menu

Source: Course Technology/Cengage Learning

To see additional programs on the Start menu, click All Programs. Figure 3-2 shows that program names have replaced the default menu items in Figure 3-1.

The Getting Started option, as shown in Figure 3-3, displays a list of links to useful places in Windows 7. Double-click the item of choice.

Here is a brief list of some of the more useful items in Getting Started:

- **Go online to find out what's new in Windows 7** takes you to a Web page that describes the new features.
- **Personalize Windows** allows you to decorate your version of Windows 7. You can choose a screen saver, replace the desktop background, adjust your monitor resolution, and so on.
- **Go online to get Windows Live Essentials** offers a free virus protection program.

Customizing the Start Menu The Start menu in Windows 7 has more customization options than in earlier versions of Windows. For instance, the menu identifies who is logged on and automatically adds the most frequently used programs to the top-level menu. Frequently used items such as the Documents, Pictures, and Music folders are accessible from the Start menu, as are shortcuts to programs you use often.

The list of programs on the left (white) side of the Start menu is divided into two parts:

- Pinned items list—These items are displayed above the separator line, where they are always available for you to click to start. This list is yours to modify; it shows

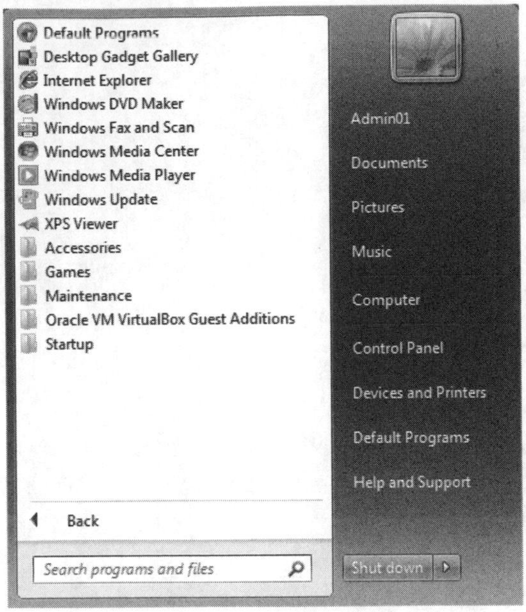

Figure 3-2 Start menu with All Programs displayed

Source: Course Technology/Cengage Learning

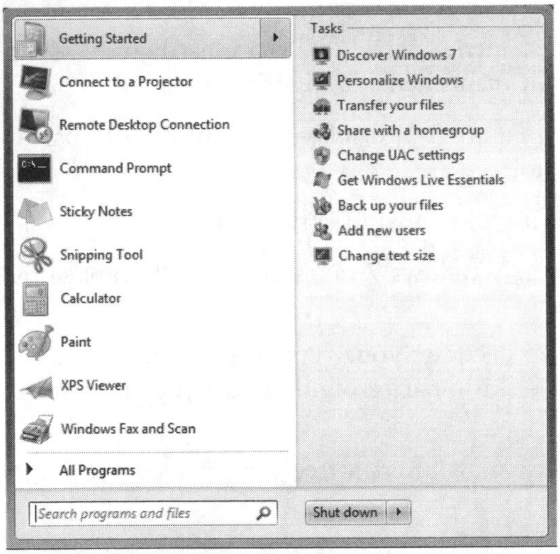

Figure 3-3 Start menu with Getting Started displayed

Source: Course Technology/Cengage Learning

programs, documents, and anything else that you want to open quickly. (You will add to this list in Activity 3-1.)

- Most frequently used programs list—These programs appear below the separator line. New programs replace less frequently used programs as needed.

If you have not used any programs, you will not see a divider line. After the first program use, the divider line will appear above the program shortcut.

The right (dark) side on the Start menu is reserved for important places on your computer. You will find folders such as Documents, Pictures, and Music. Also, you will be able to easily access media using the Computer option, configure Windows 7 options through the Control Panel, choose the programs that Windows 7 uses by default, and open Help and Support to locate the solution to a problem. Activities for these items appear throughout this chapter and subsequent chapters.

To modify the Start menu, right-click the Start menu icon and click Properties. From the Start Menu tab of the Taskbar and Start Menu Properties dialog box (see Figure 3-4), you can customize the settings for the Start menu.

On the Start Menu tab, you can click the Power button action chevron and then choose which action is taken when you press the computer's power button: Switch user, Log off, Lock, Restart, or Shut down. Also, you can control whether recently executed programs and recently opened items are displayed on the Start menu. The default action is for Windows 7 to keep links to recently used items on the Start menu.

By clicking the Customize button shown in Figure 3-4, you open the Customize Start Menu dialog box (see Figure 3-5). Use this dialog box to control how links, icons, and menus look and behave on the Start menu. For example, you can select from three choices for displaying the Computer item: Display as a link, as a menu, or not at all. You can select from these three actions for a number of items, such as the Documents folder, the Control Panel,

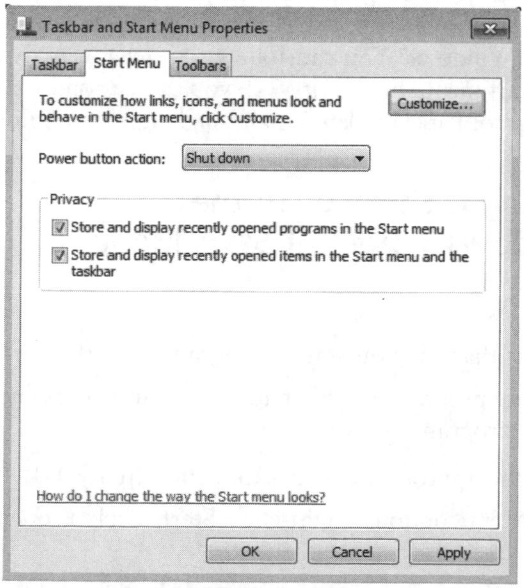

Figure 3-4 Taskbar and Start Menu Properties dialog box

Source: Course Technology/Cengage Learning

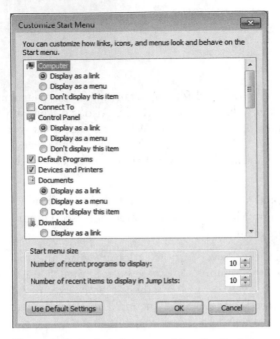

Figure 3-5 Options for customizing the Start menu

Source: Course Technology/Cengage Learning

Games, and Music. Also, you can control the number of recently executed programs and recent items you want to display.

The default Start menu has many options you can customize, so you should take some time to learn about them. These options can be a bit confusing if you have recently switched to Windows 7 from a previous version of Windows. You can follow the steps in Activity 3-1 to add a program shortcut to the default Start menu. In Activity 3-2, you can customize the default Start menu to control the display of Control Panel applets (small, single-function utilities).

Activity 3-1: Adding a Shortcut to the Windows 7 Default Start Menu

Time Required: 10 minutes

Objective: Add a shortcut that lets you start a program from the Start menu.

Description: In this activity, you add a program shortcut to the default Start menu. This activity is useful if you want to start a program quickly.

1. Start your virtual machines using the appropriate instructions in Activity 1-1.

2. To display the Customize Start Menu options, right-click **Start**, click **Properties**, and then click the **Customize** button.

3. If necessary, scroll and check the **Enable context menus and dragging and dropping** check box to permit shortcuts to be dropped on the Start menu. (You will use this feature in a later activity.)

4. Click **OK** twice.

5. To add a desktop icon for the Calculator, right-click an open area on the desktop, point to **New**, click **Shortcut**, click the **Browse** button, expand **Computer**, and expand **Local Disk (C:)**. Scroll and expand **WINDOWS**, scroll and expand **system32**, scroll and click **calc**, and click **OK**. Click **Next**, type **Calculator** over "calc", and then click **Finish**.

6. To pin the Calculator icon, right-click the icon on the desktop and then click **Pin to Start Menu**.

7. To test your addition to the Start menu, click **Start**, locate the Calculator menu shortcut on the pinned items list, and then click the **Calculator** shortcut.

8. Close the Calculator window.

9. To remove the Calculator icon from the desktop, right-click the icon, click **Delete**, and then click **Yes**.

10. Leave the virtual machines on for the next activity.

Activity 3-2: Customizing the Windows 7 Default Start Menu

Time Required: 10 minutes

Objective: Customize the Start menu.

Description: In this activity, you customize the default Start menu to control the display of Control Panel applets. This activity is useful if you want to control the display options on the Start menu.

1. If necessary, start your virtual machines using the appropriate instructions in Activity 1-1.

2. To display the Customize Start Menu options, right-click **Start**, click **Properties**, and then click the **Customize** button.

3. Clear the **Open submenus when I pause on them with the mouse pointer** check box.

4. Click **OK** twice.

5. Click **Start**, point to **All Programs**, pause, and then click **All Programs**. Notice that All Programs opens only after you click it.

6. Repeat Step 2 and then check the **Open submenus when I pause on them with the mouse pointer** check box. Click **OK** twice.

7. Click **Start**, point to **All Programs**, and then pause. Notice that All Programs opened without you having to click it.

8. To open the Pictures window, click **Start** and then click **Pictures**. Notice that the pictures appear as links.

9. Close the Pictures window.

10. Repeat Step 2 and then scroll and click the **Pictures—Display as a menu** option button. Click **OK** twice.

11. To open the Pictures menu, click **Start**, point to **Pictures**, point to **Public Pictures**, point to **Sample Pictures**, and then click the picture of your choice.

12. Close any open windows.

13. Repeat Step 2 and then scroll and click the **Pictures—Display as a link** option button. Click **OK** twice.

14. Leave the virtual machines on for the next activity.

Using the Taskbar The taskbar is the narrow box across the bottom of the screen. The taskbar (see Figure 3-6) is a key element in using the Windows 7 interface. When Windows 7 is being run in Oracle VirtualBox, the Windows 7 taskbar is above the Oracle VirtualBox taskbar.

From left to right, the taskbar has the following functions:

- Start menu—This menu is discussed earlier in the chapter.
- Open programs and windows—Switch from one open program to another.
- Open your favorite programs—Launch frequently used programs.

Figure 3-6 Windows 7 desktop showing taskbar at bottom

Source: Course Technology/Cengage Learning

- System tray (notification area)—View icons that show details about battery life, network connection status, speaker volume, and other items.
- Show Desktop button—Control the appearance of windows on the desktop.

Auto-Hiding the Taskbar To turn on the taskbar's auto-hiding feature, right-click a blank spot on the taskbar, click Properties, and then check the "Auto-hide the taskbar" check box, as shown in Figure 3-7. This feature makes the taskbar disappear when you are not using it, which permits you to have the entire desktop available for a maximized application window. To view the hidden taskbar, move the mouse pointer to the thin line at edge of the screen.

Moving and Resizing the Taskbar You can increase the size of the taskbar and change its location on the screen. To increase its size, position the mouse pointer over the taskbar's outer edge and drag the pointer. To move the taskbar, click an empty area in it and drag it to the desired location. You will move and resize the taskbar in Activity 3-3.

If you cannot resize or move the taskbar, it might be locked to prevent changes. If so, right-click an empty area of the taskbar and clear the Lock the Taskbar check box.

Likewise, changing the size of the icons on the taskbar alters its size. To do this, right-click the taskbar, click Properties, and check the Use small icons check box.

Using Toolbars on the Taskbar You can add the toolbars listed in Table 3-1 to the taskbar. These toolbars are separate sections on the taskbar that offer special features. Activity 3-4 explains how to use a toolbar.

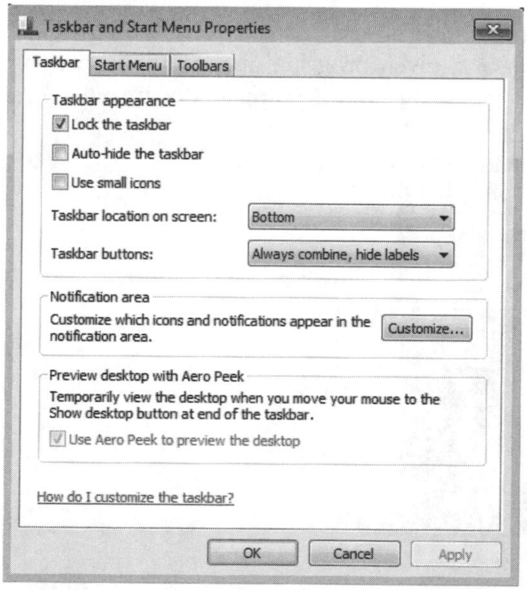

Figure 3-7 Taskbar tab in Taskbar and Start Menu Properties dialog box

Source: Course Technology/Cengage Learning

Toolbar	Content added
Address	A Web page address
Links	An Internet Explorer link or any icon
Tablet PC Input Panel	A screen to enter handwritten text on a tablet PC
Desktop	Copies of all desktop icons and frequently used places that are not on the desktop
Quick Launch	Shortcuts to start the indicated applications
New toolbar	Contents of a set of icons from a folder

Table 3-1 Toolbars you can add to the taskbar

The Links toolbar holds the links to your favorite Web sites. You can also drag any icon to this toolbar, including those for files, folders, disks, and programs, to turn them into one-click buttons. These are only shortcuts; you can delete them, rename them, and move them around on the toolbar.

Here are a few possibilities that you might consider for toolbar shortcuts:

- Three or four of the programs that you use the most
- Documents you use each day
- Folders that you frequently access for files

The Desktop toolbar provides access to the icons on your desktop; this is convenient if you need to access an icon while a program occupies the entire desktop. The toolbar also provides access to other frequently used places, such as your Personal folder, libraries, Network folders, and the Control Panel (see Figure 3-8).

Grouping Programs on the Taskbar The taskbar can become crowded with buttons when you work with multiple instances of a given program at the same time, so Windows provides a grouping feature to help you manage multiple open documents. As shown in

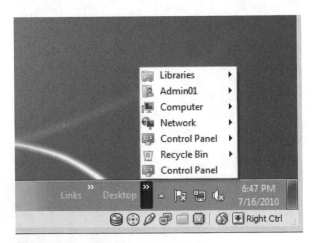

Figure 3-8 Desktop toolbar

Source: Course Technology/Cengage Learning

Figure 3-9 Taskbar showing group

Source: Course Technology/Cengage Learning

Figure 3-9, all documents opened with a particular program are combined into one button for the program.

In addition to the default taskbar behavior (Always combine, hide labels), you have two other choices for the behavior of taskbar buttons: Combine when the taskbar is full, or Never combine. To access these options, right-click an empty area of the taskbar, click Properties, and then click the Taskbar buttons list box.

Activity 3-3: Working with the Windows 7 Taskbar

Time Required: 10 minutes

Objective: Manipulate the taskbar in Windows 7.

Description: In this activity, you work with the taskbar on the desktop. This activity is useful if you want to move, resize, or hide the taskbar.

1. If necessary, start your virtual machines using the appropriate instructions in Activity 1-1.

2. Right-click an empty area of the taskbar and uncheck the **Lock the Taskbar** optionl, if necessary.

3. Position the mouse pointer over an empty area of the taskbar and then click and drag it to another location. You can move the taskbar to the top of the screen or to its left or right edge.

4. Move the taskbar back to the bottom of the screen using the technique described in Step 3.

5. Right-click an empty area of the taskbar, click **Properties**, click the **Taskbar location on screen** chevron, click **Left** in the list, and then click **OK**.

6. Repeat Step 5 to select the Right, Top, and Bottom locations.

7. Grab the edge of the taskbar with the mouse and stretch it to make it taller. Next, shrink the taskbar back to its original size.

8. Right-click an empty area of the taskbar, click **Properties**, check the **Use small icons** check box, and then click **OK**.

9. Move the mouse to the bottom of the virtual machine window.

10. Close all open windows.

11. Leave the virtual machine logged on for the next activity.

Activity 3-4: Customizing the Windows 7 Taskbar Toolbars

Time Required: 10 minutes

Objective: Customize the toolbars on the Windows 7 taskbar.

Description: In this activity, you view and customize toolbars on the taskbar, including Internet links. You may already know that the Quick Launch toolbar allows you to create shortcuts to frequently used programs without having to use the Start menu. This activity is useful if you want to customize the toolbars on the taskbar.

1. If necessary, start your virtual machines using the appropriate instructions in Activity 1-1.

2. Right-click an empty portion of the taskbar, click **Properties**, click the **Toolbars** tab, click the **Links** check box, click the **Desktop** check box, and then click **OK**.

3. Click the >> symbol next to Links on the taskbar to view the contents of the Internet links toolbar.

4. Click the >> symbol next to Desktop on the taskbar to view the contents of the Desktop toolbar.

5. To pin the Calculator to the taskbar, click **Start** and then drag the Calculator button to the taskbar.

6. To quickly open the Calculator, click the **Calculator** icon on the taskbar.

7. To unpin the Calculator from the taskbar, right-click the **Calculator** button, and then click **Unpin this program from taskbar**.

8. Close all open windows.

9. Leave the virtual machine logged on for future activities.

Customizing Fedora 13 Panels

The bars across the top and bottom of the Fedora 13 desktop are called panels. You can customize the content and position of these panels. In Fedora Core 13, the taskbar is called a **panel** and is located at the top of the screen. The major difference between a panel and the Windows 7 taskbar is the appearance of the program icons. By default, the top panel appears at the top of the desktop, as shown in Figure 3-10.

The Applications menu provides access to the applications installed on the system. When you install a new application, it is automatically added to the Applications menu.

The Places menu provides a list of locations that open in File Browser windows when selected. (For more information about these locations, see "Using the Fedora 13 File Browser" later in this chapter.) The System menu provides options for configuring the system and desktop environment.

Next on the panel are icons that launch programs. To allow faster access to applications, you can add launch icons for them to the Panel.

The right side of the panel includes the date and time, and the name of the current user. You can click the name to switch to a different user. Additional icons vary, but they permit access to different system components. For example, one icon indicates the network connectivity status.

Figure 3-10 Fedora 13 desktop showing panels

Source: Course Technology/Cengage Learning

The bottom desktop panel contains three items by default, but you can configure it as you wish. A customized panel appears at the bottom of the desktop shown in Figure 3-10. You will learn to customize the bottom panel in Activity 3-6.

Click the icon on the far left side of the panel to hide or show all windows on the desktop. The series of squares controls the currently displayed virtual workspace. Multiple workspaces may be active at any one time, with different applications visible on different workspaces. To switch to a different desktop, simply click one of the squares in the bottom toolbar. By default, four workspaces are configured, although you can change this number.

If your mouse has a scroll wheel, click a workspace in the panel and then scroll back and forth through the workspaces.

For each application running on the desktop, a button appears on the currently selected workspace. If the application's windows are currently visible on the desktop, clicking the corresponding button in the panel minimizes the windows so that they are no longer visible. Click the button again to display the windows again.

The final item on the bottom panel is the Trash, into which you can drag and drop items that you no longer need. You will learn to "take out the trash" in a later section.

Adding and Removing Panels You can control the number of panels on your desktop. To add a new panel, right-click an existing panel and click New Panel from the resulting menu. The new panel will be placed below the previous panel. To remove an existing panel, right-click it and click Delete This Panel.

Customizing Panels To customize the panel, right-click an empty area of the panel and then click Properties. The Panel Properties dialog box appears, as shown in Figure 3-11. The General tab contains options for changing the orientation, size, button, and panel characteristics. The Background tab contains options for changing a panel image: using the system theme, changing its color and style, or adding a background image. As with Windows 7, how you display windows on the panel might be important when you need to open many applications at once.

Customizing Menu Items Recall that the first area of the Fedora 13 panel contains the menu items. See Table 3-2 for options to help you customize menu items. To customize a menu item, right-click it.

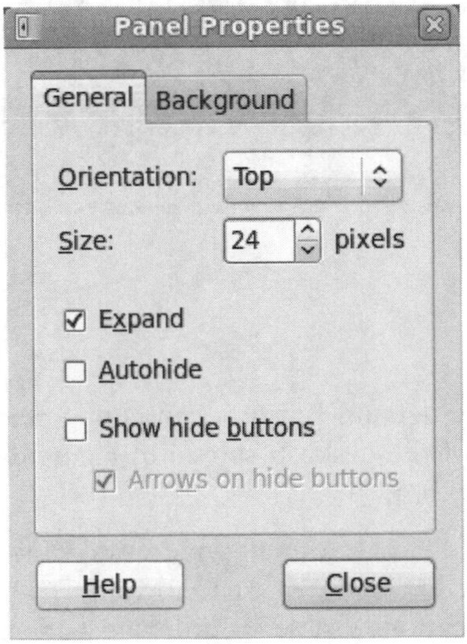

Figure 3-11 Panel Properties dialog box in Fedora 13

Source: Course Technology/Cengage Learning

Panel menu item	Options
Help	Accesses help
Remove from Panel	Removes an item from the panel
Move	Moves a panel item
Lock to Panel	Locks current panel configuration

Table 3-2 Menu item options

Adding to the Panel When Fedora Linux is first installed, a number of items are added by default to the top panel. You can add more items if you want. To add items, right-click the top panel, and then click Add to Panel. Select the desired item and click the Add button.

To add an application, you have two choices:

- Custom Application Launcher—Create an application launcher by specifying an application, an application to run in a Terminal console, or by browsing to a location.

- Application Launcher—Create a launcher (shortcut) from an existing menu item.

To add an **applet** (a small, single-function utility), locate the applet from the Add to Panel dialog box. For example, to control the brightness of your laptop display, choose the Brightness launcher.

To add a panel drawer that contains launcher icons, select the Drawer option in the Add to Panel dialog box. To add items to the drawer, right-click it, click Add to Drawer, then scroll and click an item from the Add to Drawer dialog box.

To remove an item from a panel, right-click it on the panel and then click Remove from Panel.

Activity 3-5: Adding a Launcher and Drawers to the Fedora 13 Panel

Time Required: 10 minutes

Objective: Modify the Fedora 13 panel.

Description: In this activity, you add a Terminal launcher and a drawer to the panel. Then you will remove the drawer.

1. If necessary, start your virtual machines using the appropriate instructions in Activity 1-1.

2. To open the Add to Panel dialog box, right-click an empty area of the panel and click **Add to Panel**.

3. To add the Terminal console, click **Application Launcher**, click **Forward**, expand **System Tools**, scroll and click **Terminal**, click **Add**, and then click **Close**.

4. Verify that the Terminal icon appears on the panel.

5. To open the Add to Panel dialog box again, right-click an empty area of the panel and click **Add to Panel**.

6. To add a drawer, scroll and click **Drawer**, click **Add**, and then click **Close**.

7. Verify that the Drawer icon appears on the panel.

8. To add to the drawer, right-click the **Drawer** icon, click **Add to Drawer**, scroll and click **Weather Report**, click **Add**, and then click **Close**.

9. To verify that the drawer has a Weather Report, click the **Drawer** icon, click --, and then click **Close**.

10. To remove the drawer, right-click the **Drawer** icon, click **Remove from Panel**, and then click **Delete**.

11. Verify that the Drawer icon was removed from the panel.

12. Leave the virtual machine logged on for future activities.

Activity 3-6: Customizing the Fedora 13 Bottom Panel

Time Required: 10 minutes

Objective: Modify the bottom panel in Fedora 13 to include notification icons as well as the date and time.

Description: In this activity, you modify the Fedora 13 bottom panel to include notification icons, add date and time displays, and increase the panel size. This activity is helpful if you want to customize the bottom panel in Fedora 13.

1. If necessary, start your virtual machines using the appropriate instructions in Activity 1-1.

2. To add notification icons, right-click the bottom panel, click **Add to Panel**, scroll and click **Notification Area**, and then click **Add**.

3. To add the date and time displays, scroll and click **Clock**, click **Add**, and then click **Close**.

4. To increase the size of the bottom panel, right-click the bottom panel, click **Properties**, click the arrows beside the box until **36** is displayed, and then click **Close**.

5. Leave the virtual machine logged on for the next activity.

Tailoring the Desktop

Like a physical desk, you use a computer desktop to store your electronic work equipment and give yourself easy access to current projects. The desktop is the main screen in Windows 7 and Fedora 13; you can put icons on both screens to serve as shortcuts to important programs. The following sections explain how to tailor the Windows 7 and Fedora Core 13 desktops. First, however, you will learn about some new Windows 7 desktop features.

Using the New Windows 7 Desktop Features

Based on surveys of what users wanted to see in Windows 7, Microsoft developed new features called Jump and Snap. Using a Jump list, you can go directly to the documents, pictures, songs, and Web sites you use each day. To open a Jump list, just right-click a program icon on the Start menu. The contents of a Jump list depend on the program you are using. For example, the Jump list for Internet Explorer 8 shows frequently viewed Web sites. In addition to showing file shortcuts, Jump lists can also provide quick access to commands that let you compose e-mail and play music, among other things.

Another new desktop feature is Snap, which is a quick and fun way to resize open windows simply by dragging them to the edges of your screen. Depending on where you drag a window, you can make it expand vertically, take up the entire screen, or appear side by side with another window. Snap makes it easy to read, organize, and compare windows.

Two additional new features are Peek and Shake. Peek appears to give you the power of X-ray vision—you can peer past all your open windows straight to the Windows 7 desktop.

If you simply point to the right edge of the taskbar, all open windows instantly turn transparent, revealing your hidden desktop icons. The Shake feature lets you cut through a cluttered desktop and quickly focus on a single window. Just click the desired window and give your mouse a shake; every open window except the selected one instantly disappears. Jiggle the mouse again, and the other windows reappear. (Who says an old mouse can't learn a new trick?)

Windows 7 also includes the Flip 3D feature that was introduced in Windows Vista. Flip 3D displays your open windows in a **stack**, which lets you quickly preview all of your open files, folders, and documents without having to click the taskbar. Instead, you see one open window at the top of the stack. To see the other open windows, you flip through the stack.

Shake, Peek, and Flip 3D are included in the Home Premium, Professional, Ultimate, and Enterprise editions of Windows 7. These features require Windows Aero, although not all PCs have the graphics hardware and software to run it. The virtualization software used in this text does not support Windows Aero.

Tailoring the Windows 7 Desktop

If you have difficulty reading text on the screen, you can customize the display fonts. In the following sections, you will learn to customize the desktop display fonts, choose the appearance of desktop icons, and set the display resolution (the total number of pixels displayed horizontally and vertically).

Increasing the Size of Windows Text Fonts If the text on your screen is too small for easy reading, you can increase the size of the fonts used in Windows menus, headings, and icon labels. Click Start, click Control Panel, click the Appearance and Personalization link, click "Make text and other items larger or smaller," and then click the desired size (see Figure 3-12). To change the font size, you must log off and log on again.

Choosing the Appearance of Desktop Icons With prolonged activity in Windows 7, the desktop can become cluttered. Windows 7 offers a number of ways to manage desktop clutter. To keep your desktop neat, consider the following options:

- Icon size—Choose from Large, Medium, or Small.
- Visibility—Hide all of the desktop icons when using your laptop for a presentation.
- Align to grid—All icons jump to the invisible grid.
- Consolidate—Sort and group icons to the invisible grid.
- Sort—Sort by criteria such as name and date.

To access such options, right-click the desktop and point to View. The choices are shown in Figure 3-13.

You will only see the Larger (150%) option if your screen resolution is at least 1200 x 900 pixels.

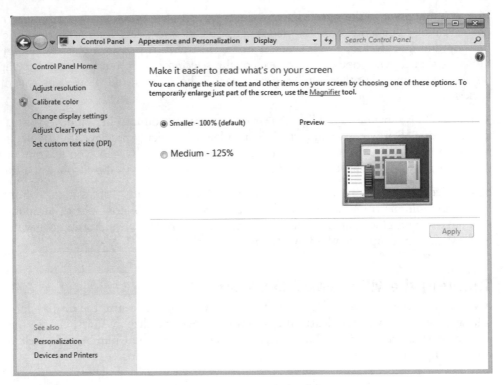

Figure 3-12 Appearance tab of Display Properties dialog box

Source: Course Technology/Cengage Learning

Figure 3-13 Desktop icon appearance choices

Source: Course Technology/Cengage Learning

Changing Screen Resolution To change the amount of information that appears on the screen, you can change the screen resolution, which modifies the apparent size of the screen fonts. To view more information, for example, increase the screen resolution. Everything on the screen will appear smaller, including text. The following activity explains how to adjust the screen resolution.

Activity 3-7: Tailoring the Windows 7 Desktop

Time Required: 10 minutes

Objective: Customize display fonts and icon sizes and adjust screen resolution in Windows 7.

Description: In this activity, you manipulate the screen fonts, change the icon sizes, and change the screen resolution. This activity is useful if you need to customize your screen display.

1. If necessary, start your virtual machines using the appropriate instructions in Activity 1-1.

2. To change the size of the desktop fonts, click **Start**, click **Control Panel,** click the **Appearance and Personalization** link, click the **Make text and other items larger or smaller** link, click the **Medium** option button, and then click **Apply**.

3. Click the **Log off now** button.

4. Log on as **User01** and enter a password of **Secret1**.

5. To change the icon size, right-click the desktop, point to **View**, and then click **Large icons**.

6. Repeat Step 5 to change the icon size to Medium.

7. To change the screen resolution, right-click an empty area on the desktop, click **Screen Resolution,** click the **Resolution** chevron, click **800 x 600**, click **Apply** twice, and then click **Keep Changes**.

 Changing to a lower screen resolution might mean that some items will no longer fit on the screen.

8. Repeat Step 7 to change the screen resolution back to 1024 x 768.

9. Drag the Screen resolution slider to change the resolution, and then click **Apply**. Wait for the screen resolution to change. If necessary, click **No** to reject the change.

10. Click **OK**.

11. Close all the open windows.

12. Leave the virtual machine logged on for future activities.

Tailoring the Fedora 13 Desktop

As previously mentioned, items that appear on the desktop are grouped as applets in the form of desktop launchers (shortcuts). To customize the Fedora 13 panel, right-click an empty area on it and then use the submenu that appears.

The three types of desktop launchers are Application, Application in Terminal, and Location (path to a file). Besides launchers, you can also create a Folders and Documents entry on the desktop by right-clicking it and selecting from the resulting **desktop context menu**. You can also clean up and align desktop icons, cut and paste desktop objects, and change the desktop background.

Activity 3-8: Working with the Fedora 13 Desktop

Time Required: 10 minutes

Objective: Modify the Fedora 13 desktop by adding a launcher to it.

Description: In this activity, you add a Terminal launcher to the desktop.

1. If necessary, start your virtual machines using the appropriate instructions in Activity 1-1.
2. Click **Applications**, click **System Tools**, right-click **Terminal**, and then click **Add this launcher to desktop**.
3. Verify that the Terminal icon appears on the desktop.
4. Leave the virtual machine logged on for future activities.

 When you right-click an icon or a file on the desktop, different menus appear depending on your selection. The menu options can be handy to know; for example, a desktop menu often allows you to move or copy a file without opening it.

Setting Appearance Preferences The Appearance Preferences dialog box contains various options for customizing your desktop's display theme, background, and fonts. To open the dialog box, click System, click Preferences, and click Appearance. The dialog box is shown in Figure 3-14.

To change the desktop background, right-click the desktop and click Change Desktop Background.

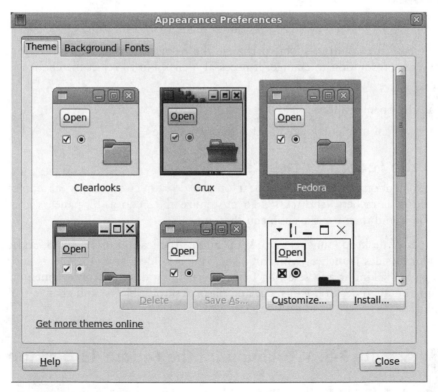

Figure 3-14 Desktop appearance preferences

Source: Course Technology/Cengage Learning

Activity 3-9: Modifying the Fedora 13 Desktop Using Appearance Preferences

Time Required: 10 minutes

Objective: Modify the desktop using the desktop context menu in Fedora Core 13.

Description: In this activity, you open the desktop context menu, select Change Desktop Background, and modify the desktop. This activity is useful if you want to modify the appearance of the Fedora 13 desktop.

1. If necessary, start your virtual machines using the appropriate instructions in Activity 1-1.

2. To open the context menu on the desktop, right-click an empty area of the desktop.

3. To open the dialog box that allows you to make changes to the desktop, click **Change Desktop Background**.

4. To select a new background for the desktop, click the **Background** tab.

5. Scroll through the background selections. Click the backgrounds you might like and observe the sample display.

6. To apply the selected background, click the background thumbnail and then click **Close**.

7. Repeat Steps 2 through 6 for the **Theme** and **Fonts** tabs.

8. Leave Fedora 13 logged on for the next activity.

Changing Display Settings The Display Settings window contains various options for customizing your display, including screen resolution, color depth, and monitor type. When you select the monitor type, the available screen resolutions are constrained for the screen resolution and color depth. To open the Display Settings window (see Figure 3-15),

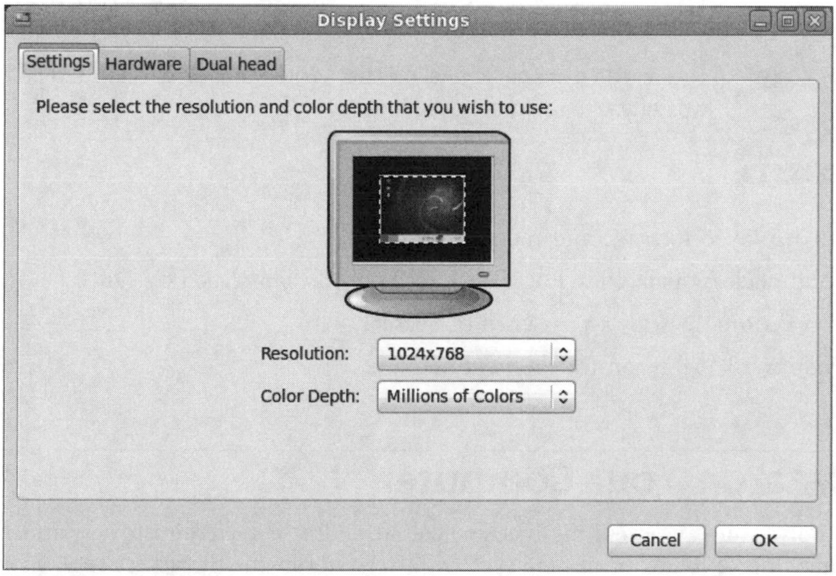

Figure 3-15 Display Settings window

Source: Course Technology/Cengage Learning

click System, point to Administration, and click Display. Changes to the display settings require the user to log out and log on again.

Activity 3-10: Modifying the Fedora 13 Display Settings

Time Required: 10 minutes

Objective: Modify the screen resolution using the Display Settings window in Fedora Core 13.

Description: In this activity, you open the Display Settings window to change the resolution. This activity is useful if you want to modify the appearance of the Fedora 13 desktop.

1. If necessary, start your virtual machines using the appropriate instructions in Activity 1-1.
2. Click **System** on the panel, click **Administration**, and click **Display**.
3. When the query dialog box appears, type **P@ssw0rd** and then click **OK**.
4. To change the screen resolution for the desktop, click the **Resolution** drop-down menu.
5. Click **800 x 600** and then click **OK**.
6. Read the displayed message and then click **OK**.
7. To log out, click **System**, click **Log Out User01**, and then click **Log Out**.
8. Log on to Fedora 13 with a password of **Secret1**.
9. Click **System** on the panel, click **Administration**, and click **Display**.
10. When the query dialog box appears, type **P@ssw0rd** and then click **OK**.
11. To select a monitor type, click the **Hardware** tab, click **Configure** for Monitor Type, expand **Generic LCD Display**, click **LCD Panel 1024x768**, click **OK**, and then click **OK**.

To prevent damage to the monitor, you need to select a monitor type after the resolution is reduced.

12. Read the displayed message and then click OK.
13. To log out, click **System**, click **Log Out User01**, and then click **Log Out**.
14. Log on to Fedora 13 with a password of **Secret1**.
15. Leave Fedora 13 logged on for the next activity.

Accessing Data on Your Computer

Using GUI tools, you can access the hierarchical structure of files, directories, and drives on your computer. In the following section, you will learn about the file access tools in Windows Explorer. You will also learn to use File Browser in Fedora 13 to access local data on your computer.

Using Windows Explorer

Windows Explorer (see Figure 3-16) is a utility in Windows 7 that enables you to locate and open files and folders. You can open it by clicking Computer or Documents on your desktop or the Start menu. This section explains how to use Windows Explorer. You will work with Explorer in Activity 3-11.

Your computer might have fewer drives than those shown in Figure 3-16.

As you can see, a lot has changed in Explorer from previous versions of Windows. The functions of the address bar are summarized in Figure 3-16; the contents list requires further explanation. This list shows the folder trail to the current folder. For example, Figure 3-17 shows the contents list to the photos in the Sample Pictures folder. The path to this folder is indicated by the ▶ symbol, which is actually a pop-up menu. Point to the symbol to see the contents of the associated folder; you can point to the symbol for any folder in the path.

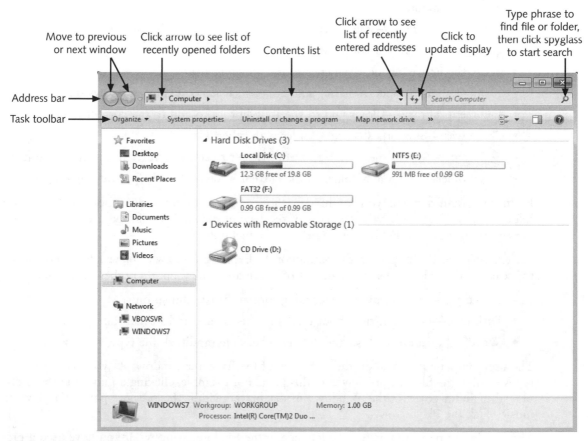

Figure 3-16 Windows Explorer

Source: Course Technology/Cengage Learning

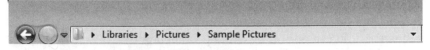

Figure 3-17 Contents list to Pictures folder

Source: Course Technology/Cengage Learning

These symbols are a type of **breadcrumb**, which are navigation aids used in an address bar and other parts of the GUI to help keep track of your locations. The term comes from the trail of crumbs left by Hansel and Gretel in the classic fairy tale.

The Task toolbar changes as different windows appear. You might encounter the following controls as you use Explorer:

- Organize—Consolidates many of the menu commands used with Explorer. Familiar commands such as Cut, Copy, Paste, Undo, Select All, Delete, and Rename appear here.
- System properties—Provides basic information about your computer.
- Uninstall or change a program—Opens a window that lets you install or remove a program.
- Map network drive—Allows you to connect a drive letter to a shared resource on another computer.
- Open Control Panel—Allows you to adjust your computer's settings.
- Change view—Allows you to switch the view.
- Show the preview pane—Switches to the previous view.
- Help—Launches Windows Help and Support, which explains Windows functions.
- Include in library—Allows you to specify a library to add to the current folder.
- Share with—Supports sharing a folder with other users.
- Slide show—Opens the Windows media viewer to show pictures in the current folder.
- New folder—Add a new folder in the current folder, which helps you organize files.

From the Organize menu, you can hide or show additional information about your files and folders. Figure 3-18 shows the contents of the Layout menu. The affected area for each layout option is indicated by the button next to the menu item.

For example, the details pane at the bottom of the Explorer window displays information about the selected item. Here are some examples of information that appears in the details pane:

- Music file—Lists the album, recording format, artist, and so on.
- Disk icon—Lists statistics about total size, free space, and formatting option.
- WordPad document—Lists the date created, date modified, file type, and size.

The preview pane is shown on the right side of the Explorer window. As you click common types of files, the files are previewed in this pane. For example, clicking a music file could display the album cover in the Windows media player within the preview pane. To play the music, click the Play arrow.

The navigation pane appears on the left side of the Explorer window. If you have used a previous version of Windows, you should be familiar with the navigation pane. In Windows 7, it works like a master map to the files and folders on your computer, as shown in Figure 3-19.

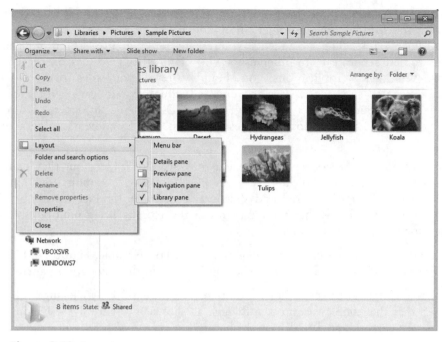

Figure 3-18 Layout menu

Source: Course Technology/Cengage Learning

Figure 3-19 Navigation pane

Source: Course Technology/Cengage Learning

Using the Libraries If you have used a previous version of Windows, you may be familiar with the My Documents folder. In Windows 7, the word *My* has been dropped from the folder name. The documents you create or save are stored in your own Documents folder, separate from other users who might also save files on the computer. As you use Windows 7 applications, you should store all your files in the Documents folder and associated subfolders. User accounts individualize Windows 7 for each person who shares a computer or network server; your Documents folder is tied to your account. You need administrator privileges to access the Documents folders of other users.

Windows 7 introduces the concept of libraries; they are like folders but they can display the contents of other folders from all over your PC. Windows 7 contains four libraries by default: Documents, Music, Pictures, and Videos. For example, the Pictures library appears to contain all of your photos, but these pictures might actually be in multiple folders that you created for different vacation trips.

To use a library, click the name in the navigation pane. For example, Figure 3-20 shows the Pictures library, which you can access by clicking Pictures in the navigation pane.

Notice that the Sample Pictures are in two locations in Figure 3-20. By clicking "2 locations" you discover that the samples are in two folders, as shown in Figure 3-21. If you click the Add button, you can add more folders to the library.

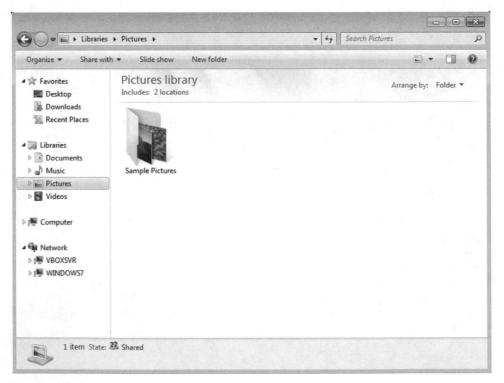

Figure 3-20 Pictures library

Source: Course Technology/Cengage Learning

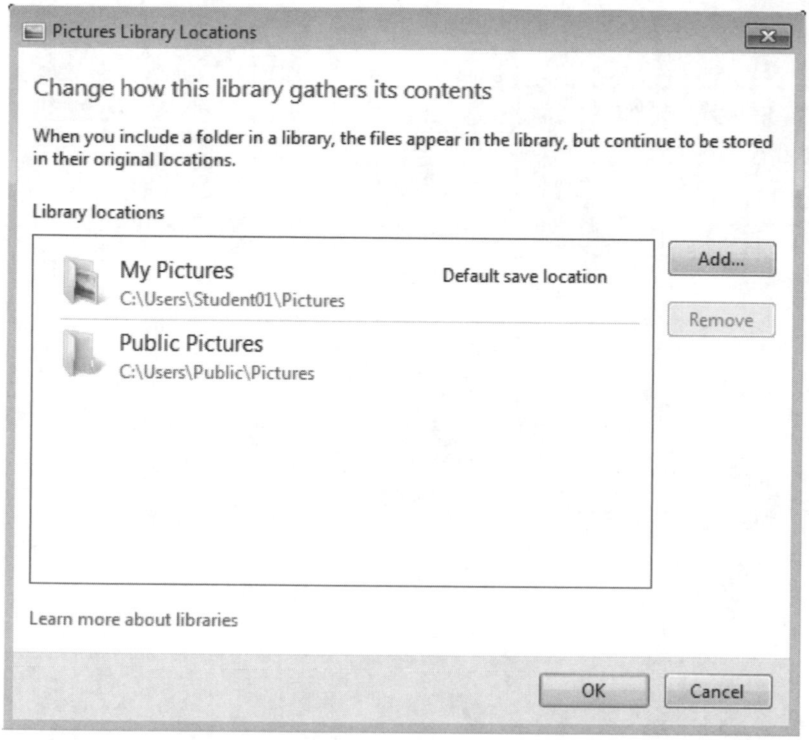

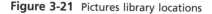

Figure 3-21 Pictures library locations

Source: Course Technology/Cengage Learning

To add a new library, right-click Libraries in the navigation pane, point to New, and then click Library. An entry called New Library is added. To name the library, right-click New Library, click Rename, and then type the library name over "New Library."

You will work with libraries in Activity 3-12.

Using the Recycle Bin The **Recycle Bin** gives you a second chance to retrieve deleted files or folders and restore them to their original location on the hard drive. You access the Recycle Bin (see Figure 3-22) by clicking its icon on the desktop. As the Recycle Bin fills with material you have deleted, older items are removed automatically to make room for newer items. More recently deleted items remain available until you decide to delete them permanently by emptying the Recycle Bin. If you are running low on hard drive space, you should empty the Recycle Bin.

Some files might be too large to delete using the Recycle Bin; you must delete such files immediately. By default, the Recycle Bin can only hold 10 percent of the hard drive's capacity.

You will work with the Recycle Bin in Activity 3-13.

Items that you delete from external drives, such as USB drives, are permanently deleted and are not sent to the Recycle Bin.

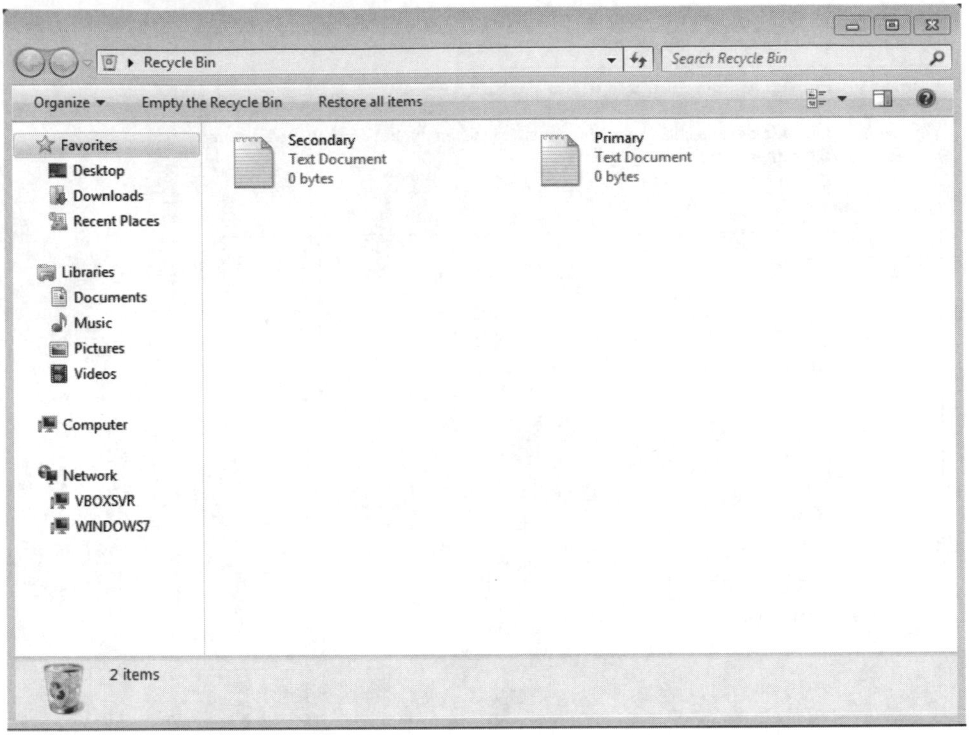

Figure 3-22 Recycle Bin

Source: Course Technology/Cengage Learning

Searching from the Start Menu You can use the Windows 7 Search feature when you need to locate a file or folder. For example, you can use it when:

- You are looking for common file types.
- You remember all or part of a filename.
- You know when you last changed a file.
- You know a word or phrase in the file.

You will use the Search option from the Start menu in Activity 3-14.

Start your search for files, folders, and programs by opening the Start menu. Type your search information in the "Search programs and files" text box. The search results start appearing as you type, and they change as you type additional characters. These changing results are called an interactive search. For example, if you are looking for a picture of a desert, typing *d* and then *de* or *des* will converge upon a picture of interest.

The results menu lists every file, folder, program, picture, movie, music file, and Web bookmark that contains your search information, regardless of filename or folder location. Depending on the applications installed, the search also includes data stored in Microsoft Office documents (Word, PowerPoint, Excel, and Outlook), e-mail messages, address book entries, and calendar appointments.

Again, Windows is not just searching file and folder names; it is searching the contents of files and folders, and it is searching metadata, which is descriptive information about files. Metadata includes file data such as height, width, size, creator, title, author, created date, and last modification date.

If you see the entry you want in your search results, double-click the entry to open it. If you choose a program or a picture, it opens on the screen. Windows will usually know which associated program to open to display the file, but occasionally a pop-up window asks you to locate the proper program.

Windows usually displays about 15 search results depending on the size of your monitor. Windows attempts to display the most likely matches to your search request, and groups them in categories such as Programs, Control Panel, Documents, and Music. Figure 3-23 shows the results of a sample search request. You can click the See more results link at the bottom of the results list to see additional matches (but not matching programs and Control Panel items).

To help locate your file, you might want to add the preview pane by clicking Organize, clicking Layout, and then clicking Preview pane. When you click an entry (such as a picture, sound, or text in a WordPad file), the file contents are shown in the preview pane. This helps locate the file you are seeking from the available candidates.

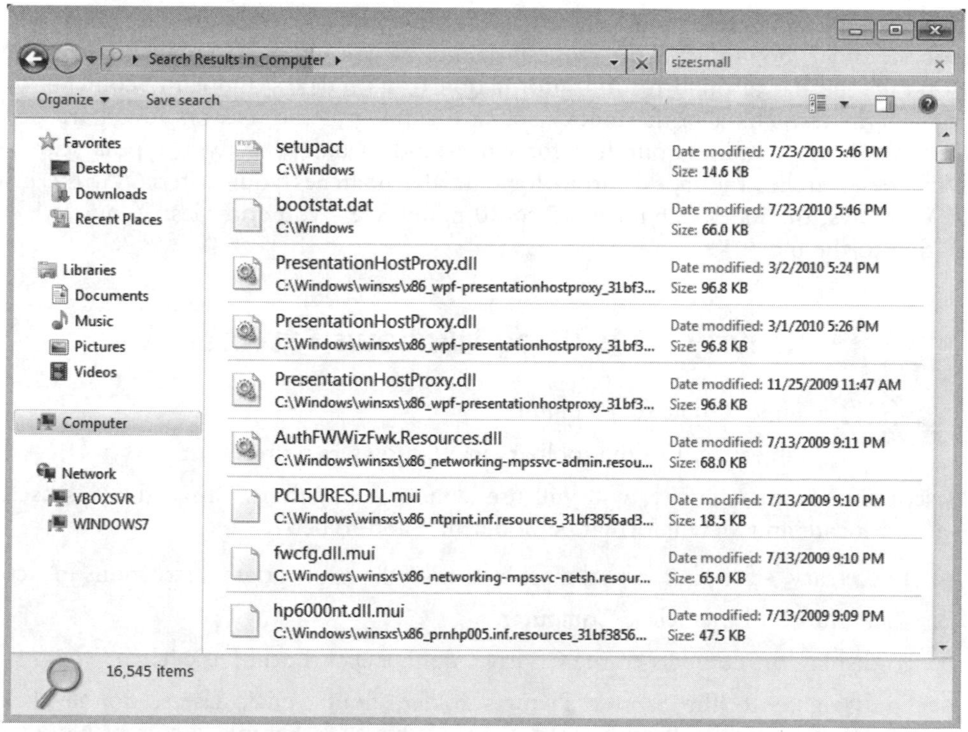

Figure 3-23 Sample search results

Source: Course Technology/Cengage Learning

Additional icons appear at the bottom of the Search Results window to help you repeat a search in just your libraries or perhaps the Internet. If you want to limit the search to a particular folder, click Custom and check the areas you want to search from the list that appears.

Searching from the Explorer Window The Search box in Explorer is located at the right end of the address bar. As with the Start menu, you type your search request into the Search box, but there is a big difference between the two. From the Start menu, you search your entire computer, but a search in Explorer is limited to the displayed Explorer window. You will perform a search from the Explorer window in Activity 3-15.

Also, an Explorer search is not limited to 15 entries, as it is in the Start menu. If a search returns a large number of results, you see a large scrollable window.

Another difference between the two searches is the Search Builder, which you can use to filter your search results. As you type in the Search text box in Explorer, a few words appear below the box—blue links to categories such as Author, Date Modified, and Size. You can use these categories to filter your search results. For example, clicking Date Modified presents a calendar with a list of date criteria you can select to refine your search.

The search filters that appear depend on the folder contents or library you are viewing. For example, if you are viewing the Pictures library, you will see search filters such as Date taken, Tags, and Type. If you are viewing the Music library, you see filters such as Album, Artists, and Genre.

You may be amazed at how quickly Windows displays results when you type a search request, and at how quickly the requests change as you type additional characters. Windows works in the background to add information to its indexes about the contents of files on your computer. Think of the **index** as a card catalog to the files on your hard disk. Recall that Windows examines your files for words and metadata. As you type a search request, Windows searches the index entries for data that matches your criteria. At the installation of Windows, the index is built in 15 to 30 minutes. As you add files, Windows adds information to the index.

Activity 3-11: Using Windows Explorer

Time Required: 10 minutes

Objective: Use the toolbars in Windows Explorer.

Description: In this activity, you will use Windows Explorer. This activity is useful if you want to locate and view information about files and folders.

1. If necessary, start your virtual machines using the appropriate instructions in Activity 1-1.

2. Click **Start** and then click **Computer**.

3. To display the contents of the C: drive, double-click **Local Disk (C:)**.

4. To navigate to the Sample Pictures folder, double-click **Users**, double-click **Public**, double-click **Public Pictures**, and then double-click **Sample Pictures**. Notice how the breadcrumbs change in the address bar.

5. To add a preview pane to the layout, click **Organize**, point to **Layout**, and then click **Preview pane**.

6. Click the picture icon of your choice. Notice the preview in the preview pane.

7. To add a details pane to the layout, click **Organize**, point to **Layout**, and then click **Details pane**. Notice the information for the selected icon at the bottom of the window.

8. To view the File Properties dialog box for the selected icon, click **Organize**, and then click **Properties**.

9. To close the File Properties dialog box without making changes, click **Cancel**.

10. To run a slide show of the pictures in this folder, click **Slide Show**.

11. To cancel the slide show, press **Esc**.

12. To see the folders available in the Public folder, click the ▶ to the right of Public.

13. To change to the Sample Music folder, click **Public Music**, and then double-click **Sample Music**.

14. Close the open windows in the virtual machine.

15. Leave the virtual machine logged on for the next activity.

Activity 3-12: Working with Libraries

Time Required: 10 minutes

Objective: View the library contents and create a new library.

Description: In this activity, you will work with an existing library, create a library, and populate it with existing folders. This activity is useful if you want to create and manage libraries.

1. If necessary, start your virtual machines using the appropriate instructions in Activity 1-1.

2. Click **Start** and then click **Computer**.

3. To view the existing libraries, click **Libraries** in the navigation pane.

4. To view the Music library, double-click **Music**.

5. To see the music with tagged information, double-click **Sample Music**.

6. To see alternative ways to organize the files, click the **Arrange by** chevron.

7. To arrange the music by artist name, click **Artist**.

8. To arrange the music by song name, click the **Arrange by** chevron, and then click **Song**.

9. To add a new library, right-click **Libraries**, point to **New**, and then click **Library**. An entry called New Library is added.

10. To name the library, type **Public Presentation** over "New Library" and then press **Enter**.

11. To populate the Public Presentation library, double-click **Public Presentation**, click **Include a Folder**, scroll and click **Computer** in the navigation pane, double-click **Local Disk (C:)**, double-click **Users**, double-click **Public**, click **Public Music**, and then click **Include Folder**.

12. To add another folder, scroll and click **Computer** in the navigation pane, double-click **Local Disk (C:)**, double-click **Users**, double-click **Public**, right-click **Public Pictures**, point to Include in Library, and then click **Public Presentation**.

13. To see the results, click **Public Presentation** on the navigation pane.

14. Close the open windows in the virtual machine.

15. Leave the virtual machine logged on for the next activity.

Activity 3-13: Managing the Recycle Bin

Time Required: 10 minutes

Objective: Delete and restore files and folders using the Recycle Bin.

Description: In this activity, you delete a document and then restore it from the Recycle Bin. Next, you empty the Recycle Bin. This activity is useful if you want to recover deleted files.

1. If necessary, start your virtual machines using the appropriate instructions in Activity 1-1.

2. Click **Start** and then click the **Documents** folder.

3. Right-click an empty area in the right pane, click **New**, click **Text Document**, type **Delete Me** over "New Text Document," and then press **Enter**.

4. Right-click the **Delete Me** icon, click **Delete**, and then click **Yes**.

5. In the Documents window, click the **Minimize** button—the first of the three buttons on the right side of the title bar—to make the window temporarily disappear and become an icon on the taskbar.

6. Double-click the **Recycle Bin** icon on the desktop.

7. Right-click the **Delete Me** icon and then click **Restore**.

8. Click the **Minimize** button in the Recycle Bin window.

9. Click the **Documents** icon on the taskbar to see the Documents window again.

10. Verify that the **Delete Me** icon has returned to the **Documents** folder.

11. Right-click the **Delete Me** icon, click **Delete**, and then click **Yes**.

12. Click the **Recycle Bin** icon on the taskbar to see the Recycle Bin window again.

13. Click **Empty the Recycle Bin** and then click **Yes**.

14. Verify that the **Delete Me** icon no longer appears in the Recycle Bin folder.

15. Close any open windows in the virtual machine.

16. Leave the virtual machine logged on for the next activity.

Activity 3-14: Searching from the Windows 7 Start Menu

Time Required: 10 minutes

Objective: Search for files from the Windows 7 Start menu.

Description: In this activity, you will search for a music file. This is useful if you want to locate a file in an unknown location.

1. If necessary, start your virtual machines using the appropriate instructions in Activity 1-1.

2. To open the Start menu, click **Start**.

3. To search for a music file when you know part of the filename, type **sle** and then click **Sleep Away**.

4. If you are prompted to choose the initial settings for Windows Media Player, click the **Recommended Setting** option button and then click **Finish**.

 Your sound might not have been configured in VirtualBox. If so, the music will not play. Click Close.

5. Close the Windows Media Player window.

6. To open the Start menu, click **Start**.

7. You can also search for a music file when you know the first few letters of the artist's name. For example, to search for the music file called *Kalimba* by Mr. Scruff, type **sc** and then locate Kalimba.

8. Close any open windows in the virtual machine.

9. Leave the virtual machine logged on for the next activity.

Activity 3-15: Searching from Windows Explorer

Time Required: 10 minutes

Objective: Search for files in Windows 7 Explorer.

Description: In this activity, you will search for a picture file. This is useful if you want to find a file in an unknown location.

1. If necessary, start your virtual machines using the appropriate instructions in Activity 1-1.

2. To open Explorer, click **Start** and then click **Computer**.

3. To focus on Pictures, click **Pictures** under Libraries on the left side of the window.

4. To search for a picture file when you know the date the picture was taken, click in the Search text box, click **Date Taken**, and then click **A long time ago**.

5. To cancel the search, click the **X** on the Search text box.

6. To search for a picture file when you know the file type, click in the Search text box, click **Type**, and then click **.jpg**.

 When searching by tags, you are limited by the tags applied by the person who created the file.

7. Close any open windows in the virtual machine.

8. To shut down the virtual machine, click **Start**, and then click the **Shut Down** button.

9. Wait a moment for the Windows 7 virtual machine to completely shut down.

10. Leave the PC logged on for the next activity.

Using the Fedora 13 File Browser

File Browser (see Figure 3-24) is a utility in Fedora 13 that enables you to locate and open files and folders. You can open it by clicking Applications, System Tools, and File Browser. The File Browser window includes basic menus, toolbars, a navigation pane, and a tabbed preview pane.

This section introduces each area in the File Browser window. You will learn to use the controls in File Browser to locate files in Activity 3-16. In Chapter 6, you will learn more about using the File Browser menus.

The menu bar in File Browser includes many helpful options. In the File menu, you can use the New Tab and New Window options to create a new tabbed preview pane and a new window, respectively. Use the Edit menu options to move, copy, and rename selected files and folders. The View menu previews pane viewing options, the Go menu provides menu access to icons on the main toolbar, the Bookmarks menu allows you to bookmark selected

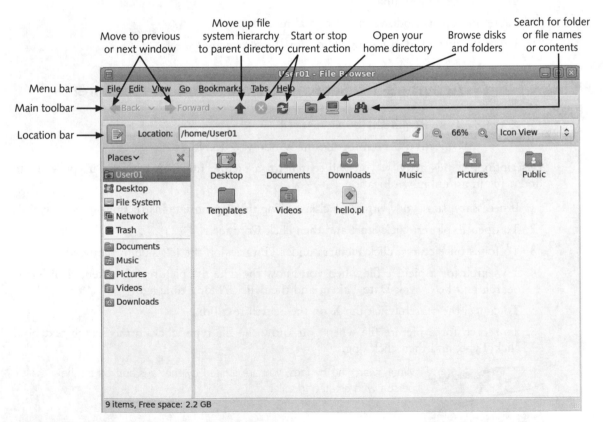

Figure 3-24 File Browser in Fedora 13

Source: Course Technology/Cengage Learning

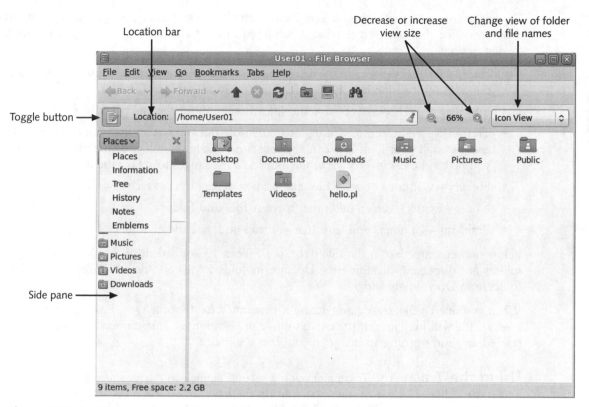

Figure 3-25 Location bar and side pane options in File Browser

Source: Course Technology/Cengage Learning

files and folders, and the Tabs menu lets you navigate preview pane tabs. If you have any questions about using these options, select the Help menu.

The functions of the main toolbar are shown in Figure 3-25. The Browse button allows you to browse all local and remote disks and folders that are accessible from your computer. (The Browse button also shows dual-OS primary drives and allows you to mount them. *Do not* mount other drives unless your instructor requests it.)

Below the main toolbar is the location bar, which corresponds to the address bar in Windows 7. Use the toggle button shown in Figure 3-25 to switch between text and button views of your location or path views. The button view displays folder items in the current path, and the text-based view shows the path location in simple text. For example, Figure 3-25 shows a text-based view of /home/User01.

The location bar contains options that let you change the view size (see Figure 3-25). Using the menu on the right side of the location bar, you can also select one of three views for folder and file names: Icon view, which lists folders and files as icons; List view, which provides detailed information with folder and file names; and Compact view, which lists folder and file names with icons.

The left side of the File Browser window contains a side pane (see Figure 3-25), which shows information about the current file or folder and enables you to navigate through your files.

To display the side pane, choose Side Pane from the View menu. The side pane contains a drop-down list that determines what is displayed in the pane. You can choose from the following options:

- Places—Displays places of particular interest, including the current user's home folder, the desktop location, file system, network location, and trash folder.

- Information—Displays an icon and information about the current folder.

- Tree—Displays a hierarchical representation of your file system that you can use to navigate through your files. You can navigate either the home folder or the file system. When you make choices in Tree view, the location bar changes to reflect the new location.

- History—Contains a list of files and folders that you have recently visited.

- Notes—Enables you to add notes to your files and folders.

- Emblems—Contains emblems that you can add to a file or folder.

Below the separator bar in the side pane, the Fedora 13 equivalent of the Windows 7 library folders are displayed, including the Documents folder, Music folder, Pictures folder, Videos folder, and Downloads folder.

When you open a file, the default action is performed for that file type. For example, opening a music file will play it with the default music application, opening a text file displays it in a text editor, and opening an image file displays the image.

Using the Trash   The Trash gives you a second chance to retrieve deleted files or folders and restore them to their original location on the hard drive. To access the Trash, click the Trash icon on the desktop. As the Trash fills with material you have deleted, older items are removed automatically to make room for newer items. More recently deleted items remain available until you delete them permanently by emptying the Trash. If you are running low on hard drive space, you should empty the trash (see Figure 3-26) to remove deleted items. You will work with the Trash in Activity 3-19.

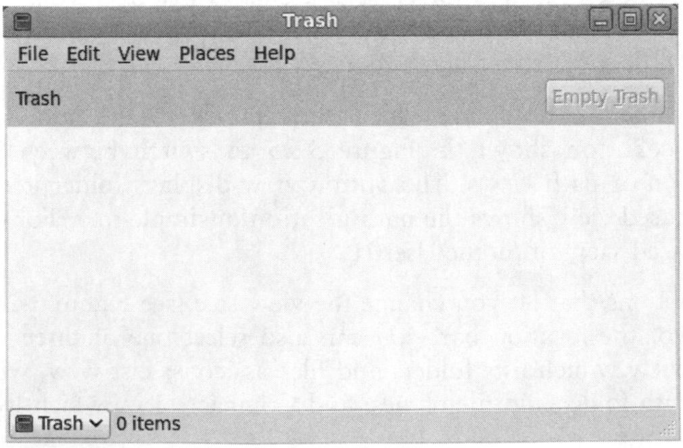

Figure 3-26 Trash in Fedora 13

Source: Course Technology/Cengage Learning

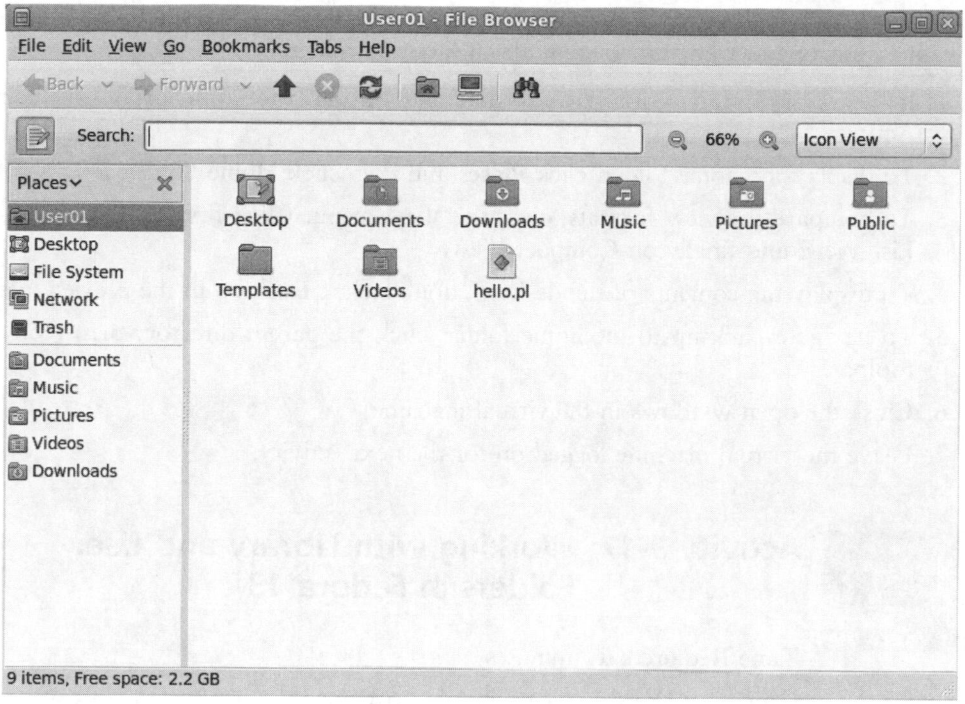

Figure 3-27 Search bar

Source: Course Technology/Cengage Learning

Items that you delete from external drives or network drives are deleted permanently and are not sent to the Trash.

Searching from the File Browser File Browser includes an easy way to search for files and folders on your computer. Like Windows 7, the Fedora Core 13 search feature lets you search by file and folder names and their contents. To begin a search, click the Search button on the main toolbar; the button looks like a pair of binoculars. The search bar replaces the location bar, as shown in Figure 3-27.

Enter a search phrase for the name or contents of the file or folder you want to find, and then press Enter. The results of your search should appear in the view pane. You will use the Search function in File Browser in Activity 3-18.

Activity 3-16: Using File Browser in Fedora 13

Time Required: 10 minutes

Objective: Use the toolbars in File Browser.

Description: In this activity, you will work with File Browser. This activity is useful if you want to locate and view information about files and folders.

1. If necessary, start your virtual machines using the appropriate instructions in Activity 1-1.
2. To display the home folder, click **Places** and then click **Home Folder**.
3. To compare the view formats, click the **View** menu. Click first on **Icon View**, then on **List View**, and finally on **Compact View**.
4. To display the contents of the desktop, double-click **Desktop** in the preview pane.
5. To navigate back up to the home folder, click the **parent directory** arrow on the main toolbar.
6. Close the open windows in the virtual machine.
7. Leave the virtual machine logged on for the next activity.

Activity 3-17: Working with Library and User Folders in Fedora 13

Time Required: 10 minutes

Objective: Use the folders in File Browser.

Description: In this activity, you will work with the Library folders in File Browser. This activity is useful if you want to locate and view information about user files and folders.

1. If necessary, start your virtual machines using the appropriate instructions in Activity 1-1.
2. Click **Places**.
3. To display the contents of the first Library folders, click **Home Folder**.
4. Repeat Step 3 using **Desktop, Documents, Music, Pictures, Videos,** and **Downloads**.
5. Close the open windows in the virtual machine.
6. Leave the virtual machine logged on for the next activity.

Activity 3-18: Searching with File Browser in Fedora 13

Time Required: 10 minutes

Objective: Search for files with File Browser.

Description: In this activity, you will search for a file that contains specific words. This activity is useful if you want to locate a file based on its content.

1. If necessary, start your virtual machines using the appropriate instructions in Activity 1-1.
2. To open gedit, click **Applications**, point to **Accessories**, and then click **gedit Text Editor**.

3. Type **Test for File Browser Search** and then press **Enter**.

4. Type **Nautilus** and then press **Enter**.

5. To save the file, click **File**, click **Save As**, type **Nautilus** in the Name text box, and then click **Save**.

6. To begin the search, click **Places** and then click **Search for Files**.

7. Type **Nautilus** in the search bar and then press **Enter**.

 If you do not see the Nautilus file in the view pane, contact your instructor.

8. Close the open windows in the virtual machine.

9. Leave the virtual machine logged on for the next activity.

Activity 3-19: Managing the Trash

Time Required: 10 minutes

Objective: Delete and restore files and folders using the Trash.

Description: In this activity, you delete a document and then restore it from the Trash. You also empty the Trash. This activity is useful if you want to recover deleted files.

1. If necessary, start your virtual machines using the appropriate instructions in Activity 1-1.

2. To create an empty file on the desktop, right-click the desktop, click **Create Document**, and then click **Empty File**.

3. To send the file to the Trash, right-click the new file and then click **Move to Trash**.

4. To see the context menu for the Trash, right-click the desktop **Trash** icon.

5. To view the contents of the Trash, click **Browse Folder**.

6. To remove the contents of the Trash, click **Empty Trash** and then click **Empty Trash** again.

7. Close the File Browser window.

8. To rename the Trash icon, right-click **Trash**, click **Rename**, type **Trash Can,** and then press **Enter**.

9. To return the name to Trash, repeat Step 8 using **Trash**.

10. To create another empty file on the desktop, right-click the desktop, click **Create Document,** and then click **Empty File**.

11. To send the file to the Trash, right-click the new file and then click **Move to Trash**.

12. To locate the deleted file in the Trash, right-click the **Trash** icon and then click **Browse Folder**.

13. To restore the file to the desktop, right-click the new file and then click **Restore**.

14. Close the File Browser window.

15. Verify that the new file is on the desktop.

16. Close any open windows in the virtual machine.

17. To shut down the virtual machine, click **System,** click **Shut Down,** and then click the **Shut Down** button.

18. Wait a moment for the Fedora 13 virtual machine to completely shut down.

19. Close any remaining open windows, log off, and shut down your PC.

Chapter Summary

- The graphical user interface (GUI) has many menus that you use to work with applications. Use the Start menu to begin applications in the Windows GUI environment; use the Applications menu to begin applications in Fedora Core 13.

- You can tailor the GUI desktop in both Windows 7 and Fedora Core 13. Besides modifying the appearance of the desktop, you can control icon placement and the behavior of windows, menus, and cursors. Each operating system has different methods for modifying the desktop.

- You have many options for accessing locally stored data in Windows 7 and Fedora Core 13. If you do not know a file or folder's exact location, use a search utility. As long as you have not cleaned out the Recycle Bin or the Trash, you can retrieve deleted files and folders from Windows 7 and Fedora Core 13, respectively. In Windows 7, you use Windows Explorer to organize and view files; in Fedora Core 13, you use File Browser to perform these tasks.

Key Terms

applet   A small, single-function utility.

Applications menu   A menu in the Fedora 13 GUI that opens applications and utilities, like the Start menu in Windows 7.

breadcrumbs   Navigation aids used in an address bar and other parts of the GUI to help keep track of your locations.

desktop context menu   The submenu that appears when you click an empty area on the Fedora 13 desktop.

File Browser   A utility in Fedora 13 that enables you to locate and open files and folders.

index   A large collection of references to information on your hard disk that helps Windows to return search results.

panel   The Fedora 13 equivalent of the taskbar used in Windows 7.

Recycle Bin   A folder that holds files and folders you delete from a hard drive in Windows 7. You can restore the deleted files and folders if necessary. The Recycle Bin is represented by a trash can icon.

shortcuts   Desktop icons that you can click to immediately access applications, text files, folders, and Web pages in a GUI environment.

stack   A Windows feature that lets you quickly preview all of your open files, folders, and documents without having to click the taskbar. Instead, you "flip" through the stack.

Start menu   A menu in Windows 7 that you use to select applications, utilities, and commands. This menu appears when you click the Start icon in the lower-left corner of the screen.

Windows Explorer   A Windows utility that enables you to locate and open files and folders.

Review Questions

1. To start applications in Windows 7, use the _____.
   a. Applications menu
   b. Start menu
   c. Launch menu
   d. Control Center

2. Windows uses the _____.
   a. default Applications menu
   b. default Start menu
   c. simple Start menu
   d. classic Start menu

3. To start applications in Fedora Core 13, use the _____.
   a. Applications menu
   b. Start menu
   c. Launch menu
   d. Configure menu

4. You can use the taskbar to _____. (Choose all that apply.)
   a. monitor current tasks
   b. quickly move between open applications
   c. change the configuration of the Start menu
   d. modify the current taskbar settings

5. If you cannot move the taskbar, _____.
   a. don't worry; the taskbar cannot be moved
   b. unlock it by right-clicking an empty area of the taskbar and clearing the Lock the Taskbar check box
   c. double-click it
   d. unlock it by right-clicking an empty area of the taskbar and checking the Unlock the Taskbar check box

6. Menus are customized to _____.

    a.   provide shortcuts to frequently used applications

    b.   remove applications that are infrequently used

    c.   change fonts, color schemes, and window behaviors

    d.   group applications by use

7. The list of programs on the Windows 7 default Start menu is divided into _____ part(s).

    a.   1

    b.   2

    c.   3

    d.   4

8. Which of the following items are commonly found on the Windows 7 taskbar? (Choose all that apply.)

    a.   Start button

    b.   File menu

    c.   Clock

    d.   open applications

9. Which of the following options appear on the Windows 7 Start menu by default? (Choose all that apply.)

    a.   Computer

    b.   Documents

    c.   Music

    d.   Pictures

10. In Fedora Core 13, the taskbar is commonly referred to as a _____.

    a.   menu

    b.   taskbar

    c.   panel

    d.   file

11. You can tailor the desktop to provide _____. (Choose all that apply.)

    a.   quick access to running applications

    b.   shortcuts to frequently used applications

    c.   an organized workspace

    d.   privacy for your desktop

12. Adding an item to the panel in Fedora 13 requires choosing from _____. (Choose all that apply.)

    a.   applets

    b.   applications

c. panels

d. drawers

13. To delete an item from a panel in Fedora 13, right-click the item and then click
_____.

a. Add to Panel

b. Move

c. Remove From Panel

d. Delete From Panel

14. Which of the following actions changes the amount of information that appears on the screen? (Choose all that apply.)

a. increasing the size of fonts

b. decreasing the size of fonts

c. increasing the screen resolution

d. decreasing the screen resolution

15. A utility that locates and opens files in Windows 7 is _____.

a. Control Center

b. File Browser

c. Search

d. Windows Explorer

16. A utility that locates and opens files in Fedora 13 is _____.

a. Control Center

b. File Browser

c. Search

d. Windows Explorer

17. When you delete files from a folder, where do they go? (Choose all that apply.)

a. Recycle Bin

b. Trash

c. File Manager

d. the Delete folder

18. To filter a search in Windows 7, you can use the _____ option. (Choose all that apply.)

a. Author

b. Date modified

c. Size

d. Date taken

19. As an aid to organization, files are grouped by _____. (Choose all that apply.)

    a. places

    b. folders

    c. libraries

    d. partitions

20. New Windows 7 desktop features include _____. (Choose all that apply.)

    a. Jump lists

    b. Snap

    c. Peek

    d. Shake

Case Projects

CASE PROJECTS

Case 3-1: Customizing the Windows Start Menu

George requested your help to customize his Windows 7 Start menu. He needs to access a limited number of applications quickly and locate previously used files. What will you suggest?

Case 3-2: Recovering Deleted Files in Fedora 13

You get a call from Susan, who has deleted a case project by mistake. She wants to know how to recover the deleted file. What do you tell her?

Case 3-3: Searching for Files

You need to help your friend locate a file on his computer, but he does not recall the name of the file. What suggestions could you make to help?

chapter 4

Installing and Configuring Applications

After reading this chapter and completing the exercises, you will be able to:

- Access Help information
- Use and configure a Web browser
- Install the ActiveState Perl application and test the installation with a test script

An application is any program designed to perform a specific function directly for the user. In some cases, an application performs a function for another program. You have already used several applications in this text, including the word processors OpenOffice Writer and WordPad.

After learning to use the Help tools in Windows 7 and Fedora 13, you will learn more about using and configuring applications. For example, you will learn to configure and use Web browsers. Windows programs have similar menus, so working with these browsers will prepare you to use and configure other applications. Later in this chapter, you will install the Community Edition of ActiveState Perl, which is available for both Windows 7 and Fedora 13.

Accessing the Help Features

If you are working in Windows 7 or Fedora 13 and you have a question about how to accomplish a task, you should check the helpful resources at your fingertips before asking your instructor or classmate for help. In the following sections, you will learn to use the GUI Help features in Windows 7 and Fedora 13.

Using the Help and Support Center in Windows 7

Help and Support is a comprehensive resource for practical advice, tutorials, and demonstrations that help you learn to use Microsoft Windows 7. Use the Search feature, index, and table of contents to view Windows 7 Help resources.

To open Help and Support, click Start and then click Help and Support. Each item on the opening screen is a link to further information or assistance (see Figure 4-1). For example, "How to get started with your computer" is a good link if you want information on setting up your new computer. While you might no longer be a neophyte, "Learn about Windows Basics" is a good link for new users of Windows.

 You can also press the F1 key to open Help and Support. If it does not open, click the desktop and press F1 again.

To get updated information from Microsoft, click the Windows link in the phrase "Check out the Windows website."

To see examples of the wide range of information available in Help and Support (as shown in Figure 4-2), click Browse Help topics.

Use the Search function in Help to locate a topic by keyword. For example, type *Internet* and click the spyglass to see information about using Windows 7 connections to the Internet. You will learn more about using Help and Support in Activity 4-1.

System Information The System Information tool (see Figure 4-3) provides summary information for your computer. You learned about the System Information tool in Chapter 1.

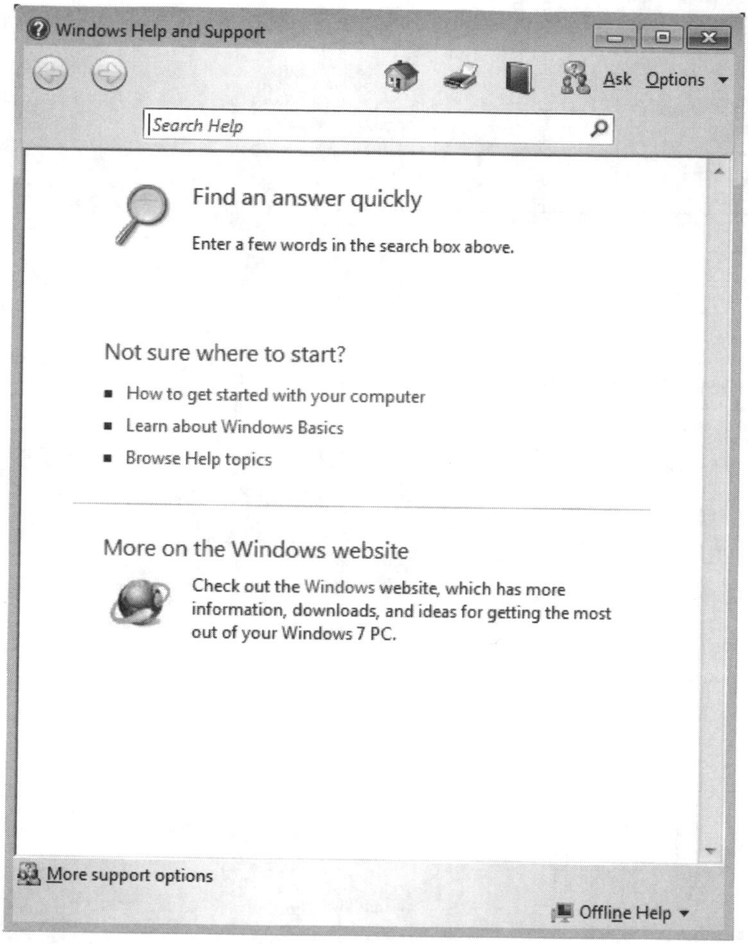

Figure 4-1 Help and Support Center

Source: Course Technology/Cengage Learning

In this chapter, you will learn more about this tool. For example, you can use the tool to confirm your system configuration. To access this tool, click Help and Support from the Start menu, type *system information* in the Search Help text box, click the spyglass, click the What is System Information link, and then click the Click to open System Information link.

Hardware Resources From the Hardware Resources section of the System Information tool, you can find information to help resolve a hardware resource problem. Click the + icon to expand Hardware Resources. For example, click Conflicts/Sharing to see hardware resources that are used by more than one device, as shown in Figure 4-4. You will learn more about using hardware resources in Activity 4-2.

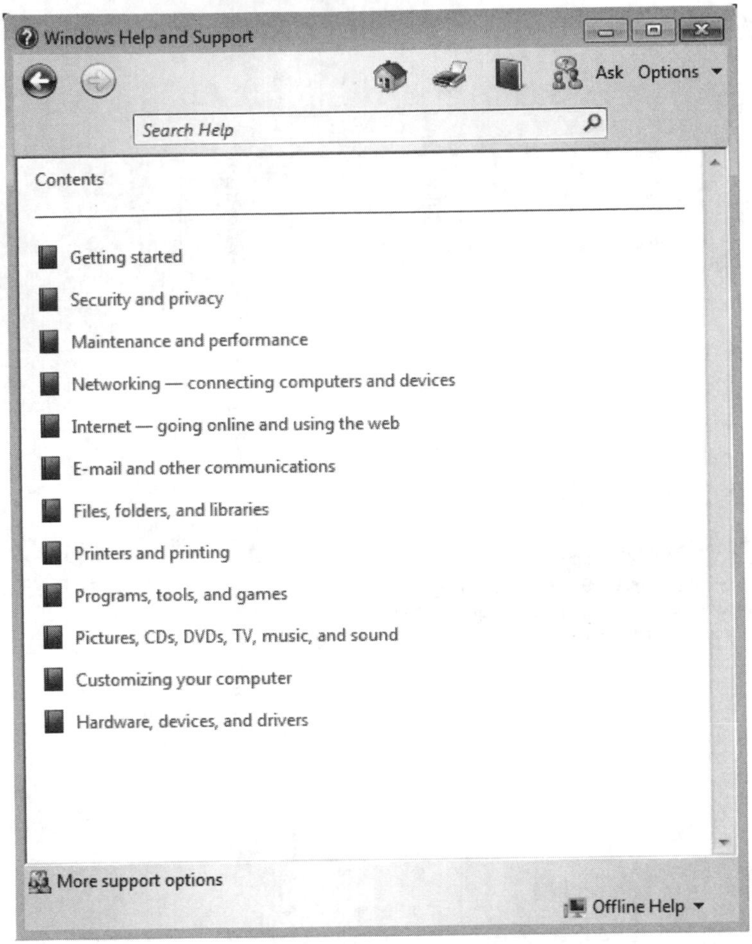

Figure 4-2 Help and Support Center showing Help topics

Source: Course Technology/Cengage Learning

Components Expanding the Components section of the System Information tool provides a detailed list of information about the hardware components on your computer system. For example, to find information about the CD-ROM drive in your computer, click CD-ROM. Figure 4-5 shows information about the CD-ROM drive in the Windows 7 virtual machine running in VirtualBox. You will learn more about this in Activity 4-2.

Software Environment If you need information about the software environment on your computer, expand Software Environment in the System Information tool. This section provides details about your operating system and applications. To view the programs running on your computer, click Running Tasks. The programs running in a Windows 7 virtual machine are shown in Figure 4-6. You will learn more about this in Activity 4-2.

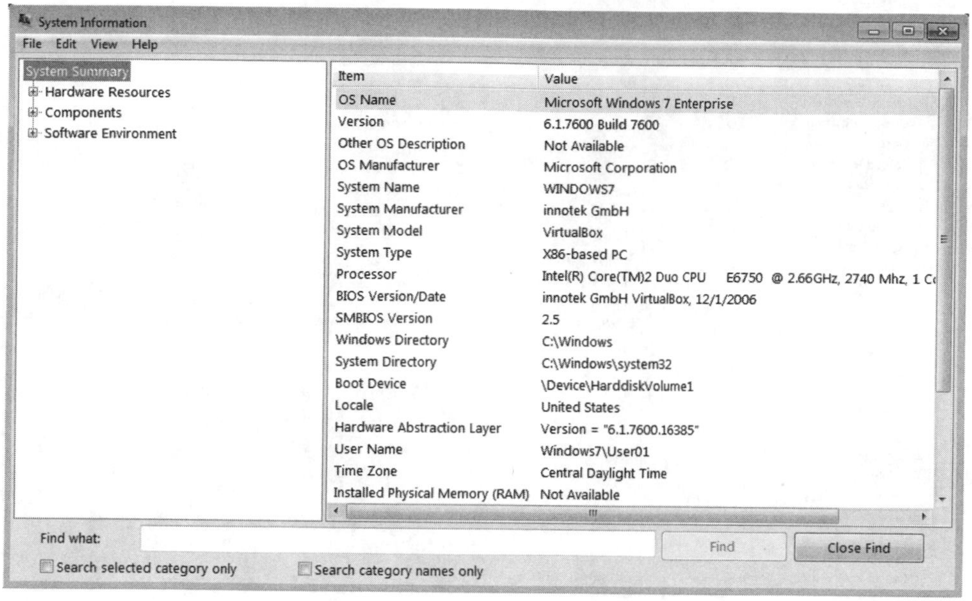

Figure 4-3 System Information tool

Source: Course Technology/Cengage Learning

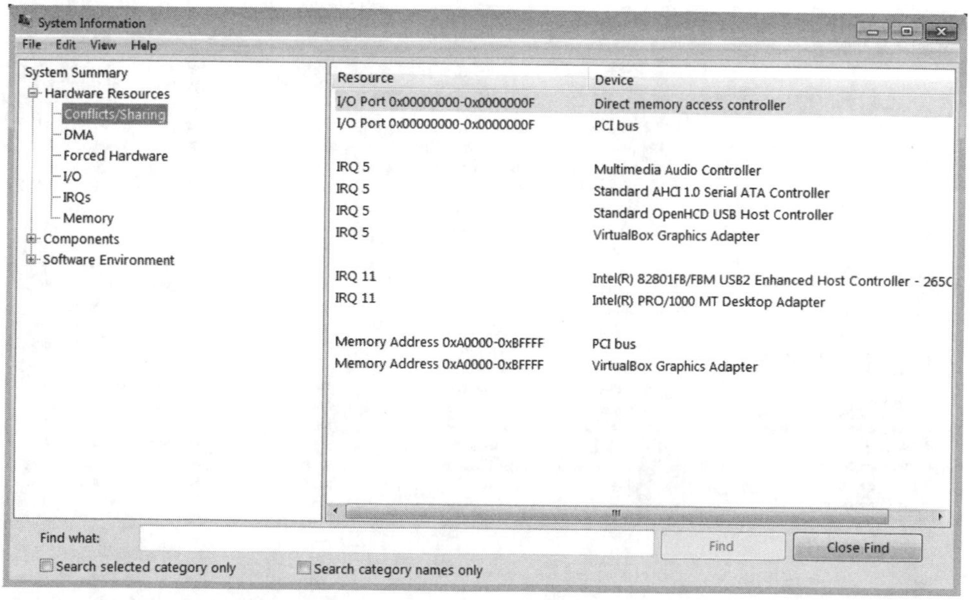

Figure 4-4 Hardware Resources showing Conflicts/Sharing

Source: Course Technology/Cengage Learning

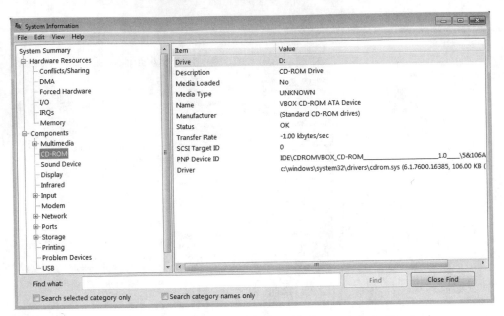

Figure 4-5 Information about CD-ROM drive displayed in System Information tool

Source: Course Technology/Cengage Learning

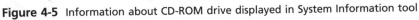

Figure 4-6 Information about running tasks displayed in System Information tool

Source: Course Technology/Cengage Learning

Activity 4-1: Using Help and Support in Windows 7

ACTIVITY

Time Required: 10 minutes

Objective: Examine the Windows 7 Help and Support.

Description: In this activity, you use the Windows 7 Help and Support. This activity is useful if you need to learn about a particular Windows 7 feature.

1. Start your virtual machines using the appropriate instructions in Activity 1-1.

2. To open Help and Support, click **Start** and then click **Help and Support**.

3. Click the **Learn about Windows Basics** link.

4. Open and read one or more topics that interest you.

5. To return to the initial Windows Help and Support window, click the **Home** icon.

6. To search for an item, type **Memory** and then click the spyglass.

7. Click the **Find out how much RAM your computer has** link and then click the **Click to open System** link.

8. Locate the Installed memory (RAM) entry.

9. Close the System window.

10. Click the **Browse Help** icon, which looks like a blue book.

11. Open and read one or more topics that interest you.

12. Close the Windows Help and Support window.

13. Leave the virtual machine logged on for the next activity.

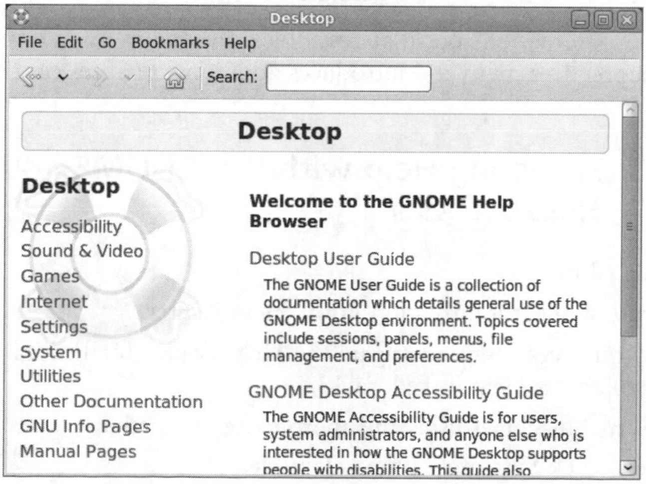

Figure 4-7 The Fedora 13 Help Center

Source: Course Technology/Cengage Learning

Activity 4-2: Viewing System Information in Windows 7

Time Required: 10 minutes

Objective: View general system information on a PC.

Description: In this activity, you view your virtual machine's system information. This activity is useful if you need to see system information to resolve problems.

1. If necessary, start your virtual machines using the appropriate instructions in Activity 1-1.
2. Click **Start**, click **Help and Support**, type **system information** in the Search Help text box, click the spyglass, click the **What is System Information** link, and then click the **Click to open System Information** link.
3. Wait for the information to appear.
4. Review the System Summary page.
5. To see the subcategories for hardware resources, expand **Hardware Resources**.
6. To view the interrupt requests (IRQs) assigned, click **IRQs**.
7. To view the memory areas assigned, click **Memory**.
8. To view the available hardware components, expand **Components**.
9. Open and read one or more topics that interest you.
10. To view the software environment, expand **Software Environment**.
11. Open and read one or more topics that interest you.
12. Close any open windows.
13. Leave the virtual machine logged on for future activities.

Using the Fedora 13 Help Center and System Information

To access the Fedora 13 Help Center (see Figure 4-7), click System and then click Help. Next, select the link for the information you need. For example, to locate information about using the GNOME desktop, click the Desktop User Guide.

Fedora 13 provides a System Information tool that resembles the one in Windows 7. You learned about this tool in Chapter 1. Activity 4-4 introduces additional features of the Fedora 13 System Information tool.

Activity 4-3: Accessing Help with the GNOME Help Browser

Time Required: 10 minutes

Objective: Access support information in the Help Center.

Description: In this activity, you access and investigate the Help Center for Fedora 13. This activity is useful if you need to access Help in Fedora 13.

1. If necessary, start your virtual machines using the appropriate instructions in Activity 1-1.
2. To access the Help Center, click **System** and then click **Help**.
3. Click **Internet** and read some of the online help information.
4. Close any open windows.
5. Leave the virtual machine logged on for the next activity.

Activity 4-4: Viewing System Information in Fedora 13

Time Required: 10 minutes

Objective: Access system information with the System Information tool.

Description: In this activity, you access and investigate system information with Fedora 13. This activity is useful if you need to access system information in Fedora 13.

1. If necessary, start your virtual machines using the appropriate instructions in Activity 1-1.

2. To open the terminal console, point to **Applications**, point to **System Tools**, and then click **Terminal**.

3. To open the System Information window, type **hardinfo** and press **Enter**.

If you see a "Command not found" message, contact your instructor.

4. To review the summary, click **Summary**.

5. To review operating system information, click **Operating System**.

6. To review processor information, click **Processor**.

7. To locate CPU resources, click **Resources**.

8. Review the I/O ports in the right pane.

9. Scroll and review the memory information in the right pane.

10. To review the input devices, click **Input Devices**.

11. To review the mounted drives, click **Storage**.

12. Close any open windows.

13. Leave the virtual machine logged on for future activities.

Using and Configuring Web Browsers

A Web browser is a software program that you use to access and navigate the Web. The first widely used browser, called NCSA Mosaic, was developed at the National Center for Supercomputing Applications in the early 1990s. Mosaic's point-and-click interface helped popularize the Web.

Browsers provide tools that allow you to travel effortlessly from Web site to Web site. If you want to visit the same site repeatedly, you can bookmark it.

In this section, you will learn to use two Web browsers—Microsoft's Internet Explorer and Mozilla's Firefox.

Using the security features and privacy options of Internet Explorer, you can create a secure environment that protects your personal information as you surf the Web.

Browsing the Web with Internet Explorer

Each page on the Web is designated by an Internet address known as a **Uniform Resource Locator (URL)**. In other words, a URL identifies the location of any Web site. Figure 4-8 shows the Internet Explorer toolbar and the address bar, which contains a URL.

The default URL for Internet Explorer is *www.msn.com*, which is Microsoft's portal to the Internet.

You can go to a Web site by typing an address in the address bar. You can also use the Back and Forward buttons on the address bar to move backward and forward through the sites you have visited during your current browsing session. To see a list of recently viewed Web pages, click the chevron next to the Forward button.

You can move from one Web page to another by clicking **hyperlinks** (usually called links) within the pages. A hyperlink takes you to a different URL that indicates a different location on the Web. The link could take you to a different Web site or to a different spot on the same page.

When you move your mouse pointer over a link, Internet Explorer detects the link and changes the pointer to a pointing finger. Hyperlinks are usually underlined or displayed in a

Figure 4-8 Internet Explorer toolbar and address bar

Source: Course Technology/Cengage Learning

different color to indicate text that is "hot," or clickable. Clickable links typically change their appearance when the pointer moves over them.

You can also use tabs in Web browsing and Web searches. Tabs permit more than one Web page to be displayed and allow you to switch rapidly between Web pages.

Randomly moving around the Web is easy, but finding your way to specific information can be trickier. When you read a book, the text flows from page to page. On the Internet, however, you must actively decide where to go next. That is why people often speak of "browsing" the Web, as if they were in a library browsing the shelves, and it is why Internet Explorer is called a browser.

To help you locate particular information in cyberspace, Internet Explorer provides a search utility. To use the default Bing search engine, type a few words into it about a topic of interest (see Figure 4-9). Bing will present a list of suggestions that you can click. If no suggestions appear, click the spyglass in the upper-right corner.

Click the Favorites button on the toolbar to return quickly to favorite sites you have specified. To save the current Web site so you can return quickly to it in the future, click the Favorites button and then click the Add to Favorites button.

Portal sites—pages with links to a variety of information—are also useful tools for getting around the Internet. For example, try *www.yahoo.com* or *www.google.com*.

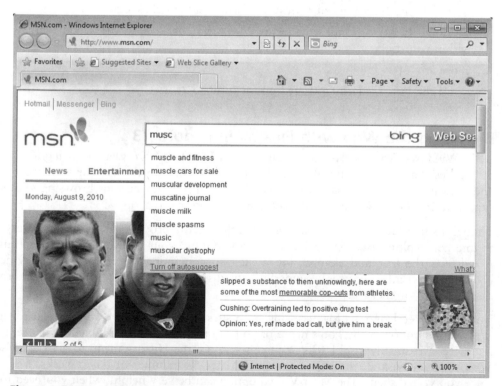

Figure 4-9 Internet Explorer Bing search engine

Source: Course Technology/Cengage Learning

Activity 4-5: Browsing the Web with Internet Explorer

Time Required: 15 minutes

Objective: Browse the Web with Internet Explorer.

Description: In this activity, you access a portal site on the Web to locate information about automobile features and pricing. This activity is useful because it shows you how to find information on the Web.

1. If necessary, start your virtual machines using the appropriate instructions in Activity 1-1.

2. To start Internet Explorer, click the **Internet** button on the taskbar.

3. If the Welcome to Internet Explorer Web page appears, click **Next**, click the **No, don't turn on** option button, click **Next**, click the **Use express settings** option button, and then click **Finish**.

4. If necessary, type **www.msn.com** in the address bar and then press **Enter**.

> **NOTE** If you are trying to access a Web site whose URL ends in ".com," type the unique part of the URL (such as "msn") and then press Ctrl+ Enter. The "www" and ".com" will be attached to the name that you typed in the address bar.

5. Point to **Money** in the menu at the top of the page, and then click the **Autos** link.

6. Complete the New Cars or Used Cars form and then click **Go**.

7. Continue browsing until you locate a car that has the features you want and stays within your budget.

8. Close any open windows.

9. Leave the virtual machine logged on for future activities.

Browsing the Web with Firefox in Fedora 13

As in Windows 7, you move to a Web site in a Fedora 13 browser by typing an address in the address bar. You use the Back and Forward buttons on the toolbar to move backward and forward through the sites you have visited during your current browsing session. You can move from one Web page to another by clicking the hyperlinks.

Though its interface and layout are different, the Firefox browser in Fedora 13 is very similar to Internet Explorer (see Figure 4-10). When you move your mouse pointer over a link, Firefox detects the link and changes the pointer to a pointing finger. As with a Windows 7 browser, hyperlinks are usually underlined or displayed in a different color to indicate text that is "hot," or clickable.

You have several options for accessing Web sites in Firefox. For example, you can use the Web Search option in the Tools menu or you can use the Bookmarks menu to store, manage, and access frequently used URLs. You can also use the History menu to access a history of Web sites you visited; the sites are organized by the number of days, weeks, and months since you visited them. The Most Visited option can be very helpful when you need to access a previously visited Web site for which you did not create a bookmark. The Show All History option displays all your bookmarks.

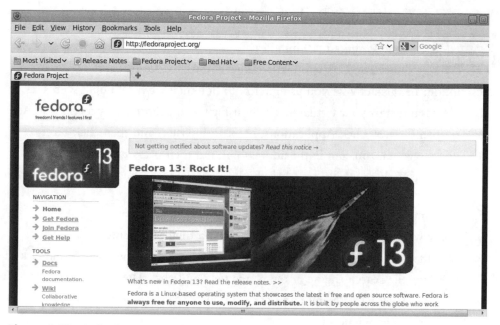

Figure 4-10 Firefox browser with navigation toolbar

Source: Course Technology/Cengage Learning

Activity 4-6: Browsing the Web with Firefox

Time Required: 15 minutes

Objective: Browse the Web with Firefox.

Description: In this activity, you access a portal site on the Web to locate information about a topic. This activity is useful because it shows you how to access catalogued information on the Web.

1. If necessary, start your virtual machines using the appropriate instructions in Activity 1-1.

2. To open Firefox, click **Applications,** point to **Internet,** and then click **Firefox.**

3. Type **www.amazon.com** in the address bar and then click the **green arrow** button.

 As with Internet Explorer, you can access the Web site in Firefox simply by typing "amazon" in the address bar and then holding down the Ctrl key while clicking Go.

4. Point to the **Electronics** link, then scroll and click the category of your choice.

5. Continue browsing to locate an electronic device that you like.

6. Close any open windows.

7. Leave the virtual machine logged on for the next activity.

Activity 4-7: Bookmarking a Page in Firefox

Time Required: 10 minutes

Objective: Create bookmarks in Firefox for future reference.

Description: In this activity, you use Firefox to bookmark two popular Web sites.

1. If necessary, start your virtual machines using the appropriate instructions in Activity 1-1.
2. To open Firefox, click **Applications**, point to **Internet**, and then click **Firefox**.
3. Type **www.amazon.com** in the address bar and then press **Enter**.
4. When the Web page appears, click the **Bookmarks** menu and then click **Bookmark This Page**.
5. Type **Amazon book store** in the Name field and click **Done**.
6. Type **www.dogpile.com** in the address bar and then press **Enter**.
7. When the Web page appears, click the **Bookmarks** menu and then click **Bookmark This Page**.
8. Type **Dogpile search engine** in the Name field and click **Done**.
9. Click the **Bookmarks** menu and note the two bookmarks you added.
10. Close any open windows.
11. Leave the virtual machine logged on for future activities.

Searching the Web with Internet Explorer

If you are looking for information on the Web that fits neatly into an obvious subject or category, go first to a Web directory. Think of a Web directory as a subject catalog—something like the catalog in your college library. Directories such as Yahoo, the Open Directory (dmoz), and the Google Directory organize the Web by dividing it into such topics as Arts, Science, Health, Business, News, and Entertainment.

Search engines use automated software programs to survey the Web and find the information you want. These programs retrieve and analyze documents that match your search criteria, and the data collected from each Web page is then added to the search engine's database. When you enter a query at a search engine site, your input is checked against the search engine's index of all the Web pages it has analyzed. The best URLs are then returned to you as "hits," with the best results listed at the top.

You need a search engine for the same reason you need the card catalog in a library. The library contains a lot of useful information, but it is impossible to examine all the books personally. Likewise, not even the most eager Web surfer could hyperlink to all the documents on the Web. Billions of Web pages are available online, and more are posted every day.

To examine the many documents on the Web, search engines use software programs known as bots, spiders, or crawlers. A **bot** is a piece of software that automatically follows hyperlinks from one document to the next around the Web. When a bot discovers a new site, it sends information back to its main site to be indexed. Because Web documents are one of the most dynamic forms of publishing, bots also update previously catalogued sites.

To rank the items in the search index, search engines use closely guarded ranking algorithms; search engine companies want to protect their methods from competitors, and they want to make it difficult for Web site owners to manipulate their rankings. A Web page's relevance ranking for a specific query depends on three factors:

- Its relevance to the words and concepts in the query
- Its overall link popularity
- Whether it is being penalized for abuse, such as linking a lot of sites to each other in a circular scam to artificially drive up the number of "hits"

A search engine has only a limited ability to understand what you want. It looks within its indexes for occurrences of the keywords or phrases you specify, but it does not understand what your keywords mean or why they are important to you. To a search engine, a keyword is just a string of characters. Read the Help files and take advantage of options that let you refine a search. Use phrases if possible.

If you are searching on a noun, keep in mind that most nouns are subsets of other nouns. Use the smallest possible subset that describes what you want. In other words, be specific. Try to help the search engine by refining your search before you begin. For example, if you want to buy a car, do not enter the keyword *car* if you can enter the keyword *Ford*. Better yet, enter the phrase "Ford dealerships" and the name of the city where you live.

Use the + character to include other keywords that you would expect to find in relevant documents, and use the − character to exclude items. Excluding text is particularly important as the Web grows and more documents are posted. If necessary, you can run your query several times, each time adding refinements to focus your list of relevant hits. For example, if you want to find out about hypertension, try querying on *hypertension* AND *treatment*. If you want to learn about lifestyle changes that could minimize the occurrence of hypertension, try entering *hypertension* AND *exercise* AND *diet* AND NOT *treatment*.

Activity 4-8: Searching the Web with Internet Explorer

Time Required: 15 minutes

Objective: Search the Web with Internet Explorer.

Description: In this activity, you access a search site using Internet Explorer to locate information about a topic. This activity is useful because you need to be able to search the Web for information, such as where to purchase a car.

1. If necessary, start your virtual machines using the appropriate instructions in Activity 1-1.
2. To start Internet Explorer, click the **Internet** button on the taskbar.
3. Type **www.google.com** in the address bar and then press **Enter**.
4. When the Google Web site appears, type your search string and then click the **Google Search** button. For example, to find pricing information for a Ford Mustang, type **Ford Mustang New Prices**.
5. Refine your search by trying additional keywords.
6. Close any open windows.
7. Leave the virtual machine logged on for future activities.

Searching the Web with Firefox

Because search engines are resident on the Internet and the Firefox browser is simply a tool to access the Web, the process for searching in Firefox is very similar to that in Internet Explorer. The Boolean syntax and phrasing of search queries are the same.

To access the search function from the Firefox browser, you can click Web Search from the Tools menu or enter a search engine's URL in the address bar and perform a search from the Firefox home page.

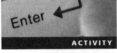 You can define the search engine you want to use by clicking the arrow beside the text box in the upper-right corner of Firefox. Google is selected by default.

Activity 4-9: Searching the Web with Firefox

Time Required: 15 minutes

Objective: Search the Web with Firefox.

Description: In this activity, you access a search site using Firefox to locate information about a topic. This activity is useful because you need to be able to search the Web for information.

1. If necessary, start your virtual machines using the appropriate instructions in Activity 1-1.

2. To open Firefox, click **Applications**, point to **Internet**, and then click **Firefox**.

3. In Firefox, click the **Tools** menu and then click **Web Search**. The cursor moves to the Search window in the Navigation toolbar.

4. Type **Fedora 13** in the Search window and press **Enter**.

5. When the search results appear, scroll up and down and look at the links.

6. Close any open windows.

7. Leave the virtual machine logged on for future activities.

Configuring Internet Explorer

Although you may assume that the default installation of Internet Explorer will suffice and that you don't need to configure the browser, that's not necessarily true. For example, if you never use the default home page that appears when you open the browser, you should select a different home page. Sometimes you might not want to leave any traces of your Web browsing on the computer you are using, such as when checking e-mail on a friend's computer or shopping for a gift on a family PC. You should also know how to regain disk space by occasionally deleting temporary Internet files that are copied to your hard drive.

Configuring Safety Settings   The InPrivate Browsing feature in Windows Internet Explorer helps protect data and privacy by preventing the browsing history, temporary Internet files, form data, cookies, user names, and passwords from being stored or retained locally by the browser, leaving virtually no evidence of the user's browsing or search history.

You can start InPrivate Browsing from the Safety menu (see Figure 4-11) by selecting InPrivate Browsing from a New Tab page. A new Internet Explorer 8 window will open with a blue and white InPrivate indicator displayed to the left of the address. You end an InPrivate session by closing the browser window.

SmartScreen Filter is a feature in Internet Explorer that helps you avoid malware sites when you browse the Web. Malware, which is short for *malicious software*, is software designed to infiltrate a computer system without the owner's informed consent. SmartScreen Filter uses the following techniques:

- Checks Web sites against a dynamically updated list of reported malware sites.
- Checks software downloads against a dynamically updated list of reported malicious software sites.
- Helps prevent you from visiting Web sites that contain malware and that can lead to identity theft.

The SmartScreen Filter is turned on by default. If you attempt to visit a Web site that has been reported, a dialog box appears and advises you not to continue to the unsafe site.

To continue configuring Internet Explorer, select Internet Options from the Tools menu. The Internet Options dialog box appears, as shown in Figure 4-12. The following sections explain the Internet Explorer configuration settings.

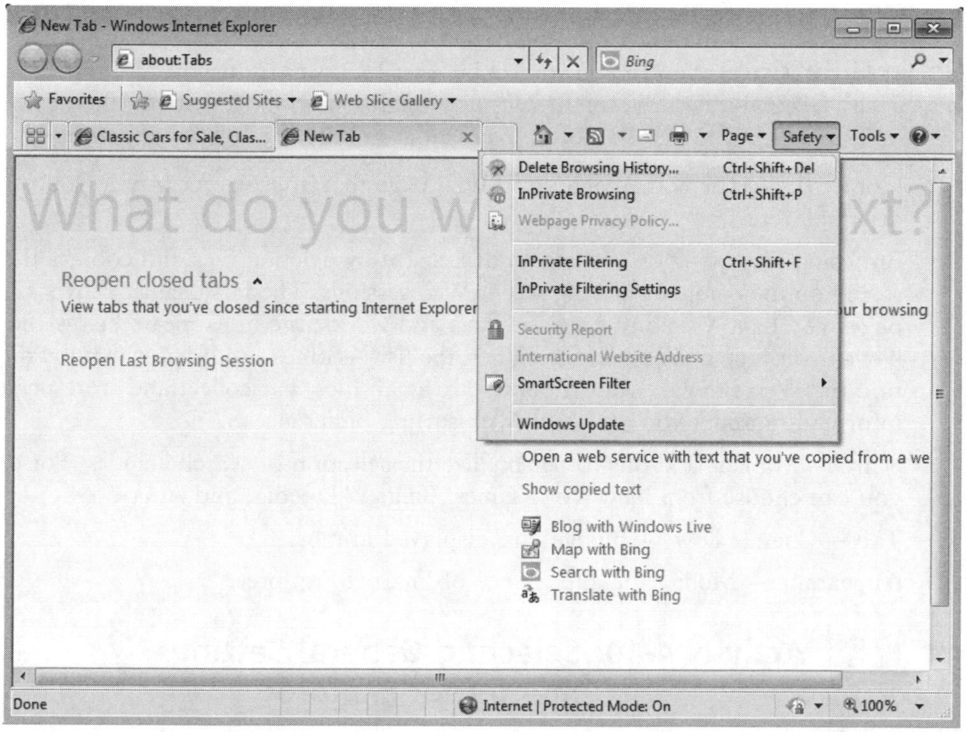

Figure 4-11 Selecting InPrivate Browsing

Source: Course Technology/Cengage Learning

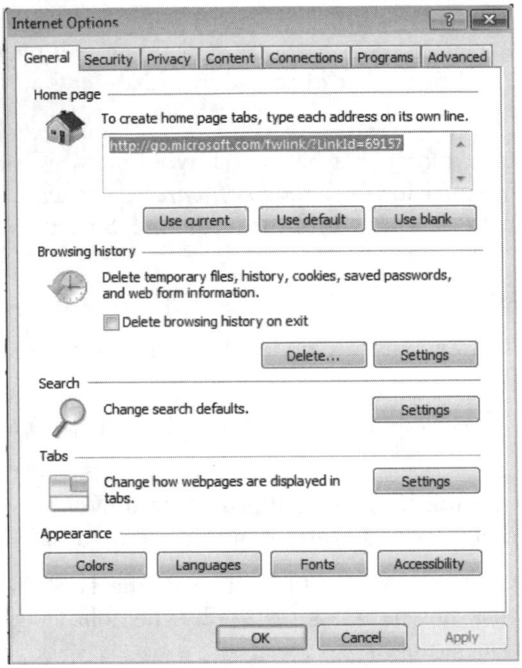

Figure 4-12 Internet Options dialog box

Source: Course Technology/Cengage Learning

General Settings You can customize Internet Explorer to fit your preferences using settings in the General tab of the Internet Options dialog box. In Activity 4-10, you will configure these settings in Internet Explorer. You can customize the following items:

- Home page—The home page is the Web page that appears every time you open Internet Explorer.

- Browsing history—You can regain disk space by deleting files and cookies that were stored on the computer during recent Web sessions. The History list shows all the Web pages you have visited in previous days and weeks; the list appears below the address bar as you type a Web address. When the list becomes too long, it may be difficult to find the Web site you want. **Cookies** are small files that collect and store personal information about you and your Web-surfing preferences.

- Search—Manage add-ons to personalize the selection of search engines. For example, you can choose from New York Times, Bing, Wikipedia, and Amazon.

- Tabs—Change how Web pages are displayed in tabs.

- Appearance—Modify the appearance of Internet Explorer.

Activity 4-10: Selecting General Settings in Internet Explorer

Time Required: 15 minutes

Objective: Configure the General tab settings in Internet Explorer.

Description: In this activity, you set the home page to a recently visited Web site. Depending on your usage, you might also need to clean up cookies, saved Internet files, and your history of recently visited Web sites. This activity is useful because it shows you how to perform basic configuration tasks for Internet Explorer.

1. If necessary, start your virtual machines using the appropriate instructions in Activity 1-1.

2. To start Internet Explorer, click the **Internet** button on the taskbar.

3. Type **www.google.com** in the address bar and then press **Enter**.

4. Click the **Tools** menu and then click **Internet Options**.

5. To set *www.google.com* as the home page, click the **Use current** button.

6. To begin the process of deleting the browsing history, click the **Delete** button.

7. Review the check boxes, check the desired items, and then click **Delete**.

8. To add a search engine, click the **Settings** button under Search, click **Find more search providers**, scroll and select a search provider, and click **Add to Internet Explorer**. Click **Add**.

9. Close the Web page, and then click **Close**.

10. To change how Web pages are displayed, click the **Settings** button under Tabs, review the check boxes, check the desired items, and then click **OK**.

11. Click **OK**.

12. Close any open windows.

13. Leave the virtual machine logged on for the next activity.

Security Zones Security **zones** offer an easy and flexible method for managing a secure Web environment. You can use these zones to implement a security policy by grouping Web sites together and assigning a security level to each zone. You can set up security zones from the Security tab of the Internet Options dialog box (see Figure 4-13).

Internet Explorer includes the following security zones:

- Internet zone—When you first install Internet Explorer 8, it corrals all Web sites into the Internet zone and stands guard with a Medium-high level of security. This level helps you browse securely, but it should prompt you before you download potentially unsafe content. If your organization is concerned about security when users browse the Web, change the security level to High. However, be aware that this change may cause some pages to malfunction or to be displayed improperly. Consider specifying a custom level that permits you to control each security decision for the zone, as explained in the next section.

- Local intranet zone—This zone applies to Web sites on an organization's intranet. You should set up this zone so that all sites in it are also inside the firewall. Obtain detailed information about your internal network from the company's network administrators. By default, this zone consists of local domain names.

- Trusted sites zone—This zone allows you to add Web sites that you trust to be safe, including those of business partners or reliable public entities. By default, this zone is assigned the Low security level; you can perform a wider range of actions on trusted Web sites.

- Restricted sites zone—Use this zone to add Web sites that you do not trust. Restricted Web sites are assigned a High security level, meaning that you can perform only minimal, very safe actions. Web pages may not function properly or may not be displayed in full.

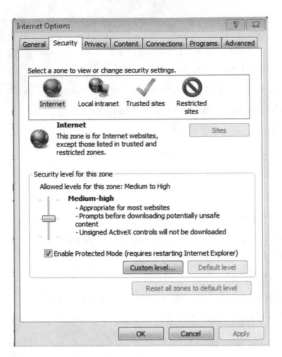

Figure 4-13 Security zones in Internet Explorer

Source: Course Technology/Cengage Learning

Figure 4-14 gives you an idea of how these zones work. A firewall acts as a protective boundary between the internal networks and the outside world. Proxy servers act as intermediaries between computers and the Internet, and filter access to Web sites. You define the location of the security zones relative to the firewall—the Local intranet zone resides behind the firewall, and the other three zones typically reside outside it.

Customizing Security Settings To set up more security for your Web browsing, click the Custom level button on the Security tab of the Internet Options dialog box. The Custom Security Settings dialog box appears, as shown in Figure 4-15.

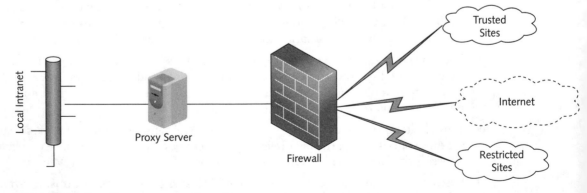

Figure 4-14 Security zones and a firewall

Source: Course Technology/Cengage Learning

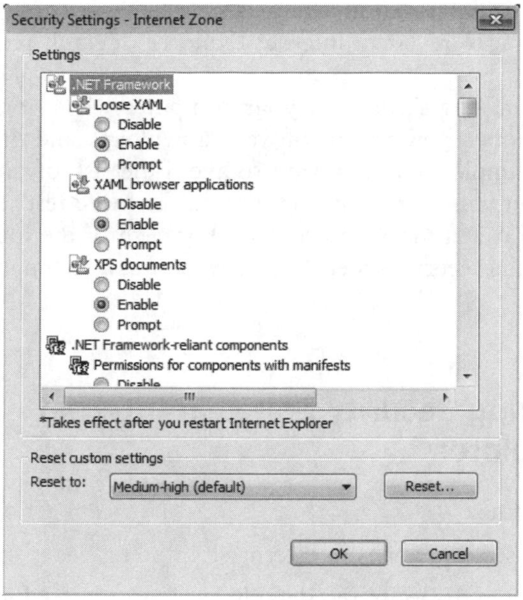

Figure 4-15 Custom Security Settings dialog box

Source: Course Technology/Cengage Learning

Use the Settings list to enable or disable specific security options that are grouped into the following categories:

- .NET Framework—You use these options to configure the behavior of applications deployed using Extensible Application Markup Language (XAML).

- .NET Framework-reliant components—You can specify how to treat programs that do not have proper Authenticode identification.

- **ActiveX controls** and plug-ins—You can use this set of custom options to approve, download, and run scripts with ActiveX controls (software components that interact with each other in a networked environment).

- Downloads—These options specify whether you can download files or fonts.

- Scripting—These options specify whether you can download scripts.

- User authentication—These options help specify the method you use to log on to a Web site.

- Miscellaneous—These options control a wide range of other actions.

Microsoft provides client-side software that monitors the downloading of supported software, such as ActiveX controls and executable files. If a piece of software has been digitally signed (that is, it uses Authenticode provisions), Internet Explorer can verify that it originated from the developer and that no one has tampered with it. However, a valid digital signature does not guarantee that the software is without problems—it simply means that the software has not been modified. Likewise, software without a signature does not prove that the software is dangerous.

You can also use the Custom Security Settings dialog box to reset any custom settings you defined. This option is useful if you want to revert to Internet Explorer's default settings.

Adjusting Security Levels Preserving the security of your computer when you browse the Web is a balancing act. The more open you are to software downloads and other content, the greater your exposure. For example, you may want to avoid the risk of downloading software that could damage data on your hard drive. However, the more restrictive you make your settings, the less usable and useful the Web becomes. For each of the four zones, you can adjust the security by moving the security slider. For each setting, a summary is provided of the security actions.

Activity 4-11: Setting Security Zones in Internet Explorer

Time Required: 20 minutes

Objective: Configure the security zones in Internet Explorer.

Description: In this activity, you review and specify the default security settings for each of the four security zones. You add the Microsoft Web site to the Trusted sites zone. This activity is useful if you need to select security settings for a security zone.

1. If necessary, start your virtual machines using the appropriate instructions in Activity 1-1.

2. To start Internet Explorer, click the **Internet** button on the taskbar.

3. To open the security options, click the **Tools** menu, click **Internet Options,** and click the **Security** tab.

4. If necessary, click the **Internet** icon.

If the Default level button is grayed out, you must activate it for this activity. Move the Security level slider.

5. Click the **Default level** button to set the security level to Medium-high.

6. Click the **Trusted sites** icon.

7. Click and drag the slider to the Low level, view the warning message, and click **OK.**

8. Click the **Default level** button to set the security level to Medium again.

9. Click the **Local intranet** icon.

10. If necessary, click the **Default level** button to set the security level to Medium-low.

11. Click the **Trusted sites** icon.

12. To add Microsoft as a trusted site, click the **Sites** button, clear the **Require server verification (https:) for all sites in this zone** check box, type **www.microsoft.com** in the "Add this Web site to the zone" text box, click the **Add** button, and then click **Close.**

13. If necessary, click the **Default level** button to set the security level to Medium.

14. Click the **Restricted sites** icon.

15. If necessary, click the **Default level** button to set the security level to High.

16. Click **OK**.

17. Close any open windows within the Windows 7 virtual machine.

18. Leave the virtual machine logged on for the next activity.

Setting Up Privacy on the Web You can configure the following privacy preferences on the Privacy tab of the Internet Options dialog box, as shown in Figure 4-16:

- Set a privacy level for the Internet zone; by default, this level is set to Medium.
- Import custom privacy settings from a preferences file.
- Customize advanced settings that override cookie handling for the privacy level you select.
- Customize your privacy settings for individual Web sites; for example, you can manage cookies differently on each Web site you visit.

The following sections discuss each privacy setting. You must have administrative rights to configure these settings.

Configuring Privacy Preferences in Internet Explorer Using the privacy features, you and your organization can create a secure environment that protects personal information on the Internet. When you use the Internet, you need the assurance that other people cannot intercept and read the information you send and receive. You do not want other

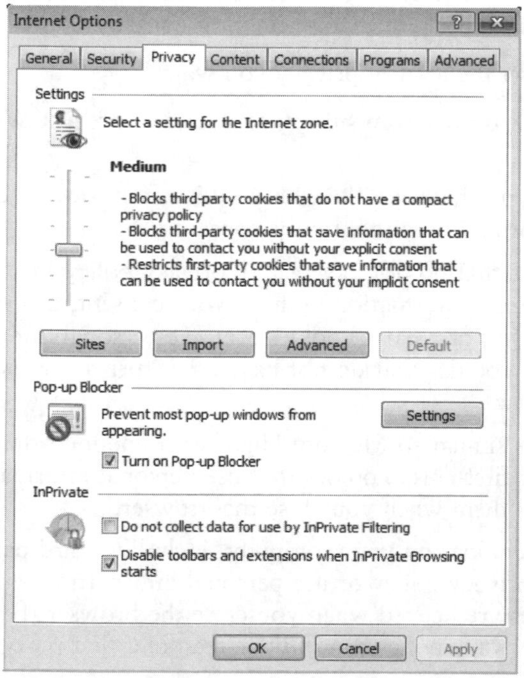

Figure 4-16 Privacy tab in Internet Options dialog box

Source: Course Technology/Cengage Learning

users to get your passwords or other private information, and you do not want Web sites to access your personal information without your knowledge.

Web sites use two types of small files, or cookies, to collect and store personal information about you and your Web-surfing preferences. These cookies are saved on your computer:

- Session cookies are deleted when you close your browser.
- Persistent cookies are more permanent. An expiration date in the cookie indicates when the browser can delete it.

Another important distinction when discussing cookies is the difference between first-party cookies and third-party cookies. First-party cookies are stored by a Web server from the same Internet domain; third-party cookies are stored by a Web server from a different domain. For example, many Web pages that contain advertising obtain it from a third-party site.

Internet Explorer supports the Platform for Privacy Preferences (P3P), which controls how personal information is used by the Web sites you visit. P3P also enables Web sites to provide policy information for the cookies they may attempt to store on your computer. Internet Explorer compares the preferences you select in the Privacy tab with the stated intentions of Web sites you visit, and then determines if the Web sites should be permitted to store cookies.

Some of the information you enter online can be used to identify or contact you, so you may not want to share your name, e-mail address, telephone number, or other personal data. However, a Web site only has access to the personal information you provide or to the entries you make while visiting the site. A site cannot determine your e-mail address unless you provide it and cannot gain access to other information on your computer.

Move the slider on the Privacy tab to set the level of privacy you want:

- Block All Cookies—Prevent all Web sites from storing cookies and prevent Web sites from reading existing cookies.
- High—Prevent Web sites that do not have a P3P privacy policy from storing cookies and from obtaining personal information without your consent.
- Medium High—Prevent Web sites that do not have a P3P privacy policy from storing third-party cookies or using personal information without your consent; this setting also prevents Web sites from storing first-party cookies that use personal information without your consent. First-party cookies that do not have a P3P privacy policy can only be read in a first-party context.
- Medium (default)—This setting is similar to Medium High, with one important difference: the Medium setting permits first-party cookies that use personal information without your consent, but deletes them when you close the browser.
- Low—Permit Web sites to store cookies on your computer, including third-party cookies that do not have a P3P privacy policy or use personal information without your consent. Third-party cookies are deleted when you close the browser. First-party cookies that do not have a P3P privacy policy can only be read in a first-party context.
- Accept All Cookies—Permit Web sites to store cookies on your computer. Web sites that create cookies can read them.

 Customized privacy settings do not override the Block All Cookies and Accept All Cookies settings, but they do override the High, Medium High, Medium, and Low privacy settings.

4

Importing Custom Privacy Settings If your organization wants to standardize the privacy settings of all its users, click the Import button in the Privacy tab to import custom privacy settings from a file. You can download files of custom settings from privacy organizations or other Web sites on the Internet, which keeps users from accessing Web sites that contain questionable content.

Advanced Privacy Settings Click the Advanced button in the Privacy tab to see the Advanced Privacy Settings dialog box, as shown in Figure 4-17. You can use these settings to override automatic first-party and third-party cookie handling for all Web sites in the Internet zone. You should check the "Always allow session cookies" box because session cookies are automatically deleted when you close Internet Explorer. This setting strikes a useful compromise between protecting privacy and letting sites recognize you during your current visit. If sites cannot recognize you as you move from page to page, you may not be able to navigate within the Web site.

After you configure privacy preferences, Internet Explorer can handle cookies in the following ways:

- Block first-party cookies (cookies stored by a Web server from the same Internet domain).
- Block third-party cookies (cookies stored by a Web server from a different domain).
- Allow all cookies to be stored without notifying you.

Controlling Pop-ups on the Web Internet Explorer 8 comes with its own pop-up blocker, which is activated by default. The browser allows you to modify some settings, such as which sites to allow pop-ups as well as notification types and preset filter levels. Figure 4-18 shows the Pop-up Blocker Settings dialog box. To access this dialog box, click the Tools menu, click Pop-up Blocker, and then click Pop-up Blocker Settings.

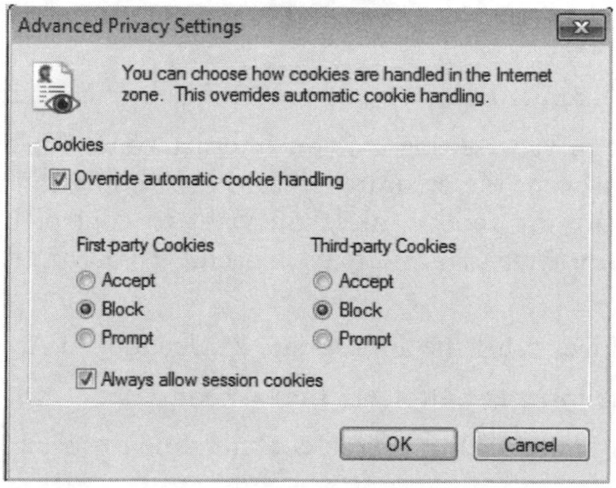

Figure 4-17 Advanced Privacy Settings dialog box

Source: Course Technology/Cengage Learning

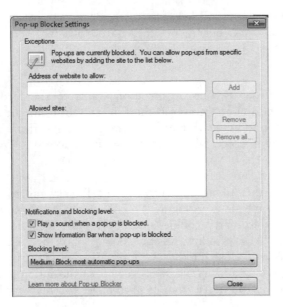

Figure 4-18 Pop-up Blocker Settings dialog box

Source: Course Technology/Cengage Learning

From this dialog box, you can perform the following tasks:

- **Allow pop-ups from selected sites.** For example, course management applications use pop-ups and would not function without this override.

- **Set notifications when a pop-up is blocked.** You can set both audible and visual notifications.

- **Choose between three blocking levels.** The levels are High: Block all pop-ups; Medium: Block most automatic pop-ups; and Low: Allow pop-ups from secure sites.

Activity 4-12: Setting Up Privacy for an Internet Zone

Time Required: 15 minutes

Objective: Configure the Internet Explorer privacy settings for an Internet zone.

Description: In this activity, you select privacy settings for an Internet zone, which protect your privacy as you surf the Web. You want the assurance that other people cannot intercept and read the information you send and receive, and you want to control how Web sites use the personal information you provide. This activity is useful if you are concerned with privacy while using the Internet.

1. If necessary, start your virtual machines using the appropriate instructions in Activity 1-1.

2. To start Internet Explorer, click the **Internet** button on the taskbar.

3. If necessary, click the **Internet** icon under "Select a Web content zone to specify its security settings."

4. To open the privacy options, click the **Tools** menu, click **Internet Options,** and then click the **Privacy** tab.

5. Click the **Default** button and then click and drag the slider to **Block All Cookies**.

6. Review the explanation for Block all cookies.

7. Click and drag the slider to **High** and view the explanation.

8. Repeat Step 7 for **Medium High, Medium, Low,** and **Accept All Cookies**.

9. Click the **Default** button to set the security level to Medium.

10. To permit cookies for the Prometric Web site (*www.2test.com*), click the **Sites** button, type **www.2test.com** in the Address of website text box, click the **Allow** button, and then click **OK**.

11. Click **OK**.

12. Close any open windows.

13. Leave the virtual machine logged on for the next activity.

Handling Web Content in Internet Explorer You can configure the following Web content preferences on the Content tab of the Internet Options dialog box, as shown in Figure 4-19:

- Parental controls of Web activity
- Settings to block objectionable Web sites

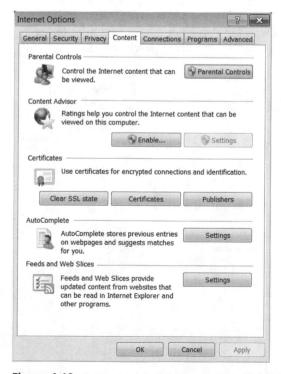

Figure 4-19 Content tab in Internet Options dialog box

Source: Course Technology/Cengage Learning

- Settings that establish the identity of other parties
- Controls for the transmission of personal information

The following sections discuss each of the content areas you can control.

Setting Parental Controls Regulating Web browsing can prevent children and employees from accessing dangerous content on the Internet and from having to make judgment calls about suitable relationships in chat rooms. To prevent access to your personal information and provide protection from unscrupulous Web sites, chat-room users, and downloaded programs, you can set up a number of parental controls.

You must use administrator access to set parental controls. You can control such parameters as time limits, access to games, and access to other programs. See Figure 4-20 for sample parental controls, which you access by clicking the Parental Controls button on the Content tab.

Using the Content Advisor Use the Content Advisor to block access to Web sites that contain objectionable material. Figure 4-21 shows ratings within the Content Advisor. For example, your organization might want to block access to Web sites that offer no business value to its employees. You can adjust the content ratings in four areas: language, nudity, sex, and violence.

You secure the Content Advisor settings by entering a supervisor password, which allows supervisors to turn the Content Advisor on or off and to change its settings for users. You can add a hint to help the supervisor remember the password; whenever Internet Explorer prompts for the password, the hint is displayed. You can also configure Internet Explorer so that users can access restricted Web pages by typing the supervisor password.

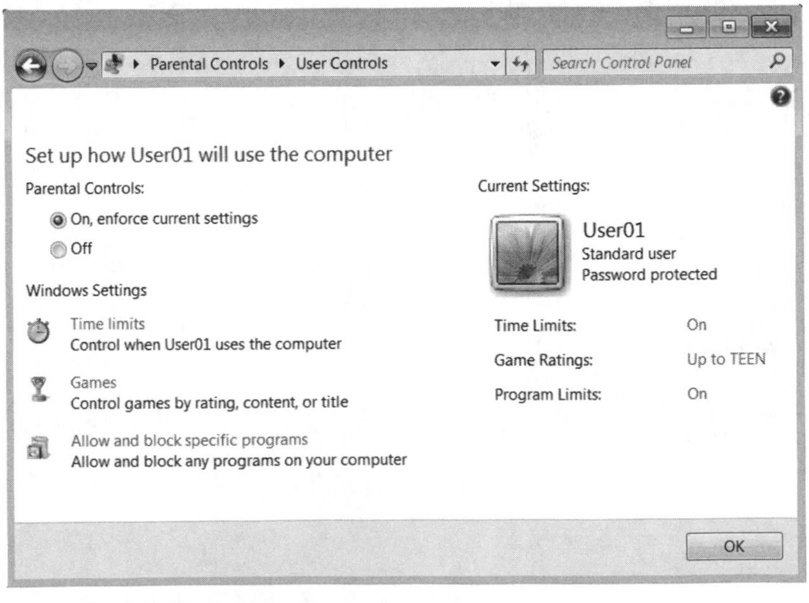

Figure 4-20 Sample parental controls

Source: Course Technology/Cengage Learning

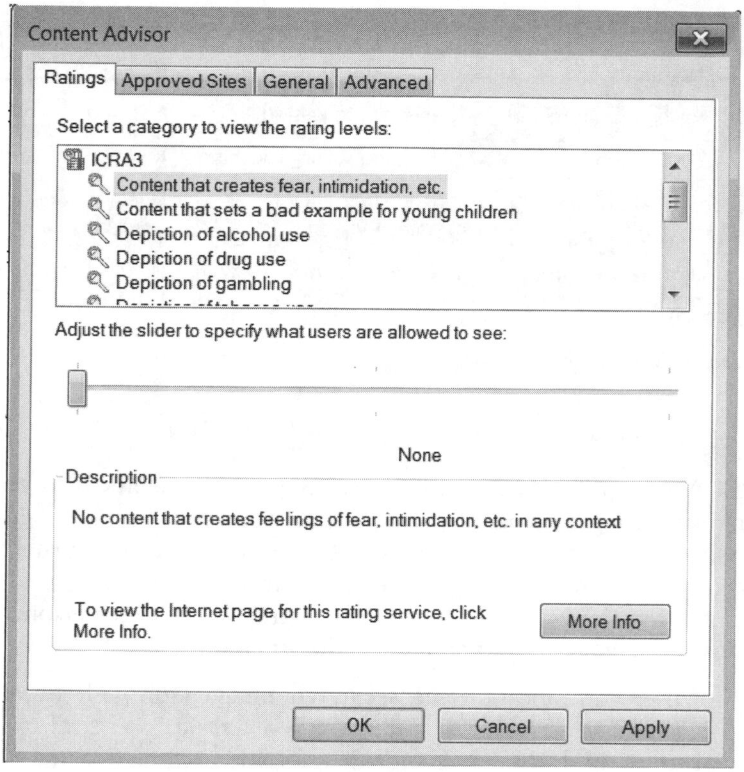

Figure 4-21 Ratings within Content Advisor

Source: Course Technology/Cengage Learning

Internet Explorer is installed with a content rating system that is based on the work of the Internet Content Rating Association (ICRA). ICRA enables users, especially parents with young children, to make informed decisions about Web content by labeling it. Web authors complete ICRA questionnaires that describe the content of their Web sites; in return, ICRA provides a small piece of HTML code that Web authors include on their Web site.

The Content Advisor examines this small piece of code to determine the levels of offensive language, nudity, sex, and violence on a Web site. Table 4-1 shows the five levels for each type of content and describes the content allowed for each level. Level 0 is the most restrictive, and Level 4 allows users to access Web sites that present explicit content.

You can set content ratings to any level for each of the four content areas. By default, all content ratings are set to Level 0. When the Content Advisor is on and the rating for a Web site exceeds the rating level you set, Internet Explorer prevents users from accessing the site. You can also configure Internet Explorer to allow or prevent access to unrated Web content.

For this rating system to work, Web authors must rate their Web pages and do so honestly. If an author posts objectionable content but does not program the page to show the rating, the Content Advisor may block the page regardless of its content. The Approved Sites feature, which is accessible when you click the Settings button, allows you to specify certain sites as approved.

Level	Language	Nudity	Sex	Violence
0	Inoffensive slang	No nudity	No sexual acts	No violence
1	Mild expletives	Revealing attire	Passionate kissing	Fighting
2	Moderate expletives	Partial nudity	Clothed sexual touching	Killing
3	Obscene gestures	Frontal nudity	Nonexplicit sexual touching	Filled with blood and gore
4	Explicit or crude language	Provocative frontal nudity	Explicit sexual activity	Wanton and gratuitous violence

Table 4-1 Levels of the Internet Explorer Content Advisor

Using Certificates When you write a check at a store, you may be asked to verify your identity by presenting your driver's license. To verify identities on the Web, Internet Explorer uses industry-standard **digital certificates**. These certificates are electronic credentials that bind the identity of the certificate owner to a pair of electronic keys (public and private). The keys ensure that the certificates belong to the correct organization or person you want to contact. You can use these keys to encrypt and sign information.

You use certificates for user authentication and secure communication with servers on the Web. If you connect to a Web server, a server authentication certificate—issued by a trusted authority—enables you to establish the server's identity. In addition, certificates enable servers to verify your identity.

You exchange certificates with servers using a secure transmission protocol, which provides encrypted and unaltered information. Secure channel transmission is typically used when you transmit credit card and purchase information on the Web.

Messages can be encrypted with the public key and decrypted with the private key, as shown in Figure 4-22 and described in the following steps:

- Step 1—The plain text message is encrypted with the public key, which is furnished by the person who receives the message.

- Step 2—The encrypted message is transferred over the Internet. The encryption process ensures that intercepted messages cannot be read.

- Step 3—The cipher text message is decrypted with the private key, which is held by the person who receives the message.

Certificates are issued, authenticated, and managed by a trusted third party called a certification authority (CA). A commercial CA must provide services that your organization and users trust. The primary responsibility of a CA is to investigate the identity of organizations and people who obtain certificates. This effort ensures the validity of the information in the certificate. When a certificate is compromised, it is revoked and added to a certificate revocation list (CRL).

To handle customer services on the Internet, your organization can obtain certificates from a commercial CA. To handle similar services on your internal intranet, your organization can obtain permission to issue its own certificates.

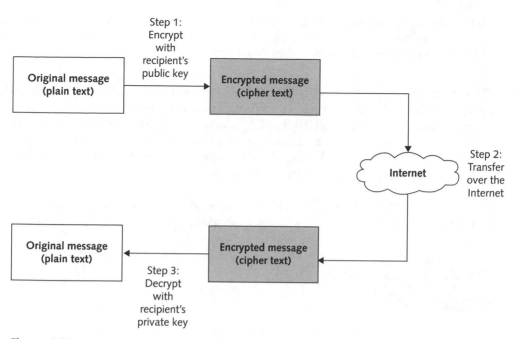

Figure 4-22 Using public and private keys

Source: Course Technology/Cengage Learning

Controlling the Completion of Data on Web pages From the AutoComplete area of the Content tab, you can click the Settings button and modify the AutoComplete settings for Web addresses and forms, as shown in Figure 4-23. You can also periodically clear your

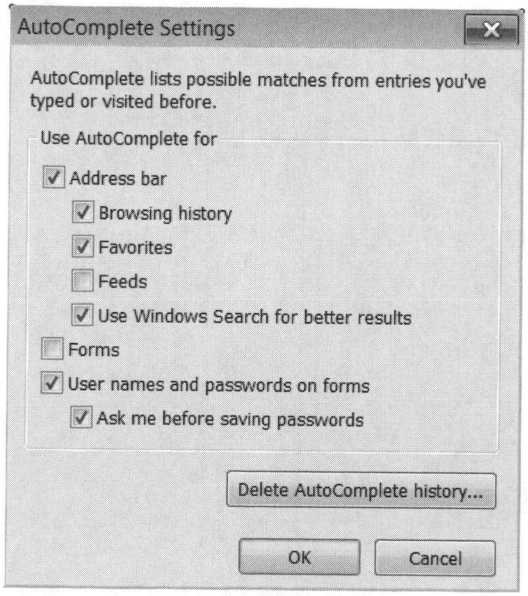

Figure 4-23 AutoComplete settings

Source: Course Technology/Cengage Learning

History folder of all user name and password entries so that no other person can view this private information. By deselecting the Forms check box, you can clear your History folder of all the entries you have made in Web pages.

Configuring Feeds and Web Slices Web Slice is a Web feed technology introduced in Internet Explorer 8 that allows you to subscribe to certain portions of a Web page. You can preview Web Slices in a special "fly-out" window. Web Slice allows you to see weather forecasts and other updates immediately, rather than having to visit a Web page and check for changes. You can control these slices by making selections in the Feed and Web Slice Settings dialog box, as shown in Figure 4-24.

Using the Connections Tab
Use the Connections tab of the Internet Options dialog box (see Figure 4-25) to set up an Internet connection and configure LAN settings.

 Setting up a dial-up Internet connection is beyond the scope of this text.

Click the LAN settings button to specify LAN connection settings for Internet Explorer. Your network administrators can configure your network so that Internet Explorer is automatically customized the first time it is started. This can help reduce administrative overhead and potentially reduce Help Desk calls about browser settings. Automatic detection of browser settings is supported by the Dynamic Host Configuration Protocol (DHCP) and the Domain Name System (DNS).

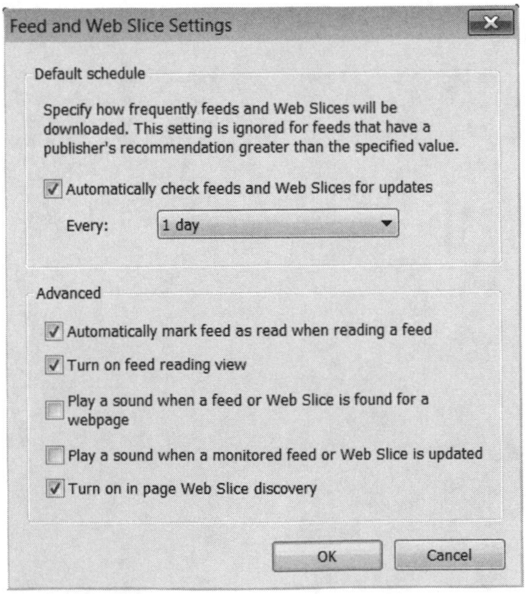

Figure 4-24 Configuring Web Slice settings

Source: Course Technology/Cengage Learning

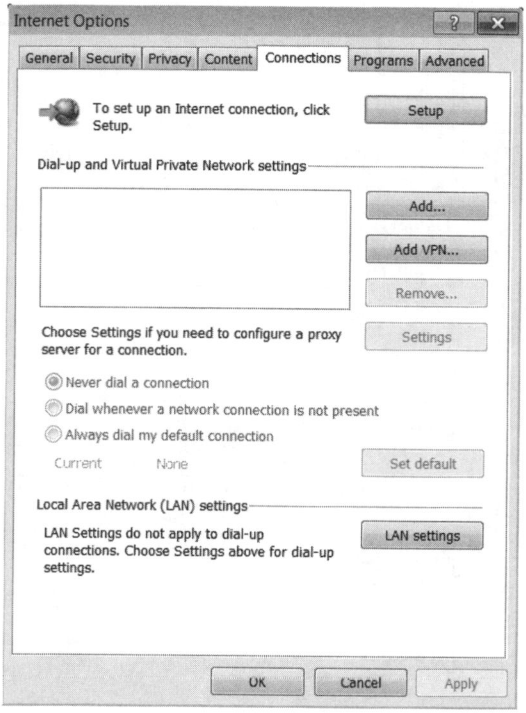

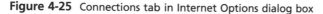

Figure 4-25 Connections tab in Internet Options dialog box

Source: Course Technology/Cengage Learning

Using the Programs Tab Using the Programs tab of the Internet Options dialog box (see Figure 4-26), you can specify which programs Windows uses for Internet services, such as e-mail and newsgroups. If you check "Tell me if Internet Explorer is not the default Web browser," Internet Explorer verifies that it is the default browser. If it is not, you are asked if you want to make Internet Explorer the default browser.

Using the Advanced Tab From the Advanced tab of the Internet Options dialog box (see Figure 4-27), you can configure options for accessibility, browsing, HTTP, multimedia, printing, and security.

If you need clarification for an option shown in Figure 4-27, click the question mark in the upper-right corner of the window; the cursor turns to a pointer with a question mark. To see Help information for an option, move the cursor to that option and click.

Configuring the Firefox Browser

Like many applications you have used in Fedora 13, you can customize Firefox according to your own preferences. For example, Firefox opens to the default home page *http://start. fedoraproject.org/*, but you can select any home page you want. The following sections explain your options for customizing Firefox.

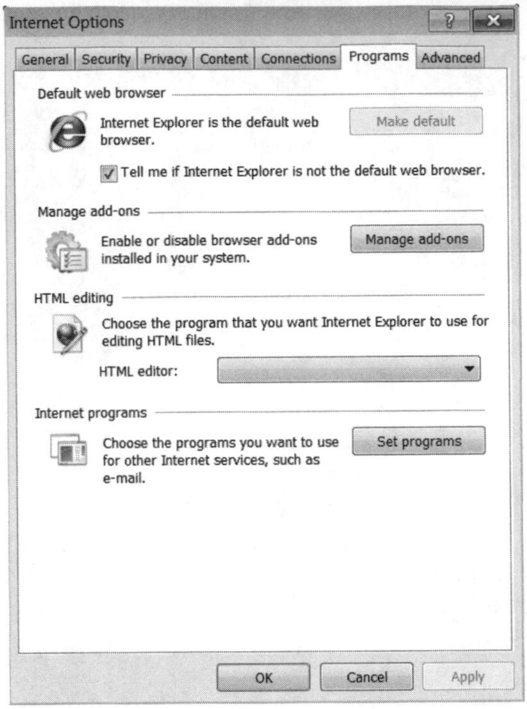

Figure 4-26 Program selections for Internet Explorer

Source: Course Technology/Cengage Learning

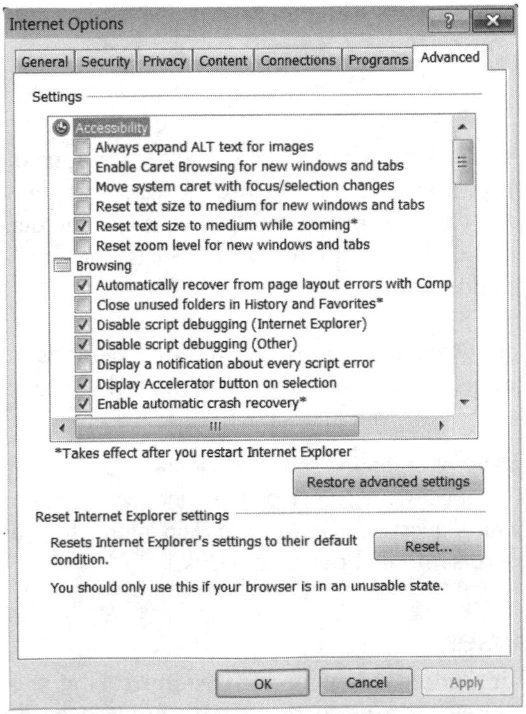

Figure 4-27 Advanced tab in Internet Options dialog box

Source: Course Technology/Cengage Learning

Customizing Text Size and Toolbars Using the View Menu You can use the View menu in Firefox to customize toolbars, the status bar, sidebars, text size, and other particulars:

- Toolbars—Display or hide the Navigation and Bookmarks toolbars in Firefox.
- Status Bar—Display or hide the status bar at the bottom of the browser window; the status bar indicates the status of requested Web pages.
- Sidebar—Display or hide sidebars on the left side of the browser window; you can display sidebars that list bookmarks of frequently used Web sites, a history of recently visited Web sites, and various add-ons.
- Text Size—Increase or decrease the default text size of Web pages; you cannot change the text size if it was **hard coded** when the Web page was developed.
- Page Source—Display the HTML code of the Web page.
- Full Screen—Make the Web page take up the entire screen.

Customizing General Settings in Firefox To customize the General settings in Firefox, click the Edit menu, and then click Preferences (see Figure 4-28).

The General settings have the following options:

- Startup section—Specify whether to show the home page or a blank page when Firefox starts. You can also select the home page you want to display whenever you open Firefox.

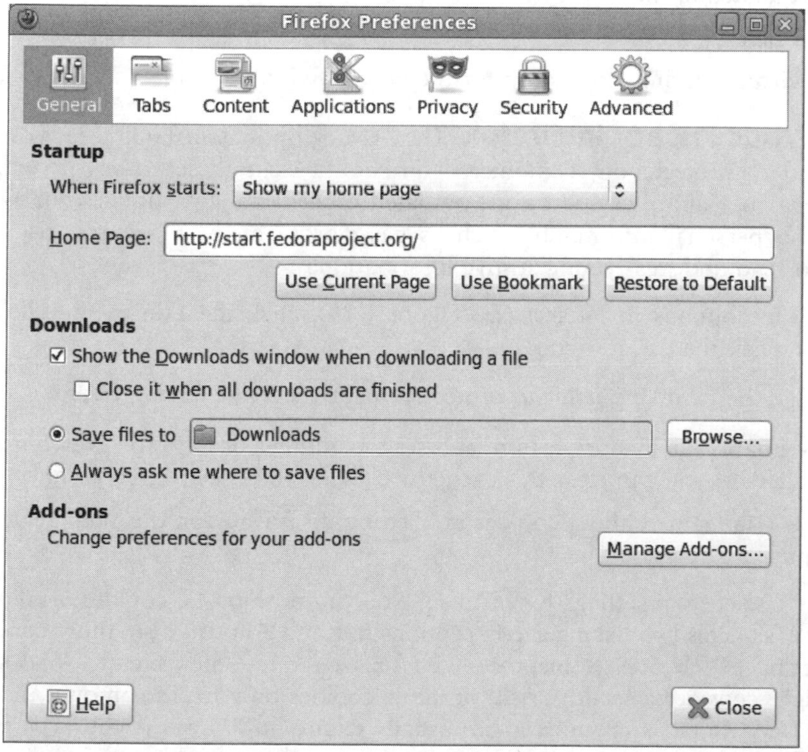

Figure 4-28 Customizing general settings in Firefox

Source: Course Technology/Cengage Learning

- Downloads section—Specify whether to show the Downloads window when downloading a file, where to save downloaded files, and whether to prompt the user to choose the download destination.

- Add-ons section—Change preferences for your add-ons.

Activity 4-13: Selecting General Settings in Firefox

Time Required: 15 minutes

Objective: Configure and note general settings for customizing Firefox.

Description: In this activity, you set the home page to a recently visited Web site.

1. If necessary, start your virtual machines using the appropriate instructions in Activity 1-1.
2. To open Firefox, click **Applications**, point to **Internet**, and then click **Firefox**.
3. Type **www.mozilla.com** in the address bar and then press **Enter**.
4. Click the **Edit** menu and then click **Preferences**.
5. To set *www.mozilla.com* as the home page, click the **General** tab, click the **Use Current Page** button, and then click **Close**.
6. Close the current browser.
7. To open Firefox again, click **Applications**, point to **Internet**, and then click **Firefox**.
8. Notice that *www.mozilla.com* is the home page.
9. Close any open windows.
10. Leave the virtual machine logged on for the next activity.

Protecting Your Privacy in Firefox The privacy options in Firefox let you manage caches designed to protect your computer. You should clear these caches periodically to improve performance and security. Large, outdated caches can slow down your Web surfing, and storing personal information such as passwords can be a security risk; hackers may be able to read and steal your sensitive information.

To set the privacy options in Firefox (see Figure 4-29), click the Edit menu, click Preferences, and then click the Privacy icon.

You can manage the following items to protect your privacy when using Firefox:

- History—Enable the History feature and set the number of days to save your history of visited URLs; you can clear this cache by clicking the "clear history" link.

- Cookies—You learned about cookies in "Setting up Privacy on the Web" earlier in this chapter.

If you choose "Use custom settings for history," you can prohibit all cookies or allow cookies for certain Web sites by clicking the Exceptions button. You can also allow cookies only from "originating" Web sites (sometimes Web sites refer to other sites to load software, which you might consider a security risk) or allow cookies only for the amount of time you specify in the Keep Cookies menu. Cookies usually expire in 30 days if you keep them (see Figure 4-30). To remove cookies, click the Show Cookies button. When the Cookies screen appears, specify the cookie and click the Remove Cookie button. You can also click the Remove All Cookies button to delete all the cookies stored in the Web browser.

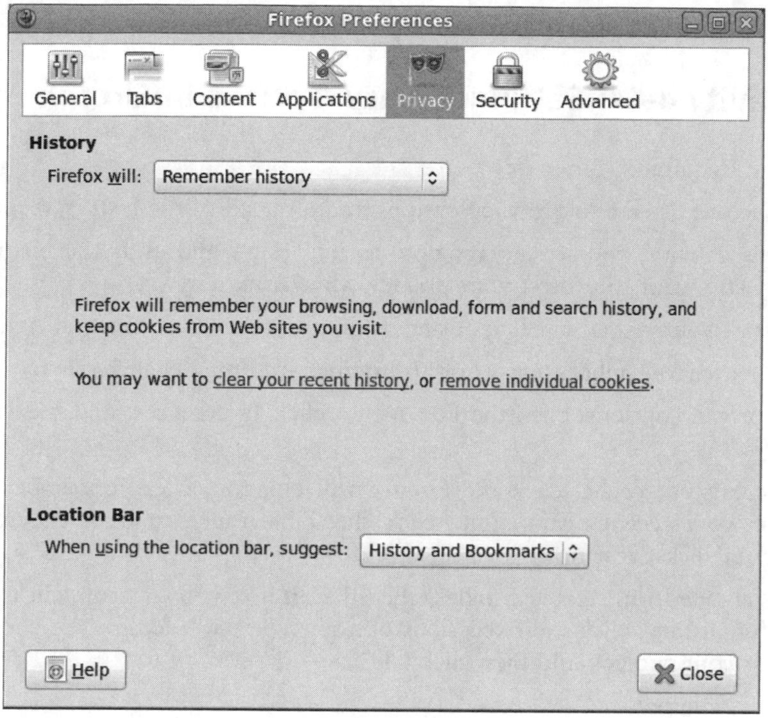

Figure 4-29 Privacy options in Firefox
Source: Course Technology/Cengage Learning

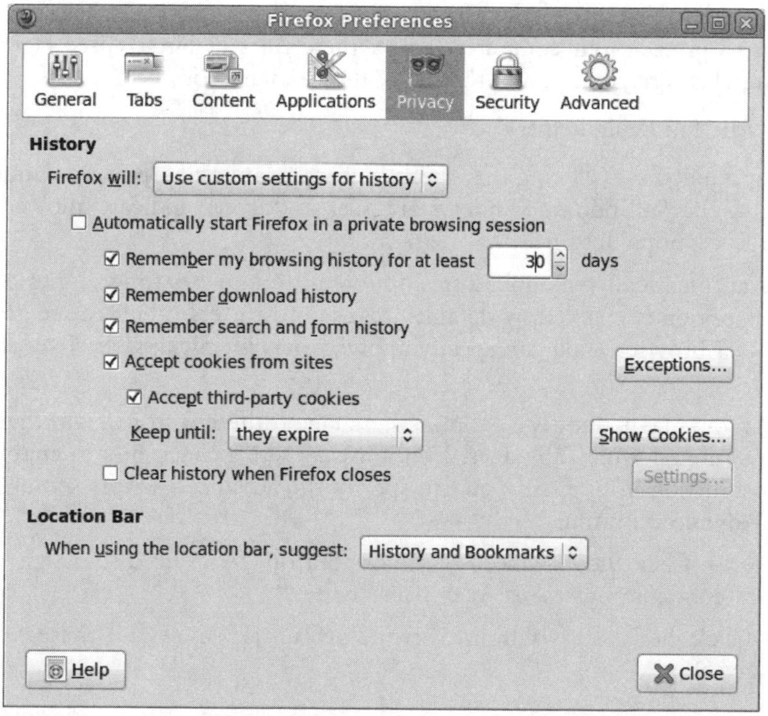

Figure 4-30 Custom history settings in Firefox
Source: Course Technology/Cengage Learning

Activity 4-14: Setting Privacy Options in Firefox

Time Required: 15 minutes

Objective: Set Firefox privacy options and clear all of the history records.

Description: In this activity, you set privacy options in Firefox and clear the history. This activity is useful if you want to protect your privacy while using Firefox.

1. If necessary, start your virtual machines using the appropriate instructions in Activity 1-1.

2. To open Firefox, click **Applications**, point to **Internet**, and then click **Firefox.**

3. To open the privacy options, click the **Edit** menu, click **Preferences**, and then click the **Privacy** icon.

4. To empty the History cache, click the **Firefox will** chevron, click **Remember history**, click the **clear your recent history** link, click the **Time range to clear** chevron, click **Today**, and then click **Clear now.**

5. To block a Web site from storing cookies, click the **Firefox will** chevron, click **Use custom settings for history**, click the **Exceptions** button, type **www.fcc.gov** (or some objectionable site of your choice), and then click **Close.**

6. Close any open windows.

7. Leave the virtual machine logged on for future activities.

Customizing Content in Firefox   The Content options in Firefox let you set behavior rules for Web sites to protect your computer. To set these rules in Firefox (see Figure 4-31), click the Edit menu, click Preferences, and then click the Content icon.

You can configure the following items:

- Block pop-up windows—Clicking this check box stops annoying pop-up windows from appearing. Not all pop-up windows are ads, so you can indicate allowed sites by using the Exceptions button.

- Load images automatically—Enabling this option allows images to load in the browser window. This option is enabled by default because most users prefer to see graphics when they use a browser. You can specify allowed sites by clicking the Exceptions button.

- Enable JavaScript—JavaScript is a scripting language (different from Java) that enables interactive functionality in Web pages. You must click this check box to enable JavaScript to function in Firefox. You can specify the advanced scripts settings by clicking the Advanced button.

- Fonts & Colors—Click the Advanced or Colors button if you need to assign special color and font combinations to see Web pages better.

- Languages—Click the Choose button to set the default language and character encoding for Firefox.

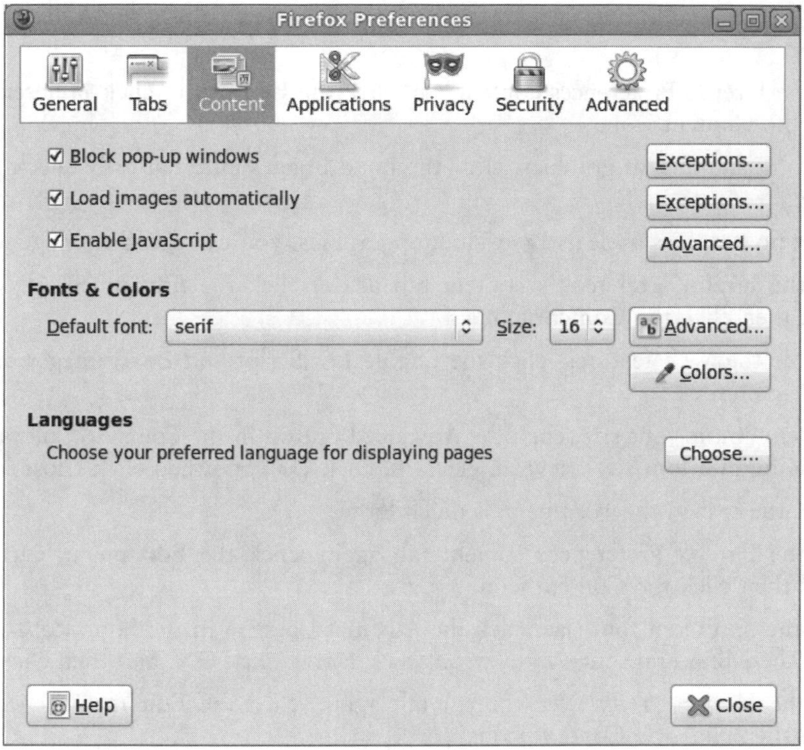

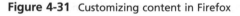

Figure 4-31 shown:

Firefox Preferences

General | Tabs | Content | Applications | Privacy | Security | Advanced

☑ Block pop-up windows   Exceptions...

☑ Load images automatically   Exceptions...

☑ Enable JavaScript   Advanced...

Fonts & Colors

Default font: serif   Size: 16   Advanced...

                              Colors...

Languages

Choose your preferred language for displaying pages   Choose...

Help   Close

Figure 4-31 Customizing content in Firefox

Source: Course Technology/Cengage Learning

Activity 4-15: Setting Content Features in Firefox

Time Required: 20 minutes

Objective: Open the Firefox Web Features window and set several options.

Description: In this activity, you set options for enabling and disabling pop-ups, image loading, and JavaScript. You also set options for fonts and languages. This activity is helpful if you need to know more about the Content features in Firefox.

1. If necessary, start your virtual machines using the appropriate instructions in Activity 1-1.

2. To open Firefox, click **Applications**, point to **Internet**, and then click **Firefox**.

3. To open the Web Features window, click the **Edit** menu, click **Preferences**, and then click the **Content** icon.

4. To stop pop-up windows, click the **Block pop-up windows** check box.

5. To disable JavaScript, clear the **Enable JavaScript** check box and then click **Close**.

After performing Step 5, you will have problems viewing Web sites that use Java applets and JavaScript to animate their pages.

6. To view a Web site that uses graphics, type **www.allposters.com** in the Address bar and press **Enter**.

7. To open the Firefox Preferences content tab, click the **Edit** menu, click **Preferences**, and then click the **Content** icon.

8. To disable the loading of graphics, clear the **Load images automatically** check box and click **Close**.

9. Verify that no graphics appear. By excluding graphics, you can speed up page loading.

10. To open the Firefox Preferences content tab again, click the **Edit** menu, click **Preferences**, and then click the **Content** icon.

11. To re-enable the Web features, click the **Enable JavaScript** and **Load images automatically** check boxes.

12. To set the minimum font size, click the **Advanced** button in the Fonts & Colors section, click the **Minimum font size** chevron, click **20**, click **OK**, and then click **Close**.

13. Verify that the text in the Web page is much larger.

14. To open the Firefox Preferences content tab again, click the **Edit** menu, click **Preferences**, and then click the **Content** icon.

15. To delete the minimum font size, click the **Advanced** button in the Fonts & Colors section, click the **Minimum font size** chevron, click **None**, click **OK**, and then click **Close**.

16. To open the Firefox Preferences content tab again, click the **Edit** menu, click **Preferences**, and then click the **Content** icon.

17. To select a language other than English, click the **Choose** button in the Languages section, click the **Select a Language to add** chevron, click a language that you want to use for displaying Web pages from another country, and then click **OK**.

18. Click **Close** to close the Firefox Preferences window.

19. Leave the virtual machine logged on for future activities.

Setting Security Features in Firefox To set the Security options in Firefox, click the Edit menu, click Preferences, and then click the Security icon.

Firefox manages the passwords you type as you access Web sites. Check the "Remember passwords for sites" check box to have Firefox prompt you to save passwords. If you want to set a master password to protect the other saved passwords, click the Change Master Password button and enter the password. You can view saved passwords by clicking the Saved Passwords button. From this dialog box, you can show passwords, remove a single password, or remove all your passwords.

Activity 4-16: Setting Security Features in Firefox

Time Required: 10 minutes

Objective: Set Firefox security options and clear all of the caches.

Description: In this activity, you set security options in Firefox and clear the caches. This activity is useful if you want to save your passwords while using Firefox.

1. If necessary, start your virtual machines using the appropriate instructions in Activity 1-1.

2. To open Firefox, click **Applications**, point to **Internet**, and then click **Firefox**.

3. To open the Security options, click the **Edit** menu, click **Preferences**, and then click the **Security** icon.

4. To view a saved password, click the **Saved Passwords** button, click the Web site, and then click the **Show Passwords** button.

5. Click **Close** and then close any open windows.

6. Leave the virtual machine logged on for future activities.

Choosing Advanced Options in Firefox   The Advanced options in Firefox refer to navigation and security features; these concepts were explained earlier in this chapter in the Internet Explorer sections. To select the Advanced options in Firefox (see Figure 4-32), click the Edit menu, click Preferences, and then click the Advanced icon. Four tabs are displayed on the Advanced options screen: General, Network, Update, and Encryption.

The following options are listed under the General tab:

- Accessibility—Select options that improve the accessibility of Firefox.

- Browsing—Select settings to make browsing more convenient, including automatic scrolling, smooth scrolling, and speller checking.

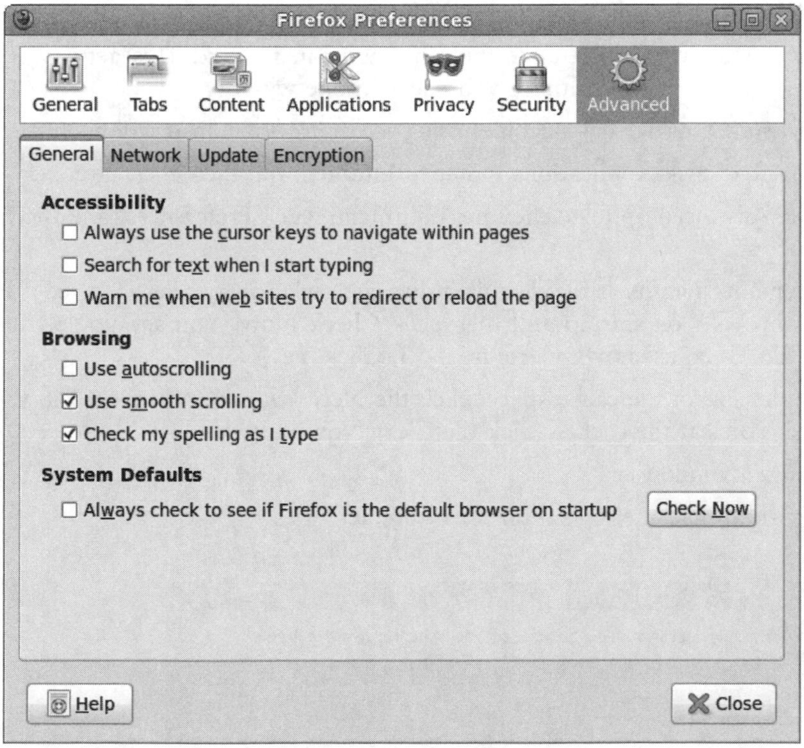

Figure 4-32 Advanced options for configuring Firefox

Source: Course Technology/Cengage Learning

- System Defaults—Check to see if Firefox is the default browser when the computer starts.

The Network tab has two sections:

- Connection—Configure how Firefox connects to the Internet.
- Offline Storage—Set the size for the cache space and offline data storage. The Firefox cache temporarily stores images, scripts, and other parts of the Web sites while you are browsing. You can specify a cache size in megabytes. To clear the cache, click the Edit menu, click Preferences, select the Advanced panel, and then click the Network tab. In the Offline Storage section, click the Clear Now button.

The Update tab specifies options for automatic Firefox updates for Firefox (which are enabled by default) and Installed Add-ons and Search engines. To list the update history, click the Show Update History button.

The Encryption tab displays two sections:

- Protocols—Set various security protocol options, such as SSL.
- Certificates—Manage certificate information, identity authentication, and security devices.

Activity 4-17: Using Advanced Options in Firefox

Time Required: 20 minutes

Objective: Use the tab feature in the Firefox browser.

Description: In this activity, you enable the tab feature in Firefox. This activity is useful if you want to open and display multiple Web pages in one window.

1. If necessary, start your virtual machines using the appropriate instructions in Activity 1-1.
2. To open Firefox, click **Applications**, point to **Internet**, and then click **Firefox**.
3. To open the Advanced options, click the **Edit** menu, click **Preferences**, and then click the **Advanced** icon.
4. To check whether Firefox is the default browser, check **Always check to see if Firefox is the default browser on startup** and then click **Check Now**. You should see the Default Browser dialog box, as shown in Figure 4-33. Click **Yes**.
5. To change the size of the cache space, click the **Network** tab and type **60** in the Use up to text box. To clear the caches, click the **Clear Now** button.
6. Close any open windows.
7. Leave the virtual machine logged on for future activities.

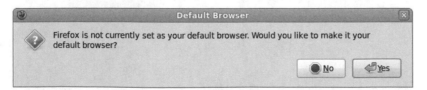

Figure 4-33 Default browser checking in Firefox

Source: Course Technology/Cengage Learning

Installing an Application

After you purchase or download an application, you must install it. You learned about the Microsoft Windows Installer and the Red Hat Package Manager (RPM) in Chapter 2; these installers typically automate most of the following tasks in an installation routine:

- Prepare the PC and complete any preinstallation steps, such as creating required directories.
- Uncompress the application. Most applications are compressed to reduce the size of the setup file.
- Run the setup or installation program to place the program modules in the proper directories and prepare them for use.
- Configure the program.
- Clean up and remove the files that are no longer needed.

The following sections provide information for installing ActiveState Perl, one of many applications you can use in both the Windows and Linux operating systems. After you install ActiveState Perl, you will use it to interpret a test script in each OS.

The Program Extraction and Reporting Language (Perl) is a highly capable, feature-rich programming language with more than 20 years of development. Perl 5 runs on more than 100 platforms from portables to mainframes. Perl is suitable for both rapid prototyping and large-scale development projects. **ActiveState Perl** is a commercial-grade language distribution that is ideal for community developers with open source projects.

Installing ActiveState Perl in Windows 7

The ActiveState Perl installation file for Windows 7 is actually a group of files that are stored together in a compressed file format. You will download the installation file. The installer extracts the individual files to a temporary folder and then runs the setup program.

Activity 4-18: Installing ActiveState Perl in Windows 7

Time Required: 15 minutes

Objective: Install the ActiveState Perl application in Windows 7.

Description: In this activity, you download ActiveState Perl from the Internet and then use the Microsoft Windows Installer utility to install the application. This activity is helpful if you want to install applications from downloaded files for use on your computer.

This activity requires an active Internet connection during the installation.

1. If necessary, start your virtual machines using the appropriate instructions in Activity 1-1.
2. To open Internet Explorer, click the **Internet Explorer** button on the taskbar.
3. Type **ActiveState Perl download** in the search text box and then click the spyglass.

4. Click the **Downloads** link. Use the link that accesses the *downloads.activestate.com* Web site.

5. Click the **ActivePerl** link, click the **Releases** link, and then click the link for the latest release.

6. Scroll and locate Windows (x86) and then click the link for the MSI installer.

7. When the Internet Explorer—Security Warning dialog box appears, click the **Run** button.

8. Wait for the download to complete, and then click **Next**.

9. Click **I accept the terms in the License Agreement**. Click **Next** three times and then click **Install**.

10. When the User Account Control dialog box appears, type **P@ssw0rd** and then click **Yes**.

11. Wait for the installation to complete and then click **Finish**.

12. Close the ActiveState Perl window.

13. Leave the virtual machine logged on; you will continue to work with ActiveState Perl in later activities.

Installing ActiveState Perl in Fedora 13

Many applications are available for use in both the Windows 7 and Linux operating systems, but their installation routines can vary depending on which OS you use. As with Windows, you download the installation files from a Web site, but Fedora 13 has different installation options. The Red Hat Package Manager (RPM) is used in the following steps to install ActiveState Perl.

Activity 4-19: Installing ActiveState Perl in Fedora 13

Time Required: 30 minutes

Objective: Install the ActiveState Perl application in Fedora 13.

Description: In this activity, you download and install ActiveState Perl with RPM. This activity is helpful if you want to install applications using RPM in Fedora 13.

This activity requires an active Internet connection during the installation.

1. If necessary, start your virtual machines using the appropriate instructions in Activity 1-1.

2. To open Firefox, click **Applications,** point to **Internet,** and then click **Firefox.**

3. Type **ActiveState Perl download** in the Google search box, and then press **Enter.**

4. Click the **ActivePerl Downloads** link. Use the link that accesses *www.activestate.com/ activeperl/downloads*.

5. Scroll down to ActiveState Perl, locate Linux (x86), and then click **RPM.**

If you are unsure about the current release number, ask your instructor.

6. When the Opening ActiveState Perl dialog box appears, click the **Save File** radio button, and then click **OK**.

7. Wait for the download to complete.

8. Right-click the ActiveState Perl rpm file that you downloaded in the **Downloads** screen, and then click **Open**.

9. When the Do you want to install this file? dialog box appears, click **Install**.

10. When the Additional confirmation required message appears, click **Continue**.

11. When the Authenticate dialog box appears, type **P@ssw0rd** and then click **Authenticate**.

12. Wait for the installation to finish. The installation screen disappears when the process is complete.

13. Close any open windows in the virtual machine.

14. Leave the virtual machine logged on for future activities.

Activity 4-20: Testing the Installation of ActiveState Perl in Windows 7

Time Required: 10 minutes

Objective: Create a Perl script to test the installation of ActiveState Perl.

Description: In this activity, you use a text editor to create the Hello World script and then test the script using ActiveState Perl. This activity is useful if you need to test the installation of ActiveState Perl.

You must complete Activity 4-18 before you can perform the following activity.

1. If necessary, start your virtual machines using the appropriate instructions in Activity 1-1.

2. To open Notepad, click **Start**, point to **All Programs**, click **Accessories**, and then click **Notepad**.

3. Type **#! /opt/bin/perl** and then press **Enter**.

4. Type **print "Hello World \n"** and then press **Enter**.

5. To save the file, click **File**, and then click **Save As**. If necessary, click Documents so that the file will be saved in the Documents folder. Click the **Save as type** chevron, click **All Files**, type **hello.pl** in the File name text box, and then click **Save**.

6. To open a Command Prompt console, click **Start**, point to **All Programs**, click **Accessories**, and then click **Command Prompt**.

7. To change to the Documents folder, type **cd documents** and then press **Enter.**

8. Type **perl hello.pl** and press **Enter.**

9. Verify that "Hello World" appears.

If "Hello World" does not appear, contact your instructor.

10. Close any open windows in the virtual machine.

11. To shut down the virtual machine, click **Start,** and then click the **Shut Down** button.

12. Wait a moment for the Windows 7 virtual machine to shut down completely.

13. Leave the PC logged on for the next activity.

Activity 4-21: Testing the Installation of ActiveState Perl in Fedora 13

Time Required: 10 minutes

Objective: Create a Perl script to test the installation of ActiveState Perl.

Description: In this activity, you use a text editor to create the Hello World script and then test the script using ActiveState Perl. This activity is useful if you need to test the installation of ActiveState Perl.

You must complete Activity 4-19 before you can perform the following activity.

1. If necessary, start your virtual machines using the appropriate instructions in Activity 1-1.

2. To open the file browser and locate the directory for the ActiveState Perl executable file, double-click **Computer,** double-click **File System,** and then double-click **opt.**

3. Record the folder name for ActiveState Perl.

4. To open gedit, point to **Applications,** point to **Accessories,** and then click **gedit Text Editor.**

5. Type **#! /opt/,** type the folder name you recorded in Step 3, type **/bin/perl,** and then press **Enter.**

In Step 5, you enter a space between ! and /opt. The remainder of the line contains no other spaces. Your entry should resemble # ! /opt/ActivePerl-5.12/bin/perl.

6. Type **print "Hello World \n"** and then press **Enter.**

7. To save the file, click **File,** click **Save As,** type **hello.pl** in the Name text box, click the Save in Folder chevron, click **Desktop,** and then click **Save.**

8. To open a Terminal console, point to **Applications**, point to **System Tools**, and then click **Terminal**.

9. To change to the Desktop directory, type **cd Desktop** and then press **Enter**.

10. To mark the perl script as executable, type **chmod 755 hello.pl** and then press **Enter**.

11. Type **./hello.pl** and then press **Enter**.

 In the previous step, enter a period and then a slash before hello.pl.

12. Verify that "Hello World" appears.

 If "Hello World" does not appear, contact your instructor.

13. To shut down the virtual machine, click **System**, click **Shut Down**, and then click the **Shut Down** button.

14. Wait a moment for the Fedora 13 virtual machine to shut down completely.

15. Close any remaining open windows, log off, and shut down your PC.

Chapter Summary

- You can obtain Help information using the Help and Support Center in Windows 7 and the Help Center in Fedora 13. Each application has Help files that are organized by topic and that contain glossaries and indexes. Tutorials in the Help Center can help new users learn new tools quickly.

- Internet Explorer and Mozilla Firefox are browsers that offer access to the Internet. Each browser has features that help you perform Internet searches, access information on the Web, and effectively manage Internet searching and URLs.

- ActiveState Perl is one of the many applications you can install in both the Windows 7 and Linux operating systems. The installation routine is different depending on which operating system you use. After you install ActiveState Perl, you should test the installation by coding and running a small test script.

Key Terms

ActiveState Perl   The leading commercial-grade distribution of the open source Perl dynamic programming language; ActiveState Perl is available in a Community Edition for Windows, Linux, and Mac OS X.

ActiveX controls   Reusable software components based on Microsoft's ActiveX technology that add interactivity and functionality to Web pages, applications, and software development tools.

bot   A program that performs a repetitive or time-consuming task on a network or the Internet. On the Internet, for example, a bot might search Web sites and newsgroups for information and then index them in a database or another record-keeping system; also called a spider.

cookies   Blocks of data that a Web server stores on a client system to identify visitors to a Web site. When a user returns to the same Web site, the browser sends a copy of the cookie back to the server. Cookies can also instruct the server to send a customized version of a requested Web page, submit account information to the user, and serve other administrative purposes.

digital certificate   An assurance that software downloaded from the Internet comes from a reputable source. A digital certificate provides information about the software, such as the author's identity and the date the software was registered with a certificate authority, as well as a measure of tamper resistance.

hard coded   Data in a program or application that is designed to handle a specific situation. Data that is hard coded into a program makes it dependent on specific values rather than on values a user can input.

hyperlink   A word, phrase, symbol, or image that you click to move from one Web location to another. A hyperlink can take you to a different part of the same Web site or to a different Web site. Hyperlinked text is usually underlined or displayed in a different color from the rest of the text.

portal site   A Web site that serves as a gateway to the Internet. A portal is a collection of links, content, and services designed to guide users to interesting information, news, weather, entertainment, commerce sites, chat rooms, and so on.

search engine   An Internet program that searches for keywords and phrases in Web files, newsgroups, and archives. Some search engines are dedicated to a single Web site. Others search multiple sites, using agents such as spiders to gather lists of available files and databases and store them for user searches.

Uniform Resource Locator (URL)   An address used in a Web browser to locate a resource on the Internet.

zone   On a LAN, a subgroup of users within a larger group of connected networks.

Review Questions

1. An application can be a _____. (Choose all that apply.)

   a.   text editor

   b.   word processor

   c.   text document

   d.   game

2. You can use the Windows 7 Help and Support Center to _____. (Choose all that apply.)

   a.   take a tutorial

   b.   obtain the latest information from Microsoft

c.   search for help on a given topic

d.   seek tips for playing computer games

e.   determine the hardware and software configuration

3. The System Information tool provides _____. (Choose all that apply.)

a.   detailed information for the computer

b.   summary information for the computer

c.   a Help and Support option

d.   information on browsers

4. The Fedora 13 equivalent of the Windows 7 Help and Support Center is _____.

a.   Support

b.   Help and Support

c.   How To

d.   Help Center

5. Mozilla Firefox and Windows Internet Explorer are both known as _____.

a.   toolbars

b.   menus

c.   Web browsers

d.   Web sites

6. URL is an acronym for _____.

a.   United Reform Language

b.   Uniform Reform Locator

c.   United Resource Locator

d.   Uniform Resource Locator

7. A URL is used to _____.

a.   identify the location of any Web site

b.   begin the browser

c.   access applications on your desktop

d.   access the browser on the desktop

8. A hyperlink is _____.

a.   used to access applications on your desktop

b.   used to identify the location of any Web site

c.   used only within browsers

d.   used to access Web sites on the Internet

9. Portal sites are _____. (Choose all that apply.)

   a. pages with links to a variety of information

   b. useful tools for getting around the Internet

   c. guides to what's available on the Internet

   d. used at Web sites such as *www.yahoo.com* or *www.msn.com*

10. You can access Web sites by using _____. (Choose all that apply.)

    a. links

    b. the browser's History option

    c. bookmarks

    d. the Web Search tool

11. Search engines are used to _____. (Choose all that apply.)

    a. survey the Web and build their Web page databases

    b. examine many documents on the Web

    c. find information from only one specific source

    d. secretly write programs

12. Other terms for a search engine include _____. (Choose all that apply.)

    a. worms

    b. crawlers

    c. bots

    d. spiders

13. RPM is an acronym for _____.

    a. Real Program Manager

    b. Resource Program Management

    c. Red Hat Package Manager

    d. Red Hat Program Manager

14. Caches should be cleared because _____. (Choose all that apply.)

    a. they are too convenient

    b. site requests and displays can be slowed down by large outdated caches

    c. stored passwords could be stolen by hackers

    d. form information can be a security risk

15. A zone is _____. (Choose all that apply.)

    a. a group of Web sites that can be separated to manage security

    b. never used to safeguard your system from potentially unsafe content

    c. used to provide security when working with Web sites

    d. used to help you browse securely

16. One type of security zone in Internet Explorer is called _____. (Choose all that apply.)

    a. Internet

    b. Local intranet

    c. Trusted sites

    d. Restricted sites

17. Cookies are used by Web sites _____.

    a. to earn money for new servers

    b. to maintain information and settings, such as your surfing preferences

    c. to keep browsers from closing

    d. to keep browsers from accessing sites

18. A file that has a zip extension _____. (Choose all that apply.)

    a. contains one or more files that have been compressed or stored

    b. needs to be processed with an archive utility to extract the files

    c. is much larger than the original file that was used to create it

    d. is generally smaller than the original file or files that were used to create it

19. Application installers are used to _____. (Choose all that apply.)

    a. prepare the PC and complete any preinstallation steps

    b. uncompress the application

    c. run the setup or installation program to place the program modules in the proper directories and prepare them for use

    d. configure the program

20. Microsoft Windows Installer and Red Hat Package Manager are known as _____.

    a. compression utilities

    b. compilers

    c. object-oriented programming languages

    d. application installers

Case Projects

CASE PROJECTS

Case 4-1: Using Microsoft Help and Support

A friend asks you to examine her computer, which has Windows 7 installed. You need to know what hardware and software are installed on the computer. Your friend logs on to the computer with administrative rights. What is the quickest way to get the "big picture" of your friend's computer?

Case 4-2: Configuring Internet Explorer

You volunteer to support a small nonprofit organization whose network consists of 10 computers, all of which have Windows 7 Professional installed. Users connect to the Internet through an Internet firewall. The manager is concerned about protecting the privacy of employees when they access Web sites. How will you configure Internet Explorer to meet the manager's concerns? Express your answer in business terms rather than technical terms.

Case 4-3: Configuring Firefox

Your boss has asked you to prepare a short presentation on Firefox security. To support your presentation, prepare a short outline of the security features in Firefox to hand out.

chapter 5

File Systems

After reading this chapter and completing the exercises, you will be able to:

- Describe the characteristics of three Windows 7 file systems
- Describe the characteristics of four Fedora 13 file systems
- Create a file system in Windows 7 and Fedora 13
- Mount a file system in Windows 7 and Fedora 13
- Manage file systems in Windows 7 and Fedora 13

A file system refers to the overall structure in which files are named, stored, and organized. File systems comprise files, directories (or folders), and the information needed to locate and access them. To prepare to use current and future operating systems, you should develop skills for using the various file systems in Windows 7 and Fedora 13. This chapter explains how.

Before storing data on a PC's hard drives, you must prepare them to accept the files. In this chapter, you will learn to create **storage areas**—areas on a disk that can be allocated and formatted for a file system—and then place a file system within a storage area. In addition, you will learn to manage file systems with standard tools in Windows 7 and Fedora 13.

Windows 7 File System Characteristics

Before you can make intelligent decisions about selecting and using a file system in Windows 7, you must know how to implement the file system. Specifically, you need to know the following information, which is explained in this section:

- Allocation of the storage areas on the hard drive
- Assignment of drive letters, which are used to access storage areas
- Characteristics of available file systems

Disk Partitions

Figure 5-1 shows the BIOS settings for the three SATA-controlled drives represented by virtual hard drives in your virtualization software. Each SATA drive has its own disk controller. The CD-ROM drive, which is not shown in the BIOS settings, has its own controller.

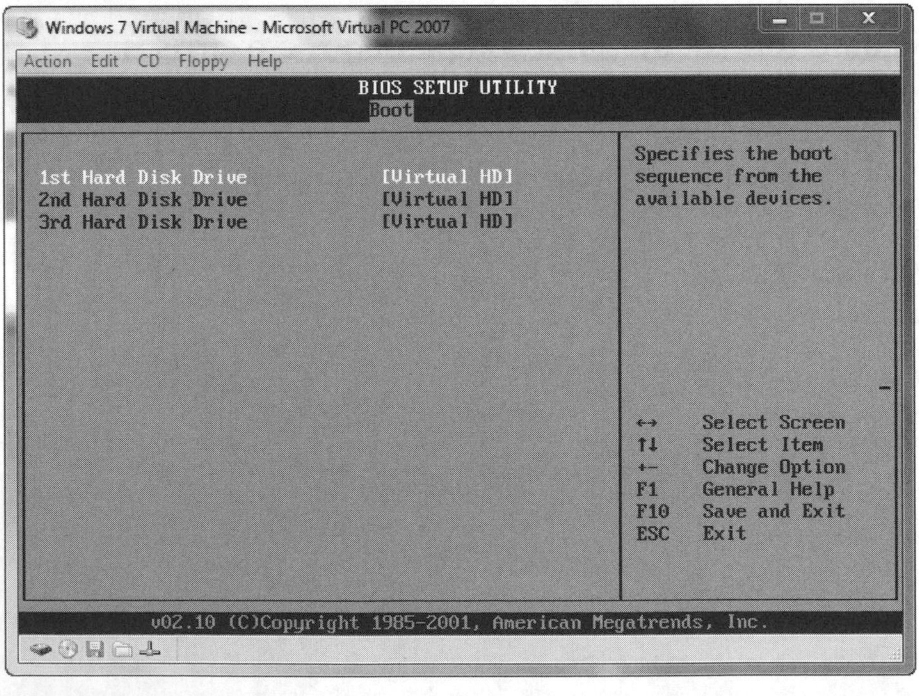

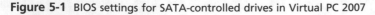

Figure 5-1 BIOS settings for SATA-controlled drives in Virtual PC 2007

Source: Course Technology/Cengage Learning

Now refer to Figure 5-2, which shows that each controller supports one device that could be a hard drive or CD-ROM drive. For purposes of illustration, consider a virtual machine with one physical hard drive on each disk controller and a CD-ROM drive on an IDE controller.

Next, consider how the same virtual machine's drives might be separated into **partitions**. These hard drives and their partitions are shown in the Disk Management console, as indicated in Figure 5-3. (The allocation of drive letters is covered in the next section.)

Windows 7 has two types of storage: basic and dynamic. Basic storage is the industry standard. Using **basic disk** storage, you can allocate primary partitions in Windows 7.

A **primary partition** normally contains an OS, such as Windows 7. The active primary partition contains the files that start an OS. You can have up to four primary partitions per physical hard drive, or three if you use an extended partition. You can only create an extended partition after creating three primary partitions.

You can allocate only one extended partition per physical hard drive, but you can allocate multiple logical drives within an extended partition. Because Z is the last available drive letter, you are limited by the number of letters.

When you install Windows 7, a single primary partition is created for the OS. This scheme offers the greatest flexibility when defining storage areas.

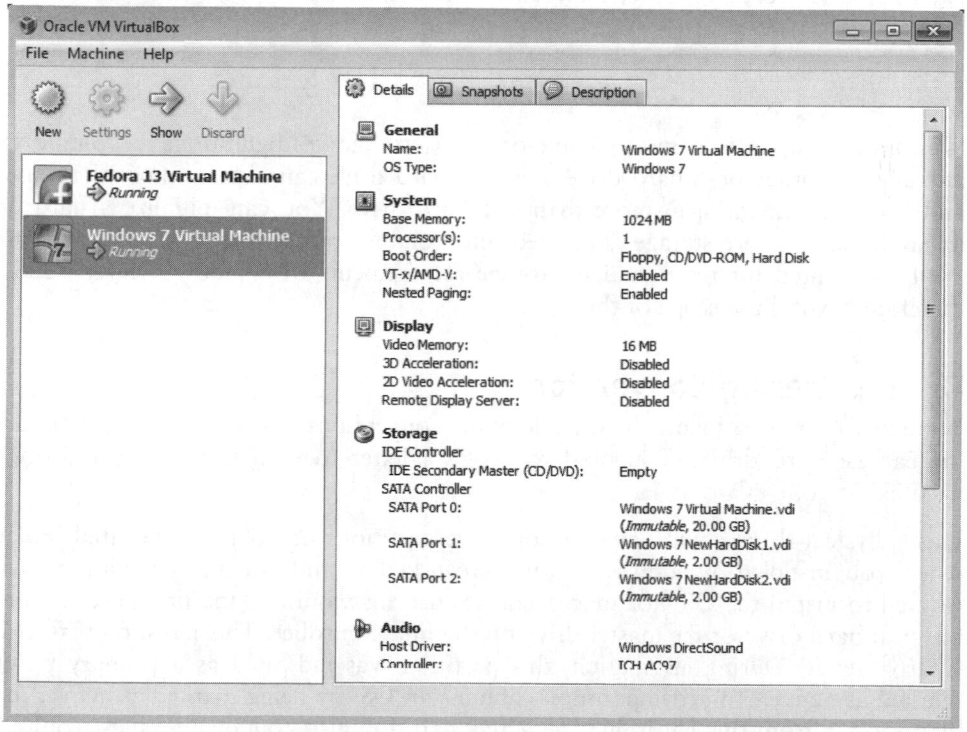

Figure 5-2 Sample devices for SATA-controlled drives

Source: Course Technology/Cengage Learning

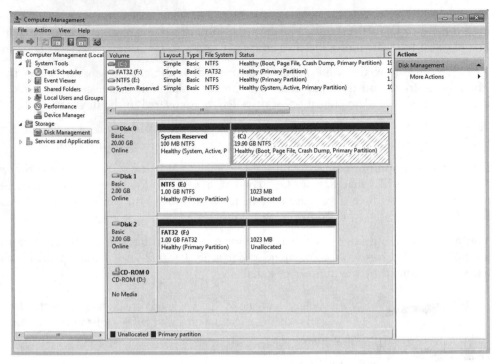

Figure 5-3 Partitions on three hard drives and a CD-ROM drive

Source: Course Technology/Cengage Learning

Windows 7 supports a new volume-oriented storage configuration. A **volume** is a fixed amount of storage on a hard drive. A single hard drive can contain more than one volume, and a volume might span more than one hard drive. You can initialize a hard drive as a **dynamic disk,** where storage is divided into volumes rather than partitions. Dynamic disks are better suited for the vast data storage requirements of Windows Server 2008, and are therefore beyond the scope of this text.

Drive-Lettering Conventions

Windows 7 tends to follow the drive-lettering conventions that were established years ago for the earliest hard drives. You need to assign a letter to each hard drive and optical drive installed in your PC.

Each physical drive could have one or more partitions or volumes allocated. For example, when you installed Windows 7, you were asked to indicate the partition in which you wanted to install the OS. For most installations, this would be the first partition on the first physical hard drive or the master drive on the first controller. This partition was assigned the C drive letter. During installation, this partition was indicated as a primary partition and marked as active. An active partition contains an OS; by being marked as active, the PC will load the OS from this partition. The active partition also contains the files required to boot the computer. The letters A and B are reserved for two floppy drives that may not exist on modern PCs.

Windows 7 assigns drive letters as you create the various partitions and logical drives. You should create multiple storage areas to separate the OS from data. For example, the partitions and logical drives in Figure 5-4 were created in the following sequence:

- The System Reserved partition, placed on the Disk 0 hard drive to facilitate system recovery, did not receive a drive letter.
- The first primary partition on the first physical drive, Disk 0, was assigned drive letter C. This partition was selected during the installation of Windows 7.
- The CD-ROM drive that was available during installation received drive letter D.
- The next primary partition, which is on Disk 1, was assigned drive letter E.
- The primary partition on the remaining drive, Disk 2, received the drive letter F.

You can view drive letters and change the CD-ROM drive letter using the Disk Management console, as shown later in Activity 5-4.

 You might be annoyed that Windows 7 assigns the letter D to the CD-ROM drive when Windows 7 is installed. If you create another partition, it is assigned drive letter E, when you probably want the disk drive letters to be C and D. To address this, you can reassign the CD-ROM drive to the letter R before allocating space for the second partition.

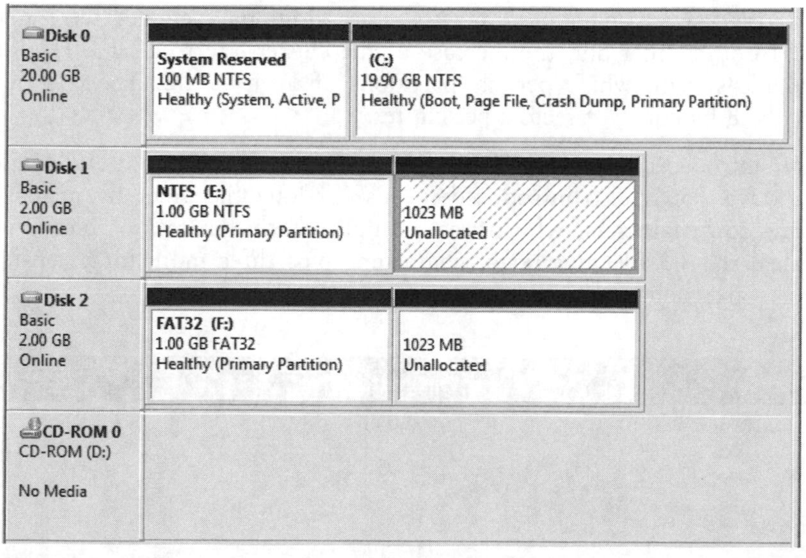

Disk 0 Basic 20.00 GB Online	System Reserved 100 MB NTFS Healthy (System, Active, P	(C:) 19.90 GB NTFS Healthy (Boot, Page File, Crash Dump, Primary Partition)
Disk 1 Basic 2.00 GB Online	NTFS (E:) 1.00 GB NTFS Healthy (Primary Partition)	1023 MB Unallocated
Disk 2 Basic 2.00 GB Online	FAT32 (F:) 1.00 GB FAT32 Healthy (Primary Partition)	1023 MB Unallocated
CD-ROM 0 CD-ROM (D:) No Media		

Figure 5-4 Disk Manager showing drive letters after additions

Source: Course Technology/Cengage Learning

FAT16 File System

The **file allocation table (FAT)** is a file system that was originally developed for early PCs running DOS. The FAT file system is relatively uncomplicated and is supported on a number of operating systems, including Windows 7 and Linux.

The smallest unit of space on a FAT disk that any OS can access is a **sector**, which usually consists of 512 bytes. Floppy diskettes store files in contiguous, 512-byte sectors. A 5,000-character file requires 10 sectors (5,000/512 = 9.76, or 10 sectors).

To manage files with relative efficiency, **FAT16** groups sectors into larger blocks called **clusters**. Cluster size is related to the size of the disk partition. Small partitions have smaller cluster sizes; large partitions require larger cluster sizes. You will encounter cluster sizes that range from 4 sectors, or 2,048 bytes, to 64 sectors, or 32,768 bytes, as shown in Table 5-1. Depending on the cluster size, a 5,000-character file might be stored in one cluster. For a cluster size of 16 sectors, the 5,000-character file fits in a cluster. However, if 8 sectors per cluster are used, the 5,000-character file requires 2 clusters (5,000/4,096 = 1.22, or 2 clusters).

The FAT16 file system has been around for a long time, and has an interesting history. The predecessor to FAT16 was **FAT12**, which was originally designed for floppy diskettes that had a capacity of about 160 KB. The disk format was called FAT12 because the counter for the **cluster address** (a number used to locate a cluster on the hard drive) was limited to 12 bits. Later, this format was used on the initial 10-MB hard drives in the IBM PC XT. When these hard drives were deployed, **subdirectories** (a logical grouping of related files) were introduced, which permitted the management of sets of files.

With the introduction of the 20-MB hard drive in the IBM PC AT, the length of the cluster address was increased to 16 bits, permitting 65,536 clusters. This change raised the limit to 32 MB per partition.

As larger hard drives were introduced for the PC, additional changes were made. The removal of the 16-bit counter and the increase of the cluster size to 32 KB resulted in the modern FAT16 file system, which permits partitions of up to 2 GB. The partition size is now limited by the 8-bit count of sectors per cluster.

When Microsoft introduced a new FAT file system called the **virtual file allocation table (VFAT)** in Windows 95, it also introduced the use of long filenames by increasing their length from 8 to 256 characters, which greatly improved the process of file naming. The short name, called the 8.3 filename (eight characters, plus three more for extensions), was retained for backward compatibility.

Number of Sectors	Cluster Size
4	2,048
8	4,096
16	8,192
32	16,384
64	32,768

Table 5-1 Cluster sizes

All Windows 7 filenames are case insensitive, meaning that their capitalization is not considered. For example, Budget, BUDGET, and budget are considered the same filename in Windows.

FAT32 File System

To support larger hard drives, Microsoft implemented the **FAT32** file system with Windows 95 OSR 2. This file system uses 32-bit cluster numbers (of which 28 bits are currently used).

In theory, the 28-bit sector address should permit about 268,435,438 clusters, which allows drive sizes of approximately 2 **terabytes** (about 2 trillion bytes). However, Microsoft chose to limit the cluster count. For Windows 7, the partition limit is 32 GB for the primary partition. FAT32 continued the use of subdirectories and long filenames.

5

NT File System

NTFS (New Technology File System) was introduced with the first version of Windows NT. NTFS is a completely different file system from FAT16 or FAT32, and is the default file system for new installations of Windows 7.

When using basic disks, NTFS supports volumes as large as 2 terabytes. For an idea of how large this is, a database that contains all of the satellite photos taken by the United States and Soviet Union during the Cold War requires about 2 terabytes. NTFS uses clusters that are similar in size to those in FATs: 512 bytes to 64 KB, with 4 KB being the default.

While FAT file systems use the file allocation table for managing access to files, NTFS uses the **master file table (MFT)**, which contains information about all the files and folders on the NTFS volume. The master file table allocates a certain amount of space for each file record. A file's attributes are written to the allocated space in the MFT. Elements such as the file's name, its security information, and even its data are all file attributes. Small files (typically 1,500 bytes or smaller) can be entirely contained within the master file table record. Fast access is assured by the use of a binary tree rather than the linear structure of FAT; NTFS does not search linearly through all table elements to find a needed file, but uses the **binary search** algorithm, a programming technique for locating an item quickly in a sequential list.

At the file level, NTFS supports many options that are not available with the FAT16 and FAT32 file systems. Because of these options, you should choose NTFS when you install Windows 7. The most notable options are:

- Journalizing—Provides a fail-safe mechanism by using transactions to ensure that data is written to the hard drive
- Compression—Reduces the space needed to store a file
- Encryption—Keeps files safe from intruders who might gain unauthorized physical access to sensitive, stored data (for example, by stealing a laptop computer)
- Security—Restricts data access to users who have permission to access the files
- Auditing—Tracks the access or attempted access to files
- Quotas—Limits the total size of files that an individual user can store on the hard drive

These options are explained in the following sections. You need this information to use NTFS effectively.

If you are running Windows 7 and another OS such as Fedora 13, you should store common data on a FAT or FAT32 partition.

Journalizing—Ensuring That Data Is Written

A file system that uses journalizing maintains data integrity for the hard drive if the OS crashes or stops abnormally. NTFS provides a fail-safe file system that can correct itself against a hard drive sector corruption or a power loss during hard drive writes. NTFS uses transactions, which means that the write action is either accomplished or canceled, that there are no incomplete hard drive writes, and that you will not lose data during a hard drive write.

If Windows 7 detects during a write operation that a sector is damaged, Windows 7 marks the sector as damaged and writes the data in another sector.

The case of a power loss is more complex. If data is being written and a power loss occurs, the OS restarts and discovers that the transaction was not completed. The transaction is then processed and the write operation is completed, ensuring that the power loss did not result in data loss.

Compression—Saving Space

The Windows 7 OS supports **compression**, a means of reducing the amount of space needed to store a block of data. With compression technology, you do not need additional software to reduce the size of files on your hard drive. For example, word-processing documents contain considerable white space and other repetitive characters, and usually yield good compression. Compressed files must be **decompressed** when they are accessed, and then must be recompressed prior to rewriting to the hard drive. This decompression and recompression requires processor cycles that can reduce the performance of your PC. For this reason, you should reserve compression for infrequently used files and folders.

Encryption—Protecting Data

When you use NTFS **encryption**, only you as the file creator can view the contents of a file. Anyone else who tries to view the file will see gibberish and will be denied access. For you, the file looks normal; it is automatically decrypted when accessed by an application.

Under normal circumstances, not even an administrator can view an encrypted file. In an emergency, however, an administrator can decrypt a file. In Windows 7, a file can be encrypted or compressed on a hard disk, but not both.

You may feel that the inability to view other users' files is a little severe, but Windows 7 is specifically designed this way for security reasons. For example, you may have heard stories of employees who left their laptops in airports; encryption keeps others from being able to view sensitive files.

Security—Restricting Access

Just as you would place valuables in a locked box to guard against theft, Windows 7 controls access to files and folders. To open the locked box, you would need the key that fit the lock. Windows 7 controls the keys (user accounts) and the locks (permissions).

In Windows 7, you need a user account and a password to access the PC. Before you can access a file, Windows 7 determines if you have permission by comparing your user ID to users who have the correct permissions to access the file (such as read, write, and modify). When a match occurs, access is permitted. As you may expect, if a match does not occur, Windows 7 displays a message indicating that access was denied.

Windows 7 is designed to provide security for files and folders accessed on an NTFS. While you may never need to specify these permissions (this is the administrator's job), you must be aware that such a security system exists to protect data on the PC. You will learn more about permissions in Chapter 11.

Auditing—Tracking Access Windows 7 deploys **auditing** to keep track of previous attempts to access data in NTFS. Because auditing requires significant processing resources and hard drive space, it is not turned on by default.

When auditing is enabled, you can configure Windows 7 to keep track of certain events. When any of these events occur, Windows 7 makes an entry in a security log. Each entry indicates information about an access event, including the type of event, the date and time that it occurred, which user triggered the event, and other relevant information.

Unless you are an administrator or another user who has been granted permission to access the security log, you will not be able to read it. However, you need to be aware that an administrator may have enabled auditing to track access to sensitive data on your work PC.

Quotas—Limiting Storage When a PC is shared by several users, Windows 7 can be configured to enforce **quotas**, which are limits on the amount of data that each user can store on each storage area on the hard drive. Quotas are set for individual users and individual storage areas (in other words, an administrator cannot limit space for a group of people). Users who attempt to store data beyond their quota will receive an error message indicating that the hard drive is full. By reviewing the log file, the administrator can determine who has reached the quota limit or the warning limit.

Optical Media File Systems

You are probably familiar with CD-ROMs, which are a form of optical disc. For example, you may have used a CD-ROM to install an OS or an application. An optical disc is a computer storage medium that operates using digitized beams of light. Windows 7 supports two file systems for optical media:

- UDF (Universal Disk Format) was developed by the Optical Storage Technology Association. It was designed for read-write interoperability among the major operating systems and for compatibility between rewritable and write-once media. DVDs are based on UDF; it is also an option for CD-Rs and CD-RWs.

- Compact Disc File System (CDFS) is not an independent file system; instead, it is a loosely used alias for ISO 9660, the CD-ROM file system standard intended to make CD-ROMs readable by many different platforms.

Activity 5-1: Finding File System Information in Windows 7

Time Required: 10 minutes

Objective: Locate information about the file systems in Windows 7.

Description: In this activity, you log on to your virtual machine and view information about file systems. This activity is useful if you need to make a decision about a file system.

1. Start your virtual machines using the appropriate instructions in Activity 1-1.

2. To open the Control Panel, click **Start** and then click **Control Panel.**

3. To open the Administrative tools, click the **System and Security** link and then click the **Administrative Tools** link.

4. To run Computer Management as an administrator, right-click **Computer Management,** click **Run as Administrator,** type **P@ssw0rd**, and then click **Yes.**

5. To see the partitions for your virtual machine, double-click **Storage,** and then double-click **Disk Management.**

To see all four disks, locate and click the bar below the horizontal slider and drag the bar up.

6. View the information about Disk 0. Note that the installation of Windows 7 occupies the entire disk.

7. View the information about Disk 1, and note that a 1-GB NTFS partition was previously allocated by your instructor. Also note that 1 GB of the disk has not been allocated, and can be used for future allocations.

8. View the information about Disk 2 and a FAT32 partition.

9. Verify that a disk was assigned for use by CD-ROM media.

The CD-ROM drive is most likely empty.

10. Close the Computer Management window.

11. Leave the virtual machine logged on for future activities.

Fedora 13 File System Characteristics

Before you can make intelligent decisions about selecting and using a file system in Fedora 13, you must know how to implement the file system. Specifically, you need to know the following information, which is explained in this section:

- Allocation of the partitions on the hard drive
- Creation of file systems on the partitions

- Creation and management of directories and files on the file systems
- Characteristics of available file systems

Each partition on a physical drive is named and then formatted for the type of file system you want to use. The file systems on the partitions are then "mounted" on mount points to enable them to be accessed, either automatically at boot time or manually when needed. Directories and files are created and managed on these file systems.

Disk Partitions

The disks on the Fedora 13 virtual machine were allocated to mimic the drives on the Windows 7 virtual machine. Figure 5-5 shows the three disks and CD drive.

You can use Table 5-2 to match partition allocations between the two operating systems for the installed virtual machines. The three Windows 7 disks (Disk 0, Disk 1, and Disk 2) match up with the corresponding Fedora 13 disks (sda, sdb, and sdc). The operating systems are installed on the first virtual disk (Disk 0 or sda). The partitions are approximately the same on the remaining two virtual disks.

Fedora 13 assigns logical storage areas called partitions on a hard drive. A partition table is located in sector 0 of the drive. Fedora 13 needs at least one partition for its root file system.

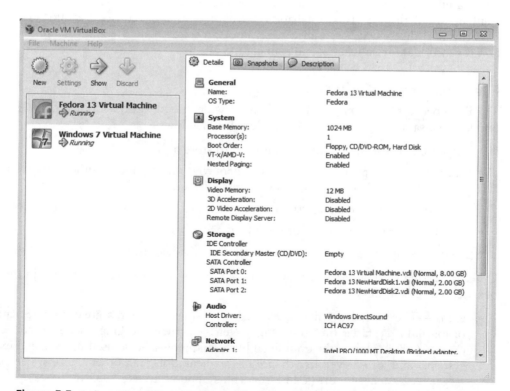

Figure 5-5 Fedora 13 partitions on three disks and a CD-ROM drive

Source: Course Technology/Cengage Learning

Windows 7		Fedora 13	
Disk 0 20 GB	System Reserved	sda 8 GB	sda1 Linux Ext4 boot partition
	Drive C: holding Windows 7 OS		sda2 LVM2 Physical volume holding Fedora 13
Disk 1 2 GB	Drive E: 1.00 GB NTFS	sdb 2.1 GB	sdb1 1.1 GB Ext3 partition
	Unallocated 1 GB		sdb2 1.1 GB Physical volume
Disk 2 2 GB	Drive F:	sdc 2.1 GB	sdc1 1.1 FAT32
	Unallocated 1 GB		sdc2 1.1 GB Physical volume
CD-ROM Drive	Empty	CD/DVD Drive	Empty

Table 5-2   Mimicked drives

Drive Partition Naming Conventions

Each partition on a hard drive is given a name, which consists of a device name followed by a partition number. Each physical drive could have one or more partitions allocated. By default, the first installed SATA drive is called sda, the second is sdb, and so on.

For example, when you install Fedora 13, you are asked to indicate the partition where you want to install the OS. This installation partition is usually the first partition on the first physical hard drive, which is named sda1. Boot processes then reference this primary partition for information on loading and running the OS.

File Systems in Fedora 13

The Extended 2 file system (ext2fs) is the most widely used file system in Fedora 13. Ext2fs provides the same functionality as NTFS does for Windows 7:

- Compression—Reduces the space needed to store a file
- Encryption—Keeps files safe from intruders who might gain unauthorized physical access to sensitive, stored data (for example, by stealing a laptop computer)
- Security—Restricts data access to users who have permission to access the files
- Auditing—Tracks the access or attempted access to files
- Quotas—Limits the total size of files that an individual user can store on the hard drive

Other file systems can also be used in Fedora 13. Many of them were discussed in the previous section on Windows 7:

- ext4fs—The Extended 4 file system adds robustness through a greater implementation of journalizing, faster time-stamping, faster file system checking, inode structure extents (which replace the traditional block mapping scheme used by ext2 and ext3 file systems, and afford even less chance of fragmentation than other Linux systems), and larger file system support (a 48-bit block as opposed to ext3's 32-bit block).
- ext3fs—The Extended 3 file system is the most widely used Linux file system; it adds robustness through its addition of journalizing to the functionality of ext2. Journalizing

provides a fail-safe mechanism, using transactions to ensure that data is written to the hard drive, as NTFS does for Windows 7.

- ext2fs—This system keeps track of the changes made to a file system, making it much easier to restore a corrupted file system.
- FAT16—This file system is typically used to read floppy diskettes.
- FAT32 (VFAT)—This file system allows long filenames.
- NTFS—Fedora 13 provides read-only access to NTFS. For copyright reasons, Fedora 13 does not automatically recognize NTFS, and sometimes it requires kernel updates for the driver.

Fedora 13 does not honor NTFS permissions, which poses a potential security breach. Because the read, write, and execute permissions are not enforced, a user who is restricted from accessing data files in Windows 7 could easily access them from Fedora 13.

- ISO 9660—This file system is used by most CD-ROMs.
- UDF—This file system is meant for use with CD-RWs and DVDs.

The Fedora 13 files and folders matched to user/group permissions are the same for all Linux file systems. The chmod, chown, and chgrp commands are used to assign these permissions, as referenced in Chapter 11.

Activity 5-2: Finding Partition Information in Fedora 13

Time Required: 10 minutes

Objective: Locate information about the partitions in Fedora 13.

Description: This activity is useful if you want to review information before making a decision about a file system.

1. Start your virtual machines using the appropriate instructions in Activity 1-1.
2. To open the Disk Utility, click **Applications**, point to **System Tools**, and then click **Disk Utility**.
3. View the information about sda, which is identified as an 8.4-GB hard disk. Note that the installation of Fedora 13 occupies the entire disk.
4. View the information about sdb, which is identified as the first 2.1-GB hard disk. Note that a 1-GB Ext3 partition was previously allocated by your instructor. Also note that 1.1 GB of the disk has not been allocated, and can be used for future file system allocations.
5. View the information about sdc and a FAT32 partition.
6. Verify that a disk was assigned for use by CD-ROM media.

The CD-ROM drive is most likely empty.

7. Close the Disk Utility window.

8. Leave the virtual machine logged on for future activities.

File System Creation

Before you can read or write to a hard drive, you must place a file system on the disk. This act, called **formatting**, prepares a storage area for use. Formatting creates the root of the directory structure and the file system for use. Prior to installing a file system, you must create a storage area.

In Windows 7, you use the Disk Management console to create the storage area and install the file system. In Linux, you use the fdisk and mkfs programs to perform the same tasks. Next, you use the file system tools in both operating systems to set up storage areas for the data to be stored on your hard drive.

This section explains how to create file systems in Windows 7 and Linux, and includes activities to take you through the individual steps.

Windows 7 File System Creation

In Windows 7, you use the Disk Management console to create a storage area and then install the file system in it. When creating the storage area, you start with an unallocated area on a physical disk. An unallocated area is one that does not contain a primary or extended partition; within an extended partition, an unallocated area does not contain a logical drive. Figure 5-6 shows areas on Disk 1; an arrow points to the unallocated area.

Use the New Simple Volume wizard to start the allocation process. Right-click the unallocated area and then click New Simple Volume. Read the information in the next window and click the Next button.

In the next dialog box, you indicate the amount of storage to set aside for the simple volume. For example, if you want to use the remainder of the virtual disk drive, you can leave the default value in the "Simple volume size in MB" field, as shown in Figure 5-7.

Windows has a number of wizards to guide you through the process of configuring various options. These wizards have a set of buttons to help you navigate through the windows. Click the Next button to accept the settings in a window and move to the next window. Click Back to return to previous windows and revise settings. Click the Finish button in the last window when you have selected and approved all the settings.

Figure 5-6   Areas on Disk 1

Source: Course Technology/Cengage Learning

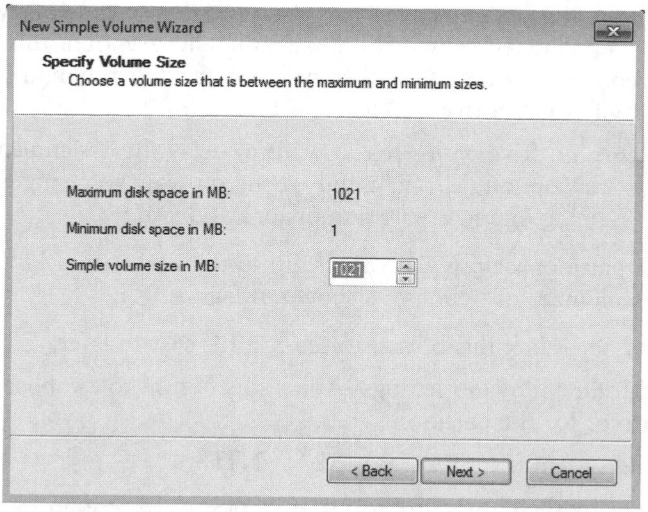

Figure 5-7 Specifying a partition size

Source: Course Technology/Cengage Learning

In the next dialog box, you can assign a letter to the drive, as shown in Figure 5-8.

You have three options in the Assign Drive Letter or Path dialog box:

- **Assign the following drive letter**—To assign a letter to a drive, click this option and then select a letter from the list box.
- **Mount in the following empty NTFS folder**—With this option, you can reference the partition or logical drive from a folder in another partition. This mount option is like

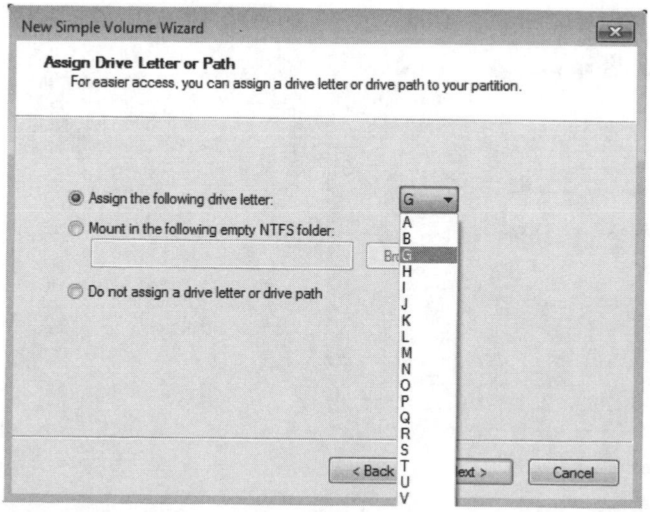

Figure 5-8 Assigning a drive letter

Source: Course Technology/Cengage Learning

the mount process in Linux. For example, you can click a folder on the C drive that links to the logical drive in an extended partition. If you intend to mount this folder, note that it should not contain any data files; they will be lost while the mount point is used. You will mount a CD-ROM drive in Activity 5-9.

- **Do not assign a drive letter or drive path**—If you want to delay the assignment of a drive letter or path, click this option. This is useful when you want to change an existing drive letter before assigning one to a partition or logical drive.

Finally, you must format the partition before you can use it. In the next dialog box, Format Partition, you can configure a number of options, as shown in Figure 5-9:

- **Do not format this volume**—Click this button to select a file system later.
- **Format this volume with the following settings**—Click this button to establish any or all of the following settings for the partition.
- **File system**—Select a file system from FAT, FAT32, or NTFS.
- **Allocation unit size**—Specify the cluster size to use (it is best to let Windows 7 make this decision).
- **Volume label**—Type the volume label that you want to appear in reference to this partition.
- **Perform a quick format**—Speed the formatting operation; you should only use this option on previously formatted partitions that are known to be in good condition.
- **Enable file and folder compression**—Indicate that files and folders are automatically compressed (only available for NT file systems).

After selecting the formatting options, click Next and then click Finish to format the drive.

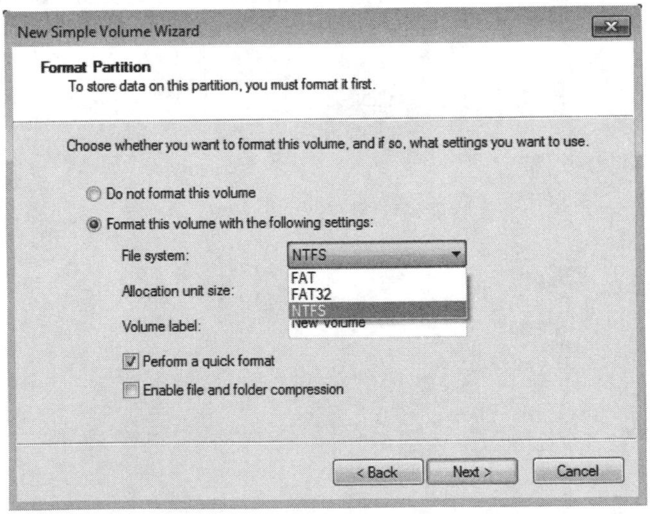

Figure 5-9 Format Partition options

Source: Course Technology/Cengage Learning

Activity 5-3: Creating a Simple Volume

Time Required: 20 minutes

Objective: Create a simple volume in Windows 7.

Description: In this activity, you open the Computer Management program and select Disk Management. Next, you create a simple volume and format the volume for use. This activity is useful if you want to create storage areas with file systems in Windows 7.

1. If necessary, start your virtual machines using the appropriate instructions in Activity 1-1.

2. To open the Control Panel, click **Start** and then click **Control Panel**.

3. To open the Administrative tools, click the **System and Security** link and then click the **Administrative Tools** link.

4. To run Computer Management as an administrator, right-click **Computer Management**, click **Run as Administrator**, type **P@ssw0rd**, and then click **Yes**.

5. To see the partitions for your virtual machine, double-click **Storage**, and then double-click **Disk Management**.

6. Locate the Unallocated area for Disk 1.

If you do not see the Unallocated area on Disk 1, inform your instructor.

7. To start the New Simple Volume wizard, right-click the **Unallocated** area on Disk 1 and then click **New Simple Volume**.

8. After reading the Welcome message, click **Next**.

9. In the Specify Volume Size dialog box, accept the recommended partition size by clicking **Next**.

10. To retain the default drive letter, click **Next**.

11. In the Format Partition dialog box, click **Format this volume with the following settings** and then type Second NTFS in the Volume label text box. Leave the other settings and click **Next**.

12. Review the setting information and then click **Finish**.

13. Wait for the simple volume to format.

If you do not see the word *Healthy* in the area that was created, inform your instructor.

14. Close the Computer Management window.

15. Leave the virtual machine logged on for future activities.

Activity 5-4: Changing a Drive Letter

Time Required: 10 minutes

Objective: Change the letter for the CD-ROM drive in Windows 7.

Description: In this activity, you open the Computer Management program, select Disk Management, and then reassign the letter for the CD-ROM drive. This activity is useful if you want to assign a different drive letter in Windows 7. For example, you may want to assign a different letter to the CD-ROM drive to remove it from the sequence of hard drive storage areas.

1. If necessary, start your virtual machines using the appropriate instructions in Activity 1-1.
2. To open the Control Panel, click **Start** and then click **Control Panel.**
3. To open the Administrative tools, click the **System and Security** link and then click the **Administrative Tools** link.
4. To run Computer Management as an administrator, right-click **Computer Management,** click **Run as Administrator,** type **P@ssw0rd,** and then click **Yes.**
5. To see the partitions for your virtual machine, double-click **Storage,** and then double-click **Disk Management.**
6. Right-click the **CD-ROM 0** button and then click **Change Drive Letter and Paths.**

> If you cannot locate the CD-ROM 0 button, inform your instructor.

7. To change the drive letter, click the **Change** button, click the **Assign the following drive letter** list box, click **R** (or the next available letter after R), and click **OK.**
8. Read the confirmation message and click **Yes.**
9. Verify that the drive letter has changed for the **CD-ROM 0** drive.
10. Close the Computer Management window.
11. Leave the virtual machine logged on for future activities.

Fedora 13 File System Creation

File systems are used for storing both system configurations and data for Fedora 13. When you install Fedora 13, you are initially required to define the "/" directory and the **swap file,** a hidden file on the hard drive used to hold parts of programs and data files that do not fit in memory. The OS moves data from the swap file to memory as needed, and moves data out of memory to the swap file to make room for new data. After the "/" directory and swap file are defined, you can add your own file systems. Table 5-3 lists the default directories created during installation.

Default Directory	Description
/	This directory contains the main file system. Every file system is attached, or "grafted," into this hierarchical "tree"; the root directory is the main node, or "root," of the file system tree.
/root	This is the home directory of the superuser (the system administrator). It is not to be confused with the system root "/," which is the directory at the highest level in the file system.
/boot	This directory contains the kernel and boot files.
/swap	This directory contains the space used on the hard drive that acts like memory, as virtual memory does in Windows 7. Note that it is sometimes advantageous to create a swap partition to improve scalability. This prevents the necessity of having to resize a swap file later.
/etc	This directory contains the system configuration files.
/dev	This directory contains files that define and point to the system devices. Device files allow user programs to access hardware devices on the system through the kernel. They are not data files, but look like files from the OS's point of view.
/sbin	This directory contains user binary programs that run administration applications.
/bin	This directory contains commonly used binary programs.
/home	This directory contains all of the user home directories (for example, /home/jmiller).
/lib	This directory contains the shared program libraries.
/proc	This virtual directory contains status information. "Virtual" means that no actual disk space is associated with the file system; it is entirely contained in memory.
/lost+found	This directory contains damaged or disconnected files.
/mnt	This directory contains various mount points for user file systems.
/usr	This directory contains various user definition files.
/var	This directory contains files that normally vary in size, such as log files, spool files, and miscellaneous dynamic files.
/tmp	This directory contains temporary files.

Table 5-3 Fedora 13 default directories

The fdisk command is called a partition table manipulator; it shows the partition table with the corresponding file systems. The command has the following syntax:

fdisk [-l] [-v] [-s partition] [device]

-v   Prints the version number of the fdisk program

-l   Lists the partition tables for /dev/sda, /dev/sdb, /dev/sdc, /dev/sdd, /dev/sde, /dev/sdf, /dev/sdg, /dev/sdh, and then exits

-s partition   If the partition is not a DOS partition (i.e., its ID is greater than 10), the size of the partition is printed on the standard output device

When you manually create a file system, you first create a new partition using the fdisk command. You need to have superuser access to use this command. You will learn to use the fdisk command with several interactive parameters in Activity 5-5.

Next, you create the file system using the `mkfs` command. This enables the file system to store files. You need to have superuser access to use this command.

With the `mount` command, you attach a file system to a partition via a mount point directory. The syntax and options for the `mount` command are:

`mount [-l] [-t type]`	Lists all mounted file systems of the type you specify; the `-l` option adds ext2 mount and ext3 labels in this listing
`-t`	Specifies the file system type
`-h`	Prints a help message
`-v`	Prints a version string

For example, you could use the following `mkfs` command to create a file system on a floppy diskette. The command defines the file system as `ext2`, but you could use the `msdos` parameter instead. The `-t` option specifies the file system type, and `/dev/fd0` names the target device.

```
mkfs -t ext2 /dev/fd0
```

In the next command, the `-c` option tells the OS to mark bad blocks and avoid writing to them.

```
mkfs -t ext3 -c /dev/hdb1
```

Activity 5-5 shows how you create a new partition with `mkfs`.

If you need to create a mount point on the current file system, you first create a directory in the file system using the `mkdir` command. This command works much like the MD command in Windows 7. For example, you can type:

```
mkdir /home/User01/mydirectory
```

To perform Activity 5-5 and create partitions on your virtual machine, you must have free space on your hard drive. Two additional hard disks—sdb and sdc—are provided by your instructor for this activity.

Activity 5-5: Creating a Fedora 13 File System

Time Required: 15 minutes

Objective: Manually create a file system in Fedora 13.

Description: In this activity, you use the `fdisk` and `mkfs` commands to create a file system in Fedora 13. This activity is useful, for example, if you need to create a new partition and file system and then set aside a storage area for data.

1. If necessary, start your virtual machines using the appropriate instructions in Activity 1-1.

2. To open a Terminal console, click **Applications**, point to **System Tools**, and then click **Terminal**.

3. To switch to superuser, type **su -** and press **Enter,** then type a password of **P@ssw0rd** and press **Enter**.

4. To start the `fdisk` utility, type **fdisk /dev/sdb** and then press **Enter**.

5. To begin creating a new partition, press **n** and then press **Enter**.

6. To specify a primary partition, press **p** and then press **Enter**.

7. To specify the second partition, press **2** and then press **Enter**.

8. To specify the starting cylinder, press **133** and then press **Enter**.

9. To use the default setting for the ending cylinder, press **Enter**.

10. To save the changes, press **w** and then press **Enter**.

11. To create the file system, type **mkfs -t ext3 -c /dev/sdb2** and then press **Enter**.

12. Notice the information for your new file system in the command output.

13. To close the Terminal console, type **exit** and then press **Enter**.

14. Leave the Fedora 13 virtual machine logged on for future activities.

Mounting a File System

Windows 7 and Fedora 13 have different approaches to mounting a file system, but each approach has merit. Windows 7, as previously discussed, assigns drive letters for various partitions, volumes, and CD-ROM drives. These "premounted" storage items, with the exception of removable drives, are routinely available to PC users without user intervention.

To understand the difference between approaches, imagine the lights in various rooms of a house. In a Windows 7 house, the lights would turn on in every room when you entered the front door. Windows 7 optimizes user convenience at the expense of PC performance by making all of the storage areas available. In a Fedora 13 house, you would turn on the lights of each room as you entered it, and turn off the lights when you left. Fedora 13 optimizes performance at the expense of user convenience by making only the needed storage area(s) available.

This section explains how to access storage areas in both operating systems.

Mounting a Windows 7 File System

Recall that Windows 7 assigns drive letters to each partition, logical drive, and CD-ROM drive. These storage areas are premounted and are available without any action by the user.

However, there is an exception. Removable drives, such as USB drives, are mounted by Windows 7 upon insertion into the USB port. Prior to removal, you must notify Windows 7 that you want to remove (dismount) the USB drive; you cannot remove the drive until Windows 7 has completed writing data to it. If you remove the USB drive too soon, you may interrupt the transfer of data to the USB drive.

Windows 7 supports mounted drives, as does Fedora 13. You can create a mounted drive in Windows 7 by using the Disk Management console. A mounted drive is a drive that is mapped to an empty folder on a volume that uses NTFS. Mounted drives function like any other drives, but they are assigned drive paths instead of drive letters. To access a mounted drive, you click the drive icon located on the other drive.

Mounted drives make your data storage more accessible and give you the flexibility to manage data storage based on your PC usage. For example, when space starts to run low on drive C, you can move the Documents folder to another drive with more available disk space, and then mount it as C:\Documents.

To create a mounted drive, start with the drive that you want to mount in the Disk Management console. For example, if you were mounting the G drive, you would start with the G drive. For a full description of how to create a mounted drive, see Activity 5-6.

Activity 5-6: Mounting a Logical Drive in Windows 7

Time Required: 10 minutes

Objective: Create a mount point to another drive in Windows 7.

Description: In this activity, you open the Computer Management program, select Disk Management, and locate the drive that you want to mount. Next, navigate to the Add Drive Letter or Path dialog box and create the mount point. As a check, you will open Windows 7 Explorer, locate the mount point icon that you created, and open the mounted drive. This activity is useful if you want to create a mount point in Windows 7. For example, you may want to move a folder to a new drive to increase the available storage on the first drive and more effectively manage storage areas.

1. If necessary, start your virtual machines using the appropriate instructions in Activity 1-1.

2. To open the Control Panel, click **Start** and then click **Control Panel.**

3. To open the Administrative tools, click the **System and Security** link and then click the **Administrative Tools** link.

4. To run Computer Management as an administrator, right-click **Computer Management,** click **Run as Administrator,** type **P@ssw0rd,** and then click **Yes.**

5. To see the partitions for your virtual machine, double-click **Storage,** and then double-click **Disk Management.**

6. Right-click the **NTFS (E:)** area and then click **Change Drive Letter and Pat**hs.

7. To add the mount point, click the **Add** button. The Add Drive Letter or Path dialog box appears, as shown in Figure 5-10.

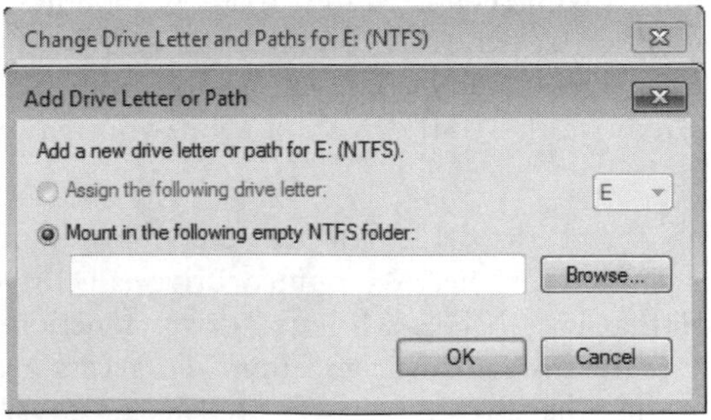

Figure 5-10 Add Drive Letter or Path dialog box

Source: Course Technology/Cengage Learning

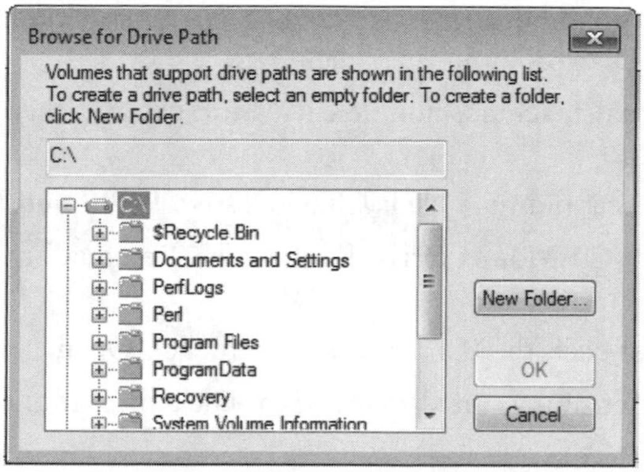

Figure 5-11 Browse for Drive Path dialog box

Source: Course Technology/Cengage Learning

8. Click the **Browse** button and then expand the **C:** drive, which is where you want to create the empty folder. See Figure 5-11.

9. To specify the mount point, click the **New Folder** button. Next, type the name of the mount point, **Mount Drive F**, over the words "New Folder" and then click **OK** twice.

10. To open Windows 7 Explorer, right-click the (C:) area and then click **Open**.

11. To open the mounted drive, double-click the gray **Mount Drive F** icon. Double-clicking this icon links you to the other drive.

12. Verify that the address changed to C:\Mount Drive F.

> If you do not see the contents of the drive, which may be empty, inform your instructor.

13. Close all the windows you opened in this activity.

14. Leave the virtual machine logged on for the next activity.

Activity 5-7: Removing a Mount Point for a Drive

Time Required: 10 minutes

Objective: Remove a mount point in Windows 7.

Description: In this activity, you open the Computer Management program, select Disk Management, and locate the drive that you want to dismount. This activity is useful if you want to remove a mount point in Windows 7.

1. If necessary, start your virtual machines using the appropriate instructions in Activity 1-1.

2. To open the Control Panel, click **Start** and then click **Control Panel.**

3. To open the Administrative tools, click the **System and Security** link and then click the **Administrative Tools** link.

4. To run Computer Management as an administrator, right-click **Computer Management**, click **Run as Administrator**, type **P@ssw0rd**, and then click **Yes**.

5. To see the partitions for your virtual machine, double-click **Storage**, and then double-click **Disk Management**.

6. Right-click the **Second NTFS (F:)** area and then click **Change Drive Letter and Paths**.

7. To remove the mount point, click **(C:)\Mount Drive F**, click the **Remove** button, and then click **Yes**.

8. To open Windows 7 Explorer, right-click the **(C:)** area and then click **Open**.

9. To remove the folder for the previously mounted drive, right-click the **Mount Drive F** folder, click **Delete**, and then click **Yes**.

10. Close all the windows you opened in this activity.

11. Leave the virtual machine logged on for the next activity.

Activity 5-8: Removing a Simple Volume

Time Required: 10 minutes

Objective: Remove a simple volume in Windows 7.

Description: In this activity, you open the Disk Management console and delete a simple volume. This activity is useful if you want to remove a volume that you no longer need.

1. If necessary, start your virtual machines using the appropriate instructions in Activity 1-1.

2. To open the Control Panel, click **Start** and then click **Control Panel.**

3. To open the Administrative tools, click the **System and Security** link and then click the **Administrative Tools** link.

4. To run Computer Management as an administrator, right-click **Computer Management**, click **Run as Administrator**, type **P@ssw0rd**, and then click **Yes**.

5. To see the partitions for your virtual machine, double-click **Storage**, and then double-click **Disk Management**.

6. To remove the volume, right-click the **Second NTFS (F:)** area, click **Delete Volume**, and then click the **Yes** button.

7. Close all the windows you opened in this activity.

8. Leave the virtual machine logged on for future activities.

Mounting a Fedora 13 File System

Recall that Fedora 13 assigns names to each partition and then mounts these partitions on mount points defined by a file system. Mounting is the process by which a file system becomes available for use. After mounting, your files are accessible at the mount point. Under normal conditions, you must have superuser access to mount a file system.

Certain partitions are created and mounted by default at installation. These same partitions are automatically mounted when the OS boots. If you want to mount another partition automatically when the OS boots, you must type an entry line in the /etc/fstab file for that partition.

As in Windows 7, mounted drives make your data storage more accessible in Fedora 13 and give you the flexibility to manage data storage based on your usage. For example, when space starts to run low on drive /dev/sba1, you can move directories to another formatted physical drive with more available disk space, and then mount it as /dev/sba2.

Mounted partitions appear to be part of the local directory structure, whether they are actually located locally or on another machine across a network. Thus, mounting Fedora 13 on another partition makes no difference to the OS.

A script in /etc/rc.d executes the mount -a command, which automatically mounts all file systems listed in /etc/fstab unless a noauto option is specified. As a result, these file systems—including hard drives and CD-ROM drives—will be mounted and available when the PC starts.

If your CD-ROM drive is not mounted automatically, it is a good idea to create a special directory such as /cdrom and mount the device there. The /mnt directory is a generic mount point under which you mount file systems or devices; it is normally used to temporarily mount file systems such as CD-ROM drives and floppy drives. You must have superuser access to use this directory unless the device is listed in the /etc/fstab file with user permission.

With the mount command, you attach a file system to a partition via a mount point directory. The syntax and options for the mount command are:

```
mount -t type device mount-point
```

`mount [-l] [-t type]`	Lists all mounted file systems of the type you specify
`-r`	Mounts the file system as read-only; a synonym is -o ro
`-w`	Mounts the file system as read/write (the default selection); a synonym is -o rw
`-t vfstype`	The argument following the -t indicates the file system type
`-h`	Prints a help message
`-V`	Prints a version string

The currently supported file system types are ext4, ext2, ext3, iso9660 (the default), msdos, ntfs, ufs, umsdos, and vfat. If you do not use the -t option with the mount command to indicate the file system type, or if you specify the auto type, the **superblock** is probed for the file system type. The superblock contains a number that identifies it as a UFS file system and includes other numbers that describe the file system's geometry, statistics, and behavioral parameters.

Normally, only a superuser can mount a file system, but if the following line is in /etc/fstab:

```
/dev/cdrom /mnt/cdrom iso9660 ro,user,noauto,unhide 0 0
```

you can mount the system even if you are not a superuser. Use the following command: mount /dev/cdrom or mount /mnt/cdrom

Figure 5-12 shows you how to display mounted file systems in Fedora 13.

Figure 5-13 and Activity 5-9 show you how to mount a file system in Fedora 13.

Figure 5-12 Displaying mounted file systems in Fedora 13

Source: Course Technology/Cengage Learning

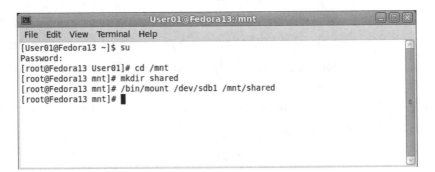

Figure 5-13 Mounting a file system in Fedora 13

Source: Course Technology/Cengage Learning

 If you want to mount a file system on a writable medium, such as a floppy disk, first mount the floppy file system, copy the files to it, and then unmount the floppy file system using the umount command. You must unmount the file system to write the data in memory to the disk. If you omit this step, the files will not be written to the floppy disk.

The umount command detaches the specified file system(s) from the file hierarchy. A file system is specified using the directory where it has been mounted.

The umount command has the following syntax:

umount [-l] [-t type]	Lists all mounted file systems of the type you specify
-h	Prints a help message
-V	Prints a version string
-v	Verbose mode
-l	"Lazy" unmount; detaches the file system from the file system hierarchy immediately, and cleans up all references to the file system as soon as it is not busy anymore (requires kernel 2.4.11 or later)

> **NOTE** A file system cannot be unmounted when it is "busy"—for example, when files are open on it, when some process has its working directory there, or when a swap file on the file system is in use. A lazy unmount avoids this problem.

Activity 5-9: Managing a Fedora 13 File System

Time Required: 10 minutes

Objective: Create a mount point to another drive in Fedora 13.

Description: In this activity, you use the mount command to mount a CD-ROM drive. Next, you will unmount the CD-ROM drive. This activity is useful if you need to use a CD-ROM drive in Fedora 13.

1. If necessary, start your virtual machines using the appropriate instructions in Activity 1-1.

2. To open a Terminal console, click **Applications**, point to **System Tools**, and then click **Terminal**.

3. To switch to superuser, type **su -** and press **Enter**, then type a password of **P@ssw0rd** and press **Enter**.

4. To make a directory to access the CD-ROM drive, type **mkdir /mnt/cdrom** and then press **Enter**.

5. Place the CD in the CD/DVD ROM drive.

> **NOTE** If there is no CD in the CD/DVD ROM drive, the mount will fail.

6. To mount the CD-ROM drive, type **/bin/mount –t iso9660 /dev/sdc /mnt/cdrom** and then press **Enter**.

7. To view the mounted file systems, type **/bin/mount** and then press **Enter**.

8. Locate your mounted file system.

9. To unmount the CD-ROM drive, type **/bin/umount /mnt/cdrom** and then press **Enter**.

10. To view the mounted file systems, type **/bin/mount** and then press **Enter**.

11. Note your unmounted file system.

12. To close the Terminal console, type **exit**, press **Enter**, type **exit** again, and press **Enter**.

13. Leave Fedora 13 logged on for the next activity.

Managing File Systems

This section shows you how to manage file systems in Windows 7 and Fedora 13. In Windows 7, you can use the Local Disk Properties dialog box to assist in file system management. In Fedora 13, you can use the `fsck` command and manage swap space.

Managing Windows 7 File Systems

Windows 7 provides a number of tools to help you manage the day-to-day operation of your file systems. Open the Computer console and use the Local Disk Properties dialog box of the selected drive as your starting point (see Figure 5-14).

You need administrative rights to view and change information in the Sharing and Quota tabs. The tools in the Local Disk Properties dialog box are grouped under several tabs, as explained in the following sections.

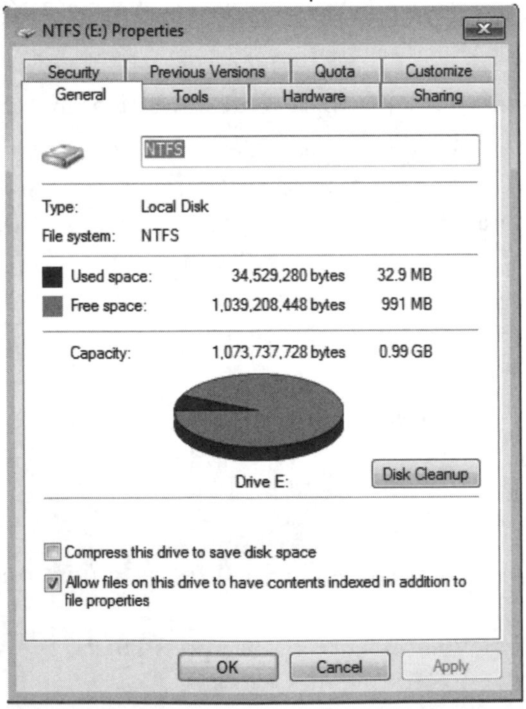

Figure 5-14 Local Disk Properties dialog box

Source: Course Technology/Cengage Learning

General Tab The General tab (see Figure 5-14) provides the following useful information and options for managing the available disk space of a given drive:

- Type—A local disk is a hard drive on the PC
- File system—Indicates the file system type on the drive
- Used space—Displays the amount of used space on the drive
- Free space—Displays the amount of unused space on the drive
- Capacity—Displays the total capacity of the disk drive
- Disk Cleanup—Removes temporary and Internet files
- Compress this drive to save disk space—Decreases the amount of space used by the files and folders stored on the drive
- Allow files on this drive to have contents indexed in addition to file properties— Enables you to rapidly search documents for key words; you can control the information included in the indexes

Tools Tab The Tools tab (see Figure 5-15) provides three tools to keep the drives on your disk tuned. You will be prompted for an administrative account password to perform error checking and defragmentation.

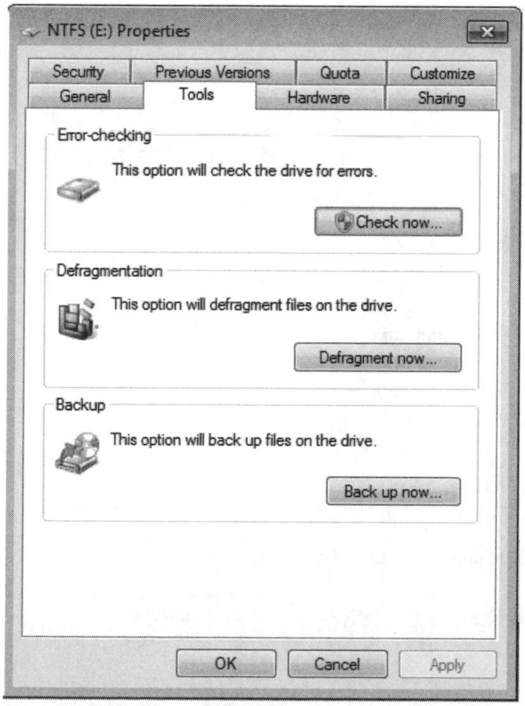

Figure 5-15 Tools tab, Local Disk Properties dialog box

Source: Course Technology/Cengage Learning

- Error-checking—Scans the volume for damage; the volume is not available during the scan, which could take a long time if the drive has a large number of files

- Defragmentation—Analyzes drives for **fragmentation** (parts of files scattered across a hard drive); the **defragmentation** tool locates fragmented files and folders and arranges them in order to improve disk performance

- Backup—Copies the contents of files and folders to safeguard valuable data; this option is not available on the Windows 7 Home edition

You can use the error-checking tool to check for file system errors and bad sectors on your hard drive. If the drive is currently in use, you will be asked if you want to reschedule the disk checking for the next time you restart your system. You should analyze drives regularly to keep them free of errors.

You can use the Disk Defragmenter (see Figure 5-16) to analyze local drives and to locate and consolidate fragmented files and folders. After defragmenting, each file and folder on your computer's hard drive will occupy a single, contiguous space on the volume. As a result, Windows 7 can access your files and folders more efficiently and save new ones more efficiently as well. Click the Analyze disk button to determine if your PC will benefit from defragmentation. After the analysis, a dialog box reports the percentage of fragmented files and folders on the drive and recommends whether to defragment the volume. You

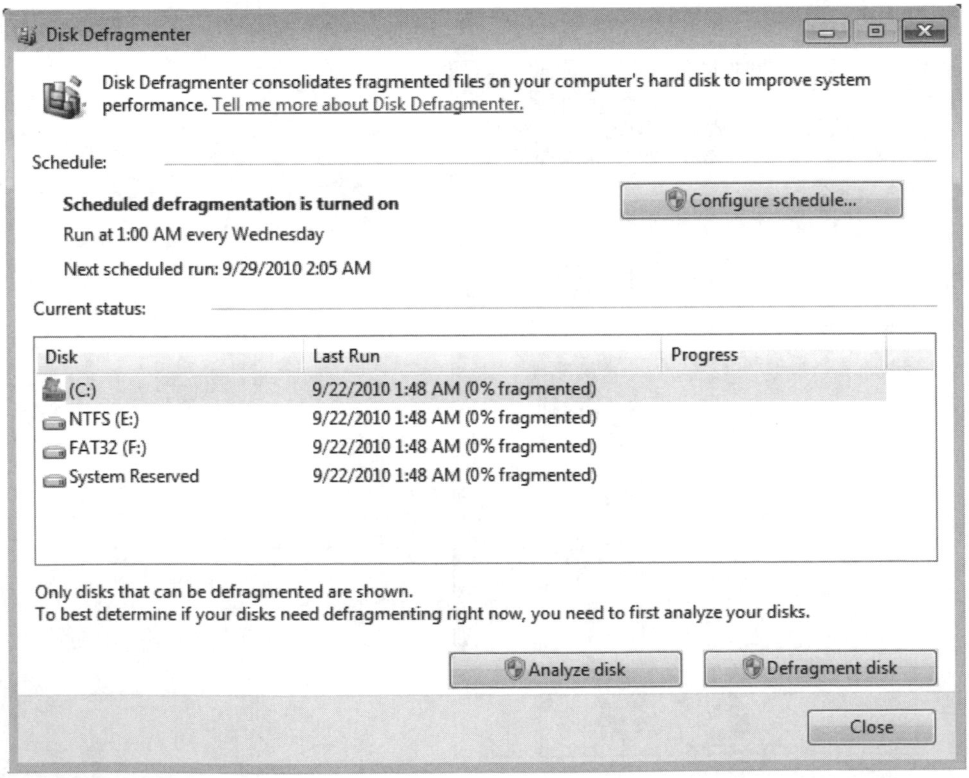

Figure 5-16 Disk Defragmenter

Source: Course Technology/Cengage Learning

should analyze volumes regularly and defragment them only when the Disk Defragmenter recommends it. To encourage the routine analysis and defragmentation of volumes, the Disk Defragmenter provides a scheduler that is on by default and runs each Wednesday at 1:00 AM.

Hardware Tab   The Hardware tab (see Figure 5-17) provides access to information and settings for all drives on a PC. You can use the following options on the Hardware tab to view information about your hard drives and keep them running efficiently:

- Name and Type—Display the drives' model names and types
- Properties button—Provides access to the Properties dialog box for a selected device

Sharing Tab   From the Sharing tab (see Figure 5-18), you can share the entire contents of a drive, and other users can access the shared drive from other computers. By default, the hidden share C$ is displayed in the dialog box. If you have administrative privileges, you can create additional shares for the entire contents of the local disk (C). To do so, click the Share button, type the name of the share in the Share name text box, click the Permissions button, check the appropriate Allow check boxes, and then click OK twice. You need to know about these settings because an administrator can create a share to your hard drive so that other users can access your files. You will be prompted for an administrative account password when you click the Advanced Sharing button.

You will learn more about file sharing in Chapter 11.

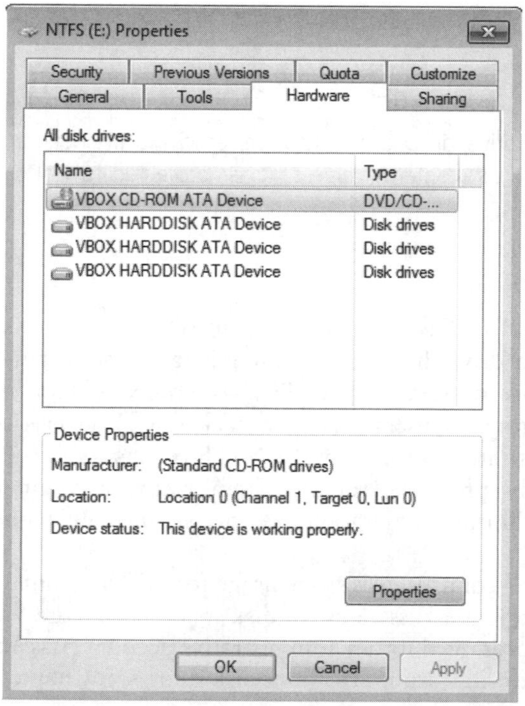

Figure 5-17 Hardware tab, Local Disk Properties dialog box

Source: Course Technology/Cengage Learning

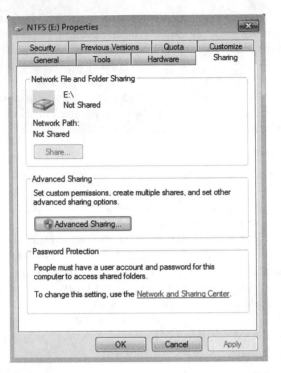

Figure 5-18 Sharing tab, Local Disk Properties dialog box

Source: Course Technology/Cengage Learning

 When you share a drive, anyone who has user access to the network can read the drive's contents unless it is protected by NTFS permissions.

Security Tab From the Security tab (see Figure 5-19), you can set the NTFS permissions that control access to data on the hard drive. If you have administrative privileges, you can manage the NTFS permissions for groups of users on your PC. To modify NTFS permissions, set the Allow check boxes for each group of users and then click OK. You need to know about these settings because an administrator can modify the NTFS permissions so that other users can access your files. You will be prompted for an administrative account password when you click the Edit button. You will learn more about security settings in Chapter 11.

Quota Tab The Quota tab tracks and controls disk space usage for NTFS volumes. Administrators can configure Windows 7 to prevent excessive use of disk space. See Figure 5-20 for an example of quota settings. You will be prompted for an administrative account password when you click the Quota Entries button. You will learn more about disk quotas in Chapter 11.

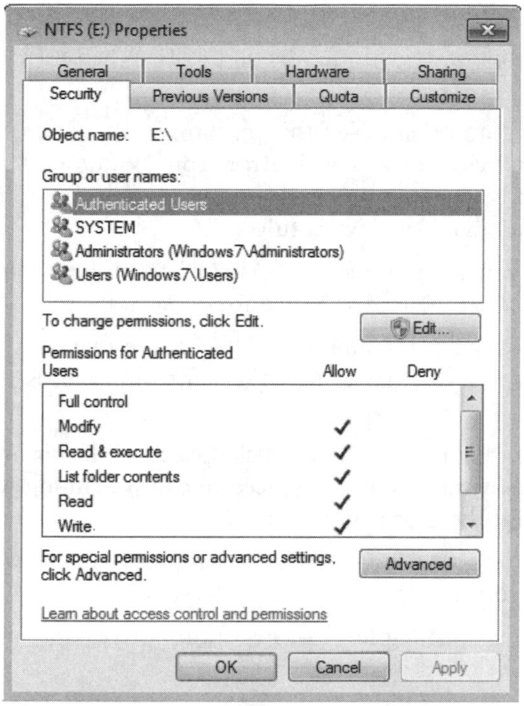

Figure 5-19 Security tab, Local Disk Properties dialog box

Source: Course Technology/Cengage Learning

Figure 5-20 Quota tab, Local Disk Properties dialog box

Source: Course Technology/Cengage Learning

The Quota tab contains the following options:

- Enable quota management—This option toggles quotas on or off. When turned on, the OS can configure disk quotas.

- Deny disk space to users exceeding quota limit—If this option is selected, a user who exceeds the limit receives an "insufficient disk space" error from Windows 7 and cannot write additional data to the drive without first deleting or moving some files from it. To affected programs, it appears that the drive is full.

- Do not limit disk usage—If this option is selected, the OS tracks disk usage. It may create a log entry when a user exceeds the limits, but it does not limit usage.

- Limit disk space to—This option specifies the amount of disk space that a new user is allowed, and the amount of disk space that has to be used before an event is written to the system log.

- Set warning level to—This option is similar to "Limit disk space to," but it only establishes a warning condition. A warning entry is placed in the system log when the warning level is exceeded; however, the user is not notified.

- Log event when a user exceeds their quota limit—This option places an entry in the system log whenever you exceed your quota limit.

- Log event when a user exceeds their warning level—This option places an entry in the system log whenever you exceed the quota warning level.

Activity 5-10: Viewing File System Properties and Analyzing the Drive for Fragmentation

Time Required: 20 minutes to two hours, depending on the size of the hard drive and the speed of the computer

Objective: Locate information about the file systems in Windows 7 and determine whether a drive has fragmented in Windows 7.

Description: In this activity, you open the Disk Management console, view the local properties for a drive, and analyze a drive for fragmentation. For example, this activity is useful if you want information about the free space on your drive and if you want to determine whether the drive needs defragmenting.

1. If necessary, start your virtual machines using the appropriate instructions in Activity 1-1.

2. To open the Control Panel, click **Start** and then click **Control Panel.**

3. To open the Administrative tools, click the **System and Security** link and then click the **Administrative Tools** link.

4. To run Computer Management as an administrator, right-click **Computer Management,** click **Run as Administrator,** type **P@ssw0rd,** and then click **Yes.**

5. To see the partitions for your virtual machine, double-click **Storage,** and then double-click **Disk Management.**

6. Right-click the **C:** area and then click **Properties.**

7. View the properties on the General tab for the C drive on your virtual machine.

8. To analyze a drive for fragmentation, click the **Tools** tab, click the **Defragment now** button, and then click the **Analyze disk** button.

9. If prompted, type **P@ssw0rd** and click **Yes**.

10. Wait for the analysis to complete.

11. Close all the windows within the Windows 7 virtual machine.

12. To shut down the virtual machine, click **Start**, and then click the **Shut Down** button.

13. Wait a moment for the Windows 7 virtual machine to shut down completely.

14. Leave the PC logged on for the next activity.

Managing Fedora 13 File Systems

This section shows you how to manage file systems in Fedora 13.

File System Checking and Repair Sometimes, power losses or abrupt shutdowns can cause file corruption and OS errors because the OS cannot synchronize the file system buffer cache with the contents of the disk. A **buffer cache** is a special memory region used for quick access to stored data items. To check for file system errors and repair them, use the fsck command.

Fedora 13 automatically checks the file systems at boot time, as Windows 7 does with the chkdsk utility, but you should also use the fsck command to check Fedora 13 file systems and correct any problems. The fsck command has syntax similar to the mkfs command, which you used earlier in the chapter. The syntax of the command is:

```
fsck [-sAVRTMNP] [-C [fd]] [-t fstype] [filesys...]
fsck -t ext3 /dev/sda2
```

You should only run the fsck command on unmounted or read-only file systems.

The exit code returned by the fsck command is the sum of the following conditions, as shown in Table 5-4. For example, if you get an exit code of 3, the file system errors were corrected and the PC needs to be rebooted.

Exit Code	Description
0	No errors
1	File system errors corrected
2	PC should be rebooted
4	File system errors left uncorrected
8	Operational error
16	Usage or syntax error
128	Shared library error

Table 5-4 Exit codes for the fsck **command**

Disk Usage Management You can use the df command to report the disk space usage of a file system. Typical output is shown in Figure 5-21. The syntax of the command is:

df [OPTION]... [FILE]...

-t, --type=TYPE	Limits the listing to file systems of the TYPE specified
-T, --print-type	Prints the file system type
-x, --exclude-type=TYPE	Excludes specified file systems from the list
–help	Prints a help message
–version	Prints a version string

You can use the du command to specify disk usage of each file or recursively for directories. Typical output is shown in Figure 5-22. The syntax of the command is:

du [OPTION]... [FILE]...

-a, --all	Writes counts for all files, not just directories
-c, --total	Produces a grand total
-h, --human-readable	Creates readable output
–help	Prints a help message
–version	Prints a version string

Swap Space Management You can use the free command to display the amount of free and used memory in the system and to manage swap space.

Swap space is used to implement paging, a process in which memory pages are written to disk when physical memory is low and read back into physical memory when needed. This process helps PC performance, enabling a number of programs to run simultaneously when they would not otherwise fit into physical memory.

This type of space was called a swap file or swap partition in the "File System Creation" section. A swap partition can yield better performance because the disk blocks are guaranteed to be contiguous. To find out how much swap space you have, type free at a command prompt. This command reports memory usage, including both memory and swap

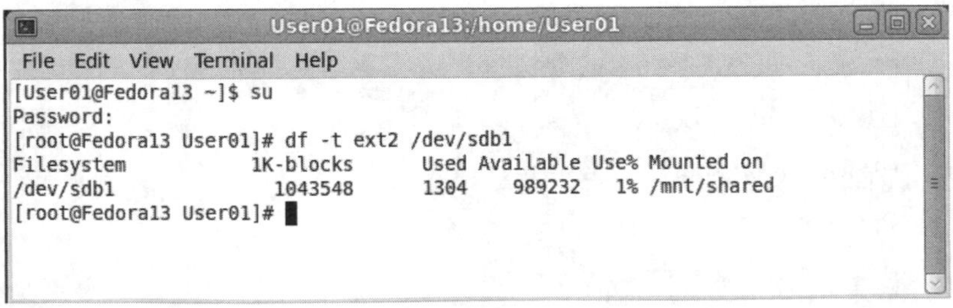

Figure 5-21 Output of df command

Source: Course Technology/Cengage Learning

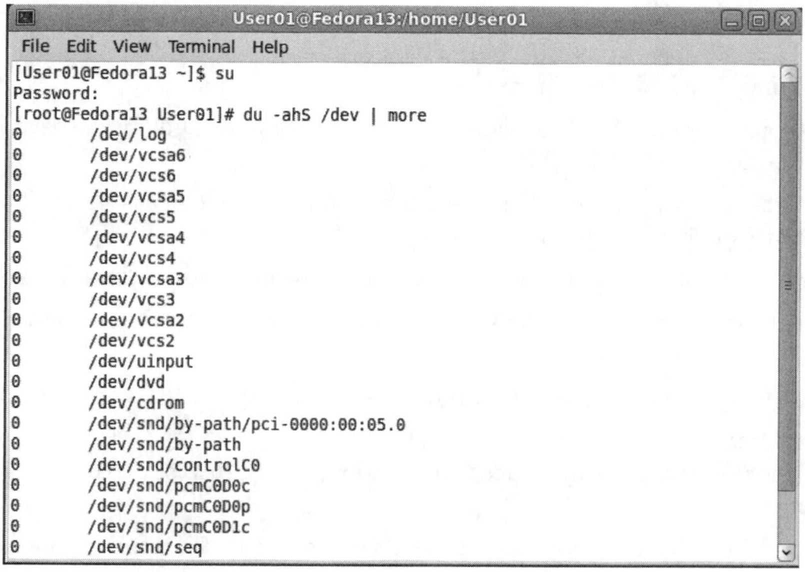

Figure 5-22 Output of du command

Source: Course Technology/Cengage Learning

space totals, along with the amount of space used, free, shared, buffered, and cached. All the numbers are reported in 1024-byte blocks. The syntax is:

`free [-b | -k | -m] [-o] [-s delay ] [-t] [-l] [-V]`

-b   Displays the amount of memory in bytes; the −k option (the default) is kilobytes, and the −m switch displays the amount in megabytes

-t   Displays a line that contains totals

-s   Activates a continuous polling delay, in seconds

-V   Prints a version string

Figure 5-23 and Activity 5-11 show how to display free space for memory and swap file systems in Fedora 13.

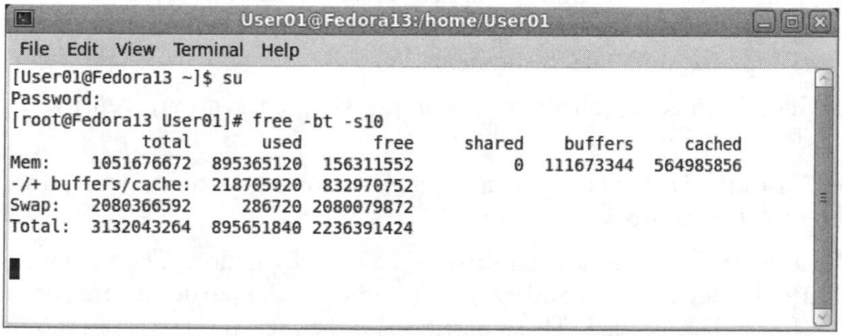

Figure 5-23 Displaying free space for memory and swap file systems

Source: Course Technology/Cengage Learning

Activity 5-11: Analyzing Available Swap Space

Time Required: 10 minutes

Objective: Use the `free` command to see memory and swap space information for a Fedora 13 OS.

Description: In this activity, you use the `free` command. This activity is useful if you need memory and swap space information.

1. If necessary, start your virtual machines using the appropriate instructions in Activity 1-1.

2. To open a Terminal console, click **Applications**, point to **System Tools**, and then click **Terminal**.

3. To switch to superuser, type **su -** and press **Enter**, then type a password of **P@ssw0rd** and press **Enter**.

4. To view memory and swap space information, type **/usr/bin/free –bt** and then press **Enter**.

5. Note the information shown for memory and swap space in the resulting output.

6. To shut down the virtual machine, click **System**, click **Shut Down**, and then click the **Shut Down** button.

7. Wait a moment for the Fedora 13 virtual machine to shut down completely.

8. Close any remaining open windows, log off, and shut down your PC.

Disk Quota Similar to the way Windows 7 supports disk quotas, Fedora 13 can restrict disk space by implementing disk quotas, which alert a system administrator before a user consumes too much disk space or a partition becomes full. You will learn more about this task in Chapter 11.

Security Administrators can configure Fedora 13 data security by adding permissions to directories and the objects they contain. You will learn more about this task in Chapter 11.

Chapter Summary

- Storage areas on hard drives are used to store programs and data. Storage areas can be implemented as primary partitions or logical drives within extended partitions. Windows 7 supports the FAT16, FAT32, and NT file systems. Fedora 13 supports the FAT16, FAT32, ext2, and ext3 file systems.

- NTFS provides options for journalizing, compression, encryption, security, auditing, and quotas.

- Windows 7 uses the Disk Management console to manage storage areas, and assigns drive letters to storage areas.

- Fedora 13 uses partitions on a hard drive to store information. The naming conventions indicate the device name and partition number. The partitions are formatted for the type of file system needed. These partitions are either automatically mounted at boot time or manually mounted when needed, which allows users to manage their data storage.

- Windows 7 and Fedora 13 take two different approaches to mounting drives on their systems. In Windows 7, you do not need to worry about mounting the drives (except for USB drives) because Windows 7 handles it. In Fedora 13, you can mount devices when they are needed, which allows you to have more memory available.

- Tools are available to manage file systems in Windows 7 and Fedora 13. Management tasks include reporting information about disk space availability, cleaning up temporary files, managing the disk space quota, and determining the file type of the drive.

Key Terms

auditing   The process an OS uses to detect and log security-related events.

basic disk   A disk that contains basic volumes, such as primary partitions, extended partitions, and logical drives.

binary search   A programming technique for quickly locating an item in a sequential list.

buffer cache   A region of memory that holds frequently used data values.

cluster   A disk-storage unit that consists of a fixed number of sectors.

cluster address   The location of a cluster on a hard drive.

compression   A means of reducing the amount of space needed to store a block of data.

decompression   The opposite of compression; restoring the contents of a compressed file to its original form.

defragmentation   The process of writing parts of a file to contiguous sectors on a hard drive to speed access and retrieval.

dynamic disk   A disk that contains dynamic volumes, such as simple volumes. Dynamic disk storage is divided into volumes instead of partitions.

encryption   The process of encoding data to prevent unauthorized access.

FAT12   A file system, first used by DOS, that uses 12-bit sector addresses.

FAT16   A file system, first used by DOS, that uses 16-bit sector addresses.

FAT32   A file system, first used by Windows 95 OSR 2, that uses 32-bit sector addresses (of which 28 bits are currently used).

file allocation table (FAT)   A data structure that DOS creates on a disk when it is formatted.

file system   The overall structure in which files are named, stored, and organized. A file system consists of files, directories (or folders), and the information needed to locate and access these items.

formatting   Preparing a file system so that a disk can be used to store programs and data.

fragmentation   The scattering of parts of the same file over different areas of a hard drive.

master file table (MFT)   A special file that contains the attributes of each file created using NTFS; used to locate a file on a hard drive.

NTFS (New Technology File System)   The default file system for new installations of Windows 7; first used by Windows NT.

partition   A logical storage area on a drive.

primary partition   A portion of a drive that functions as a physically separate allocation unit.

5

quota   A restriction on users' ability to exceed limits placed on file system resources. It allows administrators to effectively manage disk space shared by multiple users.

sector   The smallest unit of space on a disk; typically 512 bytes.

storage area   An area on a disk that can be allocated and formatted for a file system.

subdirectory   A logical grouping of related files in Windows 7.

superblock   Part of a UFS file system that contains an identifying number and other numbers that describe the file system's geometry, statistics, and behavioral parameters.

swap file   A hidden file on a hard drive that is used to hold parts of programs and data files that do not fit in memory. The OS moves data from the swap file to memory as needed and moves data out of memory to the swap file to make room for new data.

terabyte   A measurement of high-capacity storage. A terabyte is about 1 trillion bytes.

virtual file allocation table (VFAT)   A file system first used by Windows 95; the first file system to support long filenames.

volume   A fixed amount of storage on a hard drive.

Review Questions

1. You can allocate up to _____ primary partitions on a hard drive.

   a.   1

   b.   2

   c.   3

   d.   4

2. When you allocate storage areas for hard drives in Windows 7, each storage area _____. (Choose all that apply.)

   a.   is dynamically available

   b.   receives the next available drive letter

   c.   requires a file system

   d.   must be formatted

3. The FAT32 file system supports up to _____ on installation.

   a.   2 GB

   b.   16 GB

   c.   32 GB

   d.   2 terabytes

4. The NT file system supports up to _____ on installation.

   a.   2 GB

   b.   16 GB

   c.   32 GB

   d.   2 terabytes

5. Which options are available with NTFS? (Choose all that apply.)

   a. compression

   b. encryption

   c. auditing

   d. quotas

6. Which options can you use to create a storage area in Windows 7? (Choose all that apply.)

   a. free space on a hard drive

   b. unallocated area on a hard drive

   c. free space on a CD-ROM

   d. unallocated area on a CD-ROM

7. Which options can you select from the Format Partition dialog box in Windows 7? (Choose all that apply.)

   a. file system

   b. allocation unit size

   c. compression

   d. encryption

8. In Windows 7, a _____ is mapped to an empty folder on a volume that uses the NT file system.

   a. drive point

   b. drive folder

   c. mounted drive

   d. mounted folder

9. Which items can you view from the General tab of the Local Disk Properties dialog box? (Choose all that apply.)

   a. used space

   b. free space

   c. unallocated space

   d. capacity

10. Which items can you select from the Tools tab of the Local Disk Properties dialog box? (Choose all that apply.)

   a. formatting

   b. error-checking

   c. space allocation

   d. partition resizing

11. The mkfs command is used to _____.

    a.   make a file system for Windows 7

    b.   build a Fedora 13 file system on a device

    c.   manage partitions in Windows 7

    d.   do nothing; it is not a valid command

12. In Fedora 13, if you want to automatically mount another partition when the OS boots, you must include an entry line in _____ for that partition.

    a.   /dev/hba1

    b.   /dev/hba2

    c.   /etc/partition

    d.   /etc/fstab

13. In Fedora 13, you use the _____ command to create partitions.

    a.   mkfs

    b.   fsdk

    c.   dkfs

    d.   fdisk

14. Fedora 13 needs at least _____ partition(s) for its root file system.

    a.   one

    b.   two

    c.   three

    d.   four

15. Which of the following is a benefit of mounting your own drives in Fedora 13? (Choose all that apply.)

    a.   provides flexibility in data storage

    b.   makes your data storage less accessible

    c.   makes your data storage more accessible

    d.   provides inflexible data storage

16. Which options are available with the ext2 file type? (Choose all that apply.)

    a.   compression

    b.   encryption

    c.   journalizing

    d.   quotas

17. Which parameters do you interactively enter when creating a new partition with the `fdisk` command? (Choose all that apply.)

    a. n

    b. q

    c. p

    d. c

18. What information is reported by the `free` command? (Choose all that apply.)

    a. memory space used

    b. memory space free

    c. CPU cycles

    d. storage capacity

19. Which storage types can be allocated in Fedora 13? (Choose all that apply.)

    a. directories

    b. free space on a CD-ROM

    c. unallocated area on a CD-ROM

    d. primary partitions

20. Which of the following are valid file types for a CD-ROM device? (Choose all that apply.)

    a. ext3

    b. UDF

    c. ISO 9660

    d. ext2

Case Projects

CASE PROJECTS

Case 5-1: File Systems in Windows 7

Your boss has asked you to analyze the file system types that are available in Windows 7. She expects to see a summary table with the three file types as columns and the file system attributes as rows. Also, she expects you to make a recommendation. Justify your recommendation.

Case 5-2: Adding a Second File System in Fedora 13

Your client has outgrown her system and wants you to add more space to it. She needs you to design an additional file system to be accessible by Windows 7 and Fedora 13. Also, she expects you to make recommendations about the file system. Justify your recommendations.

Case 5-3: Explaining NTFS Options

Your boss has accepted your recommendation to use the NT file system. Prepare a report that lists and explains the options available in NTFS. Your target audience is company management, so the report should be relatively free of technical jargon.

Case 5-4: Fast Data Recovery in Fedora 13

Your boss has committed you to setting up and maintaining a Fedora 13 system for a new project. Fast file recovery and data integrity are of the utmost importance. Recommend which Fedora 13 file system types to use and justify your recommendations.

Case 5-5: Creating Storage Areas in Windows 7

Prepare a procedure for your company's desktop technicians to allocate storage areas in Windows 7. Your company has a standard that permits only one primary drive allocation on the two hard drives. The procedure must enable desktop technicians to create the following drive assignments:

- C—Boot/system partition
- D—Data
- R—CD-ROM

chapter 6

Directory Commands

After reading this chapter and completing the exercises, you will be able to:

- Describe directory structures
- Display directory structures
- Navigate directory structures
- Work with directories
- Work with file management commands
- Use removable drives for the storage of application data

You should learn to use directory structures to exploit the underlying technology of file systems. Knowing how to navigate directories provides great insight into how to organize files on your virtual machine. In this chapter, you will use various commands and techniques to work with directories, learn file management techniques to keep your directory structures up to date, and learn to use USB drives to store and transport data.

Directory Structures

To begin the discussion of directories, consider the example of a campus map. You probably used one when you first arrived on campus. The map in Figure 6-1 shows the buildings on a fictional campus; it is probably much more basic than the map of your school, but it demonstrates how information can be organized.

What happens to the layout when departments are added to the map? For example, what if you need to gather more information about multiple departments in each building? As you can see in Figure 6-2, your campus map becomes cluttered with the additional information. As you look closer, you may also find that not all of the departments have been listed. Campus maps often have legends with obscure letters and cryptic acronyms to distinguish buildings from each other. Also, if you needed information about courses offered by the departments, the map format would not provide the necessary information.

To store detailed information about the departments, a better approach is needed. One alternative could be a file cabinet, in which each drawer represents a building. Within the drawers, manila folders would need to be separated by dividers to keep department information from being misplaced. Many office departments still use this method to organize information. However, this system may not work for you, especially if you need access to the information at home or on a computer in the school lab.

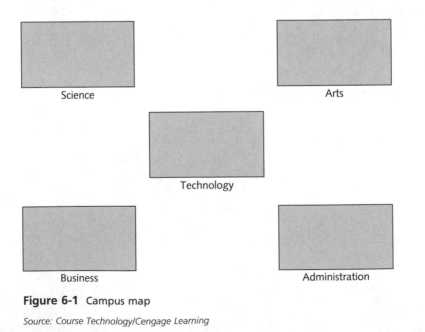

Figure 6-1 Campus map

Source: Course Technology/Cengage Learning

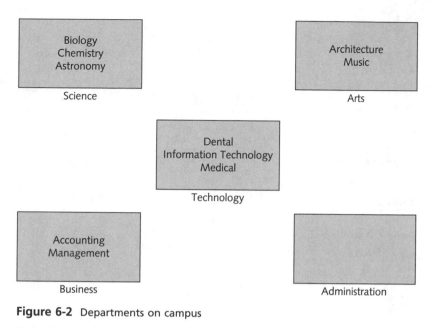

Figure 6-2 Departments on campus

Source: Course Technology/Cengage Learning

For a computer solution to be effective, campus information needs to be organized into a list, commonly referred to as a directory structure. This structure is fairly common; for example, it is similar to that of a telephone directory, where information in the yellow pages is organized alphabetically in categories, such as "Pizza" or "Restaurants." Categorizing the information makes it easier to find. When you look at Figure 6-1 again, you see that the campus map has the first group you need to begin organizing information into a directory.

In Figure 6-3, the outline of your directory begins to take shape. "Campus" is the main directory, to be followed by the buildings in alphabetical order. This ordering makes it easier to isolate information about each department when the next set of information is added.

By adding the information you gathered in Figure 6-2, you can place the departments within the correct building. In Figure 6-4, you can see that the departments have also been alphabetized for easier searching. When you need to add, delete, or modify course sections for each of the departments, you can work with the specific department or building without affecting the other stored information. The directory structure enables you to access your information efficiently.

You have many options for working with well-organized information in a computer system. Once the information is in a directory structure in Windows 7 and Fedora 13, you can use

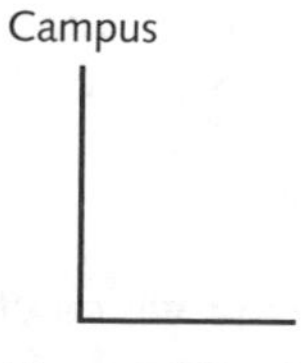

Campus

Figure 6-3 Beginning of the Campus directory

Source: Course Technology/Cengage Learning

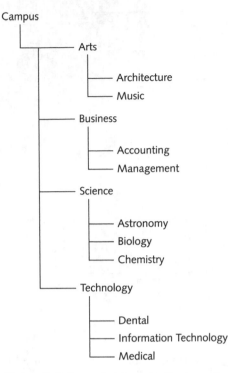

Campus
- Arts
  - Architecture
  - Music
- Business
  - Accounting
  - Management
- Science
  - Astronomy
  - Biology
  - Chemistry
- Technology
  - Dental
  - Information Technology
  - Medical

Figure 6-4 Expanded Campus directory structure

Source: Course Technology/Cengage Learning

various tools and commands to access specific areas of your stored information. The following sections show you how to work with stored information.

Displaying Directory Structures

Your OS uses directory structures, or trees, to organize files on your virtual machine. You can display the structure as well as change your focal point in it. If needed, you can display the names of files in the directory structure. The following sections address these topics.

Displaying Directory Structures in the Windows 7 CLI

From the **command-line interface (CLI)**, you can issue commands to view the directory structure and execute other tasks. Using a CLI, the user responds to a text prompt by typing a command on a specified line, receives a response back from the OS, enters another command, and so on. In Windows 7, the **command prompt** is the line area in the CLI window where the cursor is blinking.

You can choose between two commands (TREE and DIR) when you view a directory structure. When you need to locate a single file or a set of files, you can specify which characters your search must match. These topics are explained in the following sections.

Windows Command Prompt In Windows 7, you can open the command prompt console (see Figure 6-5) by clicking Start, pointing to All Programs, clicking Accessories, and clicking Command Prompt.

Using the TREE Command to Display the Directory Structure To view a graphical representation of the directories on a disk, you use the **TREE** command. Figure 6-6 displays the example directory structure explained previously in this chapter.

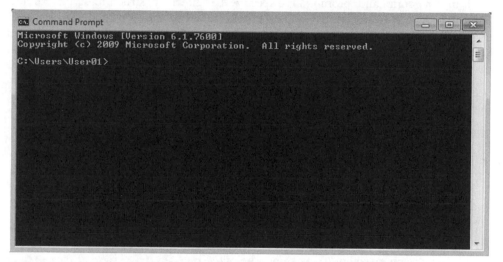

Figure 6-5 Command prompt console

Source: Course Technology/Cengage Learning

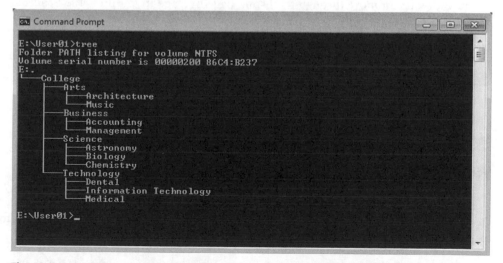

Figure 6-6 Directory structure displayed with TREE command

Source: Course Technology/Cengage Learning

The TREE command shows the current directory and all the subdirectories below it. The command has the following syntax:

TREE [drive:] [path] [/F] [/A]

/F   Displays filenames in each folder

/A   Uses ASCII characters instead of extended characters

If you omit the path, the TREE command displays the directory structure indicated by the path in the command prompt. To specify the directory structure, type the location of the directory. For example, to display the structure of the Documents folder for User01, type C:\Users\User01\Documents instead of [drive:] [path]. Because the directory is a **long filename**—a name that can contain lowercase and uppercase letters, spaces, and more than 200 characters—you may choose to enclose the drive and path in quotation marks.

Because Windows 7 does not treat spaces as delimiters, the following two commands create the same results:

TREE C:\Users\User01\Documents
TREE "C:\Users\User01\Documents"

To include filenames in the structure shown by the TREE command, you can add the /F switch. Using the /A switch, you can exclude extended characters—European characters and others that are not part of the standard ASCII set.

To page through a listing of the directories and files on a disk (or any listing that is too long for a one-screen display), use the MORE command. To pass the output of the TREE command, use the **pipe symbol** (|), as shown below.

TREE | MORE

When you use the MORE command, you can page through a listing line by line if you press Enter, and you can move through the listing page by page if you press the Spacebar.

Remember that commands are not case sensitive in Windows 7. For example, you could type the TREE command as tree or Tree.

Activity 6-1: Creating the Directory Structure in the Windows 7 CLI

Time Required: 10 minutes

Objective: Create the example directory structure in the Windows 7 CLI.

Description: In this activity, you open a command prompt and run a program file to create the example directory structure you will use in the remaining activities.

The Windows 7 activities in this chapter require the CMD files that are available at *www.cengage.com*. For further details, see the appendix for your virtualization software.

1. Start your virtual machines using the appropriate instructions in Activity 1-1.

2. Click **Start,** point to **All Programs,** click **Accessories,** and then click **Command Prompt.**

3. To run the program file that creates the directories and files you need for the Windows 7 examples in this chapter, type **MakeDS** at the command prompt and press **Enter.**

Contact your instructor if you see the following message: "MakeDS is not recognized as an internal or external command, operable program or batch file."

4. Verify that the directory tree structure appears.

5. Leave the virtual machine logged on for the next activity.

Activity 6-2: Displaying the Directory Structure in the Windows 7 CLI

6

Time Required: 15 minutes

Objective: Display a directory structure in the Windows 7 CLI.

Description: In this activity, you open a command prompt and review the directory tree for the example directory structure provided with this book. This activity is useful if you want to review the directory structure on your hard drive.

If you started a new virtual session since the last time you completed Activity 6-1, you must run Activity 6-1 again before you can complete the following activity.

1. If necessary, start your virtual machines using the appropriate instructions in Activity 1-1.

2. Click **Start,** point to **All Programs,** click **Accessories,** and then click **Command Prompt.**

3. To go to the drive that contains the College directory structure, type **E:\User01** and then press **Enter.**

4. To display the example directory structure, type **TREE** and press **Enter.**

If you do not see the example directory tree, inform your instructor.

5. Review the information in the command prompt window.

To clear the screen of previous entries, type CLS and press Enter.

6. To see the User01 directory structure with filenames, type **TREE /F** and press **Enter.**

7. Close the command prompt window.

8. Leave the virtual machine logged on for the next activity.

Displaying Filenames in the Windows 7 CLI Use the DIR (directory) command to display the names of files and subdirectories in the CLI. The DIR command has the following syntax:

DIR [drive:] [path] [filename] [/O[[:]sortorder]] [/P] [/S] [/W]

[drive:] [path] [filename]	Specifies the drive, directory, and files to list
/O	Lists files in sorted order
sortorder N	Sorts alphabetically by name
sortorder S	Sorts by size (smallest first)
sortorder E	Sorts alphabetically by extension
sortorder D	Sorts by date and time (oldest first)
sortorder G	Groups directories first
sortorder -	Adds a prefix to reverse the order
/P	Pauses after each screen of information
/S	Displays files in the specified directory and all subdirectories
/W	Uses wide list format

To list information about a file, type DIR followed by the location and filename. For instance, to list information about the example file homework.doc, you would type:

DIR C:\Users\User01\Documents\homework.doc

Using the /W switch, you can list the filenames in three columns across the screen. To pause the screen as each group of filenames is listed, use the /P switch. To control the sort order, use the /O switch. For example, to sort the files by file size, you would type the sort switch as /O:S. If you do not specify a sort order, directories are listed first, then files, in alphabetical order.

Using Wildcard Characters in the Windows 7 CLI
You may sometimes play poker or another card game that employs wild cards. If you hear "Deuces are wild!" you know that the "2" cards can be substituted for any other card in the deck.

The Windows 7 CLI uses wildcards, too. When you are entering commands, you can use two **wildcard characters** to identify groups of files: the question mark (?) and the asterisk (*, or star).

In commands, the question mark represents any single character that you want to match. For example, the following command produces a list of any files in the current directory whose name begins with "mem," followed by up to three characters.

DIR mem???.txt

This command would match any of the following filenames: memo.txt, memory.txt, mem49.txt, and memsey.txt.

The * represents any string of unknown characters. For example,*.* represents all filenames with an extension, and is the default scope of the DIR command. (You may be

Wildcard	Explanation
.	All files with any extension or no extension
*.txt	All files with a .txt extension
M.	All files starting with "M" or "m" (case does not matter)
H*.rpt	All files starting with "H" or "h" (case does not matter) and ending with an .rpt extension
?gop.*	All files starting with any character and followed by "gop"
Year??04.xls	Any file starting with "Year" and followed by two optional characters, then the digits "04," and then an .xls extension
Bud19??.xls	Any file starting with "Bud" and followed by any year in the twentieth century and an .xls extension

Table 6-1   **Examples of using wildcard characters**

6

aware that *.* is pronounced *star dot star*.) For example, the following command lists all files that have a .DOC extension in the current directory:

DIR *.DOC

To list all the .DOC files on drive C, sorted by date, you would type:

DIR *.DOC /S /O:D

Table 6-1 presents additional examples of how to use wildcard characters. To speed access when looking for files, you should learn to use wildcard characters.

Activity 6-3: Displaying Filenames in the Windows 7 CLI

Time Required: 15 minutes

Objective: Display the filenames within a directory structure in the Windows 7 CLI.

Description: In this activity, you open a command prompt and review the files within the directory structure. This activity is useful if you want to review the directory structure and file information on a hard drive.

If you started a new virtual session since the last time you completed Activity 6-1, you must run Activity 6-1 again before you can complete the following activity.

1. If necessary, start your virtual machines using the appropriate instructions in Activity 1-1.

2. Click **Start,** point to **All Programs,** click **Accessories,** and then click **Command Prompt.**

3. To display the User01 directory structure, type **DIR /S /P E:\User01\.** and press **Enter.**

If you do not see the User01 files, inform your instructor.

4. Review the information in the command prompt window and press the **Spacebar**.

5. Repeat Step 4 until the message "Press any key to continue" no longer appears.

6. To display the sorted User01 directory structure, type **DIR /S /P /O:N E:\User01\.** and press **Enter**.

7. Review the information in the command prompt window and press the **Spacebar**.

8. Repeat Step 7 until the message "Press any key to continue" no longer appears.

9. Repeat Steps 6 through 8 using the **/O:S** switch.

10. Close the command prompt window.

11. Leave the virtual machine logged on for the next activity.

Displaying the Directory Structure with Windows Explorer

Windows Explorer is a part of Windows 7 that provides a graphical user interface for accessing file systems. To open Windows Explorer, click Start, point to All Programs, click Accessories, and click Windows Explorer.

Windows Explorer uses two panes, as shown in Figure 6-7. The left pane is the Navigation pane, which can display the directory structure of one or more drives. The right pane displays the structure and files for the selected entry in the left pane.

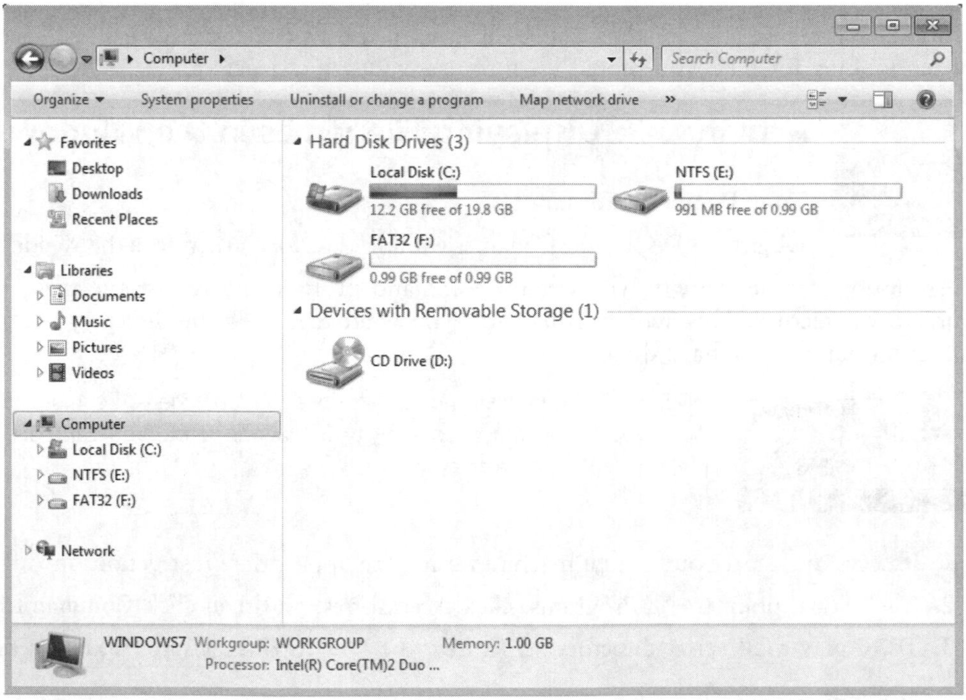

Figure 6-7 Windows Explorer

Source: Course Technology/Cengage Learning

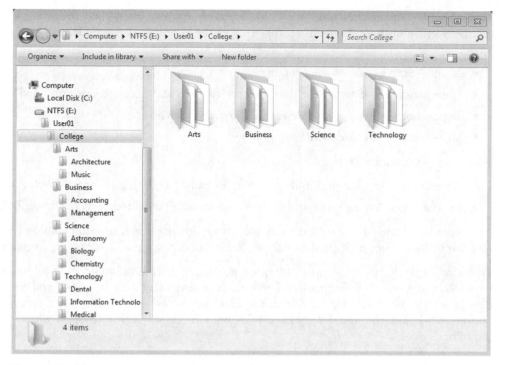

Figure 6-8 Directory structure displayed in Windows Explorer

Source: Course Technology/Cengage Learning

To display the available drives on your virtual machine, expand Computer. To see the directory structure that you used earlier in this chapter, expand NTFS (E:), expand User01, and then click College in the left pane. The results are shown in Figure 6-8.

Windows Explorer provides several ways for you to arrange and identify files when viewing them in the right pane. When a folder is open, you can access these options by right-clicking the white space in the right pane and pointing to View. The **white space** is any blank area of a window.

With the view options, you can control how files and folders are displayed:

- The four icon views (Extra Large, Large, Medium, and Small) display your files and folders as icons of varying sizes. The filename appears under the icon; however, sort information does not appear.

- The List view displays a folder's contents as a list of file or folder names preceded by small icons.

- The Details view lists the contents of the open folder and provides detailed information about your files, including their name, type, size, and date modified.

- The Tiles view displays the files and folders with a medium icon and includes the file size.

- The Content view uses medium icons and includes the date and time modified with the file size.

To locate files and folders more easily in Explorer, you can right-click the white space and use the Sort By options. You can arrange or sort the contents of the right pane using the following options:

- Name—Sort by file or folder name
- Date Modified—Sort by the date that the file was last accessed and modified
- Type—Sort by file type, as determined by the extension
- Size—Sort by the size of the file in bytes

You have two options for the sort order:

- Ascending—Arrange files and folders in ascending collating sequence (0–9, A–Z, a–z).
- Descending—Arrange files and folders in descending collating sequence (z–a, Z–A, 9–0).

A number of advanced options are available when you click the More submenu. For example, you can include more tags, such as Album, Business address, and Description, for your sort.

To more easily locate files and folders by groups, you can right-click the white space in Explorer and then click Group By. Think of grouping as adding headings and placing the files under the headings. Figure 6-9 shows files and folders grouped by type. The grouping options work like the Sort By options, with one additional choice (None), which turns off grouping.

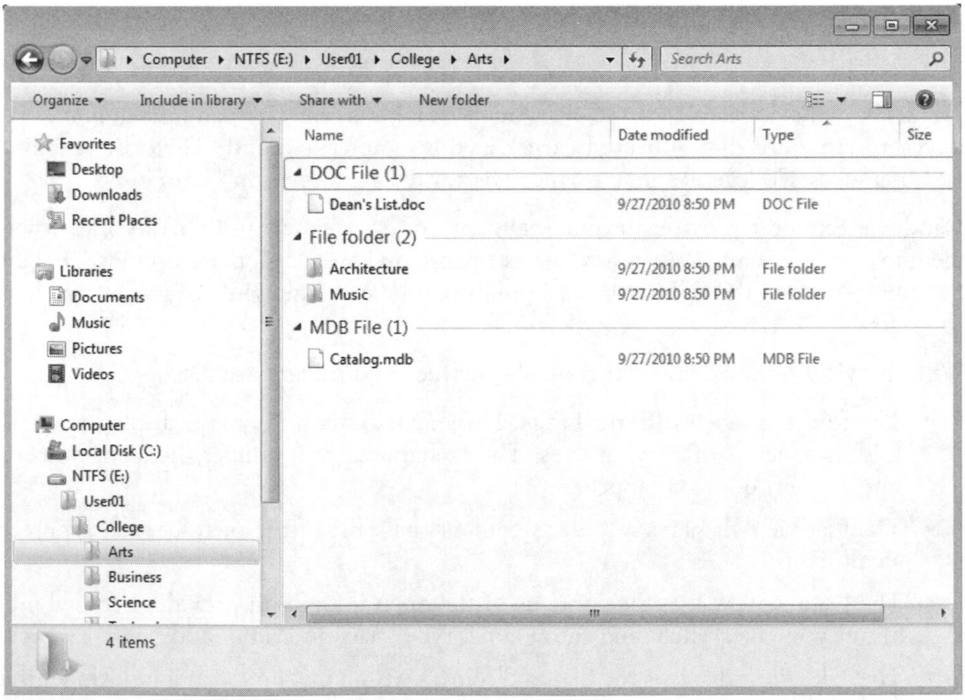

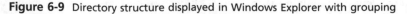

Figure 6-9 Directory structure displayed in Windows Explorer with grouping

Source: Course Technology/Cengage Learning

Activity 6-4: Displaying the Directory Structure in the Windows 7 GUI

Time Required: 15 minutes

Objective: Display the directory structure in the Windows 7 GUI.

Description: In this activity, you open Windows Explorer and review the directory structure. This activity is useful if you want to review the structure before completing other activities.

You must complete Activity 6-1 before you can complete the following activity.

1. If necessary, start your virtual machines using the appropriate instructions in Activity 1-1.
2. Click **Start**, point to **All Programs**, click **Accessories**, and then click **Windows Explorer**.
3. To go to the drive that contains the example directory structure, expand **Computer** and then double-click **NTFS (E:)**.
4. To display the example directory structure in the left pane, expand the following folders in the order shown: **User01, College, Arts, Business, Science**, and **Technology**.
5. To review files in the right pane, click **Arts**.
6. To change the way files are displayed in the right pane, right-click the white space in the right pane, point to **View**, and then click **Extra large icons**.
7. Repeat Step 6 for the remaining view options.
8. To change the order in which files are displayed in the right pane, right-click the white space in the right pane, point to **Sort By**, and then click **Name**.
9. Repeat Step 8 for the remaining sort options.
10. Close Windows Explorer.
11. Leave the virtual machine logged on for future activities.

Displaying the Directory Structure in Fedora 13

As with Windows 7, Fedora 13 directories and files are organized in a hierarchical directory structure. As the superuser, you can arrange information anywhere in this structure. As a regular user, you can manipulate directories and files in your own "branch" of the directory tree.

Fedora 13 might be configured to open to the command line. Otherwise, if the system opens to a graphical user interface (by default, GNOME), you can open a Terminal console by clicking Applications, pointing to System Tools, and then clicking Terminal.

When you first log on to Fedora 13, you are automatically positioned in the directory tree at your home directory (for example, /home/User01). The **home** directory is the conventional starting directory for all regular users, who only have permission to manipulate directories and files within their own directory. However, you can display information in the system directories if system administration permissions allow it.

6

 The paths in Fedora 13 contain forward slashes (/) as opposed to the backslashes (\) used in the Windows 7 CLI.

Fedora 13 Command Syntax

Every operating system has a general logic, or syntax, for entering commands. Consider the following command:

ls –l (the *l* is a lowercase L)

The result of the command is a detailed list of directories, files, and any errors. The ls command is explained in detail in the next section.

The general syntax for Fedora 13 commands is:

command [options] [parameter1] [parameter2] [parameter3]

The items between brackets, such as [options], are not required. You may need to enter one or more options and parameters. As an example, the following command provides a list of files in the Documents directory:

ls –l Documents

 Remember that commands are case sensitive in Fedora 13. For example, you must type the ls command in lowercase. Fedora 13 does not recognize an LS command because it has the wrong case. A command's options and parameters must also have the proper case. If you type a command that does not work in Fedora 13 and you are sure that you used the right syntax, check the case.

Displaying Directories and Files in the Fedora 13 CLI

To view a list of directories and files on a disk, use the **ls** command. By default, the command displays the current directory's contents and sorts the list alphabetically by filename. The following line shows the ls command syntax.

ls [options] [location]

The ls command has the following options:

-a   Shows hidden files

-C   Turns on colorization

-d   Lists directory entries instead of contents

-F   Appends a file type indicator to the filename; for example, "" represents an executable program, "/" represents a directory, and "@" is a symbolic link

-i   Displays the inode number of each file; in Fedora 13, an inode is used to store an application's file and directory attributes

-l   A long-listing format

-r   Lists entries in reverse sort order

-R   Lists subdirectories recursively

-S   Sorts by file size

-t   Sorts by modification time

To page through a list of directories and files on a disk (or any list that is too long for a one-screen display), use the `more` command. When you use this command, you can page through a list line by line if you press Enter, and you can move through the list page by page if you press the Spacebar.

To list your directory tree, use the `ls` command:

`ls -Rl /etc | more`

To list the size (in blocks) and inode number of the hosts file, type the following command:

`ls -iS /etc/hosts`

To list detailed information about a file or directory, type the following command:

`ls -l /etc/hosts`

Table 6-2 summarizes the long-list column definitions when using the −1 option with the `ls` command.

The `ls` command offers many useful options. For example, to list hidden files along with files that are not hidden, you would type:

`ls -a /etc/ | more`

Column (used with the `sort` command)	Description
File type	The first character in the first column denotes the file type (for example, "d" = directory, "-" = file, and "l" = link).
Access permissions	The first column also displays the permissions of a file or directory, owner, group, and any other user.
Number of links	The second column displays either the number of files linked to the file or the number of subdirectories in the directory. A directory always contains entries for "." (current directory) and ".." (parent directory). The parent directory contains the current directory and is one step higher in the directory tree structure. These notations are known as **standardized channels**.
Owner	The third column shows the owner of the file or directory.
Group	The fourth column shows the group that owns the file or directory.
Size	The fifth column shows the size of the file or directory.
Date	The sixth column displays the file's creation date or last modified date.
Time	The seventh column shows the time of creation or last modified time.
Name	The eighth column shows the directory or filename.

Table 6-2 Long-list column definitions using the `ls -1` command

To change the order of the lines in a text file, you would type:

`ls -iS /etc/hosts`

If you do not specify a sort order, files are listed alphabetically. To sort in reverse order, type the following:

`ls -r`

To page through the screen as each page of filenames is listed, you pipe the output of the ls command to a more command. For example:

`ls -l /etc | more`

To control the order in which items appear in a list, you pipe the output of the `ls` command to a **sort** command. The first `sort` command below sorts the items by the ninth field in the `ls` listing, making it the alphabetic filename. The second `sort` command reverses that sort.

```
ls -l /etc | sort -k9
ls -l /etc | sort -rk9
```

The `sort` command has many other options. Its syntax is:

`sort [options] [files]`

You can use the following switches with the `sort` command:

`-b`	Ignores leading blanks
`-d`	Considers only blanks and alphanumeric characters in a sort, as opposed to special and nonprinting characters
`-f`	Ignores case when sorting
`-r`	Reverses the result of comparisons
`-o [filename]`	Writes the result to a file instead of standard output

To display the full path filename of the current directory, use the `pwd` (print working directory) command. This command, along with the `more` command, has page definition options that are beyond the scope of this book. The syntax for the `pwd` and `more` commands is:

```
pwd [options]
more [options]
```

Using the `tree` Command to Display the Directory Structure in the Fedora 13 CLI
Tree is a recursive directory listing program that produces an indented listing of files. Like Windows 7, the Fedora 13 CLI uses the `tree` command to list contents of directories in a tree-like format. Figure 6-10 displays the directory structure in the Fedora 13 CLI.

The `tree` command itself shows the files in the current directory and its subdirectories. When directory information is given, `tree` lists all the files and/or subdirectories found in the given directories in turn.

Using Wildcard Characters in the Fedora 13 CLI
Like Windows 7, the Fedora 13 CLI uses wildcards. When entering commands, you can use wildcards to specify groups of files.

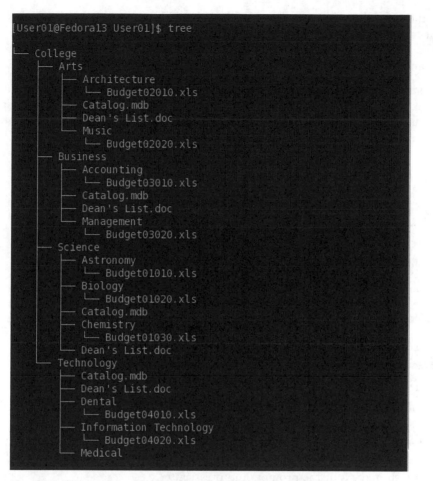

```
[User01@Fedora13 User01]$ tree
└── College
    ├── Arts
    │   ├── Architecture
    │   │   └── Budget02010.xls
    │   ├── Catalog.mdb
    │   ├── Dean's List.doc
    │   └── Music
    │       └── Budget02020.xls
    ├── Business
    │   ├── Accounting
    │   │   └── Budget03010.xls
    │   ├── Catalog.mdb
    │   ├── Dean's List.doc
    │   └── Management
    │       └── Budget03020.xls
    ├── Science
    │   ├── Astronomy
    │   │   └── Budget01010.xls
    │   ├── Biology
    │   │   └── Budget01020.xls
    │   ├── Catalog.mdb
    │   ├── Chemistry
    │   │   └── Budget01030.xls
    │   └── Dean's List.doc
    └── Technology
        ├── Catalog.mdb
        ├── Dean's List.doc
        ├── Dental
        │   └── Budget04010.xls
        ├── Information Technology
        │   └── Budget04020.xls
        └── Medical
```

Figure 6-10 Tree-style directory structure in the Fedora 13 CLI

Source: Course Technology/Cengage Learning

Fedora 13 uses the same two wildcard characters as Windows 7: the question mark (?) and the asterisk (*, or star). In commands, the ? represents any single character that you want to match. For example, the following command produces a list of any files in the current directory that have a filename beginning with "host," followed by four unknown characters.

```
ls host????
```

This command would match any of the following filenames: hostuser, hosthome, hostname, and host1234.

The * wildcard represents any string of characters. Use *.* to represent all filenames with any extension (note that the resulting list will not show the file extensions).

Linux filenames can contain extensions, but they are not used to make the same file-type associations and identifications as they do in Windows 7.

Nautilus is the official file browser for the GNOME desktop environment, which supports browsing local file systems. Nautilus uses bookmarks, window backgrounds, emblems, notes, and add-on scripts. To start Nautilus, double-click the Places icon on the desktop, or click Places and then click the directory to use.

The Nautilus file browser uses two panes. You can use the left pane to set various styles: Places, Information, Tree, History, Notes, or Emblems. The right pane displays directory and file information for the selected entry in the left pane. The user can choose an Icon, List, or Compact view.

Activity 6-5: Creating the Directory Structure in Fedora 13

Time Required: 10 minutes

Objective: Create the example directory structure in Fedora 13.

Description: In this activity, you open a Terminal console and run a script file to create the example directory structure you will use in the remaining activities.

The Fedora 13 activities in this chapter require the script files that are available at *www.cengage.com*. For further details, see the appendix for your virtualization software.

1. Start your virtual machines using the appropriate instructions in Activity 1-1.

2. To run the program file that creates the directories and files you need for the Fedora 13 examples in this chapter, click **Applications**, point to **System Tools**, and then click **Terminal**.

3. To create the directory structure with the **makeds** script, type **cd /usr/local/bin**, press **Enter**, type **sh makeds** at the prompt, and press **Enter**.

4. Leave the virtual machine logged on for the next activity.

Contact your instructor if you see the following messages: "makeds is not recognized as an internal or external command, operable program or batch file." or "… cannot execute binary file." Also, contact your instructor if you do not see the following message when running the script: "All the directories and/or files were created successfully."

Activity 6-6: Displaying the Files of the Directory Structure in the Fedora 13 CLI Using the `ls` Command

Time Required: 10 minutes

Objective: Locate information about files and directories in Fedora 13.

Description: In this activity, you use the `ls` command to find information about the file systems on a Fedora 13 system. This activity is useful if you want to review the directory structure of a hard drive.

You must complete Activity 6-5 before you can complete the following activity.

1. If necessary, start your virtual machines using the appropriate instructions in Activity 1-1.

2. To open a Terminal console, click **Applications**, point to **System Tools**, and then click **Terminal**.

3. Type **ls /etc –l | more** and then press **Enter**.

To advance the paging enabled by the more command, either press the Spacebar to review a whole page or press Enter to review one line at a time.

6

4. To close the Fedora 13 Terminal window, type **exit** and then press **Enter**.

5. Leave the virtual machine logged on for the next activity.

Activity 6-7: Displaying the Directory Structure in the Fedora 13 CLI Using the `tree` Command

Time Required: 10 minutes

Objective: Locate information about files and directories in the Fedora 13 CLI.

Description: In this activity, you use the `tree` command to find information about the file systems on a Fedora 13 system. This activity is useful if you want to review the directory structure of a hard drive.

1. If necessary, start your virtual machines using the appropriate instructions in Activity 1-1.

2. To open a Terminal console, click **Applications**, point to **System Tools**, and then click **Terminal**.

3. To change the path to the partition on sdb1, type **cd /mnt/sdb1/User01**, type **pwd**, and then press **Enter**.

4. Verify that the path is **/mnt/sdb1/User01**.

5. Type **tree** and then press **Enter** (see Figure 6-11).

If you do not see the tree structure shown in Figure 6-11, contact your instructor.

6. Leave the virtual machine logged on for the next activity.

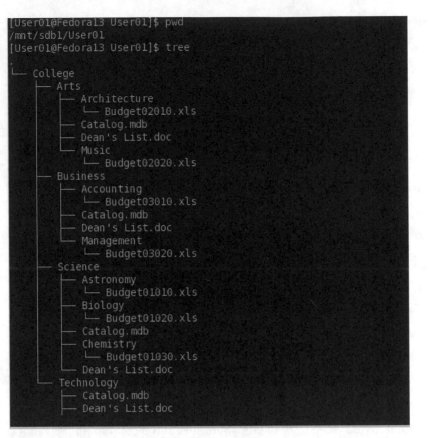

```
[User01@Fedora13 User01]$ pwd
/mnt/sdb1/User01
[User01@Fedora13 User01]$ tree
.
└── College
    ├── Arts
    │   ├── Architecture
    │   │   └── Budget02010.xls
    │   ├── Catalog.mdb
    │   ├── Dean's List.doc
    │   └── Music
    │       └── Budget02020.xls
    ├── Business
    │   ├── Accounting
    │   │   └── Budget03010.xls
    │   ├── Catalog.mdb
    │   ├── Dean's List.doc
    │   └── Management
    │       └── Budget03020.xls
    ├── Science
    │   ├── Astronomy
    │   │   └── Budget01010.xls
    │   ├── Biology
    │   │   └── Budget01020.xls
    │   ├── Catalog.mdb
    │   ├── Chemistry
    │   │   └── Budget01030.xls
    │   └── Dean's List.doc
    └── Technology
        ├── Catalog.mdb
        ├── Dean's List.doc
```

Figure 6-11 Example directory structure displayed with `tree` command

Source: Course Technology/Cengage Learning

Activity 6-8: Displaying the Files of the Directory Structure in the Fedora 13 GUI

Time Required: 15 minutes

Objective: Locate information about files and directories in Fedora 13.

Description: In this activity, you use the File Browser to find information about the file systems on a Fedora 13 system. This activity is useful if you want to review the directory structure of a hard drive.

You must complete Activity 6-5 before you can complete the following activity.

1. If necessary, start your virtual machines using the appropriate instructions in Activity 1-1.

2. Click **Places** on the top bar, and then click **Computer**.

3. To go to the disk that contains the example directory structure, click **View**, check **Side Pane** if necessary, click the down arrow next to **Places** above the left pane, and then choose **Tree** from the drop-down list.

4. To display the example directory structure in the left pane, expand the following directories in the order shown: **File System**, **mnt**, **sdb1**, **User01**, **College**, **Arts**, **Business**, **Science**, and **Technology**.

5. To review the Arts directory files in the right pane, click **Arts**.

6. To change the order in which files are displayed in the right pane, right-click the white space in the right pane, point to **Arrange Items**, and then click **By Name**.

7. To change the way files are displayed in the right pane, click the **Icon View** button on the main toolbar and choose **List View**.

8. Close the Nautilus file manager.

9. Leave the virtual machine logged on for future activities.

6

Navigating the Directory Structure

Navigating the directory structure is a bit like climbing a tree. Before climbing, you view the limbs. You can climb from limb to limb, move to smaller limbs, and retrace your steps to return to a limb. You use similar techniques to view or navigate the directory structure on your virtual machine's hard drives. The following sections explain these techniques in Windows 7 and Fedora 13.

Navigating the Directory Structure in the Windows 7 CLI

At any given time, you are working within a particular directory of the directory structure. This location is called the **working directory** or the **current directory**. You can use either the CHDIR or **CD** (change directory) command to change the location of the working directory. The CD command has the following syntax:

CD [/D] [drive:] [path]

CD ..   Specifies that you want to change to the parent directory

CD drive   Displays the current directory in the specified drive

CD   Displays the current drive and directory

/D   Changes the current drive and the current directory

As long as the CLI remains open, the **command-line interpreter** maintains a current directory for each drive on your virtual machine. The current drive and path are shown in the command prompt. When you specify the path, you are changing the working directory's location for the current drive. If you include the /D switch, you change both the drive and the path that appear. You can also use the CD command without parameters to show the current drive and path, which is useful if they are not shown in the command prompt.

To change the current directory with the CD command, you have three choices:

- CD . .—Backs up one subdirectory from the current location in the directory structure.
- CD *path*—Changes to the relative location from the current location; when navigating to a **relative path,** the current directory path is implied. A relative path does not begin with a backward slash, and its starting address is the current directory.
- CD *path*—Changes to the absolute location from the current location; to navigate to an **absolute path,** you must provide the drive and the full path name, beginning with a backward slash (\ ). The CD \ command changes to the root of the current drive.

These three choices are best illustrated by the example directory structure you used earlier in the chapter.

To change the relative location to College, you would use the CD College command. The command prompt changes from E:\User01 to E:\User01\College, as shown in Figure 6-12.

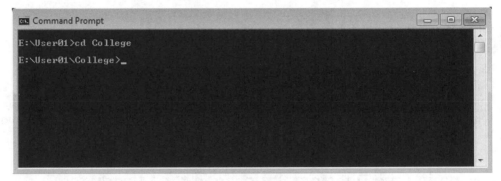

Figure 6-12 Using the CD command to change the directory location

Source: Course Technology/Cengage Learning

To change the absolute location to Technology\Information Technology, you would type the following command:

CD \User01\College\Technology\Information Technology

The command prompt changes from E:\User01\College to the path shown above.

To back up from one subdirectory to the next higher level of the tree, use the CD . . command. The command prompt changes from E:\User01\College\Technology\Information Technology to E:\User01\College\Technology.

Activity 6-9: Changing the Current Location in the Windows 7 CLI

Time Required: 15 minutes

Objective: Change the current location within a directory structure in the Windows 7 CLI.

Description: In this activity, you open a command prompt and change the current location within a directory structure. This activity is useful if you want to change locations before completing other activities. For example, you can change from one directory level to another before listing the filenames in a subdirectory.

 You must complete Activity 6-1 before you can complete the following activity.

1. If necessary, start your virtual machines using the appropriate instructions in Activity 1-1.

2. Click **Start,** point to **All Programs,** click **Accessories,** and then click **Command Prompt.**

3. To go to the example directory structure, type **CD /D E:\User01** and press **Enter.**

4. To display the example directory structure, type **TREE** and press **Enter.**

5. To change the location relative to the User01 directory structure, type **CD College** and press **Enter.**

6. Verify that the prompt is E:\User01\College.

7. To change the absolute location within the College directory structure, type **CD \User01\ College\Technology** and press **Enter.**

8. Verify that the prompt is E:\User01\College\Technology.

9. To back up one directory, type **CD ..** and press **Enter.**

10. Verify that the prompt is E:\User01\College.

11. To change the relative location within the current directory, type **CD Technology** and press **Enter.**

12. Verify that the prompt is E:\User01\College\Technology.

13. To back up one directory, type **CD ..** and press **Enter.**

14. To navigate the directory, type **CD Business** and press **Enter,** then type **CD Management** and press **Enter.**

15. Verify that the prompt is E:\User01\College\Business\Management.

16. Close the command prompt window.

17. Leave the virtual machine logged on for the next activity.

Navigating Directory Structures in Windows Explorer

To navigate the example directory structure illustrated earlier, you can click a folder in the left pane of Windows Explorer. The location changes and the right pane is refreshed. For example, to make Science the current folder, click Science in the left pane, as shown in Figure 6-13.

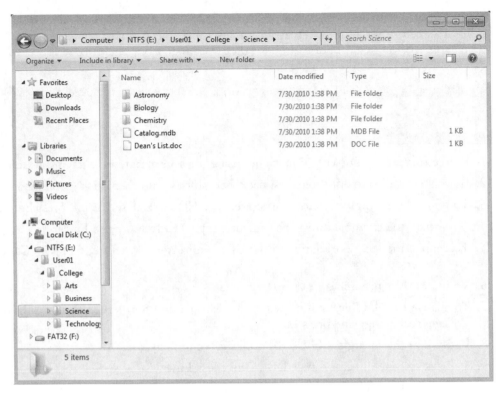

Figure 6-13 Navigating to the Science folder

Source: Course Technology/Cengage Learning

Activity 6-10: Navigating the Directory Structure in the Windows GUI

Time Required: 15 minutes

Objective: Change the current location within a directory structure in the Windows 7 GUI.

Description: This activity is similar to Activity 6-9, except that you use Windows Explorer instead of the Windows 7 CLI.

You must complete Activity 6-1 before you can complete the following activity.

1. If necessary, start your virtual machines using the appropriate instructions in Activity 1-1.

2. Click **Start,** point to **All Programs,** click **Accessories,** and then click **Windows Explorer.**

3. To go to the drive that contains the example directory structure, expand **Computer** and then expand **NTFS (E:).**

4. To display the example directory structure in the left pane, expand the following folders in the order shown: **User01, College, Arts, Business, Science,** and **Technology.**

5. To change the location relative to the User01 directory structure, click **College** in the left pane.

6. Verify that the address is E:\User01\College.

7. To change the absolute location within the College directory structure, click **Technology** in the left pane.

8. Verify that the address is E:\User01\College\Technology.

9. To back up one directory, click **College** in the left pane.

10. Verify that the address is E:\User01\College\.

11. To navigate the directory in the left pane, expand **Business** and then click **Management**.

12. Verify that the address is E:\User01\College\Business\Management.

13. Close the Windows Explorer window.

14. Leave the virtual machine logged on for future activities.

Navigating Directory Structures in Fedora 13

As with Windows 7, you can use the cd command to change the location of the working (current) directory in the Fedora 13 CLI. The cd command has page definition options that are beyond the scope of this book. The command syntax is:

```
cd [options] [location path]
```

Using Absolute and Relative Paths in the Fedora 13 CLI
As with Windows 7, you can change your current directory in the directory structure using either the absolute path method or the relative path method. Each directory also contains a "." entry that points to the current directory and a ".." entry that points to the parent directory.

For example, if your current directory is /technology/dental/ and you want to change directories to /business/accounting/, you have two options. First, you could refer to the directory structure shown in Figure 6-8 and use the absolute path method to type the following command:

```
cd /college/business/accounting
```

Second, you could refer to the previous directory structure and use the relative path method to type the following command:

```
cd ../../business/accounting
```

To back up one subdirectory and move one level higher in the structure, you would type:
```
cd ..
```

Activity 6-11: Navigating the Directory Structure in Fedora 13

Time Required: 15 minutes

Objective: Change the current directory in Fedora 13.

Description: In this activity, you use the cd command to change the current directory in a Fedora 13 directory tree. This activity is useful if you want to change levels in the directory structure before listing filenames in a subdirectory.

1. If necessary, start your virtual machines using the appropriate instructions in Activity 1-1.

2. To open a Terminal console, click **Applications**, point to **System Tools**, and then click **Terminal**.

3. To change to the /mnt/sdb1/User01 path, type **cd /mnt/sdb1/User01** and press **Enter**. Type **pwd** and then press **Enter**.

4. To list the contents of the College directory, type **ls -l** and then press **Enter**.

5. To change to the College directory, type **cd College** and then press **Enter**.

6. To list the college departments as directories, type **ls -l** and then press **Enter**.

7. To change to the Technology directory, type **cd Technology** and then press **Enter**.

8. To display the mnt/sdb1/User01/College/Technology path, type **pwd** and then press **Enter**.

9. To list the files in the Technology directory, type **ls** and press **Enter**.

10. Verify that Catalog.mdb and Dean's List.doc are displayed.

11. To move back up one directory, type **cd ..** and press **Enter**.

12. To display mnt/sdb1/User01/College, type **pwd** and then press **Enter**.

13. To close the Fedora 13 Terminal window, type **exit** and then press **Enter**.

14. Leave the virtual machine logged on for future activities.

Working with Directories

As your requirements for data storage expand, you create new directories within the structure to accommodate new files. For example, if you have enrolled in a new course or undertaken a new project at work, you might want to separate these files from the existing directory structure. Of course, you can also remove a directory when you no longer need it. The following sections explain how to create and remove directories.

Creating Directories in the Windows 7 CLI

Use the MD (make directory) command to create a subdirectory in the CLI. You may also use the MKDIR command. The MD command has the following syntax:

MD [drive:]path

The MD command syntax interprets the drive and path like the CD command described earlier. To create a subdirectory, you have two choices:

- MD *path*—Creates the subdirectory in a relative location
- MD *path*—Creates the subdirectory in an absolute location

For example, to create a Physics subdirectory relative to Science, you would first navigate to Science with the CD command and then type MD Physics, as shown in Figure 6-14. To create a Physics subdirectory using the absolute path, you would type MD \User01\ College\Science\Physics.

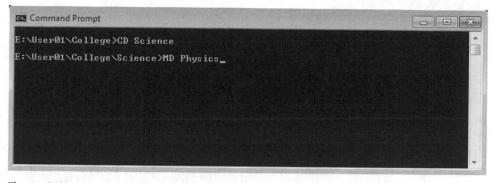

Figure 6-14 Using the MD command to make a Physics subdirectory

Source: Course Technology/Cengage Learning

6

Recall that Windows 7 CLI commands are not case sensitive. Typing MD, md, Md, or mD will produce the same results. Likewise, file or folder names such as College, college, and COLLEGE are the same.

Activity 6-12: Creating Directories in the Windows 7 CLI

Time Required: 15 minutes

Objective: Create directories within a directory structure in the Windows 7 CLI.

Description: In this activity, you open a command prompt and create directories within a directory structure.

1. If necessary, start your virtual machines using the appropriate instructions in Activity 1-1.
2. Click **Start**, point to **All Programs**, click **Accessories**, and then click **Command Prompt**.
3. If you are not at the example directory structure, type **CD /D E:\User01** and press **Enter**.
4. To display the example directory structure, type **TREE** and press **Enter**.
5. To change the location in the directory structure, type **CD \User01\College** and press **Enter**.
6. Verify that the prompt is E:\User01\College.
7. To create a new college directory, type **MD "Liberal Arts"** and press **Enter**.

When creating a directory name at the command prompt, use quotation marks to enclose names that include spaces.

8. To change the location to the new college directory, type **CD "Liberal Arts"** and press **Enter**.
9. Verify that the prompt is E:\User01\College\Liberal Arts.
10. To create the English Department directory, type **MD English** and press **Enter**.
11. To create the French Department directory, type **MD French** and press **Enter**.
12. To create the German Department directory, type **MD German** and press **Enter**.

13. To create the Spanish Department directory, type **MD Spanish** and press **Enter**.

14. To back up to College in the directory structure, type **CD ..** and press **Enter**.

15. To view the new directory structure, type **TREE** and then press **Enter**.

16. Verify that Liberal Arts and the four new language departments are present.

17. Close the command prompt window.

18. Leave the virtual machine logged on for the next activity.

Creating Directories in the Windows 7 GUI

To create a folder in the example directory structure using the Windows 7 GUI, navigate to the parent folder Science in the left pane, click Science, and then right-click the white space in the right pane. Point to New and then click Folder. Type the name over "New Folder" and press Enter. For example, the new folder in Figure 6-15 is named Physics.

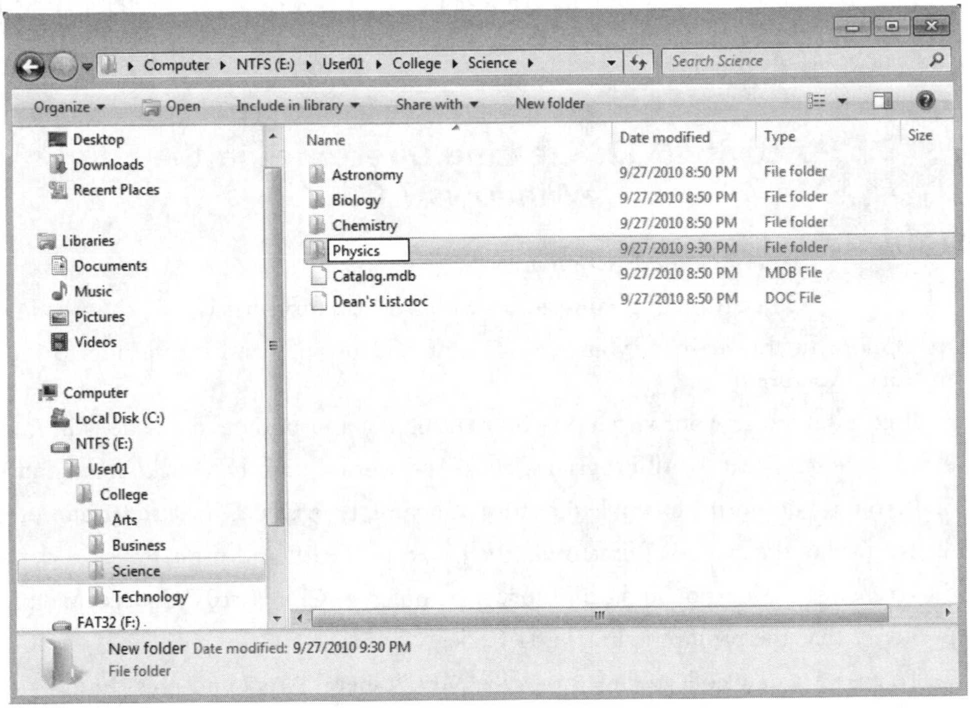

Figure 6-15 Creating the Physics directory

Source: Course Technology/Cengage Learning

Activity 6-13: Creating Directories in the Windows 7 GUI

Time Required: 15 minutes

Objective: Create directories within a directory structure in the Windows 7 GUI.

Description: In this activity, you open Windows Explorer and create directories within a directory structure.

1. If necessary, start your virtual machines using the appropriate instructions in Activity 1-1.
2. Click **Start**, point to **All Programs**, click **Accessories**, and then click **Command Prompt**.
3. To restore the example directories and files you used earlier in the chapter, type **MakeDS** at the command prompt and press **Enter**.
4. Close the command prompt window.
5. Click **Start**, point to **All Programs**, click **Accessories**, and then click **Windows Explorer**.
6. To go to the drive that contains the example directory structure, expand **Computer** and then click **NTFS (E:)**.
7. To display the example directory structure in the left pane, expand the following directories in the order shown: **User01, College, Arts, Business, Science,** and **Technology**.
8. To change the location relative to the User01 directory structure, click **College** in the left pane.
9. Verify that the address is E:\User01\College.
10. To create a new college directory, right-click the white space in the right pane, point to **New**, click **Folder**, type **Liberal Arts** over "New Folder," and then press **Enter**.
11. To change the location relative to the User01 directory structure, click **Liberal Arts** in the left pane.
12. Verify that the address is E:\User01\College\Liberal Arts.
13. To create a new department directory, right-click the white space in the right pane, point to **New**, click **Folder**, type **English** over "New Folder," and then press **Enter**.
14. Repeat Step 13 to create department directories for **French, German,** and **Spanish**.
15. Close the Windows Explorer window.
16. Leave the virtual machine logged on for future activities.

Creating Directories in Fedora 13

As in Windows 7, you sometimes need to create directories within the Fedora 13 directory structure. For example, if your college adds a Printing Department to the Arts group, you will need to add a corresponding subdirectory to the Arts directory. You must have write permission in the parent directory or be logged on as superuser to add directories in Fedora 13.

To create a directory, use the **mkdir** (make directory) command. Its command syntax is:

```
mkdir [options] [directory name]
```

The mkdir command has the following options:

-p   Makes parent directories as needed, but does not display an error if they already exist

-v   Displays a message for each created directory

For example, if your current directory is /technology/dental/ and you want to add a printing directory to the arts directory, you first need to navigate to /arts. Then, use the mkdir command to create the directory.

```
cd college/arts
mkdir printing
```

To create a printing subdirectory using the absolute path, type either of the following commands:

```
mkdir /college/arts/printing
mkdir ../../arts/printing
```

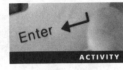

Activity 6-14: Creating Directories in Fedora 13

Time Required: 15 minutes

Objective: Create directories in Fedora 13.

Description: In this activity, you open a command prompt and use the mkdir command to create directories in a Fedora 13 directory structure.

You must repeat Activity 6-5 before you can complete the following activity.

1. If necessary, start your virtual machines using the appropriate instructions in Activity 1-1.

2. To open a Terminal console, click **Applications,** point to **System Tools,** and then click **Terminal.**

3. To display the path **/mnt/sdb1/User01,** type **cd /mnt/sdb1/User01** and press **Enter.** Type **pwd** and then press **Enter.**

4. To list the College directory, type **ls -l** and then press **Enter.**

5. To create a new directory under College, first move to the College directory by typing **cd College** and then pressing **Enter.**

6. To add the Liberal Arts directory, type **mkdir "Liberal Arts"** and then press **Enter.**

7. To verify that the Liberal Arts directory is added correctly, type **ls** and then press **Enter.**

8. To make Liberal Arts the current directory, type **cd "Liberal Arts"** and then press **Enter.**

9. Type **mkdir English** and then press **Enter.**

10. Type **mkdir French** and then press **Enter.**

11. Type **mkdir German** and then press **Enter.**

12. Type **mkdir Spanish** and then press **Enter.**

13. To verify that all four departments are listed in the Liberal Arts directory, type **ls** and then press **Enter.**

14. Close the terminal window.

15. Leave the virtual machine logged on for future activities.

Removing Directories in the Windows 7 CLI

When you no longer need a directory or the files in it, you can remove the directory. Use the RMDIR or **RD** (remove directory) command to remove a subdirectory in the CLI. The RD command has the following syntax:

```
RD [/S] [/Q] [drive:]path
```

/S   Removes all directories and files in the specified directory and the directory itself; use this command to remove a directory tree

/Q   Operates in quiet mode, meaning that the system does not ask for confirmation before removing a directory tree with the /S command

The RD command syntax interprets the drive and path like the CD command described earlier. To remove a subdirectory, you have two choices:

RD *path*   Removes the old subdirectory from the current location using the relative method

RD *path*   Removes the old subdirectory from the current location using the absolute method

If you use the /S switch to remove the indicated directory and its subdirectories, you are asked to confirm your choice by pressing the Y key. The /Q switch allows you to use the RD command in script files, where no user response is needed.

For example, to remove the Science directory, you would type RD /S \User01\College\ Science and press Enter, as shown in Figure 6-16. To confirm the deletion, press the Y key and then press Enter.

Just as you should never "cut off the limb" you are standing on, you cannot issue the RD command for a directory in the current path of the command prompt. If you try, an error message appears, as shown in Figure 6-17.

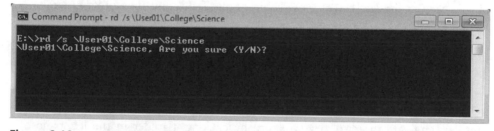

Figure 6-16 Removing the Science directory

Source: Course Technology/Cengage Learning

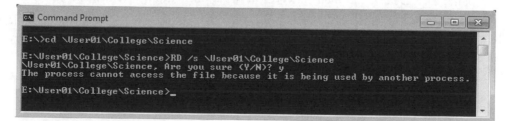

Figure 6-17 Error message generated from incorrect use of RD command

Source: Course Technology/Cengage Learning

Activity 6-15: Removing Directories in the Windows 7 CLI

Time Required: 15 minutes

Objective: Remove a directory within a directory structure in the Windows 7 CLI.

Description: In this activity, you open a command prompt and remove a directory. This activity is useful if you want to remove a directory that you no longer need.

1. If necessary, start your virtual machines using the appropriate instructions in Activity 1-1.

2. Click **Start**, point to **All Programs**, click **Accessories**, and then click **Command Prompt**.

3. To restore the example directories and files, type **MakeDS** at the command prompt and press **Enter**.

4. If you are not at the example directory structure, type **CD/D E:\User01** and press **Enter**.

5. To display the example directory structure, type **TREE** and press **Enter**.

6. To change the location relative to the directory structure, type **CD \User01\College** and press **Enter**.

7. Verify that the prompt is E:\User01\College.

8. To remove the Science directory and then confirm the deletion, type **RD /S Science**, press **Enter**, press the **Y** key, and then press **Enter**.

9. To see the changed directory structure, type **TREE** and then press **Enter**.

10. To remove the Business directory without confirmation, type **RD /S /Q Business** and then press **Enter**.

11. To see the changed directory structure, type **TREE** and then press **Enter**.

12. Close the command prompt window.

13. Leave the virtual machine logged on for the next activity.

Removing Directories in the Windows 7 GUI

You can navigate the directory structure by clicking a folder in the left pane of Windows Explorer. By doing so, the location changes and the right pane is refreshed. If you need to remove a directory, right-click its folder in the left pane, click Delete, and confirm your choice by clicking Yes. For example, to remove the Music folder, right-click Music in the left pane, click Delete, and then click Yes in the confirmation screen shown in Figure 6-18.

When you delete an item from your hard drive, Windows 7 places it in the Recycle Bin. If you change your mind about a deletion from Windows Explorer, you can retrieve the deleted item from the Recycle Bin, which provides a useful safety net.

Items that you delete from a USB drive are permanently deleted and are not placed in the Recycle Bin; neither are items you delete using the command prompt window.

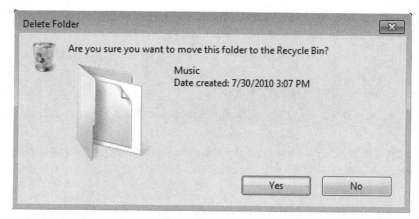

Figure 6-18 Removing a directory

Source: Course Technology/Cengage Learning

6

If you want to "undelete"—or restore—a deleted folder back to its original location, double-click the Recycle Bin icon on the desktop, right-click the deleted folder, and click Restore.

Items remain in the Recycle Bin until you permanently delete them from your computer. However, these items still take up hard drive space. When the Recycle Bin fills up, Windows 7 automatically cleans out enough space in it to accommodate the most recently deleted files and folders.

 If you are running low on hard drive space, empty the Recycle Bin. You can also restrict the size of the Recycle Bin to limit the amount of hard drive space it takes up.

Activity 6-16: Removing Directories in the Windows 7 GUI

Time Required: 15 minutes

Objective: Remove a folder within a directory structure in the Windows 7 GUI.

Description: In this activity, you open Windows Explorer and remove a folder within a directory structure. This activity is useful if you want to delete folders that you no longer need.

1. If necessary, start your virtual machines using the appropriate instructions in Activity 1-1.
2. Click **Start**, point to **All Programs**, click **Accessories**, and then click **Command Prompt**.
3. To restore the example directories and files, type **MakeDS** at the command prompt and press **Enter**.
4. Click **Start**, point to **All Programs**, click **Accessories**, and then click **Windows Explorer**.
5. To go to the drive that contains the example directory structure, expand **Computer** and then click **NTFS (E:)**.

6. To display the example directory structure in the left pane, expand **User01**, expand **College**, expand **Arts**, and then expand **Technology**.

7. To change the location relative to the User01 directory structure, click **College** in the left pane.

8. Verify that the address is E:\User01\College.

9. To remove the Arts directory, right-click the **Arts** folder in the right pane, click **Delete**, and then click **Yes**.

10. To remove the Technology directory, right-click the **Technology** folder in the right pane, click **Delete**, and then click **Yes**.

11. Close Windows Explorer.

12. Leave the virtual machine logged on for future activities.

Removing Directories in Fedora 13

To remove a directory from the tree in Fedora 13, you must have ownership permission or log on as superuser and then use the **rmdir** (remove directory) command. Its command syntax is:

```
rmdir [options] directory[s]
```

The rmdir command has the following options:

-p   Tries to remove each directory component in the path as needed

-v   Displays a message for each removed directory

For example, if your current directory is /technology/dental/ and you want to delete the printing directory from the arts directory, you first need to navigate to /arts. Then, use the rmdir command to remove the printing directory.

```
cd /college/arts
rmdir printing
```

Although you can use the absolute and relative path methods, it is usually safer to navigate directly to the parent directory.

If you created several subdirectories under a directory and now need to remove the entire branch, you can use the rmdir command with the –p option. For example, if you have a directory path of /home/User01/personal/budget/ and you need to delete the /personal/budget/ directories, you would type the following:

```
cd /home/User01
rmdir -p personal/budget
```

Unfortunately, this approach will not work if either of the directories contains files. For example, you might have created several files in the budget directory and now need to remove the entire branch. You will need to use the rm commands to remove specified files. The rm command actions can be modified with the following switches:

rm   Removes a file you specify

-f   Forces the system to ignore nonexistent files and does not prompt the user

-i   Interactively prompts the user before removing each file

-r or -R   Recursively removes directories and their contents

-v   Explains what is being done (the v stands for verbose)

Options can be combined. For example, -ir means interactive and recursive. By default, the rm command does not remove directories. Use the recursive option (-r or -R) to remove each listed directory and all of its contents:

```
.cd /home/User01
rm -ir personal OR rm -iR personal
```

Because Linux does not warn against deletions, you should use the -i options so that you are prompted to confirm each file deletion, unless you are running the command in batch mode. You will learn more about the rm command later in this chapter.

Activity 6-17: Removing Directories in the Fedora 13 CLI

Time Required: 15 minutes

Objective: Remove directories in the Fedora 13 CLI.

Description: In this activity, you use the rm command to remove directories from a Fedora 13 directory tree. This activity is useful if you want to remove a directory you no longer need.

You must repeat Activity 6-5 before you can complete the following activity.

1. If necessary, start your virtual machines using the appropriate instructions in Activity 1-1.

2. To open a Terminal console, click **Applications**, point to **System Tools**, and then click **Terminal**.

3. To display the /mnt/sdb1/User01 path, type **cd /mnt/sdb1/User01** and press **Enter**. Type **pwd** and then press **Enter**.

4. To list the College directory, type **ls -l** and then press **Enter**.

5. To change to the College directory, type **cd College** and press **Enter**.

6. To remove the Arts directory and its files, type **rm –rf Arts** and press **Enter**.

7. Type **ls Arts** and press **Enter**.

If you do not see a message similar to "ls: cannot access Arts: No such file or directory," contact your instructor.

8. Repeat Steps 6 and 7 to remove the **Technology** directory and verify its successful removal.

The `rmdir` command does not work if the target directories contain files; you cannot delete the directories without first deleting the files. Therefore, the `rm -rf` command is used here.

9. Type **ls** and then press **Enter**.

If you see either the Arts or Technology directory, contact your instructor.

10. To close the Fedora 13 Terminal window, type **exit** and then press **Enter**.

11. Leave the virtual machine logged on for the next activity.

Activity 6-18: Removing Directories in the Fedora 13 GUI

Time Required: 15 minutes

Objective: Remove directories in the Fedora 13 GUI.

Description: In this activity, you remove directories from a Fedora 13 directory tree. This activity is useful if you want to remove a directory you no longer need.

You must repeat Activity 6-5 before you can complete the following activity.

1. If necessary, start your virtual machines using the appropriate instructions in Activity 1-1.

2. Click **Places** on the top bar, and then click **Computer**.

3. To go to the disk that contains the example directory structure, click **View**, check **Side Pane**, click the down arrow next to **Places** above the left pane, and then choose **Tree** from the drop-down list.

4. To display the example directory structure in the left pane, expand the following directories in the order shown: **File System, mnt, sdb1, User01,** and then **College.**

5. Right-click the **Arts** directory and click **Move to Trash.**

6. To move the Technology directory to the trash, right-click the **Technology** directory and click **Move to Trash.**

7. Close the Nautilus file browser.

8. Leave the virtual machine logged on for future activities.

Working with Files

You can perform four tasks to keep your files up to date:

- Copy one or more files to an alternative location.
- Move files or directories from one folder to another or from one drive to another.
- Rename files and directories.
- Delete files from the computer.

The following sections explain how to perform these tasks in Windows 7 and Fedora 13.

Working with Files in the Windows 7 CLI

This section explains how to use the Windows 7 CLI to copy, move, rename, and delete files.

Copying Files in the Windows 7 CLI When copying files in the Windows 7 CLI, you can use either the **COPY** command to copy one or more files to an alternative location, or you can use the **XCOPY** command—a more powerful version of the COPY command. This section explains both commands.

Using the COPY Command in the Windows 7 CLI Use the COPY command to copy the contents of a file to a new location. The command has the following syntax:

```
COPY [/V] source [destination]
```

source	Specifies the file(s) to be copied
destination	Specifies the directory and/or filename for the new file(s)
/V	Verifies that new files are written correctly

For example, to copy the Budget.xls file from \Science to \Science\Chemistry, you would type:

```
COPY \Science\Budget.xls \Science\Chemistry
```

Although recording errors rarely occur with the COPY command, the /V switch lets you verify that critical data has been recorded correctly and that the new file can be read. This switch also slows down the COPY command because the OS must check each sector recorded on the disk.

Using the XCOPY Command in the Windows 7 CLI Use the XCOPY command when you need more control over what you copy. The XCOPY command is like the COPY command, except that it has more switches. Use this powerful command to copy files in bulk from one directory or drive to another, or to copy whole directories to a new destination. The XCOPY command has the following syntax:

```
XCOPY source [destination] [/P] [/S] [/E] [/V] [/Q] [/F] [/L]
```

source	Specifies the file(s) to copy
destination	Specifies the location and/or name of new files
/P	Prompts you before creating each destination file
/S	Copies directories and subdirectories except empty ones
/E	Copies directories and subdirectories, including empty ones

/V   Verifies each new file

/Q   Does not display filenames while copying

/F   Displays full source and destination filenames while copying

/L   Displays filenames of the selected files, but does not copy them

For example, if you needed to make a backup of the College subdirectories and files, you would type the following command, assuming that you had already created the Backup subdirectory:

```
XCOPY /S \User01\College \User01\Backup
```

If you had not already created the Backup subdirectory, you would receive this message:

```
Does \User01\Backup specify a file name
or directory name on the target
(F = file, D = directory)?
```

In this instance, you would respond by entering the letter D.

If you wanted to copy the files, duplicate the directory structure, and verify that the files were successfully copied, you would type:

```
XCOPY /E /V \User01\College \User01\Backup
```

Moving Files in the Windows 7 CLI Use the **MOVE** command to move the contents of a file to a new location and to rename files and directories. If you want to move one or more files, the command has the following syntax:

```
MOVE [/Y | /-Y] [drive:] [path]filename1 [,...] [destination]
```

If you want to rename a directory, the MOVE command has the following syntax:

```
MOVE [/Y | /-Y] [drive:] [path]dirname1 dirname2
```

[drive:] [path]filename1   Specifies the location and name of the file(s) you want to move

[destination]   Specifies the new file destination, which can include a drive letter and colon, a directory name, or a combination; if you are moving only one file, you can include a filename to rename the file as you move it

[drive:] [path]dirname1   Specifies the directory you want to rename

dirname2   Specifies the new name of the directory

The MOVE command and syntax are similar to the COPY command, with one exception: The source file is always removed from the disk with the MOVE command.

The MOVE command has the ability to move subdirectories, which is useful if you want to reorganize a directory structure. For example, to move the Architecture Department from Arts to Science, you would type:

```
MOVE \User01\College\Arts\Architecture \User01\College\Science
```

One more use for the MOVE command is to rename subdirectories. For example, to change the name of the Dental subdirectory to Dental Assistant, you would type:

```
MOVE \User01\College\Technology\Dental \User01\College\Technology\
Dental Assistant
```

Because "Dental Assistant" contains a space, you may want to use quotation marks.

Renaming Files in the Windows 7 CLI Use the **REN** (or RENAME) command to rename a file. The command has the following syntax:

```
REN [drive:] [path] filename1 filename2
RENAME [drive:] [path] filename1 filename2
```

Note that you cannot specify a new drive or path for your destination file.

For example, to rename the Budget.xls file, you would type:

```
REN Budget.xls Budget2006.xls
```

You can use wildcards such as * and ? when only part of a name is changed in a series of files, but the lengths of the old and new names must be the same. For example, to change the ".txt" extensions of all filenames in the current directory to ".bak," you would type:

```
REN *.txt *.bak
```

Deleting Files in the Windows 7 CLI Use the **DEL** (or **ERASE**) command to remove a file or files. The command has the following syntax:

```
DEL [/P] [/S] [/Q] names
ERASE [/P] [/S] [/Q] names
```

names   Specifies a list of one or more files or directories to delete; you can use wildcards to delete multiple files. If you specify a directory, all files in it are deleted.

/P   Prompts for confirmation before deleting each file

/S   Deletes specified files from all subdirectories

/Q   Operates in quiet mode, meaning that the system does not ask for confirmation before making a deletion using a global wildcard

You can delete one or more files with the DEL command. For example, to remove the homework.doc file, you would type:

```
DEL \User01\homework.doc
```

To remove all of the .doc files from the \User01 subdirectory, you would type:

```
DEL /S \User01\*.doc
```

Activity 6-19: Working with Files in the Windows 7 CLI

Time Required: 15 minutes

Objective: Work with files within a directory structure in the Windows 7 CLI.

Description: In this activity, you open a command prompt and work with files within the directory structure. This activity is useful if you copy, move, rename, and delete files.

1. If necessary, start your virtual machines using the appropriate instructions in Activity 1-1.

2. Click **Start**, point to **All Programs**, click **Accessories**, and then click **Command Prompt**.

3. To restore the example directories and files, type **MakeDS** at the command prompt and press **Enter**.

4. If you are not at the example directory structure, type **CD/D E:\User01** and press **Enter**.

5. To back up the directory structure, type **XCOPY College*.* /S /E User01\Backup**, press **Enter**, and then press the **D** key.

6. To view the files within the directory structure, type **TREE /F\Backup** and then press **Enter**.

7. To change the location relative to the directory structure, type **CD \User01\College\Arts** and press **Enter**.

8. Verify that the prompt is E:\User01\College\Arts.

9. To copy the catalog database to the Architecture subdirectory, type **COPY catalog.mdb Architecture** and then press **Enter**.

10. To move the budget file to the Arts subdirectory, type **MOVE Architecture\ budget02010.xls** and press **Enter**.

11. To change the location relative to the directory structure, type **CD \User01\College\ Science\Chemistry** and press **Enter**.

12. Verify that the prompt is E:\User01\College\Science\Chemistry.

13. To rename the budget file, type **REN Budget01030.xls BudgetChemistry.xls** and press **Enter**.

14. To change the location relative to the directory structure, type **CD \User01\College\ Science\Biology** and press **Enter**.

15. Verify that the prompt is E:\User01\College\Science\Biology.

16. To delete a budget file, type **DEL Budget01020.xls** and press **Enter**.

17. To view the files within the directory structure, type **TREE /F \User01\College** and then press **Enter**.

18. Close the command prompt window.

19. Leave the virtual machine logged on for the next activity.

Working with Files in the Windows 7 GUI

You use Windows Explorer to work with files. For example, the right pane of Windows Explorer displays important file information. The following sections explain how to copy, move, rename, and delete files using Explorer.

Copying Files in the Windows 7 GUI
You can copy files from one location to another using Windows Explorer. For example, to copy the homework.doc file, you would navigate to the subdirectory that contains the file, right-click homework.doc, and then click Copy, as shown in Figure 6-19. Next, you would navigate to the new location in the left pane, right-click the white space in the right pane, and then click Paste.

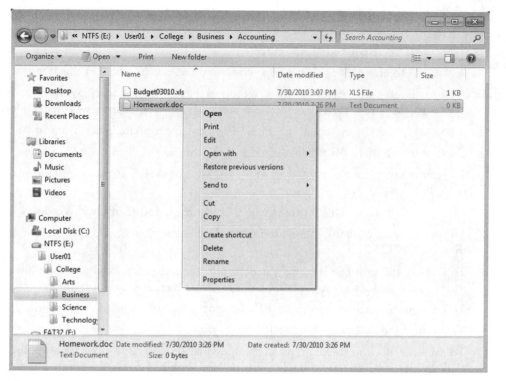

Figure 6-19 Copying files

Source: Course Technology/Cengage Learning

Moving Files in the Windows 7 GUI The steps to move files are similar to those for copying files in Windows Explorer. For example, to move the homework.doc file, you would navigate to the subdirectory that contains the file, right-click homework.doc, and then click Cut. Next, you would navigate to the new location in the left pane, right-click the white space in the right pane, and then click Paste.

Renaming Files in the Windows 7 GUI You can rename files using Windows Explorer. For example, to rename the homework.doc file, you would navigate to the subdirectory that contains the file, right-click homework.doc, click Rename, type a new name over homework.doc, and press Enter to save it.

If you attempt to change the file extension when renaming a file, you will receive a warning message. If you are sure that the new file extension is acceptable, click Yes.

Deleting Files in the Windows 7 GUI You can delete files using Windows Explorer. For example, to delete the homework.doc file, you would navigate to the subdirectory that contains the file, right-click homework.doc, and click Delete. You will receive a Confirm File Delete message. If you are sure that you want to delete the file, click Yes.

Activity 6-20: Working with Files in the Windows 7 GUI

Time Required: 15 minutes

Objective: Work with files within a directory structure in the Windows 7 GUI.

Description: In this activity, you open Windows Explorer and work with files within the directory structure. This activity is useful if you copy, move, rename, and delete files.

1. If necessary, start your virtual machines using the appropriate instructions in Activity 1-1.

2. Click **Start**, point to **All Programs**, click **Accessories**, and then click **Command Prompt**.

3. To restore the example directories and files, type **MakeDS** at the command prompt and press **Enter**.

4. Click **Start**, point to **All Programs**, click **Accessories**, and then click **Windows Explorer**.

5. To go to the drive that contains the example directory structure, expand **Computer** and then click **NTFS (E:)**.

6. To display the example directory structure in the left pane, expand the following directories in the order shown: **User01**, **College**, **Arts**, **Business**, **Science**, and **Technology**.

7. To change the location to the User01 directory structure, click **User01** in the left pane.

8. Verify that the address is E:\User01\.

9. To create a Backup folder, right-click the white space in the right pane, point to **New**, click **Folder**, and then type **Backup** over "New Folder." Press **Enter** when you finish.

10. To copy the College folder to the Backup folder, right-click the **College** folder, click **Copy**, right-click the **Backup** folder, and then click **Paste**.

11. To change the location relative to the directory structure, click **Arts** in the left pane.

12. Verify that the address is E:\User01\College\Arts.

13. To copy the catalog database to the Architecture folder, right-click **Catalog.mdb**, click **Copy**, right-click the **Architecture** folder, and click **Paste**.

14. To move the budget file to the Arts folder, click the **Music** folder, right-click **Budget02020.xls**, click **Cut**, right-click the **Arts** folder, and then click **Paste**.

15. To rename the budget file, click the **Management** folder, right-click **Budget03020.xls**, click **Rename**, enter **BudgetManagement.xls**, and then press **Enter**.

16. To delete a budget file, click **Biology**, right-click **Budget01020.xls**, click **Delete**, and then click **Yes**.

17. Close Windows Explorer.

18. Leave the virtual machine logged on for future activities.

Working with Files in Fedora 13

You can use the Fedora 13 CLI to copy, move, rename, and delete files.

Copying Files in the Fedora 13 CLI   To copy files or directories in the directory tree, use the **cp** command. Its command syntax is:

```
cp [options] [source path] [target path]
cp [options] [source path] [target directory]
cp [options] [source directory] [target directory]
```

The cp command has the following options:

-f, --force   If an existing destination file cannot be opened, this command removes it and tries again

-I   Prompts before overwriting; this option is recommended to prevent destructive mistakes

-l   Links files instead of copying them

-R or -r   Copies directories recursively

-s   Makes symbolic links instead of copying files

-v   Displays command activity as it occurs

For example, if you want to copy a Budget.xls file from /college/science/chemistry to /college/arts/music, type the following command:

```
cp /college/science/chemistry /college/arts/music
```

If you have several Budgetxxx.xls files that you want to copy, type the following command:

```
cp college/science/chemistry/* /college/arts/music
```

If you are copying a branch in a directory tree that contains several deep, nested directories, you can use either the -R or the -r option:

```
cp -r college/science/chemistry/* /college/arts/
```

Moving Files in the Fedora 13 CLI The command to move a file or directory in Fedora 13 is very similar to the Windows 7 command. You can use the **mv** command to move the contents of a file or directory to a new location. While doing so, you can also use the command to rename files. The mv command syntax is:

```
mv [options] [source] [target]
mv [options] [source] [target directory]
```

The mv command has the following options:

-f   Displays a prompt before overwriting; this command is used in batch processing to provide instructions for users

-I   Also displays a prompt before overwriting, but this command is normally used in interactive processing as a safety measure to prevent mistakes

-v   Displays command activity as it occurs

The mv command is similar to the cp command, with one exception: The source file is always removed from its directory with the mv command. The syntax is also like that of the cp command, as you must always enter a target destination. Even if you are already in the directory where you want to move the file, you must still type the directory name.

You may use the "." (the current directory metacharacter) as a relative path reference for the current location.

You can also use the mv command to move subdirectories, which is useful for reorganizing a directory structure. For example, to move the Architecture Department from Arts to Science, you would type:

`mv /User01/college/arts/architecture /User01/college/science`

Renaming Files in the Fedora 13 CLI You can use the mv command to rename a file or directory. For example, to change the name of the Dental Department to Dental Assistant, you would type:

`mv /User01/college/technology/dental /User01/college/technology/dental assistant`

Because "dental assistant" contains a space, quotation marks are required. Unlike Windows 7, which interprets spaces within filenames, Fedora 13 requires quotation marks to enclose filenames that contain spaces.

Deleting Files in the Fedora 13 CLI To remove files and directories in the directory tree, use the rm command. It does not remove directories by default. The syntax for the rm command is:

`rm [options] file[s]`

The rm command has the following options:

-I	Prompts before removing a file; this option is highly recommended for interactive program runs
-R or -r	Removes the contents of directories recursively
-v	Displays command activity as it occurs

You can delete one or more files with the rm command. For example, to remove the homework.doc file, you would type:

`rm /mnt/sdb1/User01 /homework.doc`

To remove all of the .doc files from the /User01 subdirectory, you would type:
`rm /mnt/sdb1/User01/*`

Because Linux does not warn against deletions, you should use the -i option so that you are prompted to confirm each file deletion, unless you are running the command in batch mode (for example, rm -i /User01/*).

Activity 6-21: Working with Files in the Fedora 13 CLI

Time Required: 15 minutes

Objective: Copy, move, and remove files in the Fedora 13 CLI.

Description: In this activity, you use the cp, mv, and rm commands in a Fedora 13 directory tree. This activity is useful if you need to copy, move, rename, and delete files.

You must repeat Activity 6-5 before you can complete the following activity.

1. To open a Terminal console, click **Applications,** point to **System Tools,** and then click **Terminal**.

2. To display the /mnt/sdb1/User01 path, type **cd /mnt/sdb1/User01** and press **Enter.** Type **pwd** and then press **Enter.**

3. To create a Backup directory, type **mkdir Backup** and press **Enter.**

4. To list the College and Backup directories, type **ls -l** and then press **Enter.**

5. To copy the College directory to the Backup directory, type **cp –r College Backup** and then press **Enter.**

6. To list the directories, type **ls Backup/College** and press **Enter.**

7. Repeat Step 2 for this activity to make sure that your directory path is **/mnt/sdb1/User01**.

8. To display the **/mnt/sdb1/User01/College** path, type **cd College** and press **Enter.** Type **pwd** and press **Enter.**

9. To copy the catalog database file from the Arts directory to the Architecture directory, type **cp Arts/Catalog.mdb Arts/Architecture** and then press **Enter.**

10. To list the Catalog.mdb file, type **ls Arts/Architecture** and press **Enter.** To move the budget file from the Music directory to the Arts directory, type **mv Arts/Music/Budget02020.xls Arts** and then press **Enter.**

11. To list the Budget02020.xls file, type **ls Arts** and press **Enter.**

12. Type **ls Arts/Music** and press **Enter.**

If files are listed, contact your instructor.

13. To rename the budget file in the Management directory, type mv Business/Management/Budget03020.xls Business/Management/BudgetManagement.xls and then press Enter.

14. To list the BudgetManagement.xls file, type **ls Business/Management** and then press **Enter.**

If the Budget03020.xls file is listed, contact your instructor.

15. To delete the budget file from the Biology directory, type **rm Science/Biology/Budget01020.xls** and then press **Enter.**

16. To close the Fedora 13 Terminal window, type **exit** and then press **Enter**.

17. Leave the virtual machine logged on for future activities.

Activity 6-22: Working with Files in the Fedora 13 GUI

Time Required: 15 minutes

Objective: Copy, move, and remove files in the Fedora 13 GUI.

Description: In this activity, you open the Nautilus file manager in the GNOME desktop environment in Fedora 13 and work with files within the directory structure. This activity is useful if you copy, move, rename, and delete files.

You must repeat Activity 6-5 before you can complete the following activity.

1. If necessary, start your virtual machines using the appropriate instructions in Activity 1-1.

2. To display the Nautilus file manager, click **Places** on the top bar, and then click **Computer**.

3. To go to the disk that contains the example directory structure, click **View**, check **Side Pane**, click the down arrow next to **Places** above the left pane, and then choose **Tree** from the drop-down list.

4. To display the example directory structure in the left pane, expand the following directories in the order shown: **File System, mnt, sdb1,** and then **User01**.

5. To create a Backup directory in the /mnt/sdb1/User01 folder, right-click **User01** in the left pane and then click **Create Folder**. In the untitled folder Properties window, type **Backup** in the Name text box under the Basic tab, and then press **Enter**.

If you do not see that the Backup directory is added to the /mnt/sdb1 tree, contact your instructor.

6. Close the Backup Properties window and return to the Nautilus File Browser window.

7. To copy the College directory to the Backup directory, right-click the **College** directory in the left pane in the User01 directory, click **Copy**, right-click the **Backup** directory in the same directory, and then click **Paste Into Folder**.

8. To see the copied College directory, expand the **Backup** directory. To see the list of the College directories, expand the **College** directory.

9. To copy the catalog database file to the Arts/Architecture directory from the Arts directory, expand the **College** directory under the User01 directory in the left pane. Click the **Arts** directory. Right-click **Catalog.mdb** in the right pane, click **Copy**, right-click the **Architecture** directory in the left pane, and click **Paste Into Folder**.

10. To see the **Catalog.mdb** file listed in the right pane, double-click the **Architecture** directory.

11. To move the budget file from the Arts/Music directory to the Arts directory, click the **Arts** directory, click the **Music** directory, right-click **Budget02020.xls** in the right pane, click **Cut**, right-click the **Arts** directory in the left pane, and click **Paste Into Folder**.

12. To verify that **Budget02020.xls** is listed in the right pane, click the **Arts** directory.

13. To rename the budget file in the Business/Management directory, expand the **Business** directory in the left pane, and then click the **Management** directory in the left pane. Right-click **Budget03020.xls** in the right pane, click **Rename**, replace Budget03020 with **BudgetManagement,** and then press **Enter.** You should see the BudgetManagement.xls file in the right pane.

14. To delete the budget file from the Science/Biology directory, expand the **Science** directory in the left pane, and then click the **Biology** directory in the left pane. Right-click **Budget01020.xls** in the right pane, and click **Move to Trash.** The Budget01020.xls file should be deleted now.

15. Close the Nautilus File Browser window.

16. Leave the virtual machine logged on for future activities.

Using Removable Drives for Application Data Storage

You use removable drives to store and transport data. For example, your instructor might want you to submit programming assignments on USB drives.

Normally, removable media are preformatted, but you should reformat them if you need to reuse them or if you work with two operating systems.

Using Removable Drives in the Windows 7 CLI

Before using a disk, you may want to format it to remove any existing files and improve the odds that the USB drive will accept new files without write errors. After formatting, you can copy the files from the hard drive. Also, you might want to change the file system.

Refer to the appendix for your virtualization software for specific instructions to set up your virtual machines to use USB drives.

Formatting Removable Drives in the Windows 7 CLI To format a disk for use with Windows 7, use the FORMAT command. The command has the following syntax when you format disks:

```
FORMAT volume [/V:label] [/Q]
```

volume   Specifies the drive letter (followed by a colon)

/V:label   Specifies the volume label

/Q   Performs a quick format

For example, to format a USB drive as the H drive, type FORMAT H: and press Enter. You can specify a volume label of up to 11 characters by using the /V switch. You can use the /Q switch to perform a quick format, which removes files from the disk without scanning it for bad sectors. Use this option only if the disk has been previously formatted and you are sure it is not damaged.

Copying Files to a Removable Drive in the Windows 7 CLI You can copy files to a formatted disk with the COPY command or the XCOPY command. For example, to copy the homework.doc file, you would navigate to the subdirectory that contains the file and then use the command COPY homework.doc H:.

Activity 6-23: Using Removable Drives in the Windows 7 CLI

Time Required: 15 minutes

Objective: Use a removable drive with the Windows 7 CLI.

Description: In this activity, you open a command prompt and use a removable drive. This activity is useful if you use disks to transport and store data files. For example, you might need to provide the answers to class exercises on disks.

1. If necessary, start your virtual machines using the appropriate instructions in Activity 1-1.

2. Click **Start**, point to **All Programs**, click **Accessories**, and then click **Command Prompt**.

Windows 7 will assign the next available drive letter when the USB drive is inserted. The following steps use H as the assigned drive letter, but you might use a different letter.

3. Place a USB drive in a USB port.

4. To format the disk, type **FORMAT H: /V** and press **Enter** twice.

Be sure to include the drive letter. If you do not, you might format a hard drive by mistake.

5. When prompted to enter the volume label, type **Homework** and then press **Enter**.

6. When asked if you want to format another disk, press the **N** key, and then press **Enter**.

7. To copy a file to the disk, type **COPY e:\User01\College\Arts\Catalog.mdb H:** and press **Enter**.

8. To verify that the file was copied, type **DIR H:** and press **Enter**.

9. Close the command prompt window.

10. Leave the virtual machine logged on for the next activity.

Using Removable Drives in the Windows 7 GUI

As with the Windows 7 CLI, you can format a USB drive using the Windows 7 GUI. After formatting, you can copy files from the hard drive to a USB drive or store files directly to the USB drive from an application.

Formatting Removable Drives in the Windows 7 GUI To format a USB drive, place it in the USB port. From Windows Explorer, right-click the USB option and then click Format. The Format USB dialog box appears. If you are sure that the disk is good, click the Quick Format check box. To start the format, click the Start button.

Copying Files to a Disk in the Windows 7 GUI You can copy files to a format-ted disk using Windows Explorer. For example, to copy the homework.doc file, you would navigate to the subdirectory that contains the file, right-click homework.doc, and then click Copy. Next, you would navigate to the USB drive in the left pane, right-click the white space in the right pane, and then click Paste.

6

Storing Files from an Application As an alternative to copying files from the hard drive to a USB drive, you can save files directly to the USB drive. For example, to save a file that you typed in Notepad, click the File menu, click Save As, click the Save in list box, click the USB drive, type the filename in the text box, and then click Save.

Activity 6-24: Using Removable Drives in the Windows 7 GUI

Time Required: 15 minutes

Objective: Use a removable drive with the Windows 7 GUI.

Description: In this activity, you use Windows Explorer to work with a removable drive. This activity is useful if you use disks to transport and store data files. For example, you might need to provide the answers to class exercises on disks.

1. If necessary, start your virtual machines using the appropriate instructions in Activity 1-1.

2. Click **Start,** point to **All Programs,** click **Accessories,** and then click **Windows Explorer.**

Windows 7 will assign the next available drive letter when the USB drive is inserted. The following steps use H as the assigned drive let-ter, but you might use a different letter.

3. Place a USB drive in a USB port.

4. To format the disk, expand **Computer,** right-click **USB Drive (H:),** click **Format,** and then click the **Start** button.

5. To copy a file to the disk, click **NTFS (E:),** expand **User01,** expand **College,** click **Arts,** right-click **Catalog.mdb,** click **Copy,** right-click **USB Drive (H:),** and click **Paste.**

6. To verify that the file was copied, click **USB** and review the right pane.

7. Close any open windows in the virtual machine.

8. To shut down the virtual machine, click **Start,** and then click the **Shut Down** button.

9. Wait a moment for the Windows 7 virtual machine to shut down completely.

10. Leave the PC logged on for the next activity.

Using Removable Drives in the Fedora 13 CLI

As with Windows 7, you can use removable drives in Fedora 13 to store and transport data, such as to a disk. Before using a disk, you must **unmount** and format it. Next, you **mount** the disk drive and copy the files from the hard drive. Refer to Chapter 3 for directions on using the mount and unmount commands.

Formatting Removable Drives in the Fedora 13 CLI To perform a low-level format of a disk, use the floppy command. Normally, you do not need to format disks because they are preformatted. The floppy command has the following syntax when you format disks:

floppy [options] [target device]

The floppy command has the following options:

--probe, -p	Probes for available floppy drives; the floppy command creates and displays a list of all detected floppy drives
--showrc	Lists floppy drives configured in /etc/floppy
--capacity, -c	Shows the available format capacities of the floppy drive; options are C, which shows the number of cylinders; B, which shows the number of blocks per cylinder; and S, which shows the block size, in bytes
--format, -f	Formats the disk in the floppy drive
--ext2 -	Creates an ext2 (Linux) file system on the formatted disk
--fat -	Creates a FAT (DOS) file system on the formatted disk
--noprompt, -n	Prevents the display of verbose process messages produced by the --capacity and --format commands; these messages normally appear by default
--eject	Ejects the disk from the drive (IDE floppy drives only)

Copying Files to a Removable Drive in the Fedora 13 CLI You can copy files to a formatted disk or a USB drive with the cp command. For example, to copy a file called homework.doc, you would navigate to the subdirectory that contains the file and then use one of the following commands:

cp homework.doc /dev/fd0
cp homework.doc /dev/sda0

Activity 6-25: Using Removable Drives in Fedora 13

Time Required: 30 minutes

Objective: Use a removable drive with Fedora 13.

Description: In this activity, you use Fedora 13 to work with a USB drive. You use the `fdisk` and `mkdosfs` commands to format removable disks and copy files from the sample directory tree. This activity is useful if you use disks to transport and store data files. For example, you might need to provide the answers to class exercises on disks.

You must repeat Activity 6-5 before you can complete the following activity.

1. If necessary, start your virtual machines using the appropriate instructions in Activity 1-1.

2. To open a Terminal console, click **Applications,** point to **System Tools,** and then click **Terminal.** Plug in your USB drive.

3. To list the file system disk space usage, type **df -h** and press **Enter.**

If you do not see /media in the Mounted on column, contact your instructor.

4. To switch to superuser, type **su** and press **Enter,** then type **P@ssw0rd** and press **Enter.**

5. To unmount the device and get ready for the partition and format commands, type **umount /dev/sdd1** and then press **Enter.**

If /dev/sdd1 is not the only file system associated with your USB drive when you run the `df -h` command, unmount them all now. For example, type umount /dev/sde.

6. To partition the disk, type **fdisk /dev/sdd** and press **Enter.**

Make sure to include only the disk name without any digit after it. For example, it would be incorrect to use /dev/sde1 here.

7. To create a new partition, type **n** at the command prompt and press **Enter.**

8. To create a primary partition, type **p** and press **Enter.**

Optionally, if the partition to delete is already defined, you can delete it before adding it again by typing d and pressing Enter.

9. To create the first primary partition, type **1** and press **Enter**.

10. Press **Enter** at the First cylinder prompt.

11. Press **Enter** at the Last cylinder prompt.

12. To save the changes and go back to the superuser prompt, type **w** and then press **Enter**.

13. To format the disk, type **mkdosfs -F 32 -n learnusb /dev/sdd1** and then press **Enter**.

14. To switch back to the **User01** user, type **su – User01** and then press **Enter**.

15. Make sure that all file systems associated with your USB drive are unmounted. Unplug the USB drive and then plug it back. Wait a few seconds for the system to pick up the USB drive.

16. To verify that the **learnusb** name is listed, type **ls /media** and press **Enter**.

17. Type **ls /media/learnusb** and press **Enter**. Verify that nothing is listed under this directory. Take note of the **/media/learnusb** directory; you will use the directory name when you use the **cp** command later.

18. To display **/mnt/sdb1/User01** as the current working directory, type **pwd** and then press **Enter**.

19. If you are not at the directory, type **cd /mnt/sdb1/User01** and press **Enter**.

20. To copy the Catalog.mdb file, type **cp College/Arts/Catalog.mdb /media/learnusb** and then press **Enter**.

21. To list the Catalog.mdb file, type **ls /media/learnusb** and then press **Enter**. To unmount the disk, type **umount /media/learnusb** and then press **Enter**.

22. To shut down the virtual machine, click **System**, click **Shut Down**, and then click the **Shut Down** button.

23. Wait a moment for the Fedora 13 virtual machine to shut down completely.

24. Close any remaining open windows, log off, and shut down your PC.

Chapter Summary

- You can use directory structures to organize and maintain information in files and folders. Knowing how to manage directories enables you to perform a variety of tasks with files and increases the portability of the information you store. The organization of the directory structure is similar in Windows 7 and Fedora 13.

- To help you display the contents of a directory, you can use a command-line interface (CLI). The commands you enter at the command line are executed by a command-line interpreter. You can use wildcard characters to help identify filenames in a directory, and you can add options to commands to produce more specific file lists.

- You can manage the directory structure by creating new directories to categorize folder information and by removing directories that are obsolete.

- Each operating system has its own syntax when you navigate directory structures. When navigating the absolute path, you must provide the drive and the full path name. When navigating with a relative path, the current directory path is implied.

- You can use a command prompt or a GUI to copy, move, rename, and delete files.

■ Removable drives provide portability for file management and processing. In both Windows 7 and Fedora 13, you need to format a disk for reuse. You also need to mount and unmount an external storage device with Fedora 13.

Key Terms

absolute path   A path to a file that begins with the drive identifier and root directory or with a network share and ends with the complete filename.

CD   The command that changes the current directory. The command must be lowercase in Linux or UNIX.

command-line interface (CLI)   A form of interface in which the user types commands using a special command language.

command-line interpreter   A program that accepts typed commands from the keyboard and performs tasks as directed. The command-line interpreter, which is usually part of the operating system, is responsible for loading applications and directing the flow of information between them.

command prompt   A line area within the command window, usually indicated by a blinking cursor, where you type MS-DOS or Linux commands.

COPY   An MS-DOS command used to duplicate files from one disk or directory to another.

cp   The Linux command used to copy files, similar to the COPY command in MS-DOS.

current directory   The disk directory at the end of the active directory path; it is the directory that is searched first for a requested file, and the directory in which a new file is stored unless another directory is specified.

DEL   An MS-DOS command used to permanently remove a file. The file remains stored and is recoverable until the system reuses the storage space taken by the file.

DIR   An MS-DOS command that displays a list of files and subdirectories in the current directory.

ERASE   An MS-DOS command used to permanently remove a file or folder.

home   The conventional starting directory for all regular users in Fedora 13.

long filename   A plain-text name assigned to a file that can be 200 characters or more; it can include uppercase and lowercase letters as well as spaces.

ls   The Linux command that displays a list of files and subdirectories in the current directory or the directory specified in the command.

mkdir   The Linux command that creates a directory or subdirectory in the current directory of a folder.

mount   To make a physical disk accessible to a computer's file system.

MOVE   The MS-DOS command used to transfer a file or folder from one directory to another.

mv   The Linux command used to transfer a file or folder from one directory to another; similar to the MOVE command used in MS-DOS.

pipe symbol   The vertical line symbol (|) that appears on a virtual machine keyboard as the shift character on the backslash key (\). This symbol is used in MS-DOS and Linux to transfer the output of one command to the input of a second command.

RD   The MS-DOS command to remove a directory.

relative path   A path that is implied by the current working directory. If a user enters a command that refers to a file and the full path name is not entered, the current working directory becomes the path of the file to which the user referred.

REN   The MS-DOS command to rename a file.

rmdir   The Linux command used to remove a directory. All folders need to be removed from the directory before it can be removed.

sort   The Linux command used to organize files in a particular order. Files can be organized in ascending or descending alphabetized order.

standardized channel   A path or link through which information passes between two devices.

TREE   The command used in MS-DOS to produce a graphical view of files in a directory or subdirectories.

unmount   To remove a disk or device from active use.

white space   Blank areas of a page or window that contribute to its balance and visual appeal.

wildcard character   A character you can use in a command to represent one or more unknown characters. Wildcards are useful, for example, to specify multiple filenames.

working directory   Another term for *current directory*.

XCOPY   A more powerful version of the MS-DOS COPY command, with additional features.

Review Questions

1. A directory structure is used to _____.

    a.   organize information on your virtual machine

    b.   create maps that help students navigate between campus buildings

    c.   find manila files in a file cabinet

    d.   provide detailed information about file contents

2. CLI is the acronym for _____.

    a.   core language interpreter

    b.   content line interpreter

    c.   command-line interface

    d.   command-line interpreter

3. The TREE command is used to _____.

    a.   display the contents of a single file

    b.   list the directories and subdirectories on a disk

    c.   organize the files on a disk

    d.   list the files in a directory

4. When you use a long name for a file, you may _____. (Choose all that apply.)

   a. use lowercase letters

   b. use uppercase letters

   c. have spaces between words

   d. have no more than 200 characters in the filename

5. The DIR command is used to _____. (Choose all that apply.)

   a. display the contents of a single file

   b. list the directories and subdirectories on a disk

   c. organize the files on a disk

   d. list the files in a directory

6. Wildcard characters are used in commands to _____. (Choose all that apply.)

   a. match single characters to specify groups of files

   b. match strings of characters to specify groups of files

   c. match files with the same extension

   d. speed the process of accessing files

7. Which of the following can you use to display directory structures in Windows 7? (Choose all that apply.)

   a. Windows Explorer

   b. Directory Manager

   c. Windows console or command prompt

   d. Windows directory viewer

8. You can open a _____ to access the CLI in Fedora 13.

   a. Windows console

   b. terminal window

   c. directory viewer

   d. command prompt

9. Conventional users who log on to Fedora 13 are automatically placed in the _____ directory.

   a. systems

   b. root

   c. home

   d. user

10. The _____ command in Fedora 13 displays your directories and files.

    a. dir

    b. cd

    c.   show

    d.   ls

11. When you use the `more` command with the `ls` command in Fedora 13, _____

   .

    a.   all information about files and directories appears at the same time

    b.   you can scroll through the listing page by page

    c.   nothing happens; you need to use the `less` command

    d.   you are prompted for additional file information

12. To change the directory in Windows 7, you can use which of the following commands? (Choose all that apply.)

    a.   `cddir`

    b.   `changeDIR`

    c.   `CD`

    d.   `CHDIR`

13. The relative path _____. (Choose all that apply.)

    a.   is implied to be the current working directory when a directory path is not listed in a command prompt

    b.   begins with the backslash symbol (\) before the directory path in Windows

    c.   begins with the forward slash symbol (/) before the directory path in Linux

    d.   requires no symbol before the directory path

14. The absolute path _____. (Choose all that apply.)

    a.   is a path to a file that begins with the drive identifier and root directory and ends with the complete filename

    b.   begins with the backslash symbol (\) before the directory path in Windows

    c.   begins with the forward slash symbol (/) before the directory path in Linux

    d.   requires no symbol before the directory path

15. In Fedora 13, the command to change a directory is _____. (Choose all that apply.)

    a.   the same as the command in Windows 7, and case does not matter

    b.   the same as the command in Windows 7, but it must be lowercase

    c.   complicated and not widely used

    d.   able to use standardized channels to move up and down in the directory tree structure

16. White space is _____. (Choose all that apply.)

    a.   used to help distinguish objects and text in a window

    b.   used to provide files with longer, more meaningful names

   c. used to access menus in a window

   d. not accessible by moving your arrow cursor onto it

17. To create a directory in Fedora 13, use the _____ command.

   a. `cddir`

   b. `dir`

   c. `makedir`

   d. `mkdir`

   e. `chdir`

18. Which of the following commands can you use in Windows 7 to remove a directory and its files? (Choose all that apply.)

   a. `RM`

   b. `RDDIR`

   c. `RD`

   d. `RMDIR`

19. To remove a directory in Fedora 13, _____.

   a. the directory cannot contain any files

   b. you need to use the `rm` command

   c. you use the same command that is used in Windows 7

   d. you need to use the `rmdir` command

20. The `MOVE` command in Windows 7 and the `mv` command in Fedora 13 _____.

   a. copy the contents of one file to another location, leaving the original intact

   b. can be used interchangeably

   c. move a file to another location

   d. automatically rename the file as it is processed

Case Projects

CASE PROJECTS

Case 6-1: Explaining Relative vs. Absolute Paths

You have been stopped by a peer with a question: "What is the difference between relative and absolute paths when using the CD command?" What do you tell your peer? Write a short explanation that clearly answers the question and includes examples to clarify your points.

Case 6-2: Copying Files

You have been asked to prepare a short presentation on copying files at the next technical users meeting. Prepare a handout for your audience that explains at least eight uses of the COPY and XCOPY commands.

Case 6-3: Using the `list` Command in Fedora 13

You are given a file system to clean up at work. You must delete all of the files related to the Cramden Project. A prefix of "CP" is part of the standard filename for these project files. Write a `list` command that displays every directory name and filename that begins with "CP"; be sure to include hidden files.

Case 6-4: Moving Directory Tree Branches in Fedora 13

You are in charge of the data in one of your extracurricular clubs. You need to move the "Program Meeting" files from one chairperson to another in your file system. Each chairperson has a branch in the directory tree of the club's file system. List the steps and commands you would use to move the files.

chapter 7

Files and File Attributes

After reading this chapter and completing the exercises, you will be able to:

- Describe the contents of files and identify the application that created a particular file
- Describe the use of file attributes
- Find files based on their name or content

When using applications, you work with files. You need to be able to identify a file's contents and know which application you use to open and modify a file. You also need to know how to use a file's attributes to access files.

This chapter also explains how to search for files by their filenames or contents. Searches are useful when you need information from a file but are not sure of its filename, or when you don't know a filename but know something about the file's contents.

Contents of Files

When you use a virtual machine, you work with discrete sets of information called **files**. The operating system (OS) stores program modules in file systems. As you work with applications, you save documents under **filenames** for later retrieval and use. You need to know how to recognize the contents of files and the actions a particular OS takes when opening a file.

The following sections explain the contents of files in Windows 7 and Fedora 13.

Contents of Files in Windows 7

When you save a file, you or a Windows 7 application appends an **extension** to the end of the filename. The extension is usually three letters that follow the period in the filename. File extensions typically suggest the type of data stored in a file. For example, in "default.htm," the file extension is ".htm," which identifies the file as an HTML document. The OS uses the extension to determine which program can process the file.

Thousands of file extensions are associated with programs in Windows. To view a Web site that identifies these extensions, try *www.file-ext.com.*

In the days when MS-DOS was dominant, file extensions could not exceed three characters. While this limitation no longer holds, it is still common practice; extensions that adhere to this traditional limit are commonly called short extensions. A long extension has more than three characters. For example, the short extension for an HTML document is ".htm," and the long extension is ".html."

Viewing File Extensions in Windows 7 Windows tracks the extensions that your virtual machine uses. To view the file extensions registered in Windows 7, click Start, click Control Panel, click Default Programs, and then click "Associate a file type or protocol with a program" (see Figure 7-1). For example, Microsoft WordPad documents have an extension of .rtf. Unless you have administrative rights, you cannot change these extensions.

File Associations Windows 7 uses file extensions to identify file associations. A file association also helps to specify how the OS treats different file types. These associations include:

- Which icon appears for a file in Windows Explorer
- Which commands appear in a file's shortcut menu
- Which application opens when a user double-clicks a file

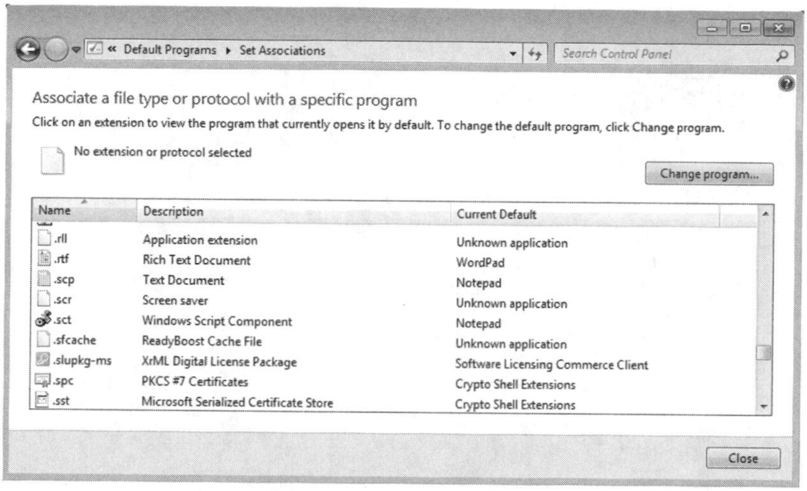

Figure 7-1 File extensions in Windows 7

Source: Course Technology/Cengage Learning

Icon Appearance in Windows Explorer Older versions of Windows Explorer display different icons for files based on the icon associated with the file type. Starting with Windows Vista, however, Microsoft eliminated this feature.

Commands in a File's Shortcut Menu When you right-click a file icon, a shortcut menu appears. The menu usually includes a list of actions that are appropriate to the object you clicked, as shown in Figure 7-2. Some menu choices appear on all shortcut menus; for example, you always have the option of creating a shortcut, deleting a file, renaming a file, or viewing its properties. However, the Open and Print menu options are specific to such files as word-processing documents, which are used in WordPad. Also, notice in Figure 7-2 that the Open option is bold, which means it is the default option when you double-click the filename. Your virtual machine might have different options on the context menu.

Opening Applications When you double-click a file icon, Windows 7 opens the file in its associated application. For example, if the user double-clicks the file Wordpad Homework.rtf, the OS opens the file in WordPad because WordPad is associated with .rtf files on the system and the default action is defined as Open. To change the default program for a given file type, right-click the file icon, and then click Open with. From the dialog box that appears, browse for the program to use with the selected file type (see Figure 7-3). If you want this file type to be associated with your choice of program, retain the check next to "Always use the selected program to open this kind of file."

Applications in Windows 7 You should know the common file extensions that you might encounter. For example, if you receive an e-mail message with an attached file from a colleague and you recognize its extension, you might be able to assess the value of the file before you open the attachment. Or, if a coworker gives you a removable drive, you can identify the applications used to create the files on it.

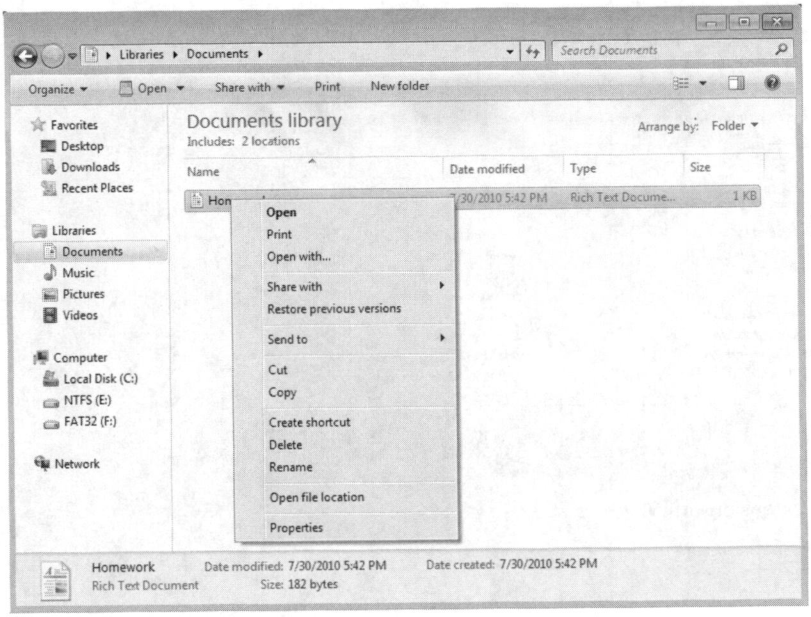

Figure 7-2 Context menu

Source: Course Technology/Cengage Learning

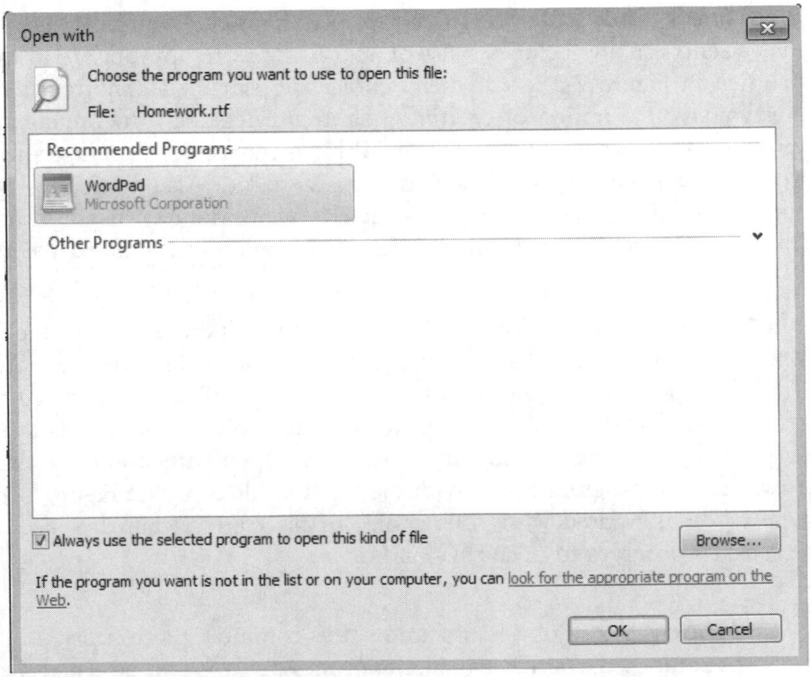

Figure 7-3 Open with dialog box showing default program for .rtf files

Source: Course Technology/Cengage Learning

Table 7-1 lists common file extensions for business applications, including brief descriptions of the extensions and the application associated with each file. With this information, you can determine whether you have the application needed to read and update a file.

Table 7-2 identifies the programming language for a particular source file, which helps you use the right compiler. Computer programming students should find this table particularly helpful.

Category	Extension	Description	Application
Database	.dbf, .mdb	dBase database, MS Access database	dBase, Access
E-mail	.pab, .pst, .wab	Personal Address Book, Post Office Box, Windows Address Book	Outlook, Outlook Express
Desktop publishing/ graphics	.cgm, .pub, .wpg	Computer Graphics Meta, Desktop publishing, WordPerfect graphic	Corel Draw, Publisher, DrawPerfect
Drawings/charts	.sda, .vsd	StarOffice drawing, Visio drawing	StarOffice, Visio
Presentations/ graphics	.cdr, .csv, .drw, .eps, .ppt, .sdc	Corel Draw graphic, Comma-separated value, Micrografx Designer graphics, Encapsulated PostScript, PowerPoint presentation, StarOffice spreadsheet	Corel Draw, Excel, Micrografx Designer, PowerPoint, StarOffice
Spreadsheet	.wk1, .wks, .xls, .xlsx	Lotus worksheet, Excel worksheet	Lotus 1-2-3, Excel
Word processing	.bps, .doc, .docx, .dot, .rtf, .sdw, .wpd, .odt, .wps	Works, Microsoft Word, Microsoft Word template, Rich text format, StarOffice word processor, WordPerfect	Works, Microsoft Word, StarOffice, WordPerfect

Table 7-1 Common business applications and their file extensions

Extension	Description
.asc	ASCII text
.txt	ASCII text
.c	C source
.cbl	COBOL program
.cpp	C++ source
.lib	Program library
.pl	PERL script
.py	Python script
.vb	VBScript

Table 7-2 Common programming source files

Extension	Description
.asp	Active Server Pages
.gif	CompuServe Graphic Interchange Format
.htm or .html	Hypertext Markup Language
.jpg or .jpeg	Joint Photographic Experts Group compression
.mid	Musical Instrument Digital Interface sound
.mov	QuickTime Movie
.mp2	Moving Picture Experts Group audio, layer 2
.mp3	Moving Picture Experts Group audio, layer 3
.mpg2	Moving Picture Experts Group Mpeg video Broadcast TV
.mpg3	Moving Picture Experts Group HDTV
.pdf	Adobe Acrobat Reader
.ra	RealAudio
.tif	Tagged Image Format

Table 7-3 Common Internet files

Table 7-3 lists some of the many Internet file extensions and formats you may encounter. This information helps you troubleshoot Internet browser problems related to particular file types.

Table 7-4 lists the files you are most likely to encounter when working with Windows 7. This table could be helpful if you need to talk to a vendor about a problem with a Windows 7 application.

Viewing the Contents of Text Files

You can view the contents of text files by using a Windows command prompt. For example, you might need to review the contents of a text file that was furnished by your instructor. This technique is particularly useful when debugging computer programs.

The **TYPE** command displays the contents of a text file line by line. For example, the following command lists the contents of the Pgm1Data.txt file, which was created in Notepad:

```
TYPE Pgm1Data.txt
```

If you had a larger text file to review, the **MORE** command would be a better choice because it displays text data files one screen at a time:

```
TYPE Pgm1Data.txt | MORE
```

 On most keyboards, the pipe character (|) is located above the Enter key.

Operating system	Extension	Description
DOS	.arc	Pkarc Compressed
DOS/Windows	.bak	Backup
DOS	.bat	Batch
Windows	.bmp	Bitmap graphic
DOS	.cfg	Configuration
Windows	.clp	Clipboard
Windows	.cmd	Command
DOS/Windows	.com	Executable
Windows	.dll	Dynamic link library
Windows	.drv	Device driver
Windows	.dun	Dial-Up Networking exported
DOS/Windows	.eps	Encapsulated PostScript
DOS/Windows	.exe	Executable
Windows	.hlp	Online Help
Windows	.ico	Icon
DOS/Windows	.ini	Program information
DOS/Windows	.iso	CD image
Windows	.lnk	Shortcut
Windows	.log	Program log
Windows	.msc	Common console
DOS/Windows	.pif	Program information
DOS/Windows	.ps	PostScript
Windows	.swp	Swap
Windows	.ttf	Windows True Type Font
Windows	.wav	Windows sound
Windows	.zip	Zip compressed

Table 7-4 Common Windows 7 files

The MORE command has the following syntax:

MORE [/E [/C] [/P] [/S] [/Tn] [+n]] < drive:] [path]filename

[drive:] [path]filename   Specifies a file to display one screen at a time

/E   Enables extended features

/C   Clears the screen before displaying the page

/P   Expands FormFeed characters

/S	Squeezes multiple blank lines into a single line
/Tn	Expands tabs to n spaces (the default is 8 spaces)
+n	Starts displaying the first file at line n

If extended features are enabled, the following commands are accepted at the -- More -- prompt:

P n	Displays next n lines
S n	Skips next n lines
F	Displays next file
Q	Quits
=	Shows line number
?	Shows help line

After one page of the text is displayed, you can press the Spacebar to display the next page or press Enter to display the next line.

To use the MORE command to display the contents of the Pgm1Data.txt file, you would type the following at a command prompt and then press Enter:

```
MORE < Pgm1Data.txt
```

The < is a required redirection symbol; it tells the OS to redirect the file into the MORE command.

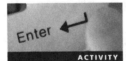

Activity 7-1: Viewing File Content with the Windows 7 CLI

Time Required: 15 minutes

Objective: Use the MORE command to view the contents of a text file.

Description: In this activity, you change to the User01 directory on the E: drive and display the contents of a file. The MakePgm1Data script sets the path to E:\User01. This activity is useful if you need to view the contents of a text file.

The Windows 7 activities in this chapter require the CMD files that are available at *www.cengage.com*. For further details, see the appendix for your virtualization software.

1. Start your virtual machines using the appropriate instructions in Activity 1-1.

2. To open a command prompt, click **Start**, point to **All Programs**, click **Accessories**, and then click **Command Prompt**.

3. To run the program file that creates the file you need for the activities in this chapter, type **MakePgm1Data** at the command prompt and press **Enter**.

Contact your instructor if you see the following message: "MakePgm1Data is not recognized as an internal or external command, operable program or batch file."

4. To display the contents of the Pgm1Data.txt file, type **MORE < Pgm1Data.txt** and then press **Enter.**

5. Verify that three lines of text appear.

6. Close the command prompt window.

7. Leave the virtual machine logged on for future activities.

Contents of Files in Fedora 13

As with Windows 7, filenames in Fedora 13 can contain file extensions, and applications in the OS contain associations that open a file in a format you can use. For example, if you open a file with an .sxw extension, OpenOffice Writer is probably the offered application that appears. However, because Fedora 13 automatically reads file headers to check a file's type, an extension is not required to open a file from the command-line interface (CLI).

More and more graphical user interfaces (GUIs) in Fedora 13 are evolving to use extensions for certain types of files and associations, as in Windows 7. Listing the default extensions for all file types is beyond the scope of this chapter, but some of the general types are shown for reference. For example, Table 7-5 lists several **Zip** file extensions that are available in Fedora 13. In Windows 7, only one such extension is available.

Table 7-6 lists extensions for multimedia files in Fedora 13; these extensions are similar to those in Windows 7.

Tables 7-7 and 7-8 list extensions for Fedora 13 system configuration files, installation packaging files, and programming files.

Unlike Windows 7, when you save a file in Fedora 13, the application stores file and directory attributes in an **inode**. The inode contains the file type (see Table 7-9) and other information about a file or directory, except its name and its actual data. A filename does not require an extension in Fedora 13 when you use a command to list, view, or execute the file.

Extension	Type
.bz2	A file compressed with bzip2
.gz	A file compressed with gzip
.tar	A file archived with tar (short for "tape archive"), also known as a tar file
.zip	A file compressed with Zip, which is commonly found in MS-DOS applications; most compressed files in Linux use gzip compression, so finding a Zip archive for Linux files is rare
.tgz	A tarred and gzipped file

Table 7-5 Extensions for Fedora 13 compressed and archived files

Extension	Type
.au	An audio file
.wav	An audio file
.gif	A GIF image file
.html or .htm	An HTML Internet file
.jpg	A JPEG image file
.pdf	An electronic image of a document
.png	A PNG image file (short for Portable Network Graphic)
.txt	A plain ASCII text file
.xpm	An image file

Table 7-6   **Extensions for Fedora 13 multimedia files**

Extension	Type
.conf	A configuration file
.rpm	A Red Hat Package Manager file used to install software

Table 7-7   **Extensions for Fedora 13 system configuration and installation packaging files**

Extension	Type
.c	A C program language source code file
.pl	A PERL script
.sh	A shell script

Table 7-8   **Extensions for Fedora 13 programming files**

When a file is created in Fedora 13, it is assigned both a name and an inode number, which is an integer that is unique within the file system. The filenames and corresponding inode numbers are stored as entries in a directory that appears to the user to contain the files. That is, the directory associates filenames with inodes.

Figure 7-4 shows another option you can use to determine the file type in Fedora 13: the ls command with the −1 option. The syntax of the ls command was explained in Chapter 4. To view a list of files in the devices folder, you use /dev. If you use the |**more** command, the output is displayed one screen at a time; the number of lines varies depending on the size of the console window:

```
ls −1 /dev | more
```

Be aware that filenames can contain files and pointers to files, not just text and multimedia.

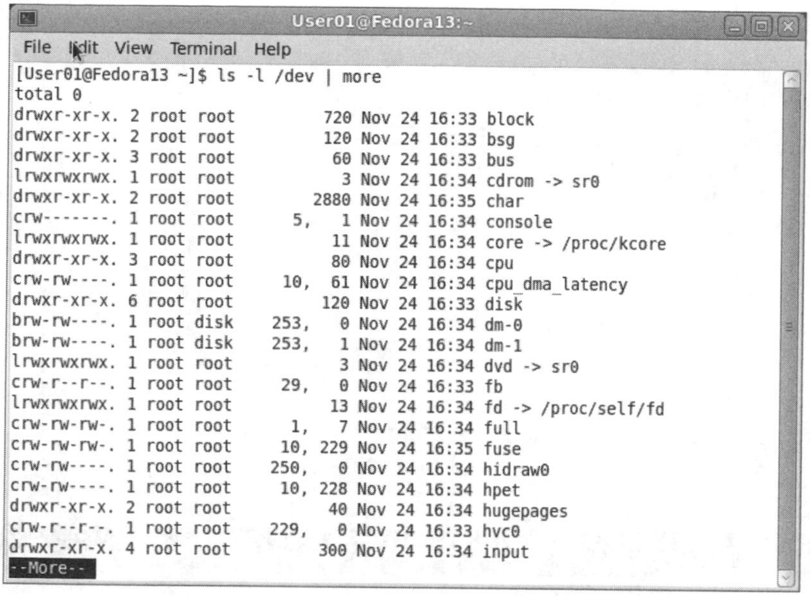

Figure 7-4 Listing Fedora 13 file types

Source: Course Technology/Cengage Learning

Symbol	Type
-	Regular file
d	Directory
l	Link
c	Special file
s	Socket
p	Named pipe

Table 7-9 Fedora 13 file types

File types you might see after running the ls command are listed in Table 7-9.

As you access files in Fedora 13, it is helpful to determine a file's contents before you try to view it. The file command is useful in this situation; you can use it to examine a file and determine its file type. The syntax for the file command is:

file[filename(s)]

For example, if you want to examine a plain text file named Pgm1Data, you can type the following:

file Pgm1Data

The Pgm1Data file then displays ASCII English text, which tells you that the file is a text file (see Figure 7-5).

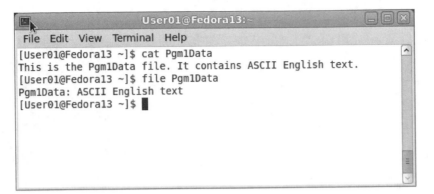

Figure 7-5 Using the Fedora 13 `file` command

Source: Course Technology/Cengage Learning

Type	Description
Text	An ASCII character file
Executable	A binary executable program
Data	All other types

Table 7-10 Fedora 13 `file` command types

Table 7-10 lists the options for the `file` command. When you display these options, you can determine whether you can view the file as a text file.

Viewing Files in Fedora 13

You can use several commands to view the contents of a Fedora 13 file, including the **cat** command (see Figure 7-6), which is short for *concatenate*. The original purpose of the cat

```
User01@Fedora13:~
File   Edit   View   Terminal   Help
[User01@Fedora13 ~]$ cat -bsT Pgm1Data
     1  This is the Pgm1Data file. It contains ASCII English text
.
[User01@Fedora13 ~]$
```

Figure 7-6 Using the Fedora 13 `cat` command

Source: Course Technology/Cengage Learning

command is to join two or more files and concatenate them into one file. When you view the contents of the file, it is concatenated to standard output.

For example, to view the contents of a file, you can type:

cat –bsT Pgm1Data

The more command, as shown in Figure 7-7, also allows you to view file contents. Sometimes it can be easier to use than the cat command, because the output does not run off the page before you can read it.

The more command has the following basic syntax and formatting options:

more [-dlfpcsu] [file ...]

-num   Specifies an integer that is the screen size (in lines)

-d   Displays *[Press 'h' for instructions]* after the more command prompts you to continue or quit

-l   Prevents the more command from treating ^L (form feed) as a special character and pausing after any line that contains a form feed

-f   Causes more to count logical lines rather than screen lines (long lines are not folded)

-p   Does not scroll, but instead clears the screen and then displays the text

-c   Does not scroll, but instead draws each screen from the top, clearing the remainder of each line as it is displayed

-s   Squeezes multiple blank lines into one

-u   Suppresses underlining

+num   Starts at line number *num*

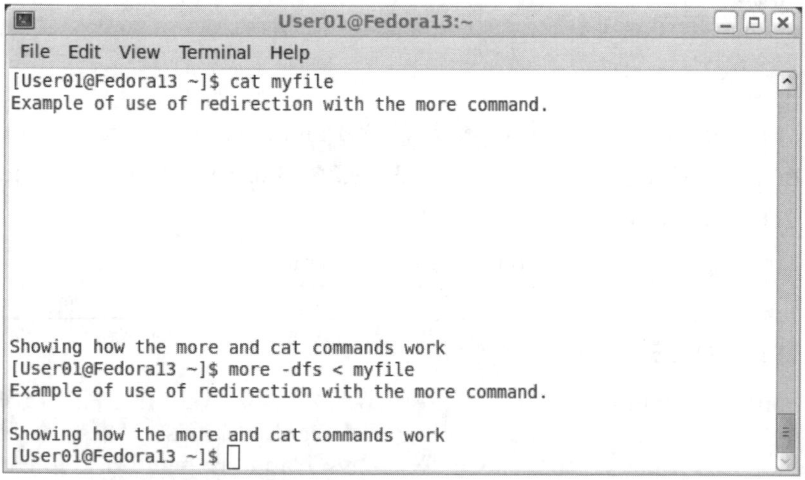

```
User01@Fedora13:~
File  Edit  View  Terminal  Help
[User01@Fedora13 ~]$ cat myfile
Example of use of redirection with the more command.




Showing how the more and cat commands work
[User01@Fedora13 ~]$ more -dfs < myfile
Example of use of redirection with the more command.

Showing how the more and cat commands work
[User01@Fedora13 ~]$ []
```

Figure 7-7 Using the Fedora 13 more and cat commands

Source: Course Technology/Cengage Learning

For example, you can type the following command to display the contents of myfile:

```
cat myfile
more -dfs myfile
```

The results are shown in Figure 7-7.

Activity 7-2: Viewing Files in Fedora 13

Time Required: 15 minutes

Objective: Use the more, file, and cat commands to view information about a file and its contents.

Description: In this activity, you display information about a file. This activity is useful if you need to view file information.

The Fedora 13 activities in this chapter require the script files that are available at *www.cengage.com.* For further details, see the appendix for your virtualization software.

1. Start your virtual machines using the appropriate instructions in Activity 1-1. To open a Terminal console, click **Applications**, point to **System Tools**, and then click **Terminal**.

2. To create the directory structure with the **makeHRS** script, type **cd /usr/local/bin**, press **Enter**, type **sh makeHRS** at the prompt, and then press **Enter**.

Contact your instructor if you see the following message: "makeHRS is not recognized as an internal or external command, operable program or batch file."

3. To display the file type of file001, type **file file001** and then press **Enter**.

Contact your instructor if you see the following message: "file001 is not an ASCII file."

4. To display the contents of file001, type **cat file001** and then press **Enter**.

5. To verify that file002 appears, type **more < Level2/file002** and then press **Enter**.

6. Close the Terminal console.

7. Leave the virtual machine logged on for future activities.

Using File Attributes

Windows 7 maintains certain attributes that are associated with every file. **File attributes** are restrictive labels attached to a file that describe and regulate its use. These attributes are mostly maintained by various components of Windows 7 and are handled automatically, so you can use Windows 7 without manipulating attributes. However, manipulating some file attributes is not difficult, and can be useful at times. The following sections explain common techniques associated with file attributes.

Using File Attributes in the Windows 7 CLI

Every file in DOS has four attributes. Each file has an entry in the directory, and the entry has four bits, one for each of the four attributes. These attributes are turned on if the bit is set to 1 and turned off if the bit is set to 0.

The four DOS file attributes are:

- **Read-only**—When set, you can read the contents of a file, but you cannot modify it.
- **Archive**—The archive bit is set to on when a file is created and then set to off when it is backed up. If the file is modified, the archive bit is turned back on so that the backup software can look at the archive bit on each file and determine if it needs to be backed up.
- **System**—The system attribute marks a file as a system file that is used only by the operating system.
- **Hidden**—The hidden attribute prevents a file from being seen by other commands. By default, the DIR command does not list files when the hidden attribute is set to on.

Viewing DOS File Attributes You can use the **ATTRIB** command to view DOS file attributes and determine how to access a particular file. The ATTRIB command has the following syntax when you display file attributes:

ATTRIB [drive:] [path] [filename] [/S]

[drive:] [path] [filename]   Specifies a file or files for ATTRIB to process

/S   Processes matching files in the current folder and all subfolders

The syntax of the ATTRIB command is similar to that of the DIR command, which you learned about in Chapter 4. For example, to view the attributes of the \Users\User01\Documents directories, you would type:

ATTRIB /S C:\Users\User01\Documents*.*

Because the ATTRIB command processes matching files, you must use the wildcard characters. Without them, no files will match. Figure 7-8 shows a sample file in the Documents folder.

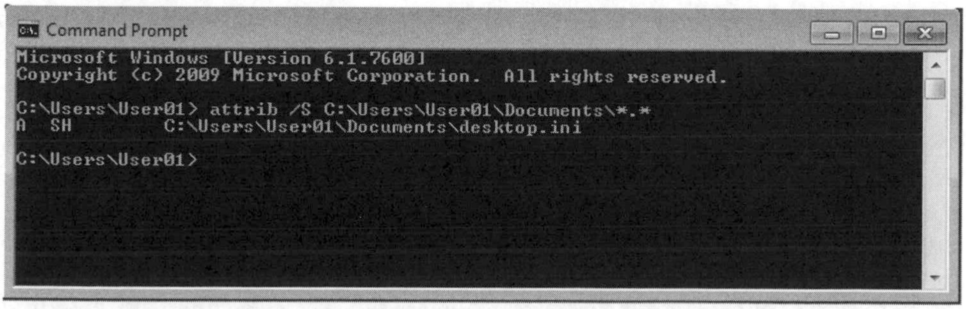

Figure 7-8 Viewing DOS file attributes

Source: Course Technology/Cengage Learning

Activity 7-3: Viewing DOS File Attributes

Time Required: 15 minutes

Objective: Display DOS file attributes in the Windows 7 CLI.

Description: In this activity, you open the command prompt, access the example files and directories you need to perform the chapter activities, and view the file attributes for two directory structures. This activity is useful if you want to view file attributes on a hard drive.

1. If necessary, start your virtual machines using the appropriate instructions in Activity 1-1.

2. Click **Start**, point to **All Programs**, click **Accessories**, and then click **Command Prompt**.

3. To create the example directories and files with attributes, type **MakeHRS** at the command prompt and then press **Enter**.

Contact your instructor if you see the following message: "MakeHRS is not recognized as an internal or external command, operable program or batch file."

4. To go to the folder for example files, type **CD /D E:\User01** and press **Enter**.

The /D switch for the CD command allows the drive letter to be set with the directory.

5. To view the file attributes at Level1, type **ATTRIB Level1*.*** and then press **Enter**.

6. Verify that nine files are listed.

7. To view the file attributes at Level2, type **ATTRIB Level1\Level2*.*.** and then press **Enter**.

8. Verify that 12 files are listed.

9. To go to a new location, type **CD \User01\Level1** and then press **Enter**.

10. To attempt to view information about an individual file, type **DIR File007.txt** and then press **Enter**.

11. Verify that you received a *File Not Found* message for the hidden file.

12. To view the attributes for an individual file, type **ATTRIB File007.txt** and then press **Enter**.

13. Verify that you received information for the hidden file.

14. To exit the command prompt, type **EXIT** and then press **Enter**.

15. Leave the virtual machine logged on for the next activity.

Setting DOS File Attributes You can use the ATTRIB command to display or change DOS file attributes. For example, you might need to reset a file attribute when working with a file. When setting the file attributes, the ATTRIB command has the following syntax:

```
ATTRIB [+R | -R] [+A | -A] [+S | -S] [+H | -H] [drive:] [path] [filename]
[/S [/D]]
```

+	Sets an attribute
-	Clears an attribute
R	Read-only file attribute
A	Archive file attribute
S	System file attribute
H	Hidden file attribute
[drive:] [path] [filename]	Specifies a file or files for ATTRIB to process
/S	Processes matching files in the current folder and all subfolders
/D	Processes folders as well as files

You can use wildcard characters with the filename parameter to change the attributes for a group of files. If a file's system or hidden attribute is set, you must clear it before you can change any other file attributes.

You can also set the file attributes on a directory. For example, to hide a directory named Secret, you would type:

ATTRIB +H Secret

When you list the directory using the DIR command, the contents of the directory entry are listed, but not the individual directory. Figure 7-9 shows the effect of hiding a directory; the Secret folder is missing from the list.

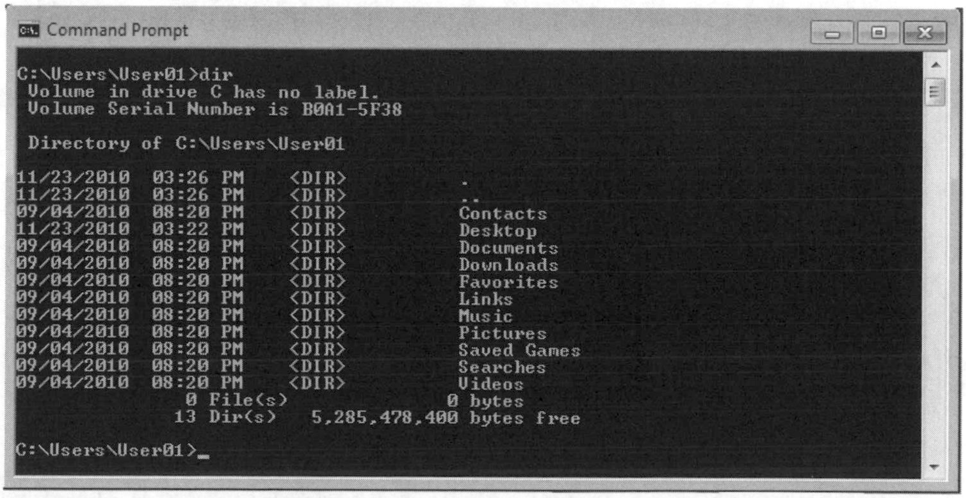

Figure 7-9 Effect of hiding a directory

Source: Course Technology/Cengage Learning

Activity 7-4: Setting DOS File Attributes

Time Required: 15 minutes

Objective: Set DOS file attributes in the Windows 7 CLI.

Description: In this activity, you open the command prompt and set the file attributes for files on two directory structures. This activity is useful if you want to set the file attributes on a hard drive.

1. If necessary, start your virtual machines using the appropriate instructions in Activity 1-1.

2. Click **Start**, point to **All Programs**, click **Accessories**, and then click **Command Prompt**.

3. If necessary, create the example directories and files with attributes by typing **MakeHRS** at the command prompt and pressing **Enter**.

4. To go to the example files at Level1, type **CD /D E:\User01\Level1** and then press **Enter**.

5. To view the file attributes, type **ATTRIB** and then press **Enter**.

6. Verify that nine files are listed.

7. To set the archive attribute for all nine files, type **ATTRIB +A** and then press **Enter**.

8. Verify that you could not set the archive attribute for six hidden files.

9. To set the archive attribute and remove the hidden attribute for all nine files, type **ATTRIB +A -H** and then press **Enter**.

10. To view the file attributes, type **ATTRIB** and then press **Enter**.

11. Verify that nine files have the archive attribute set and that four files have the read-only attribute set.

12. To set the hidden and system attributes for a single file, type **ATTRIB +H +S File007.txt** and then press **Enter**.

13. To view the attributes for an individual file, type **ATTRIB File007.txt** and then press **Enter**.

14. Verify that you saw A, S, and H for the hidden file.

15. To exit the command prompt, type **EXIT** and then press **Enter**.

16. Leave the virtual machine logged on for the next activity.

Using the `DIR` Command with File Attributes

You can use the `DIR` command when you want to view filenames with specified DOS file attributes. When using the DOS file attributes, the `DIR` command has the following syntax:

`DIR [drive:] [path] [filename] [/A[[:]attributes]]`

`[drive:] [path] [filename]`	Specifies the drive, directory, and files to list
`/A`	Displays files with specified attributes
`attributes`	D is for directories, R is for read-only files, H is for hidden files, A is for files ready for archiving, S is for system files, and "-" is a prefix meaning *not*

```
Command Prompt                                                    ─  □  ✕

C:\Users\User01\Documents>DIR *.* /A:H
 Volume in drive C has no label.
 Volume Serial Number is B0A1-5F38

 Directory of C:\Users\User01\Documents

09/04/2010  08:20 PM               402 desktop.ini
09/04/2010  08:20 PM    <JUNCTION>     My Music [C:\Users\User01\Music]
09/04/2010  08:20 PM    <JUNCTION>     My Pictures [C:\Users\User01\Pictures]
09/04/2010  08:20 PM    <JUNCTION>     My Videos [C:\Users\User01\Videos]
11/23/2010  03:38 PM                 7 SampleDocument.rtf
11/23/2010  03:39 PM                 0 SampleFile.txt
11/23/2010  03:34 PM    <DIR>          Secret
               3 File(s)            409 bytes
               4 Dir(s)    5,201,203,200 bytes free

C:\Users\User01\Documents>_
```

Figure 7-10 Files selected by file attribute

Source: Course Technology/Cengage Learning

Figure 7-10 shows files with the hidden file attribute.

Activity 7-5: Using `DIR` with DOS File Attributes

Time Required: 15 minutes

Objective: Use the `DIR` command with DOS file attributes in the Windows 7 CLI.

Description: In this activity, you open the command prompt and view file information while selecting files with DOS file attributes. This activity is useful if you want to view hidden or system files on a hard drive.

1. If necessary, start your virtual machines using the appropriate instructions in Activity 1-1. Click **Start,** point to **All Programs,** click **Accessories,** and then click **Command Prompt.**

2. To refresh the example directories and files with attributes, type **MakeHRS** at the command prompt and then press **Enter.**

3. To view the hidden files at Level1, type **DIR /AH Level1** and then press **Enter.**

4. Verify that six files are listed.

5. To view the read-only files at Level1 and Level2, type **DIR /S /AR Level1** and press **Enter.**

6. Verify that 10 files are listed.

7. To view the system files at Level1 and Level2, type **DIR /S /AS Level1** and press **Enter.**

8. Verify that three files are listed.

9. To view the hidden system files at Level1 and Level2, type **DIR /S /AHS Level1** and then press **Enter.**

10. Verify that two files are listed.

11. To exit the command prompt, type **EXIT** and then press **Enter**.

12. Leave the virtual machine logged on for the next activity.

Using the XCOPY Command with File Attributes

You can use the XCOPY command with DOS file attributes. This command is useful when you want to copy filenames with specified file attributes. When using the XCOPY command with DOS file attributes, the command has the following syntax:

XCOPY source [destination] [/A | /M] [/H] [/R] [/K]

source	Specifies the file(s) to copy
destination	Specifies the location and/or name of new files
/A	Copies only files with the archive attribute set; doesn't change the attribute
/M	Copies only files with the archive attribute set; turns off the archive attribute
/H	Copies hidden and system files
/R	Overwrites read-only files
/K	Copies attributes; normally, XCOPY resets read-only attributes

Figure 7-11 shows files with the hidden file attribute that are copied by the XCOPY command. You can copy selected files that need to be backed up by using the /A or /M switch.

Remember that commands are not case sensitive in Windows 7. For example, the XCOPY command is shown in uppercase in Figure 7-11, but you can also use lowercase.

When you use the /A switch, the system copies only files with the archive attribute set. The archive attribute is not reset. This is called a differential backup because the system backs up everything that has changed since the last full backup.

As with the /A switch, when you use the /M switch, the XCOPY command copies only files with the archive attribute set. However, when you use the /M switch, the archive attribute

Figure 7-11 XCOPY command used with file attributes

Source: Course Technology/Cengage Learning

is reset. This is called an incremental backup because it only backs up files modified since the most recent backup.

Activity 7-6: Using XCOPY with DOS File Attributes

Time Required: 15 minutes

Objective: Use the XCOPY command with DOS file attributes in the Windows 7 CLI.

Description: In this activity, you open the command prompt and copy files while selecting them with DOS file attributes. This activity is useful if you want to copy files based on the settings of DOS file attributes.

1. If necessary, start your virtual machines using the appropriate instructions in Activity 1-1.

2. Click **Start,** point to **All Programs,** click **Accessories,** and then click **Command Prompt.**

3. To refresh the example directories and files with attributes, type **MakeHRS** at the command prompt and then press **Enter.**

4. To go to the example files, type **CD /D E:\User01** and then press **Enter.**

5. To create a new directory subordinate to Level1, type the following command and then press **Enter:**

   MD E:\User01\Level1\Level2a

6. To copy the hidden files from Level2 to Level2a, type the following command and press **Enter:**

   XCOPY /H Level1\Level2*.* Level1\Level2a

7. Verify that 12 files are copied.

8. To copy the read-only files from Level2 to Level1, type the following command and then press **Enter:**

   XCOPY /R Level1\Level2 Level1

9. When the message "Overwrite E:\User01\Level1\File001.txt (Yes/No/All)?" appears, press the **A** key.

10. Verify that three files are copied.

11. To exit the command prompt, type **EXIT** and then press **Enter.**

12. Leave the virtual machine logged on for the next activity.

Using File Attributes in the Windows 7 GUI

In addition to the previously listed DOS attributes, Windows 7 offers the following attributes:

- **Index**—When set, the folder or file is indexed by the Windows Indexing Service on an NTFS volume. The Indexing Service extracts information from a set of documents and organizes it for easy access through the Windows 7 Search function. After the index is created, you can query it for documents that contain key words or phrases.

- **Compression**—When set, the folder or file is compressed on an NTFS volume.

- **Encryption**—When set, the folder or file is encrypted on an NTFS volume.

The compression and encryption attributes for disk files are mutually exclusive. For example, you must uncompress a compressed disk file before it can be encrypted.

These options appear as check boxes in the Advanced Attributes dialog box, as shown in Figure 7-12. See Activity 7-7 for directions on accessing this dialog box.

Compression and encryption are described in more detail in the following sections.

Figure 7-12 Windows 7 advanced file attributes

Source: Course Technology/Cengage Learning

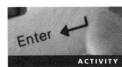

Activity 7-7: Viewing the Windows 7 File Attributes

Time Required: 15 minutes

Objective: View the attributes for files in the Windows 7 GUI.

Description: In this activity, you open Windows Explorer and view the Windows 7 attributes for a file. This activity is useful if you want to view file attributes using the properties dialog box.

1. If necessary, start your virtual machines using the appropriate instructions in Activity 1-1. Click **Start**, point to **All Programs**, click **Accessories**, and then click **Command Prompt**.

2. To refresh the example directories and files with attributes, type **MakeHRS** at the command prompt and press **Enter**.

3. To exit the command prompt, type **EXIT** and then press **Enter**.

4. Click **Start**, point to **All Programs**, click **Accessories**, and then click **Windows Explorer**.

5. To go to the folder that contains the example directory structure, expand **Computer**, expand **NTFS(E:)**, and then click the **User01** folder.

6. To go to the Level1 folder, double-click the **Level1** folder in the right pane.

7. To view the file attributes for File001, right-click the **File001** file and then click **Properties**.

8. Verify that the **Read-only** and **Hidden** check boxes are unchecked.

9. Click the **Advanced** button.

10. Verify that the **File is ready for archiving** check box is checked.

11. Click **Cancel** twice.

12. In Windows Explorer, click the **Organize** menu, click **Folder and Search Options**, click the **View** tab, click the **Show hidden files, folders and drives** option button, and then click **OK**.

13. To view the file attributes for File005, right-click the **File005** file and then click **Properties**.

14. Verify that the **Read-only** and **Hidden** check boxes are checked.

15. Click the **Advanced** button.

16. Verify that the **File is ready for archiving** check box is checked.

17. Click **Cancel** twice.

18. Close Windows Explorer.

19. Leave the virtual machine logged on for future activities.

7

Using Compression in Windows 7 Compressing files decreases their size and reduces the amount of space they use on your drives. Folder compression decreases the amount of space used by all of the files stored within a folder. Note that some files do not work as expected when compressed.

Windows 7 includes a Zip compression utility (similar to WinZip) that you can use to compress files on your hard disk. This utility uses different techniques than the file compression attribute.

Activity 7-8: Compressing Files in Windows 7

Time Required: 15 minutes

Objective: Compress the files in a folder in the Windows 7 GUI.

Description: In this activity, you open Windows Explorer and compress files. This activity is useful if you want to save space on your hard drive.

1. If necessary, start your virtual machines using the appropriate instructions in Activity 1-1. Click **Start,** point to **All Programs,** click **Accessories,** and then click **Command Prompt**.

2. To refresh the example directories and files with attributes, type **MakeHRS** at the command prompt and then press **Enter**.

3. To exit the command prompt, type **EXIT** and then press **Enter**.

4. Click **Start,** point to **All Programs,** click **Accessories,** and then click **Windows Explorer**.

5. To go to the folder that contains the example directory structure, expand **Computer,** expand **NTFS(E:),** and then click the **User01** folder.

6. To view the advanced properties for the Level1 folder, right-click the **Level1** folder and then click **Properties**.

7. Click the **Advanced** button, check the **Compress contents to save disk space** check box, click **OK,** and then click **Apply.**

8. Do not change the option to apply changes to this folder, subfolders, and files. Click **OK** twice.

9. Click the **Level1** folder.

10. Verify that the file descriptions have changed to blue from black.

11. Close Windows Explorer.

12. Leave the virtual machine logged on for the next activity.

Using Encryption in Windows 7 Encryption is provided by the **Encrypting File System (EFS),** which is installed automatically in Windows 7. Encryption prohibits unauthorized users from viewing the contents of files. Only the user who encrypted the file or an administrator can decrypt encrypted files. The administrator account is called a recovery agent because it has a global key that can decrypt any files.

The compression and encryption attributes are mutually exclusive. For example, if disk files are compressed, they must be uncompressed before encryption.

Activity 7-9: Encrypting Files in Windows 7

Time Required: 15 minutes

Objective: Encrypt the files in a folder in the Windows 7 GUI.

Description: In this activity, you open Windows Explorer and encrypt files within the directory structure. This activity is useful if you want to protect the contents of data files.

1. If necessary, start your virtual machines using the appropriate instructions in Activity 1-1.

2. Click **Start,** point to **All Programs,** click **Accessories,** and then click **Command Prompt.**

3. To refresh the example directories and files with attributes, type **MakeHRS** at the command prompt and then press **Enter.**

4. To exit the command prompt, type **EXIT** and then press **Enter.**

5. Click **Start,** point to **All Programs,** click **Accessories,** and then click **Windows Explorer.**

6. To go to the folder that contains the example directory structure, expand **Computer,** expand **NTFS(E:),** and then click the **User01** folder.

7. Click the **Level1** folder in the right pane.

8. To view the advanced properties for the Level1 folder, right-click the **Level1** folder and then click **Properties.**

9. Click the **Advanced** button, check the **Encrypt contents to secure data** check box, click **OK,** and then click **Apply.**

10. Do not change the option to apply changes to this folder, subfolders, and files. Click **OK.**

11. Read the message about having to provide administrator permission to change the attributes, click the **Continue** button, type **P@ssw0rd,** and then click **Yes.**

12. When the Error Applying Attributes dialog box appears, click **Ignore All** and then click **OK**.

13. Click the **Level1** folder.

14. Verify that the file descriptions have changed to green from black.

15. Click the **Level2** folder.

16. Verify that all the file descriptions have changed to green from black except for File010.

17. Close Windows Explorer.

18. Leave the virtual machine logged on for future activities.

Using File Attributes in Fedora 13

Like Windows 7, the file systems in Fedora 13 have file attributes. You will review them in this section. You use the `lsattr` utility to list file attributes.

Using the `lsattr` Command to View Fedora 13 File Attributes
You can view the file attributes on a Fedora 13 extended file system using the `lsattr` command. You can only set these attributes on directories and regular files:

a ("no Access time")—When you access a file or directory that has this attribute, either for reading or writing, its last access time is not updated.

A ("append only")—If this attribute is set for a file and it is open for writing, the only operation you can perform is to append data to the previous contents. If this attribute is set for a directory, you can only add files to it; you cannot rename or delete an existing file.

d ("no dump")—Dump is the standard utility for backups. When a dump is in progress, files or directories that have this attribute are not taken into account.

i ("immutable")—You cannot modify a file or directory that has this attribute.

s ("secure deletion")—When you delete a file or directory that has this attribute, the blocks it occupied on the disk are overwritten with zeroes.

S ("Synchronous mode")—When a file or directory has this attribute, all modifications are synchronous and are written to the disk immediately.

The syntax and options for the `lsattr` command are:

`lsattr [options] [file(s)]`

-R Recursively lists attributes of directories and their contents

-V Displays the program version

-a Lists all files in directories, including files that start with '.'

-d Lists directories like other files, rather than listing their contents

-v Lists the file's version/generation number

To display the attributes of files in a directory, you would type:

`lsattr`

The results are shown in Figure 7-13. The e attribute indicates that the file is using extents to map the blocks on the hard drive. You type the lsattr command using a lowercase letter *l*, not the number *1*.

```
┌──────────────────────────────────────────────────────┐
│  ▣            User01@Fedora13:~          ─ ▢ ⊗         │
│  File  Edit  View  Terminal  Help                      │
│ [User01@Fedora13 ~]$ lsattr                       ▲   │
│ ------------e- ./trash.tar.gz                          │
│ ------------e- ./Desktop                               │
│ ------------e- ./Downloads                             │
│ ------------e- ./Videos                                │
│ ------------e- ./Templates                             │
│ ------------e- ./Documents                             │
│ ------------e- ./Public                                │
│ ------------e- ./Music                                 │
│ ------------e- ./Pictures                              │
│ su----d------e- ./myfile                               │
│ [User01@Fedora13 ~]$ █                            ▼   │
└──────────────────────────────────────────────────────┘
```

Figure 7-13 Using the Fedora 13 lsattr command

Source: Course Technology/Cengage Learning

Using the ls Command to Find Hidden Files
You can use the ls command to view filenames with specified Fedora 13 file type attributes. The ls command has the following syntax:

ls [OPTION]... [FILE]...

-a, --all   Does not hide entries starting with "." (hidden files)

-l   Uses a long listing format

-p, --file-type   Appends an indicator of /, =, @, or | to entries to indicate types of files

The results of entering the following command are shown in Figure 7-14.

ls –lpa | more

```
┌──────────────────────────────────────────────────────┐
│  ▣            User01@Fedora13:~          ─ ▢ ⊗         │
│  File  Edit  View  Terminal  Help                      │
│ [User01@Fedora13 ~]$ ls -lpa |more               ▲   │
│ total 168                                              │
│ drwx------. 24 User01 User01 4096 Nov 16 17:57 ./      │
│ drwxr-xr-x.  3 root   root   4096 Aug 29 18:32 ../     │
│ -rw------.   1 User01 User01 3424 Nov 16 17:45 .bash_history │
│ -rw-r--r--.  1 User01 User01   18 Mar 31  2010 .bash_logout  │
│ -rw-r--r--.  1 User01 User01  176 Mar 31  2010 .bash_profile │
│ -rw-r--r--.  1 User01 User01  124 Mar 31  2010 .bashrc  │
│ drwxr-xr-x.  2 User01 User01 4096 Aug 29 18:34 .cache/ │
│ drwxr-xr-x.  6 User01 User01 4096 Aug 29 18:34 .config/│
│ drwx------.  3 User01 User01 4096 Aug 29 18:34 .dbus/  │
│ drwxr-xr-x.  2 User01 User01 4096 Aug 29 18:50 Desktop/│
│ -rw-r--r--.  1 User01 User01   41 Nov 16 15:07 .dmrc   │
│ drwxr-xr-x.  2 User01 User01 4096 Aug 29 18:34 Documents/ ▼ │
└──────────────────────────────────────────────────────┘
```

Figure 7-14 Using the Fedora 13 ls command to show hidden files and file types

Source: Course Technology/Cengage Learning

Activity 7-10: Using `ls` and `lsattr` with Fedora 13 File Attributes

Time Required: 15 minutes

Objective: Use the `ls` and `lsattr` commands to find the hidden file attribute in the Fedora 13 CLI.

Description: In this activity, you open the command prompt and view file information while selecting files with the hidden file attribute. This activity is useful if you want to list hidden files on a hard drive. You will also list the Linux file attributes.

The Fedora 13 activities in this chapter require the script files that are available at *www.cengage.com*. For further details, see the appendix for your virtualization software.

1. If necessary, start your virtual machines using the appropriate instructions in Activity 1-1.
2. To open a Terminal console, click **Applications**, point to **System Tools**, and then click **Terminal**.
3. To create the directory structure with the makeABC script, type **cd /usr/local/bin**, press **Enter**, type **sh makeABC** at the prompt, and press **Enter**.

Contact your instructor if you see the following message: "makeABC is not recognized as an internal or external command, operable program or batch file."

4. To display the hidden files in the directory, type **ls -la** and then press **Enter**.
5. Verify that all the files in the directory appear, including the files preceded with a ".".
6. To display the attributes of the files in the directory, type **lsattr** and then press **Enter**.
7. Verify that all the files in the directory list their attributes.
8. To display the filename additions, further indicating the file types in the directory, type **ls -lpa /dev** and then press **Enter**.
9. Verify that all the files in the directory appear, including the filenames, further illustrating the file type.
10. Close the Terminal console.
11. Leave the virtual machine logged on for future activities.

Using Compression in Fedora 13

As in Windows 7, compressing files decreases their size and reduces the amount of space they use on your drives. Folder compression decreases the amount of space used by all of the files stored in a folder. Note that some files do not work as expected when compressed.

Zip compression utility extensions correspond with the file types listed in Table 7-5.

A commonly used GNU compression utility is gzip. GNU software is the largest single component of the Fedora 13 source code, and it includes some of the major components required by the system.

By default, gzip deletes the ASCII file it compresses, and the new file contains the default extension of .gz. To decompress files, you can use a utility called **gunzip**. The **gzip** command is the basis for gunzip and zcat; both utilities are simply links to gzip.

The **zcat** utility is identical to using the gunzip -c command. By default, gzip keeps the original filename and stamp in the compressed file.

The commands have the following syntax:

```
gzip [ -acdfhlLnNrtvV19 ] [-S suffix] [ filename ... ]
gunzip [ -acfhlLnNrtvV ] [-S suffix] [ filename ... ]
zcat [ -fhLV ] [ filename ... ]
```

You can use the following switches with the preceding commands:

-a --ascii	In ASCII text mode, use this switch to convert end-of-line characters across operating system platforms using local conventions. This option is supported only on some non-UNIX systems. For MS-DOS, the CR LF character is converted to LF when compressing, and LF is converted to CR LF when decompressing. This conversion is crucial to ensuring cross-platform ASCII text compatibility.
-c --stdout --to-stdout	Writes output to standard output and keeps the original files unchanged. If there are several input files, gzip concatenates them before compressing to achieve the best compression.
-d --decompress --uncompress	Decompresses a file.
-f --force	Forces compression or decompression even if the file has multiple links, the corresponding file already exists, or the compressed data is read from or written to a terminal.
-h --help	Displays a help screen and quits.
-l --list	Lists information about the files and the compression; used in conjunction with the verbose and name switches.
-L --license	Displays the license and quits.
-n --no-name	When compressing, does not save the original filename and time stamp. This option is the default when decompressing.
-N --name	When compressing, always saves the original filename and time stamp; this is the default setting. When

	decompressing, restores the original filename and time stamp if present. This option is useful on systems that have a limit on filename lengths and when the time stamp has been lost after a file transfer.
`-q –quiet`	Suppresses all warnings.
`-r –recursive`	Traverses a directory structure recursively. If a directory is specified on the command line, gzip will compress all the files in it. If you are using the `gunzip` command, this switch decompresses the files in the specified directory.
`-S .suf --suffix .suf`	Applies the suffix .suf instead of .gz to the compressed file. You can use any suffix, but you should avoid suffixes other than .z and .gz to avoid confusion when files are transferred to other systems.
`-t –test`	Checks the compressed file's integrity.
`-v –verbose`	Displays the name and percentage reduction for each compressed or decompressed file.
`-V –version`	Displays the version number and compilation options, then quits.
`-# --fast –best`	Regulates the speed of compression; `-1` or `--fast` creates the fastest and least compression, and `-9` or `--best` creates the slowest and best compression. The default setting is `-6`.

To compress a file using the `gzip` command, you would type:

`gzip myfile`

The results are shown in Figure 7-15.

The gzip utility also decompresses files created by the gzip and zip utilities.

To decompress a file using the `gzip` command, you would type:

`gzip –d myfile`

The results are shown in Figure 7-16.
The gunzip utility decompresses files created by the gzip, zip, and compress utilities. The utility automatically detects the input format.

To decompress a file using the `gunzip` command, you would type:

`gunzip myfile`

The results are shown in Figure 7-17.

The zcat utility decompresses files created by gzip, zip, and compress, and sends the results to standard output. The utility automatically detects the input format. The compressed file is only decompressed for the display.

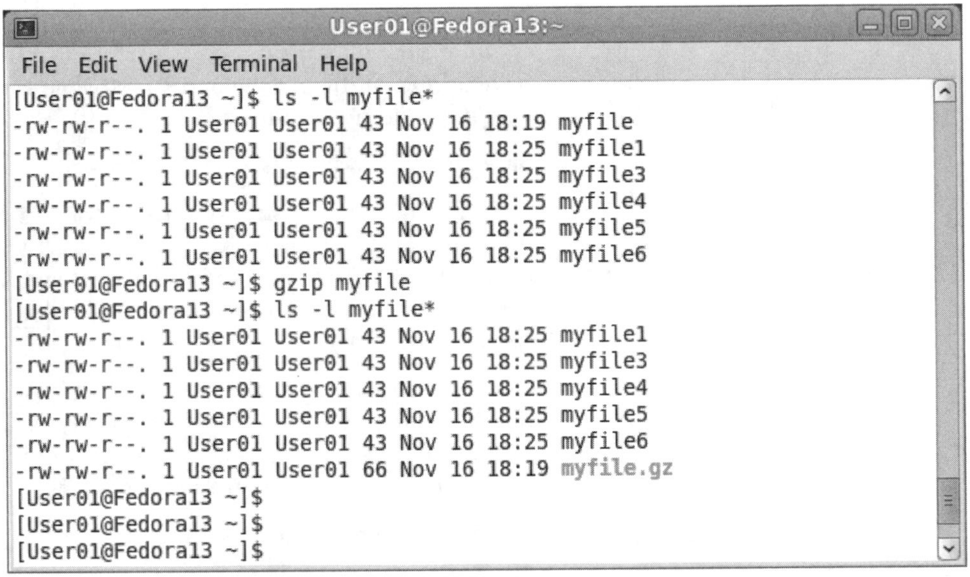

Figure 7-15 Using the Fedora 13 `gzip` command to compress files

Source: Course Technology/Cengage Learning

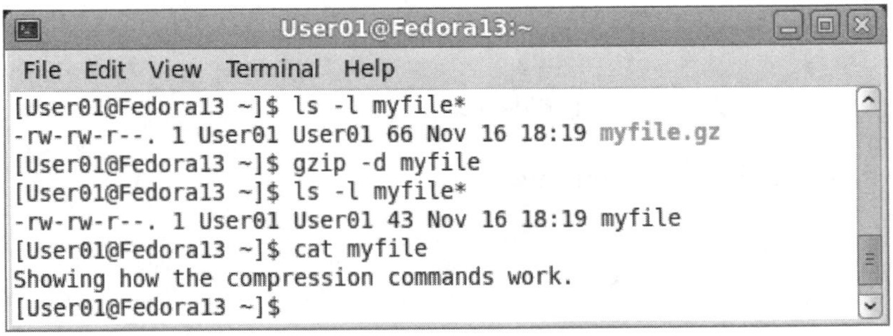

Figure 7-16 Using the Fedora 13 `gzip` command to decompress files

Source: Course Technology/Cengage Learning

To decompress a file and display its contents in ASCII form to standard output using the zcat command, you would type:

zcat myfile

The results are shown in Figure 7-18.

Compression is often used in conjunction with archiving utilities. One such utility is **tar**, which works in conjunction with gzip to package multiple files into one file.

The tar command has the following syntax:

tar [flags] archive-file-name files-to-archive

```
User01@Fedora13:~
File  Edit  View  Terminal  Help
[User01@Fedora13 ~]$ ls -l
total 56
drwxr-xr-x. 2 User01 User01 4096 Aug 29 18:50 Desktop
drwxr-xr-x. 2 User01 User01 4096 Aug 29 18:34 Documents
drwxr-xr-x. 2 User01 User01 4096 Aug 29 18:34 Downloads
drwxr-xr-x. 2 User01 User01 4096 Aug 29 18:34 Music
-rw-rw-r--. 1 User01 User01   43 Nov 16 18:25 myfile1
-rw-rw-r--. 1 User01 User01   43 Nov 16 18:25 myfile3
-rw-rw-r--. 1 User01 User01   43 Nov 16 18:25 myfile4
-rw-rw-r--. 1 User01 User01   43 Nov 16 18:25 myfile5
-rw-rw-r--. 1 User01 User01   43 Nov 16 18:25 myfile6
-rw-rw-r--. 1 User01 User01   66 Nov 16 18:19 myfile.gz
drwxr-xr-x. 2 User01 User01 4096 Aug 29 18:34 Pictures
drwxr-xr-x. 2 User01 User01 4096 Aug 29 18:34 Public
drwxr-xr-x. 2 User01 User01 4096 Aug 29 18:34 Templates
drwxr-xr-x. 2 User01 User01 4096 Aug 29 18:34 Videos
[User01@Fedora13 ~]$ gunzip myfile
[User01@Fedora13 ~]$ ls -l myfile*
-rw-rw-r--. 1 User01 User01 43 Nov 16 18:19 myfile
-rw-rw-r--. 1 User01 User01 43 Nov 16 18:25 myfile1
-rw-rw-r--. 1 User01 User01 43 Nov 16 18:25 myfile3
-rw-rw-r--. 1 User01 User01 43 Nov 16 18:25 myfile4
-rw-rw-r--. 1 User01 User01 43 Nov 16 18:25 myfile5
-rw-rw-r--. 1 User01 User01 43 Nov 16 18:25 myfile6
[User01@Fedora13 ~]$
```

Figure 7-17 Using the Fedora 13 `gunzip` command to decompress files

Source: Course Technology/Cengage Learning

```
User01@Fedora13:~
File  Edit  View  Terminal  Help
[User01@Fedora13 ~]$ ls -l myfile*
-rw-rw-r--. 1 User01 User01 66 Nov 16 18:19 myfile.gz
[User01@Fedora13 ~]$ zcat myfile
Showing how the compression commands work.
[User01@Fedora13 ~]$ ls -l myfile*
-rw-rw-r--. 1 User01 User01 66 Nov 16 18:19 myfile.gz
[User01@Fedora13 ~]$
```

Figure 7-18 Using the Fedora 13 `zcat` command

Source: Course Technology/Cengage Learning

You must use one of the following options with the `tar` command:

`-A, --catenate, --concatenate`	Appends tar files to an archive
`-c, --create`	Creates a new archive
`-d, --diff, --compare`	Finds differences between the archive and file system
`--delete`	Deletes files from the archive (do not use this command on magnetic tapes!)

-r, --append	Appends files to the end of an archive
-t, --list	Lists the contents of an archive
-u, --update	Only appends files that are updated versions of the copy in the archive
-x, --extract, --get	Extracts files from an archive
-f, --file [HOSTNAME:]F	Uses archive file or device F (the default is "-", which means standard input/output)
--recursion	Recurses into directories (the default)
-v, --verbose	Verbosely lists files processed
-z, --gzip, --gunzip, --ungzip	Filters the archive through gzip

The tar utility is used mainly for backups, and needs many different types of filters. Other options for filtering were omitted from the preceding list for the sake of simplicity.

For example, if you enter `gzip myfile.tar` at the command line, you create a file named myfile.tar.gz. If you enter `tar czvf myfile1.tgz myfile1` at the command line, you create a file named myfile1.tgz (see Figure 7-19).

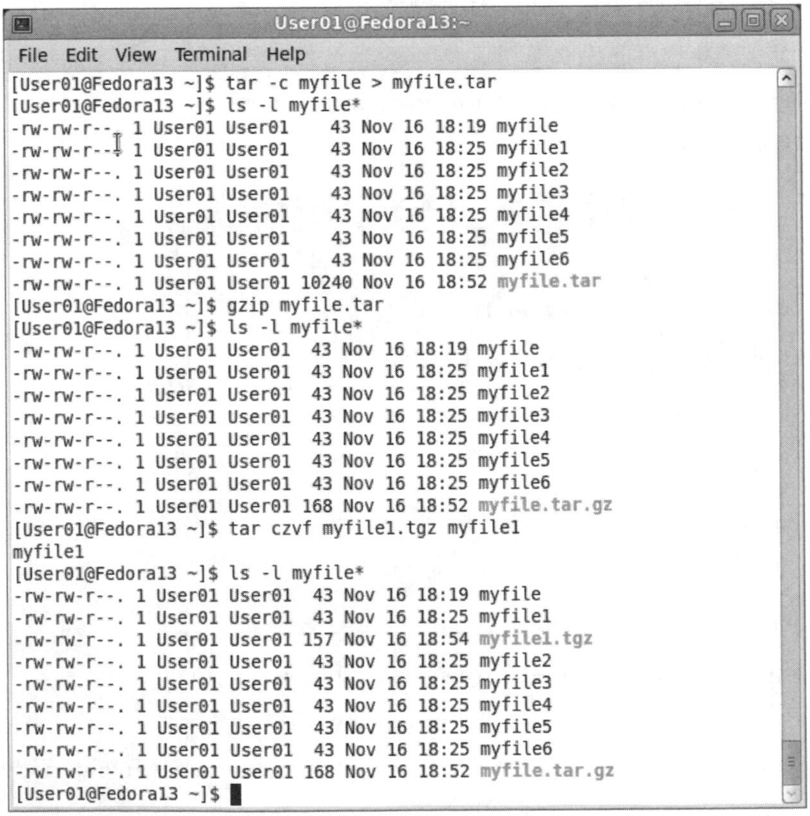

Figure 7-19 Using the Fedora 13 `tar` command with gzip compression

Source: Course Technology/Cengage Learning

Activity 7-11: Compressing Files in Fedora 13

Time Required: 15 minutes

Objective: Use the `gzip`, `gunzip`, and `zcat` utilities to compress and decompress files.

Description: In this activity, you will use several utilities to compress and decompress files. This activity is useful if you need to compress files before transmitting them or to save space on your hard drive.

The Fedora 13 activities in this chapter require the script files that are available at *www.cengage.com*. For further details, see the appendix for your virtualization software.

1. If necessary, start your virtual machines using the appropriate instructions in Activity 1-1.
2. To open a Terminal console, click **Applications**, point to **System Tools**, and then click **Terminal**.
3. To create the directory structure with the **makeQUOTE** script, type **cd /usr/local/bin**, press **Enter**, type **sh makeQUOTE** at the prompt, and press **Enter**.

Contact your instructor if you see the following message: "makeQUOTE is not recognized as an internal or external command, operable program or batch file."

4. Type **ls -l Quote0012**, press **Enter**, and note the file size.
5. Type **gzip Quote0012** and press **Enter**.
6. Type **ls -l Quote0012***, press **Enter**, and note the difference in file size.
7. Type **gunzip Quote0012** and press **Enter**.
8. Type **ls -l Quote0012***, press **Enter**, and note the difference in file name and size.
9. Type **cat Quote0012**, press **Enter**, and inspect the file contents displayed on the screen.
10. Type **gzip Quote0012** and press **Enter**.
11. Type **ls -l Quote0012*** and press **Enter**.
12. Type **zcat Quote0012**, press **Enter**, and inspect the file contents displayed on the screen.
13. Type **ls -l Quote0012***, press **Enter**, and inspect the output.
14. Close the Terminal console.
15. Leave the virtual machine logged on for future activities.

Using Encryption in Fedora 13

As with Windows 7, encryption in Fedora 13 prohibits other users from viewing the contents of files. Only the user who encrypted the file or an administrator can decrypt encrypted files.

Files must be encrypted and then compressed. Likewise, they must be uncompressed before decryption.

Entire file systems are designed for encryption, but the most popular encryption utility is gpg. If you encrypt an ASCII file, the extension is .asc; if you encrypt a binary file, the extension is .gpg.

The gpg command has the following syntax:

gpg [--homedir name] [--options file] [options] command [args]

-c	Encrypts with a symmetric cipher.
--decrypt [file]	Decrypts the file and writes it to standard output (or the file specified with --output).
-o, --output file	Writes output to a file.
-v, --verbose	Provides more information during processing. If used twice, the input data is listed in detail.
-q, --quiet	Limits the amount of detail displayed.
quit	Quits the program without updating the key rings.

If you forget your password or passphrase, you cannot recover the data, as it uses very strong encryption.

The gpg utility has many more switches, and is used with key exchange, encryption, signature validation, and trust relationships. These topics are beyond the scope of this text.

Finding Files

When working on your computer, you need to locate files quickly. For example, you might need to prepare a report for a class. You recall that you wrote a similar report last year, and you want to use its format for your new report. Unfortunately, you have 12,000 files on your hard drive, and you can't remember where you stored the report file. You think the filename contained the word *privacy* or *private*, but you're not sure.

The following sections help you find files quickly.

Finding Files in the Windows 7 CLI

The Windows 7 CLI includes commands that enable you to locate files quickly and efficiently. You can base your search on part of a filename or the contents of a file. When searching the contents of files, you can employ powerful pattern-matching techniques.

You can search for files using the DIR, FIND, and FINDSTR commands in the Windows 7 CLI, as described in the following sections.

Finding Files with the DIR Command Recall that the DIR command supports wildcards. You use two wildcard characters for searches: the question mark (?) and the asterisk (*, or star). Use the question mark to represent a single unknown character, and use the star to stand for multiple unknown characters. Use a period to extend the search to include all file extensions. Table 7-11 lists examples of multiple-character substitutions using the * wildcard.

Table 7-12 lists examples of single-character substitution using the ? wildcard.

Expression	Explanation
DIR *.cpp	Lists all files that have a .cpp extension in the current directory
DIR h*	Lists all filenames that begin with an *h* in the current directory
DIR h*.c*	Lists all filenames that begin with an *h* and have an extension that begins with a *c*
DIR *.*.	Lists all files in the current directory
DIR *.* /S .	Lists all files in the current and nested directories

Table 7-11   **Multiple-character substitutions for searches**

Expression	Explanation
DIR ?.cpp	Lists all filenames that contain one letter and have a .cpp extension in the current directory
DIR h??	Lists all filenames that begin with an *h* followed by one or two other letters (and that have no extension) in the current directory
DIR h?.c?	Lists all filenames that begin with an *h* followed by one other letter, and that have an extension beginning with a *c* followed by one other letter
DIR ???.*	Lists all filenames that contain one, two, or three letters in the current directory
DIR /S ???.*	Lists all filenames that contain one, two, or three letters in the current and nested directories

Table 7-12   **Single-character substitutions for searches**

In Figure 7-20, the DIR command is used with the *ab*.* string to find all files that start with the characters *ab* and have any extension.

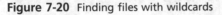

```
Command Prompt

E:\User01>dir ab*.*
 Volume in drive E is NTFS
 Volume Serial Number is 7E54-1074

 Directory of E:\User01

11/23/2010  03:57 PM                5 AB.txt
11/23/2010  03:57 PM                6 AB1.txt
11/23/2010  03:57 PM               11 ABBBBBBC.txt
11/23/2010  03:57 PM                7 ABBC.txt
11/23/2010  03:57 PM                8 AbbCC.txt
11/23/2010  03:57 PM                6 ABC.txt
              6 File(s)             43 bytes
              0 Dir(s)   1,039,253,504 bytes free

E:\User01>
```

Figure 7-20 Finding files with wildcards

Source: Course Technology/Cengage Learning

Activity 7-12: Finding Files with DIR and Wildcard Characters

Time Required: 15 minutes

Objective: Use the DIR command with wildcard characters in the Windows 7 CLI.

Description: In this activity, you open the command prompt and find files using wildcard characters. This activity is useful if you want to locate files when you know a portion of a filename.

1. If necessary, start your virtual machines using the appropriate instructions in Activity 1-1.

2. Click **Start**, point to **All Programs**, click **Accessories**, and then click **Command Prompt**.

3. To create the example files for the search activities, type **MakeABC** at the command prompt and then press **Enter**.

Contact your instructor if you see the following message: "MakeABC is not recognized as an internal or external command, operable program or batch file."

4. To view filenames that start with *ab*, type **DIR ab*.txt**, and then press **Enter**.

5. Verify that six files are listed.

6. To view filenames that contain a *b* as the third character, type **DIR ??b*.txt** and then press **Enter**.

7. Verify that four files are listed.

8. To view filenames that contain three characters, with *a* as the first character, type **DIR a??.txt** and then press **Enter**.

9. Verify that six files are listed.

10. To view filenames that contain 9 as the second character, type **DIR ?9*.txt** and then press **Enter**.

11. Verify that two files are listed.

12. Close the command prompt window.

13. Leave the virtual machine logged on for the next activity.

Finding Files with the FIND Command

Use the DOS **FIND** command to locate a specific text string in an ASCII file and then send the line that contains the information to the console or a file. This command is most useful for finding single-line data in lists; it reduces the list to a file that contains only the information you want to view.

When you are searching for files, the FIND command has the following syntax:

FIND [/V] [/C] [/N] [/I] string [[drive:] [path] filename [...]]

/V	Displays all lines that do not contain the specified string
/C	Displays only the count of lines that contain the string
/N	Displays line numbers with the displayed lines
/I	Ignores the case of characters when searching for the string
"string"	Specifies the text string to find
[drive:] [path] filename	Specifies a file or files to search

The text string for the search must be enclosed in quotation marks. The command is case sensitive unless used with the /I switch. The command finds the exact text as specified, so you can use it to search for partial words.

For example, to find files that contain *Good*, use the following command:

FIND /I "Good" *.*

The results are shown in Figure 7-21.

The greater-than and less-than signs (> and <) are used with the FIND command to redirect output and input. Recall that most DOS commands send their output to a standard output device or command prompt window. The > and < signs redirect the input or output to places other than the default standard output (the screen) or default standard input (the keyboard).

Use the > sign to redirect the output of a program. For example, consider the following command:

FIND /i "Good" *.* > dirfile

The output of the command is sent directly to the file named dirfile, overwriting anything that is already in the file. To append the redirected output to an existing file, use the "much greater than" operator (>>). If necessary, DOS creates the destination file.

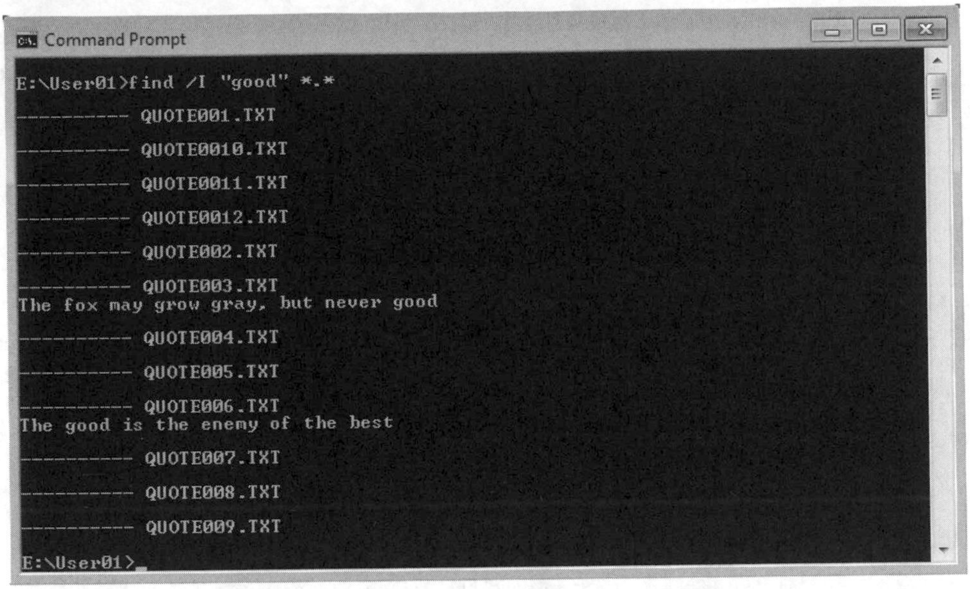

```
Command Prompt

E:\User01>find /I "good" *.*

----------- QUOTE001.TXT

----------- QUOTE0010.TXT

----------- QUOTE0011.TXT

----------- QUOTE0012.TXT

----------- QUOTE002.TXT

----------- QUOTE003.TXT
The fox may grow gray, but never good

----------- QUOTE004.TXT

----------- QUOTE005.TXT

----------- QUOTE006.TXT
The good is the enemy of the best

----------- QUOTE007.TXT

----------- QUOTE008.TXT

----------- QUOTE009.TXT

E:\User01>
```

Figure 7-21 Finding files based on content

Source: Course Technology/Cengage Learning

Use the < sign to redirect input to a command, and use the `more` command to view blocks of output one screen at a time. Thus, if the `DIR /s *.*` command produces a long list of files that scrolls off the screen, you could use the following commands:

DIR /s *.* > dirlist
MORE < dirlist

The first command creates a file called dirlist that contains the directory listing; the second command displays one screen of information, and then pauses by displaying the following line at the bottom of the screen:

- - More - -

You then press any key to see another screen of information. (You can do the same thing with the `DIR /P` command, but `MORE` has other uses.)

The redirection operators greatly enhance the flexibility of the `FIND` command. For example, the following command finds all lines that contain *Football* in a file named Winners.txt and stores the output in a file named FootballWinners.txt:

FIND /I "Football" <Winners.txt>FootballWinners.txt

Activity 7-13: Finding Files with the `FIND` Command

Time Required: 15 minutes

Objective: Use the `FIND` command to locate files by finding specified characters within the files in the Windows 7 CLI.

Description: In this activity, you open the command prompt and find files that contain specific characters. This activity is useful if you want to locate files when you know a word or part of a word contained in the files.

1. If necessary, start your virtual machines using the appropriate instructions in Activity 1-1.

2. Click **Start,** point to **All Programs,** click **Accessories,** and then click **Command Prompt.**

3. To refresh the example files for the search activities, type **MakeABC** at the command prompt and then press **Enter.**

4. To view the names of files that contain the case-sensitive characters *ab*, type **FIND "ab" *.*** and then press **Enter.**

5. Verify that two files are identified.

6. To view the names of files that contain the uppercase or lowercase characters *ab*, type **FIND /I "ab" *.*** and then press **Enter.**

7. Verify that seven files are identified.

8. To view the names of files that contain the case-sensitive characters *bbb*, type **FIND "bbb" *.*** and then press **Enter.**

9. Verify that no file is identified.

10. To view the names of files that contain the uppercase or lowercase characters *bbb*, type **FIND /I "bbb" *.*** and then press **Enter.**

11. Verify that one file is identified.

12. To view the names of files that contain the characters *123*, type **FIND "123" *.*** and then press **Enter.**

13. Verify that two files are identified.

14. To view the names of files that contain the uppercase or lowercase characters *bc*, type **FIND /I "bc" *.*** and then press **Enter.**

15. Verify that five files are identified.

16. Close the command prompt window.

17. Leave the virtual machine logged on for the next activity.

Finding Files with the FINDSTR Command

You may find the FINDSTR command more useful than the FIND command because it offers more control over the search process. When used to find text strings in files, the FINDSTR command has the following syntax:

```
FINDSTR [/B] [/E] [/L] [/R] [/S] [/I] [/X] [/V] [/N] [/M] [/O] [/P]
[/C:string] strings [[drive:] [path]filename[ ...]]
```

/B	Matches the pattern at the beginning of a line
/E	Matches the pattern at the end of a line
/L	Uses search strings literally
/R	Uses search strings as regular expressions

/S	Searches for matching files in the current directory and all subdirectories
/I	Specifies that the search is not case sensitive
/X	Prints lines that match exactly
/V	Prints only lines that do not contain a match
/N	Prints the line number before each line that matches
/M	Prints only the filename if a file contains a match
/O	Prints the character offset (the location of the character) before each matching line
/P	Skips files with nonprintable characters
/C:string	Uses a specified string as a literal search string
"Strings"	Specifies the text to search for
[drive:] [path] filename	Specifies a file or files to search

For example, to find files that contain *good* or *fool*, use the following command:

FINDSTR /I "good fool" *.*

The results are shown in Figure 7-22.

Table 7-13 shows more examples of using the FINDSTR command to find files.

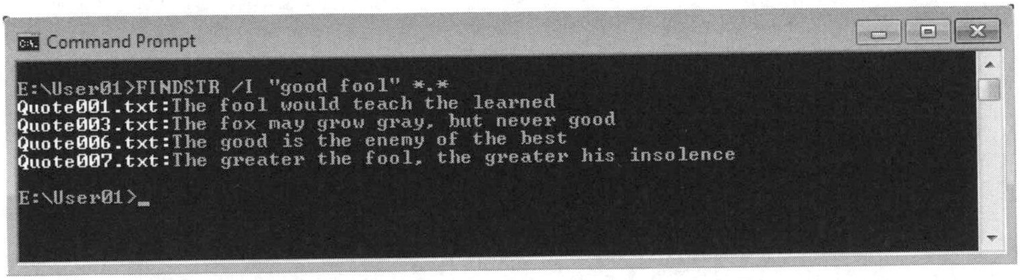

```
Command Prompt                                          _  □  ✕
E:\User01>FINDSTR /I "good fool" *.*
Quote001.txt:The fool would teach the learned
Quote003.txt:The fox may grow gray, but never good
Quote006.txt:The good is the enemy of the best
Quote007.txt:The greater the fool, the greater his insolence

E:\User01>_
```

Figure 7-22 Finding files using the FINDSTR command

Source: Course Technology/Cengage Learning

Expression	Explanation
FINDSTR "hello there" Greeting.txt	Searches for *hello* or *there* in the Greeting.txt file
FINDSTR /c: "hello there" Greeting.txt	Searches for *hello there* in the Greeting.txt file
FINDSTR Windows Proposal.txt	Searches for all occurrences of the word *Windows* (with a capital *W*) in the Proposal.txt file
FINDSTR /s /i Windows *.*	Searches every file in the current directory and all subdirectories for all occurrences of the word *Windows*, regardless of case

Table 7-13 FINDSTR examples

Activity 7-14: Finding Files with the FINDSTR Command

Time Required: 15 minutes

Objective: Use the FINDSTR command with wildcard characters in the Windows 7 CLI.

Description: In this activity, you open the command prompt and find files that contain specific characters. This activity is useful if you want to locate files when you know a word or part of a word contained in the files.

1. If necessary, start your virtual machines using the appropriate instructions in Activity 1-1.

2. Click **Start,** point to **All Programs,** click **Accessories,** and then click **Command Prompt.**

3. To create the example files for the search activities, type **MakeQUOTE** at the command prompt and then press **Enter.**

Contact your instructor if you see the following message: "MakeQUOTE is not recognized as an internal or external command, operable program or batch file."

4. To view the names of files that contain *The,* type **FINDSTR "The"** *.* and then press **Enter.**

5. Verify that 11 files are identified.

6. To view the names of files that contain *never* and/or *good,* type **FINDSTR "never good"** *.* and then press **Enter.**

7. Verify that two files are identified.

8. To view the names of files that contain *never good,* type **FINDSTR /C:"never good"** *.* and then press **Enter.**

9. Verify that one file is identified.

10. To view only the names of files that contain *rocks* and/or *rules,* type **FINDSTR /M "rocks rules"** *.* and then press **Enter.**

11. Verify that one file is identified.

12. Close the command prompt window.

13. Leave the virtual machine logged on for the next activity.

Using the FINDSTR Command with Regular Expressions The FINDSTR command can find the exact text you are looking for in any ASCII file or files. However, sometimes you only know part of the information that you want to match. For example, you might need to find a file that contains the characters *TEX.* In such cases, the FINDSTR command has the powerful ability to search for patterns of text using regular expressions.

Regular expressions are a notation for specifying patterns of text as opposed to exact strings of characters. The notation uses literal characters and **metacharacters.** Every character that does not have special meaning in the regular expression syntax is a literal character and matches an occurrence of that character. For example, letters and numbers are literal characters. A metacharacter is a symbol with special meaning (an operator or delimiter) in the regular-expression syntax.

Table 7-14 lists the metacharacters that FINDSTR accepts.

The special characters in regular expression syntax are most powerful when you use them together. Table 7-15 lists examples of regular expressions and explanations for each.

To find files containing words that start with the characters *Work*, as shown in Figure 7-23, use the following command:

```
FINDSTR /R "\<Work" *.*
```

Character	Value
.	A wildcard for any character
*	Repeats zero or more occurrences of the previous character or class
^	Line position: beginning of line
$	Line position: end of line
[class]	A character class that matches a single character out of all the possibilities offered; for example, *[abcd]* matches *a*, *b*, *c*, or *d*
[^class]	Inverse class; all characters except the listed special characters
[x-y]	Specifies a range of characters; for example, *[a-zA-Z0-9]* matches any letter or digit
\x	Specifies a metacharacter that is used as a literal character; for example, to use the metacharacter $ as a literal character, enter "\$".x
\<Xyz	Specifies characters that match the beginning of the word; for example, \<*Win* would match words that start with the characters *Win*
xyz\>	Specifies characters that match the end of the word; for example, *dows*\> would match words that end with the characters *dows*

Table 7-14 Regular expression quick reference

Expression	Explanation
.*	Matches any string of characters
w.*ing	Matches any string that begins with *w* and ends with *ing*
goo*	Matches any string that begins with *go* followed by zero or more *o*s
[ABC]	Matches any occurrence of *A*, *B*, or *C*
[^ABC]	Matches any text that does not contain an occurrence of *A*, *B*, or *C*
[A-C]	Matches only the characters *A*, *B*, or *C*

Table 7-15 Regular expression examples for FINDSTR

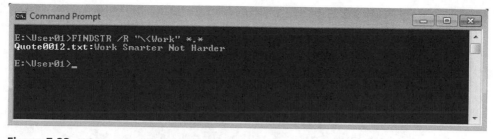

Figure 7-23 Using FINDSTR with a regular expression

Source: Course Technology/Cengage Learning

Activity 7-15: Finding Files with FINDSTR and Regular Expressions

Time Required: 15 minutes

Objective: Use the FINDSTR command with regular expressions in the Windows 7 CLI.

Description: In this activity, you open the command prompt and find files using regular expressions. This activity is useful for locating files when you know patterns contained within the file.

1. If necessary, start your virtual machines using the appropriate instructions in Activity 1-1.
2. Click **Start**, point to **All Programs**, click **Accessories**, and then click **Command Prompt**.
3. To create the example files for the search activities, type **MakeQuote** at the command prompt and then press **Enter**.
4. To view the names of files that contain the characters *x*, *y*, or *z*, type **FINDSTR /R "[xyz]" *.*.** and then press **Enter**.
5. Verify that four files are identified.
6. To view the names of files that do not contain the characters *x*, *y*, or *z*, type **FINDSTR /R "[^xyz]" *.*** and then press **Enter**.
7. Verify that 12 files are identified.
8. To view the names of files containing words that end in *r*, type **FINDSTR /R "r\>" *.*** and then press **Enter**.
9. Verify that seven files are identified.
10. To view the names of files containing words that begin with *r*, type **FINDSTR /R "\<r" *.*** and then press **Enter**.
11. Verify that one file is identified.
12. To view the names of files that contain the characters *oo*, type **FINDSTR /R "oo" *.*** and then press **Enter**.
13. Verify that four files are identified.

14. To view the names of files that contain the characters *go*, followed by zero or more *o* characters and ending in *d*, type **FINDSTR /R** "go*od" *.* and then press **Enter**.

15. Verify that four files are identified.

16. Close the command prompt window.

17. Leave the virtual machine logged on for the next activity.

Finding Files in Windows 7 with Windows Search

The Windows Search feature in Windows 7 might be the most direct way to locate a file. You first learned about Windows Search in Chapter 3. In this section, you will learn about additional features for Windows Search. Recall that you can use Windows Search if you remember all or part of the name of a file or folder you want to find. To open Windows Search, click Start. The Windows search box appears at the bottom of the Start menu, as shown in Figure 7-24. As you start to type the search term, Windows 7 displays the items that meet the initial characters of your request. As you type additional characters, Windows 7 narrows the displayed results. In addition to filename searches, you can search by specifying a word or phrase within a file.

Using Quotation Marks with Windows Search   If you want to search on more than one word, place the phrase in quotation marks. For example, you might have searched your files for documents related to an old project called the Dallas Project and got a large number of results because many files contained just the word *Dallas* or just *Project*. Searching with *"Dallas Project"* would provide the file list that you need.

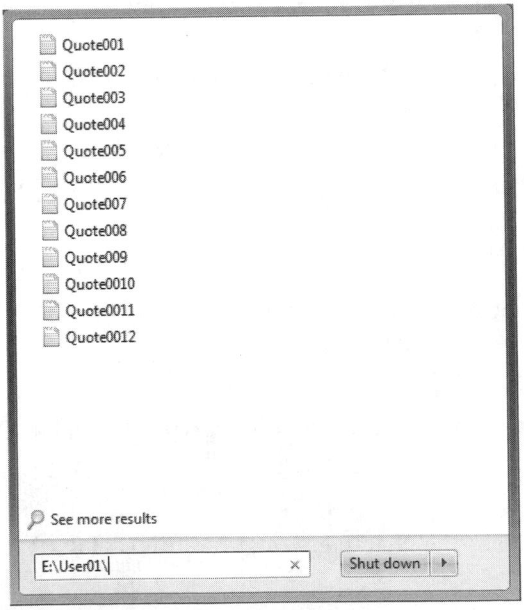

Figure 7-24 Start menu showing Windows Search

Source: Course Technology/Cengage Learning

Using Wildcards with Windows Search Windows Search can use the wildcards that you learned to use with the DOS commands. Add an asterisk (*) to a search term to represent an unknown string of letters or numbers, and use a question mark (?) as a single-character wildcard.

Unfortunately, Windows Search does not support the regular expressions that you learned to use with the FINDSTR command.

Using File Sizes with Windows Search When you know the approximate size of a file, you can include the file's size in your search by using the keyword size: For example, to find a file that is less than 100 kilobytes (KB) and that contains the word *resume*, enter the command resume size:<100KB.

To specify ranges, use the following operators:

- <   less than
- <=   less than or equal to
- >   greater than
- =>   greater than or equal to
- ..   range of file sizes

Using Dates and Date Ranges with Windows Search You can use relative dates such as today, tomorrow, or yesterday in a search. You can also combine words such as *this*, *last*, *past*, and *coming* with *week*, *month*, and *year* to create search terms such as *thisweek*, *nextmonth*, *pastmonth*, and *comingyear*. To find a file you created last week, for example, enter created:lastweek or created:pastweek.

To specify ranges, use the operators listed in the previous section.

To find a file that you created in 2010, enter created:<1/1/2011. The date format is dd/mm/year or dd/mm/yy.

To find a file created between January 31, 2011 and February 26, 2011, use created:>31/01/11 <26/02/11. Note that this search excludes files that were created on January 31, 2011 or February 26, 2011. To find those files as well, enter created:=>31/01/11 <=26/02/11 or created:31/01/11..26/02/11.

Searching by Kind Suppose you want to find all your photos that contain the word *vacation* in the filename, but you have documents and e-mails that contain *vacation* as well. Simply entering vacation is not very useful, so use the kind: command to narrow your search results. For example, enter vacation kind:photo or vacation kind:pictures to find only pictures that include *vacation* somewhere in their description.

Here is a list of possible kinds that you can use in searches:

- communications (e-mails and appointments)
- contacts (also person)
- docs (also documents)
- email

- folders
- im (for Instant Messenger conversations; for example, Windows Live Messenger)
- journal
- link
- meetings
- music (also song)
- notes
- pictures (also pics or photo)
- programs
- tasks
- videos

You can enter the search command `kind:music` to find all your mp3 files, wma files, wav files, and so on. You need to use Microsoft Outlook or Windows Live Mail to search with the following kinds: email, journal, meetings, notes, or tasks.

Searching by Type   You can use the `type:` command to narrow the search if you use the `kind:` command and receive results that are too broad. For example, if you have a large music collection and you want to find only mp3 files, not wma files, type `rock type:mp3`. If you have many photos and you want to find only files that have a .jpg extension, enter `type:jpg.?`.

Searching by File Properties   Windows Search indexes the filename and metadata for every file type and indexes the entire contents of many file types. You can search the metadata by specifying a file property. For example, suppose you want to find the song *Canon in D* by Johann Pachelbel; you know you have the song both in mp3 and wma formats, and that the wma format sounds better. But, the file has a cryptic filename, similar to 00jpcd.wma. Enter `artist:pachelbel title:canon type:wma` to find the file.

To find Word documents created by Bill Jones, enter `type:doc author:BillJones`. Another useful search would be for e-mails sent to a specific person. To find these e-mails, you could enter a command such as `type:eml to:billJones@alamo.edu`.

Here's a selection of file properties that you might find useful in searches:

- album
- artist
- author
- bitrate
- cameramake
- cameramodel

- cc
- created
- date
- datetaken
- firstname
- genre
- lastname
- modified
- rating
- size
- subject
- title
- tag
- to
- track
- year

Activity 7-16: Finding Files with the Windows Search Utility

Time Required: 15 minutes

Objective: Use the Windows Search utility to find files in Windows 7.

Description: In this activity, you search for files using the Windows Search utility. This activity is useful if you want to locate files and you know characters contained within the files.

1. If necessary, start your virtual machines using the appropriate instructions in Activity 1-1.

2. Click **Start**, point to **All Programs**, click **Accessories**, and then click **Command Prompt**.

3. To refresh the example files for the search activities, type **MakeQuote** at the command prompt and then press **Enter**.

4. To view the names of files that contain *good*, click **Start**, type **good** over "Search programs and Files," click **See more results**, expand **Computer**, expand **NTFS (E:)**, double-click **User01**, click **Search User01**, and then click **good**.

5. If you see a message that searches might be slow in non-indexed locations, click the yellow bar, click **Add to index**, and then click **Add to index**.

6. To start the search, click **Search User01**, and then click **good**.

7. Verify that two files are listed.

8. To view files that contain *lab*, type **lab** over "good."

9. Verify that two files are located.

10. Close the command prompt and Search windows.

11. Leave the PC logged on for the next activity.

Activity 7-17: Finding Files with Windows Search

Time Required: 15 minutes

Objective: Use the Windows Search utility to find files in Windows 7.

Description: In this activity, you search for files using the Windows Search utility. This activity is useful if you want to locate files and you know their properties.

1. If necessary, start your virtual machines using the appropriate instructions in Activity 1-1.

2. Click **Start**, point to **All Programs**, click **Accessories**, and then click **Command Prompt**.

3. To refresh the example files for the search activities, type **MakeQuote** at the command prompt and then press **Enter**.

4. To view files that contain the word *good*, click **Start**, type **good** over "Search programs and Files," and then click **See more results**.

5. Verify that two files are listed.

6. To view files that contain the word *good* and that were created today, click **good** in the search text box, click **date modified**, and click the highlighted date in the calendar.

7. Verify that two files are located.

8. Close any open windows in the virtual machine.

9. To shut down the virtual machine, click **Start**, and then click the **Shut Down** button.

10. Wait a moment for the Windows 7 virtual machine to shut down completely.

11. Leave the PC logged on for the next activity.

Finding Files in Fedora 13

Finding Files with the `ls` Command in Fedora 13 The `ls` command supports the same basic wildcards you use in Windows. Refer to Tables 7-11 and 7-12 for examples of how to use the asterisk and question mark wildcards.

For example, to find files using the `ls` command and a wildcard expression, you would type:

```
ls –l myfile*
```

The results are shown in Figure 7-25.

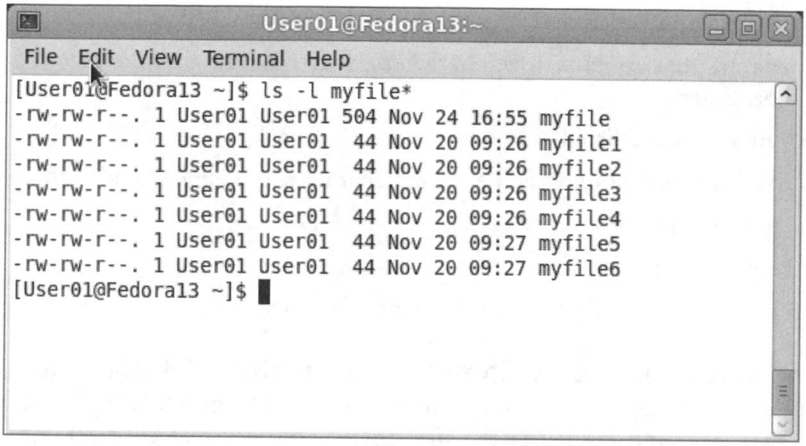

```
User01@Fedora13:~                                    _ □ ✕
File  Edit  View  Terminal  Help
[User01@Fedora13 ~]$ ls -l myfile*
-rw-rw-r--. 1 User01 User01 504 Nov 24 16:55 myfile
-rw-rw-r--. 1 User01 User01  44 Nov 20 09:26 myfile1
-rw-rw-r--. 1 User01 User01  44 Nov 20 09:26 myfile2
-rw-rw-r--. 1 User01 User01  44 Nov 20 09:26 myfile3
-rw-rw-r--. 1 User01 User01  44 Nov 20 09:26 myfile4
-rw-rw-r--. 1 User01 User01  44 Nov 20 09:27 myfile5
-rw-rw-r--. 1 User01 User01  44 Nov 20 09:27 myfile6
[User01@Fedora13 ~]$ █
```

Figure 7-25 Using the `ls` command with a regular expression

Source: Course Technology/Cengage Learning

7

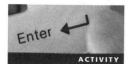

Activity 7-18: Finding Files with `ls` and Wildcard Characters in Fedora 13

Time Required: 15 minutes

Objective: Use the `ls` command with wildcard characters to find files in Fedora 13.

Description: In this activity, you open the Terminal console and find files with the help of wildcard characters. This activity is useful if you want to locate files when you know a portion of a filename.

1. If necessary, start your virtual machines using the appropriate instructions in Activity 1-1.

2. To open a Terminal console, click **Applications,** point to **System Tools,** and then click **Terminal.**

3. To create the directory structure with the **makeABC** script, type **cd /usr/local/bin,** press **Enter,** type **sh makeABC,** and then press **Enter.**

Contact your instructor if you see the following message: "makeABC is not recognized as an internal or external command, operable program or batch file."

4. To view filenames that start with *ab*, type **ls ab*** and then press **Enter.**

5. Verify that two files are listed.

6. To view filenames that contain a *b* as the third character, type **ls –a ??b*** and then press **Enter.**

7. Verify that two files are listed.

8. To view filenames that contain three characters, with *a* as the first character, type **ls a??** and then press **Enter**.

9. Verify that three files are listed.

10. To view filenames that contain *9* as the second character, type **ls ?9*** and then press **Enter**.

11. Verify that two files are listed.

12. Close the Terminal console.

13. Leave the virtual machine logged on for the next activity.

Finding Files with the `find` Command in Fedora 13

The `find` command searches the directory tree by evaluating a search expression from left to right, according to the rules of precedence, and then lists the files that match the test expression. The `find` command returns a status of 0 if all files are processed successfully, and a status of greater than 0 if errors occur. The search expression consists of the following elements:

- Options—These elements affect overall operation rather than the processing of a specific file, and always return a true value.

- Tests—These elements return a true or false value.

- Actions—These elements have side effects and return a true or false value.

These elements are separated by operators. The `-and` operator is assumed when an operator is omitted. Table 7-16 lists the order of precedence for expressions in the Fedora 13 `find` command, in ascending order.

Table 7-17 contains the test syntax used with the Fedora 13 `find` command.

Table 7-18 contains file types you can use with the Fedora 13 `find` command.

Expression	Description
(expr) parentheses	The parentheses work as they do in mathematical expressions, forcing precedence and changing the order in which operations are performed
! expr	The "!" symbol means that the inverse of the expression returns a true value; in other words, "if expr is false"
-not expr	Same as ! expr
expr1 expr2	expr2 is not evaluated if expr1 is false (in other words, an implied AND operation)
expr1 -a expr2	Same as expr1 expr2
expr1 -and expr2	Same as expr1 expr2
expr1 -o expr2	expr2 is not evaluated if expr1 is true (an OR expression)
expr1 -or expr2	Same as expr1 -o expr2
expr1 , expr2	Both expr1 and expr2 are always evaluated (a LIST expression); the value of expr1 is discarded, and the value of the list is the value of expr2

Table 7-16 Order of precedence for expressions in the Fedora 13 `find` command

Test syntax	Description
+n	For greater than *n*
−n	For less than *n*
n	For exactly *n*

Table 7-17 Test syntax used with the Fedora 13 `find` command

Type	Description
c	Character
b	Block
d	Directory
p	Named pipe
f	Regular file
l	Symbolic link
s	Socket
d	Door (Solaris)

Table 7-18 File types used with the Fedora 13 `find` command

The syntax and options for the `find` command are:

`-daystart`	Measures times (for `-amin`, `-atime`, `-cmin`, `-ctime`, `-mmin`, and `-mtime`) from the beginning of the day rather than from 24 hours ago
`-depth`	Processes each directory's contents before the directory itself
`-maxdepthlevels`	Descends at the specified number of directory *levels* (a non-negative integer) below the command-line arguments
`-mindepthlevels`	Does not apply any tests or actions beyond the specified number of *levels* (a non-negative integer)
`-xdev`	Doesn't descend into directories on other file systems
`-aminn`	File was last accessed *n* minutes ago
`-atimen`	File was last accessed *n* hours ago
`-cminn`	File's status was last changed *n* minutes ago
`-cnewer file`	File's status was last changed more recently than file was modified
`-ctimen`	File's status was last changed *n* hours ago
`-empty`	File is empty and is either a regular file or a directory
`-fstypetype`	File is on a file system of *type*; accepted types are DOS, Fat, NTFS, ext2, and ext3; use the `-printf` option to see the available types of file systems

`-gidn`	File's numeric group ID is *n*
`-inamepattern`	Searches for files with common name patterns; similar to `-name`, but the match is case insensitive
`-inum n`	File has inode number *n*
`-links n`	File has *n* links
`-name` *`pattern`*	Looks for a certain pattern in a filename; uses the metacharacters , ?, and []
`-size n[bckw]`	File uses *n* units of space; the units are 512-byte blocks by default
`-type c`	The type of file, where *c* represents the type
`-user uname`	File is owned by user *uname* (numeric user ID allowed)
`-print True`	Prints the full filename on the standard output device, followed by a newline character
`-prune`	If `-depth` is not given, true; does not descend into the current directory

For example, to locate directories using the `find` command, you can type:

`find /etc –type d | more`

The results are shown in Figure 7-26.

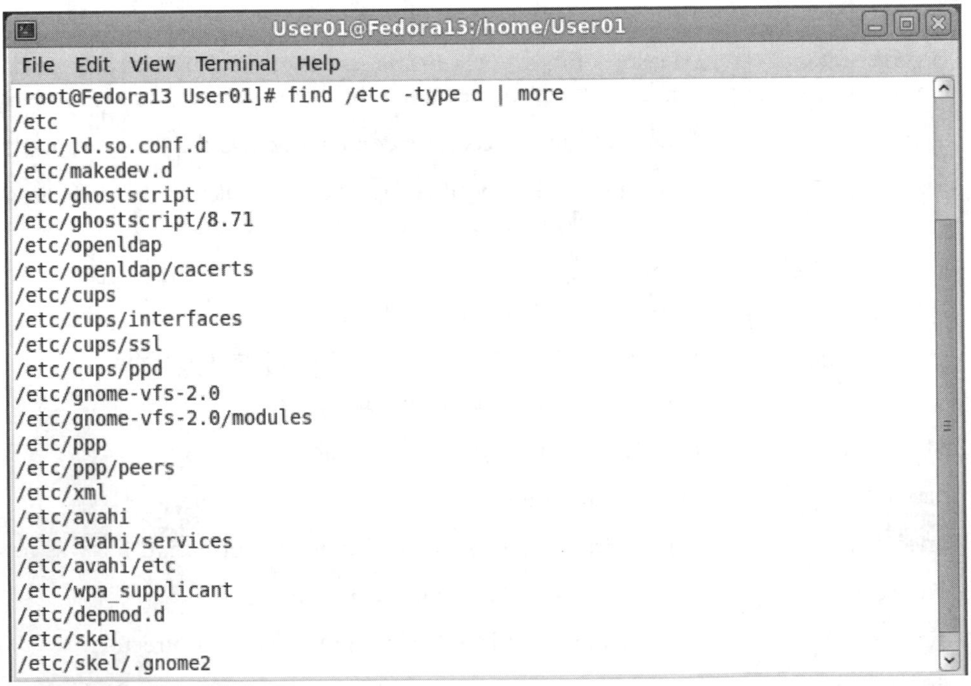
User01@Fedora13:/home/User01
File Edit View Terminal Help
[root@Fedora13 User01]# find /etc -type d | more
/etc
/etc/ld.so.conf.d
/etc/makedev.d
/etc/ghostscript
/etc/ghostscript/8.71
/etc/openldap
/etc/openldap/cacerts
/etc/cups
/etc/cups/interfaces
/etc/cups/ssl
/etc/cups/ppd
/etc/gnome-vfs-2.0
/etc/gnome-vfs-2.0/modules
/etc/ppp
/etc/ppp/peers
/etc/xml
/etc/avahi
/etc/avahi/services
/etc/avahi/etc
/etc/wpa_supplicant
/etc/depmod.d
/etc/skel
/etc/skel/.gnome2

Figure 7-26 Using the Fedora 13 `find` command for directories

Source: Course Technology/Cengage Learning

To locate links using the `find` command, you can type:

`find /etc -type l | more`

The results are shown in Figure 7-27.

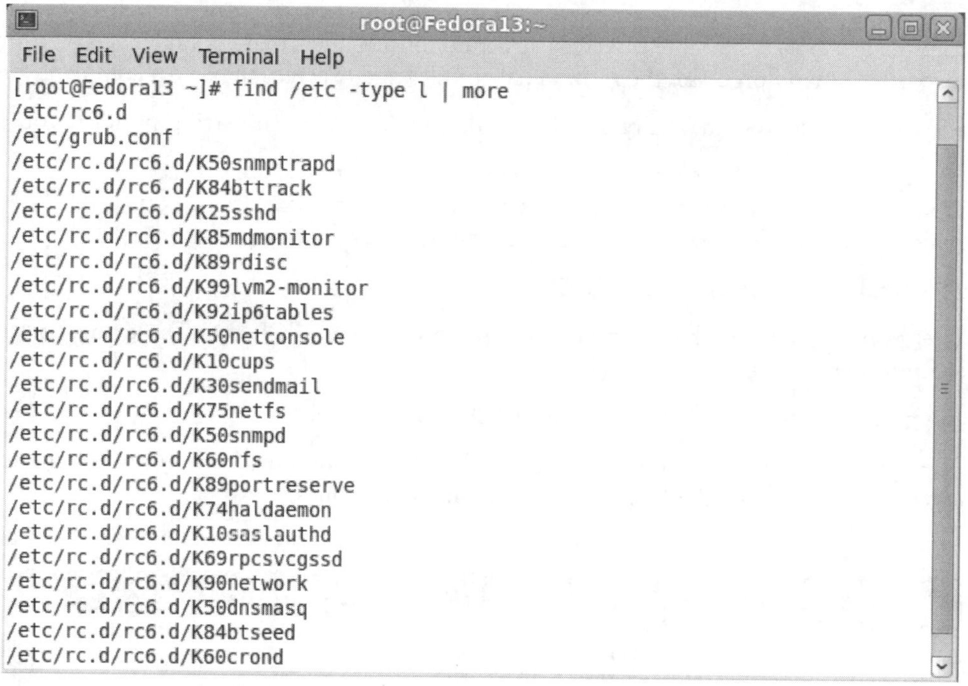

```
root@Fedora13:~
File  Edit  View  Terminal  Help
[root@Fedora13 ~]# find /etc -type l | more
/etc/rc6.d
/etc/grub.conf
/etc/rc.d/rc6.d/K50snmptrapd
/etc/rc.d/rc6.d/K84bttrack
/etc/rc.d/rc6.d/K25sshd
/etc/rc.d/rc6.d/K85mdmonitor
/etc/rc.d/rc6.d/K89rdisc
/etc/rc.d/rc6.d/K99lvm2-monitor
/etc/rc.d/rc6.d/K92ip6tables
/etc/rc.d/rc6.d/K50netconsole
/etc/rc.d/rc6.d/K10cups
/etc/rc.d/rc6.d/K30sendmail
/etc/rc.d/rc6.d/K75netfs
/etc/rc.d/rc6.d/K50snmpd
/etc/rc.d/rc6.d/K60nfs
/etc/rc.d/rc6.d/K89portreserve
/etc/rc.d/rc6.d/K74haldaemon
/etc/rc.d/rc6.d/K10saslauthd
/etc/rc.d/rc6.d/K69rpcsvcgssd
/etc/rc.d/rc6.d/K90network
/etc/rc.d/rc6.d/K50dnsmasq
/etc/rc.d/rc6.d/K84btseed
/etc/rc.d/rc6.d/K60crond
```

Figure 7-27 Using the Fedora 13 `find` command for links

Source: Course Technology/Cengage Learning

To locate files with certain permissions using the `find` command, you can type:

`find /dev/input/* -perm 777`

The results are shown in Figure 7-28.

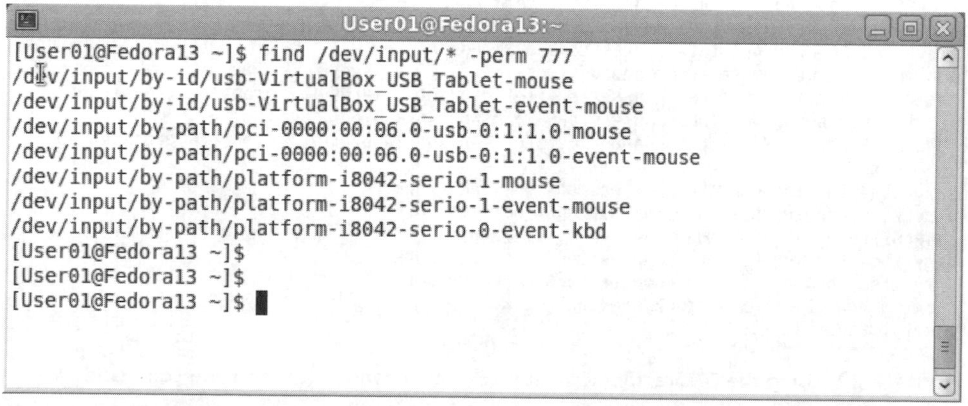

```
User01@Fedora13:~
[User01@Fedora13 ~]$ find /dev/input/* -perm 777
/dev/input/by-id/usb-VirtualBox_USB_Tablet-mouse
/dev/input/by-id/usb-VirtualBox_USB_Tablet-event-mouse
/dev/input/by-path/pci-0000:00:06.0-usb-0:1:1.0-mouse
/dev/input/by-path/pci-0000:00:06.0-usb-0:1:1.0-event-mouse
/dev/input/by-path/platform-i8042-serio-1-mouse
/dev/input/by-path/platform-i8042-serio-1-event-mouse
/dev/input/by-path/platform-i8042-serio-0-event-kbd
[User01@Fedora13 ~]$
[User01@Fedora13 ~]$
[User01@Fedora13 ~]$
```

Figure 7-28 Using the Fedora 13 `find` command with permission filter

Source: Course Technology/Cengage Learning

The **xargs** command is often piped with the find command to construct an argument list using standard input from the find command. The xargs command has the following syntax:

```
xargs [options] [command]
```

In the following example, xargs executes a command once for each piped record. The find command searches the entire directory structure for filenames that contain a specified string. The xargs command processes the resulting list of files and executes the grep command for each.

For example, to systematically locate files that include a certain string pattern, you can type:

```
find . -name 'myfile*' -print | xargs -n2 grep 'compression'
find . -name 'myfile*' -print | xargs -n2 grep 'compression6'
find . -name 'myfile*' -print | xargs -n2 grep 'compression[46]'
```

The results are shown in Figure 7-29.

The grep utility finds character or string patterns in an ASCII file. The **grep** command has the following syntax:

```
grep [options] [-e PATTERN | -f FILE] [FILE...]
```

The grep command searches the named input files for lines that contain a match of the given PATTERN. By default, grep prints the matching lines.

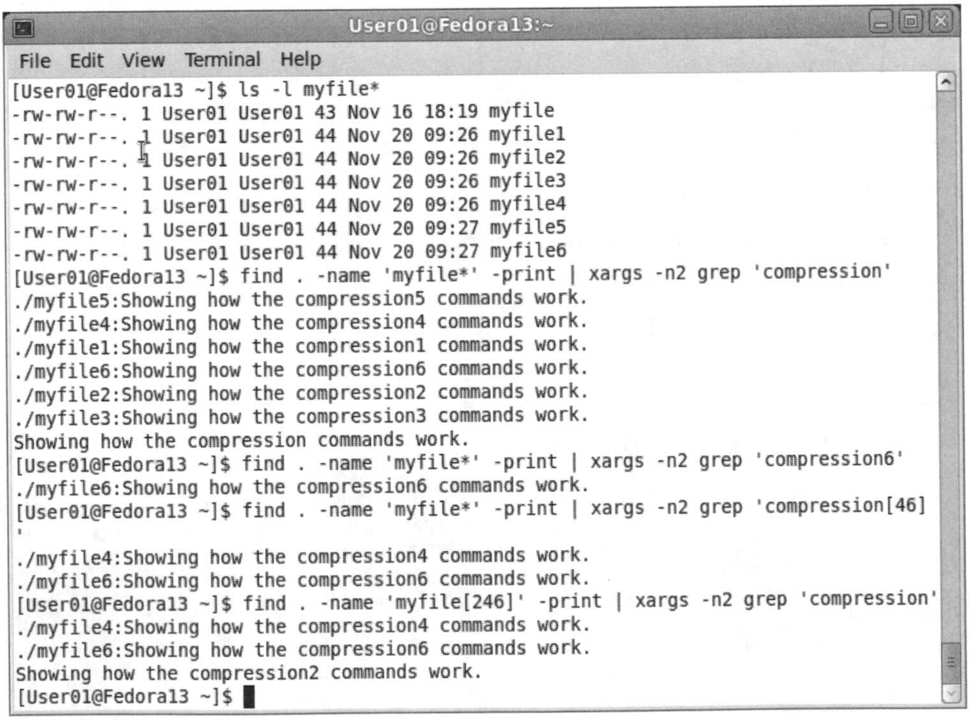

Figure 7-29 Using the Fedora 13 xargs and grep commands with the find command

Source: Course Technology/Cengage Learning

The grep command has the following options:

-a –text	Does not suppress output lines that contain binary data. Normally, the first few bytes of a file indicate that the file contains binary data. This option causes grep to treat the file like a text file, even if it would otherwise be treated as binary. Note that the result might be binary garbage printed to the terminal, which can create problems if the terminal driver interprets some of it as commands.
-c –count	Suppresses normal output; instead prints a count of matching lines for each input file.
-e *PATTERN* --regexp=*PATTERN*	Uses *PATTERN* as the pattern; this option is useful for protecting patterns that begin with a -.
-f *FILE* --file=*FILE*	Obtains patterns from *FILE*, one per line.
-H --with-filename	Prints the filename for each match.
-r --recursive	For each directory mentioned in the command line, reads and processes all files in the directories recursively.
-v --invert-match	Reverses the matching to select nonmatching lines.
-V --version	Prints the grep version number to the standard output stream.

To use the grep command to select files that contain certain string patterns, you can type:

```
grep –c compression myfile5
grep –c compression myfile4
grep –c compression myfile3
```

The results are shown in Figure 7-30.

```
[User01@Fedora13 ~]$ cat myfile*
Showing how the compression commands work.
Showing how the compression1 commands work.
Showing how the compression2 commands work.
Showing how the compression3 commands work.
Showing how the compression4 commands work.
Showing how the compression5 commands work.
Showing how the compression6 commands work.
[User01@Fedora13 ~]$ grep -c compression myfile5
1
[User01@Fedora13 ~]$ grep -c compression myfile4
1
[User01@Fedora13 ~]$ grep -c compression myfile3
1
[User01@Fedora13 ~]$
```

Figure 7-30 Using the Fedora 13 grep command

Source: Course Technology/Cengage Learning

Activity 7-19: Finding Files in Fedora 13

Time Required: 15 minutes

Objective: Use the find, xargs, and grep commands to find files.

Description: In this activity, you open the Terminal console and find files with the help of wildcard characters and a string (pattern) search. This activity is useful if you want to locate files when you know a portion of a filename or a string of characters in a file.

1. If necessary, start your virtual machines using the appropriate instructions in Activity 1-1.

2. To open a Terminal console, click **Applications**, point to **System Tools**, and then click **Terminal**.

3. To create the directory structure with the **makeHRS** script, type **cd /usr/local/bin**, press **Enter**, type **sh makeHRS** at the prompt, and press **Enter**.

> Contact your instructor if you see the following message: "makeHRS is not recognized as an internal or external command, operable program or batch file."

4. To display symbolic links, type **find /etc type l | more** and press **Enter**.

5. To display directories, type **find /etc type d | more** and press **Enter**.

6. To find files that contain certain filename strings, type **find /etc –name cro*** and press **Enter**.

7. Verify that 11 files are listed.

8. To find files that contain certain strings, type **find /rc | xargs grep mode***. and press **Enter**.

9. Verify that the rc file includes two lines that contain the word *mode*.

10. To close the Terminal window, type **exit** and then press **Enter**.

11. To shut down the virtual machine, click **System**, click **Shut Down**, and then click the **Shut Down** button.

12. Wait a moment for the Fedora 13 virtual machine to shut down completely.

13. Close any remaining open windows, log off, and shut down your PC.

Chapter Summary

- Files can have different types of contents. You can determine file types by their extensions in Windows 7 or by their file header information in Fedora 13. Knowing the contents of a file helps with error processing, application selection, troubleshooting, and other file processing. You can view a file's contents as a whole or in sections, on a standard display, or within another file.

- File attributes provide information about a file's access privileges. Files in Windows 7 and Fedora 13 have different file attributes. The most common Windows 7 file attributes are archive, read-only, hidden, compression, and encryption.

- As directories are built, more files are added. Many options are available to help you locate these files quickly. For example, when you don't know the exact name of a file you need, you can use wildcards to represent unknown characters in the filename or file type. You can search for files by their name, type, or content. Use the FIND and FINDSTR commands to locate needed information in a file. Regular expressions permit pattern searching of file contents.

- Using the Search feature in Windows 7, you can locate files by their contents, as you can with the FINDSTR command. You can also search for files by their type, kind, size, and date.

- File compression saves disk space by removing duplicated data in files. In Windows 7, the compression attribute indicates that the file has been compressed. In Fedora 13, the gzip and gunzip commands are used to compress and uncompress files.

Key Terms

archive A Windows 7 file attribute that indicates a file is available for archiving or backup.

ATTRIB A command used to view DOS file attributes.

cat A command used to display file contents by directing the entire contents of a compressed file to an output device in one pass.

compression A Windows 7 file attribute that indicates a file is compressed.

Encrypting File System (EFS) A system that Windows 7 uses to store data using file encryption.

encryption A Windows file attribute that indicates a file is protected using the Encrypting File System.

extension A set of characters that a user or program adds to a filename to help describe or categorize a file.

file A basic unit of storage that enables a computer to distinguish one set of information from another.

file attribute A restrictive label attached to a file that describes and regulates its use; examples include hidden, system, read-only, and archive. In MS-DOS, this information is stored as part of the file's directory entry.

filename The set of letters, numbers, and allowable symbols assigned to a file to distinguish it from all other files in a particular directory on a disk. A filename is the label under which a user saves and requests a block of information.

FIND A command used in DOS to locate a specific text string in an ASCII file. The information is sent either to the console or a file.

find A command used in Fedora 13 to search the root directory for files.

FINDSTR A command used in DOS to locate an exact text string in any ASCII file. The information is sent either to the console or a file.

grep A command used to find string patterns in files.

gunzip The sister utility to gzip that decompresses gzip files.

gzip A command used to compress Fedora 13 files.

hidden   A Windows 7 file attribute that indicates a file is hidden from directory commands.

index   A Windows 7 file attribute that indicates a file should be indexed.

inode   A place where Fedora 13 applications store file and directory attributes. The inode contains information about a file or directory, including its type.

`lsattr`   A command used in Fedora 13 to view file attributes.

metacharacter   A character embedded in a program source or a data stream that conveys information about other characters rather than itself.

`MORE`   A Windows command that displays text files one screen at a time.

`more`   A command used in Fedora 13 to display text one screen at a time.

read-only   A Windows 7 file attribute that indicates a file cannot be modified.

regular expression   A combination of symbols, identifiers, values, and operators that yields a result upon evaluation.

system   A Windows 7 file attribute that indicates a file belongs to the operating system.

tar   An archive or backup utility that selects and packages files according to filters and is often used in conjunction with the gzip compress utility.

`TYPE`   A Windows 7 command used to display the text contained in files.

`xargs`   A command often piped with the `find` command to construct an argument list using standard input from the `find` command.

zcat   A utility that decompresses gzip files and redirects the output to standard output.

Zip   A format for compressed data files.

Review Questions

1. A file extension _____. (Choose all that apply.)
   a. is required in both the Windows 7 and Fedora 13 operating systems
   b. is usually three letters and comes after the comma
   c. is usually three letters and comes after the period
   d. typically suggests the type of data in the file
   e. is used by the OS to determine which program could be used to process the file

2. File associations _____.
   a. specify certain aspects of the operating system's treatment of different directories
   b. specify the operating system you are using
   c. refer to left-over information that does not help you
   d. specify certain aspects of the operating system's treatment of different file types
   e. are only used in the Windows 7 OS

3. When working with files, knowing the file extension helps you _____.
   (Choose all that apply.)
   a. determine if you need to load the application to read or update the file
   b. determine the value of the file before you begin working with it

   c.   determine the correct compiler to use

   d.   troubleshoot problems you may encounter with downloaded files from the Internet

   e.   in no way; it is only for decorative purposes

4. In Fedora 13, file extensions _____.

   a.   are required

   b.   are not necessary because the OS can read the file header to check for the file type

   c.   are identical to those used in the Windows 7 OS

   d.   do not help in determining the contents of the file

5. To view a file in Fedora 13, use the _____ command. (Choose all that apply.)

   a.   `FIND`

   b.   `cat`

   c.   `find`

   d.   `more`

   e.   `less`

6. The `cat` command displays a file's contents _____. (Choose all that apply.)

   a.   by concatenating them to the standard output device or another file

   b.   and requires a file operand to do so

   c.   and can use the redirection symbol >

   d.   one page at a time when the `more` command is also used

7. Every file in DOS has _____ attributes.

   a.   one

   b.   two

   c.   three

   d.   four

8. Use the `more` command to _____.

   a.   copy file contents

   b.   determine file attributes

   c.   view file contents

   d.   view hardware configuration

9. The hidden attribute _____. (Choose all that apply.)

   a.   causes your files to become invisible

   b.   cannot be seen unless you use the `DIR UNHIDE` command

   c.   is used to prevent a file from being seen by other commands

   d.   is not listed by the `DIR` command by default

10. Use the _____ command to view attributes in DOS.

   a. VIEW

   b. FIND

   c. ATTRIB

   d. FILE_ATTRIB

11. Compressing files _____. (Choose all that apply.)

   a. decreases a file's size

   b. decreases the amount of space used by all the files stored within a folder

   c. may result in a loss of performance

   d. is not recommended and should not be considered

   e. cannot be done prior to encryption

12. Encryption of files _____. (Choose all that apply.)

   a. cannot occur if the files are compressed

   b. is the same as compression

   c. prohibits other users from viewing the contents of encrypted files

   d. is not available in Windows 7

   e. is used to decrease file size

13. File attributes in Fedora 13 _____. (Choose all that apply.)

   a. are different from those in Windows 7

   b. are seldom used

   c. can be viewed with the lsattr command

   d. are the same as those in Windows 7

14. A regular expression _____. (Choose all that apply.)

   a. uses literal characters and metacharacters

   b. is a notation for specifying patterns of text, as opposed to exact strings of characters

   c. is helpful when searching for exact text matches in an ASCII file

   d. example is "[A-C]"

15. Use the _____ command to search for an exact text match in an ASCII file.

   a. find

   b. SEEK

   c. SEARCH

   d. FIND

   e. FINDSTR

16. The DIR command in Windows 7 is similar to the _____ command in Fedora 13.

    a. find

    b. more

    c. file

    d. ls

17. Which standard search criteria can you use with the Windows 7 Search feature? (Choose all that apply.)

    a. all of a filename

    b. part of a filename

    c. date

    d. author

18. When using the Windows 7 Search feature, which of the following criteria can you use to narrow your search? (Choose all that apply.)

    a. date modified

    b. author

    c. program

    d. size

19. You use the find command in Fedora 13 to search for _____. (Choose all that apply.)

    a. text within a file

    b. directories

    c. links

    d. files based on file type

20. You use the grep command in Fedora 13 to search for _____.

    a. text within a file

    b. directories

    c. links

    d. files based on file type

Case Projects

Case 7-1: Copying Files for an Associate with Windows 7

You want to give an associate a disk that contains a copy of all the files in the default directory, except files with the .bak extension. The disk is in drive A. Your virtual machine also has a B drive. You plan to use the XCOPY command to copy only the files you have marked with the archive attribute. Describe the steps to achieve this objective. Provide examples of the commands you plan to use.

Case 7-2: Preparing for a Presentation on DOS File Attributes

You have been asked to give a short presentation on DOS file attributes. The presentation should include handouts that provide definitions of the file attributes and at least three examples of setting them.

Case 7-3: Selecting Files for a Forensics Investigation with Fedora 13

Your law firm is investigating a company's files and inventories. The company is suspected of doctoring its inventory records. Your firm asks you to find and display all inventory files that were last modified after a certain date. You must also keep the directory structure intact. List and explain the steps you need to perform, and include plausible commands to do the job. Keep in mind that you may find many directories full of files and that you must consider resource efficiencies.

Case 7-4: Designing Backup Plans with Fedora 13

You work for a system administration company that specializes in backup and recovery for small to medium-sized businesses. Your boss asks you to design a backup system for a new client. List and explain the steps you need to perform, including details on backup timing and plausible command lines to select files for the last week. Keep in mind that you may find many directories full of files and that you must consider resource efficiencies.

You only have to design the command lines needed to select files for backup, not the actual backup commands.

chapter 8

Text Editors

After reading this chapter and completing the exercises, you will be able to:

- Understand the functions of common text editors
- Work with individual files and multiple files in text editors
- Work with lines of text in files using cut, copy, and paste commands
- Search for character strings in documents
- Search and replace character strings in documents

You use text editors to create and revise text files, which contain important system configuration data and program source information. In this chapter, you will learn to use three text editors: DOS Edit, Windows 7 TextPad, and Fedora 13 Vim. The DOS Edit and Vim programs are installed by default when you install the operating system. The third program, **Text-Pad**, is a full-featured text editor that you can download for a free trial and use in Windows 7.

After a brief overview, you will begin learning to use the three text editors, including working with multiple files, searching for character strings, and replacing character strings. You will also continue to learn the power of regular expressions, to which you were introduced in Chapter 7.

Overview of Common Text Editors

This chapter starts with a brief overview of three text editors: DOS Edit, TextPad, and Vim. Do not overlook the value of DOS Edit; it could be your only choice on a PC if the operating system has crashed. The skills you learn while using DOS Edit also make it easier to make the transition to the Vim editor.

Overview of DOS Edit

DOS Edit is a text editor that allows you to create, edit, save, and print ASCII text files. For example, you can edit program files for compilers or script files that the OS uses. DOS Edit is only available in the 32-bit versions of Windows 7.

Use the menu options in DOS Edit (see Figure 8-1) to choose commands, enter data, and specify preferences. The menu commands are explained throughout the chapter. DOS Edit also includes a Help menu that explains program techniques and commands in more detail.

Use the keyboard arrow keys to navigate through menus. You can select menu items by pressing the Spacebar or by holding down the Alt key and pressing a second key that

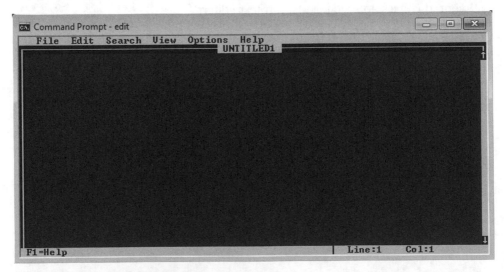

Figure 8-1 The DOS Edit program window

Source: Course Technology/Cengage Learning

corresponds to the menu option. For example, you can save a document in DOS Edit by holding down the Alt key and pressing the S key. This key combination (abbreviated Alt+S) is called a shortcut.

Although DOS Edit works with a mouse, you should learn to use the program with the keyboard in case a mouse is not available. Using the keyboard with DOS Edit prepares you to use the Vim editor in Fedora 13, which does not support a mouse.

Overview of TextPad

TextPad is a full-featured text editor that offers a wide range of options, including many that you would expect to find in a word processor. For professional programmers who work in Windows, TextPad is the editor of choice.

You can download a free copy of TextPad for evaluation from *www.textpad.com*. You must pay for the software if you decide to keep it.

In addition to the usual cut-and-paste capabilities, you can correct common typing errors with TextPad; use commands to change the case of words; and transpose words, characters, and lines. Other commands let you indent blocks of text, split or join lines, and insert whole files. You can undo or redo any change or any number of changes, back to the first change you made. You can also insert visible bookmarks on lines to mark your place in a file, and then apply editing commands to lines with bookmarks.

TextPad was created according to Windows 7 user-interface guidelines, so both beginners and experienced users should find it easy to use. If you know how to use a Windows application, you should feel comfortable with TextPad (see Figure 8-2).

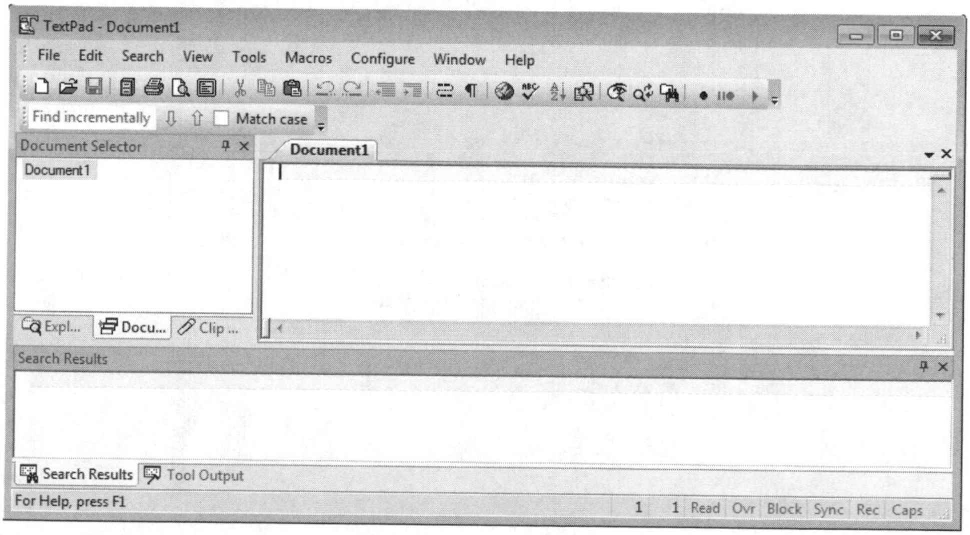

Figure 8-2 The TextPad editor window

Source: Course Technology/Cengage Learning

Overview of Vim

Vim is a powerful, cross-platform editor that many computer professionals use to write computer programs and text documents. (Vim, shown in Figure 8-3, is short for Visual editor Improved.) Unlike the editors to which you have been introduced so far, you do not use the Vim editor via menus. However, the same text-editing options and features are available.

If you question why you need to learn yet another text editor, be aware that Vim offers some advantages. For example, the documents you write for your classes will be scripts, data files, and source code that a computer reads and processes, so you need an editor that allows you to do more than just "type it in." Vim offers several editing options depending on your task. In Edit mode, for instance, you can make minor changes to a file without having the entire document available for editing.

After writing a few programs, you will discover that you do not spend all of your time typing new text, but that you frequently edit existing text. The Vim editor has three modes with distinct features that help you accomplish specific tasks during an editing session:

- **Command/Edit mode**—This is the default mode of the editor; use it to modify text. This mode allows you to modify only the part of the text you need to change without exposing the entire document to changes. (In many texts, this option is called the Normal/Command mode. This book uses the term *Edit mode* because it is used to edit text documents.)

- **Insert mode**—Use this mode to enter text; type i to begin typing your text in this mode.

- **Visual mode**—Use this mode to highlight text and perform copy-and-paste operations. The cursor is placed on the text; when the arrow moves the cursor, the text is highlighted.

To toggle between the modes, press the Esc key. This is important to remember because you can only quit the editor from the Edit mode.

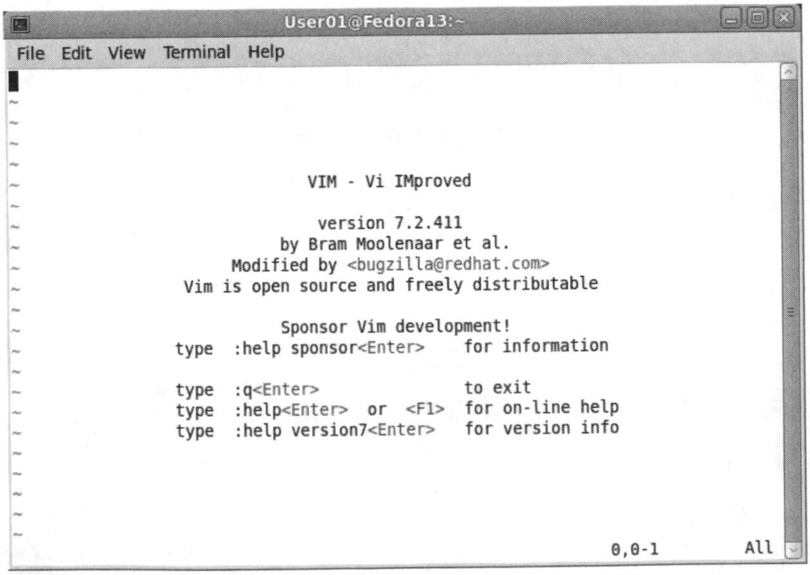

Figure 8-3 The Vim editor

Source: Course Technology/Cengage Learning

Working with Files

When you need to work with a file, you open it in a document editor, as shown in Figure 8-4. After you finish editing the file, you must save it—if not, your changes will be lost.

Of course, you can also start by creating a new document. Or, you may find it advantageous to open multiple files and work among them.

The editors used in this text are line editors—you create or edit one line of a document at a time. When you complete a line, press Enter to end the line and go to the start of the next one. Because you use the text editor to create a script or source program, creating a line at a time is the proper approach.

You will learn these techniques and others when using each of the three editors in the following sections.

Working with Files in DOS Edit

You work with files in the DOS Edit program using document windows. You can begin by creating a file or opening an existing file. To create a file, type `edit` at the command prompt to start DOS Edit, and then begin typing in the document window. Press Enter when you complete a line.

To open an existing file, press Alt+F and then press the O key. When the Open dialog box appears, as shown in Figure 8-5, type the name of the file you want to open. You can also press Alt+F to switch to the Files list, use the arrow keys to highlight the desired file, and press Enter. If you need to change the directory before selecting a file, press Alt+D to switch to the Directories list. Use the arrow keys to highlight the desired directory and press Enter.

To open a second window, press Alt+V and then press the S key. From the second window, you can see another part of the document. When the same lines appear in both open documents, changes you make in the second window appear in the first window. Press the F6 key to move between the two windows while editing the document.

In many editing operations, you need access to another file. Before opening this file, open a second window and then press F6 to switch to it. Use the previous instructions to open the file in the second document window.

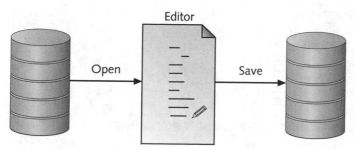

Figure 8-4 Working with files

Source: Course Technology/Cengage Learning

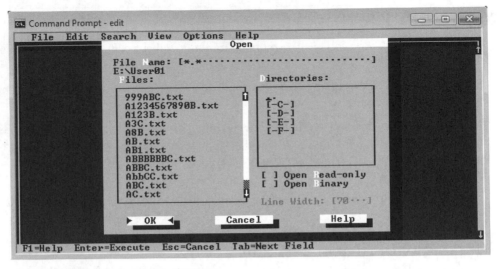

Figure 8-5 Open dialog box in DOS Edit

Source: Course Technology/Cengage Learning

Unless you want to reject the changes you make in a document window, save the file before exiting DOS Edit or opening a new file. To save an existing file, press Alt+F and then press the S key. To save a new file or save a file under a new name, press Alt+F, press the A key, and then enter the name in the File Name field of the Save As dialog box (see Figure 8-6). If you need to save the file in a different directory, press Alt+D to switch to the Directories list. Use the arrow keys to highlight the desired directory and press Enter.

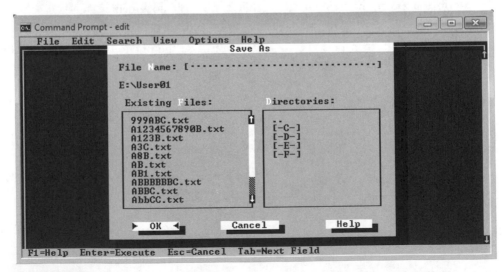

Figure 8-6 Save As dialog box in DOS Edit

Source: Course Technology/Cengage Learning

Activity 8-1: Creating and Using Multiple Files in DOS Edit

Time Required: 15 minutes

Objective: Create files with the DOS Edit text editor in the Windows 7 command-line interface (CLI).

Description: In this activity, you open the command prompt, open DOS Edit, and enter two short program files. This activity is useful if you want to create files in DOS Edit.

If you make typing mistakes, do not correct them. You will correct them in Activity 8-5.

1. Start your virtual machines using the appropriate instructions in Activity 1-1. To open a Command Prompt window, click **Start**, point to **All Programs**, click **Accessories**, and then click **Command Prompt**.

2. To open DOS Edit, type **edit** at the command prompt and then press **Enter**.

3. Type the statements from Table 8-1, pressing **Enter** at the end of each line.

4. To save the file, press **Alt+F** and then press the **A** key.

5. To change to the E: drive, press **Alt+D**, use the arrow keys to move to the [-E-] entry, and then press **Enter**.

6. To enter the filename and save the file, press **Alt+N**, type **doctype.htm** on the File Name text line, and then press **Enter**.

7. To open a second window, press **Alt+V** and then press the **S** key.

8. To start a new document, press **Alt+F** and then press the **N** key.

9. Type the statements from Table 8-2, pressing **Enter** at the end of each line.

10. To save the file, press **Alt+F** and then press the **A** key.

11. To enter the filename and save the file, press **Alt+N**, type **program1.htm** on the File Name text line, and then press **Enter**.

12. To switch between windows, press **F6**. Note that the cursor moves to the other window, and the filename is highlighted in the window.

13. To close DOS Edit, press **Alt+F** and then press the **X** key.

14. At the command prompt, type **exit** and then press **Enter**.

15. Leave the virtual machine logged on for the next activity.

<!DOCTYPE HTML PUBLIC "-//W3C/DTD XHTML 1.0 Transitional//EN"
"http://www.w3.org/TR/xhtml1/DTD/xhtml1-transitional.dtd">
<html xmls="http://www.w3.org/1999/xhtml">

Table 8-1 First program in HTML

8

<head>
<title>My first program</title>
</head>
<body>
Hello World
</body>
</html>

Table 8-2 **Second program in HTML**

Working with Files in TextPad

You have two choices when creating a file in TextPad:

- To create an unnamed document, click the File menu and then click New, or click the New Document button on the toolbar. You can name the new document later using the Save As command on the File menu.

- To create a named document, click the File menu and then click Open, or click the Open button on the toolbar. The File Open dialog box appears. In the Directories box, double-click a folder where you want to store the source file (or move up or down a path to the appropriate folder). Type the filename in the File name text box and click Open. The default file extension is .txt, but you can specify a different extension. Click Yes when prompted to create the file. You can create more files by repeating these steps.

Use the TextPad document window to type the contents of the file. Press Enter after each line you complete.

To facilitate switching between files, click the View menu and then click Document Tabs. To switch to a document, click the appropriate tab.

When working with two or more documents, you can arrange them horizontally, vertically, or in a cascaded (overlapped) pattern for ease of viewing. To create a horizontal arrangement, as shown in Figure 8-7, click the Window menu and then click Tile Horizontally. To switch between documents, click the document you want to use. To select a document and turn off a viewing arrangement, double-click the document's title bar.

You should periodically save the document to avoid losing your work. You can save a file by clicking the File menu and then clicking Save, pressing Ctrl+S, or clicking the Save button on the toolbar.

If you create a file in TextPad to use as input to the C++ compiler in Fedora 13, you must save the file in a format that is compatible with the compiler. For example, each line must end in a line feed, so TextPad's default setting is to save files in DOS PC format with a carriage return/line feed at the end of each line. When working with C++ files, you save them by selecting UNIX from the File Format list box in the Save As dialog box.

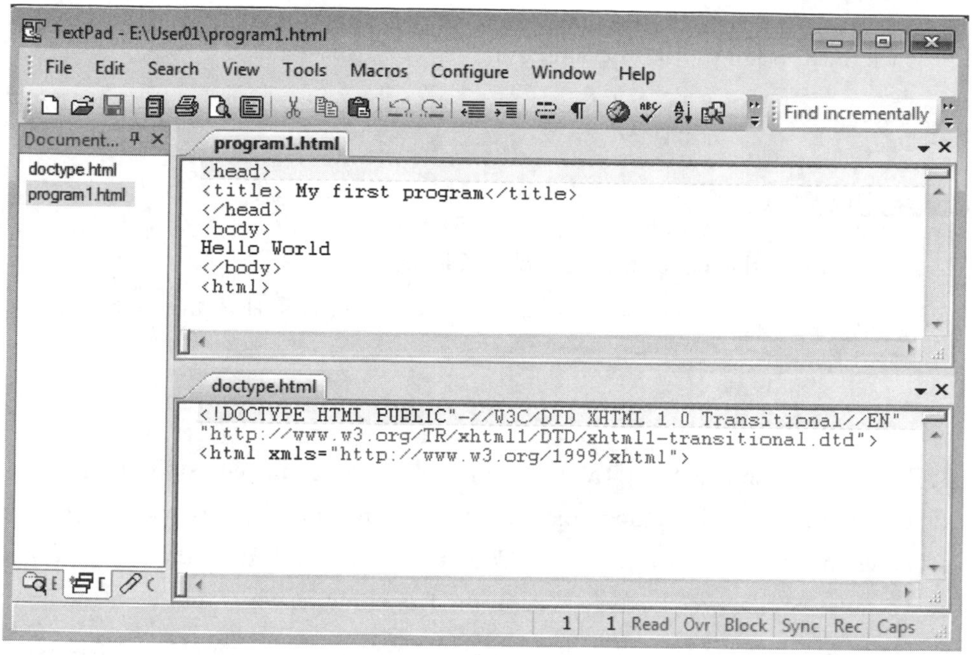

```
TextPad - E:\User01\program1.html

File   Edit   Search   View   Tools   Macros   Configure   Window   Help

Document...    program1.html
doctype.html      <head>
program1.html     <title> My first program</title>
                  </head>
                  <body>
                  Hello World
                  </body>
                  <html>

                  doctype.html
                  <!DOCTYPE HTML PUBLIC"-//W3C/DTD XHTML 1.0 Transitional//EN"
                  "http://www.w3.org/TR/xhtml1/DTD/xhtml1-transitional.dtd">
                  <html xmls="http://www.w3.org/1999/xhtml">

                                        1    1  Read  Ovr  Block  Sync  Rec  Caps
```

8

Figure 8-7 TextPad showing horizontal documents

Source: Course Technology/Cengage Learning

If you repeatedly work with the same set of files, you should use a **workspace**. Open all the files you need and then create the workspace by clicking File, Workspace, and then Save As. When you finish working with the documents, close the workspace, which saves the individual files. To close the workspace, click File, point to Workspace, and then click Close. To open the workspace, click File, point to Workspace, and then click Open.

If you are using a workspace and you close one of its files instead of the workspace itself, the file is removed from the workspace. No data is lost, but the file is no longer managed by the workspace. If you open a file after opening the workspace, it is managed by the workspace.

Activity 8-2: Creating and Using Multiple Files in TextPad

Time Required: 15 minutes

Objective: Create files in the TextPad editor in the Windows 7 graphical user interface (GUI).

Description: In this activity, you open TextPad and create two short program files. You also create a workspace for the two files. This activity is useful if you need to create files in TextPad.

> If you make typing mistakes, do not correct them. You will correct them in Activity 8-6.
>
> NOTE

1. If necessary, start your virtual machines using the appropriate instructions in Activity 1-1. Click **Start**, point to **All Programs**, and then click **TextPad**.

If TextPad does not appear on the All Programs menu, contact your instructor.

2. After reading the Tip of the Day, click **Close**.

If you find the Tip of the Day annoying, clear the "Show tips on start-up" check box.

3. Type the statements from Table 8-1, pressing **Enter** at the end of each line.
4. To open the Save As dialog box, click the **File** menu and then click **Save As**.
5. To change to the E: drive, expand **Computer** and double-click the **NTFS (E:)** entry.
6. To save the file, type **doctype.html** in the File name text box and then click **Save**.

Click Yes if the following message appears: "E:\doctype.html already exists. Do you want to replace it?"

7. To open a second document, click the **File** menu and then click **New**.
8. To tile the windows, click the **Window** menu and then click **Tile Horizontally**.
9. Type the statements from Table 8-2, pressing **Enter** at the end of each line.
10. To save the file, click the **File** menu and then click **Save As**.
11. Type **program1.html** in the File name text box and then click **Save**.
12. To save the workspace, click the **File** menu, point to **Workspace**, and then click **Save As**.
13. Type **FirstProgram** in the File name text box and then click **Save**.
14. To exit TextPad, click the **File** menu and then click **Exit**.
15. Leave the virtual machine logged on for future activities.

Working with Files in Vim

You can open the Vim editor from the terminal in Fedora 13 by typing the `vi` command. If you specify a filename with the command, the file opens in Normal/Command mode—the Vim editing mode (which is called *Edit mode* in this text). Edit mode is useful for editing existing files, but you can change to Insert mode if you need to enter new text or Visual mode if you want to highlight text and perform copy-and-paste operations.

If you type `vi` and then type more than one filename, multiple files open for editing, although only the first file in the list is available for immediate viewing. To access the other open files, you must be in Edit mode; press Esc to change modes, type `:w` to save the content in the first file, and then type `:next` to see the next file in the list. To go back to the previous file, type `:w` to save the content in the second file and then type :previous. If you try to go beyond the number of open files, Vim tells you there are no more in the list, as shown in Figure 8-8.

Cut, copy, and paste operations work with multiple open files because they share the same buffered area. After you copy or cut text from one file, you can paste it into another open file. If you aren't sure which file you are using, type :args; brackets appear around the active file, as shown in Figure 8-9.

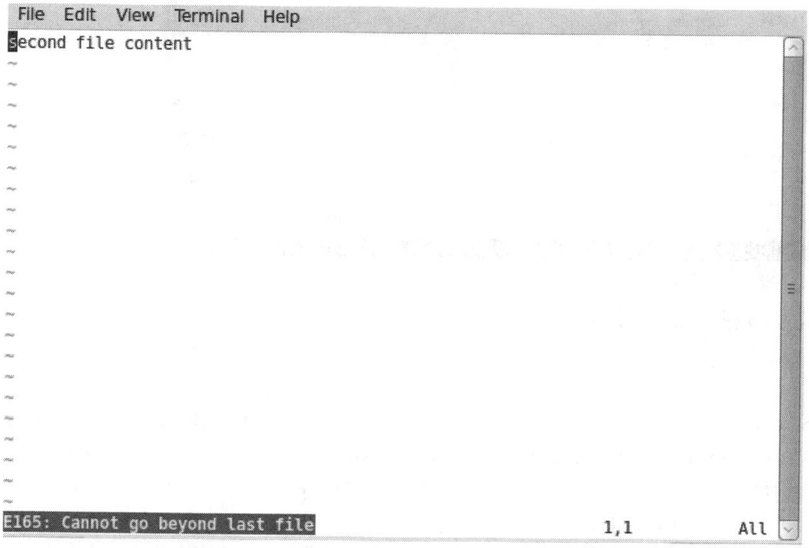

Figure 8-8 Using the :next command in Vim

Source: Course Technology/Cengage Learning

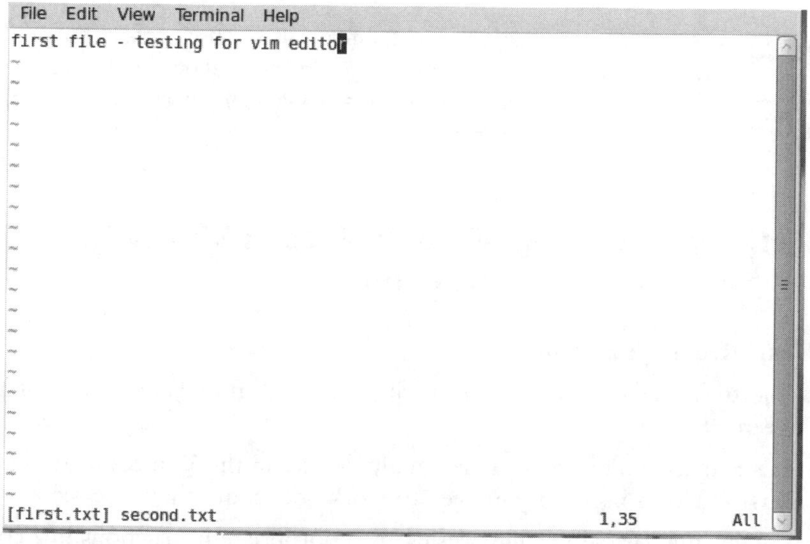

Figure 8-9 Results of using the :args command

Source: Course Technology/Cengage Learning

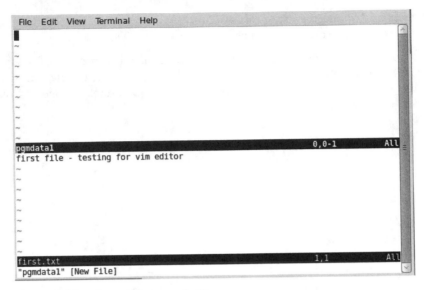

Figure 8-10 Using a split screen in Vim

Source: Course Technology/Cengage Learning

You can also open multiple files using the `:split` command, which is useful when you already have an open file and need to open or create another. For example, if you type `:split pgmdata1`, another window opens, as shown in Figure 8-10. The cursor moves to the new file called pgmdata1 in the top window, and the file you were editing moves to the bottom window. When you use split screens, you must keep track of which file you are editing by reading the file status bar below each text-entry area. The edit command line applies to both windows, so it is not always helpful for determining which window you are using. To move between the windows, type Ctrl+W twice.

Be careful when using the split screen. Although it is useful to work with multiple files, nothing stops you from creating more than one split. You can easily open too many windows, become confused, and ruin your documents.

Activity 8-3: Using Multiple Files in Vim with a Split Screen

Time Required: 20 minutes

Objective: View multiple files in the Vim editor in Fedora 13 using a split screen.

Description: In this activity, you open and view multiple files in the Vim editor using the split-screen option. This activity is useful if you need to work with more than one file at a time.

1. If necessary, start your virtual machines using the appropriate instructions in Activity 1-1. To open a Terminal console, click **Applications**, point to **System Tools**, and then click **Terminal**.

2. To create your first file and open the Vim editor without seeing the introductory text, type **vi doctype.html** at the command line and then press **Enter**.

3. You are in Edit mode. To begin inserting text, type **i**. The word *INSERT* appears at the bottom of the editor.

4. Type the statements from Table 8-1, pressing **Enter** at the end of each line.

5. To save the file, you must be in Edit mode. Press **Esc**. The word *INSERT* disappears from the bottom of the screen.

6. To save the file and quit the editing session, type **:wq** and then press **Enter**.

7. To see the new file, type **ls** at the command prompt and then press **Enter**.

8. To create the second file, type **vi program1.html** and then press **Enter**. To begin Insert mode, type **i** and then type the text from Table 8-2, pressing **Enter** at the end of each line.

9. To save the file, press **Esc** to move from Insert mode to Edit mode, type **:wq**, and then press **Enter**.

10. To view the files in your directory, type the **ls** command at the command prompt and then press **Enter**. Your two new files are listed in the directory.

11. Re-open program1.html in the Vim editor by typing **vi program1.html** at the command line and pressing **Enter**. Instead of a blank screen, your program appears. Because you are already in Edit mode, you do not need to press **Esc**.

If you accidentally enter Insert mode, press Esc to go back to Edit mode.

12. To open the other file, type **:split doctype.html** and then press **Enter**.

13. To toggle between the top and bottom windows, press **Ctrl+W** twice.

14. To quit, type **:q** and then press **Enter**.

15. To quit editing without saving the other file, type **:q** and then press **Enter**.

16. If prompted to save changes, type **:q!** and then press **Enter**.

This exercise was designed to illustrate the split-screen view, so you shouldn't have made any changes.

17. Close the Terminal window.

18. Leave the virtual machine logged on for the next activity.

Activity 8-4: Opening Two Files in Vim from the Command Line

Time Required: 15 minutes

Objective: View multiple files in the Vim editor in Fedora 13 by opening two files at one time with the vi command on the command line.

Description: In this activity, you open two files at the same time using the vi command. Use Edit mode commands to move from one file to another. This activity is useful if you want to work with multiple files but you don't need to view them at the same time.

You must complete Activity 8-3 before starting this activity.

1. If necessary, start your virtual machines using the appropriate instructions in Activity 1-1.

2. To open a Terminal console, click **Applications,** point to **System Tools,** and then click **Terminal.**

3. To open two files, type **vi doctype.html program1.html** at the command line and then press **Enter.**

4. Verify that the name of the first file, doctype.html, appears at the bottom of the editor window when the file opens.

5. To display the other file, type **:next** and press **Enter.**

6. Verify that the program1.html file appears in the editor window.

7. To return to the last viewed file, type **:previous** and press **Enter.**

8. Type **:previous** again and press **Enter.** Verify that the error message "Cannot go before first file" appears in the Edit command line at the bottom of the editor.

9. To determine the name of the file you are viewing, type **:args** and press **Enter.** Verify that the two filenames appear in the Edit command line at the bottom of the editor; the brackets indicate that you are viewing doctype.html.

10. To quit and return to the command line, type **:q** and press **Enter.** If you made changes, you are prompted to save them by typing **:q!** and then pressing **Enter.**

If you accidentally enter Insert mode, press Esc to go back to Edit mode.

11. Close the Terminal window.

12. Leave the virtual machine logged on for future activities.

Working with Lines of Text

In the following sections, you learn to work with individual lines of text in the three editors. For example, you can use the cut, copy, and paste commands when working with lines of text. The principles behind these commands are similar to using physical tools like scissors and tape to cut and paste paper. Once you learn to cut and paste, your editing becomes much more productive. Of course, if you need to copy text, you can copy and paste instead.

Working with Lines of Text in DOS Edit

The cut, copy, and paste operations work as shown in Figure 8-11. All three operations use a temporary holding area called an edit buffer. Placing an item in the buffer overwrites the previous entry in it. When working with DOS Edit, you can cut, copy, and paste one line of text or multiple lines. When you cut highlighted text, it is removed from the document and placed in the buffer.

A copy operation is similar to a cut. However, the copy leaves the highlighted text in the document and places the same text in the buffer. After you cut or copy the text, use the paste operation to insert the text from the buffer into the document at the cursor location. If you highlighted text in the document before making the paste, the text from the buffer replaces the highlighted text.

To highlight text you want to cut or copy, first position your cursor at the first character using the arrow keys or cursor movement keys (see Table 8-3). Next, use the arrow keys or cursor movement keys in conjunction with the Shift key to highlight the text. For example, press Shift+End to highlight all the characters from the cursor to the end of a line. To cut text, press Alt+E and then press the T key. To copy, press Alt+E and then press the C key.

You can only use the Paste command to place text from the edit buffer after first using the Cut or Copy command. Indicate the new text location by moving the cursor with the arrow keys or cursor movement keys. To paste text, press Alt+E and then press the P key.

NOTE Using the shortcut keys Ctrl+X, Ctrl+C, and Ctrl+V is convenient when you cut, copy, and paste text, respectively. These key combinations work with DOS Edit, TextPad, and other Windows 7 applications.

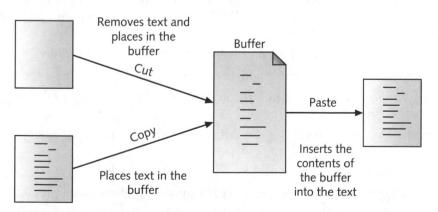

Figure 8-11 Cut, copy, and paste operations

Source: Course Technology/Cengage Learning

Home	Moves the cursor to the beginning of the current line
End	Moves the cursor to the end of the current line
Up	Scrolls up one line
Down	Scrolls down one line
Page Up	Scrolls up one screen
Page Down	Scrolls down one screen
Ctrl+Home	Scrolls to the top of the document
Ctrl+End	Scrolls to the bottom of the document
Ctrl+Left	Moves left one word
Ctrl+Right	Moves right one word

Table 8-3 Cursor movement keys

Activity 8-5: Working with Lines of Text in DOS Edit

Time Required: 15 minutes

Objective: Work with lines of text in DOS Edit in the Windows 7 CLI.

Description: In this activity, you open DOS Edit and edit the program you typed earlier. This activity is useful if you want to edit files in DOS Edit.

You must complete Activity 8-1 before starting this activity.

1. If necessary, start your virtual machines using the appropriate instructions in Activity 1-1. To open a Command Prompt window, click **Start**, point to **All Programs**, click **Accessories**, and then click **Command Prompt**.

2. To open DOS Edit, type **edit** at the command prompt and then press **Enter**.

3. To open the Open dialog box for the first file, press **Alt+F** and then press the **O** key.

4. To change to the E: drive, press **Alt+D**, use the arrow keys to move to the [-E-] entry, and then press **Enter**.

5. To open the file, press **Alt+F**, use the arrow keys to move to **doctype.htm**, and then press **Enter**.

6. To open a second window, press **Alt+V** and then press the **S** key.

7. To open the Open dialog box for the second file, press **Alt+F** and then press the **O** key.

8. To open the file, press **Alt+F**, use the arrow keys to move to **program1.htm**, and then press **Enter**.

9. Press **F6** to change to the doctype.htm window.

10. Review the text that you typed previously against Table 8-1.

11. Using the cursor movement keys, move to any error you find and then type the correction.

 To toggle between insert mode and overtype mode, press the Insert key. In overtype mode, the cursor changes to a block.

12. Press **F6** to change to the program1.htm window.

13. Review the text that you typed previously against Table 8-2.

14. Using the cursor movement keys, move to any error you find and then type the correction.

15. Press **F6** to change to the doctype.htm window.

16. Using the Shift key with the cursor movement keys, highlight all the text in the doctype.htm file.

17. To copy the highlighted text to the text buffer, press **Alt+E** and then press the **C** key.

18. Press **F6** to change to the program1.htm window.

19. To position the cursor at the first character in the file, press **Ctrl+Home**.

20. To create a blank line and position the cursor at the first character on the first line, press **Enter** and then press the **Up arrow** key.

21. To paste the text from the text buffer, press **Alt+E** and then press the **P** key.

22. To save the file, press **Alt+F** and then press the **S** key.

23. To close DOS Edit, press **Alt+F** and then press the **X** key.

24. Type **exit** at the command prompt and press **Enter**.

25. Leave the virtual machine logged on for the next activity.

Working with Lines of Text in TextPad

TextPad works with the Windows Clipboard to store or retrieve text. The cut, copy, and paste functions in TextPad are similar to those in DOS Edit. However, the Windows Clipboard rather than the edit buffer is used to hold text in transition, meaning that you can move text between TextPad and other Windows 7 applications.

You must highlight text before using the Cut or Copy command. Use the arrow keys or cursor movement keys to move to the first character you want to select, and then highlight text using the arrow keys or cursor movement keys in conjunction with the Shift key. You can also select text for cutting or copying by dragging the mouse over it. To drag the mouse, click and hold the left mouse button while moving over the text.

To cut the highlighted text, you have the following choices:

- Click the Edit menu and then click Cut.
- Right-click and then click Cut from the menu.
- Press Ctrl+X.
- Click the Cut button on the toolbar.

To copy the highlighted text, you have the following choices:

- Click the Edit menu and then click Copy.
- Right-click and then click Copy from the menu.
- Press Ctrl+C.
- Click the Copy button on the toolbar.

Before issuing the Paste command, use the cursor movement keys or the mouse to move to the new text location. To paste the text from the Windows Clipboard, you have the following choices:

- Click the Edit menu and then click Paste.
- Right-click and then click Paste from the menu.
- Press Ctrl+V.
- Click the Paste button on the toolbar.

Activity 8-6: Working with Lines of Text in TextPad

Time Required: 15 minutes

Objective: Edit text using the Windows TextPad editor.

Description: In this activity, you open TextPad and edit the files you created earlier in the chapter. This activity is useful if you want to edit files in TextPad.

You must complete Activity 8-2 before starting this activity.

1. If necessary, start your virtual machines using the appropriate instructions in Activity 1-1. Click **Start**, point to **All Programs**, and then click **TextPad**.
2. After reading the Tip of the Day, click **Close**.
3. To open the workspace, click the **File** menu, point to **Workspace**, and then click **1 E:\FirstProgram.tws**.
4. Click within the E:\doctype.html window.
5. Review the text that you typed previously against Table 8-1.
6. Using the cursor movement keys, move to any error you find and then type the correction.
7. Click within the E:\program1.html window.
8. Review the text that you typed previously against Table 8-2.
9. Using the cursor movement keys, move to any error you find and then type the correction.
10. To go to the doctype.html window, click the first character of the first line in the E:\doctype.html window.

11. To highlight the text, click the **Edit** menu and then click **Select All**.

12. To copy the text, click the **Edit** menu and then click **Copy**.

13. To go to the program1.html window, click the first character of the first line in the E:\program1.html window.

14. To create a blank line and position the cursor at the first character on the first line, press **Enter** and then press the **Up arrow** key.

15. To paste the text from the Windows Clipboard, click the **Edit** menu and then click **Paste**.

16. To save the files, click the **File** menu and then click **Save All**.

17. To save the workspace, click the **File** menu, point to **Workspace**, and then click **Save**.

18. To go to the program1.html window, click within the E:\program1.html window.

19. To view the program in your Web browser, click the **View** menu and then click **In Web Browser**.

20. Close Internet Explorer and TextPad.

21. Leave the virtual machine logged on for future activities.

8

Working with Lines of Text in Vim

One of the Vim editor's strengths is how well it works for editing text documents. The key is to practice the variety of line-editing options that Vim provides. To cut a line from a document, for example, use the arrow keys to position the cursor anywhere on the line you want to cut and then type the dd command. If you have more than one line to cut, you can enter a number before typing dd; the number of lines you specify are cut and placed in the buffer area. For example, type 20dd to remove 20 lines of text from your document. If you make a mistake—for example, if you type 2 instead of 20—type u for undo before you move on.

 Do not try to use the mouse to cut text in Vim. The cursor will not position correctly and you could inadvertently delete lines that you do not want to cut.

Before pasting lines you cut, you must first decide if you want to paste before the cursor or after it. Type a capital P to paste the text before the cursor and a lowercase p to paste the text after the cursor. Again, if you make a mistake, you can undo your action by typing u.

You should copy text in Visual mode. First, position your cursor where you want the copy to start, press Esc, and type v. You should see the word *VISUAL* at the bottom of the screen. Use the arrow keys to highlight the text you want to copy. To place the text into the buffer, type y (which is short for *yank*). The text is ready to be pasted. As with the other editors you have used in this chapter, you should paste text from the buffer as soon as possible after cutting or copying it.

Unlike other editors, the entire document is not exposed to editing commands in Vim. Figure 8-12 illustrates how a text document appears in Edit mode. Think of the document as having a protective layer over it—when you revise text, the remainder of the document is not affected.

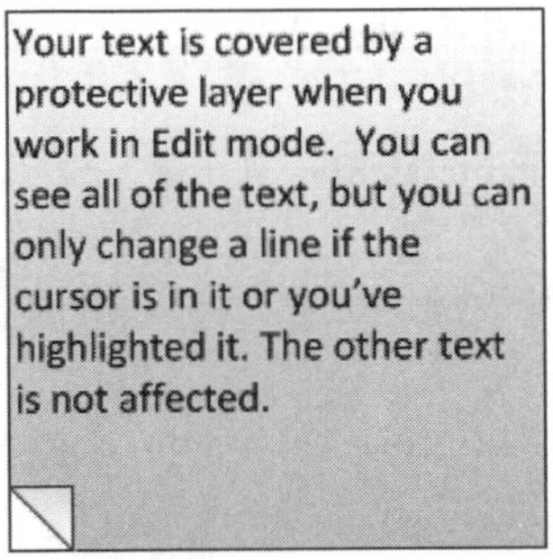

Your text is covered by a protective layer when you work in Edit mode. You can see all of the text, but you can only change a line if the cursor is in it or you've highlighted it. The other text is not affected.

Figure 8-12 Edit mode in Vim

Source: Course Technology/Cengage Learning

As with other editors you have already used, you can store cut or copied text in the buffer. However, it will be overwritten by the next text you cut. When you decide to cut or copy text, you should paste it immediately; otherwise, you might forget the text and then overwrite it in the buffer the next time you make a cut.

Activity 8-7: Working with Lines of Text in Vim

Time Required: 20 minutes

Objective: Edit text in the Vim editor in Fedora 13.

Description: In this activity, you edit lines of text using Vim. Open the files you created earlier in the chapter and then use editing commands to modify lines of text and undo the modifications. This activity is useful if you need to modify text documents and undo unwanted edits.

You must complete Activity 8-3 before you start this activity.

1. If necessary, start your virtual machines using the appropriate instructions in Activity 1-1. To open a Terminal console, click **Applications**, point to **System Tools**, and then click **Terminal**.

2. To open a file in the Vim editor, type **vi program1.html** at the command line and press **Enter**.

3. Verify that the name of the file, program1.html, appears at the bottom of the editor window.

4. To practice cutting a line of text, use the arrow keys to move the cursor anywhere within the line that contains *Hello World* and then type **dd**.

5. To paste the line back into the text, type **p**.

6. To undo the edits (because the text was pasted incorrectly), type **u**.

7. To paste the text in the correct location, type a capital **P**.

8. Verify that the text is pasted between the body tags.

9. To create another line that contains *Hello World*, type **P**.

10. Move the cursor to the **H** on the first line that contains *Hello World*.

11. To enter Visual mode, type **v**.

12. Verify that *VISUAL* appears at the bottom of the screen.

13. To highlight the entire first line that contains *Hello World*, press **End**.

14. To "yank" the text into the buffer, type **y**.

15. To paste the text, type **p**.

16. Verify that the text is pasted to the right of the cursor, which makes the first line incorrect.

17. To undo the paste and then paste the text correctly, type **u** and then type **P**.

 If the text does not align correctly when you paste it, shift it into place using the > or < keys. You may need to press the keys a few times to align the text properly.

18. Place the cursor on the first line that contains *Hello World*.

19. To delete the extra lines from your file, type **2dd**.

20. Take a few moments to review your file.

21. If you need to remove an extra character, place your cursor over the character and type **x**.

22. If you need to delete a word, move the cursor to the beginning of the word and then type **cw**. The editor is in Insert mode now.

23. If you need to return to Edit mode, press **Esc**.

24. To save your file and quit the editor, type **:wq** and then press **Enter**.

25. Close the Terminal window.

26. Leave the virtual machine logged on for the next activity.

Searching for Text Strings

A handy feature in text editors is the Search or Find command, which lets you locate a **text string** (a series of characters) in a document. Because the text may appear more than once in a document, you may have to repeat the search to find the occurrence of the text you want.

In the following sections, you learn to search for text strings in each of the three editors.

Searching for Text Strings in DOS Edit

To search for text strings in DOS Edit, press Alt+S and then press the F key. The Find dialog box appears, as shown in Figure 8-13. Type the text string that you want to search for in the Find What field. If you are searching for a word, press Alt+W to match the whole

Command Prompt - edit

```
File   Edit   Search   View   Options   Help
                    E:\User01\program1.htm
<head>
<title> My first program</title>
</head>
<body>
Hello World
</body>
<html>
                         ┌─────────────── Find ───────────────┐
                         │                                     │
                         │  Find What: [-·····················]│
                         │                                     │
                         │    [ ] Match Whole Word Only        │
                         │    [ ] Match Case                   │
                         │                                     │
                         │  ► OK ◄        Cancel        Help    │
                         └─────────────────────────────────────┘



F1=Help   Enter=Execute   Esc=Cancel   Tab=Next Field
```

Figure 8-13 Finding text strings in DOS Edit

Source: Course Technology/Cengage Learning

word. If you need to search with a text string that has both uppercase and lowercase characters, press **Alt+C** to match the case of the text string. Press **Enter** to start the search and **F3** to repeat it.

Activity 8-8: Searching for Text Strings in DOS Edit

Time Required: 15 minutes

Objective: Search for text in DOS Edit in the Windows 7 CLI.

Description: In this activity, you search for text strings in a file you typed earlier. This activity is useful if you want to search for text using DOS Edit.

> You must complete Activities 8-1 and 8-5 before starting this activity.

1. If necessary, start your virtual machines using the appropriate instructions in Activity 1-1. To open a Command Prompt window, click **Start**, point to **All Programs**, click **Accessories**, and then click **Command Prompt**.
2. To open DOS Edit, type **edit** at the command prompt and then press **Enter**.
3. To open the Open dialog box for the first file, press **Alt+F** and then press the **O** key.
4. To change to the E: drive, press **Alt+D**, use the arrow keys to move to the [-E-] entry, and then press **Enter**.
5. To open the file, press **Alt+F**, use the arrow keys to move to **program1.htm**, and then press **Enter**.

6. To search for the first occurrence of *title*, press **Alt+S**, press the F key, type **title**, and then press **Enter**.

7. Verify that the word *title* is highlighted.

8. To return to the start of the document, press **Ctrl+Home**.

9. To search for the first occurrence of *html*, press **Alt+S**, press the F key, type **html**, press **Alt+C**, and then press **Enter**.

10. Verify that the first occurrence of *html* is highlighted.

11. To search for *html* as a whole word, press **Alt+S**, press the F key, press **Alt+W**, and then press **Enter**.

12. Verify that the next occurrence of *html* is highlighted.

13. To repeat the search for additional occurrences of *html*, press **F3**.

14. Verify that no more matches fit the search criteria and then press **Enter**.

15. To search and replace the word *Hello* with *Goodbye*, press **Alt+S**, press the R key, press **Alt+W**, press **Alt+N**, type **Hello** in the Find What field, press **Tab**, type **Goodbye** in the Replace With field, and then press **Enter**.

16. To skip the replacement, press the S key and then press **Enter**.

17. To close DOS Edit, press **Alt+F** and then press the **X** key.

18. Type **exit** at the command prompt and press **Enter**.

19. Leave the virtual machine logged on for the next activity.

Searching for Text Strings in TextPad

To open the Find dialog box shown in Figure 8-14, you have the following options. The dialog box remains on the screen until you close it.

- Click the Search menu and then click Find.
- Press Alt+S and then press the F key.
- Press the F5 key.

Type the text string in the Find what text box. To use a previous search string, click the Find what list arrow and then click the text string.

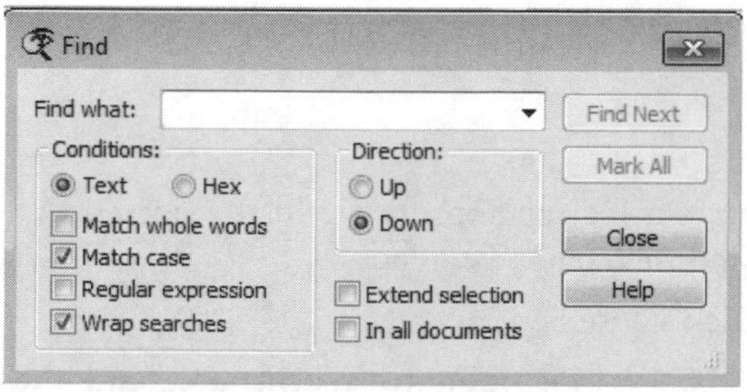

Figure 8-14 Find dialog box in TextPad

Source: Course Technology/Cengage Learning

If you highlight a text string before opening the Find dialog box, the text string appears in the Find what text box.

After entering the search string, you have the following options for tailoring your search:

- Text—Specify a text search string.
- Hex—Specify a search string in **hexadecimal**, a numbering system that uses a base of 16.
- Match whole words—Find occurrences of the text as whole words.
- Match case—Find text that has the given pattern of uppercase and lowercase letters.
- Regular expression—Specify that the search string is a regular expression.
- Wrap searches—If you are searching down, continue searching from the beginning of the document after reaching the end. If you are searching up, continue searching from the end of the document after reaching the beginning.
- Up—Search the document above the location of the cursor.
- Down—Search the document below the location of the cursor.
- Extend selection—Extend the selection from the cursor position to the matched text; this highlights the text in the document.
- In all documents—Find the next instance of the search pattern in all open documents simultaneously; this option works best when documents are tiled.

To repeat a search, click the Search menu and then click Find Next, or press Ctrl+F. If you are searching backward, click the Search menu and then click Find Previous, or press Ctrl+Shift+F.

Activity 8-9: Searching for Text Strings in TextPad

Time Required: 15 minutes

Objective: Search for text using the Windows TextPad editor.

Description: In this activity, you open TextPad and search for text in the files you created earlier. This activity is useful if you want to learn to search for text using TextPad.

You must complete Activities 8-2 and 8-6 before starting this activity.

1. If necessary, start your virtual machines using the appropriate instructions in Activity 1-1. Click **Start,** point to **All Programs,** and then click **TextPad.**
2. After reading the Tip of the Day, click **Close.**
3. To open the workspace, click the **File** menu, point to **Workspace,** and then click **1 E:\FirstProgram.tws.**
4. Click within the E:\program1.html window.

5. To search for the title line, click the **Search** menu, click **Find**, type **title** in the Find what text box, and then click **Find Next**.

6. Verify that *title* is highlighted and then click **Close**.

7. To return to the start of the document, press **Ctrl+Home**.

8. To search for all occurrences of the title line, click the **Search** menu, click **Find**, and then click the **Mark All** button.

9. Verify that the line containing *title* is highlighted and then click **Close**.

10. To search for all occurrences of *html*, click the **Search** menu, click **Find**, type **html** in the Find what text box, and then click the **Mark All** button.

11. Verify that the lines containing *html* are highlighted and then click **Close**.

12. To clear the bookmarks, click the **Search** menu and then click **Clear All Bookmarks**.

13. To search for all lowercase occurrences of *html*, click the **Search** menu, click **Find**, click the **Match whole words** check box, click the **Match case** check box, and then click the **Mark All** button.

14. When you see that all lines containing the lowercase *html* are highlighted, click **Close**.

15. To search and replace the word *Hello* with *Goodbye*, click the **Search** menu, click **Replace**, type **Hello** in the Find what text box, press the **Tab** key, type **Goodbye** in the Replace with text box, and then click **Find Next**.

16. To skip the replacement, click **Find Next** and then click **OK**.

17. Click **Close**.

18. To close all the files, click the **File** menu and click **Close All**. If prompted to replace a file, click **No**.

19. Close the TextPad window.

20. Leave the virtual machine logged on for the next activity.

As you learned in Chapter 7, regular expressions help you describe patterns in search strings when using the FINDSTR command. Table 8-4 gives you more examples for using regular expressions to search for character patterns.

Expression	Explanation
.	Finds a single character (for example, *b.t* matches *bat, bet, bit, bot,* and *but*)
[ ]	Finds any one of the characters in the brackets, or any of a range of characters separated by a hyphen or a character class operator (for example, *b[aeiou][a-z]* matches *bat, ben, bit, bop,* and *but*; *[A-Za-z]* matches any single letter; and *x[0-9]* matches *x0, x1, …, x9*)
[^]	Finds any characters except those after the caret (^); for example, *b[^u]t* matches *bat, bit,* and *bot,* but not *but*
^	Finds characters at the start of a line (for example, *^the* only matches *the* when it is the first word on a line)

Table 8-4 Regular expressions used in TextPad (*continues*)

Expression	Explanation
$	Finds characters at the end of a line, excluding line-break characters (for example, *end$* only matches *end* when it is the last word on a line)
\\<	Finds the start of a word
\\>	Finds the end of a word
\\t	Finds the tab character
\\f	Finds the page break (form feed) character
\\n	Finds a newline character, which is useful for matching expressions that span line boundaries; this cannot be followed by operators such as *, +, or {}
\\xdd	*dd* is the two-digit hexadecimal code for any character
*	Matches zero or more of the preceding characters (for example, *bo*p* matches *bp*, *bop*, and *boop*)
?	Matches zero or one of the preceding characters (for example, *bo?p* matches *bp* and *bop*, but not *boop*)
+	Matches one or more of the preceding characters (for example, *bo+p* matches *bop* and *boop*, but not *bp*)
\\{count\\}	Matches the specified number of preceding characters (for example, *bo\\{2\\}p* matches *boop*, but not *bop*)
\\{min,\\}	Matches at least the specified number of preceding characters (for example, *bo\\{1,\\}p* matches *bop* and *boop*, but not *bp*)
\\{min,max\\}	Matches between the minimum and maximum numbers of the preceding characters (for example, *bo\\{1,2\\}p* matches *bop* and *boop*, but not *bp* or *booop*)
\\|	Matches either the expression to its left or its right (for example, *bop\\|boop* matches *bop* or *boop*)
\\	"Escapes" the special meaning of the above expressions, so that they can be matched as literal characters; hence, to match a literal "\\", you must use "\\\\" (for example, "\\<" matches the start of a word, but "\\\\<" matches "\\<")

Table 8-4 Regular expressions used in TextPad (*continued*)

When studying regular expressions, the RegEx Coach is helpful. The coach is available for free at *www.weitz.de/regex-coach/*.

Activity 8-10: Searching for Text Strings Using Regular Expressions in TextPad

Time Required: 15 minutes

Objective: Search for text using regular expressions in the Windows TextPad editor.

Description: In this activity, you open TextPad and search for text using regular expressions. This activity is useful if you want to learn to search for text using regular expressions in TextPad.

1. If necessary, start your virtual machines using the appropriate instructions in Activity 1-1.

2. Click **Start,** point to **All Programs,** and then click **TextPad.**

3. After reading the Tip of the Day, click **Close.**

4. Type the statements in Table 8-5, pressing **Enter** at the end of each line.

5. To open the Save As dialog box, click the **File** menu and then click **Save As.**

6. To change to the E: drive, expand **Computer** and double-click the **NTFS (E:)** entry.

7. To save the file, type **expressions.txt** in the File name text box and then click **Save.**

8. To search for lines containing strings that start with a *b* and are followed by a vowel and a *t*, click the **Search** menu, click **Find,** type **b[aeiou]t** in the Find what text box, click the **Regular expression** check box, and then click the **Mark All** button.

9. Verify that three lines are marked.

10. To clear the bookmarks, click **Search** and then click **Clear All Bookmarks.**

11. To search for lines containing three characters that start with a *b* and are followed by a vowel and an additional character, type **b[aeiou].** in the Find what text box, and then click the **Mark All** button.

12. Verify that all six lines are marked.

13. To clear the bookmarks, click **Search** and then click **Clear All Bookmarks.**

14. To search for lines containing strings that start with a *b* and are followed by an *e* or an *o* and then a *b* or a *t*, type **b[eo][bt]** in the Find what text box, and then click the **Mark All** button.

15. Verify that two lines are marked.

16. To clear the bookmarks, click **Search** and then click **Clear All Bookmarks.**

17. To position the cursor at the top of the document, press **Ctrl+Home.**

18. To search for lines containing words that start with a *b* and are followed by *ee* or *oo*, type **b[eo]\{2,\}** in the Find what text box, clear the Match case check box, and then click **Find Next.**

Statement
I bet a bit on the big red bag.
Ben went to bat in the bottom of the fourth.
The boy at the bay was bitten by a bug.
I want to buy a boa for my wife.
Was it a bug or a bee?
A big box was sent from the Boo and Bop.

Table 8-5 Sample text strings

19. Verify that *bee* is highlighted.

20. Click **Find Next**.

21. Verify that *Boo* is highlighted.

22. To close the Find dialog box, click **Close**.

23. Close the TextPad window.

24. Leave the virtual machine logged on for future activities.

Searching for Text Strings in Vim

You have many search options in the Vim editor. The option you use depends on the object of your search. For example, when you know the exact spelling of a word, you can use either of the following quick options:

- Type `: /` (a colon and then a forward slash) followed by the word you want to find. If the word exists in the file, all instances of it will be highlighted.

- Place the cursor on a word and then press the `*` key. All matching words will be highlighted.

If you need to perform multiple searches and remove all of the highlighting, type either `:noh` or `:nohl` and press Enter. The `nohighlight` command is useful to remember, especially when using the Vim editor in a student lab where other students may have performed searches and left text highlighted. Highlighting is considered "sticky"; it remains from one session to the next and can be distracting if you are not doing searches.

To search for more than one word or command, use regular expressions. As with the other editors, you can substitute characters for other characters, locate the beginning and end of a line, and find special characters in programming documents.

Table 8-6 contains a partial list of expressions that you may find useful when doing text searches in the Vim editor.

Expression	Explanation
.	Finds a single character (for example, *b.t* matches *bat*, *bet*, *bit*, *bot*, and *but*)
[ ]	Finds any one of the characters in the brackets, or any of a range of characters separated by a hyphen or a character class operator (for example, *b[aeiou][a-z]* matches *bat*, *ben*, *bit*, *bop*, and *but*; *[A-Za-z]* matches any single letter; and *x[0-9]* matches *x0*, *x1*, ..., *x9*)
[^]	Finds any characters except those after the caret (^); for example, *b[^u]t* matches *bat*, *bit*, and *bot*, but not *but*
^	Finds characters at the start of a line (for example, *^the* only matches *the* when it is the first word on a line)
$	Finds characters at the end of a line, excluding line-break characters (for example, *end$* only matches *end* when it is the last word on a line)
\<	Finds the start of a word

Table 8-6 Regular expressions used in Vim editor

Expression	Explanation
\>	Finds the end of a word
\t	Finds the tab character
\f	Finds the page break (form feed) character
\n	Finds a newline character, which is useful for matching expressions that span line boundaries; this cannot be followed by operators such as *, +, or {}
*	Matches zero or more of the preceding characters (for example, *bo*p* matches *bp*, *bop*, and *boop*)
\{count\}	Matches the specified number of preceding characters (for example, *bo\{2\}p* matches *boop*, but not *bop*)
\{min,\}	Matches at least the specified number of preceding characters (for example, *bo\{1,\}p* matches *bop* and *boop*, but not *bp*)
\{min,max\}	Matches between the minimum and maximum numbers of the preceding characters (for example, *bo\{1,2\}p* matches *bop* and *boop*, but not *bp* or *booop*)
|	Matches either the expression to its left or its right (for example, *bop|boop* matches *bop* or *boop*)
\	"Escapes" the special meaning of the above expressions, so that they can be matched as literal characters; hence, to match a literal "\", you must use "\\" (for example, "\<" matches the start of a word, but "\\<" matches "\<")

Table 8-6 Regular expressions used in Vim editor (*continued*)

Activity 8-11: Searching for Text Strings in Vim

Time Required: 10 minutes

Objective: Search for text strings in the Vim editor in Fedora 13.

Description: In this activity, you search documents for text strings using Vim. Open a file and search the text using complete words and single letters. Remove highlighting after a search to prepare for the next search. This activity is useful if you need to find particular words, letters, or special characters in a Vim document.

You must complete Activity 8-3 before starting this activity.

1. If necessary, start your virtual machines using the appropriate instructions in Activity 1-1. To open a Terminal console, click **Applications**, point to **System Tools**, and then click **Terminal**.

2. To open the file in the Vim editor, type **vi program1.html** at the command line and press **Enter**.

3. Verify that the name of the file, program1.html, appears at the bottom of the editor window when the file opens.

4. To find the word *World*, type **:/World** and press **Enter**. To turn off the highlighting, type either **:noh** or **:nohl** and press **Enter**.

5. To find all instances of the letter *e* in the text, type **:/e** and press **Enter**. Notice that all embedded characters are highlighted. (In the next activity, you use regular expressions to narrow your search when the text you are looking for is embedded within other text.)

6. Use the arrow keys to place your cursor on the first HTML tag at the letter *h*.

7. To search for the one set of HTML tags in the document, type **:/\<html\>**. Two tags should be highlighted. The bottom of the screen shows the regular expression (/\<html\>) that was used to search for the text string.

8. To quit the editing session, type **:q** and press **Enter**.

9. Close the Terminal window.

10. Leave the virtual machine logged on for the next activity.

Activity 8-12: Searching for Text Strings Using Regular Expressions in Vim

Time Required: 15 minutes

Objective: Search for text using regular expressions in the Vim editor.

Description: In this activity, you search a text document in Vim using regular expressions. This activity helps you learn to search for text when you are not sure about exact spelling or the correct characters to use. Knowing how to work with highlighted text also helps in future text searches using Vim.

1. If necessary, start your virtual machines using the appropriate instructions in Activity 1-1. To open a Terminal console, click **Applications**, point to **System Tools**, and then click **Terminal**.

2. To begin creating the file for this activity, type **vi expressions.txt** at the command prompt and press **Enter**.

3. To enter Insert mode, press **i**.

4. Type the statements in Table 8-5, pressing **Enter** at the end of each line. This is the same text you used in Activity 8-10.

5. To enter Edit mode, press **Esc**.

6. To save the file, type **:w** and press **Enter**.

7. To search for lines containing strings that start with a *b* and are followed by a vowel and a *t*, type **:/b[aeiou]t** and press **Enter**.

8. Verify that the first three lines in the text have the correct highlighted text.

9. To clear the highlighting, type either **:noh** or **:nohl** and press **Enter**.

10. To search for lines containing three characters that start with a *b* and are followed by a vowel and an additional character, type **:/b[aeiou].** and press **Enter**.

11. Verify that all six lines have the correct text highlighted.

12. To clear the highlighting, type **:noh** or **:nohl** and press **Enter**.

13. To search for lines containing strings that start with a *b* and are followed by an *e* or an *o* and then a *b* or a *t*, type **:/b[eo][bt]** and press **Enter**.

14. Verify that the first two lines in the text have the correct text highlighted.

15. To clear the highlighting, type either **:noh** or **:nohl** and press **Enter**.

16. To search for lines containing words that start with *b* and are followed by a pair of the letters *e* or *o*, type **:/b[eo]\{2,\}** and press **Enter**.

17. Verify that *bee* is highlighted.

18. To search for lines containing words that start with *B* and are followed by a pair of the letters *e* or *o*, type **:/B[eo]\{2,\}** and press **Enter**.

19. Verify that *Boo* is highlighted.

20. To close the Vim editor, type **:q** and then press **Enter**.

21. Close the Terminal window.

22. Leave the virtual machine logged on for future activities.

Searching and Replacing Text Strings

Another handy tool when you work with text strings is the search-and-replace operation, also known as Find and Replace. A search-and-replace operation lets you replace a text string with another string throughout a document. For example, if you repeatedly assigned the wrong name to an item in a document, you can use a search-and-replace operation to fix the problem quickly.

Most text editors have two search-and-replace modes. In the first mode, the text editor automatically makes all the replacements in the document. In the second mode, the text editor requires you to approve each replacement. The latter method is better when you do not want to make the change everywhere in the document.

Searching and Replacing Text Strings in DOS Edit

To search and replace text strings in DOS Edit, press Alt+S and then press the R key. The Replace dialog box appears, as shown in Figure 8-15. Type the text string you want to

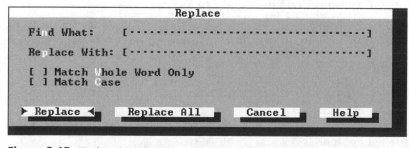

Figure 8-15 Find and Replace text strings in DOS Edit

Source: Course Technology/Cengage Learning

search for in the Find What field, and then type the replacement text string in the Replace With field. If you are searching for a word, press Alt+W to match a whole word. If you need to search with a text string that has uppercase and lowercase characters, press Alt+C to match the case of the text string. Press Enter to start the search. When a match is found, press Enter to accept the change or press the right arrow key and then press Enter to reject the change.

To replace all of the matches, press the Down arrow key until Replace is highlighted, press the right arrow key to highlight Replace All, and then press Enter.

Activity 8-13: Searching and Replacing Text Strings in DOS Edit

Time Required: 15 minutes

Objective: Search and replace text in DOS Edit in the Windows 7 CLI.

Description: In this activity, you search for one text string and replace it with another. This activity is useful if you want to replace the same text several times in a DOS Edit file.

1. If necessary, start your virtual machines using the appropriate instructions in Activity 1-1.
2. To open a Command Prompt window, click **Start**, point to **All Programs**, click **Accessories**, and then click **Command Prompt**.
3. To open DOS Edit, type **edit** at the command prompt and then press **Enter**.
4. To open an existing file, press **Alt+F** and then press the **O** key.
5. To change to the E: drive, press **Alt+D**, use the arrow keys to move to the [-E-] entry, and then press **Enter**.
6. To open the file, press **Alt+F**, use the arrow keys to move to **expressions.txt**, and then press **Enter**.
7. To replace the first instance of *bit* with *five*, press **Alt+S**, press the **R** key, type **bit**, press **Tab**, type **five**, press **Enter** twice, and then press **Esc**.
8. Verify that the first sentence changed to "I bet a five on the big red bag."
9. To replace each occurrence of the word *bug* with *wasp*, press **Alt+S**, press the **R** key, type **bug**, press **Tab**, type **wasp**, press **Alt+A**, and then press **Enter**.
10. Verify that two occurrences of *bug* changed to *wasp*.
11. To replace each occurrence of the word *Boo* with *Boot*, press **Alt+S**, press the **R** key, type **Boo**, press **Tab**, type **Boot**, press **Alt+C**, press **Alt+A**, and then press **Enter**.
12. Verify that one occurrence of *Boo* was changed.
13. To exit DOS Edit without saving the file, press **Alt+F**, press the **X** key, and then press **Alt+N**.
14. Type **exit** at the command prompt and press **Enter**.
15. Leave the virtual machine logged on for the next activity.

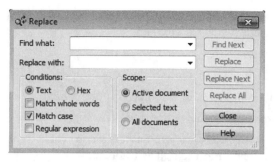

Figure 8-16 Replace dialog box in TextPad

Source: Course Technology/Cengage Learning

Searching and Replacing Text Strings in TextPad

To open the Replace dialog box (see Figure 8-16), you have the following options. The dialog box remains on the screen until you finish making replacements.

- Click the Search menu and then click Replace.
- Press Alt+S and then press the R key.
- Press the F8 key.

Type the search string in the Find what text box. If you want to use a previous search string, click the Find what list arrow and then click the text string. Type the replacement text string in the Replace with text box. To use a previous replacement string, click the Replace with list arrow and then click the text string.

After entering the search and replacement text strings, you have a number of options for tailoring your search. Many of these options are similar to those in the Find dialog box in TextPad, which you learned about earlier in this chapter. The Replace dialog box includes the following additional buttons to help you search and replace text:

- Click the Find Next button to find the next occurrence of the text.
- Click the Replace button to replace the current text selection.
- Click the Replace Next button to replace the current selection and find the next occurrence.
- Click the Replace All button to replace all occurrences of the search text in the specified search area.

Activity 8-14: Searching and Replacing Text Strings in TextPad

Time Required: 15 minutes

Objective: Search and replace text strings using the Windows TextPad editor.

Description: In this activity, you search for one text string and replace it with another. This activity is useful if you want to replace the same text several times in a TextPad file.

1. If necessary, start your virtual machines using the appropriate instructions in Activity 1-1. Click **Start,** point to **All Programs,** and then click **TextPad.**

2. After reading the Tip of the Day, click **Close.**

3. To open the Open dialog box, click the **File** menu and then click **Open.**

4. To change to the E: drive, expand **Computer** and double-click the **NTFS (E:)** entry.

5. To open the file, double-click **expressions** in the right pane.

6. To replace the first instance of *bit* with *five,* click the **Search** menu, click **Replace,** type **bit,** press **Tab,** type **five,** click **Find Next,** and then click **Replace.**

7. Verify that the first sentence changed to "I bet a five on the big red bag."

8. To replace each occurrence of the word *bug* with *wasp,* click in the **Find what** text box, type **bug,** press **Tab,** type **wasp,** and then click **Replace All.**

9. Verify that two occurrences of *bug* changed to *wasp.*

10. To replace each occurrence of the word *Boo* with *Boot,* click in the **Find what** text box, type **Boo,** press **Tab,** type **Boot,** click the **Match case** check box, and then click **Replace All.**

11. Verify that one occurrence of *Boo* was changed.

12. Click **Close.**

13. To exit TextPad without saving the file, click the **File** menu, click **Exit,** and then click **No.**

14. Leave the virtual machine logged on for the next activity.

Searching and Replacing Text Strings Using Regular Expressions in TextPad

You can use TextPad's search-and-replace feature with regular expressions to extend the power of your searches. You can use the replacement expressions in Table 8-7 to substitute text in conjunction with the regular search expressions you learned earlier in this chapter.

For example, you can find the word *paste:*

Find what: `paste`

and replace it with the contents of the Clipboard:

Replace with: `\p`

Next, you can find any word that starts with an uppercase letter:

Find what: `[A-Z][a-z]+`

and replace it with the same word, all in uppercase letters:

Replace with: `\U&`

Or, you can position the cursor at the start of each line:

Find what: `^`

and insert consecutive line numbers:

Replace with: `\i`

Expression	Definition
&	Substitutes the text matching the entire search pattern
\0 to \9	Substitutes the text matching a tagged expression 0 through 9 (\0 is equivalent to &)
\f	Substitutes a page break (form feed)
\i	Substitutes a sequence number
\n	Substitutes a newline character
\p	Substitutes the contents of the Clipboard
\t	Substitutes a tab
\xdd	Substitutes the character with the hexadecimal code *dd* (must be two hex digits, excluding *00*)
\u	Forces the next substituted character to be in uppercase
\l	Forces the next substituted character to be in lowercase
\U	Forces all subsequent substituted characters to be in uppercase
\L	Forces all subsequent substituted characters to be in lowercase
\E or \e	Turns off the previous \U or \L expression

Table 8-7 Replacement expressions in TextPad

If the line numbers start at 1, use \i. If they start at 100, use \i*(100)*.

Replacements that use regular expressions can also exploit the concept of tagged expressions, which indicate the location of the text to be substituted. A tagged expression is a regular expression that starts with the character pair "\(" and ends with the pair "\)". A regular expression can have up to nine tagged expressions, numbered according to their order in the regular expression. The corresponding replacement expression is \x, where x is a number in the range of 1 to 9.

For example, if \(*[a-z]*+\) \(*[a-z]*+\) matches *way wrong*, then \2 \1 would replace it with *wrong way*.

Activity 8-15: Searching and Replacing Text Strings Using Regular Expressions in TextPad

Time Required: 15 minutes

Objective: Search and replace text using regular expressions with TextPad.

Description: In this activity, you open the TextPad editor and then search and replace text using regular expressions. This activity is useful if you want to use regular expressions to replace text in TextPad.

1. If necessary, start your virtual machines using the appropriate instructions in Activity 1-1.

2. Click **Start**, point to **All Programs**, and then click **TextPad**.

3. After reading the Tip of the Day, click **Close**.

4. To open the Open dialog box, click the **File** menu and then click **Open**.

5. To change to the E: drive, expand **Computer** and double-click the **NTFS (E:)** entry.

6. To open the file, double-click **expressions** in the right pane.

7. To capitalize each word that starts with a *b*, click the **Search** menu, click **Replace**, type **b[a-z]+**, press the **Tab** key, type **\u&**, clear the **Match case** check box, check the **Regular expression** check box, and then click **Replace All**.

8. Verify that each word that started with a *b* now starts with a *B*.

9. To switch the words *Big* and *red* in the first sentence, click in the **Find what** text box, type **\(Big\) +\(red\)**, press the **Tab** key, type **\2 \1**, and then click **Replace All**.

10. Verify that the words *red* and *Big* appear switched in the first sentence.

11. To number the lines in the document, click in the **Find what** text box, type **^**, press **Tab**, type **\i -**, and then click **Replace All**.

12. Verify that the lines are numbered with a hyphen after the line numbers.

13. Click **Close**.

14. To exit TextPad without saving the file, click the **File** menu, click **Exit**, and then click **No**.

15. Close any open windows in the virtual machine.

16. To shut down the virtual machine, click **Start**, and then click the **Shut Down** button.

17. Wait a moment for the Windows 7 virtual machine to shut down completely.

Searching and Replacing Text Strings in Vim

In Vim, the term used for search-and-replace operations is *substitution*; you need to know this before using the Vim help manual. The placement of the cursor causes most of the frustration with the :substitute command, though some users blame the command itself. The basic command syntax used for searching and replacing is often one of the following, in which a user does not specify a range:

```
:substitute  /pattern/string
:sub  /pattern/string
:s  /pattern/string
```

Figure 8-17 shows a program before any changes are made. The cursor is located at the line to change. Figure 8-18 shows the effect of the search-and-replace operation without a specified range. Notice that *World* is replaced with *There*.

You can become frustrated if Vim does not find a pattern and make replacements. If so, consider whether to search the whole document or just a range of lines in it. A basic search does not encompass the entire document; it only searches for the pattern on the line that contains the cursor, and then displays an error message if the search finds nothing. Figure 8-19 displays the original program without any changes. The cursor is located at the beginning of the program. To perform a search-and-replace operation on the entire document, place a % sign before the :substitute command (see Figure 8-20). Notice that the word *World* is replaced with *There*.

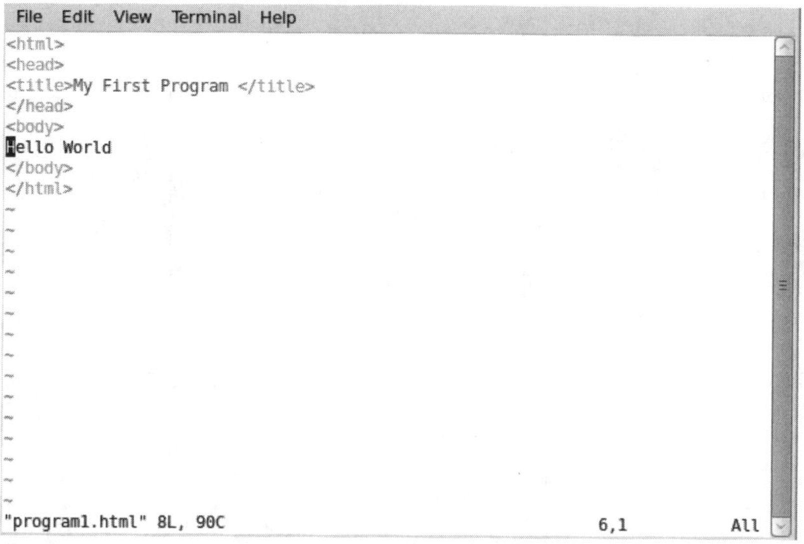

Figure 8-17 The original program for the `:substitute` command used with no range

Source: Course Technology/Cengage Learning

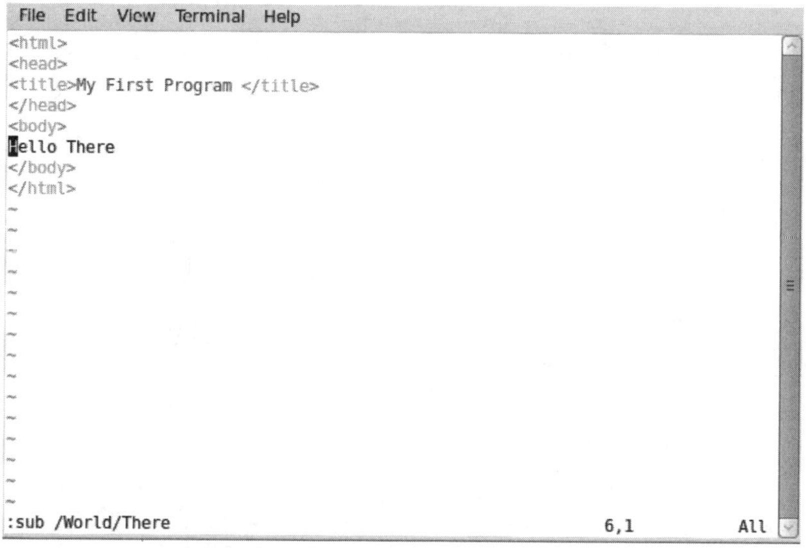

Figure 8-18 The `:substitute` command used with no range

Source: Course Technology/Cengage Learning

You can use the following search-and-replace syntax and options:

`:[range]sub  /{pattern}/{string} [&] [c] [g]`

[range]   Specifies which lines you want to search for the pattern; if you are uncertain about the range of lines to specify, use a wildcard like %, which starts the search from the beginning of the document. The following example would replace all occurrences of *bug* with *wasp*:

`:% sub /bug/wasp`

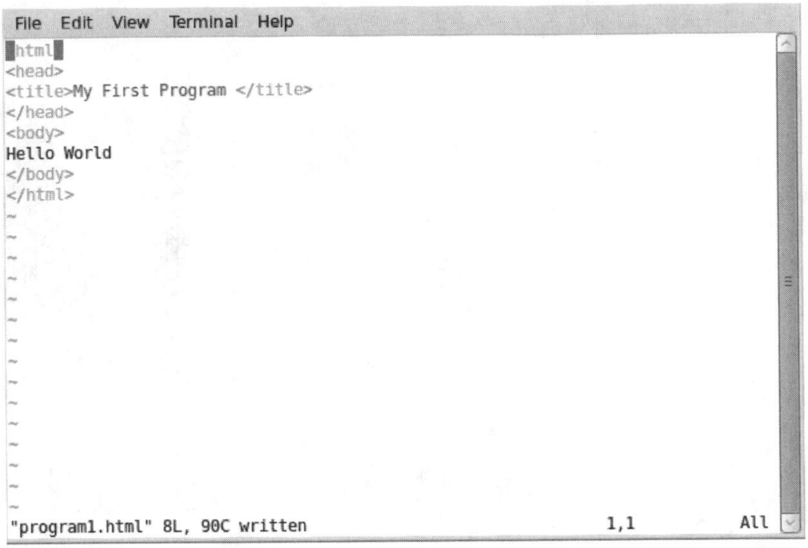

Figure 8-19 The original program for the :substitute command with %

Source: Course Technology/Cengage Learning

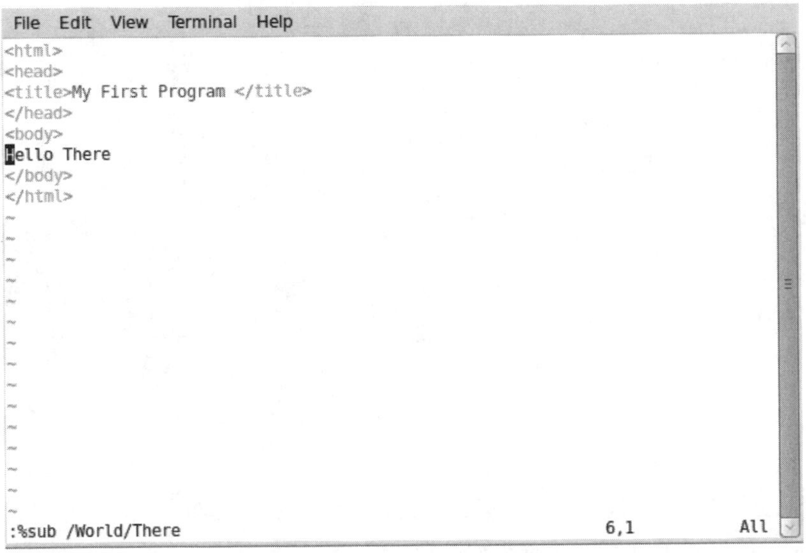

Figure 8-20 The :substitute command used with %

Source: Course Technology/Cengage Learning

A few of the flags that you can use to improve a search-and-replace operation are more helpful with a little explanation:

[&]   Uses the previous search pattern; if you used flags in the previous search, the search works differently. To keep the same flags in your search, use the following command:

          :sub &&

[c]   Confirms each substitution; this flag displays a question with one-letter choices:

      'y'   Yes, substitute this match

      'l'   Yes, substitute this match

      'n'   Skips this match and goes to the next match

     Esc   Quits substituting

      'a'   Substitutes this and all remaining matches

      'q'   Quits substituting

^E   Scrolls the screen up (same as Ctrl+E)

^Y   Scrolls the screen down (same as Ctrl+Y)

[g]   Performs a global replacement in a line or within a specified range

Search-and-replace operations are more effective when you use regular expressions; in fact, some advanced searches are nearly impossible without them. Learning the many combinations of these options can seem daunting at first, but eventually you will discover favorites and use them frequently. Special characters, also known as "magic" characters in the Vim editor, are used as wildcards in search patterns and strings. Table 8-8 lists some common magic characters used in regular expressions.

The following examples show you how to use some of these special characters in regular expressions to perform a search and replace:

`:s/a|b/xxx\0xxx/g`	Modifies *a b* to *xxxaxxx xxxbxxx*
`:s/\([abc]\)\([efg]\)/\2\1/g`	Modifies *af fa bg* to *fa fa gb*
`:s/abcde/abc^Mde/`	Modifies *abcde* to *abc*; *de* will be placed on the next line

Magic character	Special meaning
\0	Replaces text with the whole matched pattern
\1	Replaces text with the matched pattern in the first pair of ()
\2	Replaces text with the matched pattern in the second pair of ()
\n	Replaces text with the matched pattern in the nth pair of ()
\9	Replaces text with the matched pattern in the ninth pair of ()
\u	Makes the next character uppercase
\	Makes the next character lowercase
^M	Splits a line in two; to enter this command, press Ctrl+V and then press Enter
\b	Inserts a Backspace character (which may appear as ^H in the text)
\t	Inserts a Tab character
\\	Inserts a single backslash

Table 8-8   Magic characters for search-and-replace operations

Activity 8-16: Searching and Replacing Text Strings in Vim

Time Required: 20 minutes

Objective: Search and replace text strings in the Vim editor.

Description: In this activity, you search and replace text strings using the :substitute command on a single line, an entire document, and a range of lines. This activity is useful if you need to modify a text document by replacing incorrect text; it also demonstrates that you can retract changes with the undo command if you make errors during editing.

You need to complete Activity 8-12 before starting this activity.

1. If necessary, start your virtual machines using the appropriate instructions in Activity 1-1. To open a Terminal console, click **Applications**, point to **System Tools**, and then click **Terminal**.

2. To open the file you created in a previous Vim activity, type **vi expressions.txt** at the command prompt and press **Enter**.

3. Place the cursor within the first line. To replace *bit* with *five*, type **:sub /bit/five/c** and press **Enter**.

4. In response to the confirmation question, type **y**.

5. Verify that the first sentence changed to "I bet a five on the big red bag."

6. To replace each occurrence of *bug* with *wasp*, type **:%sub /bug/wasp/c** and press **Enter**.

7. In response to the confirmation question, type **a** for all.

8. Verify that two occurrences of *bug* were changed to *wasp*.

9. To change a range of lines, type **:1,3 sub /I/You** and press **Enter**.

10. Verify that only the first line was changed.

11. To undo the last search-and-replace operation, type **u**.

12. To recall the last typed command, type **:** and then press the **Up arrow** key.

13. Use the **left arrow** key to move the cursor to the white space after the 3, press the **Backspace** key to remove the 3, and type **4**. Press **Enter**.

14. Verify that you have changed two lines from *I* to *You*.

15. To save the file and quit the editing session, type **:wq** and press **Enter**.

16. Close the Terminal window.

17. Leave the virtual machine logged on for the next activity.

Activity 8-17: Searching and Replacing Text Strings Using Regular Expressions in Vim

Time Required: 15 minutes

Objective: Search and replace text strings using regular expressions in the Vim editor.

Description: In this activity, you use the :substitute command with regular expressions in the Vim editor to search and replace text strings. This activity is useful if you want to use regular expressions to replace text in the Vim editor.

You need to complete Activity 8-12 before starting this activity.

1. If necessary, start your virtual machines using the appropriate instructions in Activity 1-1. To open a Terminal console, click **Applications**, point to **System Tools**, and then click **Terminal**.

2. To open the file you created in a previous Vim activity, type **vi expressions.txt** at the command prompt and press **Enter**.

3. Type **:%sub /a/xxx\0xxx/g** and press **Enter**.

4. To undo the substitution, press **Enter** and then **u** until all instances of the letter *a* no longer have the *x*'s.

5. Notice that the letter *a* is still highlighted. To turn off the highlighting, type either **:nohl** or **:noh** and press **Enter**.

6. Type **:%sub /wasp/bugs^MWow/** and press **Enter**.

To type the ^M correctly, you must press Ctrl+V and then press Ctrl+M. The ^M appears on the command line. Only then can you type the remainder of the command.

7. Verify that one line contains only *Wow* and another later line begins with *Wow*.

8. To quit without saving your changes in this activity, type **:q!** and press **Enter**.

9. Close the Terminal window.

10. To shut down the virtual machine, click **System**, click **Shut Down**, and then click the **Shut Down** button.

11. Wait a moment for the Fedora 13 virtual machine to shut down completely.

12. Close any remaining open windows, log off, and shut down your PC.

8

Chapter Summary

- Text editors do more than allow you to edit files. For example, you can use them to create files, modify them, search for text within a file, and save files under new names. The same basic editing capabilities exist in DOS Edit, TextPad, and Vim.

- Each text editor discussed in this chapter allows you to work with multiple files at the same time. When working with multiple files, be careful not to inadvertently change the wrong one.

- Text editors allow you to rearrange words and lines in your text files. Use cut-and-paste operations to define text in one section of a document and move it to another section. Copy-and-paste operations are beneficial because you don't have to retype similar phrases or lines over and over. You can also move text between multiple files.

- Use a text editor's search feature to locate information quickly. You can find text in an entire document or on a particular line. Knowing how a particular editor performs a search operation helps you perform the corresponding replace operation.

- Search-and-replace operations are especially powerful when you use regular expressions. When you only know part of a text string, you can use wildcards and "magic characters" to make a search more precise, which is useful in large documents. You can also use wildcards when searching for text that contains special characters.

Key Terms

Command/Edit mode   The state in which the Vim editor accepts changes to a file.

hexadecimal   A number system that uses 16 for the base instead of 10. Hexadecimal uses the digits 0–9 and the uppercase letters A–F to represent the numbers 0–15.

Insert mode   A mode of operation in which the Vim editor pushes characters to the right of the screen rather than overwriting them. Use Insert mode to first enter information into a file.

TextPad   A full-featured text editor used in the Windows OS.

text string   A sequence of characters in a file that you can display, print, or process.

Visual mode   A mode of operation in which the Vim editor highlights characters in a document. Visual mode is most useful when you select text for a copy or paste operation.

workspace   A file or area in TextPad where you can place common resources to more easily manage a project or a project environment.

Review Questions

1. Text editors are used to _____. (Choose all that apply.)
   a.   edit files
   b.   create files
   c.   execute files
   d.   compile files

2. Common text editors include _____. (Choose all that apply.)
   a. DOS Edit
   b. Vim editor
   c. Windows 7
   d. TextPad

3. Learning DOS Edit prepares you to use _____.
   a. TextPad
   b. the Vim editor
   c. Windows 7
   d. No editor is comparable.

4. Common File menu options in DOS Edit are _____. (Choose all that apply.)
   a. Find
   b. Save
   c. New
   d. Exit

5. Common Edit menu options in DOS Edit are _____. (Choose all that apply.)
   a. Clear
   b. Copy
   c. Cut
   d. Paste

6. Copy, cut, and clear commands require _____. (Choose all that apply.)
   a. text of more than three characters
   b. the use of Edit mode
   c. highlighting
   d. special characters

7. TextPad is _____. (Choose all that apply.)
   a. similar to DOS Edit
   b. a powerful word processor
   c. a full-featured text editor
   d. a Windows 7 text editor that is easy for new users to learn

8. When you cut or copy text in TextPad, it is placed in _____.
   a. a special buffer within the editor
   b. the buffer stack within the editor
   c. the Windows Clipboard
   d. a file within your editing session

9. You can use TextPad to _____. (Choose all that apply.)

   a. create and edit text documents

   b. create and edit computer programs

   c. run Java applications

   d. compile Java programs

10. The Windows Clipboard can be used with the Copy, Cut, and Paste commands to _____. (Choose all that apply.)

   a. copy text within a text file edited in DOS Edit

   b. cut text within a text file edited in TextPad

   c. copy text from a text file edited in TextPad to another Windows application

   d. copy text within a text file edited in DOS Edit to a file edited in Vim

11. You can use the Vim editor to _____. (Choose all that apply.)

   a. create and edit text documents

   b. create and edit computer programs

   c. run Java applications

   d. compile Java programs

12. Which of the following is a mode in the Vim editor? (Choose all that apply.)

   a. Insert

   b. Visual

   c. Edit

   d. Application

13. To save a file in the Vim editor, type _____. (Choose all that apply.)

   a. `:w`

   b. `:wq`

   c. `:s`

   d. `:wf`

14. Which of the following editors work with a mouse? (Choose all that apply.)

   a. DOS Edit

   b. TextPad

   c. the Vim editor

   d. all of the above

15. To close a file in the Vim editor, you must first be in _____ mode before you type the `quit` command.

   a. Edit

   b. Visual

    c. Insert

    d. The mode does not matter.

16. To move from Insert mode to Edit mode in the Vim editor, press the _____ key.

    a. i

    b. Insert

    c. Enter

    d. Esc

17. In TextPad, which of the following are options for viewing multiple files? (Choose all that apply.)

    a. Horizontal

    b. Vertical

    c. Cascaded

    d. Hidden

18. To save C++ files in TextPad for compiling in Fedora 13, _____.

    a. choose the C++ option in the Options menu

    b. just save them like any other files

    c. select UNIX from the File Format list box

    d. select Program from the File Format list box

19. Use the `:split` command in the Vim editor to _____. (Choose all that apply.)

    a. divide your time between assignments

    b. view multiple files at one time

    c. use one buffer between multiple files to store cut or copied text

    d. create files without closing the file you are working on

20. You can use regular expressions to _____. (Choose all that apply.)

    a. search for strings

    b. search and replace strings

    c. make mathematical calculations

    d. make complex comparisons

Case Projects

Case 8-1: Comparing Text Editors

You are walking between classes and overhear a conversation between two of your classmates. They are discussing the advantages of the text editors they use in their Parallel Operating Systems course. One classmate asks, "Why would I ever need a text editor other than TextPad?" What would you say in reply?

Case 8-2: Using the Keyboard Commands in DOS Edit

You are preparing a short presentation to discuss the DOS Edit text editor. You anticipate that someone will ask you about using the mouse in DOS Edit, but you do not plan to cover this topic. How will you justify your decision to emphasize the keyboard commands?

Case 8-3: Why Purchase TextPad?

Windows 7 comes with two programs you can use to edit text files—Notepad and Word-Pad. Why might you want to purchase another Windows text editor, such as TextPad?

chapter 9

The Command Line

After reading this chapter and completing the exercises, you will be able to:

- Describe the features of command-line interpreters
- Use the command line
- Access Help files for commands
- Display the contents of files
- Create script files to automate simple tasks

Depending on your level of technical expertise, you may have experience using a command-line interface (CLI). As computers evolved, many users moved away from the CLI and began depending on the graphical user interface (GUI). Although GUIs allow you to control an operating system without memorizing commands and key combinations, there are still many reasons to learn to work "under the hood" of the PC:

- Using the CLI often offers a faster way to perform a task, such as renaming multiple files or folders.

- Using the CLI might be your only option if the PC fails and you need to troubleshoot the problem.

- Working from the CLI uses fewer resources than working from the GUI.

- Creating powerful, multifaceted instructions by stringing commands together is easy from the command line.

- Working from the CLI may even inspire you to become a computer programmer!

You have used the CLI in previous chapters. This chapter fills in many of the remaining details for using the CLI.

Features of Command-Line Interpreters

A **command interpreter** is the part of a computer operating system that understands and executes commands entered by a human being or from a program. In some operating systems, the command interpreter is called the **shell**.

To visualize what happens in a command console, whether it is a command prompt in Windows 7 or a terminal console in Fedora 13, consult Figure 9-1 and the following steps:

1. Type a command on your keyboard. After passing through the **STDIN** (standard input), the characters are echoed on the console.

2. When you press Enter, the command processor takes over and performs the appropriate action.

3. If the command produces errors when processed, the error message is passed through the **STDERR** (standard error) for display on your monitor. Other output passes through the **STDOUT** (standard output) for display on your monitor.

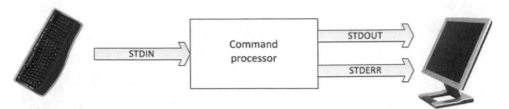

Figure 9-1 Consoles

Source: Course Technology/Cengage Learning

You can redirect input or output—for example, you can type commands in a text file and use it for input to the command processor by passing the file through standard input. Likewise, you can redirect output from the command processor and have a text file accept the standard output. Redirection is explained later in this chapter.

Using the Command Line with the Windows 7 CLI

You can use the Windows 7 CLI to configure your command prompt, copy and paste text using the command prompt, explore the command history, and complete filenames and directory names. The following sections explain these topics.

Customizing the CLI Window
You can use the CLI menu in the command prompt to customize the window. To access this menu, right-click the title bar of the command prompt (see Figure 9-2). From this menu, you have the following options for manipulating the CLI:

- Restore—Restore the command prompt from the taskbar, a graphical toolbar used in Windows 7 to select open applications.
- Move—Move the command prompt with the arrow keys.
- Size—Resize the command prompt with the arrow keys.
- Minimize—Minimize the command prompt to the taskbar.
- Maximize—Maximize the command prompt.
- Close—Close the command prompt.
- Edit—Edit lines in the command prompt; the options in the Edit submenu are explained in "Using the Command Prompt Edit Menu in Windows 7" later in this chapter.

9

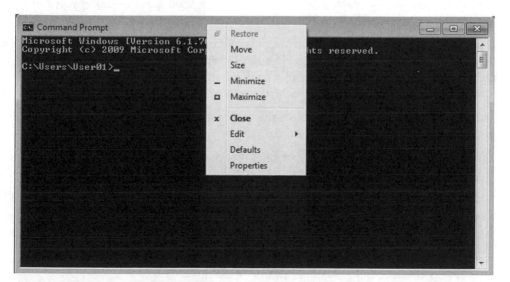

Figure 9-2 Command prompt menu

Source: Course Technology/Cengage Learning

- Defaults—Permanently change the default settings in the command prompt; the changes don't appear in the current window, but appear in subsequent command prompts.
- Properties—Use the Properties dialog box to change settings for the current window only; however, you can subsequently choose to make your changes permanent for any command prompt you open from the same shortcut.

You can click the Defaults menu option to open the Console Windows Properties dialog box and change default settings that affect all future command prompts. For example, this dialog box is helpful if you need to increase the vertical size of the command prompt.

From the Options tab of the Console Windows Properties dialog box, you can set the following options:

- Cursor Size—Change the cursor size to a line, a half-block, or a full block.
- Display Options—Choose a window to share text with other programs or a full screen to run DOS programs that display graphics; press Alt+Enter to toggle between the window and full-screen modes.
- Buffer Size—Indicate the number of commands that can be stored in the buffer. (Recall that a buffer is a memory location that holds data while it is being moved or copied from one place to another.)
- Number of Buffers—Specify how many processes can have distinct buffers.
- Discard Old Duplicates—Eliminate duplicate commands in the buffer to conserve buffer space.
- QuickEdit Mode—Use the mouse to mark text without using the Mark tool on the Edit menu.
- Insert Mode—Enable text to be inserted at the cursor as you type instead of using Overtype mode.
- AutoComplete—Enable commands to be completed automatically; you can press the Tab key to cycle through the available items in a directory.

Click the Properties menu option from the command prompt menu to open the "Command Prompt" Properties dialog box (see Figure 9-3) and make changes that affect only the current command prompt. From the Font tab of this dialog box, you can select the display font's pixel size and shape and then verify your selection in the Selected Font window.

From the Layout tab, you can select the screen buffer and window sizes of the command prompt. You have the following choices:

- Screen Buffer Size – Width—Set the number of characters stored in a line in the buffer.
- Screen Buffer Size – Height—Set the number of lines stored in memory; if the height of the screen buffer size is smaller than the current window size, scroll bars appear.
- Window Size – Width—Set the number of characters that can fit in a line on the screen.
- Window Size – Height—Set the number of lines that can fit on the screen.
- Window Position – Left and Top—Indicate the pixel position of the command prompt if you check the "Let system position window" check box.
- Let system position window—Allow the operating system to automatically position the window.

Figure 9-3 "Command Prompt" Properties dialog box

Source: Course Technology/Cengage Learning

9

From the Colors tab of the "Command Prompt" Properties dialog box, you can select colors for screen text, the screen background, pop-up text, and the pop-up background.

NOTE

To add a shortcut to the command prompt, click Start, point to All Programs, click Accessories, right-click Command Prompt, and then click Pin to Start Menu.

ACTIVITY

Activity 9-1: Customizing the Command Prompt in Windows 7

Time Required: 15 minutes

Objective: Customize the command prompt in the Windows 7 CLI.

Description: In this activity, you log on to your virtual machine, pin the command prompt to the Start menu, open the command prompt, and customize its look and behavior. This activity is useful if you want to modify the command prompt for your own needs.

1. Start your virtual machines using the appropriate instructions in Activity 1-1.

2. To add a shortcut to the command prompt on the Start menu, click **Start**, point to **All Programs**, click **Accessories**, right-click **Command Prompt**, and then click **Pin to Start Menu**.

3. Click **Start** and then click **Command Prompt**.

4. To display the "Command Prompt" Properties dialog box, right-click the title bar of the command prompt and then click **Properties**.

5. To change the cursor size, click the **Options** tab if necessary and then click the **Medium** or **Large** option button.

6. To increase the buffer size for the command history, click the **Buffer Size up arrow**.

7. To enable use of the mouse for copy-and-paste operations, check the **QuickEdit Mode** check box.

8. To enable the use of Insert mode rather than Overtype mode for typing, verify that the **Insert Mode** check box is checked.

9. To set the previous selections for the current window only, click **OK**.

10. To display the "Command Prompt" Properties dialog box again, right-click the title bar of the command prompt and then click **Properties**.

11. To change the font size, click the **Font** tab, click the desired font size in the Size list box, and then view the size in the Selected Font preview box. Adjust the Size list box until you find a suitable font size.

12. To increase the screen buffer size, click the **Layout** tab, and increase the appropriate Height value by clicking the **up arrow**. Adjust the height until you find a suitable size.

13. To increase the window size, increase the appropriate Height value by clicking the **up arrow**, and then view the size in the Window Preview box. Adjust the height until you find a suitable size.

14. To change the color scheme for the screen text in the command prompt, click the **Colors** tab, click the **Screen Text** option button, click the **blue** box, click the **Screen Background** option button, and then click the **yellow** box. If these colors are not suitable, repeat this step and try other combinations.

15. To change the color scheme for the pop-up text in the command prompt, click the **Colors** tab, click the **Popup Text** option button, click the **black** box, click the **Popup Background** option button, and then click the **white** box. If these colors are not suitable, repeat this step and try other combinations. When the colors are suitable, click **OK**.

16. At the command prompt, type **exit** and then press **Enter**.

17. Leave the virtual machine logged on for the next activity.

Using the Command Prompt Edit Menu in Windows 7 To display the Edit menu of the command prompt (see Figure 9-4), right-click its title bar and then click Edit.

You can perform the following tasks with the Edit menu:

- Mark—Mark text in the command prompt using the Shift key and cursor movement keys.
- Copy—Copy marked text to the Windows Clipboard.
- Paste—Paste copied text from the Windows Clipboard.
- Select All—Mark all of the text in the command prompt.

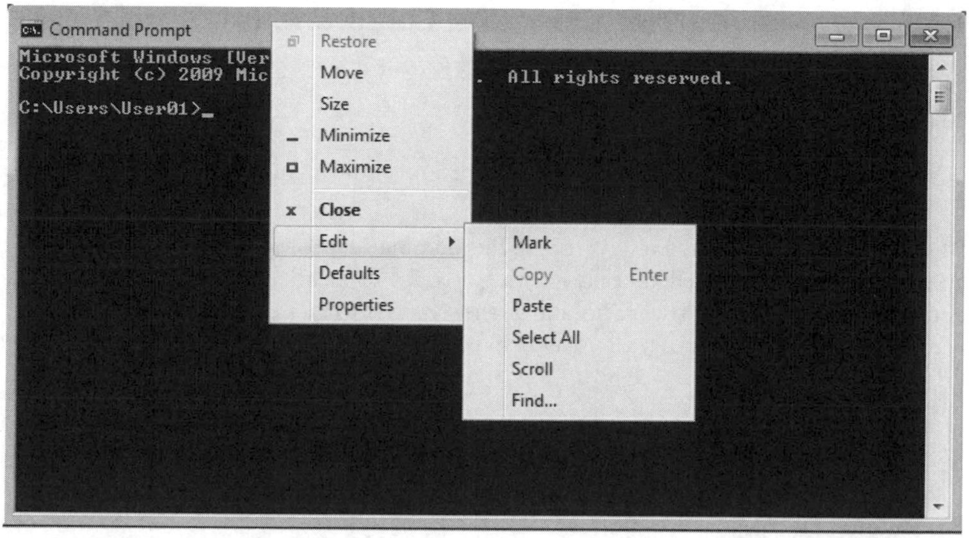

Figure 9-4 Command prompt Edit menu

Source: Course Technology/Cengage Learning

- Scroll—Turn on scrolling; when *Scroll Command Prompt* appears in the title bar, use the arrow keys to scroll within the window. Press the Esc key to turn off scrolling.
- Find—Display a dialog box to find a text string within the command prompt.

You cannot cut text from a command prompt.

If you want to use a mouse in the command prompt, check the QuickEdit Mode check box, as discussed earlier in this chapter. To copy text when you have enabled QuickEdit mode, drag your mouse to select the text and then press Enter to place it in the Windows Clipboard. To paste text in a command prompt, position your cursor at the insertion point and then right-click.

If you want to copy text and you have not enabled QuickEdit mode, right-click the title bar of the command prompt, choose Edit, and then click Mark. Position your cursor at the beginning of the text you want to copy and hold down the Shift key while repeatedly pressing the arrow keys. Press Enter to place the selected text in the Windows Clipboard. To paste text in the command prompt, position your cursor where you want to insert the text, right-click the command prompt's title bar, and then select Paste from the menu that appears.

Use the Find option to locate text in the command prompt. Right-click the title bar of the command prompt, choose Edit, and then click Find. Type the text string in the Find what text box and then click the Find Next button. If you need to locate other occurrences of the text, repeatedly click the Find Next button. Click Cancel when you finish.

Activity 9-2: Using the Command Prompt Edit Menu in Windows 7

Time Required: 15 minutes

Objective: Use the command prompt Edit menu to copy text to the Windows 7 Clipboard.

Description: In this activity, you open the command prompt, copy text to the Clipboard, and then view the copied text by pasting it into TextPad. In TextPad, create a command and copy it to the Windows Clipboard, then return to the command prompt and paste the command there. This activity is useful if you want to practice copying and pasting text in the command prompt.

You must complete Activity 9-1 before starting this activity.

1. If necessary, start your virtual machines using the appropriate instructions in Activity 1-1.

2. Click **Start** and then click **Command Prompt**.

3. To fill the text window with sample text, type **DIR** and then press **Enter**.

4. Use the mouse to highlight five lines of text in the command prompt.

5. Right-click the title bar of the command prompt, click **Edit**, and then click **Copy**.

6. To open the TextPad text editor, click **Start**, point to **All Programs**, and then click **TextPad**.

7. To paste the contents of the Clipboard, click the **Edit** menu in TextPad and then click **Paste**.

8. To open a second window in TextPad, click the **File** menu and then click **New**.

9. To create a command line in the second TextPad window, type **DIR** and then press **Enter**.

10. To copy the command to the Clipboard, click the **Edit** menu, click **Select All**, click the **Edit** menu, and then click **Copy**.

11. Close all the TextPad windows. If necessary, click **Save None**.

12. Return to the command prompt, type **CLS** at the command prompt, and then press **Enter**.

13. To paste the command from the Windows Clipboard, right-click the title bar of the command prompt, click the **Edit** menu, and then click **Paste**.

14. Verify that the DIR command displayed a directory listing.

15. At the command prompt, type **exit** and then press **Enter**.

16. Leave the virtual machine logged on for future activities.

Working with the Terminal Window in Fedora 13

As with the Windows 7 command prompt, you can choose how you want to work with the Terminal window in Fedora 13. For example, to scroll through previous commands and output, use one of the following methods:

- Use the scroll bar, which is usually displayed on the right side of the terminal window.
- Press the Shift+Page Up, Shift+Page Down, Shift+Home, or Shift+End keys.
- Scroll up or down one line at a time by pressing Control+Shift+Up or Control+Shift+Down.

You can select text in any of the following ways:

- To select a group of characters, click on the first character that you want to select and drag the mouse to the last character you want to select.
- To select a group of words, double-click on the first word that you want to select and drag the mouse to the last word you want to select. Symbols are selected individually.
- To select a line or lines, triple-click on the first line that you want to select and drag the mouse to the last line you want to select.

For all text selections, the Terminal window copies the selected text into the clipboard when you release the mouse button. Of course, you could also highlight text with your mouse, right-click the selected text, and then click Copy.

After you have copied text to the clipboard, you can paste the text into a Terminal window by clicking the middle mouse button at the command prompt. If you do not have a middle mouse button, press both the left and right mouse buttons at the same time. Of course, you could also right-click at the command prompt and then click Paste.

To change the size of text in the Terminal window, click View and then click Zoom Out or Zoom In. To restore characters to their default size, click View and then click Normal Size.

If you are using multiple Terminal window sessions, you might want to change the title of the currently displayed Terminal window. Click Terminal, click Set Title, type the new title, and then close the dialog box. The change is applied immediately.

Other changes, such as changes to colors, require that you edit window preferences. To access these preferences, click the Edit menu, click Profile Preferences, and then click Colors.

Activity 9-3: Working with the Terminal Window in Fedora 13

Time Required: 10 minutes

Objective: Use Terminal window commands and tailor the Terminal window.

Description: In this activity, you open the Terminal window and practice using copy and paste commands. You also will customize the appearance of the Terminal window.

1. Start your virtual machines using the appropriate instructions in Activity 1-1.

2. To open a console, click **Applications**, point to **System Tools**, and then click **Terminal**.

3. To display directories, type **ls** and then press **Enter**.

4. To copy the word *Public*, double-click **Public**.

5. To change to the public directory, type **cd** and point to a location that is at least one space from the cd command. If you have a middle mouse button, click it; otherwise, press the left and right mouse buttons at the same time, and then press **Enter**.

6. To make the displayed characters larger, click **View** and then click **Zoom In**.

7. To make the displayed characters smaller, click **View** and then click **Zoom Out**.

8. To change the colors used in the window, click **Edit**, click **Profile Preferences**, click **Colors**, and clear the **Use Colors from system theme** check box.

9. Experiment with the text color and background colors.

10. To see the new color scheme, click **Close**.

11. If you are not satisfied with your color choices, go back to Step 8.

12. Leave the virtual machine logged on for future activities.

Using the Command History in Windows 7

Both Windows 7 and Fedora 13 allow the reuse of commands. By reusing existing commands in the command history, you can save time when entering many commands in a command prompt or terminal session. You will learn how to use the Windows 7 command history in this section, and you will learn how to use the Fedora 13 command history later in this chapter.

If you want to reuse a command that you used in the current session in the command prompt, click within the window and then press the up arrow. The first press displays the previous command, the second the command before that, and so on. If you go back too far, press the down arrow to go back through the list.

To review a list of previous commands, press F7 (see Figure 9-5). Use the arrow keys to move up and down the list and then press Enter to copy the highlighted command to the prompt. Press the Esc key to close the window.

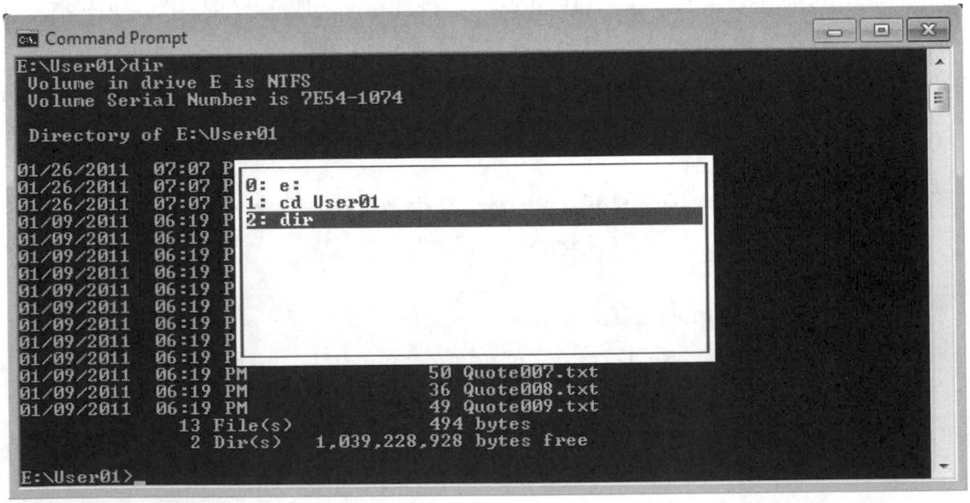

Figure 9-5 Command history list

Source: Course Technology/Cengage Learning

Using Shortcut Keys in Windows 7

As you improve your skills with the command prompt, you can use function keys to speed the entry of commands. Table 9-1 lists the function keys you can use at the command prompt and the actions they perform.

As an example of using shortcut keys, consider F2, which is handy for repeating parts of lengthy or complex command lines. You can use F2 to copy the current command in the history buffer to the command prompt, up to the first occurrence of the character you specify.

For example, suppose that the current command in the history buffer is CD \Program Files\TextPad 5 and you want to move one directory level up to the Program Files directory. Directories with spaces in their names are cumbersome to type because they require quotation marks. To save time, press F2 and type *T* to copy the line up to but not including the *T*, as shown in Figure 9-6. The command line then contains CD \Program Files\. Press Enter to execute the command.

Key	Action
F1	Brings back the last command one character at a time (same as right arrow)
F2	Copies the current command from the history buffer to the command prompt, up to the character you specify
F3	Brings back the last command
F4	Deletes characters to the right of the cursor, up to the character you specify
F5	Shows the previous command in the history buffer and stops at the top of the list (same as up arrow)
F6	Inserts the end-of-file character (^Z)
F7	Shows the command history list and executes the highlighted command
Alt+F7	Clears the command history buffer
F8	Shows the previous command in the history buffer and cycles from the bottom when it reaches the top; also searches for matching commands in the history buffer if you enter the first few characters of a command
F9	Retrieves commands by number from the history buffer
Esc	Clears the command line
Insert	Toggles Insert mode on and off
Home	Moves the cursor to the beginning of the line
End	Moves the cursor to the end of the line
Delete	Deletes characters above the cursor
Backspace	Deletes the character to the left of the cursor
Up arrow	Shows the previous command in the history buffer and stops at the top of the list (same as F5)
Down arrow	Shows the next command in the history buffer and stops at the bottom of the list
Right arrow	Brings back the last command one character at a time (same as F1)
Left arrow	Moves the cursor to the left one character at a time

Table 9-1 Command prompt shortcut keys

9

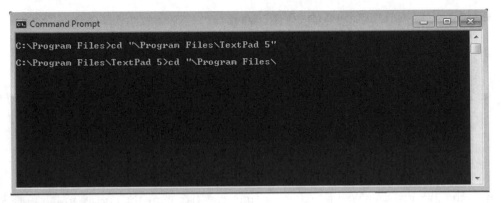

Figure 9-6 Command completion

Source: Course Technology/Cengage Learning

Activity 9-4: Using the Command History in Windows 7

Time Required: 15 minutes

Objective: Use the command history to locate, modify, and reuse previously entered commands.

Description: In this activity, you open the command prompt and then practice using the command history. This activity is useful if you want to reuse commands.

1. If necessary, start your virtual machines using the appropriate instructions in Activity 1-1.

2. Click **Start** and then click **Command Prompt**.

3. Type each of the lines in Table 9-2 at the command prompt, pressing **Enter** at the end of each line.

The redirection operator (>) is explained in the section on console redirection later in this chapter. Also, the ECHO command is used to display text to the console, as explained later in this chapter.

4. To obtain a listing of the sales files, press the **up arrow** until the DIR Sales*.txt command appears, and then press **Enter**.

5. To find the files that contain information on 2010 expenses, press the **down arrow** until the FIND 10 exp*.* command appears, and then press **Enter**.

6. To find the files that contain sales information, press the **down arrow** until the FINDSTR Sales *.* command appears, and then press **Enter**.

7. To recall the last command, press **F3**.

8. To recall the last command up to a particular character, press **F2** and then press **Shift+S**.

9. To change the FINDSTR command to a FIND command, repeatedly press **F1** until Sales *.* appears, and then press **Enter**. To view the command history and select a command, press **F7**, use the arrow keys to locate FINDSTR Sales *.*, and then press **Enter**.

10. Leave the command prompt open for the next activity.

CD /D E:\User01
MD Accounting
CD Accounting
ECHO Budget 2010 > Budget10.txt
ECHO Budget 2011 > Budget11.txt
ECHO Sales 2010 > Sales10.txt
ECHO Sales 2011 > Sales11.txt
ECHO Expenses 2010 > Expense10.txt
ECHO Expenses 2011 > Expense11.txt
DIR Sales*.txt
FIND "10" exp*.*
FINDSTR "Sales" *.*
CLS

Table 9-2   **Commands to practice using the command history**

If you close the command prompt window, you will need to re-enter Table 9-2 before continuing with Activities 9-5, 9-8, and 9-10.

Completing Filenames and Directory Names in Windows 7

A helpful feature at the command line is filename and directory name completion. You can use it when you enter a command and are unsure of the directory name or filename that you need.

The completion feature is not enabled by default, but you can type the following command to use it during an editing session:

```
CMD /F:ON
```

After you execute the command, the title bar changes to indicate that filename and directory name completion is on.

To use the completion feature, type a partial directory name or filename and then a key combination at a command prompt; the system automatically completes the entry. Press Ctrl+D to complete a directory entry and Ctrl+F to complete a filename entry.

For example, you can type the following partial command:

```
CD \pro
```

and then press Ctrl+D to supply the Program Files directory (see Figure 9-7).

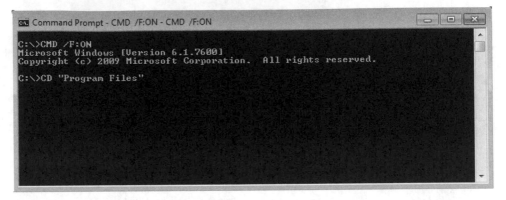

Figure 9-7 Directory name completion

Source: Course Technology/Cengage Learning

You can also type the following:

DIR myf

and then press Ctrl+F to complete myfile.txt.

If multiple directory names or filenames match the characters you enter, press the key combination again to move to the next instance. When you find the file or directory you want, press Enter to complete the command. If you don't find a match, the system beeps.

Activity 9-5: Using Filename and Directory Name Completion in Windows 7

Time Required: 10 minutes

Objective: Use the filename and directory name completion feature to locate files and directories.

Description: In this activity, you open the command prompt and practice using the filename and directory name completion feature. This activity is useful if you need help completing directory names and filenames.

You must complete Activity 9-4 before starting this activity. If you closed the command prompt, repeat Steps 2 and 3 in Activity 9-4.

1. Return to the command prompt you used in Activity 9-4.
2. To turn on filename and directory name completion for the current session, type **CMD /F:ON** and then press **Enter**.
3. To change the directory to E:\User01, type **CD ..** and then press **Enter**.
4. To see the files in the Accounting directory, type **DIR Acc**, press **Tab**, and then press **Enter**.
5. To change to the Accounting directory, type **CD Acc**, press **Tab**, and then press **Enter**.

6. To complete the filename using the FINDSTR command, type **FINDSTR "10" bud**, press **Ctrl+F**, and then press **Enter**.

7. Leave the command prompt open for activities later in this chapter.

Using the Command History in Fedora 13

It doesn't take long before typing the same command over and over becomes unappealing. One solution is to use the command line history. By scrolling with the up and down arrow keys, you can find previously typed commands and reuse them.

Activity 9-6: Using the Command Prompt History in Fedora 13

Time Required: 15 minutes

Objective: Use the command prompt history to locate, modify, and reuse previously entered commands.

Description: In this activity, you open the Terminal window and practice using the command history and completion keys. This activity is useful if you want to learn to use the command prompt history.

1. If necessary, start your virtual machines using the appropriate instructions in Activity 1-1.

2. To open a console, click **Applications**, point to **System Tools**, and then click **Terminal**.

3. Type each of the lines in Table 9-3 at the command prompt, pressing **Enter** at the end of each line.

mkdir accounting
cd accounting
echo Budget 2010 > budget10
echo Budget 2011 > budget11
echo Sales 2010 > sales10
echo Sales 2011 > sales11
echo Expenses 2010 > expense10
echo Expenses 2011 > expense11
cat budget10
echo Update 2010 >> budget10
cat budget10
ls
ls exp*
ls s*

Table 9-3 Commands to illustrate command prompt history

4. To obtain a listing of all the files created, press the **up arrow** until the `ls` command appears, and then press **Enter**.

5. To find the files that begin with an *s*, press the **up arrow** until the `ls s*` command appears, and then press **Enter**.

6. To see the first entered command, press the **up arrow** until the `mkdir accounting` command appears.

7. To view the contents of the **budget10** file, press the **down arrow** until the `cat budget10` command appears, and then press **Enter**.

8. To begin a command, type **cat b** and then press **Tab**.

9. To view a list of all the files that begin with a *b*, press **Tab** again.

10. To complete the command and display the contents of the file, type 0 and then press **Enter**.

11. To close the Terminal window, type **exit** and then press **Enter**.

12. Leave the virtual machine logged on for future activities.

Environment Variables

Environment variables have long been used in computer operating systems, and are present in Windows 7 and Fedora 13. In this context, **environment** refers to various features of the computer system and certain basic system data.

The environment exists in memory during program execution. Some of the environment can be tweaked or adapted by the running programs (with permission, of course) through the use of commands within the programs.

Picture a parent who teaches a child to ride a bicycle. The parent (administrator) provides an environment of a driveway (space), custom instruction (input), practice assistance (processing), standard instruction (libraries), doctor phone numbers, first aid, street monitoring, steadying the bike (security), and letting go (output). The parent might need to adapt this environment, perhaps by using an empty street instead of a steeply sloped driveway or by using training wheels. The parent could also schedule the lesson on a sunny, clear day, or increase the amount of emotional support.

Using Environment Variables in Windows 7
Environment variables are strings that contain information such as drives, paths, or filenames. They control the behavior of various programs. For example, the TEMP environment variable specifies the location in which programs place temporary files.

Values for some environment variables are established at login; these variables are sometimes called predefined variables. They include such parameters as the path and the name of the current user; a **parameter** is a variable that has a specific value for the operating system. Table 9-4 shows some of the more useful variables for Windows 7. The variables are enclosed by percent signs when used in scripts or at the command line, as shown in the table. Although the variables are shown in uppercase, they are not case sensitive in Windows 7.

In Windows 7, you can use the `set` command without any arguments to display all environment variables along with their values.

Variable	Typical value
%COMPUTERNAME%	{*computername*}
%DATE%	Current date
%HOMEDRIVE%	C:
%HOMEPATH%	\Users\{*username*}
%PATH%	Varies, but can include C:\Windows\System32\, C:\Windows\, and C:\Windows\System32\Wbem
%PROMPT%	Code for current command prompt format; usually PG
%PUBLIC%	C:\Users\Public
%TEMP% and %TMP%	C:\Users\{*Username*}\AppData\Local\Temp
%TIME%	Current time
%USERNAME%	{*username*}

Table 9-4 **Useful Windows 7 environment variables**

To see the current value of a particular variable, use the following format:

SET *VARIABLE*

where VARIABLE is a variable name or the initial characters of one or more variables.

For example, the SET P command shows the current setting for environment variables that start with *p*.

```
C:\Users\User01>set p
Path=C:\Windows\system32;C:\Windows;C:\Windows\System32\Wbem;
C:\Windows\System32
\WindowsPowerShell\v1.0\
PATHEXT=.COM;.EXE;.BAT;.CMD;.VBS;.VBE;.JS;.JSE;.WSF;.WSH;.MSC
PROCESSOR_ARCHITECTURE=x86
PROCESSOR_IDENTIFIER=x86 Family 6 Model 37 Stepping 5,
GenuineIntel
PROCESSOR_LEVEL=6
PROCESSOR_REVISION=2505
ProgramData=C:\ProgramData
ProgramFiles=C:\Program Files
PROMPT=$P$G
PSModulePath=C:\Windows\system32\WindowsPowerShell\v1.0\Modules\
PUBLIC=C:\Users\Public
```

To set a variable to a particular value, use the following format:

SET *VARIABLE*=*value*

For example, to create a variable for your school name, you would type:

SET SCHOOL=San Antonio College

This value will remain stored in SCHOOL until you log out from the virtual machine or exit the current command session.

To delete the SCHOOL variable, type:

SET SCHOOL=

Activity 9-7: Viewing Environment Variables in Windows 7

Time Required: 10 minutes

Objective: Display the contents of environment variables.

Description: In this activity, you open the Environment Variables dialog box, display the current user variables, create an environment variable, and display the contents. This activity is useful if you want to view environment variables in the Windows 7 GUI.

1. If necessary, start your virtual machines using the appropriate instructions in Activity 1-1.
2. Click **Start**, right-click **Computer**, click **Properties**, click the **Advanced system settings** link, and then click **Environment Variables**. Scroll and view the user variables for User01.
3. To add an environment variable, click the **New** button under User variables for User01, type **Mascot** in the Variable name text box, type a mascot name in the Variable value text box, and then click **OK** three times.
4. Close the open window.
5. Leave the virtual machine logged on for the next activity.

Activity 9-8: Using Environment Variables in Windows 7

Time Required: 10 minutes

Objective: Create and display the contents of environment variables.

Description: In this activity, you open the command prompt, create new environment variables, and display their contents. This activity is useful if you want to practice working with environment variables.

1. Return to the command prompt you used in Activity 9-4.
2. To create an environment variable for your first name, type **SET FNAME=***John* and then press **Enter**. Type your own first name instead of *John*.
3. To create an environment variable for your last name, type **SET LNAME=***Doe* and then press **Enter**. Type your own last name instead of *Doe*.
4. To display a message with environment variables, type the following:

    `ECHO %FNAME% %LNAME% is %USERNAME% on computer %COMPUTERNAME%`

    Press **Enter** when you finish.
5. Leave the command prompt open for a later activity in this chapter.
6. Leave the virtual machine logged on for future activities.

The Fedora 13 Shell and Environment Variables In Fedora 13, the shell interprets the commands in a terminal session. The default shell for Fedora 13 is bash—the Bourne Again shell. Bash is an extension of the original UNIX Bourne shell.

As with Windows 7, Fedora 13 supports environment variables (see Tables 9-5 and 9-6). Most default environment variables can be read-only, changed, or added.

Variable	Description
SHELL	Returns the location where applications store data by default
PS1	The primary prompt string
PATH	A colon-separated list of directories in which the shell looks for commands
HOME	The current user's home directory; the default for the cd built-in command

Table 9-5 Some predefined Bourne shell environment variables

Variable	Description
BASH	The full path name used to execute the current instance of bash
BASH VERSION	The version number of the current instance of bash
EDITOR	The name of the default text editor
HISTFILE	The name of the file to which the command history is saved; the default value is ~/.bash_history
HISTFILESIZE	The maximum number of lines contained in the history file. When this variable is assigned a value, the history file is truncated if necessary by removing the oldest entries to contain no more than the specified number of lines. The history file is also truncated to this size after it is saved when an interactive shell exits. The default value is 500.
HISTSIZE	The maximum number of commands to remember in the history list; the default value is 500
HOSTNAME	The name of the current host
LINES	A variable used by the selected built-in command to determine the column length for printing selection lists
PWD	The current working directory as set by the cd built-in command
RANDOM	Each time this parameter is referenced, a random integer between 0 and 32767 is generated; assigning a value to this variable seeds the random number generator
SECONDS	This variable expands to the number of seconds since the shell was started
SHELL	The full path name to the shell is kept in this environment variable; if it is not set when the shell starts, bash assigns it the full path name of the current user's login shell
UID	The numeric real user ID of the current user; this variable is read only

Table 9-6 Some predefined bash shell environment variables

As an example of manipulating a shell environment variable, consider the following command syntax to temporarily set the value of the **shell variable** VARNAME:

VARNAME="ABC Company"

This value will remain stored in VARNAME until you log out from the virtual machine or exit from the current shell session. In other words, it is shell session-based.

If you type the following command and press Enter, other programs that use the variable are made aware of the new value:

export VARNAME

To delete the variable, use the unset command:

unset VARNAME

Activity 9-9: Using Environment Variables in Fedora 13

Time Required: 10 minutes

Objective: Use the shell environment variables.

Description: In this activity, you open the Terminal window and practice using the shell environment variables. This activity is useful if you want to learn to use shell environment variables.

1. If necessary, start your virtual machines using the appropriate instructions in Activity 1-1.
2. To open a console, click **Applications**, point to **System Tools**, and then click **Terminal**.
3. To display the current user's home directory, type **echo $HOME** and then press **Enter**.
4. To display the computer name, type **echo $HOSTNAME** and then press **Enter**.
5. To establish a variable called CITY, type **CITY="San Antonio"** and then press **Enter**.
6. To display the city, type **echo $CITY** and then press **Enter**.
7. To remove the city variable, type **unset CITY** and then press **Enter**.
8. Close the Terminal window.
9. Leave the virtual machine logged on for future activities.

Console Redirection

Instead of displaying the output of a command on the screen, you can **redirect** the output to a file or printer. The following sections explain how to redirect output in Windows 7 and Fedora 13.

Console Redirection in Windows 7
For example, you can redirect the output of the DIR command to a file named dirlist with a > switch, as shown in the following command:

DIR /S *.* > dirlist

You can use this technique when you need to document the files in a directory. Using a text editor, you can then read the contents of the redirected file. Or, you can use the output to produce a report.

To send the output to a local printer, use a printer port in your command:

```
DIR /S *.* > prn
```

You can use the local printer ports (such as PRN, LPT1, LPT2, and LPT3) or a network printer in your redirection command. To redirect the output to a network printer, specify the printer using the **UNC (Universal Naming Convention) format** of *servername**printername*, in which you substitute the actual server name and printer name, respectively:

```
DIR /S *.* > \\Windows99\Printer
```

You can just as easily redirect input by using an < after the command:

```
MORE < dirlist
```

The MORE filter is discussed later in the chapter.

Console Redirection in Fedora 13 As with Windows 7, you can redirect output to a file or printer in Fedora 13 instead of displaying the output of a command on the screen. You might be creating a report, a printout of the contents of a directory, or a printout of an ASCII file. For example, you can redirect the output of the ls command to a file named myReport with a > symbol, as shown in the following command:

```
ls -l *.* > myReport
```

If you need to append subsequent reports to this same file each day, you can redirect the output using an append (>>) redirection symbol. For example, you can redirect the output of the ls command and append it to the file named myReport with a >> symbol, as shown in the following command:

```
ls -l *.* >> myReport
```

If myReport does not exist, it will be created depending on the user's directory permissions.

To quickly create a text file, type:

```
echo "I am creating a new file on the fly." > newFile
```

You can use both input and output redirection with the same command, as you will see later in this chapter.

Using Filter Commands for Redirection in Windows 7 Filter commands take input from a file, change the input in some way, and send the output to a file or the standard output device. They are called filter commands because they work like physical filters, removing unnecessary material and returning the material you need. This section discusses the following three filter commands:

- FIND—Searches for a string of characters
- MORE—Temporarily pauses display output to give you time to read the lines
- SORT—Arranges lines in ascending or descending order

Using the* FIND *Filter The **FIND** filter searches lines of input for a text string you specify. The filter has the following syntax:

FIND [/V] [/C] [/N] [/I] *string* [[*drive:*] [*path*] *filename* [...]]

/V	Displays all lines that do *not* contain the specified string
/C	Displays only the count of lines that contain the string
/N	Displays line numbers with the displayed lines
/I	Ignores the case of characters when searching for the string
string	Specifies the text string to find
[*drive:*] [*path*] *filename*	Specifies a file or files to search

For example, to find all of the lines that contain the .txt extension, you can use the FIND filter with the input from a file called dirlist that you used earlier:

FIND txt dirlist

The output from the FIND filter provides the names of the files in multiple directories, as shown:

```
-------- DIRLIST
11/04/2010  03:49 PM                 7 File001.txt
11/04/2010  03:49 PM                 7 File002.txt
11/04/2010  03:49 PM                 7 File003.txt
11/04/2010  03:49 PM                 7 File001.txt
11/04/2010  03:49 PM                 7 File002.txt
11/04/2010  03:49 PM                 7 File003.txt
```

You can also find the lines that do not contain a particular string by including the /V switch. For example, the following command finds lines that do not contain the string *txt*:

FIND /V txt dirlist

You can redirect output of the FIND filter to a printer. For example, to redirect lines in a file that contain the string *txt*, use the following command:

FIND txt dirlist > prn

Using the* SORT *Filter The **SORT** filter arranges, or sorts, lines of input and sends the sorted output to the standard output device unless you redirect it. The SORT filter has the following syntax:

SORT [/R] [/+n] [[*drive1:*] [*path1*] *filename1*]
[/O [*drive2:*] [*path2*] *filename2*]

/+n	Specifies the character number *n* at which to begin each comparison; for example, "/+3" indicates that each comparison should begin at the third character in each line. Lines with fewer than *n* characters collate before other lines. By default, comparisons start at the first character in each line.

/R	Reverses the sort order—that is, sorts from Z to A and then from 9 to 0.
[[*drive1*:] [*path1*] *filename1*]	Specifies the file to be sorted; otherwise, the standard input is sorted. Specifying the input file is faster than redirecting the same file as standard input.
[/O [*drive2*:] [*path2*] *filename2*]	Specifies the file where the sorted input is to be stored; otherwise, data is written to standard output. Specifying the output file is faster than redirecting standard output to the same file.

The simplest use of the SORT filter is to sort a file in ascending order starting in the first column:

```
SORT < dirlist
```

The sorted output is displayed on the standard output device. To sort the output in descending (reverse) order on column 40, for example, you would type the following command:

```
SORT /+40 /R < dirlist
```

If you want to redirect both input and output, follow the filter name with < and the name of the input file, and then type > followed by the name of a file or a printer.

```
SORT < dirlist > prn
```

Connecting Commands with a Pipe   A filter is useful for redirecting the output of a command as input to a filter command. In effect, the two commands are connected, with the output of one command routed directly into a filter command. This connection is called a **pipe** (|).

Type a pipe symbol between the two commands to form the connection between them. For example, you will frequently use the MORE filter with a pipe.

The MORE filter displays one screen (24 lines) of information at a time followed by -- More --. After reviewing the screen, press the Spacebar to see another screen. For example, to display the files in a directory one screen at a time, use the following command:

```
DIR /s *.* | MORE
```

The MORE filter has the following syntax:

```
command-name | MORE [/E] [/C] [/P] [/S] [/Tn] [+n]
```

command-name	Specifies a command whose output will be displayed
/E	Enables extended features
/C	Clears the screen before displaying the page
/P	Expands form-feed characters
/S	Squeezes multiple blank lines into a single line
/T*n*	Expands tabs to *n* spaces (the default value is 8)
+*n*	Starts displaying the output at line *n*

If extended features are enabled, the following commands are accepted at the -- More -- prompt:

P *n*   Displays next *n* lines

S *n*   Skips next *n* lines

F   Displays next file

Q   Quits

=   Shows line number

?   Shows help information

<space>   Displays next page

<enter>   Displays next line

You can combine filter commands—for example, one technique is to feed the output of one FIND filter into another FIND filter. Because you know that the /V switch selects lines that do not contain a specified string, you could use the following series of piped filters to display filenames and omit lines that contain <DIR> or *File(s)* or *Total*:

FIND /V <DIR>dirlist | FIND /V File(s) | FIND /V Total

The first FIND command removes the lines that contain the <DIR> characters and passes the remaining lines to the next FIND command. The second FIND command removes the lines that contain *File(s)*. The third FIND command acts on the output of the second FIND command, removes the lines that contain *Total*, and displays the resulting lines.

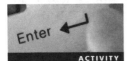

Activity 9-10: Using the Command Prompt Filters in Windows 7

Time Required: 10 minutes

Objective: Use the FIND, SORT, and MORE filters with redirection and piping.

Description: In this activity, you open the command prompt and practice using common filters. This activity is useful if you want to learn to use the FIND, SORT, and MORE filters.

You must complete Activity 9-4 before starting this activity. If you closed the command prompt, repeat Steps 2 and 3 in Activity 9-4.

1. Return to the command prompt you used in Activities 9-4 and 9-8.

2. To redirect the directory listing to a file, type **DIR > list** and then press **Enter**.

3. To redirect and display the contents of the list file, type **MORE < list** and then press **Enter**.

4. To eliminate the lines that contain <DIR> and pipe the results, type **FIND /V "<DIR>" list | MORE** and then press **Enter**.

The string for the FIND command is case sensitive. Type DIR, not dir.

5. To eliminate the lines that contain *<DIR>* and sort on the filenames, type **FIND /V "<DIR>" list | SORT /+40 | MORE** and then press **Enter**.

6. To eliminate the lines that contain *<DIR>* and *bytes* and sort on the filenames, type **FIND /V "<DIR>" list | FIND /V "bytes" | SORT /+40 | MORE** and then press **Enter**.

7. At the command prompt, type **exit** and then press **Enter**.

8. Leave the virtual machine logged on for future activities.

Accessing Help for Commands

As you work with the CLI, you will become more familiar with its commands and techniques. Many users might be able to type commands without turning to a reference, but others might need to refresh their memory or discover new commands to help them complete new tasks. In Windows 7, you use Help to learn command information. In Fedora 13, Help files are called **man pages** (short for *manual*). This section describes both references.

Accessing Help with the Windows 7 CLI

To see a list of available commands at the Windows 7 command prompt, type HELP at the command prompt and press Enter. The commands are listed in alphabetical order and briefly described (see Figure 9-8).

```
Command Prompt - CMD /F:ON - CMD /F:ON

C:\>help
For more information on a specific command, type HELP command-name
ASSOC           Displays or modifies file extension associations.
ATTRIB          Displays or changes file attributes.
BREAK           Sets or clears extended CTRL+C checking.
BCDEDIT         Sets properties in boot database to control boot loading.
CACLS           Displays or modifies access control lists (ACLs) of files.
CALL            Calls one batch program from another.
CD              Displays the name of or changes the current directory.
CHCP            Displays or sets the active code page number.
CHDIR           Displays the name of or changes the current directory.
CHKDSK          Checks a disk and displays a status report.
CHKNTFS         Displays or modifies the checking of disk at boot time.
CLS             Clears the screen.
CMD             Starts a new instance of the Windows command interpreter.
COLOR           Sets the default console foreground and background colors.
COMP            Compares the contents of two files or sets of files.
COMPACT         Displays or alters the compression of files on NTFS partitions.
CONVERT         Converts FAT volumes to NTFS.  You cannot convert the
                current drive.
COPY            Copies one or more files to another location.
DATE            Displays or sets the date.
DEL             Deletes one or more files.
DIR             Displays a list of files and subdirectories in a directory.
DISKCOMP        Compares the contents of two floppy disks.
DISKCOPY        Copies the contents of one floppy disk to another.
DISKPART        Displays or configures Disk Partition properties.
DOSKEY          Edits command lines, recalls Windows commands, and
                creates macros.
```

Figure 9-8 Windows 7 Help

Source: Course Technology/Cengage Learning

9

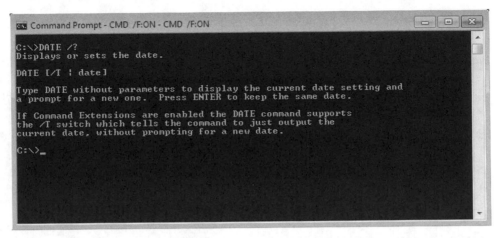

Figure 9-9 Help for the **DATE** command

Source: Course Technology/Cengage Learning

You can display Help information for a specific command by typing the command followed by /?. For example, type DATE /? and press Enter to produce the output shown in Figure 9-9.

In addition to describing the form of the command, Help also shows tips for using the command.

Activity 9-11: Using Windows 7 Help from the CLI

Time Required: 20 minutes

Objective: Use the Windows 7 CLI Help.

Description: In this activity, you open the command prompt and explore Help. This activity is useful if you need help using a Windows 7 command.

1. If necessary, start your virtual machines using the appropriate instructions in Activity 1-1.

2. Click **Start** and then click **Command Prompt**.

3. To see a list of commands, type **HELP | MORE** and then press **Enter**.

4. To advance through the Help listing, repeatedly press the **Spacebar**.

5. To see information about the XCOPY command, type **XCOPY /? | MORE** and then press **Enter**.

6. If necessary, press the **Spacebar** to see the remaining information.

7. To scroll through the commands, click and drag the slider on the right scroll bar.

8. Repeat Steps 5 through 7 for the following commands: COPY, DATE, DEL, DIR, FIND, FINDSTR, MD, MOVE, PRINT, RD, RENAME, RMDIR, SORT, TIME, TREE, TYPE, and VER.

9. At the command prompt, type **exit** and then press **Enter**.

10. Leave the virtual machine logged on for future activities.

Accessing the Man Pages in Fedora 13

The man pages (short for *manual*) are the Help files you use to reference commands in Fedora 13. The man pages are structured differently from the Help files you work with in Windows 7. The man pages can be a little overwhelming at first; however, once you understand their structure and what you need to look for, the man pages become very helpful.

The man pages display the following information for a command:

- Name—The name of the command
- **Synopsis**—The syntax of the command
- Description—The description or use of the command
- Options—The variety of switches you can use with the command
- Specific definitions—The regular expressions or environment variables
- Diagnostics—The return codes associated with the command
- Bugs—Links to or descriptions of any known errors associated with the command

The number of available command options can be intimidating at first. For example, Figure 9-10 shows the list of information that appears when you type man man at the command prompt.

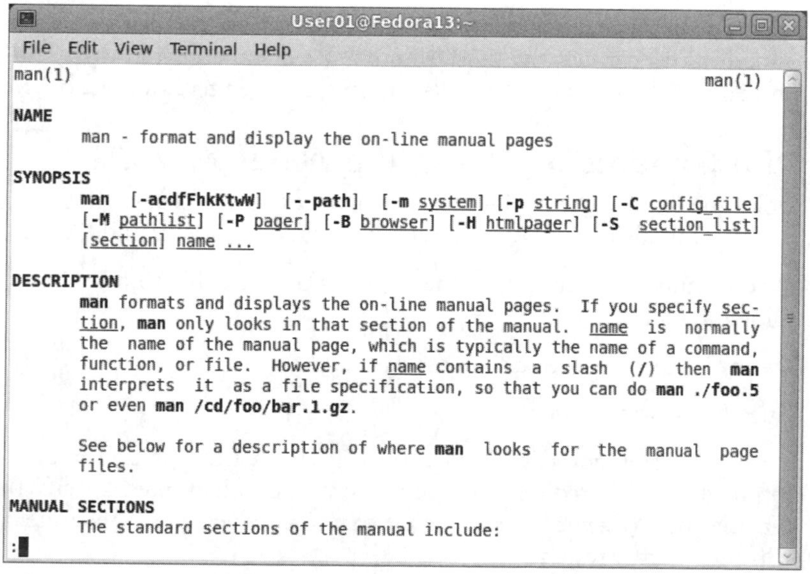

Figure 9-10 Man page information

Source: Course Technology/Cengage Learning

Activity 9-12: Using the Fedora 13 Man Pages

Time Required: 15 minutes

Objective: Use the man pages to research the grep command and its −c, −l, −m, −n, and −v switches. (You will learn more about using the grep command and its switches later in this chapter.)

Description: In this activity, you open the Terminal window and use the man command with a switch to view the descriptions, syntax, and options of the grep command. This activity is useful if you need to access the man pages and research different commands and their options.

1. If necessary, start your virtual machines using the appropriate instructions in Activity 1-1.

2. To open a console, click **Applications**, point to **System Tools**, and then click **Terminal**.

3. To access the man pages for the grep command, type **man grep** and then press **Enter**.

4. To find information about one of the command switches, press **Page Down** until you find the –c switch and then read what it does.

5. Repeat Step 4 for the –l, –m, –n, and –v switches.

6. To exit the man pages, type **q**.

7. To close the Terminal window, type **exit** and then press **Enter**.

8. Leave the virtual machine logged on for future activities.

Displaying the Contents of Files

This section discusses some of the commands you can use to display a file's contents in Windows 7 and Fedora 13. You can use the PRINT and TYPE commands to display file contents in Windows 7. In Fedora 13, you can use the less, cut, head, tail, and grep commands.

Displaying the Contents of Files in the Windows 7 CLI

Earlier in the book, you learned to display the contents of text files using the FINDSTR and MORE commands. You can also use two additional commands—PRINT and TYPE.

With the **PRINT command**, you can output the contents of a text file to a printer. The command has the following syntax:

PRINT [/E:*device*] [[*drive:*] [*path*] *filename* […]]

/E:*device*   Specifies a print device

You can use the local printer ports (such as PRN, LPT1, LPT2, and LPT3) or a network printer as the output device. To redirect the output to a network printer, specify the printer using the UNC format of \\servername\printername, where you substitute the actual server name and printer name, respectively.

Use the **TYPE command** to display the contents of a text file on the standard output device. The command has the following syntax:

TYPE [*drive:*] [*path*] *filename*

Activity 9-13: Displaying the Contents of Files in the Windows 7 CLI

Time Required: 10 minutes

Objective: Display the contents of files.

Description: In this activity, you open the command prompt and explore several techniques for displaying the contents of a text file. This activity is useful if you want to evaluate alternatives for viewing a text file's contents.

1. If necessary, start your virtual machines using the appropriate instructions in Activity 1-1.

2. Click **Start** and then click **Command Prompt**.

3. To open the DOS Edit text editor, type **EDIT** at the command prompt and then press **Enter**.

4. Type a short text file of at least five lines.

5. To save the file, press **Alt+F** and then press the **A** key.

6. To change to the E: drive, press **Alt+D**, use the arrow keys to move to the [-E-] entry, and then press **Enter**.

7. To select the User01 directory, use the arrow keys to move to the **User01** entry, and then press **Enter**.

8. To enter a filename and save the file, press **Alt+N**, type **sample.txt** on the File Name text line, and then press **Enter**.

9. To exit DOS Edit, press **Alt+F** and then press the **X** key.

10. To change the directory, type **CD /D E:\User01** and then press **Enter**.

11. To display the contents of the sample.txt file with the TYPE command, type **TYPE** **sample.txt** and then press **Enter**.

12. To display the contents of the sample.txt file with the MORE command, type **MORE <** **sample.txt** and then press **Enter**.

13. To display the contents of the sample.txt file with the FINDSTR command, type **FINDSTR /R "."** **sample.txt** and then press **Enter**.

14. If you do not have a printer, continue with Step 16.

15. To print the contents of the sample.txt file with the PRINT command, type **PRINT /E:** *printer* **sample.txt**, substituting your printer port for *printer*, and then press **Enter**.

16. At the command prompt, type **exit** and then press **Enter**.

17. Leave the virtual machine logged on for future activities.

Displaying the Contents of Files in Fedora 13

The **cat command** displays the contents of an ASCII file to the standard output device. The command has the following syntax:

```
cat [FILE] filename [-n] [-b] [-u] [-s] [-v] [-e] [-t]
```

Some of the options for using the `cat` command are:

`-n`	Precede each line of output with its line number
`-b`	Number the lines, as with the `-n` option, but omit numbers from blank lines
`-u`	The output is not buffered (the default is buffered output)
`-v`	Nonprinting characters except for tabs, new lines, and form feeds are printed visibly. ASCII control characters (octal 000-037) are printed as ^n, where *n* is the corresponding ASCII character in the range octal 100-137
`-e`	A $ character will be printed at the end of each line (prior to the new line)
`-t`	A tab will be printed as `^I` and a form feed will be printed as `^L`

The `-e` and `-t` switches will be ignored if used with the `-v` switch.

Figure 9-11 illustrates the results of using the following `cat` command to display the contents of an ASCII file and preceding each line of output with its line number:

```
cat -n /etc/inittab
```

```
[User01@Fedora13 ~]$ cat -n /etc/inittab
     1  # inittab is only used by upstart for the default runlevel.
     2  #
     3  # ADDING OTHER CONFIGURATION HERE WILL HAVE NO EFFECT ON YOUR SYSTEM.
     4  #
     5  # System initialization is started by /etc/init/rcS.conf
     6  #
     7  # Individual runlevels are started by /etc/init/rc.conf
     8  #
     9  # Ctrl-Alt-Delete is handled by /etc/init/control-alt-delete.conf
    10  #
    11  # Terminal gettys are handled by /etc/init/tty.conf and /etc/init/serial.conf,
    12  # with configuration in /etc/sysconfig/init.
    13  #
    14  # For information on how to write upstart event handlers, or how
    15  # upstart works, see init(5), init(8), and initctl(8).
    16  #
    17  # Default runlevel. The runlevels used are:
    18  #   0 - halt (Do NOT set initdefault to this)
    19  #   1 - Single user mode
    20  #   2 - Multiuser, without NFS (The same as 3, if you do not have networking)
    21  #   3 - Full multiuser mode
    22  #   4 - unused
    23  #   5 - X11
    24  #   6 - reboot (Do NOT set initdefault to this)
    25  #
    26  id:5:initdefault:
[User01@Fedora13 ~]$
```

Figure 9-11 Fedora 13 `cat` command results

Source: Course Technology/Cengage Learning

The **less command** is like the more command in that it allows you to move forward through a file, but you can also use less to move backward through a file. (You learned about the Fedora 13 more command in Chapter 6.) Because the less command does not have to read the entire file, you can access larger files faster. The command has the following syntax:

less [-[+]NpsS] [FILE]

Some of the options for using the less command are:

-p *pattern*	Causes the file to be read starting at the first occurrence of the matched *pattern*
-s	Causes multiple blank lines to be compressed into a single blank line for display
-S	Causes the excess of a long line to be discarded
-N	Displays the line number

Figure 9-12 illustrates the results of using the following less command to display the contents of a file starting at the first occurrence of a pattern:

less –Np runlevel /etc/inittab

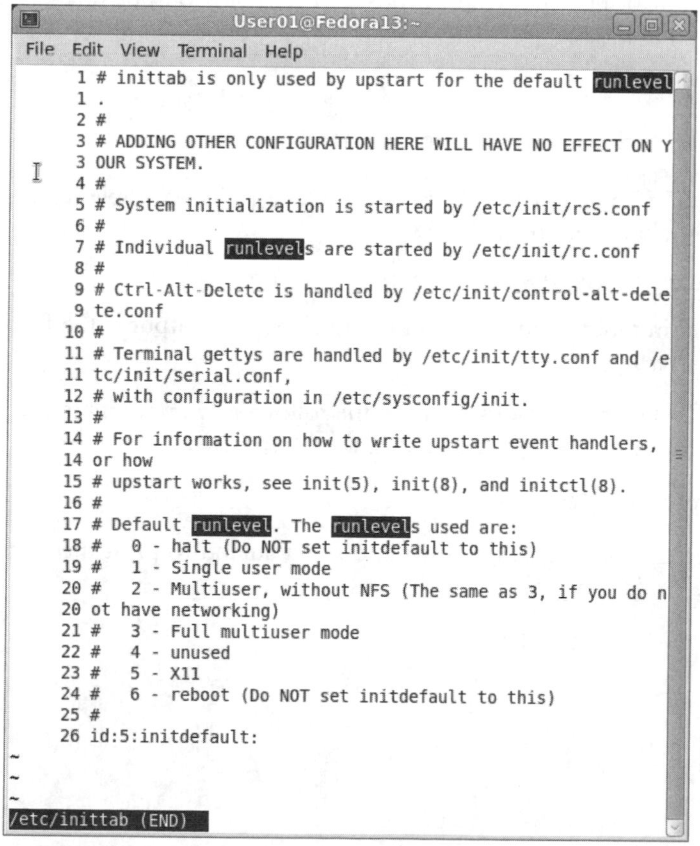

Figure 9-12 Fedora 13 **less** command results

Source: Course Technology/Cengage Learning

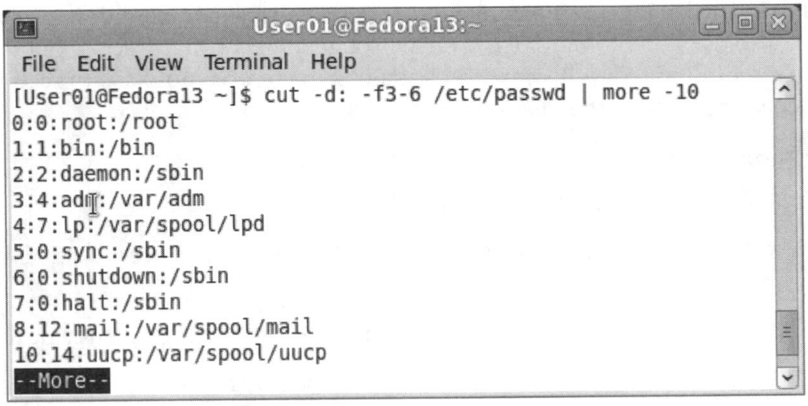

Figure 9-13 Using the Fedora 13 `cut` command to print a specific field

Source: Course Technology/Cengage Learning

Use the **cut command** to extract fields from a file line (record). The command mainly uses the −d and −f options and prints the extracted fields to standard output unless redirected. The syntax for the `cut` command is:

`cut [OPTION] ... [FILE] ...`

You can use the following options with the `cut` command:

- `-c`   Defines the cut by the line's starting character and length; for example, `cut −c1-30` outputs the first 30 characters of each line

- `-d`   Specifies the delimiter to use; the default selection is Tab

- `-f`   Designates the field number, counting from left to right; the output is the field only, as opposed to the entire line

For example, Figure 9-13 shows the results of using the following `cut` command to print the third field (delimited by the : symbol) of the lines in the /etc/passwd file:

`cut −d: −f3-6 /etc/passwd | more -10`

Figure 9-14 shows the results of using the following `cut` command to print the first 15 characters of the lines in the /etc/passwd file:

`cut −c1-15 /etc/passwd | more -10`

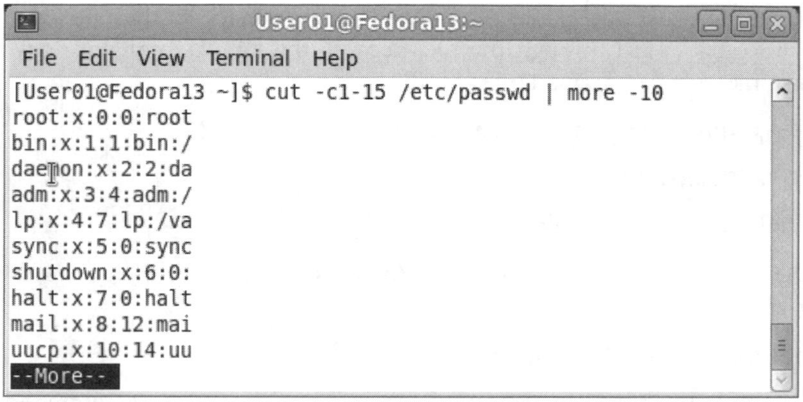

Figure 9-14 Using the Fedora 13 `cut` command to print specific characters

Source: Course Technology/Cengage Learning

The **head command** prints the first 10 lines from a file to standard output. The syntax and options for the head command are:

head [OPTION]... [FILE]...

-n   Prints the first *n* lines instead of the first 10; to change the default setting of 10, type a different number after -n

For example, Figure 9-15 shows the results of using the following head command to print the first 15 lines from the /etc/passwd file:

head –n15 /etc/passwd

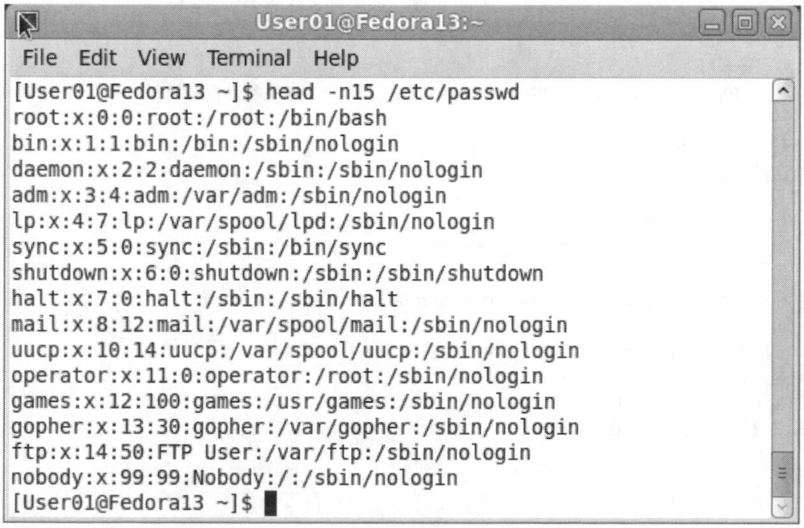

Figure 9-15 Fedora 13 `head` command results

Source: Course Technology/Cengage Learning

The **tail command** prints a specified number of lines or bytes at the end of a file and allows you to move backward through the file. Because the tail command does not have to read the entire file, you can access larger files faster.

The syntax and options of the tail command are:

tail [OPTION]… [FILE]…

-c*N*   Prints the last *N* bytes in a file

-n*N*   Prints the last *N* lines of a file; to change the default setting of 10, type a different number after −n

-v   Prints headers that list the filenames involved

For example, Figure 9-16 shows the results of using the following tail command to print the last 20 lines of the /etc/passwd file:

tail −n20 −v /etc/passwd | more

You can use the **grep command** to search a file and then print all the lines that match your search. You can also list line numbers and counts to summarize your search results. If necessary, you can use wildcard metacharacters such as * and ? to refine your search. The syntax and options for the grep command are:

grep [options] *PATTERN* [FILE…]

-C *N*   Prints *N* lines from the file; used for formatting

-c   Suppresses normal output and instead prints a count of matching lines for each input file

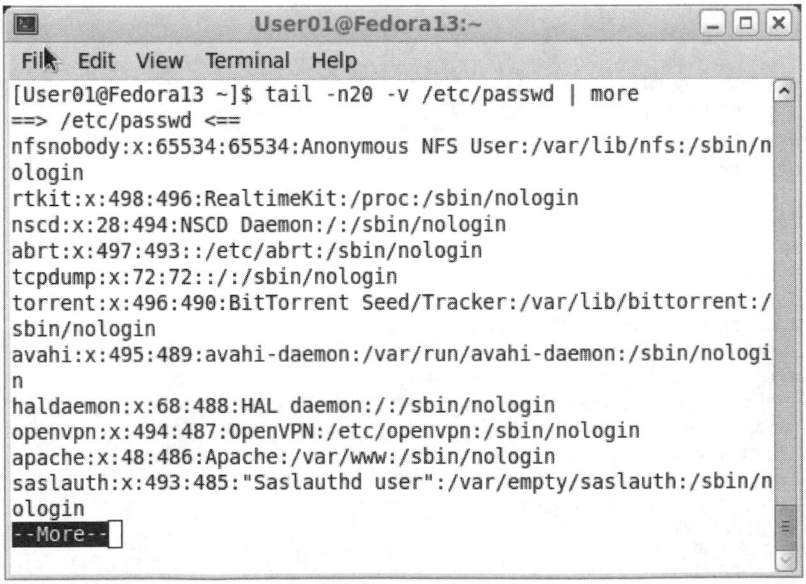

Figure 9-16 Fedora 13 **tail** command results

Source: Course Technology/Cengage Learning

-I	Ignores case in both the search pattern and input files
-L	Suppresses normal output and instead prints the name of each file from which there is no match
-l	Suppresses normal output and instead prints the name of each file from which there is at least one match; the command stops after one match
-m *N*	Stops processing the file after *N* matches
-n	Adds the line number to the beginning of each matching line
-o	Prints only the matching part of the line
-R or -r	Reads all files under each directory recursively; you can use this option to process an entire branch of a file system
--include=*PATTERN*	Indicates the pattern a file must contain before it can be searched
--exclude=*PATTERN*	Indicates the pattern a file must contain so it will *not* be searched
-v	Inverts the match pattern
-x	Selects only exact matches of whole lines

For example, Figure 9-17 shows the results of a grep command that prints the line numbers, count, and actual lines of text that contain the "root" pattern in the /etc/ passwd file:

```
grep -n root /etc/passwd
```

When many lines will be displayed as a result of the grep command, you may want to use the more command to help display the information. You can pipe the two commands together to view the information without it scrolling past:

```
grep -n nologin /etc/passwd | more -10
```

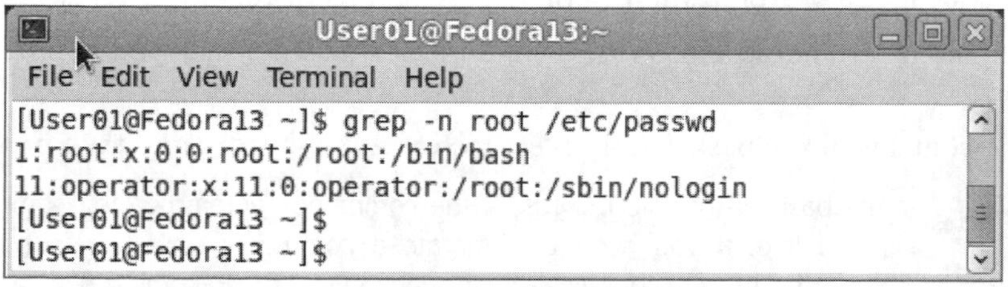

Figure 9-17 Fedora 13 grep command results

Source: Course Technology/Cengage Learning

```
┌──────────────────────────────────────────────────────┐
│ ▣              User01@Fedora13:~              ⊟ □ ✕   │
├──────────────────────────────────────────────────────┤
│  File  Edit  View  Terminal  Help                      │
│ [User01@Fedora13 ~]$ grep -n nologin /etc/passwd | more -10  ▲│
│ 2:bin:x:1:1:bin:/bin:/sbin/nologin                     │
│ 3:daemon:x:2:2:daemon:/sbin:/sbin/nologin              │
│ 4:adm:x:3:4:adm:/var/adm:/sbin/nologin                 │
│ 5:lp:x:4:7:lp:/var/spool/lpd:/sbin/nologin             │
│ 9:mail:x:8:12:mail:/var/spool/mail:/sbin/nologin       │
│ 10:uucp:x:10:14:uucp:/var/spool/uucp:/sbin/nologin     │
│ 11:operator:x:11:0:operator:/root:/sbin/nologin        │
│ 12:games:x:12:100:games:/usr/games:/sbin/nologin       │
│ 13:gopher:x:13:30:gopher:/var/gopher:/sbin/nologin     │
│ 14:ftp:x:14:50:FTP User:/var/ftp:/sbin/nologin       ▒ │
│ --More--█                                            ▼ │
└──────────────────────────────────────────────────────┘
```

Figure 9-18 Results of using the `grep` command with a pipe

Source: Course Technology/Cengage Learning

The results of using the command are shown in Figure 9-18. Notice that `--More--` is highlighted at the end of the displayed information. The user can press Enter and view the information 10 lines at a time.

Activity 9-14: Listing and Viewing Files in Fedora 13

Time Required: 10 minutes

Objective: List all files, including hidden files within a directory, and view the contents of the hidden files.

Description: In this activity, you open the Terminal window and practice using the `ls` command with a switch to view all the files in a directory. You also use the `cat` command with a pipe symbol to view the contents of hidden files and become acquainted with the bash history and profile files. This activity is useful if you need to view hidden files and use a pipe symbol to help control large scrolling displays of file contents.

1. If necessary, start your virtual machines using the appropriate instructions in Activity 1-1.

2. To open a console, click **Applications**, point to **System Tools**, and then click **Terminal**.

3. To list all files in the home directory, including the hidden files, type **ls –a** and then press **Enter**.

4. To view the contents of the bash history file, type **cat .bash_history** and then press **Enter**.

The bash history file records all the commands entered at the command line. If you need to duplicate a command, you can do so using the bash history file with special commands. Becoming familiar with the history file can save you time.

5. To view the contents of the bash history file one line at a time, type **cat .bash_history | more**. Keep pressing the **Spacebar** until you reach the command prompt.

6. To view the contents of the bash history file one page at a time, type **cat .bash_history | less** and then press **Enter**. Next, press **Page Down** until *END* appears at the bottom of the list.

7. To return to the command prompt, type **q**.

8. To view the bash profile file, type **cat .bash_profile** and then press **Enter**.

The bash profile file allows you to set up the shell environment, which includes the command prompt and shortcuts for frequently used command combinations.

9. To close the Terminal window, type **exit** and then press **Enter**.

10. Leave the virtual machine logged on for the next activity.

Activity 9-15: Displaying the Contents of Files in Fedora 13

Time Required: 10 minutes

Objective: Display the contents of files using a variety of commands.

Description: In this activity, you open the Vim editor and then use several commands to display the contents of a text file. This activity is useful if you want to evaluate alternatives for displaying a text file's contents.

1. If necessary, start your virtual machines using the appropriate instructions in Activity 1-1.

2. To open a console, click **Applications**, point to **System Tools**, and then click **Terminal**.

3. To open the Vim editor without the introductory text, type **vi courselist** at the command prompt and then press **Enter**.

4. To begin Insert mode, type **i** and then type the text from Table 9-7, pressing **Enter** at the end of each line.

| botany |
| biology |
| accounting |
| finance |
| chemistry |
| english |
| programming |
| engineering |
| art |
| calculus |
| networking |

Table 9-7 Text of the courselist file

5. To save the file, press **ESC**, type **:wq**, and then press **Enter**.

6. To display the contents of the courselist file with the `cat` command, type **cat courselist** and then press **Enter**.

7. To display the contents of the courselist file with the `less` command, type **less < courselist** and then press **Enter**.

8. To quit the `less` command and return to the command line, type **q**.

9. To display the file contents sorted in ascending order, type **sort –f courselist** and then press **Enter**.

10. To display the file contents sorted in descending order, type **sort –r courselist** and then press **Enter**.

11. To close the Terminal window, type **exit** and then press **Enter**.

12. Leave the virtual machine logged on for the next activity.

Activity 9-16: Displaying the Contents of Files Using grep in Fedora 13

Time Required: 10 minutes

Objective: Display the contents of files using the `grep` command.

Description: In this activity, you use the `grep` command and switches to select text from a previously created file. This activity is useful if you want to learn to use the `grep` command.

1. If necessary, start your virtual machines using the appropriate instructions in Activity 1-1.

2. To open a console, click **Applications**, point to **System Tools**, and then click **Terminal**.

3. To find course names in the file that contain a *b*, type **grep "b" courselist** and then press **Enter**.

4. To determine if case matters with the `grep` command, type **grep "B" courselist** and then press **Enter**. No courses should be listed.

5. To ignore the case of the search argument, use the `–i` switch with the `grep` command. Type **grep –i "B" courselist** and then press **Enter**. The course names that contain a *b* or a *B* appear.

6. To find courses in the file that contain an *a* and the lines that include those courses, type **grep –n "a" courselist** and then press **Enter**.

7. To find courses in the file that do not contain the letter *e*, type **grep –v "e" courselist** and then press **Enter**.

8. To find the lines in the /etc/passwd file that *do not* contain the phrase *nologin*, type **grep –nv "nologin" /etc/passwd | more** and then press **Enter**.

9. To quit the `more` command, press **q**.

10. To close the Terminal window, type **exit** and then press **Enter**.

11. Leave the virtual machine logged on for future activities.

Creating Script Files

Script files are lists of CLI instructions that are batched together in one document or small program to help you automate repetitive tasks. You could manually type the lines each time you need to accomplish a task and get the same results, but script files make this work easy. In this section, you will learn to build script files and enhance them by adding decision-making capabilities and repetition.

Because script files are acts of programming, you will benefit from learning a problem-solving process before you start building example files for the CLIs in Windows 7 and Fedora 13.

The Six-Step Problem-Solving Process

For most of us, the ability to solve problems is acquired, not innate. Developing a systematic, logical process for solving problems can greatly enhance your ability to develop effective script files.

Good problem solvers find the following six-step process useful for examining problems and creating successful solutions. Obviously, these guidelines are general—certain problems will require you to adapt the process to the situation.

1. Read the problem statement and then name the programming project.
2. Read the problem statement and then write a descriptive summary of the problem.
3. Read the problem summary and then list the known input elements.
4. Read the problem summary and then list the display (output) elements.
5. Read the problem summary and then identify and list the processing steps.
6. Read the problem summary and then define the constants and variables.

To illustrate the six-step process, suppose that you need to create a script program that lists all filenames with a .txt extension and a *10* in the Accounting directory.

You begin by listing the contents of the Accounting directory:

```
Directory of E:\User01\Accounting
10/12/2011  02:11 PM    <DIR>          .
10/12/2011  02:11 PM    <DIR>          .
10/12/2011  02:07 PM                14 Budget09.txt
10/12/2011  02:07 PM                14 Budget10.txt
10/12/2011  02:07 PM                16 Expense09.txt
10/12/2011  02:07 PM                17 Expense10.txt
10/12/2011  02:18 PM               704 list
10/12/2011  02:07 PM                13 Sales09.txt
10/12/2011  02:07 PM                13 Sales10.txt
              8 File(s)          1,450 bytes
              2 Dir(s)  27,859,718,144 bytes free
```

- After reading the problem statement, you name the programming project "Text files for '10".

- You reread the problem statement and then write a descriptive summary of the problem: "Change to the Accounting directory and find the files that have a .txt extension with the digits *10* in the filename."
- You read the problem summary and then state that no information is needed as input to the script file.
- You reread the problem summary and then list the items that will be displayed: Filenames with a .txt extension and the digits *10* in the filename.
- You reread the problem summary and then list the processing steps: Change to the Accounting directory and find the .txt files for the year 2010.
- You reread the problem summary and then state that no variables are needed.

Using available information from the six-step problem-solving process, you write the required statements:

```
CD accounting
FIND 10 *.txt
```

Creating Batch Programs in Windows 7

A **batch program**, or batch file, is an unformatted text file that contains one or more Windows 7 commands and has a .cmd extension. When you type the name of the batch program at the command prompt, the commands in the file are carried out as a group.

Any Windows 7 command you use at the command prompt can also be used in a batch program. In addition, some Windows 7 commands are specially designed for batch programs, including CALL, ECHO, FOR, GOTO, IF, PAUSE, REM, SET, and SHIFT.

In the following sections, you will learn to create batch programs to automate repetitive tasks.

Using Batch Parameters   Batch parameters can contain any information you need to pass to a batch program when you execute the program. The parameters %0 through %9 are separated by spaces, commas, or semicolons. The parameter %0 has the name of the batch command as it appears on the command line when the batch is executed. The parameter %1 represents the first string typed after the batch command, %2 the second string, and so on.

For example, to copy the contents of Folder1 to Folder2, where %1 is replaced by the value Folder1 and %2 is replaced by the value Folder2, type the following in a batch file called mycopy.cmd:

```
XCOPY %1\*.* %2
```

To run the file, type the following command:

```
mycopy.cmd C:\folder1 E:\folder2
```

This command has the same effect as typing the following command in the batch file:

```
XCOPY C:\folder1\*.* E:\folder2
```

You can also use modifiers with batch parameters. Modifiers use current drive and directory information to expand the batch parameter as a partial or complete filename or directory name. For example, you can type %~ and then an appropriate modifier. Table 9-8 lists the modifiers you can use with this expansion.

Modifier	Description
%~1	Expands %1 and removes any surrounding quotation marks
%~f1	Expands %1 to a fully qualified path name
%~d1	Expands %1 to a drive letter
%~p1	Expands %1 to a path
%~n1	Expands %1 to a filename
%~x1	Expands %1 to a file extension
%~s1	Expands %1 to a path that contains short names only
%~a1	Expands %1 to file attributes
%~t1	Expands %1 to date and time of file
%~z1	Expands %1 to size of file

Table 9-8 Batch parameter modifiers

Modifier	Description	Example
%~dp1	Expands %1 to a drive letter and path	C:\Shared\
%~nx1	Expands %1 to a filename and extension	Program1.html
%~ftza1	Expands %1 to a DIR-like output line	10/24/2011 08:28 PM 94 Program1.html

Table 9-9 Samples of compound results

Table 9-9 lists possible combinations of modifiers and qualifiers with examples that you can use to get compound results.

Displaying Text with the ECHO Command Use the ECHO command to display text to the standard output device. The syntax for the command is:

```
ECHO [{on|off}] [message]
```

{on|off}   Specifies whether to turn the command-echoing feature on or off

message   Specifies text you want to display on the screen

When used without parameters, the ECHO command displays the current echo setting. The ECHO message command is useful when echo is turned off; for example, to display a message that is several lines long without displaying other commands, you can include several ECHO message commands after the ECHO off command in your batch program. To prevent echoing of a line, insert an @ in front of a command in a batch program. To echo a blank line on the screen, type ECHO followed by a period.

The following example shows a small batch program that includes a three-line message both preceded and followed by a blank line:

```
@ECHO off
ECHO.
ECHO this batch program
ECHO formats and checks
ECHO new disks
ECHO.
```

Repeating Commands with the FOR Command The FOR command lets you execute a command for a specific set of items, such as text strings, filenames, and directories. The syntax for this command is:

FOR {%%variable} IN (set) DO command [CommandLineOptions]

{%%variable}	A required part of the syntax that represents a replaceable parameter; variables are case sensitive and must be represented with an alphabetical value, such as %%A, %%B, or %%C
(set)	A required part of the syntax that specifies one or more files, directories, ranges of values, or text strings that you want to process with the specified command (the parentheses are also required)
Command	A required part of the syntax that specifies the command you want to carry out on each file, directory, range of values, or text string included in the specified (set)
CommandLineOptions	Specifies any command-line options that you want to use with the specified command

The set parameter can represent a series of text strings. When you use the FOR command, the first value in set replaces %%variable, and then the specified command processes this value. This process continues until all of the items that correspond to the set value are processed. The IN and DO keywords are required when you use the FOR command; if you omit either keyword, an error message appears.

The following sample program, called SAMPLEPROGRAM.CMD, illustrates the use of text strings:

FOR %%V IN (Blue Green Red) DO @ECHO %%V

The output is shown in Figure 9-19.

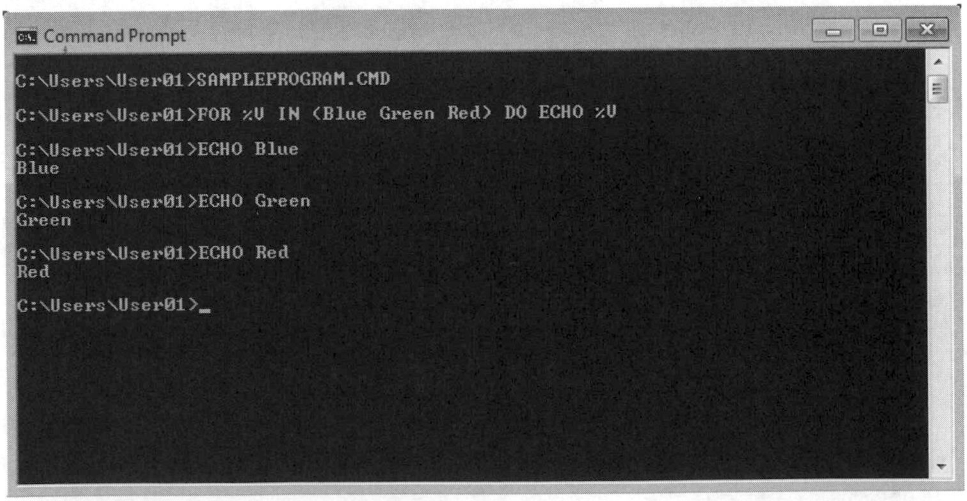

Figure 9-19 Sample output of the FOR command

Source: Course Technology/Cengage Learning

The set parameter can represent a single group of files or several groups of files. You can use wildcards such as * and ? to specify a file set. The following examples are valid file sets:

```
(*.doc)
(*.doc *.txt *.me)
(jan*.doc jan*.rpt feb*.doc feb*.rpt)
(ar??2009.* ap??2009.*)
```

To display the contents of all the files in the current directory that have the extension .doc or .txt using the replaceable variable %%F, use the following batch file:

```
FOR %%F IN (*.doc *.txt) DO TYPE %%F
```

Branching with the GOTO Command Within a batch program, the GOTO command directs Windows 7 to a line identified by a label. When Windows 7 finds the label, it processes the commands that begin on the next line. The GOTO command has the following syntax:

```
GOTO label
```

label   Specifies the line in a batch program where you want to go.

The label value you specify must match a label in the batch program. The label within the batch program must begin with a colon (:). Windows 7 recognizes a batch program line that begins with a colon as a label and does not process it as a command. If a line begins with a colon, any commands on that line are ignored. If your batch program does not contain the label that you specify, the batch program stops and displays the following message:

```
Label not found
```

Making Decisions with the IF Command You can use the IF command to perform conditional processing and make decisions in batch programs. The command has the following syntax:

```
IF [not] errorlevel number command [else expression]
IF [not] string1==string2 command [else expression]
IF [not] exist FileName command [else expression]
```

The correct name for errorlevels would be return codes. However, because the DOS command to determine the return code is IF **ERRORLEVEL,** most people use the name *errorlevel*.

Errorlevels are not a standard feature of every command. A certain errorlevel may mean anything the programmer wants it to mean. However, most programmers agree that an errorlevel of 0 means the command executed successfully, and an errorlevel that is not equal to zero usually indicates trouble. For example, the following command line would issue an error message when a nonzero return code occurred:

```
IF %ERRORLEVEL% NEQ 0 THEN ECHO Trouble has occurred in script
```

Command extensions are enabled by default in Windows 7. If you need to disable them before running a particular process, type CMD /e:off. If command extensions are enabled, use the following syntax:

```
IF [/i] string1 CompareOp string2 command [else expression]
```

not	Specifies that the command should be carried out only if the condition is false
errorlevel number	Specifies a true condition only if the previous program returned an exit code equal to or greater than number
command	Specifies the command to carry out if the preceding condition is met
string1==string2	Specifies a true condition only if string1 and string2 are the same; these values can be literal strings or batch variables (for example, %1). You do not need to use quotation marks around literal strings.
existFileName	Specifies a true condition if the filename exists
CompareOp	Specifies a three-letter comparison operator; see Table 9-10 for a list of valid operator values
/i	Forces string comparisons to ignore case; you can use /i on the string1==string2 form of IF. These comparisons are generic—if string1 and string2 are both made up of all numeric digits, the strings are converted to numbers and a numeric comparison is performed.
expression	Specifies a command-line command and any parameters to be passed to it in an ELSE clause

If the condition specified in an IF command is true, the command that follows the condition is carried out. If the condition is false, the command that follows the condition is ignored and any command specified in the ELSE clause is executed.

The following examples demonstrate how to use the IF command. For instance, you can use comparison operators in the following command to verify that the errorlevel is not zero:

```
IF %errorlevel% NEQ 0 GOTO okay
```

Operator	Description
EQU	Equal to
NEQ	Not equal to
LSS	Less than
LEQ	Less than or equal to
GTR	Greater than
GEQ	Greater than or equal to

Table 9-10 CompareOp **values**

You must use the ELSE clause on the same line as the command after the IF. For example:

```
IF EXIST filename. (
DEL filename.
) ELSE (
ECHO filename. missing.
)
```

The following code does not work because you must terminate the DEL command by a new line:

```
IF EXIST filename. DEL filename.ELSE ECHO filename.missing
```

The following code does not work because you must use the ELSE clause on the same line as the end of the IF command:

```
IF EXIST filename. DEL filename.
ELSE ECHO filename.missing
```

If you want to format everything on a single line, use the following form of the original statement:

```
IF EXIST filename. (DEL filename.)ELSE ECHO filename.missing
```

If the product.dat file cannot be found, the following message appears:

```
if not exist product.dat ECHO product.dat missing
```

You cannot use the IF command to test directly for a directory, but the null (NUL) device does exist in every directory. As a result, you can test for the null device to determine whether a directory exists. The following example tests for the existence of a directory:

```
IF EXIST c:\mydir\nul GOTO process
```

Calling Other Batch Programs You use the **CALL command** to call one batch program from another without stopping the parent batch program. The syntax for the call is:

```
CALL [[Drive:][Path] FileName [BatchParameters]]
```

[Drive:][Path] FileName	Specifies the location and name of the batch program you want to call; the FileName parameter must have a .bat or .cmd extension
BatchParameters	Specifies any command-line information required by the batch program, including batch parameters (%0 through %9) or variables (for example, %option%)

For example, to run the child.bat program from another batch program, type the following command in the parent batch program:

```
CALL child
```

If the parent batch program accepts two batch parameters and you want it to pass the parameters to child.bat, use the following command in the parent batch program:

```
CALL child %1 %2
```

Pausing for User Response Use the PAUSE command to suspend processing of a batch program and display a message that prompts the user to press any key to continue. The PAUSE command has the following syntax:

```
PAUSE
```

When you pause within a batch program, the following message appears:

```
Press any key to continue …
```

If you suspect that a batch program is "running away" because of an infinite loop, or you change your mind about allowing the program to complete, press Ctrl+C to stop the program. The following message appears:

```
Terminate batch job (Y/N)?
```

If you press Y (for yes) in response, the batch program ends and control returns to the OS. You can then insert the PAUSE command before running a section of the batch file you may not want to process.

Adding Comments to a Batch Program The REM command enables you to include comments (remarks) in a batch file. The syntax is:

```
REM [comment]
```

After typing REM, you can specify any string of characters you want to include as a comment. This is a good programming practice for documenting your batch files. For example, you should add remarks like the following to each batch program file:

```
REM Program: Backup
REM Author: Ron Carswell
REM Date: November 10, 2010
REM Purpose: Copy chapters to removable USB drive
```

Changing the Position of Batch Parameters The SHIFT command changes the position of batch parameters in a batch file. The command does not require any parameters:

```
SHIFT
```

The SHIFT command changes the values of the batch parameters %0 through %9 by copying each parameter into the previous one. In other words, the value of %1 is copied to %0, the value of %2 is copied to %1, and so on. This command is useful for writing a batch file that performs the same operation on any number of parameters.

 There is no backward SHIFT command. After you use the command, you cannot recover the first batch parameter (%0) that existed before.

For example, to create a batch program that displays the contents of the files listed in the batch parameters, starting with the first parameter and shifting through the remaining parameters, use the following command:

```
:loop
TYPE %1 | MORE
```

```
SHIFT
IF %1 == GOTO end
GOTO loop
:end
```

Using Environment Variables in Scripts

You first learned about environment variables earlier in this chapter. In this section, you will learn how they are used in scripts. You can define this behavior by using two types of environment variables—system and local. System environment variables define the behavior of the global operating system environment. Local or user environment variables define the behavior of the environment in the current instance of the command prompt.

System environment variables are preset in the operating system and are available to all Windows 7 processes. Only users with administrative privileges can change system variables.

You use local environment variables to control the operation of your batch files. These environment variables are only available as long as you remain logged on to the computer with the same command prompt open.

You can use a number of predefined environment variables in your batch files (see Table 9-4). For example, to display the current date and time, you could use the following command:

```
@ECHO Today is %DATE% at %TIME%
```

You use the **SET command** to display, create (set), or remove environment variables. You can also store numeric or text values for later use; variable names are not case sensitive but their contents can be. Variables can also contain spaces.

When used without parameters, the SET command displays the current environment settings. The syntax is:

```
SET [[/A [expression]] [/P [variable=]] string]
```

/A   Sets the string to a numerical expression that is evaluated.

/P   Sets the value of the variable to a line of input.

variable   Specifies the variable you want to set or modify.

string   Specifies the string you want to associate with the specified variable.

If you use the /A switch with the SET command, you can perform arithmetic operations. Table 9-11 lists the arithmetic operators for the SET command.

You can use the modulus (%) operator to obtain the remainder from dividing two specified integers. For example, 12 % 5 returns a remainder of 2.

Windows 7 includes an environment variable called %RANDOM%. This variable contains a random number from 0 to 32767 that changes at each execution of %RANDOM%. You can use random numbers to automatically generate temporary filenames, but you can also have some fun with this variable. Take a random number, perform some arithmetic, and then use a command to simulate a random dice roll:

```
SET /A dice=%RANDOM% % 6 + 1
ECHO %dice%
```

Operation	Operator
Multiply	*
Divide	/
Add	+
Subtract	-
Modulus	%

Table 9-11 Arithmetic operators for the SET command

To have a batch file wait for user input, you could use the following command:

SET /P Choice=Enter your option number

The /P switch allows you to set a variable equal to a line of input the user enters. The prompt string appears before the user input is read. Although the prompt string can be empty, it is not a good programming practice because the batch file halts without displaying a message to the user.

To implement a menu that permits a user to control variables, you could use the following lines:

```
@ECHO OFF
ECHO 1. Set a variable
ECHO 2. Clear a variable
ECHO 3. Show a variable's contents
SET /P Choice=Enter your choice (1, 2, 3)
```

Activity 9-17: Creating Interactive Batch Files for File Manipulation in Windows 7

Time Required: 15 minutes

Objective: Create and execute two batch files.

Description: In this activity, you open the command prompt, open the DOS Edit text editor, and then type and execute a batch file. Modify the first batch file in DOS Edit and then execute a second one. This activity is useful if you want to learn to create batch files that manipulate directories and files.

1. If necessary, start your virtual machines using the appropriate instructions in Activity 1-1.

2. Click **Start** and then click **Command Prompt**.

3. To open DOS Edit, type **EDIT** at the command prompt and then press **Enter**.

4. To turn off the display of command lines, type **@ECHO OFF** and then press **Enter**.

5. To document the program, type **REM This BAT file lists folders and files** and then press **Enter**.

6. To continue with the program documentation, type **REM that match a typed parameter** and then press **Enter**.

7. To display the entered parameter, type **ECHO You typed %1** and then press **Enter**.

8. To display the folder or filename(s), type **DIR /P /S %1** and then press **Enter**.

9. To save the file, press **Alt+F** and then press the **A** key.

10. To change to the E: drive, press **Alt+D**, use the arrow keys to move to the [-E-] entry, and then press **Enter**.

11. To select the User01 directory, use the arrow keys to move to the **User01** entry, and then press **Enter**.

12. To enter the filename and save the file, press **Alt+N**, type **activity1.cmd** on the File Name text line, and then press **Enter**.

13. To exit DOS Edit, press **Alt+F** and then press the **X** key.

14. To change the directory, type **CD /D E:\User01** and then press **Enter**.

15. To run the batch program, type **activity1** at the command prompt and then press **Enter**. If necessary, press the **Spacebar**.

16. Verify that the filenames were displayed.

17. To open DOS Edit again, type **EDIT** at the command prompt and then press **Enter**.

18. To open the file you created, press **Alt+F** and then press the **O** key.

19. To select the filename and open the file, press **Alt+F**, use the arrow keys to move to **activity1.cmd**, press the **Spacebar** if necessary, and then press **Enter**.

20. Edit the first comment to read **REM This BAT file creates a folder**.

21. Edit the second comment to read **REM and two files**.

22. Edit the next statement to read **ECHO You typed %1%2 and %3**.

23. Remove the **DIR /P /S %1** statement.

24. To create a subdirectory, type **MD %1** and then press **Enter**.

25. To change to the subdirectory, type **CD %1** and then press **Enter**.

26. To create a file in the subdirectory, type **ECHO This is the first file > %2** and then press **Enter**.

27. To create another file in the subdirectory, type **ECHO This is the second file > %3** and then press **Enter**.

28. To display the filenames, type **DIR /P /S** and then press **Enter**.

29. To save the file, press **Alt+F** and then press the **S** key.

30. To exit DOS Edit, press **Alt+F** and then press the **X** key.

31. Type **activity1 Work FileA FileB** at the command prompt and then press **Enter**. If necessary, press the **Spacebar**.

32. At the command prompt, type **exit** and then press **Enter**.

33. Leave the virtual machine logged on for the next activity.

Activity 9-18: Creating Interactive Batch Files for File Creation and Deletion in Windows 7

Time Required: 15 minutes

Objective: Create and execute two batch files.

Description: In this activity, you open DOS Edit and then type and execute a batch file that uses an input variable to control program processes. This activity is useful if you want to learn to create batch files that make decisions regarding the creation and deletion of files.

1. If necessary, start your virtual machines using the appropriate instructions in Activity 1-1.

2. Click **Start** and then click **Command Prompt**.

3. To open DOS Edit, type **EDIT** at the command prompt and then press **Enter**.

4. To turn off the display of command lines, type **@ECHO OFF** and then press **Enter**.

5. To document the program, type **REM This BAT file creates a list of files** and then press **Enter**.

6. Type **REM or removes a list of files** and then press **Enter**.

7. To echo the parameter, type **ECHO You typed %1** and then press **Enter**.

8. To test for the Delete parameter, type **IF [%1] == [Delete] GOTO delete** and then press **Enter**.

9. To test for the Create parameter, type **IF [%1] == [Create] GOTO create** and then press **Enter**.

10. To issue an error message, type **ECHO The correct syntax is activity2 Create or activity2 Delete** and then press **Enter**.

11. To continue the error message, type **ECHO Create and Delete are case sensitive** and then press **Enter**.

12. To complete the error message, type **ECHO Retry the command with the correct parameter** and then press **Enter**.

13. To transfer control to the end of the program, type **GOTO end** and then press **Enter**.

14. To enter a label, type **:delete** and then press **Enter**.

15. To delete the previously created file, type **FOR %%A IN (File1 File2 File3 File4 File5) DO DEL %%A** and then press **Enter**.

16. To transfer control to the end of the program, type **GOTO end** and then press **Enter**.

17. To enter a label, type **:create** and then press **Enter**.

18. To create the files, type **FOR %%A IN (File1 File2 File3 File4 File5) DO ECHO This is the file > %%A** and then press **Enter**.

19. To enter a label, type **:end** and then press **Enter**.

20. To save the file, press **Alt+F** and then press the **A** key.

21. To change to the E: drive, press **Alt+D**, use the arrow keys to move to the [-E-] entry, and then press **Enter**.

22. To select the User01 directory, use the arrow keys to move to the **User01** entry, and then press **Enter**.

23. To enter the filename and save the file, press **Alt+N**, type **activity2.cmd** on the File Name text line, and then press **Enter**.

24. To exit DOS Edit, press **Alt+F** and then press the **X** key.

25. To change to the E:\User01 folder, type **CD /D E:\User01** and then press **Enter**.

26. To test file creation, type **activity2 Create** and then press **Enter**. If necessary, press the **Spacebar**. To verify that the files were created, type **dir** and press **Enter**.

27. To test file deletion, type **activity2 Delete** and then press **Enter**. If necessary, press the **Spacebar**. To verify that the files were deleted, type **dir** and press **Enter**.

28. At the command prompt, type **exit** and then press **Enter**.

29. Close any open windows in the virtual machine.

30. To shut down the virtual machine, click **Start**, and then click the **Shut Down** button.

31. Wait a moment for the Windows 7 virtual machine to shut down completely.

Creating Scripts in Fedora 13

Earlier in this chapter, you learned how to work with batch files to manipulate files in Windows 7. The purpose behind creating these files is the same in Fedora 13. Although scripts can be complex, they are usually small programs that you write quickly. In the following sections, you will create scripts to handle simple tasks in Fedora 13.

Solving a problem with a script in Fedora 13 uses the same six-step process you learned for Windows 7. You write scripts in Fedora 13 using a text editor such as Vim. The basic design of a well-written script should include the following components.

Header Line The **header line** is the first line in a script. This statement indicates the type of shell environment under which the script is run. When you write a script, you should include a header line to ensure that the script is run under the correct shell. For example, the following line shows a header line for a bash script:

```
#!/bin/bash
```

Exit Return Code The statement exit 0 is needed to end the script if all goes well because a code must be returned from the script. A return code of zero indicates success.

Executable Permission When you are creating and executing shell scripts, you must change the permissions on the file before running it; normally, the default permissions do not include execution permissions.

The **chmod command** modifies the permissions of a file. The following command sets myScript as executable:

```
chmod 755 myScript
```

You will learn more about Linux permissions in Chapter 11.

File Extensions As with the other file types you have used in Fedora 13, using an extension on script files is optional. However, to avoid confusion with other file types, some system administrators prefer to use an .sh extension on their scripts.

Script Parameters As in Windows 7, script parameters can contain any information that you need to pass to a batch program when you execute it. The parameters $0 through $9 are separated by spaces, commas, or semicolons. The parameter $0 has the name of the batch command as it appears on the command line when the batch is executed. The parameter $1 represents the first string typed after the batch command, $2 represents the second string, and so on. Table 9-12 contains a list of command-line reference parameters.

For example, to copy the contents of myFile1 to myFile2, in which $1 is replaced by the value myFile1 and $2 is replaced by myFile2, type the following cp command:

```
cp /home/myFile1 /home/myFile2
```

Conditional Execution In Fedora 13, many programmers develop small, simple script routines that they can use generically and within multiple scripts. These scripts require structures that allow repetitive and conditional processing. The structures should have two important properties:

- Command lines that are executed multiple times should be written only once to avoid errors in consistency. This simplicity also makes scripts easy to maintain.
- Structures must provide a clear selection between command lines when conditions in a script are tested.

The following sections introduce you to three common conditional commands in Fedora 13.

***if* Command** The if command enables decision making in scripts when a program contains different sets of instructions to execute based on a conditional test result. For example, *if* the result of the test is true, the script executes a set of instructions. Two formats are used when you need to set up decisions within scripts. The first format is sometimes referred to as the **if then...fi** construct; use it when only one decision path is needed. The construct has the following syntax:

```
if [decision placed here]; then
[command list here]
fi
```

Modifier	Description
$1, $2, ...$n	How command-line parameters are referenced in a script
$#	Shows the command-line parameter count (used for display and iteration delimiters)
$@	Represents the list of actual command-line parameters with quotation marks around each parameter (used for display and iteration delimiters)
$*	Represents the list of actual command-line parameters (used for display and iteration delimiters)

Table 9-12   Command-line parameter reference in a Fedora 13 script

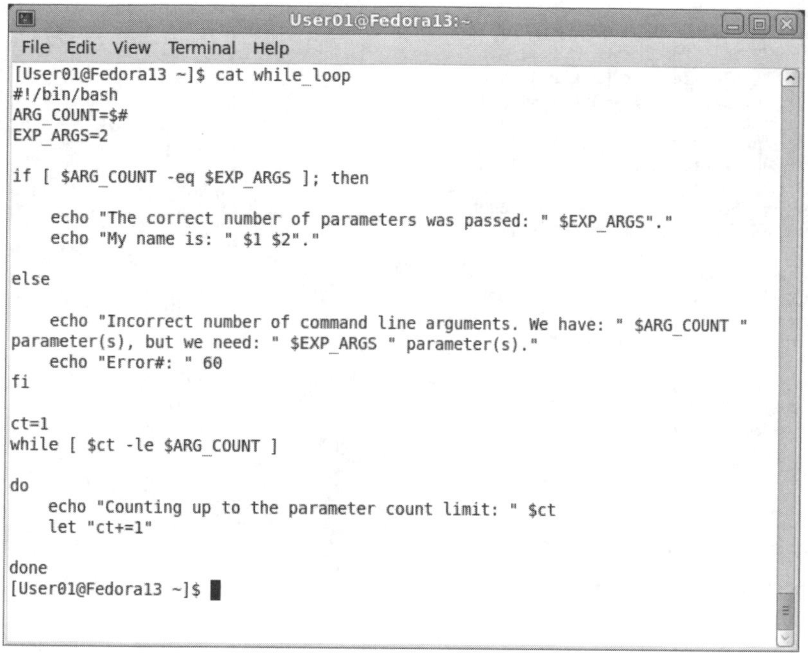

Figure 9-20 Fedora 13 `if else fi` script

Source: Course Technology/Cengage Learning

The other common syntax used with the `if` command is the **`if else fi`** construct. Use it when you need to take two distinctly different paths based on the results of a decision. The syntax for this construct is:

```
if [decision]; then
[command list here]
else
[command list here]
fi
```

With both `if` command constructs, the decision is made by testing a variable. This variable may change as the script is run. To illustrate the use of the `if else fi` construct, you can type the script shown in Figure 9-20. This script also illustrates the management, testing, and use of command-line arguments.

`while` Command Use the **`while`** command to enable multiple executions of a set of instructions while a certain condition exists. The general syntax of the `while` construct is:

```
while [ loop decision ] do
done
```

The limit for the loop comes from testing a changing variable. Figure 9-20 illustrates how you can use the `while` loop in a script; the results of the script are shown in Figure 9-21.

```
[User01@Fedora13 ~]$ ./while_loop Mary Jones
The correct number of parameters was passed:  2.
My name is:  Mary Jones .
Counting up to the parameter count limit:  1
Counting up to the parameter count limit:  2
[User01@Fedora13 ~]$ ./while_loop Mary
Incorrect number of command line arguments. We have:  1
parameter(s), but we need:  2  parameter(s).
Error#:  60
Counting up to the parameter count limit:  1
[User01@Fedora13 ~]$ ./while_loop Mary Lee Jones
Incorrect number of command line arguments. We have:  3
parameter(s), but we need:  2  parameter(s).
Error#:  60
Counting up to the parameter count limit:  1
Counting up to the parameter count limit:  2
Counting up to the parameter count limit:  3
[User01@Fedora13 ~]$
[User01@Fedora13 ~]$ █
```

Figure 9-21 Fedora 13 `while` script output

Source: Course Technology/Cengage Learning

It is good programming practice to test for the presence of input parameters before using them in the `while` construct. This is best accomplished with an `if` test.

for in Command Use the **for in command** to execute a number of instructions based on a maximum count you specify. (You will use the command in Activity 9-20.) The syntax for the command is:

```
for [some value] in [limitation variable] do
done
```

The limitation variable for the loop can either come from a single number or operate on a list of items. The bottom of Figure 9-22 illustrates a script using the `for in` loop; the results of the script are shown in Figure 9-23.

It is good programming practice to test for the presence of input parameters before using them in the `for in` construct. This is best accomplished with an `if` test.

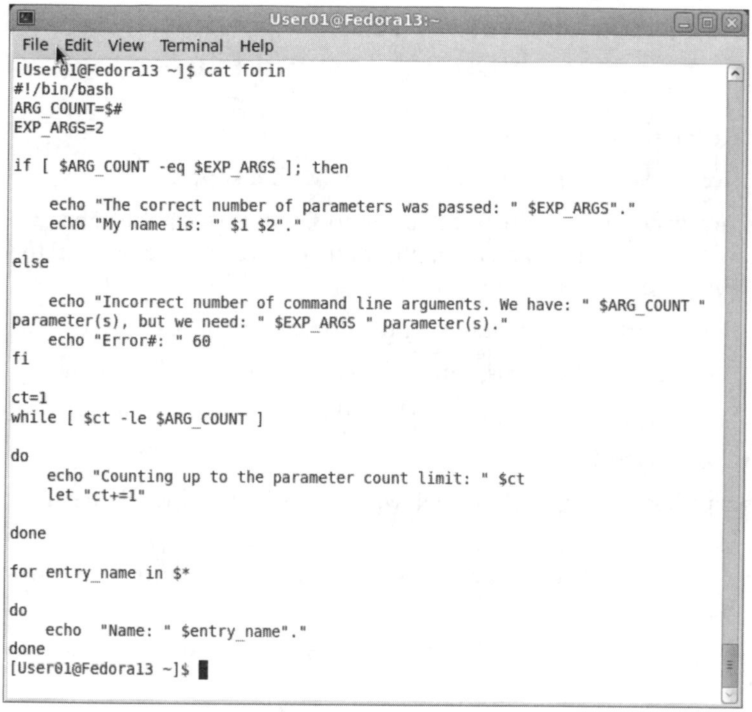

Figure 9-22 Fedora 13 `for in` script

Source: Course Technology/Cengage Learning

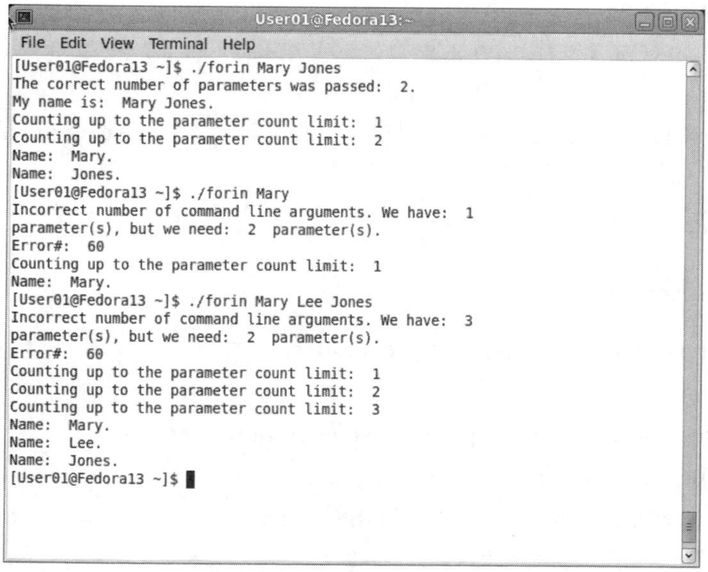

Figure 9-23 Fedora 13 `for in` script output

Source: Course Technology/Cengage Learning

Activity 9-19: Creating a Script in Fedora 13 to Work with Directories and Files

Time Required: 15 minutes

Objective: Create a directory and text file with a script.

Description: In this activity, you use the Vim editor to create a script file that adds a new directory, adds a new file within the directory, and adds text to the file. This activity is useful if you want to develop skills for creating scripts.

1. If necessary, start your virtual machines using the appropriate instructions in Activity 1-1.

2. To open a console, click **Applications**, point to **System Tools**, and then click **Terminal**.

3. To open the Vim editor, type **vi createNew.sh** at the command prompt and press **Enter**.

4. To begin Insert mode, type **i.**

5. To begin the script header, type **#!createNew.sh** on the first line of the file and press **Enter**.

6. To enter program documentation, type **#This script creates a directory and new file** and press **Enter**.

7. To finish the program documentation, type **#Text is entered and appended to the new file** and press **Enter**.

8. To create the directory, type **mkdir newone** and press **Enter**.

9. To create a new file and enter text in it, type **echo "This is text entered into a new file in the new directory" > ./newone/testing.txt** and press **Enter**.

10. To append text to the new file, type **echo "Another line has been added to the test file text." >> ./newone/testing.txt** and press **Enter**.

11. To add some blank lines to the file, press **Enter** three times.

12. To provide a program exit, type **exit 0.**

13. To save the file and return to the command line, press **Esc**, type **:wq**, and then press **Enter**.

14. Type the following command and press **Enter** to change the permissions of the new script:

    ```
    chmod 755 createNew.sh
    ```

15. To run the script, type **./createNew.sh** and press **Enter**.

16. To view the new directory, type **ls** and press **Enter**.

17. To change to the newone directory, type **cd newone** and press **Enter**.

18. To list the files in the directory, type **ls** and press **Enter**.

19. To view the contents of the new file and verify that it contains the two lines of information, type **cat testing.txt** and press **Enter**.

20. To close the Terminal window, type **exit** and then press **Enter**.

21. Leave the virtual machine logged on for the next activity.

Activity 9-20: Creating a Script in Fedora 13 to Illustrate the `for in` Construct

Time Required: 15 minutes

Objective: Create a script that uses the `for in` construct.

Description: In this activity, you open the Terminal window and then use the Vim editor to create a script file. The script displays a screen listing within a `for in` loop. This activity is useful if you want to develop skills for creating scripts that use loops.

1. If necessary, start your virtual machines using the appropriate instructions in Activity 1-1.

2. To open a console, click **Applications**, point to **System Tools**, and then click **Terminal**.

3. To open the Vim editor, type **vi createlist.sh** at the command prompt and then press **Enter**.

4. To begin Insert mode, type **i**. Next, type the text from Table 9-13, pressing **Enter** at the end of each line.

5. To save the file and return to the command prompt, press **Esc**, type **:wq**, and then press **Enter**.

6. Type the following command and press **Enter** to change the permissions of the new script:

   chmod 755 createlist.sh

7. To run the script, type **./createlist.sh** and press **Enter**.

8. Note the standard output display from the script.

9. To close the Terminal window, type **exit** and then press **Enter**.

10. To shut down the virtual machine, click **System**, click **Shut Down**, and then click the **Shut Down** button.

11. Wait a moment for the Fedora 13 virtual machine to shut down completely.

12. Close any remaining open windows, log off, and shut down your PC.

9

```
#!/bin/bash
# for arg in "$var1" "$var2" "$var3" ... "$varN"
for plant in Daisy Geranium Grass Oak Juniper Rose Fern
do
echo $plant # Each plant on a separate line.
done
exit 0
```

Table 9-13 Text for createlist.sh script

Chapter Summary

- Use the command line to perform tasks quickly. Knowing how to use the command line is helpful if you cannot access the GUI and the command line is the only interface available.

- A command interpreter is the part of a computer operating system that understands and executes commands entered by a human being or from a program. Environment variables are strings that contain information and control the behavior of various programs.

- The Help files in Windows 7 and the man pages in Fedora 13 provide reference information for using OS commands, including command descriptions, syntax, usage, possible errors, and other helpful links.

- Each operating system has its own methods for displaying the contents of a file; learning to display this information becomes important when you don't need to see the entire file. You can sort the information you want to display or open files in a read-only view to help protect the original contents.

- Scripts and batch command files can help you automate directory and file management tasks that you need to perform often. Developing a systematic, logical process to solve problems can greatly enhance your ability to create effective and efficient script files that perform no unexpected actions.

Key Terms

batch program   A program that executes without interacting with the user.

CALL   A Windows 7 command used to call one batch program from another without stopping the parent batch program.

cat   A command in Fedora 13 that displays the contents of an ASCII file on the standard output device.

chmod   A command in Fedora 13 that changes file permissions.

command interpreter   A computer program that reads lines of text entered by a user and interprets them in the context of a given operating system or programming language.

CompareOp   A three-letter comparison operator used by the IF command in Windows 7.

cut   A command in Fedora 13 that extracts fields from a line in a file or extracts an entire record from a file.

ECHO   A command in Windows 7 that displays text to the standard output device.

environment   The software configuration or mode of operation of a computer system.

environment variable   A set of dynamic named values that can affect the way running processes behave on a computer.

ERRORLEVEL   In Windows 7, the return code of a script that can be tested to determine whether a command executed correctly.

FIND   A command or filter in Windows 7 that provides the lines to match a prescribed pattern.

FOR   A command in Windows 7 that executes a section of code a specified number of times. Command syntax can vary depending on the task the loop needs to perform.

for in   The Fedora 13 version of the for command. You can use the command without the in and vary the syntax depending on the task the loop needs to perform.

GOTO   A command you use in Windows 7 programs to transfer execution to some other statement; the high-level equivalent of a branch or jump instruction.

grep **(global regular expression print)**   A command in Fedora 13 that searches a file or files by keyword.

head   A command in Fedora 13 that prints the first 10 lines (by default) from a file to standard output.

header line   A construct in Fedora 13 scripts that signals that a file is an executable script.

IF   A Windows 7 command that executes a block of statements if a decision expression evaluates as true; when an ELSE clause is included, its statements execute if the decision evaluates as false.

if else fi   A command in Fedora 13 that works like the IF command in Windows 7 when the ELSE clause is included.

if then...fi   A command in Fedora 13 that is used when only one decision path is needed.

less   A command that allows backward movement when you view file contents.

man pages   The Help file documents in Fedora 13.

parameter   In programming, a value given to a variable at the beginning of an operation or before a program evaluates an expression. The parameter can be a string, a number, or another parameter name.

PAUSE   A Windows 7 command that temporarily stops the operation of a program or command.

pipe   A temporary connection between two commands, represented by the | symbol.

PRINT   A Windows 7 command that outputs text to the console.

redirect   To change the direction of command output or input from the standard location.

REM   A Windows 7 command to add comments (remarks) to a program or batch file.

script   A program that consists of a set of instructions to control some function of an application or utility program; these instructions typically use the rules and syntax of the application or utility.

SET   A Windows 7 command that displays, creates, or removes environment variables.

shell   In Fedora 13, an invoked interface that parses and interprets command lines and code for execution on behalf of a user interface or program process.

shell variable   In Fedora 13, a variable that is local to the shell in which it is defined for its specific feature availability and efficiencies. It is locally scoped and not available to other shells. Shell variables are usually represented in lowercase format.

SHIFT   A Windows 7 command that changes the position of batch parameters in a batch file.

SORT   A Windows command or filter that arranges lines in a directed order.

STDERR   A standard device that accepts error messages.

STDIN   A standard device that accepts input.

STDOUT   A standard device that accepts output.

synopsis   A term used in the Fedora 13 man pages to describe the syntax of commands.

tail   A command in Fedora 13 that typically prints the last 10 lines or bytes of a file. For large files, this command can provide faster access to data within the file.

TYPE   A Windows 7 command that displays the contents of a text file on the standard output device.

UNC (Universal Naming Convention) format   A system of naming files on a network so that they have the same path name when accessed from any of the networked computers.

while   A command in Fedora 13 that enables you to execute a group of statements a specified number of times.

9

Review Questions

1. Why should you use the CLI? (Choose all that apply.)

   a. It offers a faster way to perform a task, such as renaming multiple files.

   b. It may inspire you to stay away from computer programming.

   c. It uses fewer resources than the graphical user interface.

   d. It allows you to create powerful, multifaceted commands.

2. The command history is _____.

   a. a historical document of a virtual machine's specifications

   b. useful if you need to recall a previously used command

   c. nonexistent in Fedora 13

   d. unreliable and should be used with caution

3. The man pages in Fedora 13 display _____. (Choose all that apply.)

   a. the synopsis of a command

   b. the description of a command

   c. the known bugs associated with a command

   d. options you can use with a command

4. Which of the following commands should you use in a Fedora 13 script to print the last bytes of a file?

   a. `tail`

   b. `last`

   c. `lastbytes`

   d. `head`

5. Use the _____ command to place comments in Windows 7 batch files.

   a. `#`

   b. `/`

   c. `Comments:`

   d. `REM`

6. In its basic form, the `grep` command in Fedora 13 _____.

   a. prints to the standard output device

   b. erases data from a file

   c. searches a file for a particular pattern

   d. appends data to a file

7. Environment variables in Windows 7 are classified as _____. (Choose all that apply.)

   a. user

   b. system

   c. character

   d. fundamental

8. By default, the `head` command in Fedora 13 _____.

   a. provides a detailed description of the header record

   b. only outputs the first, or head, record

   c. outputs the first 10 lines of a file

   d. only works with the `tail` command

9. You can use the `SET` command in Windows 7 to _____ environment variables. (Choose all that apply.)

   a. print

   b. create

   c. remove

   d. display

10. The six-step problem-solving process _____. (Choose all that apply.)

   a. helps provide a solution to a problem

   b. cannot be used to write scripts

   c. helps organize information to provide solutions

   d. can be adapted to any set of problems

11. Use the `PAUSE` command in Windows 7 batch programs to _____. (Choose all that apply.)

   a. temporarily stop the program to keep it from going out of control

   b. temporarily stop the program to ask a question

   c. permanently stop the program from executing from that point

   d. provide a point of escape for the program

12. Scripts or batch files are written to _____. (Choose all that apply.)

   a. organize commonly used commands

   b. provide complex logical statements that maintain files

   c. provide more work

   d. use specific commands

13. To display the contents of a file in Windows 7, you can use the _____ command. (Choose all that apply.)

   a. SET

   b. REM

   c. PRINT

   d. TYPE

14. To display the contents of a file in Fedora 13, you can use the _____ command. (Choose all that apply.)

   a. cat

   b. head

   c. tail

   d. less

15. Which of the following symbols do you use to redirect output from a screen display to a file in Windows 7 or Fedora 13?

   a. <

   b. >

   c. ->

   d. <>

16. Which of the following symbols do you use to redirect input from a file to a screen display in Windows 7 or Fedora 13?

   a. <

   b. >

   c. ->

   d. <>

17. Which command should you use to perform branching within a batch program in Windows 7?

   a. BRANCH

   b. GO

   c. GOTO

   d. TO

18. Which of the following file extensions can you use on batch program files in Windows 7? (Choose all that apply.)

   a. .exe

   b. .cmd

   c. .bat

   d. .sh

19. Which of the following file extensions can you use on scripts in Fedora 13?

    a. .exe

    b. .cmd

    c. .bat

    d. .sh

20. Which of the following are considered filter commands in Windows 7? (Choose all that apply.)

    a. FOR

    b. FIND

    c. MORE

    d. SORT

Case Projects

CASE PROJECTS

Case 9-1: Displaying System Environment Variables in Windows 7

Use the six-step problem-solving process to create a command file that displays the account of a user who logs on to a computer. Include the computer name, operating system, and processor architecture. Display the environment variables with appropriate identifying text.

Case 9-2: Creating a Demonstration Menu for the Windows 7 CLI

Use the six-step problem-solving process to create a command file that displays the following user instructions:

```
A - Text for item A
B - Text for item B
C - End
```

The user should be able to enter an uppercase or lowercase A, B, or C. Use IF commands to select the location of the appropriate GOTO command. Provide sample code commands for the A, B, and C labels.

Case 9-3: Displaying a Computer's IP Address in Windows 7

Use the six-step problem-solving process to create a command file that displays a computer's IP address information using the output of the IPCONFIG command. Use the following example as a guide:

```
C:\>IPCONFIG
Windows IP Configuration
Ethernet adapter Local Area Connection:
    Connection-specific DNS Suffix . : satx.rr.com
    IP Address . . . . . . . . . . . : 192.168.0.8
    Subnet Mask . . . . . . . . . . . : 255.255.255.0
    Default Gateway . . . . . . . . . : 192.168.0.1
```

9

You can determine the IP address (192.168.0.8 in this example) by piping the output of the IPCONFIG command to another command that finds the line that contains the address.

Case 9-4: Creating Demonstration Command Files in Windows 7 for Called Programs

Use the six-step problem-solving process to create three command files. The main program will call one of two other programs and display an appropriate message. When the user enters ECHOHI to execute the main program, call a program to display a greeting message. Otherwise, call a program to display a goodbye message when the user enters ECHOBYE.

Case 9-5: Creating a Script in Fedora 13 to Process Files

Using the six-step problem-solving process, create a script in Fedora 13 that uses the createlist.sh script in this chapter. The revised script must write the information to a file and then display the information to the user in descending sorted order.

Case 9-6: Creating a Script in Fedora 13 to Back up Files

Using the six-step problem-solving process, create a script in Fedora 13 to list the /etc directory and redirect the listing output to a file called dir_list in your home directory. List the file contents and modify the script to make changes to filenames within the dir_list file.

 Do not modify the actual /etc directory in this case; modify the contents of the dir_list file.

chapter 10

Operating System Management

After reading this chapter and completing the exercises, you will be able to:

- Manage tasks
- Monitor performance
- Monitor reliability

Operating system management is the general area of information technology that deals with the configuration and management of computer resources. In this chapter, you will learn to manage the processes that are executed on your virtual machine and measure the virtual machine's performance. Also, you will monitor your virtual machine's reliability.

Managing Tasks

Sometimes your computer might seem slow and unresponsive for reasons you don't understand. Using the task management tools in Windows 7 and Fedora 13, you can explore the factors that affect your virtual machine's performance.

Managing Tasks in Windows 7

As you learned in Chapter 2, the Windows 7 Task Manager provides information about the programs and processes running on your computer and displays common performance measurements for these processes. The following section provides a more comprehensive explanation of Task Manager.

Before you learn to use Task Manager, you will learn a technique for running a system tool when you do not have the administrative privileges to execute it.

Using the Run As Feature   You can use the Run As feature to access system tools that require administrative privileges and determine the cause of a problem. This feature works like the su command in Fedora 13. Knowing the cause of a problem might help you resolve it. See Activity 10-1 for details on using the Run As feature.

Activity 10-1: Running a Computer Management Tool without Administrative Privileges

Time Required: 15 minutes

Objective: Run a program that requires administrative privileges from an account with limited rights.

Description: In this activity, you practice using the Run As feature to run a program that requires administrative privileges. This activity is useful for troubleshooting problems without disturbing users by having them log off their user accounts.

1. Start your virtual machines using the appropriate instructions in Activity 1-1. To open the Administrative Tools, click **Start** and then click **Control Panel**. If necessary, click **View By** and then click **Small icons**. Click **Administrative Tools**.

2. In the Administrative Tools folder, right-click **Computer Management** and then click **Run as administrator**. Click the **The following user** option button. If necessary, type **Administrator** in the User name text box, type **P@ssw0rd** in the Password text box, and then click **OK**.

3. Click **Device Manager**.

4. Click **View**, click **Resources by type**, and then expand **Interrupt request (IRQ)**.

5. Review the IRQs.

6. Close the Computer Management window.

7. Leave the virtual machine logged on for the next activity.

Using Task Manager Use Task Manager to monitor active applications and processes on your computer. You can also stop a hung application or process, which helps your computer run better. You can start Task Manager on your virtual machine (see Figure 10-1) in one of two ways:

- Right-click an empty area of the taskbar and click Task Manager.
- Press Right-Ctrl+Delete and click Task Manager.

Consult your virtualization software for the actions needed to key the Ctrl+Alt+Delete sequence.

If you need to access Task Manager from a native installation of Windows 7, you have another alternative: press Ctrl+Shift+Esc.

Use the five tabs in Task Manager to control applications, processes, and services, as well as view system and network performance. The following sections describe each tab.

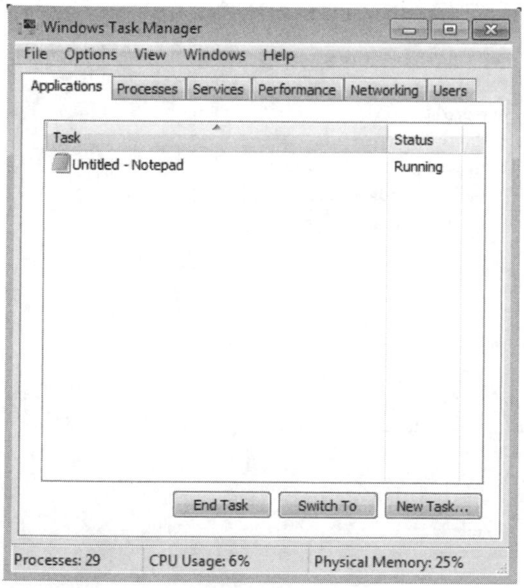

10

```
Windows Task Manager                          [ — ][ □ ][ ✕ ]
File  Options  View  Windows  Help
┌─────────────┬──────────┬─────────┬─────────────┬────────────┬───────┐
 Applications │ Processes │ Services │ Performance │ Networking │ Users │

  Task                             ▲       Status
  ▨ Untitled - Notepad                     Running




                [ End Task ]  [ Switch To ]  [ New Task... ]
 Processes: 29      CPU Usage: 6%      Physical Memory: 25%
```

Figure 10-1 Task Manager

Source: Course Technology/Cengage Learning

NOTE

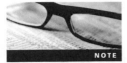

A sixth tab, called Users, is available if your computer is in a Windows workgroup or is a stand-alone system with no networking capabilities installed. This tab is not available to computer systems in a domain network.

Using the Applications Tab in Task Manager From the Applications tab (see Figure 10-1), you can determine if a program is not responding. You can kill the program by selecting it and clicking the End Task button. The other two buttons allow you to switch to a listed program or start a new program.

Using the Processes Tab in Task Manager You can use the Processes tab in Task Manager (see Figure 10-2) to list all the processes that are running on the computer. Additional information is shown beside each process, including the user name under which each process is running, processor usage (in the CPU column), and memory usage (in the Memory column). The display depends on which columns are visible. You can sort each column of data by clicking the column name. To include the System, Local Service, and Network Service accounts, check the "Show processes from all users" check box.

You can customize Task Manager to display specific columns of information to meet your particular requirements. Open Task Manager, click the Processes tab, click the View menu,

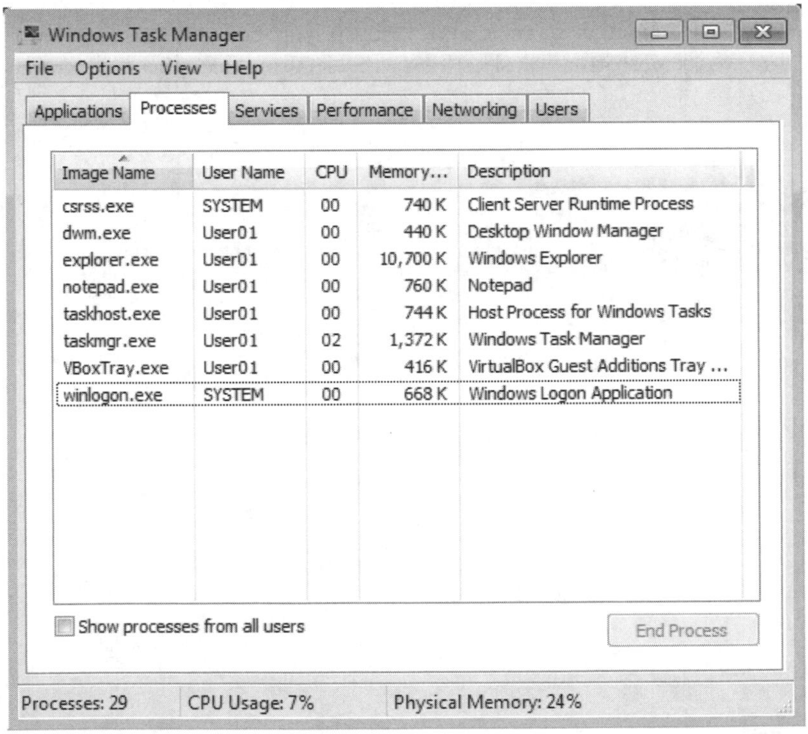

Windows Task Manager
File Options View Help
Applications Processes Services Performance Networking Users
Image Name User Name CPU Memory... Description
csrss.exe SYSTEM 00 740 K Client Server Runtime Process
dwm.exe User01 00 440 K Desktop Window Manager
explorer.exe User01 00 10,700 K Windows Explorer
notepad.exe User01 00 760 K Notepad
taskhost.exe User01 00 744 K Host Process for Windows Tasks
taskmgr.exe User01 02 1,372 K Windows Task Manager
VBoxTray.exe User01 00 416 K VirtualBox Guest Additions Tray ...
winlogon.exe SYSTEM 00 668 K Windows Logon Application
Show processes from all users
End Process
Processes: 29
CPU Usage: 7%
Physical Memory: 24%

Figure 10-2 Processes tab in Task Manager

Source: Course Technology/Cengage Learning

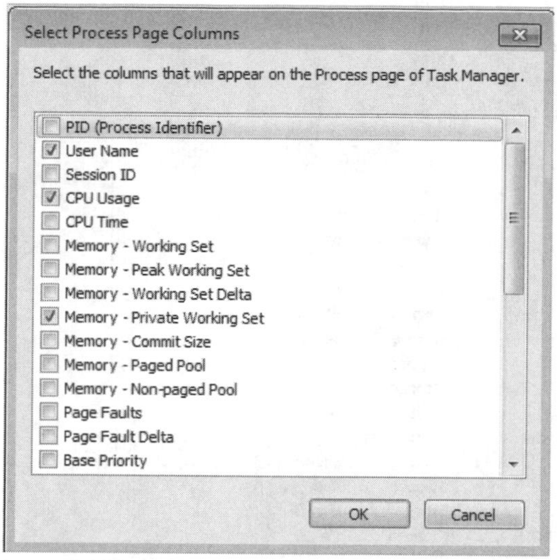

Select Process Page Columns

Select the columns that will appear on the Process page of Task Manager.

- ☐ PID (Process Identifier)
- ☑ User Name
- ☐ Session ID
- ☑ CPU Usage
- ☐ CPU Time
- ☐ Memory - Working Set
- ☐ Memory - Peak Working Set
- ☐ Memory - Working Set Delta
- ☑ Memory - Private Working Set
- ☐ Memory - Commit Size
- ☐ Memory - Paged Pool
- ☐ Memory - Non-paged Pool
- ☐ Page Faults
- ☐ Page Fault Delta
- ☐ Base Priority

[OK]   [Cancel]

Figure 10-3 Selecting columns to display in Task Manager

Source: Course Technology/Cengage Learning

and then click Select Columns. From the dialog box that appears (see Figure 10-3), place a check beside the columns you want to display and click OK.

By default, Task Manager displays a minimal set of process data. You can choose more columns, but the following selections are the most essential for day-to-day use:

- Memory Usage—The "working set" of a process, or the amount of memory it is actively using.
- Peak Memory Usage—The maximum amount of memory this process has used since it has been running.
- Page Faults—The number of times this process has been forced to reload memory pages from the page file.
- Virtual Memory Size—The amount of the process's less frequently used memory that has been paged to disk.
- Base Priority—The priority of this process.

To help troubleshoot your computer, you can determine which programs use the most processor resources or memory. For example, a program with an abnormally high CPU value could be hung, or a program with an extremely large amount of memory usage might have a **memory leak,** meaning that a process uses memory without bounds. To stop a process, select the program and click the End Process button.

Be careful when killing processes. You could render your computer unstable or lose valuable data in memory.

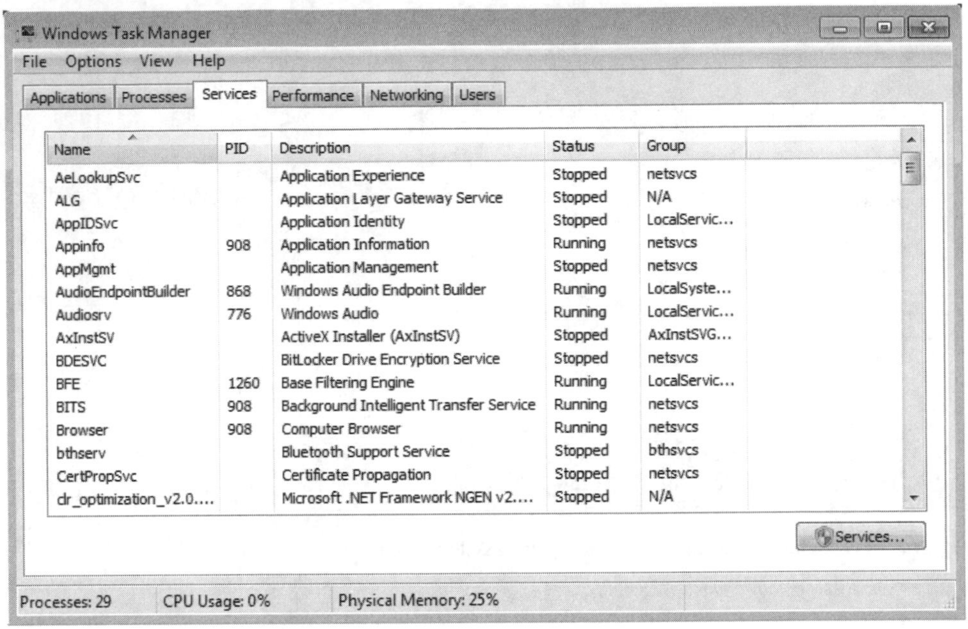

Figure 10-4 Services tab in Task Manager

Source: Course Technology/Cengage Learning

Using the Services Tab in Task Manager The Services tab, as shown in Figure 10-4, provides a convenient way to quickly view the services that are running while you troubleshoot your virtual machine.

If you want to investigate whether a running service is tied to a particular process, you can right-click the service name and select the Go to Process command. When you do, Task Manager will switch to the Processes tab and list the associated process(es).

Using the Performance Tab in Task Manager From the Performance tab (see Figure 10-5), you can get a quick view of your computer's CPU and memory usage.

The Performance tab includes four graphs. The top two graphs show how much of the CPU is being used, both currently and for the past few minutes. A high percentage means that programs or processes are requiring a lot of CPU resources, which can slow your computer. If the percentage appears frozen at or near 100%, then a program might not be responding.

The bottom two graphs display the number of megabytes (MB) being used by RAM, or physical memory, both currently and for the past few minutes. If memory use seems consistently high or slows your computer's performance noticeably, try reducing the number of programs you have open at one time, or configure the virtual machine to use more RAM.

Using the Networking Tab in Task Manager You can use the Networking tab (see Figure 10-6) to view a graph of network activity related to your computer's network card. The tab only appears when a network card is present.

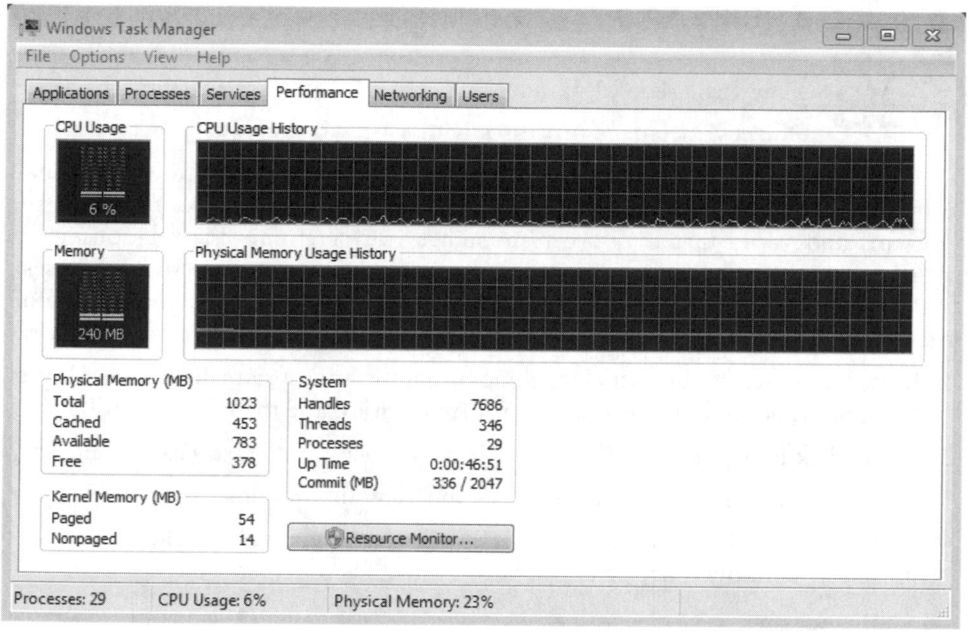

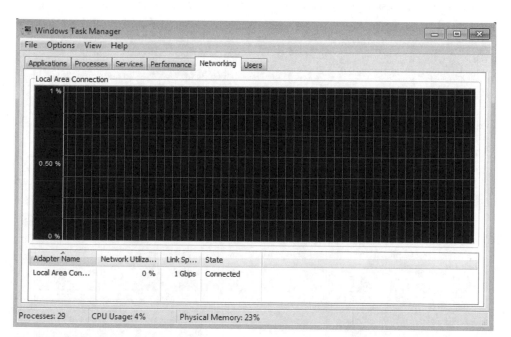

Figure 10-5 Performance tab in Task Manager

Source: Course Technology/Cengage Learning

10

Figure 10-6 Networking tab in Task Manager

Source: Course Technology/Cengage Learning

Activity 10-2: Controlling Processes in Windows 7

Time Required: 15 minutes

Objective: Manage processes with Task Manager.

Description: In this activity, you practice controlling processes with Task Manager and a 16-bit program called winhelp—a Windows 3.1 legacy application. You view the running programs and verify that they are responding; you determine the relationship among the ntvdm, wowexec, and winhelp programs by terminating the respective processes; and you check the performance of the processor, RAM, and network. This activity is useful for troubleshooting problems related to applications, processes, performance, and networking.

1. If necessary, start your virtual machines using the appropriate instructions in Activity 1-1. Click **Start,** point to **All Programs,** click **Accessories,** and then click **WordPad.**

2. Right-click an empty spot on the taskbar and then click **Start Task Manager.**

3. If necessary, click the **Applications** tab and view the running programs.

4. Click the **New Task** button, type **winhelp** in the Open list box, click **OK,** and then minimize the Windows Help window.

Running winhelp starts the 16-bit version of Windows Help—an old Help program—which appears as a black window. You will kill the application later.

5. Click the **Processes** tab to view the active processes (see Figure 10-7).

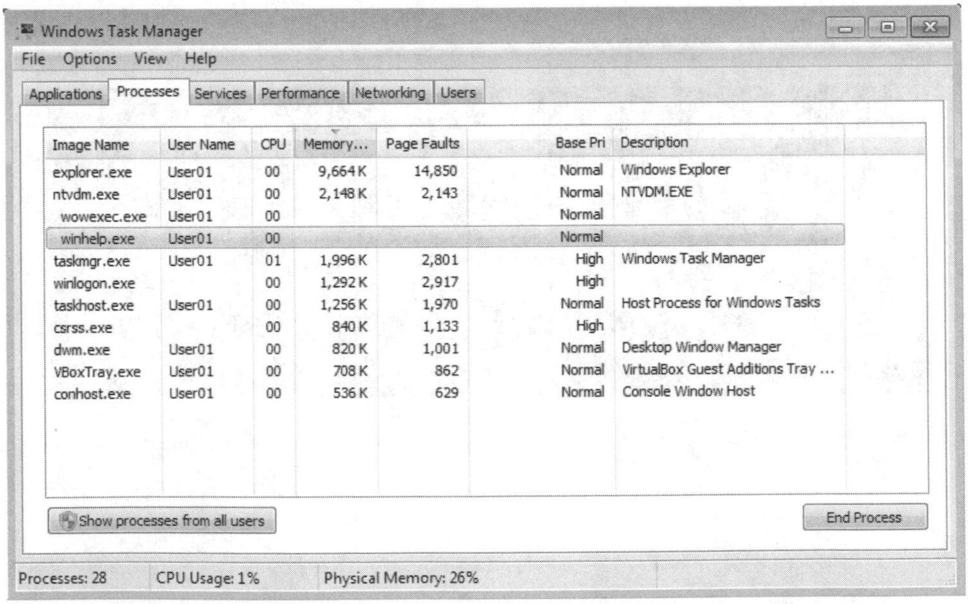

Windows Task Manager

File Options View Help

Applications | Processes | Services | Performance | Networking | Users

Image Name	User Name	CPU	Memory...	Page Faults	Base Pri	Description
explorer.exe	User01	00	9,664 K	14,850	Normal	Windows Explorer
ntvdm.exe	User01	00	2,148 K	2,143	Normal	NTVDM.EXE
wowexec.exe	User01	00			Normal	
winhelp.exe	User01	00			Normal	
taskmgr.exe	User01	01	1,996 K	2,801	High	Windows Task Manager
winlogon.exe		00	1,292 K	2,917	High	
taskhost.exe	User01	00	1,256 K	1,970	Normal	Host Process for Windows Tasks
csrss.exe		00	840 K	1,133	High	
dwm.exe	User01	00	820 K	1,001	Normal	Desktop Window Manager
VBoxTray.exe	User01	00	708 K	862	Normal	VirtualBox Guest Additions Tray ...
conhost.exe	User01	00	536 K	629	Normal	Console Window Host

☑ Show processes from all users   End Process

Processes: 28   CPU Usage: 1%   Physical Memory: 26%

Figure 10-7 Active processes

Source: Course Technology/Cengage Learning

6. Locate the ntvdm.exe, wowexec.exe, and winhelp.exe processes, which are shown near the top of the list in Figure 10-7.

The ntvdm.exe program (NT Virtual Machine) creates a virtual DOS machine to run DOS programs. The ntvdm program may fail on processors that do not support the Virtual Mode Extensions. The wowexec.exe program (Windows on Windows executive) creates the environment that is required to run 16-bit (Windows 3.1) programs.

7. Click the **winhelp.exe** process, click the **End Process** button, read the caution message, and then close the message window. Note that the wowexec.exe and ntvdm.exe processes remain.

8. Click the **ntvdm.exe** process, click the **End Process** button, read the caution message, and then close the message window. Note that the wowexec.exe and ntvdm.exe processes are removed.

9. Click the **View** menu and then click **Select Columns**. If necessary, click the **Memory Usage** check box. Next, click the following check boxes: **Memory - Peak Working Set**, **Page Faults**, and **Base Priority**. When you finish, click **OK**.

10. Expand the Windows Task Manager and view the process statistics.

11. To see which program is using the most CPU (processor cycles), click the **CPU** button twice.

12. To see which program is using the most memory, click the **Memory** button twice.

13. Click the **Performance** tab and view the CPU Usage and CPU Usage History graphs.

14. Click the **Windows Task Manager** title bar and drag the window to another location.

15. Observe the CPU spike that occurred when you moved the Windows Task Manager window.

16. Click the **Networking** tab and view the network use.

17. Close all open windows.

18. Leave the virtual machine logged on for future activities.

Managing Tasks in Fedora 13

The task management tool in Fedora 13 is called System Monitor on the GNOME desktop. You first learned about System Monitor in Chapter 2. It provides system information and monitors system processes running on the computer. The following sections provide a more comprehensive explanation of System Monitor.

Using System Monitor   You use System Monitor to monitor active applications, view graphs, and manipulate the running applications on your computer. System Monitor also displays information about available resources, such as CPU and memory usage on your system (see Figure 10-8). You can access System Monitor by clicking Applications, System Tools, and then System Monitor.

The four tabs in System Monitor are System, Processes, Resources, and File Systems.

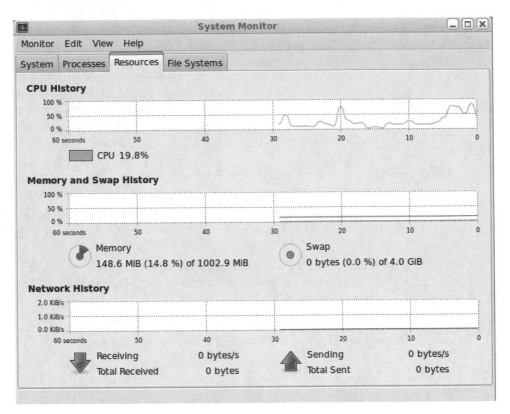

Figure 10-8 GNOME System Monitor

Source: Course Technology/Cengage Learning

Using the System Tab in System Monitor The System tab shows the computer name, the amount of memory and available disk space, and the type of CPU on your system. It also shows the current kernel and GNOME version of the system (see Figure 10-9).

Using the Processes Tab in System Monitor You use the Processes tab in System Monitor (see Figure 10-10) to list all the processes that are running on your computer. Information is shown for each process. To sort the information by a specific column in ascending order, click the name of the column. To toggle the sort between ascending and descending order, click the column name again.

Two menus on the Processes tab are worth noticing: the Edit and View menus (see Figures 10-11 and 10-12, respectively).

To stop a process, click Edit and then choose Stop Process. Alternatively, you can right-click a process row and select Stop Process.

From the View menu, you can control which processes are displayed (All, My, or Active). If you select the Dependencies option, the parent processes are indicated by a triangle symbol to the left of the process name. If you select the Memory Maps option, maps are displayed when you point to a process.

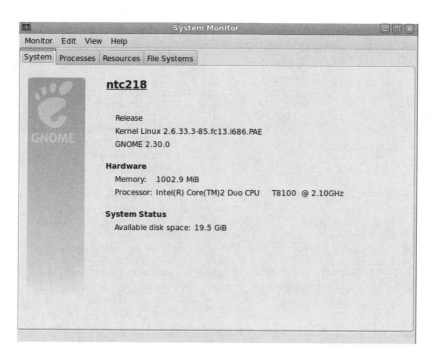

Figure 10-9 System tab in System Monitor

Source: Course Technology/Cengage Learning

10

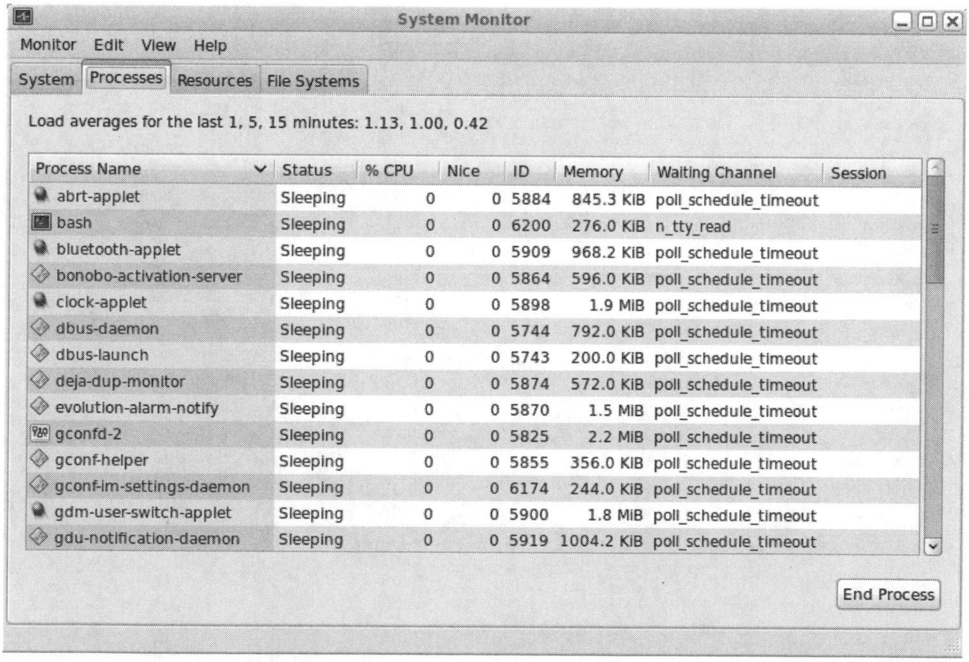

Figure 10-10 Processes tab in System Monitor

Source: Course Technology/Cengage Learning

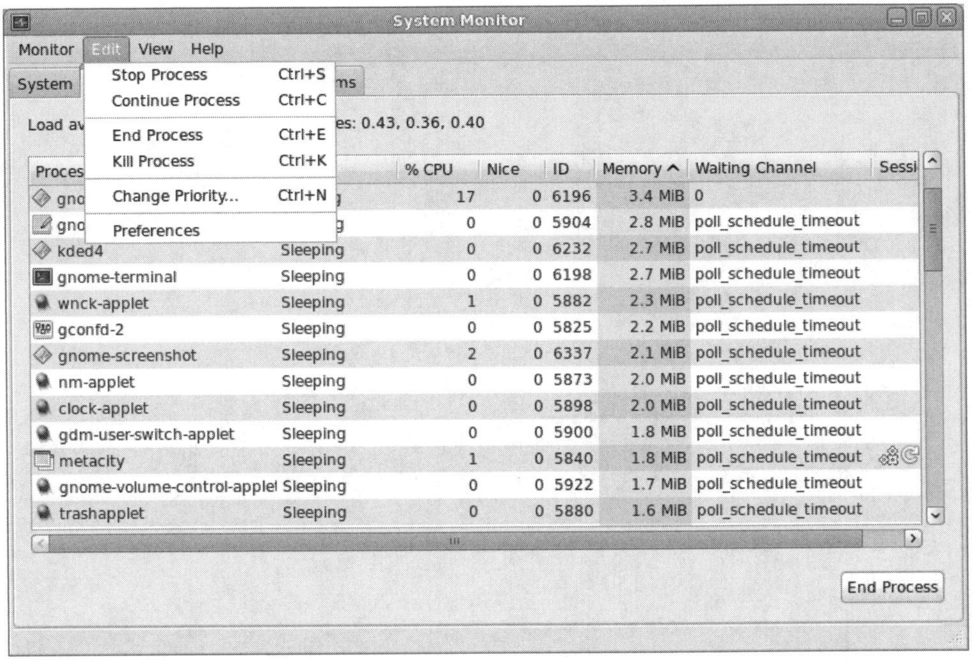

Figure 10-11 Edit menu in Processes tab

Source: Course Technology/Cengage Learning

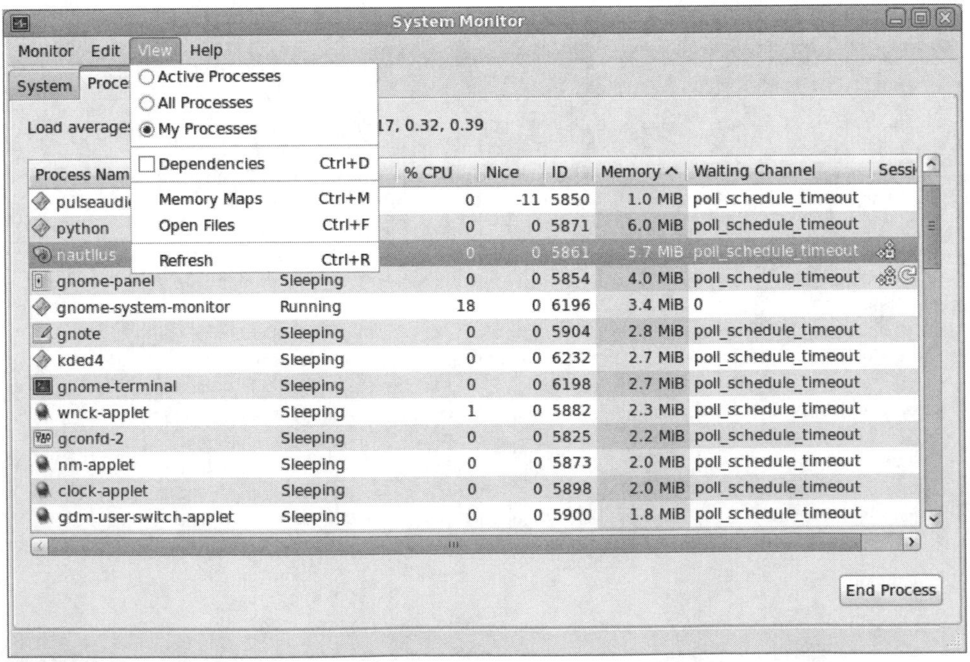

Figure 10-12 View menu in Processes tab

Source: Course Technology/Cengage Learning

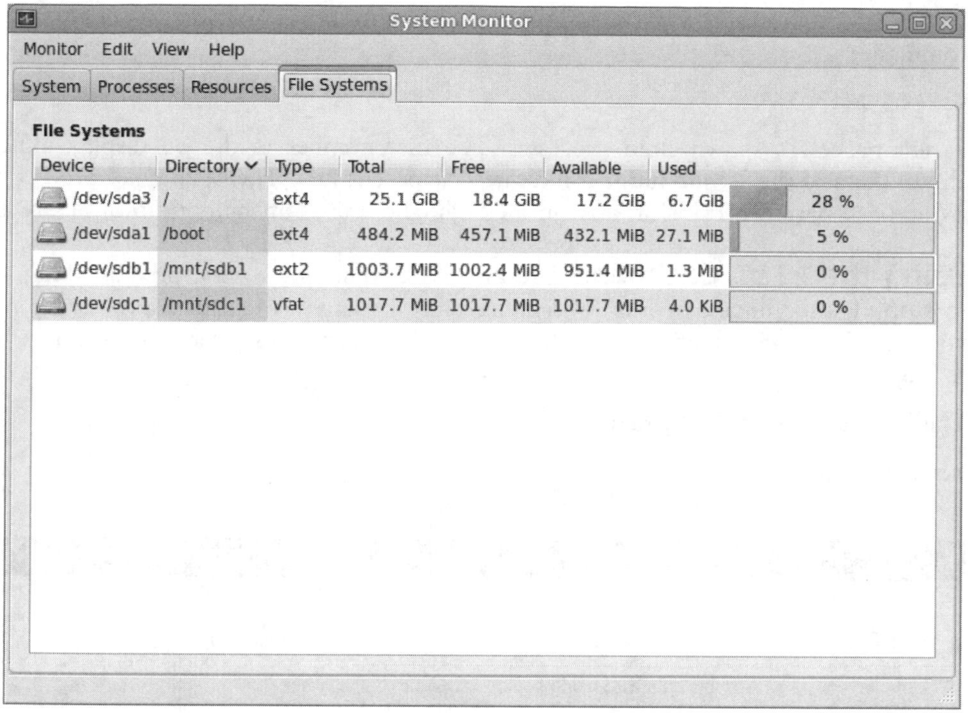

Figure 10-13 File Systems tab in System Monitor

Source: Course Technology/Cengage Learning

10

Using the Resources Tab in System Monitor The Resources tab displays the usage history of your CPU, memory, swap memory, and network in graphical format (see Figure 10-8).

Using the File Systems Tab in System Monitor The File Systems tab displays information about your file systems, including where they are mounted and what their types are. The tab also shows how much disk space is being used and how much is free (see Figure 10-13). The Device, Directory, and Type columns are displayed alphabetically. The Total, Free, Available, and Used columns can be listed in ascending or descending order.

The next sections explain a number of commands you can use to manage tasks in Fedora 13, including ps and kill.

Using the Process Command The **ps command** lists the system processes that are running, identifies who owns them, and shows the amount of system resources being used. You can control these processes at the command line. Whenever a program or command is executed, the kernel assigns an identification number called a **PID** (process ID) to the process. The syntax for the ps command is:

ps [*options*]

Table 10-1 lists the options you can use with the ps command.

Figure 10-14 shows how to access the processes for your ID when you type the following command:

`ps -fu User01`

Parent processes spawn child processes. The first number in the `ps` display indicates the child PID, and the second number indicates the parent PID. The 4625 child process indicates a /bin/bash parent process of 4624 in the highlighted lines at the bottom of Figure 10-15.

Using the `kill` Command   Use the `kill` command to end processes that you need to stop. The command works by sending one of many signals to a process or processes; you must be specific (and very careful) about which processes, users, or terminals you want to stop.

The basic syntax of the `kill` command is:

`kill` *option PID*

Entry	Description
e	Selects all processes
f	Displays a full, detailed listing
P	Selects specific processes by PID
t	Selects processes associated with a particular tty (physical terminal)
u	Selects processes by user

Table 10-1   Fedora 13 `ps` command options

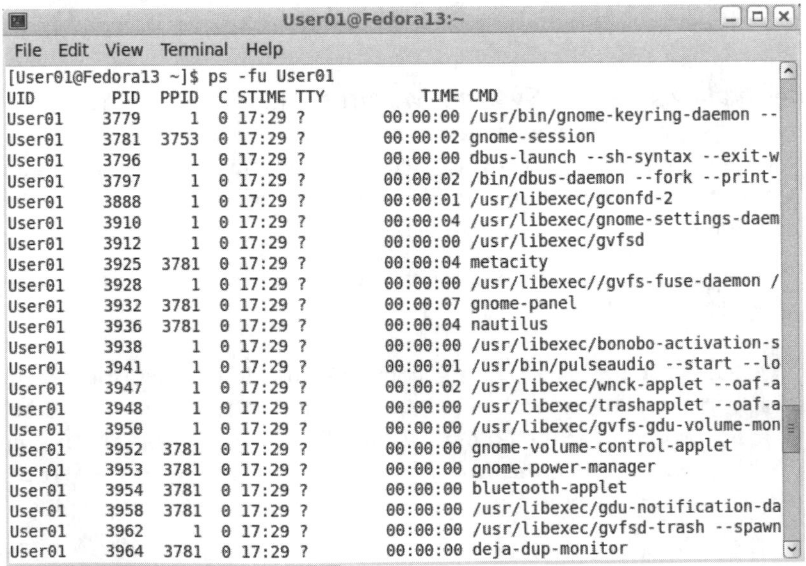

```
                          User01@Fedora13:~                       _ □ ×
 File  Edit  View  Terminal  Help
[User01@Fedora13 ~]$ ps -fu User01
UID        PID  PPID  C STIME TTY        TIME CMD
User01    3779     1  0 17:29 ?      00:00:00 /usr/bin/gnome-keyring-daemon --
User01    3781  3753  0 17:29 ?      00:00:02 gnome-session
User01    3796     1  0 17:29 ?      00:00:00 dbus-launch --sh-syntax --exit-w
User01    3797     1  0 17:29 ?      00:00:02 /bin/dbus-daemon --fork --print-
User01    3888     1  0 17:29 ?      00:00:01 /usr/libexec/gconfd-2
User01    3910     1  0 17:29 ?      00:00:04 /usr/libexec/gnome-settings-daem
User01    3912     1  0 17:29 ?      00:00:00 /usr/libexec/gvfsd
User01    3925  3781  0 17:29 ?      00:00:04 metacity
User01    3928     1  0 17:29 ?      00:00:00 /usr/libexec//gvfs-fuse-daemon /
User01    3932  3781  0 17:29 ?      00:00:07 gnome-panel
User01    3936  3781  0 17:29 ?      00:00:04 nautilus
User01    3938     1  0 17:29 ?      00:00:00 /usr/libexec/bonobo-activation-s
User01    3941     1  0 17:29 ?      00:00:01 /usr/bin/pulseaudio --start --lo
User01    3947     1  0 17:29 ?      00:00:02 /usr/libexec/wnck-applet --oaf-a
User01    3948     1  0 17:29 ?      00:00:00 /usr/libexec/trashapplet --oaf-a
User01    3950     1  0 17:29 ?      00:00:00 /usr/libexec/gvfs-gdu-volume-mon
User01    3952  3781  0 17:29 ?      00:00:00 gnome-volume-control-applet
User01    3953  3781  0 17:29 ?      00:00:00 gnome-power-manager
User01    3954  3781  0 17:29 ?      00:00:00 bluetooth-applet
User01    3958  3781  0 17:29 ?      00:00:00 /usr/libexec/gdu-notification-da
User01    3962     1  0 17:29 ?      00:00:00 /usr/libexec/gvfsd-trash --spawn
User01    3964  3781  0 17:29 ?      00:00:00 deja-dup-monitor
```

Figure 10-14   User01's processes

Source: Course Technology/Cengage Learning

```
                              User01@Fedora13:~                        _ □ x
 File  Edit  View  Terminal  Help
User01   4237  4158  0 17:32 ?      00:00:01 /usr/bin/akonadi_ical_resource -
User01   4240     1  0 17:32 ?      00:00:00 /usr/bin/nepomukserver
User01   4241     1  0 17:32 ?      00:00:00 kdeinit4: kdeinit4 Running...
User01   4242  4241  0 17:32 ?      00:00:00 klauncher --fd=8
User01   4244     1  0 17:32 ?      00:00:01 kded4
User01   4247     1  0 17:32 ?      00:00:00 /usr/libexec/gam_server
User01   4252  4240  0 17:32 ?      00:00:02 /usr/bin/nepomukservicestub nepo
User01   4253     1  0 17:32 ?      00:00:01 /usr/bin/knotify4
User01   4256  4252  0 17:32 ?      00:00:00 [nepomukservices] <defunct>
User01   4259  4252  0 17:32 ?      00:00:04 /usr/bin/virtuoso-t +foreground
User01   4262  4158  0 17:32 ?      00:00:00 /usr/bin/akonadi_maildir_resourc
User01   4270  4240  0 17:32 ?      00:00:03 /usr/bin/nepomukservicestub nepo
User01   4271  4240  0 17:32 ?      00:00:00 /usr/bin/nepomukservicestub nepo
User01   4272  4240  0 17:32 ?      00:00:02 /usr/bin/nepomukservicestub nepo
User01   4273  4240  0 17:32 ?      00:00:00 /usr/bin/nepomukservicestub nepo
User01   4274  4240  0 17:32 ?      00:00:00 /usr/bin/nepomukservicestub nepo
User01   4577     1  2 18:14 ?      00:00:07 ksnapshot -caption KSnapshot
User01   4578  4241  0 18:14 ?      00:00:00 kdeinit4: kio_trash [kdeinit] tr
User01   4579  4241  0 18:14 ?      00:00:00 kdeinit4: kio_file [kdeinit] fil
User01   4624     1 17 18:19 ?      00:00:01 gnome-terminal
User01   4625  4624  0 18:19 ?      00:00:00 gnome-pty-helper
User01   4626  4624  1 18:19 pts/0  00:00:00 bash
User01   4642  4626  0 18:19 pts/0  00:00:00 ps -fu User01
[User01@Fedora13 ~]$
```

Figure 10-15 Parent and child processes

Source: Course Technology/Cengage Learning

One common use of the `kill` command is with the process ID. Type the following command to stop the process with the associated PID:

`kill PID`

When you use `-9`, the `kill` command is considered stronger. Its associated signal name is SIGKILL. Use the following command when the one shown previously doesn't work:

`kill -9 PID`

Another `kill` command, SIGHUP, is the signal to "hang up," or stop, a process. Its associated signal number is –1. It is cleaner than the –9 SIGKILL signal because it cleans up all associated processes as well.

`kill -SIGHUP PID`

As you become proficient at process control and job control, you will understand the usefulness of a number of `kill` options. You can find a full list of signal options on the signal man page.

To display the User01 associated processes, as shown in Figure 10-16, type the following command:

`ps –ef | grep User01 | more –d20`

Refer back to Figure 10-15, which shows a later screen of User01's associated processes. Note the 4624, 4625, and 4642 child processes listed after User01 at the bottom of the figure. All of them were "spawned" by the parent process 4624 associated with your bash shell, /bin/bash; this PID is listed after its child PIDs in Figure 10-15. Your bash shell was spawned by PID 1, and so on.

```
                              User01@Fedora13:~                              _ □ X
File  Edit  View  Terminal  Help
[User01@Fedora13 ~]$ ps -ef | grep User01 | more -d20
User01   3779      1  0 17:29 ?        00:00:00 /usr/bin/gnome-keyring-daemon --daemonize --login
User01   3781   3753  0 17:29 ?        00:00:02 gnome-session
User01   3796      1  0 17:29 ?        00:00:00 dbus-launch --sh-syntax --exit-with-session
User01   3797      1  0 17:29 ?        00:00:02 /bin/dbus-daemon --fork --print-pid 5 --print-address 7 --session
User01   3888      1  0 17:29 ?        00:00:01 /usr/libexec/gconfd-2
User01   3910      1  0 17:29 ?        00:00:05 /usr/libexec/gnome-settings-daemon
User01   3912      1  0 17:29 ?        00:00:00 /usr/libexec/gvfsd
User01   3925   3781  0 17:29 ?        00:00:06 metacity
User01   3928      1  0 17:29 ?        00:00:00 /usr/libexec//gvfs-fuse-daemon /home/User01/.gvfs
User01   3932   3781  0 17:29 ?        00:00:08 gnome-panel
User01   3936   3781  0 17:29 ?        00:00:06 nautilus
User01   3938      1  0 17:29 ?        00:00:00 /usr/libexec/bonobo-activation-server --ac-activate --ior-output-fd=19
User01   3941      1  0 17:29 ?        00:00:01 /usr/bin/pulseaudio --start --log-target=syslog
User01   3947      1  0 17:29 ?        00:00:03 /usr/libexec/wnck-applet --oaf-activate-iid=OAFIID:GNOME_Wncklet_Facto
ry --oaf-ior-fd=18
User01   3948      1  0 17:29 ?        00:00:00 /usr/libexec/trashapplet --oaf-activate-iid=OAFIID:GNOME_Panel_TrashAp
plet_Factory --oaf-ior-fd=26
User01   3950      1  0 17:29 ?        00:00:00 /usr/libexec/gvfs-gdu-volume-monitor
User01   3952   3781  0 17:29 ?        00:00:00 gnome-volume-control-applet
User01   3953   3781  0 17:29 ?        00:00:01 gnome-power-manager
--More--[Press space to continue, 'q' to quit.]
```

Figure 10-16 The first screen of the User01 process display

Source: Course Technology/Cengage Learning

You must be very careful with `kill` commands that use PIDs. If you kill processes using a PID, you also kill the processes it has spawned. For example, if you kill the bash shell (PID 1), you also kill PIDs 4624, 4625, and 4642; in this case, the Terminal window that contains the bash shell also closes.

Activity 10-3: Displaying Processes in Fedora 13

Time Required: 20 minutes

Objective: Display and trace processes in Fedora 13.

Description: In this activity, you display system processes using the `ps` command. This activity is useful when you need to view system processes running in Fedora 13.

1. Start your virtual machines using the appropriate instructions in Activity 1-1.

2. To open a console, click **Applications**, point to **System Tools**, and then click **Terminal**.

3. Type **ps –ef | more –d20** and press **Enter**.

4. Take notes on the processes, their child PIDs, and their parent PIDs.

5. Press the **Spacebar** to scroll through the list of processes and trace the spawning of child processes. Notice the pattern and sequence of which processes create others.

6. To find your own processes, type **ps** at the command prompt and trace the relationships of the processes attached to your PID.

7. Close any open windows.

8. Leave the virtual machine logged on for the next activity.

Activity 10-4: Killing Processes in Fedora 13

Time Required: 15 minutes

Objective: Kill system processes in Fedora 13.

Description: In this activity, you kill system processes using the ps and kill commands.

1. If necessary, start your virtual machines using the appropriate instructions in Activity 1-1. To open a console, click **Applications**, point to **System Tools**, and then click **Terminal**.

2. To spawn another bash shell within your original bash shell, type **bash** and then press **Enter**. Type **ps –ef** and then press **Enter**.

3. Note the two bash shell processes. Note the child PID on the latest bash shell and how it is attached to your PID and the ps –ef process.

4. To kill the latest bash shell process you spawned, type **kill -9** *child_PID_value,* substituting the correct PID for *child_PID_value* in the command, and then press **Enter**.

5. Verify that the message *Killed* appears on the screen.

6. To verify that the later bash process is gone, type **ps –ef** and press **Enter**. Note that only one bash process is displayed.

7. Close any open windows.

8. Leave the virtual machine logged on for future activities.

Monitoring Performance

By using the performance-monitoring tools in Windows 7 and Fedora 13 for real-time and periodic observation, you can acquire important information about the health of your virtual machine. In general, acceptable performance is a subjective judgment that can vary significantly from one virtual machine to another. To use the tools efficiently, you need to know how data is collected, what types of data are collected, and how to use the data to keep your system performing at its best.

Routine performance monitoring starts with establishing a default set of counters to track. You can use these counters to establish a performance **baseline**—the level of performance you can reliably expect during typical usage and workloads.

A **bottleneck** is anything that slows down a virtual machine's performance. A systematic approach to investigating bottlenecks is important in determining the correct solution.

Monitoring System Performance in Windows 7

Use Performance Monitor in Windows 7 to collect and view real-time data about a system's memory, disk, processor, network, and other activities. You can view these activities as a graph, histogram, or report. To open Performance Monitor, click Start and then click Control Panel. If necessary, click View By and then click Small icons. Click Administrative Tools, double-click Performance Monitor, and then click Performance Monitor. By default, Performance Monitor shows the % Processor Time (see Figure 10-17).

10

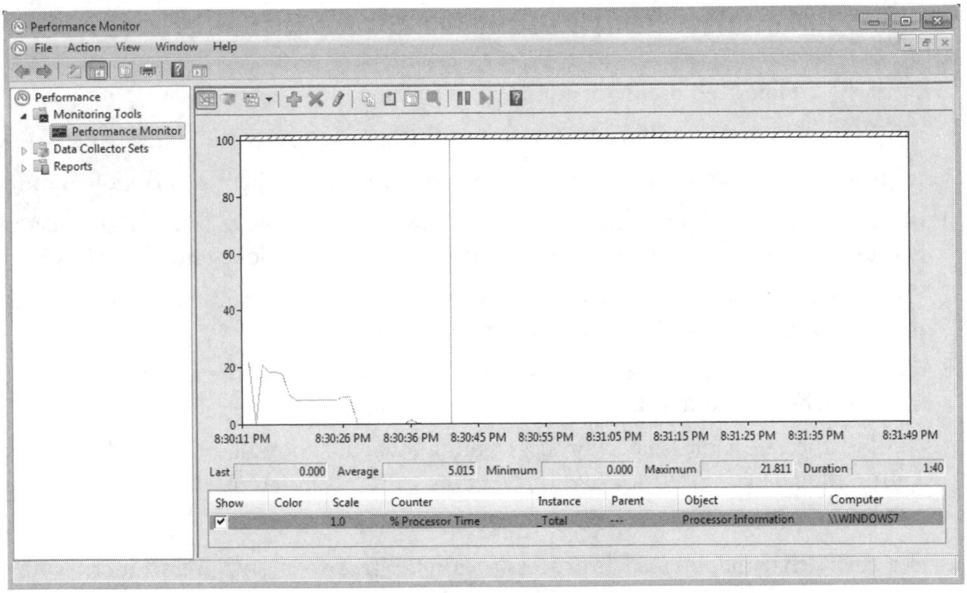

Figure 10-17 Viewing processor performance

Source: Course Technology/Cengage Learning

The % Processor Time measures how much time the processor actually spends working on productive threads versus how often it is busy servicing requests; if this counter's value continually exceeds 85 percent, you might need to upgrade the processor.

To add a counter, click the + button on the toolbar. The Add Counters dialog box appears, as shown in Figure 10-18. The dialog box contains options for the following items:

- Computers—Use the controls at the top of the dialog box to specify the source virtual machine of the item you select as the performance object; you can select the local computer or another computer on your network by typing the computer name in the appropriate box.

- Performance object—From this list, select the area of the virtual machine that you want to monitor. You can select Memory, Processor, or Physical Disk. Click the chevron to expand the performance object and view its counters.

- Counters—Select all counters or select particular counters for the performance object you choose for monitoring; the counters depend on the performance object you select.

- Instances—Select all instances or the specific instance to measure when multiple objects of the same type exist on a single system; for example, if you select the Processor performance object, the instances list displays all the active processors on the specified computer. If you have multiple processors, you will see *Total, 0, 1* in the list.

To view a description for each individual counter during the selection steps, check the Show description check box.

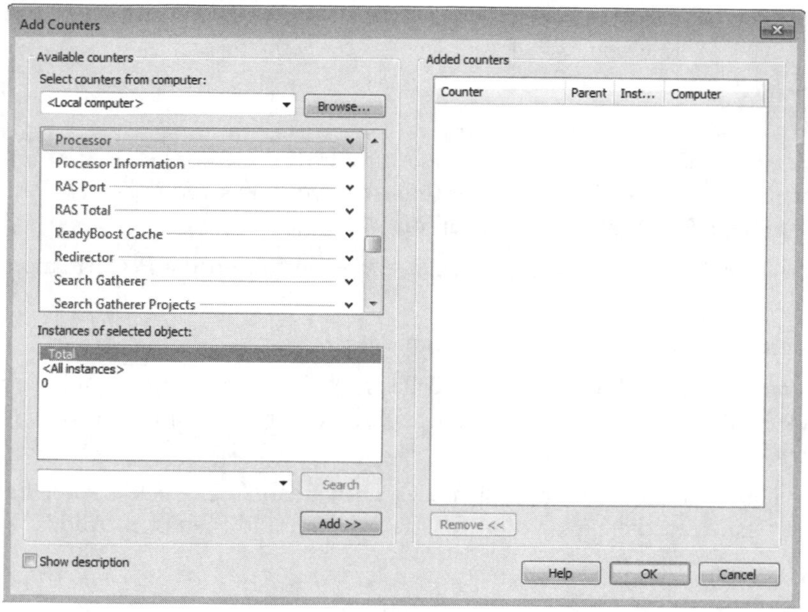

Figure 10-18 Add Counters dialog box

Source: Course Technology/Cengage Learning

When you have completed your selection for a counter, click the Add button. Your choice appears in the right pane. If you change your mind about a counter, click the Remove button. After you have added the last counter, click OK.

Monitoring Disk Performance Disk usage statistics help you balance the workload of your virtual machine. Performance Monitor provides physical disk counters for troubleshooting and measuring activity on a physical volume. Microsoft recommends using the following physical disk counters, which you can access and set in Activity 10-5:

- % Disk Time—A general indicator of how busy the disk is; if the value of the counter exceeds 90 percent, check the Current Disk Queue Length.

- Disk Reads/sec—The number of reads that the disk can accomplish per second; this count should not exceed the manufacturer's specifications for the disk drive.

- Disk Writes/sec—The number of writes that the disk can accomplish per second; again, this count should not exceed the manufacturer's specifications.

Activity 10-5: Monitoring Disk Performance in Windows 7

Time Required: 10 minutes

Objective: Manage disk performance with Performance Monitor.

Description: In this activity, you add recommended counters to practice monitoring disk performance using Performance Monitor.

 Because the peaks on the graphs are limited by the amount of disk activity, you may see only limited activity on the graphs.

1. If necessary, start your virtual machines using the appropriate instructions in Activity 1-1. Click **Start**, click **Control Panel**, click **Administrative Tools**, double-click **Performance Monitor**, and then click **Performance Monitor**.

2. To open the Add Counters dialog box, click the **+** button on the Performance Monitor toolbar.

3. To view the counter descriptions, check **Show description**.

4. To add a counter, scroll down and expand **Physical Disk**. Scroll again and click **% Disk Time**. Click **<All instances>** in the instances list, read the explanation for the counter, and then click **Add**.

5. To add the next counter, scroll and then click **Disk Reads/sec**. Click **<All instances>** in the instances list, read the explanation for the counter, and then click **Add**.

6. Repeat Step 5 for Disk Writes/sec.

7. Click **OK** and observe the changes in the counters.

8. To simulate activity, click **Start**, point to **All Programs**, click **Accessories**, and then click **WordPad**.

9. To view the counter statistics, click the **Highlight** button, which is just to the right of the **+** and X buttons in the toolbar shown in Figure 10-17. Click the **Disk Reads/sec** counter and observe the changes in the statistics. Note that the line for Disk Reads/sec is highlighted on the graph.

10. Repeat Step 9 for Disk Writes/sec.

11. Close all open windows.

12. Leave the virtual machine logged on for the next activity.

Managing Memory If your virtual machine is paging frequently, it may have a memory shortage. Paging occurs when the virtual machine accesses the hard drive to store or retrieve a memory page. Although some paging activity is acceptable because it enables Windows 7 to use more memory than actually exists, constant paging is a drain on performance. Therefore, you can reduce paging to significantly improve your virtual machine's responsiveness. The following counters are recommended for monitoring memory and paging; you can access and set them using Performance Monitor in Activity 10-6:

- Available MBytes—Indicates the amount of memory that is left after operating system allocations; if the value drops below 4 MB or 5 percent of RAM for several minutes at a time, your computer may have a memory shortage.

- Cache Bytes—Monitors the number of bytes used by the file system cache; use this counter in association with the Available MBytes counter. If the value exceeds 4 MB, you may need to add more RAM.

- Pages/sec—A general indication of how often a virtual machine uses the hard drive to store or retrieve memory-associated data; if the value exceeds 20, you need to analyze paging activity. A high degree of page file activity indicates that more RAM is required.

- Page Faults/sec—Gives you a general idea of how often requested information must be retrieved from another memory location or the page file; although a sustained value might indicate trouble, you should be more concerned with hard page faults that represent actual reads or writes to the disk. Remember that disk access is much slower than RAM.

Activity 10-6: Monitoring Memory Performance in Windows 7

Time Required: 10 minutes

Objective: Manage memory performance with Performance Monitor.

Description: In this activity, you add recommended counters to practice monitoring memory performance with Performance Monitor.

Because the peaks on the graphs are limited by the amount of memory activity, you may see only limited activity on the graphs.

1. If necessary, start your virtual machines using the appropriate instructions in Activity 1-1. Click **Start**, click **Control Panel**, click **Administrative Tools**, double-click **Performance Monitor**, and then click **Performance Monitor**.

2. To open the Add Counters dialog box, click the **+** button on the Performance Monitor toolbar.

3. If necessary, check **Show description** to view the counter descriptions.

4. To add a counter, scroll down and click **Memory**. Scroll again and click **Available MBytes**. Read the explanation for the counter, and then click **Add**.

5. To add the next counter, scroll and then click **Cache Bytes**, read the explanation for the counter, and then click **Add**.

6. Repeat Step 5 for Pages/sec and Page Faults/sec.

7. Click **OK** and observe the changes in the counters.

8. To simulate activity, click **Start**, point to **All Programs**, click **Accessories**, and then click **WordPad**.

9. To view the counter statistics, click the **Highlight** button, which is just to the right of the **+** and X buttons in the toolbar shown in Figure 10-17. Click the **Cache Bytes** counter and observe the displayed changes in the statistics.

10. Repeat Step 9 for Pages/sec and Page Faults/sec.

11. Close all open windows.

12. Leave the virtual machine logged on for the next activity.

10

Monitoring Processor Use The Processor and System object counters provide valuable information about the use of your processors. You need this information to effectively tune your virtual machine. You should monitor the following counters; to access and set them in Performance Monitor, see Activity 10-7.

- % Processor Time—Measures how much time the processor actually spends working on productive threads versus how often it is busy servicing requests; if this counter's value continually exceeds 85 percent, you might need to upgrade the processor.
- Interrupts/sec—The average rate, in incidents per second, at which the processor receives and services hardware interrupts.
- Processor Queue Length—The number of threads in the processor queue that are ready to be executed; this counter is located under the System object. A sustained processor queue of less than 10 threads per processor is normally acceptable.

Activity 10-7: Monitoring Processor Use in Windows 7

Time Required: 10 minutes

Objective: Manage processor use with Performance Monitor.

Description: In this activity, you add recommended counters to analyze and monitor processor use with Performance Monitor.

Because the peaks on the graphs are limited by the amount of processor activity, you may see only limited activity on the graphs.

1. If necessary, start your virtual machines using the appropriate instructions in Activity 1-1. Click **Start,** click **Control Panel,** click **Administrative Tools,** double-click **Performance Monitor,** and then click **Performance Monitor.**

2. To open the Add Counters dialog box, click the **+** button on the Performance Monitor toolbar.

3. If necessary, check **Show description** to view the counter descriptions.

4. To add a counter for % Processor Time, scroll and expand **Processor,** then scroll and click **% Processor time.** Read the explanation for the counter, and then click **Add.**

5. To add the next counter, scroll through the counters list, click **Interrupts/sec,** read the explanation for the counter, and then click **Add.**

6. Collapse the **Processor** list.

7. To add the last counter, scroll down and expand **System.** Scroll again and click **Processor Queue Length,** read the explanation for the counter, and then click **Add.**

8. Click **OK** and observe the changes in the counters.

9. To simulate activity, click **Start,** point to **All Programs,** click **Accessories,** and then click **WordPad.**

10. To view the counter statistics, click the **Highlight** button, which is just to the right of the + and X buttons in the toolbar shown in Figure 10-17. Click the **Interrupts/sec** counter and observe the changes in the statistics.

11. Repeat Step 10 for the Processor Queue Length counter.

12. Close all open windows.

13. Leave the virtual machine logged on for future activities.

Monitoring System Performance in Fedora 13

When you monitor performance, you typically look at such statistics as memory usage, CPU usage, input/output usage, delay times, and queuing. The commands in the following sections describe these statistics and provide an introduction to monitoring system performance.

/Proc File System Fedora 13 contains a command-line reporting and control information system known as the **/proc file system**. To access this information, use the cat command and different kernel parameters. The kernel, or system, information is contained in files in the /proc directory. The /proc file system is known as a **pseudo-file system**, which directly interfaces with the kernel and is stored in memory.

This chapter covers only a few of the many kernel parameters; see Table 10-2 for a partial list of kernel values. To see a complete list and descriptions of the available kernel values, consult the proc man page.

You can use the /proc file system for the following types of system-related tasks:

- Performance and memory information
- Viewing and modifying run-time parameters
- Viewing hardware information
- Viewing and modifying network parameters
- Viewing statistical information

You can see the available kernel value statistics, as shown in Figure 10-19, by changing to the /proc directory and typing ls:

```
cd /proc
ls
```

Entry	Description
iomem	Memory input/output statistics
mounts	Mounted file system statistics
stat	Process status in readable format
diskstats	Disk statistics
swaps	Swap file statistics (swap files are used in the way that virtual memory is used in Windows 7)
loadavg	The average number of processes ready to run during the last 1, 5, and 15 minutes

Table 10-2   Kernel system values

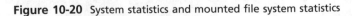

```
                          User01@Fedora13:/proc
 File   Edit   View   Terminal   Help
1        1273   1608   1699   2048   36    942        ioports        scsi
10       1275   1613   17     2051   37    948        irq            self
1001     1294   1616   1702   2052   380   956        kallsyms       slabinfo
1061     1297   1622   1704   2056   4     982        kcore          softirqs
1070     13     1623   1705   2089   40    989        keys           stat
1071     1312   1628   1712   2097   41    acpi       key-users      swaps
11       1382   1632   1713   21     42    asound     kmsg           sys
1100     1388   1633   1714   2102   43    buddyinfo  kpagecount     sysrq-trigger
1111     14     1635   1716   2121   5     bus        kpageflags     sysvipc
1132     1424   1640   1754   22     6     cgroups    latency_stats  timer_list
1196     1426   1646   18     23     688   cmdline    loadavg        timer_stats
12       1436   1647   19     25     689   cpuinfo    locks          tty
1212     1441   1649   1943   26     7     crypto     mdstat         uptime
1221     1462   1650   1946   27     740   devices    meminfo        version
1231     1464   1654   1953   277   8      diskstats  misc           vmallocinfo
1239     1465   1655   1954   28     862   dma        modules        vmstat
1250     1491   1656   1955   284   897    driver     mounts         zoneinfo
1258     1498   1671   1984   29     9      execdomains mtrr
1265     15     1682   2      293   908    fb          net
1267     1508   1692   20     294   917    filesystems pagetypeinfo
1269     1509   1693   2015   3     928    fs          partitions
1270     16     1696   2016   327   935    interrupts  sched_debug
1271     1602   1698   2017   35    941    iomem       schedstat
[User01@Fedora13 proc]$ █
```

Figure 10-19 List of /proc directory contents

Source: Course Technology/Cengage Learning

To see performance information for system and mounted file system statistics, as shown in Figure 10-20, change to the /proc directory and type the following commands:

```
cd /proc
cat stat
cat mounts
```

```
                          User01@Fedora13:/proc
 File   Edit   View   Terminal   Help
[User01@Fedora13 proc]$ cat stat
cpu  84667 17987 117808 956906 54352 7285 3874 0 0 0
cpu0 84667 17987 117808 956906 54352 7285 3874 0 0 0
intr 2773420 536 3342 0 0 0 169990 0 0 1 0 49876 38178 140 0 0 175053 0 0 0 0
0 0 0 0 0 0 0 0 0 0 0 0 0 0 0 0 0 0 0 0 0 0 0 0 0 0 0 0 0 0 0 0 0 0 0 0 0
0 0 0 0 0 0 0 0 0 0 0 0 0 0 0 0 0 0 0 0 0 0 0 0 0 0 0 0 0 0 0 0 0 0 0 0 0
0 0 0 0 0 0 0 0 0 0 0 0 0 0 0 0 0 0 0 0 0 0 0 0 0 0 0 0 0 0 0 0 0 0 0 0 0
0 0 0 0 0 0 0 0 0 0 0 0 0 0 0 0 0 0 0 0 0 0 0 0 0 0 0 0 0 0 0 0 0 0 0 0 0
0 0 0 0 0 0 0 0 0 0 0 0 0 0 0 0 0 0 0 0 0 0 0 0 0 0 0 0 0 0 0 0 0 0 0 0 0
0 0 0 0 0 0 0 0 0 0 0 0 0 0 0 0 0 0 0 0 0 0 0 0 0 0 0 0 0 0 0 0 0 0 0 0 0
0 0 0 0 0 0 0 0 0 0 0 0 0 0 0 0 0 0 0 0 0 0 0 0 0 0 0 0 0 0 0 0 0 0 0 0 0
0 0 0 0 0 0 0 0 0 0 0 0 0 0 0 0 0 0 0 0 0 0 0 0 0 0 0 0 0 0 0 0 0 0 0 0 0
0 0 0 0 0 0 0 0 0 0 0 0 0 0 0 0 0 0 0 0 0 0 0 0 0 0 0 0 0 0 0 0 0 0 0 0 0
0 0 0 0 0 0 0 0 0 0 0 0 0 0 0 0 0 0 0 0 0 0 0 0 0 0 0 0 0 0 0 0 0 0 0 0 0
0 0 0 0 0 0 0 0 0 0 0 0 0 0 0 0 0 0 0 0 0 0 0 0 0 0 0 0 0 0 0 0 0 0 0 0 0
0 0 0 0 0 0 0 0 0 0 0 0 0 0 0 0 0 0 0 0 0 0 0 0 0 0 0 0 0 0 0 0 0 0 0 0 0
0 0 0 0 0 0 0 0 0 0 0 0 0 0 0 0 0 0 0 0 0 0 0 0 0 0 0 0 0 0 0 0 0 0 0 0 0
0 0 0 0 0 0 0 0 0 0 0 0 0 0 0 0 0 0 0 0 0 0 0 0 0 0 0 0 0 0 0 0 0 0 0 0 0
0 0 0 0 0 0 0 0 0 0 0 0 0 0 0 0 0 0 0 0 0 0 0 0 0 0 0 0 0 0 0 0 0 0 0 0 0
0 0 0 0 0 0 0 0 0 0 0 0 0 0 0 0 0 0 0 0 0 0 0 0 0 0 0 0 0 0 0 0 0 0 0 0 0
0 0 0 0 0 0 0 0 0 0 0 0 0 0 0 0 0 0 0 0 0 0 0 0 0 0 0 0 0 0 0 0 0 0 0 0 0
```

Figure 10-20 System statistics and mounted file system statistics

Source: Course Technology/Cengage Learning

```
User01@Fedora13:/proc                          _ □ ✕
File  Edit  View  Terminal  Help
[User01@Fedora13 proc]$ cat mounts
rootfs / rootfs rw 0 0
/proc /proc proc rw,relatime 0 0
/sys /sys sysfs rw,seclabel,relatime 0 0
udev /dev devtmpfs rw,seclabel,relatime,size=507744k,nr_inodes=126936,mode=75
5 0 0
devpts /dev/pts devpts rw,seclabel,relatime,gid=5,mode=620,ptmxmode=000 0 0
tmpfs /dev/shm tmpfs rw,seclabel,relatime 0 0
/dev/mapper/vg_fedora13-lv_root / ext4 rw,seclabel,relatime,barrier=1,data=or
dered 0 0
none /selinux selinuxfs rw,relatime 0 0
/proc/bus/usb /proc/bus/usb usbfs rw,relatime 0 0
/dev/sda1 /boot ext4 rw,seclabel,relatime,barrier=1,data=ordered 0 0
/dev/sdb1 /mnt/sdb1 ext2 rw,seclabel,relatime,errors=continue 0 0
/dev/sdc1 /mnt/sdc1 vfat rw,relatime,fmask=0111,dmask=0000,allow_utime=0022,c
odepage=cp437,iocharset=ascii,shortname=mixed,errors=remount-ro 0 0
none /proc/sys/fs/binfmt_misc binfmt_misc rw,relatime 0 0
sunrpc /var/lib/nfs/rpc_pipefs rpc_pipefs rw,relatime 0 0
gvfs-fuse-daemon /home/User01/.gvfs fuse.gvfs-fuse-daemon rw,nosuid,nodev,rel
atime,user_id=500,group_id=500 0 0
[User01@Fedora13 proc]$ ▮
```

Figure 10-20 (Continued)

To see performance information for the disk statistics, as shown in Figure 10-21, change to the /proc directory and type the following commands:

```
cd /proc
cat diskstats
```

10

```
User01@Fedora13:/proc                          _ □ ✕
File  Edit  View  Terminal  Help
[User01@Fedora13 proc]$ cat diskstats
   1    0 ram0 0 0 0 0 0 0 0 0 0 0 0
   1    1 ram1 0 0 0 0 0 0 0 0 0 0 0
   1    2 ram2 0 0 0 0 0 0 0 0 0 0 0
   1    3 ram3 0 0 0 0 0 0 0 0 0 0 0
   1    4 ram4 0 0 0 0 0 0 0 0 0 0 0
   1    5 ram5 0 0 0 0 0 0 0 0 0 0 0
   1    6 ram6 0 0 0 0 0 0 0 0 0 0 0
   1    7 ram7 0 0 0 0 0 0 0 0 0 0 0
   1    8 ram8 0 0 0 0 0 0 0 0 0 0 0
   1    9 ram9 0 0 0 0 0 0 0 0 0 0 0
   1   10 ram10 0 0 0 0 0 0 0 0 0 0 0
   1   11 ram11 0 0 0 0 0 0 0 0 0 0 0
   1   12 ram12 0 0 0 0 0 0 0 0 0 0 0
   1   13 ram13 0 0 0 0 0 0 0 0 0 0 0
   1   14 ram14 0 0 0 0 0 0 0 0 0 0 0
   1   15 ram15 0 0 0 0 0 0 0 0 0 0 0
   7    0 loop0 0 0 0 0 0 0 0 0 0 0 0
   7    1 loop1 0 0 0 0 0 0 0 0 0 0 0
   7    2 loop2 0 0 0 0 0 0 0 0 0 0 0
   7    3 loop3 0 0 0 0 0 0 0 0 0 0 0
   7    4 loop4 0 0 0 0 0 0 0 0 0 0 0
   7    5 loop5 0 0 0 0 0 0 0 0 0 0 0
   7    6 loop6 0 0 0 0 0 0 0 0 0 0 0
   7    7 loop7 0 0 0 0 0 0 0 0 0 0 0
   8    0 sda 48651 9712 2603568 562837 121869 527590 5079884 3816927 0 830827 4381446
   8    1 sda1 208 83 1614 600 8 0 28 175 0 775 775
   8    2 sda2 48408 9626 2601650 561942 106880 527590 5079856 3650456 0 663508 4214085
   8   16 sdb 196 348 1548 619 1 0 8 0 0 618 618
   8   17 sdb1 128 344 972 391 1 0 8 0 0 390 390
   8   32 sdc 222 2550 3543 693 1 0 1 71 0 673 764
```

Figure 10-21 Disk statistics

Source: Course Technology/Cengage Learning

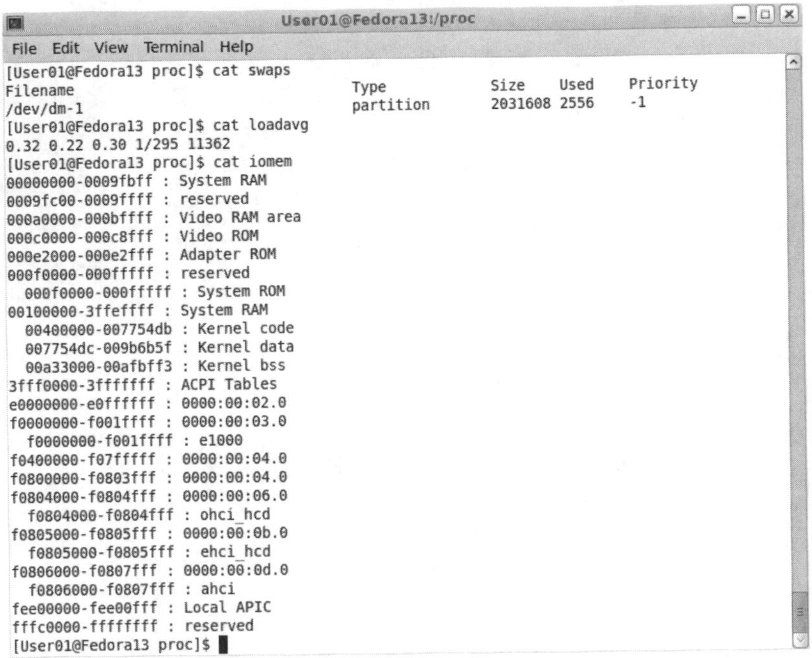

Figure 10-22 Swap statistics, average load, and input/output memory usage

Source: Course Technology/Cengage Learning

To see performance information for swap statistics, average load, and input/output memory usage, as shown in Figure 10-22, change to the /proc directory and type the following commands:

```
cd /proc
cat swaps
cat loadavg
cat iomem
```

Using the `top` Command The `top` command displays system statistics continuously in real time, with a five-second delay by default. The command constantly updates console-based output for the most CPU-intensive processes that are running. The basic syntax of the top command is:

`top - display top CPU processes`

The basic fields for the `top` command are:

- `uptime`—The amount of time the system has been up and the system's three average loads: the average number of processes ready to run during the last 1, 5, and 15 minutes
- `processes`—The total number of processes running at the time of the last update
- `CPU states`—The percentage of CPU time in user mode, system mode, niced tasks, iowait, and idle (a niced task is a task run with a modified scheduling priority); time

spent in niced tasks is also counted in system and user time, so the total will be more than 100 percent

- Mem—Statistics on memory usage, including total available memory, free memory, used memory, shared memory, and memory used for buffers
- Swap—Statistics on swap space, including total swap space, available swap space, and used swap space
- PID—The process ID of each task
- PPID—The parent process ID of each task
- UID—The user ID of the task's owner
- USER—The user name of the task's owner
- SHARE—The amount of shared memory used by the task

To start the top utility with five iterations and a delay of 10 seconds (see Figure 10-23), type the following command with the default abbreviated field names:

top –n5 –d10.00

The top command uses a large amount of memory, so you should only use the command for troubleshooting and tuning; don't keep it running all the time. When you finish, press q to quit the top display.

Using the free Command The **free command** indicates the amounts of free, used, and swap memory in the system. The amounts of free and used memory are shown in kilobytes; use the –m option with free if you want to see the readings in megabytes. To use the free command, as shown in Figure 10-24, simply type free.

10

```
                        User01@Fedora13:/proc
 File  Edit  View  Terminal  Help
top - 18:16:36 up 50 min,  3 users,  load average: 0.00, 0.00, 0.00
Tasks: 143 total,    1 running, 142 sleeping,   0 stopped,   0 zombie
Cpu(s):  0.1%us,  0.2%sy,  0.0%ni, 99.6%id,  0.0%wa,  0.0%hi,  0.1%si,  0.0%st
Mem:   1027028k total,   641932k used,   385096k free,    28032k buffers
Swap:  2031608k total,        0k used,  2031608k free,   458416k cached

  PID USER      PR  NI  VIRT  RES  SHR S %CPU %MEM    TIME+  COMMAND
 1297 root      20   0 46116  22m 7192 S  0.2  2.2  0:32.99 Xorg
 1655 root      20   0  5732  584  384 S  0.1  0.1  0:00.66 udisks-daemon
 2125 User01    20   0  2696 1152  896 R  0.1  0.1  0:00.04 top
    1 root      20   0  2828 1400 1196 S  0.0  0.1  0:00.89 init
    2 root      20   0     0    0    0 S  0.0  0.0  0:00.00 kthreadd
    3 root      RT   0     0    0    0 S  0.0  0.0  0:00.00 migration/0
    4 root      20   0     0    0    0 S  0.0  0.0  0:00.01 ksoftirqd/0
    5 root      RT   0     0    0    0 S  0.0  0.0  0:00.00 watchdog/0
    6 root      20   0     0    0    0 S  0.0  0.0  0:00.05 events/0
    7 root      20   0     0    0    0 S  0.0  0.0  0:00.00 cpuset
    8 root      20   0     0    0    0 S  0.0  0.0  0:00.00 khelper
    9 root      20   0     0    0    0 S  0.0  0.0  0:00.00 netns
   10 root      20   0     0    0    0 S  0.0  0.0  0:00.00 async/mgr
   11 root      20   0     0    0    0 S  0.0  0.0  0:00.00 pm
   12 root      20   0     0    0    0 S  0.0  0.0  0:00.00 sync_supers
   13 root      20   0     0    0    0 S  0.0  0.0  0:00.00 bdi-default
   14 root      20   0     0    0    0 S  0.0  0.0  0:00.00 kintegrityd/0
```

Figure 10-23 The top command with delay and iteration defined

Source: Course Technology/Cengage Learning

User01@Fedora13:/proc
File Edit View Terminal Help
[User01@Fedora13 proc]$ free
total used free shared buffers cached
Mem: 1027220 1004416 22804 0 51892 659672
-/+ buffers/cache: 292852 734368
Swap: 2031608 2556 2029052
[User01@Fedora13 proc]$

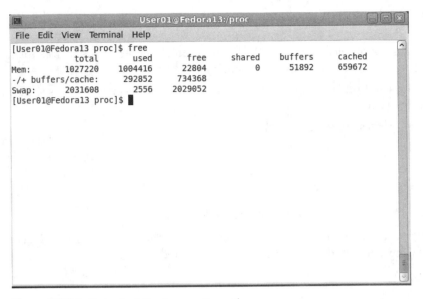

Figure 10-24 Output of the `free` command

Source: Course Technology/Cengage Learning

Using the `watch free` Command Line The **`watch free` command** line produces real-time statistics on the amount of free space in the system. The default for the delay is two seconds. You can control the frequency of the output by setting the interval time, and you can terminate the output by pressing Ctrl+C. To use the command line, as shown in Figure 10-25, type the following command:

```
watch free
```

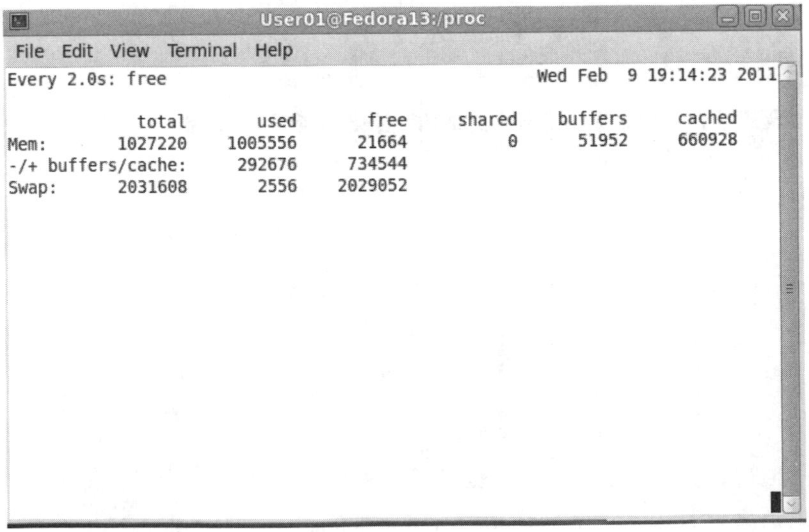

User01@Fedora13:/proc
File Edit View Terminal Help
Every 2.0s: free
Wed Feb 9 19:14:23 2011
total used free shared buffers cached
Mem: 1027220 1005556 21664 0 51952 660928
-/+ buffers/cache: 292676 734544
Swap: 2031608 2556 2029052

Figure 10-25 Output of the `watch free` command line

Source: Course Technology/Cengage Learning

Using the `vmstat` Command The `vmstat` command reports on process status, memory consumption, paging activity, I/O operations, and CPU usage. It typically provides an average since the last reboot, or it can report usage for a current period of time if you specify the time interval in seconds and the number of iterations you need. The command continues reporting until you interrupt it.

The basic fields for the `vmstat` command are:

- `procs`—Number of processes running and sleeping
- `swap`—Amount of memory paged for input and output
- `us`—Percentage of total processor time consumed by user space
- `sy`—Percentage of total processor time consumed by the kernel
- `wa`—Percentage of total processor time spent in I/O wait
- `id`—Percentage of total processor time spent idle

Figure 10-26 shows how the `vmstat` command begins to execute a delay of five seconds and 10 iterations after you type the following command:

vmstat 5 10

Figure 10-27 shows the results of the `vmstat` command after a delay of five seconds.

Using the `uptime` Command The `uptime` command displays the amount of time since the last system reboot, shows the CPU average load for the past 1, 5, and 15 minutes, and shows how many users are logged on (see Figure 10-28). To use the command, simply type uptime.

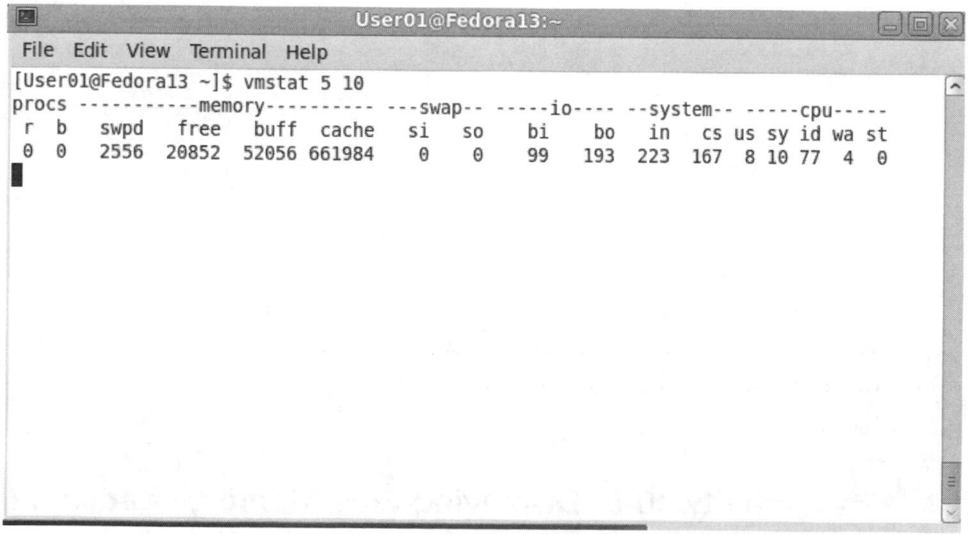

10

```
[User01@Fedora13 ~]$ vmstat 5 10
procs -----------memory---------- ---swap-- -----io---- --system-- -----cpu-----
 r  b   swpd   free   buff  cache   si   so    bi    bo   in   cs us sy id wa st
 0  0   2556  20852  52056 661984    0    0    99   193  223  167  8 10 77  4  0
```

Figure 10-26 The `vmstat` command with a five-second delay and 10 iterations

Source: Course Technology/Cengage Learning

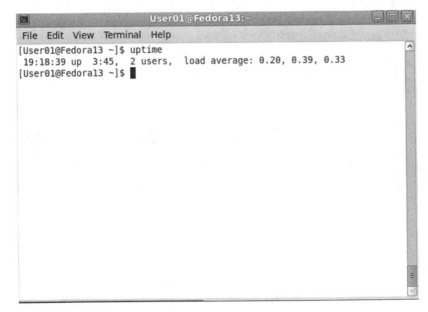

Figure 10-27   The **vmstat** display after a five-second delay

Source: Course Technology/Cengage Learning

Figure 10-28   Output of the **uptime** command

Source: Course Technology/Cengage Learning

Activity 10-8: Displaying Free Memory Statistics in Fedora 13

Time Required: 5 minutes

Objective: Display free memory statistics.

Description: In this activity, you display free memory statistics using the `free` command. The activity is useful if you need to view and monitor the memory on your Fedora 13 system.

1. If necessary, start your virtual machines using the appropriate instructions in Activity 1-1. To open a console, click **Applications**, point to **System Tools**, and then click **Terminal**.

2. To display memory statistics, type **free** and then press **Enter**.

3. Note the system's average loads for the past 1, 5, and 15 minutes.

4. Close all open windows.

5. Leave the virtual machine logged on for the next activity.

Activity 10-9: Real-Time Monitoring of System Performance in Fedora 13

Time Required: 15 minutes

Objective: Display real-time, continuous system statistics.

Description: In this activity, you display system processes using the `top` command. The system statistics are updated every five seconds for 10 iterations. This activity is useful if you need to establish a real-time system monitor for statistics.

1. If necessary, start your virtual machines using the appropriate instructions in Activity 1-1. To open a console, click **Applications**, point to **System Tools**, and then click **Terminal**.

2. Type **top −n5 −d10.00** and then press **Enter**.

3. Note the different system statistics and how they change as the display iterates.

4. Close any open windows.

5. Leave the virtual machine logged on for the next activity.

10

Activity 10-10: Viewing System Statistics Straight from the Kernel in Fedora 13

Time Required: 10 minutes

Objective: Display up-to-date system statistics straight from the kernel.

Description: In this activity, you display system processes using the `cat` command with /proc files. This activity is useful if you want to view statistics on swap files, average CPU load, and memory input/output.

1. If necessary, start your virtual machines using the appropriate instructions in Activity 1-1.

2. To open a console, click **Applications**, point to **System Tools**, and then click **Terminal**.

3. To change to the /proc directory, type **cd /proc** and then press **Enter**.

4. To view swap file statistics, type **cat swaps** and then press **Enter**.

5. To view average CPU load statistics, type **cat loadavg** and then press **Enter**.

6. To view memory input/output statistics, type **cat iomem** and then press **Enter**.

7. Close all open windows.

8. To shut down the virtual machine, click **System,** click **Shut Down,** and then click the **Shut Down** button.

9. Wait a moment for the Fedora 13 virtual machine to shut down completely.

Monitoring Reliability

The following sections introduce you to two tools that help you check the reliability of your system: the Reliability Monitor in Windows 7 and the Automatic Bug Reporting Tool in Fedora 13.

Using the Reliability Monitor in Windows 7

The Windows 7 "Reliability Monitor (shown in Figure 10-29) is an advanced tool that measures hardware and software problems and other changes to your computer. It provides a stability index that ranges from 1 to 10, where 10 is most stable. You can use the index to help evaluate the reliability of your computer. Any change you make to your computer and any problem that occurs on your computer affects the stability index. To open the Reliability Monitor, click Start, type *reliability* in the search text box, and then click View reliability history.

The main goal of the Windows 7 Reliability Monitor is to keep track of "reliability events," which are changes to your system that could alter its stability or other events that might indicate system instability.

Events monitored include:

- Windows updates
- Software installations and uninstalls

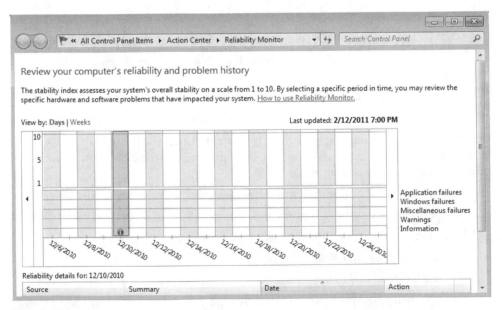

Figure 10-29 Windows 7 Reliability Monitor

Source: Course Technology/Cengage Learning

- Device driver installations, updates, rollbacks, and uninstalls
- Application hangs and crashes
- Device drivers that fail to load or unload
- Disk and memory failures
- Windows failures, including boot failures, system crashes, and sleep failures

The Stability Index rating gives you a visual indication of how reliably your system performs over time. You are given an overall Stability Index score. Ten is a perfect score, and one is the lowest. The Reliability Monitor retains data for up to a year so you can see how your system has been performing over time. Recent events will only be displayed in the Reliability Monitor after 24 hours.

If you see a drop in stability for your virtual machine, you can check the date that the drop began and then see if the decline was due to one of the following issues:

- Application failures
- Windows failures
- Miscellaneous failures
- Warnings

Figure 10-29 shows one informational event, which is indicated by a blue circle that contains the letter *i*. Warning messages are indicated by a yellow triangle that contains a black exclamation mark. Error messages appear as red circles with a white X. To see information about a warning message, click on the day that the warning occurred. Figure 10-30 shows summary information about the events on the chosen day.

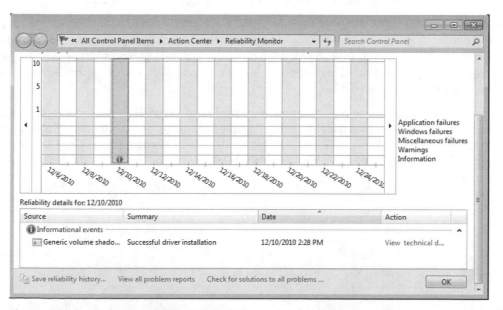

Figure 10-30 Windows Reliability Monitor showing information for events

Source: Course Technology/Cengage Learning

Activity 10-11: Viewing the Reliability History for Windows 7

Time Required: 10 minutes

Objective: View the reliability history of your virtual machine.

Description: In this activity, you will open the Reliability Monitor and view the history of your virtual machine. This activity is useful if you want to view recent changes to your virtual machine and the possible consequences of these changes.

1. If necessary, start your virtual machines using the appropriate instructions in Activity 1-1.

2. To open the Reliability Monitor, click **Start**, type **reliability** in the search text box, and then click **View reliability history**.

There is a 24-hour delay for the display of events in the Reliability Monitor. For this reason, you may not see any warnings or other failures.

3. Close any open windows in the virtual machine.

4. To shut down the virtual machine, click **Start,** and then click the **Shut Down** button.

5. Wait a moment for the Windows 7 virtual machine to shut down completely.

Automatic Bug Reporting in Fedora 13

Fedora 13 has an Automatic Bug Reporting Tool (ABRT) for regular, nonadministrative users. ABRT is one of the easiest tools to use for reporting bugs (see Figure 10-31). The abrt daemon resides in the background and watches for application crashes.

When a crash occurs, the abrt daemon collects the crash-related data and an icon appears in the notification area on the desktop. When you click the Bug Report icon, the Automatic Bug Reporting Tool screen appears. Highlight the corresponding reported application, and then click the Report button. The Reporter Selector screen allows you to choose where to send the report (see Figure 10-32).

If you select Logger, the report is sent to a local hard drive. If you select Bugzilla, a ticket is generated in Red Hat Bugzilla. Logger is simpler to use because it does not require login credentials and no follow-up is needed. Figure 10-33 shows the process screen that appears when Logger is selected from the Reporter Selector screen. Figure 10-34 displays the corresponding analysis result.

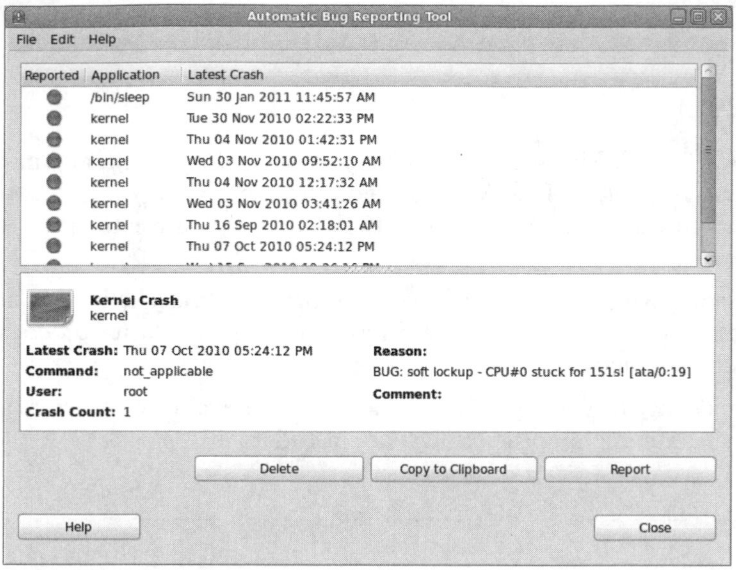

Figure 10-31 ABRT

Source: Course Technology/Cengage Learning

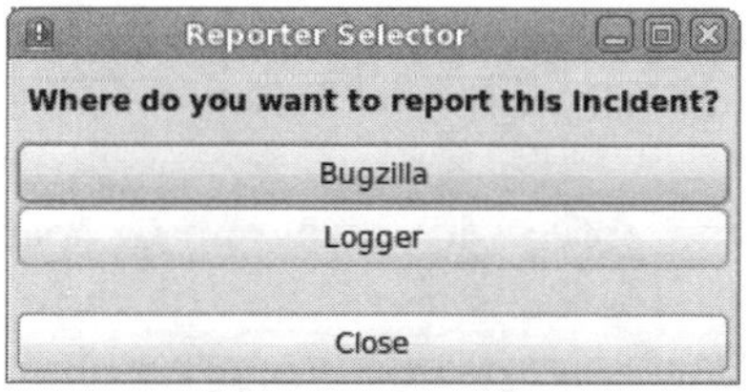

Figure 10-32 Reporter Selector

Source: Course Technology/Cengage Learning

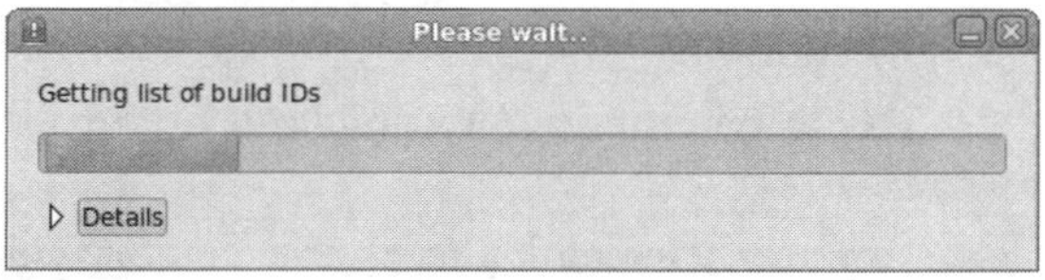

Figure 10-33 ABRT report to Logger

Source: Course Technology/Cengage Learning

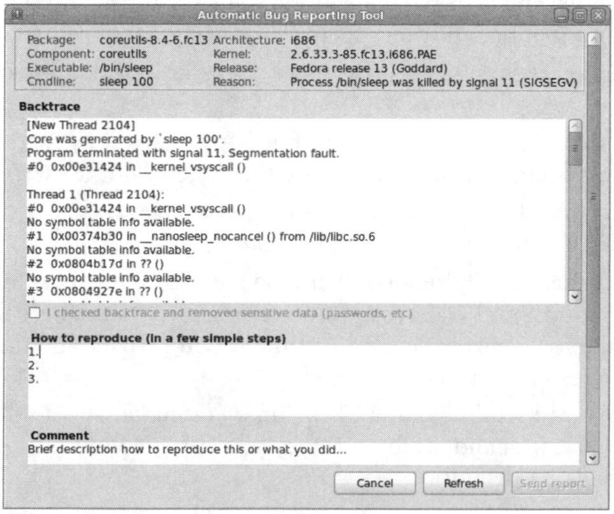

Figure 10-34 ABRT Logger report result

Source: Course Technology/Cengage Learning

Chapter Summary

- Use the Windows 7 Task Manager to maintain your computer system and monitor the processes that are running. If Task Manager indicates a problem, you can correct it so that other tasks can use necessary resources. In Fedora 13, you use the ps and kill commands to manage tasks.

- Monitoring system performance can help you run processes more efficiently and quickly, and can help determine if you need more memory or a faster processor for tasks that are not working properly.

- To check the reliability of your system, you can use the Reliability Monitor in Windows 7 and the Automatic Bug Reporting Tool in Fedora 13.

Key Terms

baseline   The level of performance that you can expect during typical usage and workloads.

bottleneck   A performance problem that occurs when multiple processes are competing for resources and all of them converge on the same resource at once.

free command   A command used to display the amount of free and used memory in Fedora 13.

kill command   A command used to stop or abort a process in a program or operating system.

memory leak   Unnecessary memory consumption caused by a computer program or process that is not properly releasing memory. Leaks can diminish the performance of a computer.

PID   A number used by Fedora 13 to uniquely identify a process.

/proc file system   A command-line reporting and control information system in Fedora 13 that directly interfaces with the kernel and is stored in memory. It is used for such system-related tasks as performance, memory information, and viewing and modifying run-time parameters.

ps command   A command used in Fedora 13 to provide a "snapshot" of the processes that are running.

pseudo-file system   A system that acts like a file system but is specially constructed to interface with specific areas in a system; it is maintained by the system, not a user.

uptime command   A command that displays the amount or percentage of time a computer system or associated hardware is functioning and available for use.

vmstat command   A command that usually reports average values on process status, memory consumption, I/O operations, and CPU usage since the last reboot. You can also use the command to report usage for a current period of time if you provide the time interval in seconds and the number of iterations you need.

watch free command   A command used in Fedora 13 to run a command repeatedly. When you combine watch with another command, such as free, you can view output on the Terminal screen every two seconds by default.

Review Questions

1. Use Windows 7 Task Manager to _____. (Choose all that apply.)

   a. install Windows 7 applications

   b. provide information about programs running on your computer

   c. display common performance measurements for processes running on your computer

   d. provide information about processes running on your computer

2. The Run As feature in Windows 7 is similar to the _____ command in Fedora 13.

   a. run

   b. go

   c. su

   d. runs

3. You can use the Run As feature in Windows 7 to _____. (Choose all that apply.)

   a. access system tools that require administrative privileges for execution

   b. run an administrative tool to determine what caused a problem

   c. run all applications in Windows 7

   d. resolve problems

4. Use the Processes tab in Task Manager to view _____. (Choose all that apply.)

   a. the names of processes running on the computer

   b. the processor

   c. the memory usage

   d. conflicts that are occurring

5. In Fedora 13, you use the _____ command to list the running processes.

   a. view

   b. kill

   c. ps

   d. top

6. In Fedora 13, you use the _____ command to stop processes.

   a. ps

   b. kill

   c. top

   d. stop

10

7. In Windows 7, disk usage statistics help _____.
   a. determine which applications can't run on your system
   b. determine whether upgrades are necessary
   c. balance uploading to your virtual machine
   d. balance the workload of your virtual machine

8. You can use the /proc file system in Fedora 13 to _____. (Choose all that apply.)
   a. view and modify run-time parameters
   b. view performance and memory information
   c. view hardware information
   d. view statistical information

9. In Fedora 13, the top command _____. (Choose all that apply.)
   a. monitors system statistics and displays them in real time
   b. constantly updates console-based output for the most CPU-intensive processes that are running
   c. is used to kill processes
   d. is used to monitor processes

10. In Fedora 13, the top command _____. (Choose all that apply.)
   a. uses a large amount of memory
   b. is mainly used for troubleshooting and tuning
   c. is very efficient for viewing processes
   d. should be kept running all the time

11. Frequent paging _____.
   a. is a normal occurrence
   b. indicates that you may have a memory shortage
   c. indicates that you have a lot of memory available
   d. does not drain performance

12. High CPU usage is _____. (Choose all that apply.)
   a. indicated by a value that is consistently greater than 85 percent
   b. an indication that the processor speed is inadequate
   c. an indication that your system needs more RAM
   d. indicated by a high rate of page file activity

13. A high rate of page file activity is _____.
   a. indicated by a value that is consistently greater than 85 percent
   b. an indication that the processor speed is inadequate
   c. an indication that your system needs more RAM
   d. indicated by high CPU usage

14. The GUI task management tool in Fedora 13 is _____.
   a. Task Management
   b. System Monitor
   c. GNOME System Tool
   d. KDE System Monitor

15. Which of the following displays CPU-related system information in System Monitor?
   a. System tab
   b. Resources tab
   c. Processes tab
   d. Both the System and Resources tabs
   e. Both the System and Processes tabs

16. If you want to report a bug when using the Automatic Bug Reporting Tool, which of the following should you use?
   a. Bugzilla
   b. Logger
   c. Either Bugzilla or Logger
   d. None of the above

17. By default, the Windows 7 Performance Monitor displays the _____.
   a. % Disk Time
   b. % Processor Time
   c. Disk Reads/Sec
   d. Disk Writes/Sec

18. The Windows 7 Reliability Monitor tracks _____. (Choose all that apply.)
   a. hardware problems
   b. software problems
   c. changes to the computer
   d. user errors

10

19. Events monitored in the Windows 7 Reliability Monitor include _____. (Choose all that apply.)

    a. Windows updates

    b. software installations and uninstalls

    c. application hangs and crashes

    d. disk and memory failures

20. Reporting of events in the Windows 7 Reliability Monitor is delayed _____ hours.

    a. 8

    b. 24

    c. 48

    d. 168

Case Projects

CASE PROJECTS

Case 10-1: Observing Performance with Task Manager

You are interning for a local firm and respond to a user's complaint about the performance of her Windows 7 computer, which she says seems "sluggish." Which features will you use in Task Manager to research her problem? Explain each of your choices in detail.

Case 10-2: Investigating a Performance Problem in Fedora 13

You are working for a company that provides financial services to clients. An employee tells you that his Fedora 13 computer is running slowly. Explain how you would investigate this performance problem.

Case 10-3: Investigating System Reliability

You are interning for a local firm and respond to a user's complaint about the stability of his Windows 7 computer. How will you use the Reliability Monitor to research the problem? Explain each of your choices in detail.

chapter 11

Networking

After reading this chapter and completing the exercises, you will be able to:

- Explain networking terminology
- View TCP/IP settings
- Access network resources
- View folder and file sharing permissions

Simply stated, a network **is a series of computer devices or nodes interconnected by** communication paths. Networks can range in size from a pair of PCs in your den to thousands of computers linked throughout a multinational corporation.

Because entire books are dedicated to networking topics, this chapter is intended only to provide a quick overview.

Networking Terminology

This section presents basic terminology used to explain networking.

Client/Server Networks

The **client/server** model has become a central idea of networking. The term describes the relationship between two computers in which a desktop computer (the client) makes a service request of another computer (the server), which fulfills the request.

In Figure 11-1, the client is a desktop computer that accesses or uses network resources. A switch provides connectivity for the two computers. A server provides network resources such as files to other computers and their users. In addition, the client can send a request to print to the server's attached printer.

Peer-to-Peer Networks

You also may be familiar with **peer-to-peer networks,** which employ desktop computers that are equally capable of being both clients and servers. An example is a small office/home office (SOHO) network, which serves the needs of small office environments and the self-employed. A typical SOHO network is shown in Figure 11-2; at the top is a DSL/cable modem, which connects to the Internet. The router secures the local network and provides connectivity for the three computers.

Fedora 13 provides peer-to-peer networking with **Samba,** which is based on the common client/server protocol of **Server Message Block (SMB).** The name *Samba* was created by

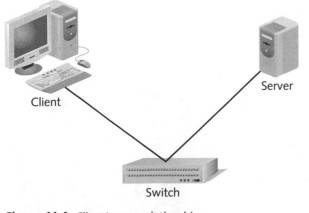

Figure 11-1 Client/server relationship

Source: Course Technology/Cengage Learning

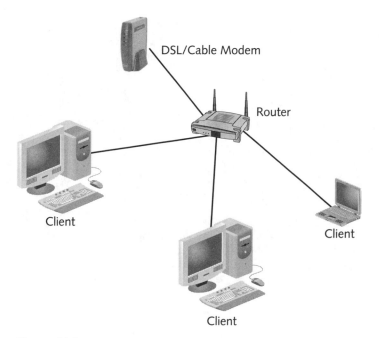

Figure 11-2 Peer-to-peer network

Source: Course Technology/Cengage Learning

adding two *A*s to SMB. Samba is functionally identical to the protocols provided by Windows 7, which allows Windows 7 and Fedora 13 to share files. In Activity 11-4, you will connect to a share on the Windows 7 host computer from the Fedora 13 virtual machine.

LANs (Local Area Networks)

LANs are networks that are usually confined to a geographic area, such as a single building or a college campus. As shown in Figure 11-3, LANs can be small, linking as few as two or three computers, but often they link hundreds of computers used by many people. The development of standard networking protocols and media has resulted in worldwide proliferation of LANs throughout business and educational organizations.

WANs (Wide Area Networks)

Figure 11-4 shows a system that combines multiple, geographically separate LANs to form a wide area network, or **WAN**. A WAN connects different LANs using services such as dedicated, leased data lines, satellite links, and data packet carrier services. Wide area networking can be as simple as a modem and remote access server for employees to dial into, or it can be as complex as hundreds of branch offices globally linked over data communication lines to send data over vast distances.

Internet

In Chapter 4, you first learned that the Internet is a system of linked networks that are worldwide in scope and facilitate data communication services that permit access to the World Wide Web and e-mail.

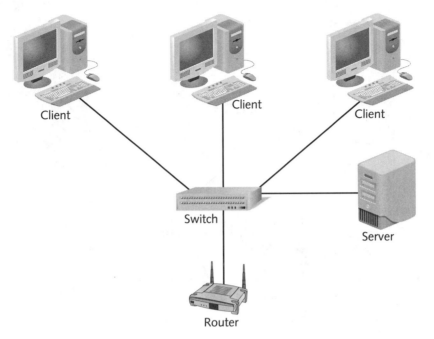

Figure 11-3 Local area network

Source: Course Technology/Cengage Learning

With the rapid rise in demand for connectivity, the Internet has become a communications highway for millions of users. Social media, which include Myspace, Facebook, Twitter, and LinkedIn, could not have become popular without the Internet.

Intranet

With the advancements made in browser-based software for the Internet, many private organizations are implementing intranets. An intranet is a private network that uses Internet-type applications, but is available only within a single organization. For large organizations, an intranet allows easy access to Web-based applications to provide corporate information for employees.

VPN

A **VPN (virtual private network)** uses a technique known as tunneling to transfer data securely on the Internet to a remote access server on your workplace network. Using a VPN helps you save money by using the public Internet to connect securely with your private network instead of requiring you to make long-distance dial-up calls. Data is routed over the Internet from your Internet service provider (ISP) to your organization.

Internet Protocol

The **Internet Protocol** (or IP) is the main networking protocol that allows for the communication of data across a network. Using this protocol, computers can deliver **packets**, or units of

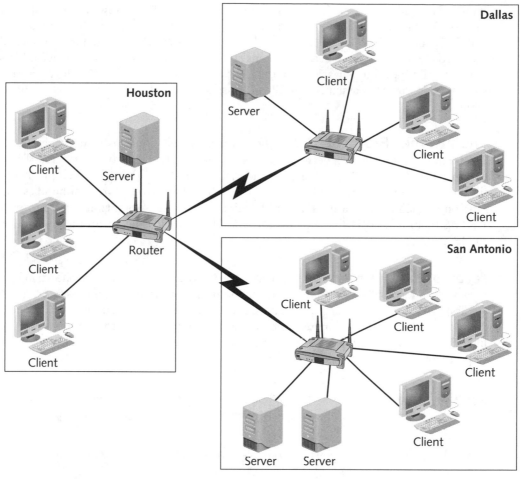

Figure 11-4 Wide area network

Source: Course Technology/Cengage Learning

data, to other computers and devices based on their unique IP addresses. This protocol is the standard used by home and business computers and all networking software, and is the foundation of the Internet Protocol Suite.

Protocols

A protocol is a set of rules that enables two computers to talk to each other. It is a computing standard that defines the syntax and regulations of a connection across a network: how to detect the other computer, how to send a message to it, how to format that message, and so on.

Internet Protocol Addresses The Internet Protocol uses unique addresses, simply called **IP addresses**, to identify two computers or devices in a network. There are two standards of IP addresses. The most common is IPv4 (IP Address Version 4), which consists of 32 bits divided into four octets. Each octet is represented by a value between 0 and 255, and each value is separated by a period—192.168.0.10, for example. A newer standard, IPv6, has also emerged; it consists of 128 bits, resulting in longer addresses and more possibilities for variation. In this text, you use IP Version 4 addresses. Every networked computer is assigned an IP address, although servers can provide IP addresses dynamically.

The Internet Protocol Suite The Internet Protocol Suite is a set of protocols used in combination for different networking tasks. The Internet Protocol and the Transmission Control Protocol (TCP) are the two underlying standards that all other protocols use, so the suite is commonly referred to as TCP/IP. While the Internet Protocol handles each transmission of each packet of data, the TCP is like an overseer, organizing data into packets and sending them to the IP. On the flip side, the TCP rebuilds files from the individual packets the IP sent.

Layers of the Internet Protocol Suite The Internet Protocol Suite, as shown in Figure 11-5, is divided into four "layers" of communication from bottom to top: the Network (or Network Access) layer, the Internet layer, the Transport layer, and the Application layer. Very simply, the Network layer links the computers, the Internet layer allows the IP to transfer packets across the link, the Transport layer uses the TCP to organize the packets, and the Application layer consists of protocols for specific types of transfer.

Application Layer Protocols While the Internet Protocol itself is the foundation for network communication, many other popular protocols exist in the topmost Application layer:

- HTTP (Hypertext Transfer Protocol), which allows Web users to request Web sites from remote servers
- FTP (File Transfer Protocol), which allows for the rapid transfer of files across the Web
- POP3 (Post Office Protocol 3), for sending and receiving e-mail
- SMTP (Simple Mail Transfer Protocol), for sending and receiving e-mail

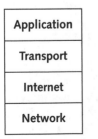

Figure 11-5 Internet Protocol Suite

Source: Course Technology/Cengage Learning

Viewing TCP/IP Settings

To assist in troubleshooting TCP/IP-related problems, you need to know how to view TCP/IP settings. In this text, you will view IP Version 4 addresses. To communicate effectively on a routed network, such as a WAN, computers require four TCP/IP settings:

1. The IP address is a numerical label assigned to devices participating in a computer network that uses the Internet Protocol for communication between its nodes.

2. The subnetwork, or subnet, is a logically visible, distinctly addressed part of a single IP network. Subnetting is the division of a network into groups of computers that have a common, designated IP address routing prefix. The bits for the network are indicated by the subnet mask.

3. The gateway IP address is a node (a router) on a TCP/IP network that serves as an access point to another network.

4. The final item is the DNS IP address of the server that provides domain name resolution. Most importantly, this server translates domain names that are meaningful to people into numerical (binary) identifiers associated with networking equipment for the purpose of locating and addressing these devices worldwide. For example, *www.google.com* translates to 74.125.227.51.

The **Dynamic Host Configuration Protocol (DHCP)** is a computer networking protocol used by hosts (DHCP clients) to retrieve IP address assignments and other configuration information. DHCP uses a client/server architecture. The client sends a broadcast request for configuration information; the DHCP server receives the request and responds with the needed information from its configuration database.

In the absence of DHCP, all hosts on a network must be manually configured with static IP addresses—a time-consuming and error-prone undertaking.

11

Viewing TCP/IP Settings in Windows 7

You can use Windows 7 GUI tools or execute commands from the command line to view TCP/IP settings in Windows 7.

Figure 11-6 shows the Network Connection Details window, which is a convenient way to view TCP/IP settings. By default, the Network icon is not on the Start menu. To add the Network icon, right-click Start, click Properties, click the Start Menu tab, and then click Customize. Scroll and check the Network check box, and then click OK twice.

To display the Network Connection Details window, click Start, right-click Network, click Properties, click the Local Area Connection link, and then click Details. A No value for the DHCP Enabled property indicates that an administrator assigned a static configuration. All four required entries are present: an IPv4 address of 192.168.0.10, an IPv4 subnet mask of 255.255.255.0, an IPv4 default gateway of 192.168.0.1, and an IPv4 DNS server of 192.168.0.1.

The IPCONFIG /ALL command provides similar information, as shown in Figure 11-7. To access this information, click Start, point to All Programs, click Accessories, click Command Prompt, type IPCONFIG /ALL, and then press Enter.

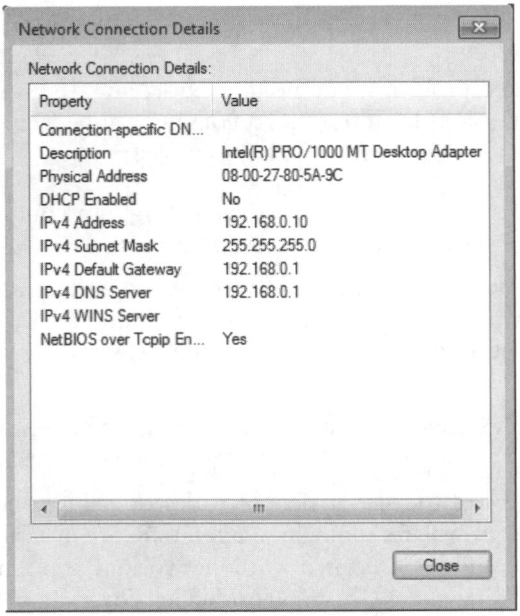

Figure 11-6 Network Connection Details window

Source: Course Technology/Cengage Learning

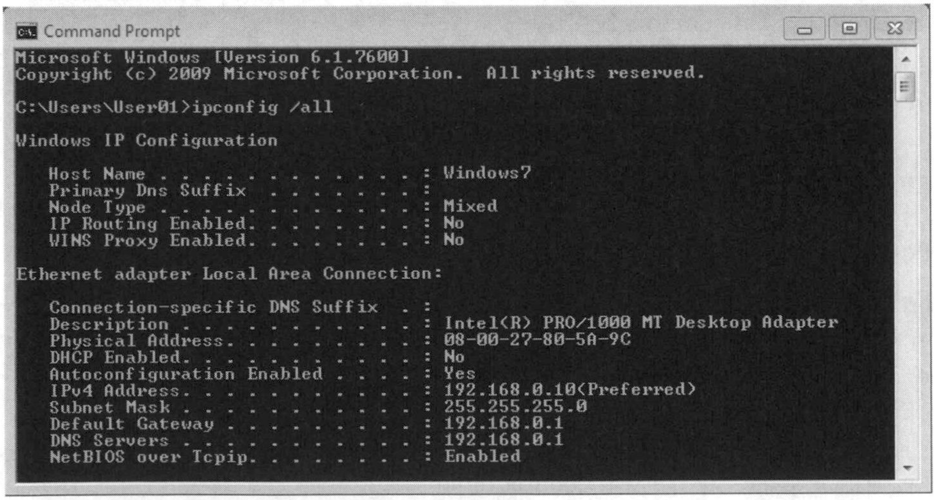

Figure 11-7 Network connection details

Source: Course Technology/Cengage Learning

Activity 11-1: Viewing TCP/IP Settings in Windows 7

Time Required: 10 minutes

Objective: View TCP/IP settings in Windows 7.

Description: In this activity, you will investigate alternative ways to view the TCP/IP settings. First, you will use the Network Connection Details window to view the settings. Later in the activity, you will execute the IPCONFIG /ALL command. This activity is useful if you want to view your TCP/IP settings.

1. Start your virtual machines using the appropriate instructions in Activity 1-1.

2. To add the Network icon, right-click **Start,** click **Properties,** click the **Start Menu** tab, and then click **Customize.** Scroll and check the **Network** check box, and then click **OK** twice.

3. To display the Network Connection Details window, click **Start,** right-click **Network,** click **Properties,** click the **Local Area Connection** link, and then click **Details.**

4. Record your TCP/IP settings.

5. Close the open windows.

6. To open a command prompt, click **Start,** point to **All Programs,** click **Accessories,** and then click **Command Prompt.**

7. To view the IP configuration, type **IPCONFIG /ALL** and then press **Enter.**

8. Compare your settings with the ones you recorded in Step 4.

9. Close the Command Prompt window.

10. Leave the virtual machine logged on for future activities.

Viewing TCP/IP Parameters in Fedora 13

As in Windows 7, you can use Fedora 13 GUI tools or execute commands from the Terminal window to view TCP/IP settings. The Ethernet Device settings, as shown in Figure 11-8, follow the same sequence as Windows 7.

To display the Ethernet Device settings, click System, point to Administration, click Network, type your password, and then click Edit.

Another way to view the IPv4 settings is to use the nm-tool command in a Terminal window. The results are shown in Figure 11-9.

Another alternative for displaying the IP configuration is the ifconfig -a command. However, the ifconfig command does not display the IP address for the DNS server.

11

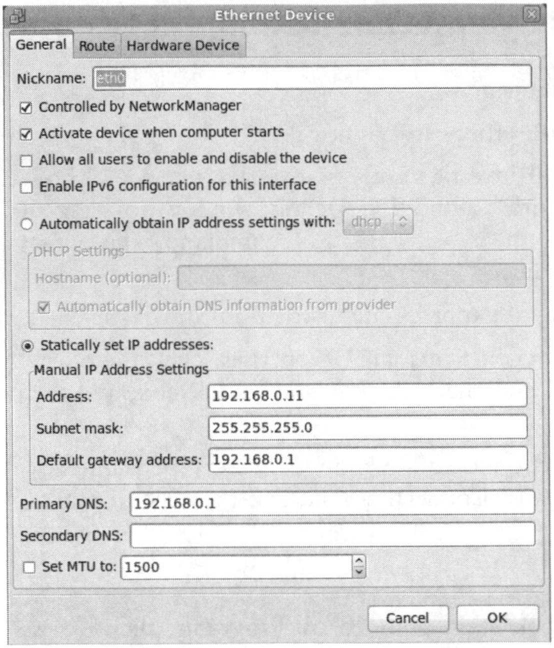

Figure 11-8 Ethernet Device settings

Source: Course Technology/Cengage Learning

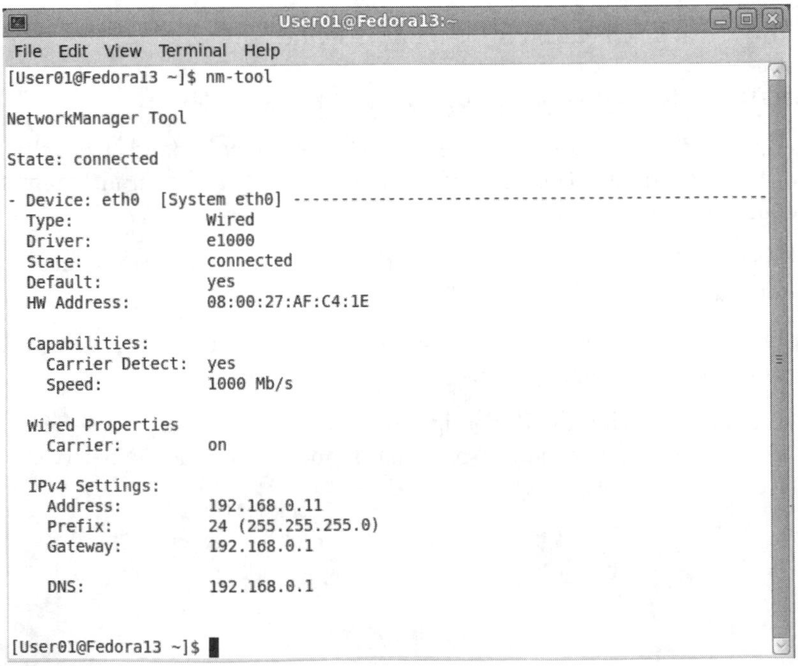

Figure 11-9 Network Manager tool

Source: Course Technology/Cengage Learning

Activity 11-2: Viewing TCP/IP Settings in Fedora 13

Time Required: 10 minutes

Objective: View TCP/IP settings using Fedora 13.

Description: In this activity, you will investigate alternative ways to view the TCP/IP settings in Fedora 13. First, you will use the Ethernet Device window to view the settings. Later in the activity, you will execute the `nm-tool` and `ifconfig` commands. This activity is useful if you want to view your TCP/IP settings.

1. If necessary, start your virtual machines using the appropriate instructions in Activity 1-1.

2. To display the Ethernet Device settings, click **System**, point to **Administration**, click **Network**, type **P@ssw0rd**, and then click **Edit**.

3. Compare your settings with the ones you recorded in Step 4 of Activity 11-1.

4. Close the open windows.

5. To use the Network Manager tool to view the TCP/IP settings, click **Applications**, point to **System Tools**, click **Terminal**, type **nm-tool**, and then press **Enter**.

6. Compare your settings with the ones you recorded in Step 4 of Activity 11-1.

7. To use the `ifconfig` command to view the TCP/IP settings, click **Applications**, point to **System Tools**, click **Terminal**, type **ifconfig -a**, and then press **Enter**.

8. Compare your settings with the ones you recorded in Step 4 of Activity 11-1.

9. Leave the virtual machine logged on for future activities.

Accessing Network Resources

When you speak of network resources, you are usually referring to shared folders and files on file servers, shared resources and files on other people's computers, and shared printers.

Accessing Network Resources in Windows 7

When you set up a peer-to-peer network, Windows automatically creates a workgroup and gives it a name. A **workgroup** provides a basis for file and printer sharing. You can join an existing network workgroup, by default called WORKGROUP, or you can create a new one.

Also, you can create or join a homegroup in Windows 7, which automatically turns on file and printer sharing on home networks. A **homegroup** makes it easy to share your libraries and printers on a home network. You can share pictures, music, videos, documents, and printers with other people in your homegroup. The homegroup is protected with a password, so you can always choose what you share with the group. If you have a home network, you should create or join an existing homegroup.

You should only use a homegroup when all of the computers in the peer-to-peer network are running Windows 7. For Windows operating systems prior to Windows 7, you should use a workgroup.

The Network option on the Start menu displays shortcuts to shared computers, printers, and other resources on the network. These shortcuts are created automatically in the Network area whenever you open a shared network resource, such as a printer or shared folder.

To open the Network window, click Start and then click Network. Windows Explorer shows the computers in the network that are participating in the shared network resources (see Figure 11-10).

To see the shares that another computer is offering, type *servername*\ in the Windows Search text box and then click the server name. In place of *servername* in the preceding command, you can use the name of the other computer. If your computer cannot resolve the server name (which may occur on a home network), use the IP address, as shown at the top of Figure 11-11.

Also, you can type NET VIEW *servername* at a command prompt to see the shares that another computer is offering. Again, for *servername* you can use the name of the other computer. If your computer cannot resolve the server name, use the IP address (see Figure 11-12).

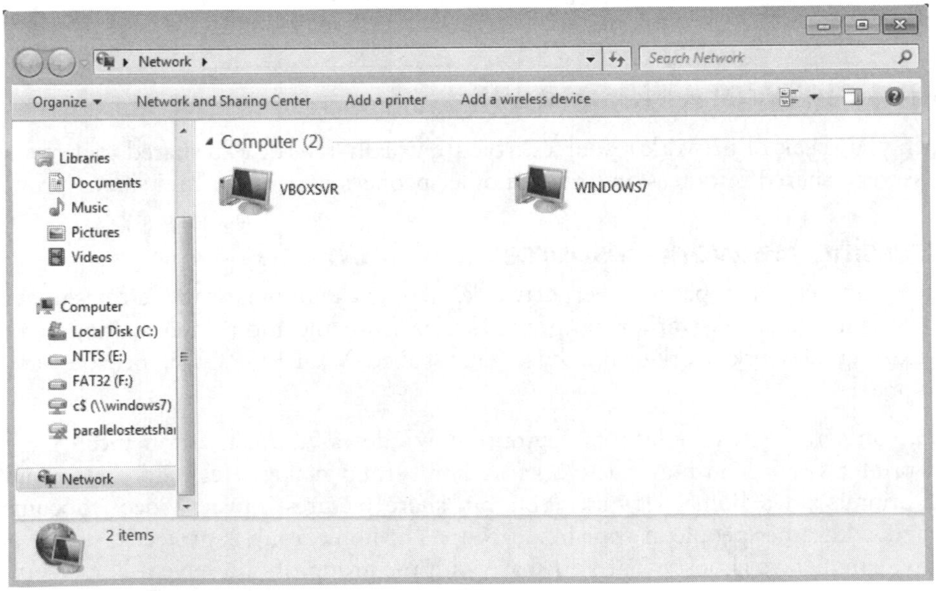

Figure 11-10 Network resources shown in workgroup

Source: Course Technology/Cengage Learning

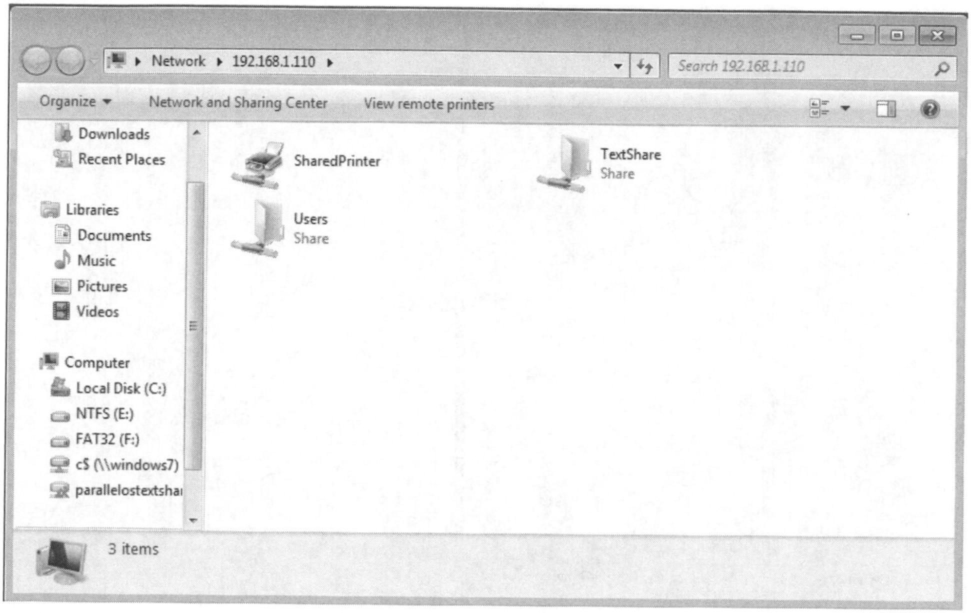

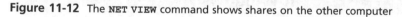

Figure 11-11 Shares on the Host01 computer

Source: Course Technology/Cengage Learning

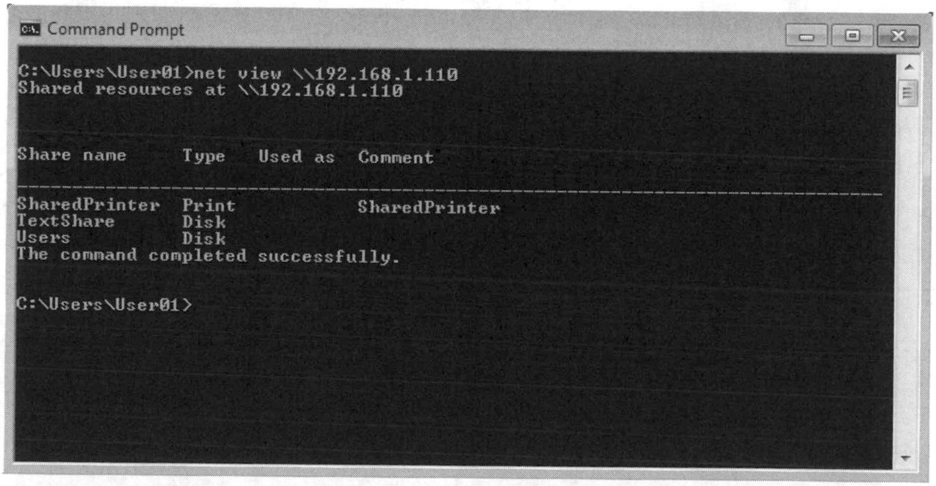

Figure 11-12 The **NET VIEW** command shows shares on the other computer

Source: Course Technology/Cengage Learning

Windows 7 allows you to refer to network shares through the use of syntax known as **UNC (Universal Naming Convention)** notation. Using UNC notation requires that you know the name or IP address of the server and share. You can then open a folder to a network location by typing the UNC in the search text box, as shown in Figure 11-13. To access the files, click the UNC displayed in the search results text box.

No items match your search.

⌕ See more results

| \\192.168.1.110\ | ✕ | Shut down ▸ |

Figure 11-13 Accessing a network share from the Search window

Source: Course Technology/Cengage Learning

Also, you can access a network share from the command prompt by double-clicking the Command Prompt icon on the desktop and using the following syntax for the NET USE command:

NET USE [*drive letter* | *] *computer name**share name*

You may specify a drive letter or permit Windows 7 to provide one. If you do not provide a drive letter, Windows 7 will assign drive letters in reverse order starting with Z:. For example, to connect the N: drive to the Windows 7 virtual machine and the History share, type:

NET USE N: \\Windows7\History

The N: drive is available in Windows Explorer. Of course, you can use the DIR directory command to view the files.

Activity 11-3: Connecting to a Network Share in Windows 7

Time Required: 10 minutes

Objective: Connect to a network share using Windows 7.

Description: In this activity, you will investigate alternative ways to connect to a shared folder. First, you will need to determine the IP address for your host computer. Next, you will use the search text box to locate and connect to the TextShare folder on your host computer. The TextShare folder was installed on the host computer when you followed the instructions in Appendix B, C, or D for your virtualization software. Later in the activity, you will connect to the share using a UNC. This activity is useful if you want to access network data.

1. If necessary, start your virtual machines using the appropriate instructions in Activity 1-1. You will need to perform Steps 2 through 5 on your host computer to determine the IP address for accessing that computer.

2. Minimize your virtual machines.

3. To display the Network Connection Details window, click **Start** on your host computer, right-click **Network**, click **Properties**, click the **Local Area Connection** link, and then click **Details**.

4. Record the IPv4 address for your host computer.

5. Close the open windows.

6. To display the shared files for the TextShare folder on your host computer, click **Start**, type **\\IPv4 Address** in the search text box, and then click the **TextShare** folder on your host computer.

 If you are unable to connect to the TextShare folder, contact your instructor.

7. Close the Windows Explorer window.

8. To open a command prompt, click the **Command Prompt** icon on the desktop.

9. To use the UNC to locate the shared files, type the following and press **Enter**:

   `NET USE * \\IPv4 Address\TextShare`

10. Verify that Windows 7 assigned the Z: drive for the shared folder.

11. To change to the Z: drive, type **Z:** and then press **Enter**.

12. To view the filenames, type **DIR** and press **Enter**.

13. Close the Command Prompt window.

14. To view the contents of the Z: drive in Windows Explorer, click **Start**, click **Computer**, and then double-click **TextShare (\\IPv4 Address) (Z:)**.

15. To view the contents of the Article12.txt file in Notepad, double-click **Article12.txt**.

16. Close the open windows.

17. Leave the virtual machine logged on for future activities.

Accessing Network Resources in Fedora 13

Fedora 13's methods for accessing shared files are similar to the methods used in Windows 7. To access a share, you must mount the share. After you create a directory for the mount destination, you can type the `mount` command and specify the UNC for the share, the logon credentials, and the destination directory. Once the share completes, you change the directory to the mount destination and issue an `ls` command to view the files (see Figure 11-14).

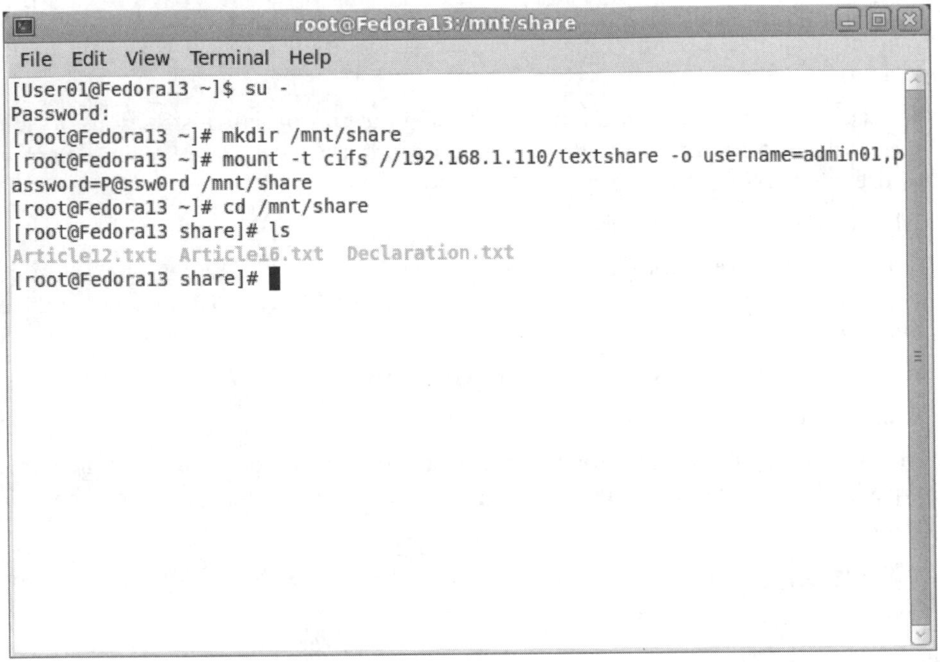

```
root@Fedora13:/mnt/share
File  Edit  View  Terminal  Help
[User01@Fedora13 ~]$ su -
Password:
[root@Fedora13 ~]# mkdir /mnt/share
[root@Fedora13 ~]# mount -t cifs //192.168.1.110/textshare -o username=admin01,p
assword=P@ssw0rd /mnt/share
[root@Fedora13 ~]# cd /mnt/share
[root@Fedora13 share]# ls
Article12.txt  Article16.txt  Declaration.txt
[root@Fedora13 share]# █
```

Figure 11-14 Mounting a Windows share in Linux

Source: Course Technology/Cengage Learning

Once the mount is completed, you can use File Browser to see the file entries. You will access these files in Activity 11-4.

Activity 11-4: Connecting to a Network Share in Fedora 13

Time Required: 10 minutes

Objective: Connect to a network share using the mount command.

Description: In this activity, you will open a Terminal session, change to the superuser, mount the Windows share on your Host01 computer, list the files with the ls command, and view the file browser. The TextShare folder was installed on the host computer when you followed the instructions in Appendix B, C, or D for your virtualization software. This activity is useful if you want to access network data.

1. If necessary, start your virtual machines using the appropriate instructions in Activity 1-1.

2. To open a Terminal session, click **Applications**, point to **System Tools**, and then click **Terminal**.

3. To switch to the superuser, type **su –** and press **Enter**, then type **P@ssw0rd** and press **Enter**.

4. To create a destination directory, type **mkdir /mnt/share** and then press **Enter**.

5. To mount the share on the Host01 computer, type the following command and then press **Enter**:

```
mount -t cifs //IPv4 Address/textshare -o username=admin01,
password=P@ssw0rd /mnt/share
```

If you are unable to connect to the TextShare folder, contact your instructor.

6. To change to the destination directory, type **cd /mnt/share** and then press **Enter**.

7. To view the files, type **ls** and then press **Enter**.

8. To view the files in File Browser, click **Places**, click **Computer**, double-click **File System**, double-click **mnt**, and then double-click **share**.

9. Close the open windows.

10. To open the gedit text editor, click **Applications**, point to **Accessories**, and then click **gedit Text Editor**.

11. To view the contents of the Article12.txt file, click **File**, click **Open**, click **File System**, double-click **mnt**, double-click **share**, and then double-click **Article12.txt**.

12. Close the open windows.

13. Leave the virtual machine logged on for future activities.

Accessing Network Printers

It makes good economic sense to share a printer and make it available to several users on a network. Network administrators are responsible for setting up shared printers on the network. The following activities explain how to connect and access a network printer in Windows 7 and Fedora 13, respectively.

Activity 11-5: Connecting a Network Printer in Windows 7 Using the Add Printer Wizard

Time Required: 10 minutes

Objective: Connect to a network printer using the Add Printer Wizard.

Description: In this activity, you use the Add Printer Wizard to connect to a network printer. This activity is useful if your network has a shared printer.

1. If necessary, start your virtual machines using the appropriate instructions in Activity 1-1.

2. Click **Start** and then click **Control Panel**. If necessary, click the **View By** chevron and then click **Small icons**. Click **Devices and Printers**, and then click the **Add a printer** link.

3. Click the **Add a network, wireless or Bluetooth printer** link.

4. Click **The printer that I want is not listed**.

5. Click the **Select a shared printer by name** option button.

6. In the Name text box, type ***IPv4 Address**SharedPrinter***, substituting your IP address for *IPv4 Address*. When you finish, click **Next**.

7. Wait for the printer to be detected and then click **Next** twice.

8. Review the summary information and then click **Finish**.

9. Close any open windows.

10. Leave the virtual machine logged on for future activities.

Activity 11-6: Accessing Network Printers in Fedora 13

Time Required: 10 minutes

Objective: Connect to a Windows shared printer in Fedora 13.

Description: In this activity, you will open a Terminal session, change to the superuser, and connect to the Windows shared printer on your Host01 computer. This activity is useful if you want to connect to a Windows network printer.

1. If necessary, start your virtual machines using the appropriate instructions in Activity 1-1.

2. To open a Terminal session, click **Applications**, point to **System Tools**, and then click **Terminal**.

3. To switch to the superuser, type **su –** and press **Enter**, then type **P@ssw0rd** and press **Enter**.

4. To open the printer dialog box, type **system-config-printer** and then press **Enter**.

5. To select the new printer, click **Add**, click **Yes**, click **Network Printer**, scroll through the list, and then click **Windows Printer via SAMBA**.

6. Type **IP *address*/SharedPrinter** in the smb:// text box, substituting your IP address for *IP address*. When you finish, click **Forward**.

7. Wait for the driver search to complete.

8. To specify the driver, click **Generic**, click **Forward**, click **Generic Text-only printer**, click **Forward**, and then click **Apply**.

9. When asked if you want to print a test page, click **No**.

10. Close the open windows.

11. Leave the virtual machine logged on for future activities.

Folder and File Sharing Permissions

When administrators share files and folders with you and other computer users on the network, you can open and view those files and folders just as if they were stored on your own computers. Any changes that administrators allow users to make to a shared file or folder will change the file or folder on your computer. However, administrators can restrict people to just viewing your shared files without having the ability to change them.

This section explains how to view file permissions in Windows 7 and Fedora 13. To troubleshoot problems related to file sharing, you need to know how to view these settings.

Managing Windows NT File System Permissions

Because system access and security are so crucial, you must be able to view folder and file permissions and make sure that only authorized users can access local and network folders and files.

NT File System Required The NTFS is required to share folders and files with other network users. Although the FAT and FAT32 file systems permit folders to be shared, they do not provide the required permissions to properly secure the files. Only NTFS permits user accounts and user groups to be linked to folder and file permissions, which are required to implement the needed security.

Using Local User Groups Administrators use local user groups to simplify the management and authorization of network resources. Groups are created to define sets of user accounts that require access to the same resources. For example, users who conduct sales activities can be placed in the Sales group, and newly hired salespeople can be added to the group as new user accounts, so that all salespeople have access to the same network resources. Likewise, if a person switched jobs from sales to advertising, her user account in the Sales group would need to be closed and then added to the Advertising group.

Activity 11-7: Viewing Local User Groups in Windows 7

11

Time Required: 15 minutes

Objective: View local user groups.

Description: In this activity, you view a local user group that consists of the local user accounts. This activity is useful because it will help you answer questions about using local user groups.

1. If necessary, start your virtual machines using the appropriate instructions in Activity 1-1.

2. Click **Start**, click **Control Panel**, click **Administrative Tools**, and then double-click **Computer Management**.

3. Expand **Local Users and Groups** in the left pane and then click **Groups**, which displays the window shown in Figure 11-15.

User accounts have single-headed icons and user groups have two-headed icons.

4. Close any open windows.

5. Leave the virtual machine logged on for future activities.

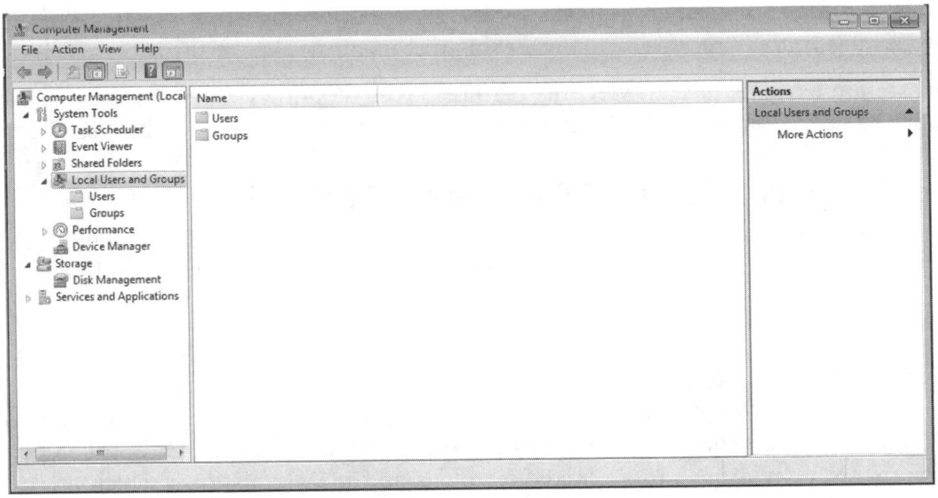

Figure 11-15 Local Users and Groups window

Source: Course Technology/Cengage Learning

Shared folder permission	Definition
Read	Displays folders and files within a shared folder and executes programs contained in the folder
Change	Has all of the permissions associated with the Read permission; also allows you to add folders and files to the shared folder, and to append to or delete existing files
Full Control	Has all of the permissions associated with the Change permission; also allows you to change file permissions and take ownership of the file resources (if you have the proper NTFS permissions)

Table 11-1 Windows 7 shared folder permissions

Viewing Shared Folder Permissions When sharing a folder with users on a network, administrators must specify the level of access that they are willing to assign to specific users. They must also balance security with functionality by allowing access to appropriate resources and prohibiting unauthorized access. To support shared access, Windows 7 provides the shared folder permissions listed in Table 11-1.

Activity 11-8: Viewing Share Permissions in Windows 7

Time Required: 15 minutes

Objective: View share permissions on a folder.

Description: In this activity, you view the share permissions on an existing folder. This activity is useful because it will help you answer user questions about using share permissions.

1. If necessary, start your virtual machines using the appropriate instructions in Activity 1-1.

2. To view shared resources, click **Start**, click **Control Panel**, click **Administrative Tools**, and then double-click **Computer Management**.

3. Double-click **Shared Folders** and then double-click **Shares**.

4. Right-click **Shared Folder**, click **Properties**, and then click the **Shared Permissions** tab.

5. Close any open windows.

6. Leave the virtual machine logged on for future activities.

Assigning NTFS Permissions Administrators secure the folders and files on an NTFS volume. It is worth repeating that the NT file system is required to use NTFS permissions. Unless you are a member of a group with assigned permissions, you cannot access the files for that account or group.

You can view folder permissions that control access to folders and the files in them. Table 11-2 lists the NTFS permissions that can be assigned to a folder.

You assign file permissions to control access to files. Table 11-3 lists the NTFS permissions that can be assigned to a file.

Permission	Description
List Folder Contents	Allows you to view the names of subfolders and files
Read	Allows you to view files and subfolder names and to view folder attributes, ownership, and permissions
Read & Execute	Has all of the permissions associated with the List Folder Contents and Read permissions; also allows you to traverse folders
Write	Allows you to create files and subfolders within the folder, change folder attributes, and view ownership and permissions
Modify	Has all of the permissions associated with the Read & Execute and Write permissions; also allows you to delete folders
Full Control	Allows you to change permissions, take ownership of folders, delete subfolders and files, and perform the actions granted by the other permissions

Table 11-2 NTFS folder permissions

Permission	Description
Read	Allows you to read files and view file attributes, ownership, and permissions
Read & Execute	Allows you to run applications and perform the actions permitted by the Read permission
Write	Allows you to overwrite existing files, change file attributes, and view ownership and permissions
Modify	Has all of the permissions associated with the Read & Execute and Write permissions; also allows you to modify and delete files
Full Control	Allows you to change permissions, take ownership of folders, delete files, and perform the actions granted by the other permissions

Table 11-3 NTFS file permissions

Multiple NTFS Permissions Although permissions can be assigned to individual user accounts, it is more effective to assign them to user groups. Being a member of a local user group entitles a user to the same permissions as the other group members. If you have memberships in multiple groups, the permissions associated with each group are combined. The exception to this rule is Deny. When Deny appears as the Read permission, for example, it overrides any other Read permission.

NTFS permissions are assigned to all of the files on the NTFS volume. When determining a user's effective permissions, you must examine the permissions assigned to particular resources. Remember that permissions assigned at the file level override those assigned at the folder level.

Permission Inheritance When you create or copy a subfolder or a file, it inherits the permissions of the parent folder by default. This concept, known as permission inheritance, is illustrated in Figure 11-16. After the Accounting folder was created, the indicated permissions were assigned. When the General Ledger folder was created as a subfolder in the Accounting folder, its permissions were inherited from the Accounting folder. Likewise, Accounts Receivable inherited the permissions of the General Ledger folder.

Administrators can prevent subfolders and files from inheriting the parent's permissions if they do not want changes to the parent folder to affect its subfolders and files. When administrators elect to prevent inheritance, they must choose one of the following options:

- Copy the inherited permissions from the parent folder.
- Remove the inherited permissions and retain only the assigned permissions.

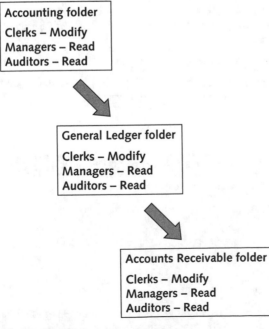

Figure 11-16 Permission inheritance

Source: Course Technology/Cengage Learning

Combining Shared Folder and NTFS Permissions Administrators use share permissions to grant access to resources over a network. In a previous section, you encountered shared folder permissions, which provide limited security. Shared folder permissions provide access to an entire directory structure, from the shared folder down to the subfolders, so administrators seldom use these permissions without also using NTFS permissions.

By combining shared folder permissions and NTFS permissions, administrators gain the highest level of security and control. To effectively use these permissions together, administrators must combine them to control access to network resources. Administrators can use shared folder permissions to grant access to folders over the network and then use NTFS permissions to secure the resources in your file system. NTFS offers the most flexible level of control and can be assigned to resources on an individual basis.

To determine your effective permissions for a given network resource, you need to complete the following three steps:

1. Combine the shared folder permissions (recall that Deny prevents access and overrides other permissions).
2. Combine the NTFS folder permissions (again, Deny overrides other permissions).
3. Determine which permission is the most restrictive—this is the effective permission.

Figure 11-17 illustrates these three steps. The shared folder permissions have a combined permission of Full Control. The NTFS permissions—Read, Write, and Modify—combine as Modify. Between Full Control and Modify, the more restrictive permission is Modify.

 To demonstrate these three steps, you can write the shared folder permissions on the left side of a marker board and the NTFS permissions on the right. To indicate how shared folder permissions are combined, make a trickling motion. Repeat this motion for the NTFS permissions. To indicate the most restrictive permission, join your hands together.

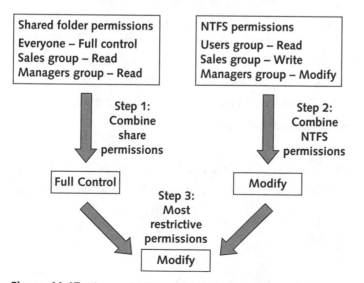

Figure 11-17 The result of combining shared folder and NTFS permissions

Action/target	Same volume	Different volume
Move	Retain	Inherit
Copy	Inherit	Inherit

Table 11-4   Effects of move and copy actions on permissions

Moving and Copying Files in NTFS Volumes   When you copy or move files and folders within or between NTFS volumes in Windows 7, remember that the files or folders will inherit permissions from the destination folder. When files or folders are moved within an NTFS partition, they don't need to be re-created, meaning that they retain their original permissions after the move.

When you move a file or folder between NTFS volumes, it must be created on the destination volume, meaning that the moved file or folder will inherit the destination folder's permissions.

Be aware that neither the FAT16 nor the FAT32 file system supports NTFS permissions—only NTFS does. Likewise, NTFS permissions are removed when a file or folder is moved or copied to a FAT16 or FAT32 formatted partition.

Table 11-4 summarizes the permission inheritance for move and copy actions on the same volume or different volumes. Note that a move on the same volume is the only option that retains permissions.

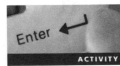

Activity 11-9: Viewing NTFS Permissions in Windows 7

Time Required: 15 minutes

Objective: View the NTFS permissions for a folder.

Description: In this activity, you view the NTFS permissions assigned to a folder. This activity is useful because it will help you answer user questions about using NTFS permissions.

1. If necessary, start your virtual machines using the appropriate instructions in Activity 1-1.

2. Click **Start**, click **Computer**, and then double-click **NTFS (E:)**.

3. Right-click the **Shared Folder** folder and then click the **Security** tab.

4. Review the NTFS permissions and then click **OK**.

5. Close any open windows.

6. To shut down the virtual machine, click **Start**, and then click the **Shut Down** button.

7. Wait a moment for the Windows 7 virtual machine to shut down completely.

Activity 11-10: Analyzing Share and NTFS Permissions

Time Required: 10 minutes

Objective: Analyze share and NTFS permissions to determine the effective permissions.

Description: In this activity, you combine share permissions, combine NTFS permissions, and determine the effective permission for a given scenario. This activity is useful because it will help you answer user questions regarding security.

1. Using Figure 11-18 and Table 11-5 as guides, specify the combined permissions and the effective permission for a scenario in which Sally is a member of the Everyone, Executive, and Finance groups.

Shared folder permissions	NTFS folder permissions
Everyone – Read	Everyone – Read
Accounting – Deny all access	Accounting – Modify
Executive – Read	Executive – Read
Finance – Change	Finance – Modify
Marketing – Read	Marketing – Write

Figure 11-18 Combining share and NTFS permissions

Source: Course Technology/Cengage Learning

Combined share permissions	Combined NTFS permissions	Most restrictive permission

Table 11-5 Combined permissions and effective permission

2. Using Figure 11-18 and Table 11-6 as guides, use your project log to specify the combined permissions and the effective permission for a scenario in which Bob is a member of the Everyone, Executive, and Accounting groups.

Combined share permissions	Combined NTFS permissions	Most restrictive permission

Table 11-6 Combined permissions and effective permission

3. Using Figure 11-18 and Table 11-7 as guides, use your project log to specify the combined permissions and the effective permission for a scenario in which Roger is a member of the Everyone, Executive, and Marketing groups.

Combined share permissions	Combined NTFS permissions	Most restrictive permission

Table 11-7 Combined permissions and effective permission

4. Using Figure 11-18 and Table 11-8 as guides, use your project log to specify the combined permissions and the effective permission for a scenario in which Susan is a member of the Everyone, Accounting, Executive, and Finance groups.

Combined share permissions	Combined NTFS permissions	Most restrictive permission

Table 11-8 Combined permissions and effective permission

5. Using Figure 11-18 and Table 11-9 as guides, use your project log to specify the combined permissions and the effective permission for a scenario in which George is a member of the Everyone, Finance, and Marketing groups.

Combined share permissions	Combined NTFS permissions	Most restrictive permission

Table 11-9 Combined permissions and effective permission

Viewing Fedora 13 File Permissions

When specifying Fedora 13 permissions, you basically define them by files and directories. Throughout this book, you have used the ls command with the –l option to see detailed lists of directories and files in a file system.

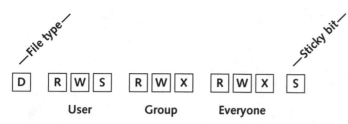

Figure 11-19 File permissions in Fedora 13

Source: Course Technology/Cengage Learning

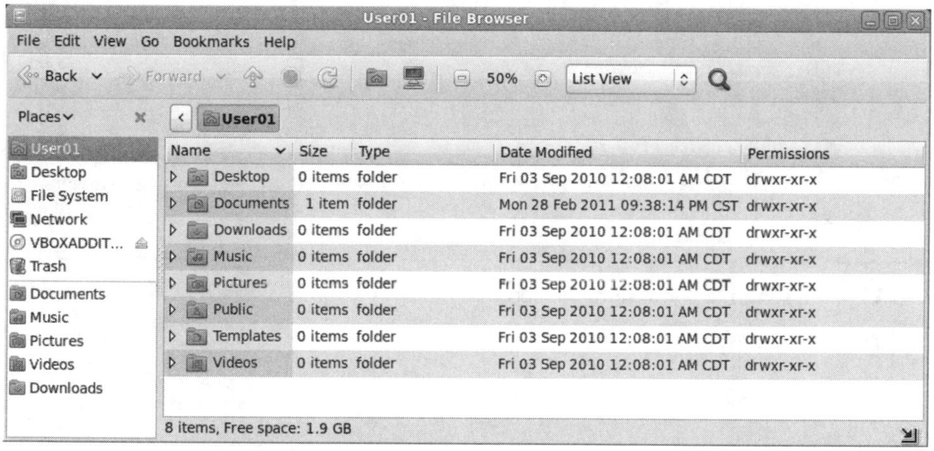

Figure 11-20 Viewing file permissions in Fedora 13

Source: Course Technology/Cengage Learning

Each file and directory has permissions for the owner, group, and everyone else, as shown in Figure 11-19. The permissions for each group consist of three (binary) bits. The 10th bit is the sticky bit, as you will learn later. The bits are assigned as RWX.

You can view these file permissions from the Properties dialog box in File Browser (see Figure 11-20).

Use the `ls` command with the `-l` option to show the file permissions. When you type the following command, you see the output shown in Figure 11-21.

`ls -l`

Figure 11-22 shows how these file permissions are displayed.

The first character in the permissions column is the file type. The available file types are listed in Table 11-10. Table 11-11 lists some combinations of permissions for files and directories.

11

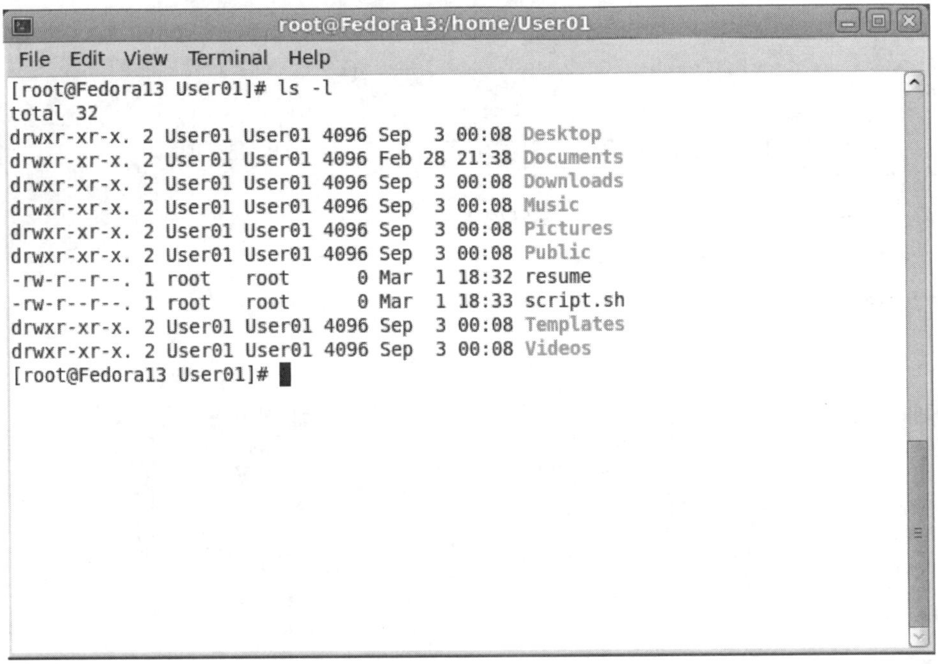

root@Fedora13:/home/User01
File Edit View Terminal Help
[root@Fedora13 User01]# ls -l
total 32
drwxr-xr-x. 2 User01 User01 4096 Sep 3 00:08 Desktop
drwxr-xr-x. 2 User01 User01 4096 Feb 28 21:38 Documents
drwxr-xr-x. 2 User01 User01 4096 Sep 3 00:08 Downloads
drwxr-xr-x. 2 User01 User01 4096 Sep 3 00:08 Music
drwxr-xr-x. 2 User01 User01 4096 Sep 3 00:08 Pictures
drwxr-xr-x. 2 User01 User01 4096 Sep 3 00:08 Public
-rw-r--r--. 1 root root 0 Mar 1 18:32 resume
-rw-r--r--. 1 root root 0 Mar 1 18:33 script.sh
drwxr-xr-x. 2 User01 User01 4096 Sep 3 00:08 Templates
drwxr-xr-x. 2 User01 User01 4096 Sep 3 00:08 Videos
[root@Fedora13 User01]#

Figure 11-21 Listing file permissions in Fedora 13

Source: Course Technology/Cengage Learning

File type
D
R W X
R W X
R W X
Owner
Group
Everyone

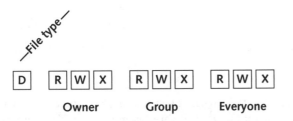

Figure 11-22 Displaying file permissions in Fedora 13

Source: Course Technology/Cengage Learning

File Type	Symbol
d	Directory
-	Regular file
c	Character device
b	Block device
l	Link
s	Socket
p	Named pipe

Table 11-10 Fedora 13 file types

Display	Permissions
r--	Read only
r-x	Read and execute
rw-	Read and write

Table 11-11 Fedora 13 file and directory permissions

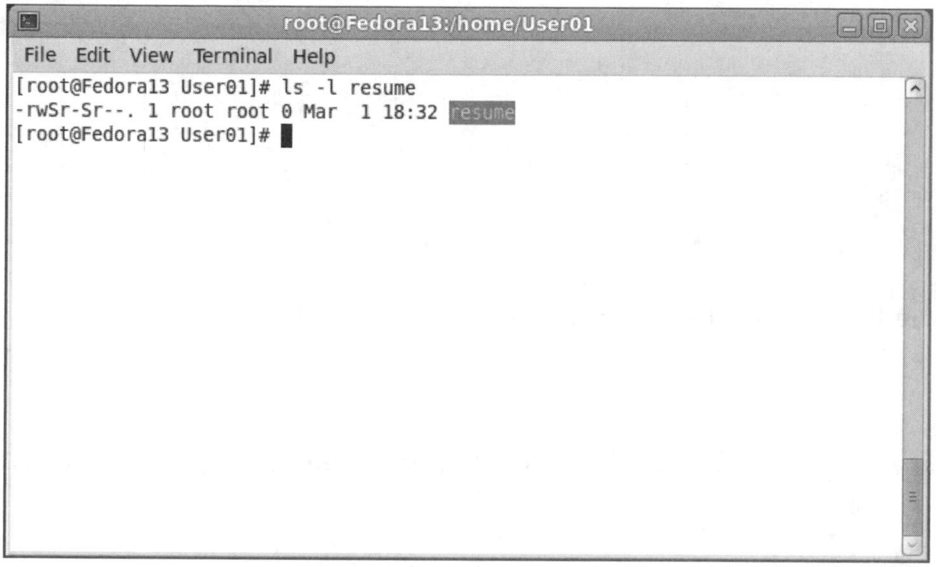

```
root@Fedora13:/home/User01
File  Edit  View  Terminal  Help
[root@Fedora13 User01]# ls -l resume
-rwSr-Sr--. 1 root root 0 Mar  1 18:32 resume
[root@Fedora13 User01]#
```

Figure 11-23 Viewing the User Identification attribute

Source: Course Technology/Cengage Learning

The User Identification Attribute The file permissions bits include an execute permission bit for the file owner, the group, and others. When the execute bit is set for the owner, the SUID bit (short for *set user ID*) is set to *s*. This permission allows any users or processes that run the file to have the same access to system resources as the owner of the file. This permission is important if a program must use the same environment as the owner's. (See Figure 11-23.)

This permission can be dangerous because the ability to run someone else's programs allows other users to enjoy the permissions for the duration of the program run. This is how hackers get superuser rights; they break out of the running program and keep the resource permissions.

The Sticky Bit Setting the **sticky bit** ensures that only the owner (and root, of course) who created a file in his directory can delete the file and prevent malicious or accidental deletion by others. A *t* appears as the third character of the Others permission bits when the sticky bit is set, as shown in Figure 11-24.

Figure 11-24 Viewing the sticky bit in Fedora 13

Source: Course Technology/Cengage Learning

Activity 11-11: Viewing File Permissions in Fedora 13

Time Required: 10 minutes

Objective: View the permissions for a file in Fedora 13.

Description: In this activity, you view the permissions for two files. This activity is helpful when you want to check file permissions.

1. If necessary, start your virtual machines using the appropriate instructions in Activity 1-1.

2. To open a Terminal console, click **Applications**, point to **System Tools**, and then click **Terminal**.

3. To view the file permissions for the resume file, type **ls –l resume** and then press **Enter**.

4. To view the file permissions for the script.sh file, type **ls –l script.sh** and then press **Enter**.

5. To shut down the virtual machine, click **System**, click **Shut Down**, and then click the **Shut Down** button.

6. Wait a moment for the Fedora 13 virtual machine to shut down completely.

7. Close any remaining open windows, log off, and shut down your PC.

Chapter Summary

- A network is a series of computers interconnected by communication paths. Common network organizations are client/server, peer-to-peer, local area networks, and wide area networks. The Internet Protocol Suite is the de facto standard for network communications.

- To enable communications in a routed network, a computer must have an IP address, subnet mask, gateway IP address, and DNS IP address.

- Network resources, folders, files, and printers are shared on the network. In Windows 7, you can access these resources from Windows Explorer and the Add Printer Wizard. In Fedora 13, network resources are accessed using the `mount` command and the `system-config-printer` command.

- File permissions enable users to access needed files and enable groups to share project files and folders. A file's owner and the system administrator determine a file's level of access. Be careful not to give blanket permissions to users who may not need access to your files.

Key Terms

client/server   A network architecture in which each computer or process on the network is either a client or a server.

Dynamic Host Configuration Protocol (DHCP)   An auto-configuration protocol used on IP networks.

homegroup   A feature unique to Windows 7 that permits a simple password-protected network with other Windows 7 systems through which you can easily share printers and folders.

Internet Protocol (IP)   The principal communications protocol used for relaying packets across the Internet.

IP address   Usually a numeric label assigned to each computer, printer, and other device in a computer network.

LAN (local area network)   A network that is usually confined to a small geographic area.

network   A series of computer devices or nodes interconnected by communication paths.

packets   Units of data traveling over a network.

peer-to-peer network   A type of network in which each workstation has equivalent capabilities and responsibilities.

Samba   The Fedora 13 implementation of peer-to-peer networking.

Server Message Block (SMB)   A network protocol used by Windows 7 and Fedora 13 computers that allows systems within the same network to share files.

sticky bit   An access flag that you can assign to files and directories on UNIX systems. When the sticky bit is set for a directory, a user can only modify and delete files and subdirectories in the directory he owns.

UNC (Universal Naming Convention)   A naming convention used primarily to specify and map network drives.

VPN (virtual private network)   A secured private network connection built on top of publicly accessible infrastructure.

WAN (wide area network)   Two or more local area networks (LANs). Computers connected to a WAN are often connected through public networks.

workgroup   A collection of computers on a LAN that share common resources and responsibilities.

Review Questions

1. A _____ employs desktop computers that are capable of being both clients and servers.

   a.   client/server network

   b.   peer-to-peer network

   c.   LAN

   d.   WAN

   e.   VPN

2. The four layers of the Internet Protocol Suite are arranged in the following order from top to bottom.

   a.   Application, Internet, Transport, Network

   b.   Application, Transport, Internet, Link

   c.   Link, Internet, Transport, Application

   d.   Application, Link, Transport, Network

3. TCP/IP normally requires which of the following settings to communicate on a routed network? (Choose all that apply.)

   a.   IP address

   b.   Subnet mask

   c.   Router address

   d.   DNS IP address

   e.   Web server address

4. _____ is a computer networking protocol used by hosts to retrieve IP address assignments.

   a.   DNS

   b.   Workgroup

   c.   DHCP

   d.   Homegroup

5. In Windows 7, the _____ command displays TCP/IP settings.

   a.   DHCP

   b.   DNS

   c.   ifconfig -a

   d.   IPCONFIG /ALL

6. In Fedora 13, the _____ command displays TCP/IP settings. (Choose all that apply.)

   a.   DHCP

   b.   DNS

    c. `ifconfig -a`

    d. `nm-tool`

    e. `IPCONFIG /ALL`

7. In Windows 7, the _____ makes it easy to share libraries with a single password.

    a. peer-to-peer network

    b. client/server

    c. homegroup

    d. workgroup

8. In Windows 7, the NET USE command maps a _____ to a shared folder.

    a. path

    b. drive letter

    c. homegroup

    d. computer

9. In Windows 7, the correct format for the UNC is _____.

    a. *\\driveletter\sharename*

    b. *\\servername\sharename*

    c. *\\servername\driveletter*

    d. *\\sharename\servername*

10. To securely share folders and files with required permissions in Windows 7, use the _____ file system.

    a. NT

    b. FTS

    c. FAT32

    d. FAT

11

11. Folder permissions are used to _____.

    a. keep paging at a minimum

    b. control access to folders and their files

    c. maintain processors

    d. control memory usage

12. Which of the following statements is true of NTFS? (Choose all that apply.)

    a. It is required to support NTFS permissions.

    b. Its permissions are not supported by FAT16 and FAT32 file systems.

    c. Its permissions are removed when a file folder is moved or copied to a FAT16 or FAT32 formatted partition.

    d. Its permissions are supported by FAT16 and FAT32 file systems.

13. In Fedora 13, the file type is a _____ when the first bit in the permissions column is a "-".
    a. directory
    b. socket
    c. link
    d. regular file

14. In Fedora 13, the file type is a _____ when the first bit in the permissions column is a *d*.
    a. directory
    b. socket
    c. link
    d. regular file

15. To switch to the superuser in Fedora 13, use the _____ command.
    a. su–
    b. SU–
    c. SUPERUSER
    d. Superuser

16. In Windows 7, the shared folder permissions are _____. (Choose all that apply.)
    a. Read
    b. Write
    c. Change
    d. Full Control

17. In Windows, the NTFS file permissions are _____. (Choose all that apply.)
    a. Read
    b. Write
    c. Change
    d. Full Control

18. When a file is moved to an existing folder on the same partition, the permissions _____.
    a. are copied with the folder
    b. are inherited
    c. must be reentered by the administrator
    d. are ignored

19. Fedora 13 has permissions for _____. (Choose all that apply.)

    a. Owner

    b. User

    c. Group

    d. Everyone

20. In Fedora 13, the `r-x` file and directory permissions represent _____.

    a. Read only

    b. Read and change

    c. Read and execute

    d. Read and write

Case Projects

Case 11-1: Accessing File Shares

You have been asked to give a short presentation on accessing file shares from Windows 7 and Fedora 13. Prepare a one-page handout to support your presentation.

Case 11-2: Using Share and NTFS Permissions

You are interviewing for a summer job as a desktop support technician. All client computers at the company run Windows 7. Before moving to the Finance Department, Upali was a member of the Accounting Department. He is a member of the Accounting and Finance groups, and is attempting to gain access to the Schedules folder, which has the share and NTFS permissions shown in Figure 11-25. How will you give Upali access to the Schedules folder?

Shared folder permissions	NTFS folder permissions
Everyone – Full control	Everyone – Read
Accounting – Deny all access	Accounting – Modify
Executive – Read	Executive – Read
Finance – Change	Finance – Modify
Marketing – Read	Marketing – Write

Figure 11-25 Share and NTFS permissions

Source: Course Technology/Cengage Learning

Case 11-3: Investigating a User Access Problem

Your company's Programming Department installed a new client notes system last weekend. You get a call from Janey, who cannot use the new system. She can log on and access the initial screen, but when she clicks the calendar, she gets an error message that reads "No calendar found." Your associate tells you that the calendar module is installed on the server and that all interfaces have been tested by the Development Department. How will you investigate this access problem using the ls command?

Numbering Systems and Data Representation

After reading this appendix and completing the exercises, you will be able to:

- Convert numbers from one base to another (decimal, binary, and hexadecimal)
- Use an ASCII reference table to see the decimal and hexadecimal equivalents for a specified character
- Describe the data types for Boolean, character, integer, and floating-point data

Probably the biggest stumbling block that beginning programmers encounter is the common use of binary and hexadecimal numbering systems in programming languages. Most people have used the decimal numbering system all their lives, so using systems with different "base" numbers can be disconcerting. Knowing the binary and hexadecimal systems can simplify other complex topics, including Boolean algebra, signed numeric representation, and character codes.

This appendix explains the relationships among decimal, binary, and hexadecimal numbering systems, and explains how to convert numbers from one base to another. It also provides information about the ASCII character set.

Numbering Systems

PCs do not represent numeric values using the well-known decimal system. Instead, PCs typically use a binary numbering system and represent large binary values using hexadecimal numbers. When programming for the PC, you should be familiar with the three numbering systems listed in Table A-1. These numbering systems are described in the following sections.

Name	Base	Symbol
Decimal	Base 10	none or D
Binary	Base 2	B
Hexadecimal	Base 16	H or 0x

Table A-1   Numbering systems

Decimal Numbers

You've been using the decimal numbering system for so long that you probably take it for granted. In the decimal system (base 10), there are 10 different symbols to represent values: 0, 1, 2, 3, 4, 5, 6, 7, 8, and 9. Because the "base" of the system is 10, you can represent all values of less than 10 with single numbers. Once you reach 10, however, you need a second column of numbers to represent the value. When you reach 100, you need a third column, and so on. Each column is distinguished by a greater power of 10, which is why the decimal system is called base 10.

The only real difference between the decimal, binary, and hexadecimal systems is that a different base is used to distinguish these columns. Throughout this appendix, the values of these columns are called *positional values*.

The values for each base 10 position are shown in the following columns. The caret symbol (^) represents an exponent—for example, $10\text{^}2$ is 10 to the 2nd power, or 10×10, which equals 100.

$10\text{^}4$	$10\text{^}3$	$10\text{^}2$	$10\text{^}1$	$10\text{^}0$
10000	1000	100	10	1

When you see a number like 123, you probably don't think much about the composition of the value. Remember from elementary school, however, that 1 is the number in the hundreds

A

position, 2 is the number in the tens position, and 3 is the value in the ones position. A new column or position is required each time the numeric value surpasses a power of 10:

```
1 * 10^2 + 2 * 10^1 + 3 * 10^0 =
1 * 100 + 2 * 10 + 3 * 1 =
100 + 20 + 3 =
123
```

In the United States and other countries, every three decimal digits are separated with a comma to make larger numbers easier to read. For example, the number 123,456,789 is much easier to read and comprehend than 123456789.

Binary Numbers

The binary numbering system (base 2) has only two symbols to represent values: 0 and 1. Because the hardware for modern digital computers uses electronic circuits called gates, which represent information using only the two values of On and Off, binary is a convenient numbering system for computers to use.

The values for each binary column position are shown in Table A-2. Note that these positions operate on the same principle as those in base 10; the only difference is that a new column or position is required each time the numeric value surpasses a power of 2.

2^7	2^6	2^5	2^4	2^3	2^2	2^1	2^0
128	64	32	16	8	4	2	1

Table A-2 Powers of 2

Just as commas are used to separate decimal numbers and make them more readable, spaces are added after every fourth number in the binary system. For example, the following binary value:

```
1010111110110010
```

is written:

```
1010 1111 1011 0010
```

Hexadecimal Numbers

Because binary numbers use only two values, representing large amounts in binary quickly becomes unwieldy. To represent the value 911, for example, you need 10 binary digits. The hexadecimal numbering system solves this problem. In the hexadecimal system (base 16), there are 16 different symbols to represent values instead of just two: 0, 1, 2, 3, 4, 5, 6, 7, 8, 9, A, B, C, D, E, and F. Because hexadecimal has a much larger "base" number than binary, you can represent a value like 911 with just three symbols (38F) instead of 10 binary digits.

Notice that hexadecimal uses the letters A through F to represent single digits of more than 9.

Binary	Decimal	Hexadecimal
0000B	00	00H
0001B	01	01H
0010B	02	02H
0011B	03	03H
0100B	04	04H
0101B	05	05H
0110B	06	06H
0111B	07	07H
1000B	08	08H
1001B	09	09H
1010B	10	0AH
1011B	11	0BH
1100B	12	0CH
1101B	13	0DH
1110B	14	0EH
1111B	15	0FH

Table A-3 **Number conversions**

Table A-3 shows relationships between the binary, decimal, and hexadecimal numbering systems. The table shows all the conversions for the decimal values of 0 to 15 into binary and hexadecimal.

In programming, most compilers require the first digit of a hexadecimal number to be 0 and require an H at the end to denote the use of hexadecimal.

As with binary numbers, programmers make hexadecimal numbers more readable by adding a space every four digits. For example, the hexadecimal value 3287092778E3 is written 3287 0927 78E3.

Converting Between Numbering Systems

Students of programming are expected to be able to convert between the decimal, binary, and hexadecimal numbering systems. The following sections show you how.

A

Converting Binary Numbers to Decimal Numbers

To begin converting a binary number to a decimal number, simply separate the number into columns and write the positional value of each column above each binary digit. The positional values are calculated using the powers of 2 that you saw in Table A-2. Keep in mind that the equivalent positional values in the decimal system are ones, tens, hundreds, and so on; because the binary system uses a smaller base number, its positional values are ones, twos, fours, and so on.

For example, take the following binary number:

    1001B =

Disregard the B, which merely represents a binary number, and write the positional value above each binary digit:

8	4	2	1
1	0	0	1

Discard the positional values that result in zero and add the positions that have 1s; in other words, $8 + 1 = 9$. The conversion of 1001 results in a decimal value of 9.

When you think about this operation, keep in mind that binary and decimal systems operate on the same principle—only the base is different. For example, in decimal, a 1 in the thousands column plus a 1 in the ones column equals 1001.

Activity A-1: Converting Binary Numbers to Decimal Numbers

Time Required: 10 minutes

Objective: Convert binary numbers to decimal numbers.

Description: In this activity, you practice converting binary numbers to decimal numbers. To perform this conversion, simply separate the binary number into columns and write the positional value of each column above each binary digit. Next, add the positional values wherever a binary 1 appears.

Complete Table A-4 by providing the decimal equivalents for each binary number. Use scratch paper for your calculations.

Binary	Decimal
1011B	
1100B	
0011B	
0110B	
1001 1110B	
1011 0111B	

Table A-4 Answers for binary to decimal conversions

Keep in mind that the B merely represents a binary number; it does not play a part in the conversion.

Converting Decimal Numbers to Binary Numbers

One way to convert decimal numbers to binary numbers is to use long division, as demonstrated in Figure A-1. Follow these steps:

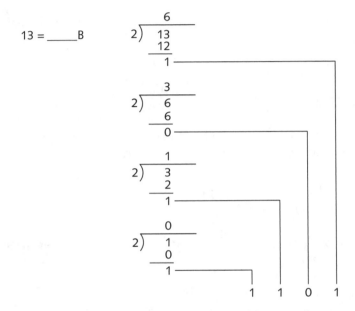

Figure A-1 Converting decimal numbers to binary numbers

Source: Course Technology/Cengage Learning

1. Repeatedly divide the decimal number by 2, using the remainder of each division operation as part of your binary answer. Record the remainders from right to left.

2. Each quotient becomes the dividend of the next division operation. For example, dividing 13 by 2 produces a quotient of 6, which becomes the dividend for the next step. Dividing 6 by 2 produces a quotient of 3, and so on.

3. Continue dividing until you get a quotient of zero, which will yield the last (far left) digit of your binary answer.

Study this procedure thoroughly; you will use a similar procedure later in this appendix for decimal to hexadecimal conversions.

Activity A-2: Converting Decimal Numbers to Binary Numbers

A

Time Required: 10 minutes

Objective: Convert decimal numbers to binary numbers.

Description: In this activity, you practice converting decimal numbers to binary numbers. To perform this conversion, you repeatedly divide the decimal number by 2, using the procedure explained in the previous section.

Complete Table A-5 by providing the binary equivalents for each decimal number. Use scratch paper for your calculations.

Decimal	Binary
5	
10	
16	
25	
31	
49	

Table A-5 **Answers for decimal to binary conversions**

Converting Hexadecimal Numbers to Decimal Numbers

To begin converting from hexadecimal to decimal, simply separate the hexadecimal number into columns and write the positional value of each column above each hexadecimal digit. Because the hexadecimal system uses a base number of 16, the positional values are calculated using powers of 16, as shown in Table A-6.

16^6	16^5	16^4	16^3	16^2	16^1	16^0
16,777,216	1,048,576	65,536	4,096	256	16	1

Table A-6 **Powers of 16**

Take the following number:

0239H =

Disregard the H at the end and write the positional value above each hexadecimal digit:

256	16	1
2	3	9

Multiply each digit by its column value and then add the products for each position:

$2 \times 256 + 3 \times 16 + 9 \times 1$
$512 + 48 + 9 = 569$

Activity A-3: Converting Hexadecimal Numbers to Decimal Numbers

Time Required: 10 minutes

Objective: Convert hexadecimal numbers to decimal numbers.

Description: In this activity, you practice converting hexadecimal numbers to decimal numbers. To perform this conversion, write the positional value of each column above each hexadecimal digit, multiply each digit by its column value, and add the products.

Complete Table A-7 by providing the decimal equivalents for each hexadecimal number. Use scratch paper for your calculations.

Hexadecimal	Decimal
5H	
10H	
1AH	
2EH	
31H	
4BH	

Table A-7 Answers for hexadecimal to decimal conversions

Converting Decimal Numbers to Hexadecimal Numbers

One way to convert decimal numbers to hexadecimal numbers is to use long division, as demonstrated in Figure A-2 and explained in the following steps. You used a similar method to convert decimal numbers to binary numbers.

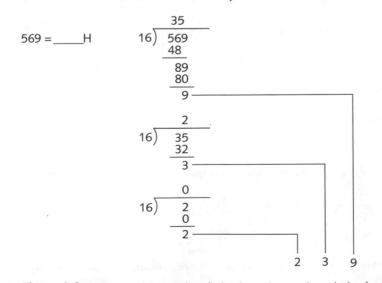

$$569 = \underline{\quad} H$$

Figure A-2 Example of converting decimal numbers to hexadecimal numbers

Source: Course Technology/Cengage Learning

A

1. Divide the decimal number by 16, using the hexadecimal remainder of each division operation as part of your answer. Record the remainders from right to left.

2. Each quotient becomes the dividend of the next division operation. For example, dividing 569 by 16 provides 35, which becomes the next number to divide by 16.

3. Continue dividing until you get a quotient of zero, which will yield the last (far left) digit of your hexadecimal answer.

If a remainder is between 10 and 15, you must convert it to the corresponding hexadecimal value between A (10) and F (15) in your answer. For another example of converting decimal numbers to hexadecimal numbers, as well as a helpful conversion chart, see Figure A-3. The remainder for the first division is 10, which is represented by the hexadecimal number A.

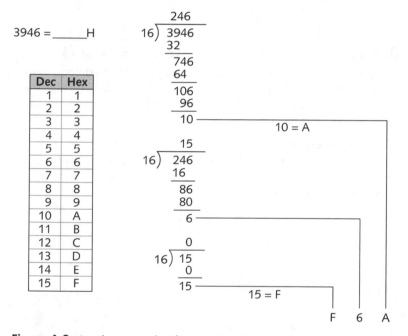

Figure A-3 Another example of converting decimal numbers to hexadecimal numbers

Source: Course Technology/Cengage Learning

Activity A-4: Converting Decimal Numbers to Hexadecimal Numbers

Time Required: 10 minutes

Objective: Convert decimal numbers to hexadecimal numbers.

Description: In this activity, you practice converting decimal numbers to hexadecimal numbers. To perform this conversion, repeatedly divide the decimal number by 16, using the remainder of each division as part of your hexadecimal answer. Record the remainders from right to left.

Complete Table A-8 by providing the hexadecimal equivalents for each decimal number. Use scratch paper for your calculations.

Decimal	Hexadecimal
5	
10	
75	
88	
126	
500	

Table A-8 Answers for decimal to hexadecimal conversions

Converting Binary Numbers to Hexadecimal Numbers

A bit is a binary digit—either a zero or a one. To make a binary number more readable, place a blank between each set of four bits, as shown in Figure A-4. Group the bits from right to left. If you are left with a group of less than four bits, pad the group with zero bits on the left. For example, the bit pattern 111 is padded as 0111.

When converting binary numbers to hexadecimal numbers, there is a simple rule: Each group of four bits is converted to one hexadecimal character, as shown in the conversion chart in Figure A-4. For example, to convert the binary number 0101, scan the conversion table to find the equivalent hexadecimal number: 5.

0111 1010 0101B = _____H

Bin	Hex
0000	0
0001	1
0010	2
0011	3
0100	4
0101	5
0110	6
0111	7
1000	8
1001	9
1010	A
1011	B
1100	C
1101	D
1110	E
1111	F

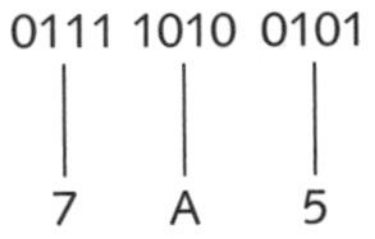

0111 1010 0101

7   A   5

Figure A-4 Converting binary numbers to hexadecimal numbers

Source: Course Technology/Cengage Learning

ACTIVITY

Activity A-5: Converting Binary Numbers to Hexadecimal Numbers

Time Required: 10 minutes

Objective: Convert binary numbers to hexadecimal numbers.

Description: In this activity, you practice converting binary numbers to hexadecimal numbers. To perform this conversion, use the procedure explained in the previous section and the conversion table in Figure A-4.

Complete Table A-9 by providing the hexadecimal equivalents for each binary number. Use scratch paper for your calculations.

Binary	Hexadecimal
1100B	
1000 0111B	
0110 0100B	
0001 0011 0110B	
1001 1101 1000B	
1111 0011 1100B	

Table A-9   Answers for binary to hexadecimal conversions

Converting Hexadecimal Numbers to Binary Numbers

To accomplish this conversion, use the inverse of the rule in the previous section. Each hexadecimal character can be converted to four bits, as shown in Figure A-5. For

9BAH = _____B

Bin	Hex
0000	0
0001	1
0010	2
0011	3
0100	4
0101	5
0110	6
0111	7
1000	8
1001	9
1010	A
1011	B
1100	C
1101	D
1110	E
1111	F

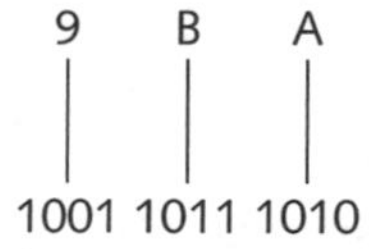

```
9    B    A
|    |    |
|    |    |
1001 1011 1010
```

Figure A-5   Converting hexadecimal numbers to binary numbers

Source: Course Technology/Cengage Learning

example, to convert the hexadecimal character A, scan the conversion table to find the equivalent binary number: 1010. Repeat the search for the remaining hexadecimal characters.

Activity A-6: Converting Hexadecimal Numbers to Binary Numbers

Time Required: 10 minutes

Objective: Convert hexadecimal numbers to binary numbers.

Description: In this activity, you practice converting hexadecimal numbers to binary numbers. To perform this conversion, use the procedure explained in the previous section and the conversion table in Figure A-5.

Complete Table A-10 by providing the binary equivalents for each hexadecimal number. Use scratch paper for your calculations.

Hexadecimal	Binary
05H	
1CH	
75H	
8FH	
126H	
500H	

Table A-10   Answers for hexadecimal to binary conversions

Converting Numbers Using the Windows 7 Calculator

You can use the calculator (see Figure A-6) in Windows 7 to check your answers. To open the calculator, click Start, point to All Programs, click Accessories, and then click Calculator. In the Standard view, you can perform decimal calculations.

When checking number conversions, the Programmer view is more useful. To switch to this view, click the View menu and then click Programmer (see Figure A-7).

Start by selecting the base of the number you want to convert. Choose from Hex (base 16), Dec (base 10), or Bin (base 2) near the top of the calculator. Next, enter the number you want to convert. (If you're more comfortable entering numbers with the numeric keypad on

Figure A-6 Calculator in Standard view

Source: Course Technology/Cengage Learning

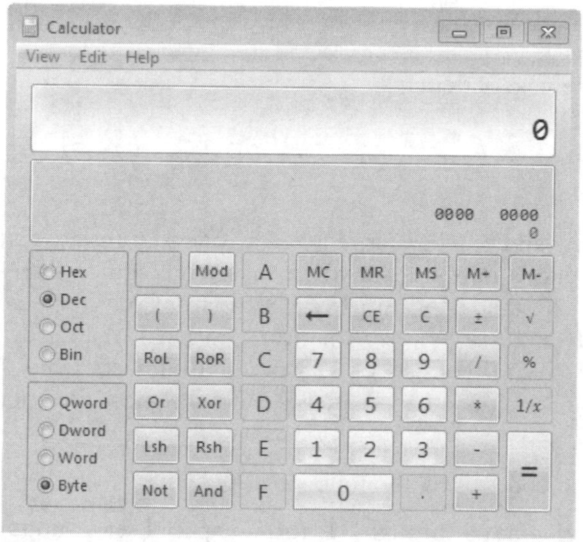

Figure A-7 Calculator in Programmer view

Source: Course Technology/Cengage Learning

your keyboard, press NUM LOCK and then enter the number.) To convert the number, click the Hex, Dec, or Bin option button.

If you want to see hexadecimal and binary numbers with separating spaces, click the View menu and then click Digit grouping.

Activity A-7: Converting Numbers Using the Windows 7 Calculator

Time Required: 10 minutes

Objective: Convert numbers from one base to another using the Windows 7 calculator.

Description: In this activity, you enter a decimal number into the calculator and convert it to a hexadecimal or binary number.

1. Start your virtual machines using the appropriate instructions in Activity 1-1.
2. Click **Start,** point to **All Programs,** click **Accessories,** and then click **Calculator.**
3. To turn on the Programmer view, click the **View** menu and then click **Programmer.**
4. Click the **Dec** option button.
5. Press the **2** key, press the **0** key twice, and then press the **6** key.
6. Click the **Hex** option button.
7. Click the **View** menu and then click **Digit grouping.**
8. Click the **Bin** option button.
9. Close any open windows.
10. Leave the PC logged on for the next activity.

Using ASCII Characters

Because a computer can only understand numbers, it requires a code to translate text characters such as *a* or @ and certain actions into numbers. The most common of these codes is ASCII (pronounced *ask-key*), which stands for American Standard Code for Information Interchange. ASCII was finalized in 1968 by the American National Standards Institute (ANSI). The standard ASCII character set consists of 128 decimal numbers from 0 to 127, which are assigned to letters, numbers, punctuation marks, and the most common special characters.

The ASCII characters were assigned codes using the following guidelines:

- The first 32 characters, ASCII codes 0 through 31, form a special set of nonprinting characters called the control characters. These control characters, now obsolete, once controlled how text was printed.
- The second group of 32 codes comprises various punctuation symbols, special characters, and numbers.
- The third group of 32 codes is reserved for uppercase alphabetic characters and six special symbols.
- The fourth and final group of 32 codes is reserved for lowercase alphabetic symbols, five additional special symbols, and another control character (delete).

Table A-11 shows the ASCII character codes with their equivalent decimal and hexadecimal values. The obsolete control characters are not included.

Character	Dec	Hex	Character	Dec	Hex	Character	Dec	Hex
(sp)	32	0x20	@	64	0x40	`	96	0x60
!	33	0x21	A	65	0x41	a	97	0x61
"	34	0x22	B	66	0x42	b	98	0x62
#	35	0x23	C	67	0x43	c	99	0x63
$	36	0x24	D	68	0x44	d	100	0x64
%	37	0x25	E	69	0x45	e	101	0x65
&	38	0x26	F	70	0x46	f	102	0x66
'	39	0x27	G	71	0x47	g	103	0x67
(	40	0x28	H	72	0x48	h	104	0x68
)	41	0x29	I	73	0x49	i	105	0x69
*	42	0x2a	J	74	0x4a	j	106	0x6a
+	43	0x2b	K	75	0x4b	k	107	0x6b
,	44	0x2c	L	76	0x4c	l	108	0x6c
-	45	0x2d	M	77	0x4d	m	109	0x6d
.	46	0x2e	N	78	0x4e	n	110	0x6e
/	47	0x2f	O	79	0x4f	o	111	0x6f
0	48	0x30	P	80	0x50	p	112	0x70
1	49	0x31	Q	81	0x51	q	113	0x71
2	50	0x32	R	82	0x52	r	114	0x72
3	51	0x33	S	83	0x53	s	115	0x73
4	52	0x34	T	84	0x54	t	116	0x74
5	53	0x35	U	85	0x55	u	117	0x75
6	54	0x36	V	86	0x56	v	118	0x76
7	55	0x37	W	87	0x57	w	119	0x77
8	56	0x38	X	88	0x58	x	120	0x78
9	57	0x39	Y	89	0x59	y	121	0x79
:	58	0x3a	Z	90	0x5a	z	122	0x7a
;	59	0x3b	[	91	0x5b	{	123	0x7b
<	60	0x3c	\	92	0x5c	|	124	0x7c
=	61	0x3d	]	93	0x5d	}	125	0x7d
>	62	0x3e	^	94	0x5e	~	126	0x7e
?	63	0x3f	_	95	0x5f	(del)	127	0x7f

Table A-11 ASCII characters and equivalent decimal and hexadecimal values

Table A-11 uses the alternative symbol 0x for hexadecimal values.

Because most modern computers work with 8-bit bytes, which can represent 256 different values, the ASCII character set now offers an additional 128 characters known as extended ASCII. These extended character sets are platform- and locale-dependent, so more than one set is available. One example of an extended ASCII character set is available in TextPad, as you will see in Activity A-9.

Activity A-8: Using ASCII Character Codes

Time Required: 10 minutes

Objective: Look up the character codes for ASCII characters.

Description: In this activity, you practice looking up the decimal and hexadecimal codes for ASCII characters. Use the conversions in Table A-11 to fill in the appropriate codes in Table A-12 for the given ASCII characters.

Character	Decimal	Hexadecimal
*		
4		
Q		
f		
(sp)		

Table A-12   Decimal and hexadecimal codes for ASCII characters

Activity A-9: Entering ASCII Characters Using TextPad

Time Required: 10 minutes

Objective: Enter ASCII characters into a document using TextPad.

Description: In this activity, you enter ASCII characters using the Clip Library in TextPad. The Clip Library supports 256 characters, including the extended ASCII character set.

1. Start your virtual machines using the appropriate instructions in Activity 1-1.

2. Click **Start**, point to **All Programs**, and then click **TextPad**.

3. If necessary, display the Clip Library by clicking **View** and then clicking **Clip Library**.

4. Press the " key.

5. Locate and double-click the ¡ character (located at 161) in the Clip Library.

6. Type **Cuidado! grit**.

7. Locate and double-click the ó character (located at 243) in the Clip Library.

8. Type **."** **"Careful!" he shouted.** and then press **Enter.**

9. Review the text and make any necessary corrections. The TextPad window should look like Figure A-8.

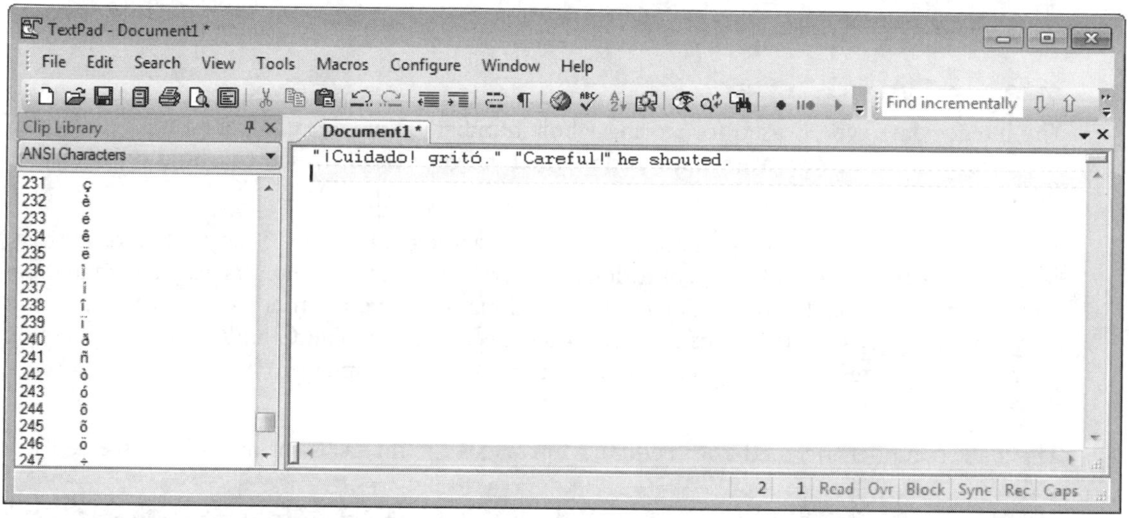

Figure A-8 Entering ASCII characters in TextPad

Source: Course Technology/Cengage Learning

10. Close any open windows, click **Start,** and then click the **Shut Down** button.

11. Wait a moment for the Windows 7 virtual machine to shut down completely.

Representing Data Types

In a PC, the hardware stores data items and software applications perform operations on them. The values of these data items are called bits (short for *binary digits*); each bit represents a discrete piece of information.

Bits are grouped together, and the pattern of values within the group is used to represent a symbol. For example, a group of 8 bits (called a byte) can have 256 different patterns and can therefore represent 256 different symbols. In modern computers, groupings of 2 or 4 bytes, called words, can represent larger "chunks" of information.

Understanding internal binary representation is not required for programming, but it is helpful to know. The following sections explain common data types.

Character Type

You learned previously about the representation of ASCII characters. Two types of character data are defined:

- Signed characters—These characters store integers in the range of +128 to –127.

- Unsigned characters—These characters store whole integers in the range of 255 to 0; they are also used to store ASCII characters.

Boolean Type

The Boolean type can have only one of two values: true or false. (In some cases, the two values are 0 or non-0.)

Integer Type

The integer data type is used for storing whole numbers. You can use signed integers, which can hold positive or negative values, or unsigned integer values, which can hold only positive values.

The most common source of confusion when discussing an integer type is its size and the range of values it can hold. The confusion stems from the fact that languages leave many features of integer types for particular implementations to define themselves, meaning that each program compiler can determine its own exact specifications. The C and C++ compilers do set minimum requirements for each integer type, but the implementation is free to exceed these limits.

The g++ compiler included with Fedora 13 provides the integer sizes listed in Table A-13.

Type	Length	Maximum value	Minimum value
char	1 byte	128	−127
unsigned char	1 byte	255	0
short	2 bytes	32,768	−32,767
short unsigned	2 bytes	65,535	0
long	4 bytes	2,147,483,648	−2,147,483,647
long unsigned	4 bytes	4,294,967,295	0

Table A-13   Integer sizes

Floating-Point Type

A floating-point number is a number that can contain a fractional part. For example, floating-point numbers can contain decimal values, such as 3.14, −0.982, or −0.087. The term *floating point* means that there is no fixed number of digits before or after the decimal point; that is, the decimal point can float. In general, floating-point calculations are slower and less accurate than fixed-point (integer) calculations, but they can handle a larger range of numbers.

Floating-point representation is similar to scientific notation, which is a useful way to represent numbers that are very large or very small. The following are examples of scientific notation:

```
47,300 = 4.73 × 4
0.000000021 = 2.1 × 10 −8
```

Floating-point numbers come in two sizes: float (single-precision) and double (double-precision). The g++ compiler included with Fedora 13 provides the floating-point sizes listed in Table A-14.

Type	Length	Maximum
float	4 bytes	$3.4E \pm 38$ (7 digits)
double	8 bytes	$1.7E \pm 308$ (15 digits)

Table A-14 Floating-point sizes

Activity A-10: Providing a Data Type

Time Required: 10 minutes

Objective: Given example data, provide the proper data type to store it.

Description: In this activity, you practice specifying data types for example data by completing Table A-15.

Data example	Data type
A	
1024	
66	
1023.996	
#	
−32700	
−88888.778	
65000	
−2,000,000,000	
777777789	

Table A-15 Answers for data types

Working with Virtual PC 2007

Getting Started with Virtual PC 2007

Microsoft Virtual PC 2007 is an x86 virtualization software package that is installed on an existing host operating system; within this application, additional guest operating systems can be loaded and run, each with its own virtual environment.

Microsoft Virtual PC 2007 includes the following features:

- The virtualization architecture has been optimized for the Windows 7 family of operating systems to improve performance, system resource usage, and stability.

- It provides support for 64-bit host operating systems. You can run Virtual PC 2007 on 64-bit versions of Windows 7 family operating systems.

- It provides support for sound devices in Windows 7 guest operating systems. Virtualized sound device drivers are available to the Windows 7 family of guest operating systems, which allows them to play sound through the host operating system sound devices.

- It supports USB device access.

Configuring the Host Computer

To enable the two virtual machines to communicate with the Internet and with each other, you will install Internet Connection Sharing (ICS). First, you connect the existing network adapter in your Host01 computer to the Internet. Next, you install a second network adapter—the Microsoft Loopback adapter—which has a separate connection to the virtual machines. You will enable ICS on the Internet connection to share the Internet with the Microsoft Loopback adapter.

To enable future activities, you will share and populate the TextShare folder with files from the Cengage Learning Web site. In addition, you will set up a shared generic printer.

Complete the following steps to prepare the Windows 7 host computer to support the virtual environment.

1. Log on to your host PC with **Admin01** and a password of **P@ssw0rd**.
2. To open the Add Hardware dialog box, click **Start**, click **Control Panel**, click the **View by** chevron, click **Small icons**, and then click **Device Manager**.

3. Right-click **Host01** and click **Add legacy hardware**.

4. Click **Next**, click **Install the hardware that I manually select from a list (Advanced)**, and then click **Next**.

5. Scroll through the common hardware types, click **Network adapters**, and then click **Next**.

6. To select the Microsoft Loopback adapter, click **Microsoft** under Manufacturer, scroll the Network Adapter list, click **Microsoft Loopback Adapter**, and then click **Next**.

7. To install the Microsoft Loopback adapter, click **Next**.

8. Wait for the installation to complete, and then click **Finish**.

9. In the Control Panel, click **Network and Sharing Center**.

10. To display the Local Area Connection Properties dialog box, click **Change adapter settings**, right-click **Local Area Connection** (do not use Local Area Connection 2), and then click **Properties**.

11. To enable Internet Connection Sharing (ICS), click the **Sharing** tab, click **Allow other network users to connect through this computer's Internet Connection**, and then click **OK**.

12. Close the Network Connections window.

13. If asked about the connection type, click **Work**, click **Next**, and then click **Close**.

14. Verify that the Internet Globe is blue/green, and is not grayed out. If it is, contact your instructor.

15. Close all open windows.

16. To share a printer on the Host01 computer, click **Start**, click **Control Panel**, click the **View by** chevron, and click **Small icons**. Click **Devices and Printers**, click **Add a printer**, click **Add a local printer**, and click **Next**. Scroll the Manufacturer list, click **Generic**, click **Generic/Text Only**, and click **Next** twice. Type **SharedPrinter** in the Printer name text box, click **Next** twice, and then click **Finish**.

17. To create the TextShare folder on the host computer, click **Start**, click **Computer**, and double-click **Local Disk (C:)**. Note that your operating system drive might have a different name. Right-click the white space in the right pane, point to **New**, click **Folder**, type **TextShare**, and press **Enter**. Right-click **TextShare**, click **Properties**, click the **Sharing** tab, and click **Share**. Type **Everyone**, click **Add**, click **Share**, click **Done**, and then click **Close**.

18. To access this book's text on the Cengage Learning Web site, click the **Internet Explorer** icon on the taskbar, type **www.cengage.com** in the Address bar, and press **Enter**. Click the **Higher Education** link on the left, scroll down and click the **Course Technology** link under "Browse by Publisher," type **carswell** over "Enter author, title, ISBN, or keyword," and click **Search**.

19. To download the student data files, click **Guide to Parallel Operating Systems with Windows 7 and Linux, 2nd Edition**, click **Instructor Companion Site**, click the **Data Files for Students (TextShareFiles)** link on the left, click the entry after Download Now, and click **Run** twice. Click **Browse**, click **Local Disk (C:)**, double-click **TextShare**, click **OK**, click **Unzip**, click **OK**, and then click **Close**.

Downloading Virtual PC 2007

Complete the following steps to download the current version of Virtual PC 2007 from the Microsoft Virtual PC site.

1. Log on to your host PC with **Admin01** and a password of **P@ssw0rd**.
2. To start Internet Explorer, click the **Internet Explorer** icon on the taskbar.
3. To locate the download Web site for Virtual PC 2007, type **download virtual pc 2007** in the Internet Explorer search box, and then press **Enter**.
4. Click the appropriate Virtual PC 2007 link, which is the version that matches your host operating system: either **32 BIT/setup.exe** or **64 BIT/setup.exe**. Click **Save** twice.
5. Wait for the download to complete.
6. Leave the Download complete window open.

Installing Virtual PC 2007

The installation of Virtual PC 2007 uses the Microsoft Software Installer. Complete the following steps to install the program.

1. To start the Virtual PC 2007 Setup wizard, click **Run** in the Download complete dialog box.
2. Click **Yes** in the next dialog box, which asks if you want to allow the following program to make changes to this computer.
3. Click **Next** in the next dialog box, which welcomes you to the installation wizard.
4. Click **I accept the terms in the License Agreement**, click **Next** twice to move through the subsequent windows, click **Install**, and then click **Next**.
5. Type your **Username** and **Organization** in the Customer Information dialog box, leave the **Anyone who uses this computer** (**All users**) setting as is, and click **Next**.
6. Click **Next** and then click **Finish** when the installation is finished.

Installing Operating Systems in Virtual PC 2007

In the following sections, you will create virtual machines and virtual hard drives, and you will configure network adapters. When you finish, you will be ready to install a guest operating system. Recall that the virtual machines look like physical machines to the operating system installers.

Creating the First Virtual Machine for Windows 7

Here is a brief overview of the tasks required to create a virtual machine for Windows 7.

1. Start Virtual PC.
2. Create the Windows 7 virtual machine, which will use Disk0.
3. Create two additional virtual disks (Disk1 and Disk2) for future lab activities.
4. Connect the network adapter to the virtual machine.

Because each chapter in the text starts with Windows 7 activities first, you will create a virtual machine for Windows 7 first. Complete the following steps to create the first virtual machine.

1. If necessary, log on to your host PC with **Admin01** and a password of **P@ssw0rd**.

2. If necessary, click **Start**, click **All Programs**, and click **Microsoft Virtual PC** to start the Virtual PC console.

3. Click **New** to start the New Virtual Machine Wizard, and then click **Next**.

4. Click **Create a Virtual Machine**, and then click **Next**.

5. Name the machine **Windows 7** and click **Next**. Note that the default location is Libraries\Documents\My Virtual Machines\Windows 7.

6. Choose **Other** from the Operating System menu, and click **Next**.

7. Select **Adjusting the RAM**, enter **1024** MB, and click **Next**.

8. Select **A new virtual hard disk**, and click **Next**.

9. Select **Virtual Hard Disk Size**, enter **20000** MB, click **Next**, and click **Finish**.

10. Click the Windows 7 virtual machine and then click **Settings**. A Windows 7 virtual machine entry appears in the Virtual PC console.

11. To create the second virtual hard disk (Disk1) for future lab activities, click **Hard Disk 2**, click the **Virtual Disk Wizard** button, and click **Next**.

12. Click **Create a new virtual disk**, and click **Next**.

13. Click **A virtual hard disk**, and click **Next**.

14. Click the **Browse** button, click **Libraries**, click **Documents**, click **My Virtual Machines**, and click **Windows 7**. You should see the Windows 7 virtual machine file you just created.

15. Type **Windows 7 HardDisk2** in the File name text box, click **Save**, and click **Next**.

16. Select **Fixed size** and click **Next**.

17. Enter **2048** as the Virtual hard disk size, click **Next**, and click **Finish**.

18. Wait for the Virtual Hard Disk Wizard to finish successfully and click **Close**.

19. Click the **Virtual hard disk file** option button, click the **Browse** button, select the **Windows 7 Hard Disk1** file, and click **Open**.

20. To create the third virtual hard disk for Windows 7, click **Hard Disk 3**, click the **Virtual Disk Wizard** button, and click **Next**.

21. Click **Create a new virtual disk**, and click **Next**.

22. Click **A virtual hard disk**, and click **Next**.

23. Click the **Browse** button, click **Libraries**, click **Documents**, click **My Virtual Machines**, and click **Windows 7**. You should see both the Windows 7 virtual machine file and the Windows 7 HardDisk1 file you just created.

24. Type **Windows 7 HardDisk3** in the File name text box, click **Save**, and click **Next**.

25. Select **Fixed size** and click **Next**.

26. Enter **2048** as the Virtual hard disk size, click **Next**, and click **Finish**.

27. Wait for the Virtual Hard Disk Wizard to finish successfully and click **Close**.

28. Select **Networking** and click **Shared network (NAT)** next to Adapter 1.

29. Select **Hardware Virtualization** to enable it and then check **Enable hardware assisted virtualization** if it is available on your computer.

30. Click **OK**.

31. Leave Virtual PC 2007 open for the next activity.

Installing Windows 7

Installing Windows 7 on a virtual machine is not fundamentally different from installing on a physical machine. Perform the following steps to install the Windows 7 virtual machine, which ensures that your virtual environment corresponds to the environment used throughout the text.

1. If necessary, log on to your host PC with **Admin01** and a password of **P@ssw0rd**.

2. If necessary, click **Start**, click **All Programs**, and click **Microsoft Virtual PC** to open the Virtual PC console.

3. Double-click the Windows 7 virtual machine.

To free the mouse pointer from the virtual machine window, press the right Alt key.

4. Click within the Windows 7 Virtual Machine window.

Do not install the 64-bit version of Windows 7; it does not have the DOS Edit text editor that is required for various activities in Chapter 8.

5. To get to the DVD or the image that contains your guest operating system, insert the Windows 7 32-bit DVD in the DVD/CD drive. Click the **CD** menu, and then click **Use Physical Drive D:**.

6. Verify and correct the language and other settings as needed, and then click **Next**.

7. To continue with the installation of Windows 7, click the **Install now** button.

8. Wait for the Setup program to start.

9. When the license terms appear, click **I accept the license terms**, and then click **Next**.

10. When asked to select the type of installation you want, click **Custom (advanced)**, click **Disk 0 Unallocated Space**, and then click **Next**.

11. Wait for the files to be copied and expanded.

12. When prompted to choose a user name for your account, type **Admin01** in the "Type a user name" text box, type **Windows7** in the "Type a computer name" text box, and then click **Next**.

13. When the account password dialog box appears, type **P@ssw0rd** in the "Type a password (recommended)" text box, press **Tab**, type **P@ssw0rd** in the Retype your password text box, type **It's a Microsoft password** in the "Type a password hint (required)" text box, and then click **Next**.

14. Get the product key provided by your instructor, type the number in the product key text box, and then click **Next**.

15. When prompted to help protect your computer and improve Windows automatically, click **Install important updates only**.

16. When the time and date settings appear, click the **Time zone** arrow, scroll and click your time zone, click and change the time as required, and then click **Next**.

17. When prompted to select your computer's current location, click **Work network**.

18. Wait for Windows to prepare your desktop.

19. Wait for the installation to finish.

20. To release the Windows 7 DVD, press the **right Alt** key, click the **CD** menu, and then click **Release CD**.

21. Wait for any Windows updates to be installed.

Installing the Virtual PC 2007 Virtual Machine Additions and Completing Windows 7 Configuration

Next, you install the Virtual PC 2007 Virtual Machine Additions, which is special software for Windows virtual machines that improves performance and makes integration much more seamless.

Also, you will prepare the two hard disks (Disk1 and Disk2) for use in the text activities by partitioning and formatting them. As part of disk creation, you will download a set of script files to Disk1.

You will configure the network protocol, and then you will go to *www.textpad.com* and download a trial version of the TextPad text editor.

Next, you will create the User01 Standard user account, which is used by some activities in the text. It is not a good practice to use the Administrator accounts for day-to-day computer activities.

You will create the proper Virtual PC 2007 settings so that you can repeat the lab activities, because the changes will be discarded every time you start your virtual machines.

Perform the following steps to configure the Windows 7 virtual machine, which ensures that your virtual environment corresponds to the environment used throughout the text.

1. Log on with the **Admin01** account and a password of **P@ssw0rd**.

2. Click the **right Alt** key.

3. To start installing the Virtual PC 2007 Virtual Machine Additions, click the **Action** menu, and then click **Install or Update Virtual Machine Additions**.

4. Click **Continue**.

B

5. If the CD/DVD Drive window appears, click **Run Setup** to run the setup from your Windows 7 CD/DVD.

6. Wait for the setup to complete, click **Finish**, and click **Yes** to restart.

7. Log on with the **Admin01** account and a password of **P@ssw0rd**.

8. To start Disk Management, click **Start**, click **Control Panel**, click the **System and Security** link, and then click the **Create and format hard disk partitions** link under Administrative Tools.

9. When the Initialize Disk dialog box appears, review the settings and then click **OK**.

In the following steps, you will create disk volumes for future activities. For other future activities, you will need unallocated space on these two disks. It is important that you do not create the volume over the entire disk.

10. To create and format an NTFS volume, scroll the bottom pane until Disk 1 appears, right-click in the **2.00 GB Unallocated** box, click **New Simple Volume**, and click **Next**. Type **1024** over the 2045 in the "Simple volume size MB" spinner box, and click **Next** twice. Type **NTFS** over "New Volume" in the Volume label box, click **Next**, and then click **Finish**.

11. Wait for the E: drive to be formatted.

12. To create and format a FAT32 volume, scroll the bottom pane until Disk 2 appears, right-click in the **2.00 GB Unallocated** box, click **New Simple Volume**, and click **Next**. Type **1024** over the 2045 in the "Simple volume size MB" spinner box, and click **Next**. Click **File system** under the "Format this volume with the following settings" arrow, click **FAT32**, type **FAT32** over "New Volume" in the Volume label box, click **Next**, and then click **Finish**.

13. Wait for the F: drive to be formatted.

14. Close all open windows in the Windows 7 virtual machine.

15. To configure the Internet Protocol, click **Start**, click **Control Panel**, and click **Network and Internet**. Click **View Network Status and Tasks**, click **Change Adapter Settings**, right-click **Local Area Connection**, and click **Properties**. Clear the **Internet Protocol Version 6 (TCP/IPv6)** check box, click **Internet Protocol Version 4 (TCP/IPv4)**, and click **Properties**. Click **Use the following DNS server addresses**, type **192.168.131.254** in the Preferred DNS server text box, click **OK**, and then click **Close**.

16. To open User accounts management, click **Start**, click **Control Panel**, and then click **Add or Remove user accounts** under User Accounts and Family Safety.

17. To create a user account, click the **Create a new account** link, type **User01** over "New account name," retain the **Standard user** option, and then click the **Create Account** button.

18. To set the password, click **User01**, click the **Create a password** link, type **Secret1** over "New password," and press **Tab**. Type **Secret1** over "Confirm new password," type **It's one Secret** over "Type a password hint," and then click **Create password**.

19. Close the User accounts window.

20. To access this book's text on the Cengage Learning Web site, click the **Internet Explorer** icon on the taskbar, type **www.cengage.com** in the Address bar, and press **Enter**. Click the **Higher Education** link on the left, scroll down and click the **Course Technology** link under "Browse by Publisher," type **carswell** over "Enter author, title, ISBN, or keyword," and click **Search**.

21. To download the student data files, click **Guide to Parallel Operating Systems with Windows 7 and Linux, 2nd Edition**, click **Instructor Companion Site**, click the **Data Files for Students (Windows)** link on the left, click the entry after Download Now, and click **Run** twice. Click **Browse**, click **NTFS (E:)**, click **OK**, click **Unzip**, click **OK**, and then click **Close**.

22. To move the files to a folder in the path of executables, double-click **NTFS (E:)**, click **MakeABC**, hold down the **Shift** key, and click **MakeQUOTE**. Right-click in the highlighted area, click **Cut**, expand **Computer**, and double-click **Local Disk (C:)**. Right-click **Windows**, click **Paste**, click **Continue**, type **P@ssw0rd**, and then click **Yes**.

23. To access the TextPad text editor, click the **Internet Explorer** icon on the taskbar, type **www.textpad.com** in the Address bar, and press **Enter**.

24. To start the download, click the **Download** button, click the **TextPad Downloads** link, and then click the **FTP (USA)** link.

25. When the File Download – Security Warning appears, click **Save**.

26. When the Save As dialog box appears, click **Save**.

27. Wait for the download to complete, and then click **Run**.

28. When the Internet Explorer – Security Warning appears, click **Run**.

29. Wait for the installation to start and then click **Next**.

30. Click **I accept the terms in the license agreement**, click **Next** to move through the next three windows, and then click **Install**.

31. When the User Account Control dialog box appears, click **Yes**.

32. Wait for the installation to complete and then click **Finish**.

33. Close any open windows.

34. To open TextPad, click **Start**, point to **All Programs**, and then click **TextPad**.

35. To close the Tip of the Day, click Close.

36. To close the clip library, click the **X** on the Clip Library pane.

37. To close the search results, click the **X** on the Search Results pane.

38. To force Windows 7 updates to be installed, click **Start**, click **Control Panel**, click **Review your computer's status** under System and Security, click **Windows Update**, and then click **Check for updates**.

39. Wait for a response from Windows Update, and then click **Install updates**.

40. Click the **I accept the license terms** option button, and then click **Finish**.

41. Wait for the updates to install and then click the **Restart** button.

42. Click **Start** and then click **Shut down**.

43. Wait for any updates to be installed and then click **Restart now**.

44. Wait for the remaining updates to be installed.

45. Log on with the **User01** account and a password of **Secret1**.

46. Wait for the desktop to be prepared.

47. Click **Action** on the CLI menu toolbar, click **Close**, select **Shut down Windows 7 and save changes**, check **Commit changes to the virtual hard disk**, and click **OK**.

 The next steps must be completed through Virtual PC 2007. After these steps are completed, all changes to the Windows 7 virtual operating environment will be discarded each time Windows 7 starts. This includes all Virtual PC 2007 virtual disks (Hard Disk 1, Hard Disk 2, and Hard Disk 3).

48. Click **Start**, click the **Documents** menu, click the **My Virtual Machines** directory, and click **Windows 7**. You should see the Windows 7 virtual machine file, the Windows 7 HardDisk1 file, and the Windows 7 HardDisk2 file.

49. Hold down the **Ctrl** key and select *only* the Virtual Machine Hard Drive Image files. The Windows image files are Windows 7 HardDisk1 and Windows 7 HardDisk2.

50. Right-click the selected files, select **Properties** from the shortcut menu, and check **Read-only**.

51. Click **Start**, click **All Programs**, and click **Microsoft Virtual PC** to open the Virtual PC console.

52. Click the Windows 7 virtual machine and click **Settings**.

53. Select **Undo Disks** and check **Enable undo disks**.

54. Click **Close**, select **Automatically close without a message**, select **Turn off and delete changes**, and click **OK**.

Creating a Second Virtual Machine for Fedora 13

Here is a brief overview of the tasks required to create a virtual machine for Fedora 13:

1. Start Virtual PC.

2. Create the Fedora 13 virtual machine, which will use sda.

3. Create two virtual disks (sdb and sdc) for future lab activities.

4. Connect the network adapter to the virtual machine.

Complete the following steps to create the virtual machine:

1. If necessary, log on to your host PC with **Admin01** and a password of **P@ssw0rd**.

2. If necessary, click **Start**, click **All Programs**, and click **Microsoft Virtual PC** to open the Virtual PC console.

3. Click **New** to start the New Virtual Machine Wizard, and click **Next**.

4. Select **Create a Virtual Machine**, and then click **Next**.

5. Name the machine **Fedora 13** and click **Next**. Note that the default location is Libraries\Documents\My Virtual Machines\Fedora 13.

6. Choose **Other** from the Operating System menu, and click **Next**.

7. Select **Adjusting the RAM**, enter **1024** MB, and click **Next**.

8. Select **A new virtual hard disk**, click **Next**, click **Next**, and click **Finish**. A Fedora 13 virtual machine entry appears in the Virtual PC console.

9. Click the Fedora 13 virtual machine and click **Settings**.

10. To create the first virtual hard disk (sdb) for future lab activities, click **Hard Disk 2**, click the **Virtual Disk Wizard** button, and click **Next**.

11. Click **Create a new virtual disk**, and then click **Next**.

12. Click **A virtual hard disk**, and click **Next**.

13. Click the **Browse** button, click **Libraries**, click **Documents**, click **My Virtual Machines**, and click **Fedora 13**. You should see the new Fedora 13 virtual machine file you just created.

14. Type **Fedora 13 HardDisk1** in the File name text box, click **Save**, and click **Next**.

15. Select **Fixed size** and click **Next**.

16. Enter **2048** as the Virtual hard disk size, click **Next**, and click **Finish**.

17. Wait for the Virtual Hard Disk Wizard to finish successfully and click **Close**.

18. Click the **Virtual hard disk file** option button, click the **Browse** button, select the **Fedora 13 Hard Disk1** file, and click **Open**.

19. To create the second virtual hard disk (sdc) for future lab activities, click **Hard Disk 3**, click the **Virtual Disk Wizard** button, and click **Next**.

20. Click **Create a new virtual disk**, and click **Next**.

21. Click **A virtual hard disk**, and click **Next**.

22. Click the **Browse** button, click **Libraries**, click **Documents**, click **My Virtual Machines**, and click **Fedora 13**. You should see both the Fedora 13 virtual machine file and the Fedora 13 HardDisk1 file you just created.

23. Type **Fedora 13 HardDisk2** in the File name text box, click **Save**, and then click **Next**.

24. Select **Fixed size** and click **Next**.

25. Enter **2048** as the Virtual hard disk size, click **Next**, and click **Finish**.

26. Wait for the Virtual Hard Disk Wizard to finish successfully and click **Close**.

27. Click the **Virtual hard disk file** option button, click the **Browse** button, select the **Fedora 13 Hard Disk2** file, and click **Open**.

28. Select **Undo Disk** and check **Enable undo disks**.

29. Select **Networking** and click **Shared network (NAT)** next to Adapter 1.

30. Select **Hardware Virtualization** to enable it and check **Enable hardware assisted virtualization** if it is available on your computer.

31. Click **OK**.

32. Leave Virtual PC 2007 open for the next activity.

Installing Fedora 13

Installing Fedora 13 on a virtual machine is not fundamentally different from installing on a physical machine. Perform the following steps to install the Fedora 13 machine, which ensures that your virtual environment corresponds to the environment used throughout the text.

1. If necessary, log on to your host PC with **Admin01** and a password of **P@ssw0rd**.

2. If necessary, click **Start,** click **All Programs,** and click **Microsoft Virtual PC** to open the Virtual PC console.

3. Double-click the Fedora 13 virtual machine.

 To free the mouse pointer from the virtual machine window, press the right Alt key.

4. Click within the Fedora 13 Virtual Machine window.

5. Insert the Fedora 13 32-bit DVD in the DVD/CD drive. Click the **CD** menu, and then select **Use Physical Drive D:.**

6. When the Welcome to Fedora 13 window appears, press **Enter.**

7. When the Disk Found window appears, press **Tab,** and then press **Enter.**

8. When the Fedora splash screen appears, click **Next.**

9. When asked to select a language, scroll and click an appropriate language, and then click **Next.**

10. When asked to select a keyboard, scroll and click an appropriate keyboard, and then click **Next.**

11. When asked what type of devices your installation will involve, click **Next.**

12. Select the drives where you want to install the operating system, as well as any drives you want to mount to your system automatically, and then click **Next.**

13. When the drive initialization warning appears, click **Re-initialize.**

14. When prompted to name the computer, type **Fedora13**, and then click **Next.**

15. When the time zone request appears, click **America/Chicago**, scroll and select an appropriate time zone, and then click **Next.**

16. When requested to supply the root password, type **P@ssw0rd**, press **Tab,** type **P@ssw0rd**, and then click **Next.**

17. When the Weak Password message appears, click **Use Anyway.**

18. When asked which type of installation you want, click **Next.**

19. When the "Writing storage configuration to disk" window appears, click **Write changes to disk.**

20. Wait for the file systems to be created.

21. Review the package choices for the installation, and then click **Next**.

22. Wait for the installation to start and install selected packages.

23. When the congratulations splash screen appears, press the **right Alt** key, click the **CD** menu, and then click either **Release CD**.

24. Click in the Fedora 13 Virtual Machine window, and then click **Reboot**.

25. When the Welcome splash screen appears, click **Forward**.

26. Read the license information, and then click **Forward**.

27. To create a user, type **User01** in the Username text box, type **Parallel OS Student** in the Full Name text box, type **Secret1** in the Password text box, type **Secret1** in the Confirm Password text box, and then click **Forward**.

28. When the Weak Password message appears, click **Yes**.

29. Verify the date and time, correct them as needed, and then click **Forward**.

30. When the Hardware Profile summary appears, click **Finish** and then click **No, do not send**.

31. Log on to Fedora 13 as **Parallel OS Student** with a password of **Secret1**.

32. Click **Action** on the CLI menu toolbar, click **Close**, select **Turn off and save changes**, check **Commit changes to the virtual hard disk**, and click **OK**.

Completing Fedora 13 Configuration

Perform the following steps to finish configuring the Fedora 13 virtual machine, which ensures that your virtual environment corresponds to the environment used throughout the text. You will prepare the two hard disks (sdb and sdc) for use in the text activities by partitioning and formatting them. You also will configure the proper Virtual PC 2007 settings so that you can repeat the lab activities, because the changes will be discarded every time you start your virtual machines.

1. If necessary, log on to your host PC with **Admin01** and a password of **P@ssw0rd**.

2. If necessary, click **Start**, click **All Programs**, and click **Microsoft Virtual PC** to open the Virtual PC console.

3. Double-click the Fedora 13 virtual machine.

4. Log on to Fedora 13 as **Parallel OS Student** with a password of **Secret1**.

5. Click the **Network** icon on the menu bar, and click **System eth0**.

6. Wait for the connection to finish.

7. To open a Terminal session, click **Applications**, point to **System Tools**, and then click **Terminal**.

8. Type **su –** and press **Enter**.

9. Type **P@ssw0rd** and press **Enter**.

10. To obtain an IP address, type **dhclient –v eth0** and press **Enter**.

11. To start the search for the system configuration display, type **yum search system-config-display** and press **Enter**.

12. Wait for the search to finish.

13. To install the system configuration display, type **yum install system-config-display.i686** and press **Enter**.

14. When prompted to confirm that the changes are OK, press **y** and press **Enter**.

15. If you are prompted to confirm the changes again, press **y** and press **Enter**.

16. To modify the monitor type, type **system-config-display** and press **Enter**, click the **Hardware** tab, and click **Configure** for Monitor Type. Expand **Generic LCD Display**, click **LCD Panel 1024x768**, click **OK**, click **Settings**, click the **Resolution** chevron, click **1024x768**, and then click **OK** twice.

17. Close the Terminal window.

18. To restart the system, click **System**, click **Shut Down**, and then click **Restart**.

19. Log on to Fedora 13 as **Parallel OS Student** with a password of **Secret1**.

20. To reset the resolution, click **System**, click **Preferences**, and click **Monitors**. Click the **Resolution** chevron, click **1024 x 768**, click **Apply**, click **Keep This configuration**, and then click **Close**.

21. To open the Ethernet Device dialog box, click **System**, point to **Preferences**, and click **Network Connections**. Select the **Wired** tab, and click **System etho**. Click the **Edit** button and click **IPv4 Settings**. Select **Automatic (DHCP) addresses only**, type **192.168.131.254** in the **DNS servers** text box, and click **Apply**.

22. Enter **P@ssw0rd**, click **Authenticate**, and click **Close**.

23. To restart the system, click **System**, click **Shut Down**, and then click **Restart**.

24. Log on to Fedora 13 as **Parallel OS Student** with a password of **Secret1**.

25. To open a Terminal session, click **Applications**, point to **System Tools**, and then click **Terminal**.

26. Type **su –** and press **Enter**.

27. Type **P@ssw0rd** and press **Enter**.

28. Type **yum search hardinfo** and press **Enter**.

29. Wait for the search to finish.

30. Wait for the download to finish.

31. Type **yum install hardinfo.i686**, and press **Enter**.

32. When prompted to confirm that the changes are OK, press **y** and press **Enter**.

33. Repeat Steps 28 through 32 for **system-config-network, system-config-samba, system-config-printer**, and **system-config-lvm**.

Continue the configuration by preparing the two hard disks created earlier in Virtual PC 2007 (sdb and sdc) for use in the text activities by partitioning and formatting them.

34. To start partitioning the sdb disk, type **fdisk /dev/sdb** and press **Enter**.

35. Ignore the warning message.

36. To create the first primary partition on sdb, type **n** and press **Enter**, type **p** and press **Enter**, type **1** and press **Enter**, type **1** and press **Enter**, and then type **+1G** and press **Enter**.

37. To review the partition and write to the partition table, type **p** and press **Enter**, then type **w** and press **Enter**.

38. To format the partition as Ext2, type **mkfs /dev/sdb1** and press **Enter**.

39. To label the partition, type **e2label /dev/sdb1 Ext2** and press **Enter**.

40. To start partitioning the sdc disk, type **fdisk /dev/sdc** and press **Enter**.

41. Ignore the warning message.

42. To create the first primary partition on sdc, type **n** and press **Enter**, type **p** and press **Enter**, type **1** and press **Enter**, type **1** and press **Enter**, and then type **+1G** and press **Enter**.

43. To review the partition and write to the partition table, type **p** and press **Enter**, then type **w** and press **Enter**.

44. To format the partition, type **mkfs –t vfat /dev/sdc1** and press **Enter**.

45. To position to the /mnt directory, type **cd /mnt** and press **Enter**.

46. To make the directory for sdb1, type **mkdir sdb1** and press **Enter**.

47. To mount the sdb1 partition, type **mount ./dev/sdb1 –t ext2 /mnt/sdb1** and press **Enter**. (The command runs without the period.)

48. To make the directory for sdc1, type **mkdir sdc1** and press **Enter**.

49. To mount the sdc1 partition, type **mount ./dev/sdc1 –t vfat /mnt/sdc1** and press **Enter**. (The command runs without the period.)

50. To return to the root folder, type **cd ..** and press **Enter**.

51. To open the /etc/fstab file for editing, type **nano /etc/fstab** and press **Enter**.

52. Use the arrow key to move down to a new line.

53. To add the mount line for sdb1, type **/dev/sdb1 /mnt/sdb1 ext2 defaults 0 0** and press **Enter**.

54. To add the mount line for sdc1, type **/dev/sdc1 /mnt/sdc1 vfat defaults,dmask=000, fmask=111 0 0** and press **Enter**.

55. To write the file to disk, press **Ctrl+O** and then press **Enter**.

56. To exit nano, press **Ctrl+X**.

57. To remount the devices, type **mount –a** and press **Enter**.

58. To verify that the mount worked, double-click **Computer**, double-click **Filesystem**, double-click **mnt**, verify that the sdb1 and sdc1 folders appear, and then close the open windows.

59. To access this book's text on the Cengage Learning Web site, click the **Mozilla Firefox** icon on the taskbar, type **www.cengage.com** in the Address bar, and press **Enter**. Click the **Higher Education** link on the left, scroll down and click the **Course Technology** link under "Browse by Publisher," type **carswell** over "Enter author, title, ISBN, or keyword," and click **Search**.

60. To download the student data files, click **Guide to Parallel Operating Systems with Windows 7 and Linux, 2ⁿᵈ Edition**, click **Instructor Companion Site**, and click the **Data Files for Students (FedoraFiles)** link on the left. Choose the **Save File** option, and

then click **OK**. When the download is complete, right-click the **tar.gz** file, click **Open Containing Folder**, and verify that the file was downloaded into the Downloads directory.

61. Open a terminal, type **cd Downloads**, and then press **Enter**. Type **su** and press **Enter**. Enter the **root** password and press **Enter**. To decompress the file to the /usr/local/bin/ directory, type **tar –zxvf makes.tar.gz –C /usr/local/bin/**.

62. **Type cd /usr/local/bin/** and press **Enter**. Type **chmod 555 [mM]ake[dAHQ]*** and press **Enter**.

63. Click **Action** on the CLI menu toolbar, click **Close**, select **Shut down and save changes**, check **Commit changes to the virtual hard disk**, and click **OK**.

The next steps must be completed through Virtual PC 2007. After these steps are completed, all changes to the Fedora 13 virtual operating environment will be discarded each time Fedora 13 starts. This includes all Virtual PC 2007 virtual disks (Hard Disk 1, Hard Disk 2, and Hard Disk 3).

64. Click **Start**, click the **Documents** menu, click the **My Virtual Machines** directory, and click **Fedora 13**. You should see the Fedora 13 virtual machine file, the Fedora 13 HardDisk1 file, and the Fedora 13 HardDisk2 file.

65. Hold down the **Ctrl** key and select *only* the Virtual Machine Hard Drive Image files. Do not select the Fedora 13 Virtual Machine Settings file. The Fedora image files are Fedora 13 HardDisk1 and Fedora 13 HardDisk2.

66. Select **Properties** on the shortcut menu, and check **Read-only**.

67. Click **Start**, click **All Programs**, and click **Microsoft Virtual PC** to open the Virtual PC console.

68. Click the Fedora 13 virtual machine and click **Settings**.

69. Select **Undo Disks** and check **Enable undo disks**.

70. Click **Close**, click **Automatically close without a message**, select **Turn off and delete changes**, and click **OK**.

Working with VirtualBox

Getting Started with VirtualBox

Oracle VirtualBox is an x86 virtualization software package that was originally created by the German software company innotek GmbH. VirtualBox was purchased by Sun Microsystems and is now developed by Oracle Corporation as part of its family of virtualization products. It is installed on an existing host operating system; within this application, additional guest operating systems can be loaded and run, each with its own virtual environment.

VirtualBox includes the following features:

- The full VirtualBox package comes under a proprietary Personal Use and Evaluation License (PUEL), which allows use of the software free of charge for personal and educational purposes and for product evaluation.

- Several guest operating systems can be loaded. Each can be started, paused, and stopped independently. The host operating system and guest operating systems can communicate with each other through a common clipboard or using the network facility provided, as can guest operating systems if more than one is running.

- VirtualBox supports Intel's hardware virtualization VT-x and AMD's AMD-V.

- Hard disks are emulated in a disk image format—a VirtualBox-specific container format called Virtual Disk Image (VDI), which is stored as files with a .vdi extension on the host operating system.

- Both ISO images and host-connected physical devices can be mounted as CD/DVD drives. For example, the DVD image of a Linux distribution can be downloaded and used directly by VirtualBox.

- By default, VirtualBox provides graphics support through a custom virtual graphics card that is VESA compatible. The Guest Additions for Windows and Linux come with a special video driver that allows for better performance and features such as dynamic adjustment of the guest resolution when the VM window is resized.

- When used with an Ethernet network adapter, VirtualBox virtualizes a variety of network interface cards.

- When used with a sound card, VirtualBox virtualizes an Intel ICH AC'97 device or a SoundBlaster 16 card.

Configuring the Host Computer

To enable the two virtual machines to communicate with the Internet and with each other, you will install Internet Connection Sharing (ICS). First, you connect the existing network adapter in your Host01 computer to the Internet. Next, you install a second network adapter—the Microsoft Loopback adapter—which has a separate connection to the virtual machines. You will enable ICS on the Internet connection to share the Internet with the Microsoft Loopback adapter.

To enable future activities, you will share and populate the TextShare folder with files from the Cengage Learning Web site. In addition, you will set up a shared generic printer.

Complete the following steps to prepare the Windows 7 host computer to support the virtual environment.

1. Log on to your host PC with **Admin01** and a password of **P@ssw0rd**.

2. To open the Add Hardware dialog box, click **Start**, click **Control Panel**, click the **View by** chevron, click **Small icons**, and then click **Device Manager**.

3. Right-click **Host01** and click **Add legacy hardware**.

4. Click **Next**, click **Install the hardware that I manually select from a list (Advanced)**, and then click **Next**.

5. Scroll through the Common hardware types, click **Network adapters**, and then click **Next**.

6. Click **Microsoft** under Manufacturer, scroll through the Network Adapter list, click **Microsoft Loopback Adapter**, and then click **Next**.

7. To install the Microsoft Loopback Adapter, click **Next**.

8. Wait for the installation to complete, and then click **Finish**.

9. In the Control Panel, click **Network and Sharing Center** to display it.

10. To display the Local Area Connection Properties dialog box, click **Change adapter settings**, right-click the **Local Area Connection** entry (do not use Local Area Connection 2), and then click **Properties**.

11. To enable Internet Connection Sharing (ICS), click the **Sharing** tab, click the **Allow other network users to connect through this computer's Internet Connection** check box, click **OK**, and then close the Network Connections window.

12. If asked about the connection type, click **Work**, click **Next**, and then click **Close**.

13. Verify that the Internet Globe is blue/green, and is not grayed out. If it is, contact your instructor.

14. Close all open windows.

15. To share a printer on the Host01 computer, click **Start**, click **Control Panel**, click the **View by** chevron, and click **Small icons**. Click **Devices and Printers**, click **Add a printer**, click **Add a local printer**, and click **Next**. Scroll the Manufacturer list and click **Generic**, click **Generic/Text Only**, and click **Next** twice. Type **SharedPrinter** in the Printer name text box, click **Next** twice, and then click **Finish**.

16. To create the TextShare folder on the Host computer, click **Start**, click **Computer**, and double-click **Local Disk (C:)**. Note that your operating system drive might have a

different name. Right-click the white space in the right pane, point to **New**, and click **Folder**. Type **TextShare**, press **Enter**, right-click **TextShare**, click **Properties**, and click the **Sharing** tab. Click **Share**, type **Everyone**, click **Add**, click **Share**, click **Done**, and then click **Close**.

17. To access this book's text on the Cengage Learning Web site, click the **Internet Explorer** icon on the taskbar, type **www.cengage.com** in the Address bar, and press **Enter**. Click the **Higher Education** link on the left, scroll down and click the **Course Technology** link under "Browse by Publisher," type **carswell** over "Enter author, title, ISBN, or keyword," and click **Search**.

18. To download the student data files, click **Guide to Parallel Operating Systems with Windows 7 and Linux, 2nd Edition**, click **Instructor Companion Site**, click the **Data Files for Students (TextShareFiles)** link on the left, click the entry after Download Now, and click **Run** twice. Click **Browse**, click **Local Disk (C:)**, double-click **TextShare**, click **OK**, click **Unzip**, click **OK**, and then click **Close**.

Downloading VirtualBox

Complete the following steps to download the current version of VirtualBox from the Oracle Web site.

1. Log on to your host PC with **Admin01** and a password of **P@ssw0rd**.

2. To start Internet Explorer, click the **Internet Explorer** icon on the taskbar.

3. To locate the download Web site for VirtualBox, type **download virtualbox for windows** in the Internet Explorer search box, and then press **Enter**.

4. Click a **Downloads – VirtualBox** link, click **Download**, click the **x86/amd64** link after VirtualBox for Windows hosts, and then click **Save** twice.

5. Wait for the download to complete.

6. Leave the Download complete window open.

Installing VirtualBox

The installation of VirtualBox uses the Microsoft Software Installer. As a last simple task, you will configure Internet Connection Sharing (ICS) to permit virtual access to the Internet. Complete the following steps to install VirtualBox.

1. To start the Oracle VM VirtualBox Setup wizard, click **Run** twice.

2. Click **Next** three times, click **Yes**, and then click **Install**.

3. To install USB device support, click **Install**.

4. To install the Network Service, click **Install**.

5. To install the network adapters, click **Install** twice.

6. To exit the wizard, click **Finish**.

7. Close the Internet Explorer window.

8. To open the Network and Sharing Center, click **Start**, click **Control Panel**, and then click the **Network and Sharing Center** link.

9. To enable Internet Connection Sharing, click the **Local Area Connection** link, click **Properties**, clear the **Internet Protocol Version 6 (TCP/IPv6)** check box, click the **Sharing** tab, click the **Allow other network users to connect through this computer's Internet connection** check box, click **OK**, and then click **Close**.

10. Close the Network and Sharing Center window.

Installing Operating Systems in VirtualBox

In the following sections, you will create virtual machines, create virtual hard drives, and configure network adapters. When you finish, you will be ready to install a guest operating system. Recall that the virtual machines look like physical machines to the operating system installers.

Creating the First Virtual Machine for Windows 7

Here is a brief overview of the tasks required to create a virtual machine for Windows 7:

1. Start VirtualBox.

2. Create the Windows 7 virtual machine, which will use Disk0.

3. Create two virtual disks (Disk1 and Disk2) for future lab activities.

4. Connect the network adapter to the virtual machine.

Because each chapter in the text starts with Windows 7 activities first, you will create a virtual machine for Windows 7 first. Complete the following steps to create the first virtual machine:

1. If necessary, log on to your host PC with **Admin01** and a password of **P@ssw0rd**.

2. If necessary, double-click the **Oracle VM VirtualBox** icon on the desktop.

3. To start creating the Windows 7 virtual machine, click **New**, click **Next**, type **Windows 7 Virtual Machine** in the Name text box, click the **Version** arrow, scroll and click **Windows 7**, and then click **Next**.

4. To configure memory, type **1024** over the 512 in the MB text box, and then click **Next**.

5. Verify and accept the default settings in the Virtual Hard Disk dialog box, and then click **Next**.

6. To create the virtual hard disk for your virtual machine (Disk0), click **Next**, accept the default settings in the Hard Disk Storage Type dialog box, and then click **Next**.

7. Verify and accept the default settings for the virtual hard disk location and size, and then click **Next**.

8. Review the Summary window and then click **Finish** twice.

9. To create the second virtual hard disk (Disk1) for future lab activities, click **Storage**, click **SATA Controller**, and click the **Add Hard Disk** icon (the second green + icon). Click **Create new disk**, click **Next**, review the default settings in the Hard Disk Storage Type dialog box, and then click **Next**.

10. To specify the virtual hard disk location and settings, type **Windows 7 NewHardDisk1.vdi** over "NewHardDisk1.vdi," type **2 GB** over "20.00 GB," and then click **Next**.

11. Review the Summary window and then click **Finish**.

12. To create the third virtual hard disk (Disk2) for future lab activities, click **Storage**, click **SATA Controller**, and click the **Add Hard Disk** icon (the second green + icon). Click **Create new disk**, click **Next**, review the default settings in the Hard Disk Storage Type dialog box, and then click **Next**.

13. To specify the virtual hard disk location and settings, type **Windows 7 NewHardDisk2.vdi** over "NewHardDisk1.vdi," type **2 GB** over "20.00 GB," and then click **Next**.

14. Review the Summary window and then click **Finish**.

15. To enable a connection to the Internet, click the **Network** link, click the **Attached to** chevron, click **Bridged Adapter**, click the **Name** chevron, click **Microsoft Loopback adapter**, and then click **OK**.

16. Close the open windows.

17. Leave the machine logged on for the next activity.

Installing Windows 7

Installing Windows 7 on a virtual machine is not fundamentally different from installing it on a physical machine. Perform the following steps to install the Windows 7 virtual machine, which ensures that your virtual environment corresponds to the environment used throughout the text. To install Windows 7, you will need the 32-bit version of Windows 7. Also, you will need to ask your instructor for the product key.

1. If necessary, log on to your host PC with **Admin01** and a password of **P@ssw0rd**.

2. If necessary, double-click the **Oracle VM VirtualBox** icon on the desktop.

3. Insert the Windows 7 32-bit DVD in the DVD/CD drive.

Do not install the 64-bit version of Windows 7; it does not include the DOS Edit text editor that is required for various activities in Chapter 8.

4. To mount the DVD, click the **Storage** link, click **Empty** under IDE Controller, click the **CD/DVD Device** arrow, click **Host Drive 'D:'**, and then click **OK**.

5. To start the Windows 7 virtual machine, click the green **Start** arrow.

6. To show the Windows 7 virtual machine, click the green **Show** arrow.

7. Read the information about the Autocapture keyboard, click the **Do not show this message again** check box, and then click **OK**.

To free the mouse pointer from the virtual machine window, press the right Ctrl key.

8. Review the 32-bit color message, click the **Do not show this message again** check box, and then click **OK**.

9. Wait for the Windows 7 installation to start.

10. Review the information about mouse pointer integration, click the **Do not show this message again** check box, and then click **OK**.

11. Click within the Windows 7 Virtual Machine window.

12. Review the host key information, click the **Do not show this message again** check box, and then click **Capture**.

13. Verify and correct the language and other settings as needed, and then click **Next**.

14. To continue with the installation of Windows 7, click the **Install now** button.

15. Wait for the Setup program to start.

16. When the "Please read the license terms" dialog box appears, click the **I accept the license terms** check box, and then click **Next**.

17. When asked to select the type of installation you want, click **Custom (advanced)**, click **Disk 0 Unallocated Space**, and then click **Next**.

18. Wait for the files to be copied and expanded.

19. When prompted to choose a user name for your account, type **Admin01** in the "Type a user name" text box, type **Windows7** in the "Type a computer name" text box, and then click **Next**.

20. When the "Set a password for your account" dialog box appears, type **P@ssw0rd** in the "Type a password (recommended)" text box, press **Tab**, type **P@ssw0rd** in the Retype your password text box, press **Tab**, type **It's a Microsoft password** in the "Type a password hint (required)" text box, and then click **Next**.

21. Get the product key from your instructor, type the number in the product key text box, and then click **Next**.

22. When prompted to help protect your computer and improve Windows automatically, click **Install important updates only**.

23. When the time and date settings appear, click the **Time zone** arrow, scroll and click your time zone, click and change the time as required, and then click **Next**.

24. When prompted to select your computer's current location, click **Work network**.

25. Wait for Windows to prepare your desktop.

26. Wait for the Windows updates to be installed and then click the **Restart now** button.

27. Wait for the remaining Windows updates to be installed.

28. To unmount the Windows 7 DVD, press the **right Ctrl** key, click the **Devices** menu, click **CD/DVD Devices**, and then click **Unmount CD/DVD Device**.

Installing the VirtualBox Guest Additions and Completing Configuration

Next, you install the VirtualBox Guest Additions, which is special software for Windows and Linux virtual machines that improves performance and makes integration much more seamless. The Guest Additions include features such as mouse pointer integration and screen resizing.

Also, you will prepare the two hard disks (Disk1 and Disk2) for use in the text activities by partitioning and formatting them. As part of disk creation, you will download a set of script files to Disk1.

Next, you will go to *www.textpad.com* and download a trial version of the TextPad text editor, which you will use in Chapter 8.

Next, you will create the User01 Standard user account, which is used by some activities in the text. It is not a good practice to use the Administrator accounts for day-to-day computer activities.

Finally, you will configure your hard disks to be immutable, which means that you can repeat the lab activities because the changes will be discarded every time you start your virtual machines.

Perform the following steps to configure the Windows 7 virtual machine, which ensures that your virtual environment corresponds to the environment used throughout the text.

1. Log on with the **Admin01** account and a password of **P@ssw0rd**.
2. To start installing the Guest Additions, press the **right Ctrl** key, click the **Devices** menu, and then click **Install Guest Additions**.
3. When the Autoplay window appears, click in the Windows 7 Virtual Machine window, click **Run VBoxWindowsAdditions.exe**, click **Yes**, click **Next**, click **I Agree**, click **Next** twice, and then click **Install**.
4. When asked if you want to install this device software's display adapters, click **Install**.
5. When asked if you want to install this device software's system devices, click **Install**.
6. When the Completing the Oracle VM VirtualBox Guest Additions window appears, click **Finish**.
7. When the mouse pointer integration information appears, click the **Do not show this message again** check box and then click **OK**.
8. Log on with the **Admin01** account and a password of **P@ssw0rd**.
9. To start Disk Management, click **Start**, click **Control Panel**, click the **System and Security** link, and then click the **Create and format hard disk partitions** link under Administrative Tools.
10. When the Initialize Disk dialog box appears, review the settings and then click **OK**.

 In Steps 11 through 14, you will create disk volumes for future activities. For other future activities, you will need unallocated space on these two disks. It is important that you do not create the volume over the entire disk.

11. To create and format an NTFS volume, scroll the bottom pane until Disk 1 appears, right-click in the **2.00 GB Unallocated** box, click **New Simple Volume**, and click **Next**. Type **1024** over the 2045 in the "Simple volume size MB" spinner box, click **Next** twice, type **NTFS** over "New Volume" in the Volume label box, click **Next**, and then click **Finish**.
12. Wait for the E: drive to be formatted.

13. To create and format a FAT32 volume, scroll the bottom pane until Disk 2 appears, right-click in the **2.00 GB Unallocated** box, click **New Simple Volume,** and click **Next.** Type **1024** over the 2045 in the "Simple volume size MB" spinner box, click **Next,** click **File system** under the "Format this volume with the following settings" arrow, and click **FAT32.** Type **FAT32** over "New Volume" in the Volume label box, click **Next,** and then click **Finish.**

14. Wait for the F: drive to be formatted.

15. Close all open windows in the Windows 7 virtual machine.

16. To configure the Internet Protocol, click **Start,** click **Control Panel,** click **Network and Internet,** click **Network Status and Tasks,** and click **Change Adapter Settings.** Right-click **Local Area Connection,** click **Properties,** clear the **Internet Protocol Version 6 (TCP/IPv6)** check box, and click **Internet Protocol Version 4 (TCP/IPv4).** Click **Properties,** click **Use the following IP address,** type **192.168.0.10** in the IP address text box, and press **Tab** twice. Type **192.168.0.1** in the Default gateway text box, press **Tab,** type **192.168.0.1** in the Preferred DNS server text box, and click **OK.** When you finish, click **Close.**

17. To open the user accounts management window, click **Start,** click **Control Panel,** and then click **Add or Remove user accounts** under User Accounts and Family Safety.

18. To create a user account, click the **Create a new account** link, type User01 over "New account name," retain the **Standard user** option, and then click the **Create Account** button.

19. To set the password, click **User01,** click the **Create a password** link, and type Secret1 over "New password." Press **Tab,** type Secret1 over "Confirm new password," type **It's one Secret** over "Type a password hint," and then click **Create password.**

20. Close the User accounts window.

21. To access this book's text on the Cengage Learning Web site, click the **Internet Explorer** icon on the taskbar, type **www.cengage.com** in the Address bar, and press **Enter.** Click the **Higher Education** link on the left, scroll down and click the **Course Technology** link under "Browse by Publisher," type **carswell** over "Enter author, title, ISBN, or keyword," and click **Search.**

22. To download the student data files, click **Guide to Parallel Operating Systems with Windows 7 and Linux, 2ⁿᵈ Edition,** click **Instructor Companion Site,** click the **Data Files for Students (Windows)** link on the left, click the entry after Download Now, and click **Run** twice. Click **Browse,** click **NTFS (E:),** click **OK,** click **Unzip,** click **OK,** and then click **Close.**

23. To move the files to a folder in the path of executables, double-click **NTFS (E:),** click **MakeABC,** hold down the **Shift** key, and click **MakeQUOTE.** Right-click in the highlighted area, click **Cut,** expand **Computer,** double-click **Local Disk (C:),** right-click **Windows,** click **Paste,** click **Continue,** type **P@ssw0rd,** and then click **Yes.**

24. To access the TextPad text editor, click the **Internet Explorer** icon on the taskbar, type **www.textpad.com** in the Address bar, and press **Enter.**

25. To start the download, click the **Download** button, click the **TextPad Downloads** link, and then click the **FTP (USA)** link.

26. When the File Download – Security Warning appears, click **Save**.

27. When the Save As dialog box appears, click **Save**.

28. Wait for the download to complete, and then click **Run**.

29. When the Internet Explorer – Security Warning appears, click **Run**.

30. Wait for the installation to start and then click **Next**.

31. Click **I accept the terms in the license agreement**, click **Next**, click **Next** in each of the next two windows, and then click **Install**.

32. When the User Account Control dialog box appears, click **Yes**.

33. Wait for the installation to complete and then click **Finish**.

34. Close any open windows.

35. To open TextPad, click **Start**, point to **All Programs**, and then click **TextPad**.

36. To close the Tip of the Day, click **Close**.

37. To close the clip library, click the **X** on the Clip Library pane.

38. To close the search results, click the **X** on the Search Results pane.

39. To force updates to be installed, click **Start**, click **Control Panel**, click **Review your computer's status** under System and Security, click **Windows Update**, and then click **Check for updates**.

40. Wait for a response from Windows Update, and then click **Install updates**.

41. Click the **I accept the license terms** option button, and then click **Finish**.

42. Wait for the updates to install and then click the **Restart** button.

43. Click **Start** and then click **Shut down**.

44. Wait for any updates to be installed and then click **Restart now**.

45. Wait for the remaining updates to be installed.

46. Log on with the **User01** account and a password of **Secret1**.

47. Wait for the desktop to be prepared.

48. Close any open windows in the virtual machine.

49. To shut down the virtual machine, click **Start**, and then click the **Shut Down** button.

50. Wait a moment for the Windows 7 virtual machine to shut down completely.

NOTE Steps 51 through 67 must be completed from the Host01 computer. After these steps are completed, all changes to the Windows 7 operating environment will be discarded each time the Windows 7 virtual machine starts. This includes all virtual disks (Disk 0, Disk 1, and Disk 2).

51. To open the Storage link and disconnect the virtual drives, click the **Windows 7 virtual machine** entry, click **Settings**, and click **Storage**. Click **Windows 7 Virtual Machine.vdi**, click the **–disk** icon, click **Windows 7 NewHardDisk1.vdi**, click the **–disk** icon, click **Windows 7 NewHardDisk2.vdi**, click the **–disk** icon, and then click **OK**.

52. Close the Oracle VM VirtualBox window.

53. To open a Command Prompt window, click **Start**, point to **All Programs**, click **Accessories**, and then click **Command Prompt**.

54. To change to the VirtualBox folder, type **cd ** and press **Enter**, type **cd program files** and press **Enter**, type **cd Oracle** and press **Enter**, then type **cd Virtualbox** and press **Enter**.

55. To mark the Disk0 virtual hard drive as immutable, type **vboxmanage modifyhd** **"Windows 7 Virtual Machine.vdi" -type immutable**, and then press **Enter**.

56. To mark the Disk1 virtual hard drive as immutable, type **vboxmanage modifyhd** **"Windows 7 NewHardDisk1.vdi" -type immutable**, and then press **Enter**.

57. To mark the Disk2 virtual hard drive as immutable, type **vboxmanage modifyhd** **"Windows 7 NewHardDisk2.vdi" -type immutable**, and then press **Enter**.

58. Type **exit** and then press **Enter**.

59. To start the VirtualBox console, double-click the **Oracle VM VirtualBox** icon on the desktop.

60. To reconnect the Windows 7 NewHardDisk1.vdi file, click the **Storage** link, click **SATA Controller**, and click the **+disk** icon. Click the **Slot** arrow, click **SATA Port 1**, and then click **OK**.

61. To reconnect the Windows 7 NewHardDisk2.vdi file, click the **Storage** link, click **SATA Controller**, and click the **+disk** icon. Click the **Slot** arrow, click **SATA Port 2**, and then click **OK**.

If an entry appears more than once, right-click one of the duplicate entries and click Remove Attachment.

62. To reconnect the Windows 7 Virtual Machine.vdi file, click the **Storage** link, click **SATA Controller**, and click the **+disk** icon. Click the **Slot** arrow, click **SATA Port 0**, and then click **OK**.

63. Verify that the disks are in the following order: Windows 7 Virtual Machine.vdi, Windows 7 NewHardDisk1.vdi, and Windows 7 NewHardDisk2. Click **OK**.

64. To start the Windows 7 virtual machine, click the green **Start** arrow.

65. To show the Windows 7 virtual machine, click the green **Show** arrow.

All changes made to the virtual hard drives will be discarded when you start the Windows 7 virtual machine.

66. Log on with the **User01** account and a password of **Secret1**.

67. Continue with the lab activities in the text.

Creating a Second Virtual Machine for Fedora 13

Here is a brief overview of the tasks required to create a virtual machine for Fedora 13:

1. Start VirtualBox.
2. Create the Fedora 13 virtual machine, which will use sda.

3. Create two virtual disks (sdb and sdc) for future lab activities.

4. Connect the network adapter to the virtual machine.

Complete the following steps to create the second virtual machine for Fedora 13.

1. If necessary, log on to your host PC with **Admin01** and a password of **P@ssw0rd**.

2. If necessary, double-click the **Oracle VM VirtualBox** icon on the desktop.

3. To start creating the Fedora 13 virtual machine, click **New**, click **Next**, type **Fedora 13 Virtual Machine** in the Name text box, verify that the operating system is Linux and the version is Fedora, and then click **Next**.

4. To configure memory, type **1024** over the 512 in the MB text box, and then click **Next** twice.

5. Verify and accept the default settings in the Virtual Hard Disk dialog box, and then click **Next**.

6. To create the virtual hard disk for your virtual machine, click **Next**, accept the default settings in the Hard Disk Storage Type dialog box, and then click **Next**.

7. Verify and accept the default settings for the virtual hard disk location and size, and then click **Next** twice.

8. Review the Summary window and then click **Finish**.

9. To enable a connection to the Internet, scroll and click the **Network** link, click the **Attached to** chevron, click **Bridged Adapter**, click the **Name** chevron, click **Microsoft Loopback adapter**, and then click **OK**.

10. To create the second virtual hard disk (sdb) for future lab activities, click **Storage**, click **SATA Controller**, and click the **Add Hard Disk** icon (the second green + icon). Click **Create new disk**, click **Next**, review the default settings in the Hard Disk Storage Type dialog box, and then click **Next**.

11. To specify the virtual hard disk location and size settings, type **Fedora 13 NewHardDisk1.vdi** over "NewHardDisk1.vdi," type **2 GB** over "8.00 GB," and then click **Next**.

12. Review the Summary window and then click **Finish**.

13. To create the third virtual hard disk (sdc) for future lab activities, click **Storage**, click **SATA Controller**, and click the **Add Hard Disk** icon (the second green + icon). Click **Create new disk**, click **Next**, review the default settings in the Hard Disk Storage Type dialog box, and then click **Next**.

14. To specify the virtual hard disk location and size settings, type **Fedora 13 NewHardDisk2.vdi** over "NewHardDisk1.vdi," type **2 GB** over "8.00 GB," and then click **Next**.

15. Review the Summary window and then click **Finish**.

16. Leave the machine logged on for the next activity.

Installing Fedora 13

Installing Fedora 13 on a virtual machine is not fundamentally different from installing it on a physical machine. Perform the following steps to install the Fedora 13 machine, which ensures that your virtual environment corresponds to the environment used throughout the text.

1. If necessary, log on to your host PC with **Admin01** and a password of **P@ssw0rd**.

2. If necessary, double-click the **Oracle VM VirtualBox** icon on the desktop.

3. Insert the Fedora 13 DVD in the DVD/CD drive.

4. To mount the DVD, click the **Storage** link, click **Empty** under IDE Controller, click the **CD/DVD Device** arrow, click **Host Drive 'D:'**, and then click **OK**.

5. To start the Fedora 13 virtual machine, click the green **Start** arrow.

6. When the Welcome to Fedora 13 window appears, press **Enter**.

7. When the Disk Found window appears, press **Tab**, and then press **Enter**.

8. When the Fedora splash screen appears, click **Next**.

9. When asked to select a language, scroll and click an appropriate language, and then click **Next**.

10. When asked to select a keyboard, scroll and click an appropriate keyboard, and then click **Next**.

11. When asked in the next window what type of devices your installation will involve, click **Next**.

12. Select the drives where you want to install the operating system, as well as any drives you want to mount to your system automatically, and click **Next**.

13. When the drive initialization warning appears, click **Re-initialize**.

14. When prompted to name the computer, type **Fedora13**, and then click **Next**.

15. When the time zone request appears, click **America/Chicago**, scroll and select an appropriate time zone, and then click **Next**.

16. When requested to supply the root password, type **P@ssw0rd**, press **Tab**, type **P@ssw0rd**, and then click **Next**.

17. When the Weak Password message appears, click **Use Anyway**.

18. When asked which type of installation you would like, click **Next**.

19. When the "Writing storage configuration to disk" window appears, click **Write changes to disk**.

20. Wait for the file systems to be created.

21. Review the package choices for the installation, and then click **Next**.

22. Wait for the installation to start and install selected packages.

23. When the congratulations splash screen appears, press the **right Ctrl** key, click **Devices**, click **CD/DVD Devices**, click **Unmount CD/DVD device**, remove the Fedora 13 DVD, click in the Fedora 13 Virtual Machine window, and then click **Reboot**.

24. When the Welcome splash screen appears, click **Forward**.

25. Read the license information, and then click **Forward**.

26. To create a user, type **User01** in the Username text box, type **Parallel OS Student** in the Full Name text box, type **Secret1** in the Password text box, type **Secret1** in the Confirm Password text box, and then click **Forward**.

27. When the Weak Password message appears, click **Yes**.

28. Verify the date and time, correct them as needed, and then click **Forward**.

29. When the Hardware Profile summary appears, click **Finish** and then click **No, do not send**.

30. Log on to Fedora 13 as **Parallel OS Student** with a password of **Secret1**.

31. To shut down the Fedora 13 virtual machine, click **System**, click **Shut Down**, and then click **Shut Down** again.

Configuring Fedora 13

Next, you prepare the two hard disks (sdb and sdc) for use in the text activities by partitioning and formatting them. Also, you will install the VirtualBox Guest Additions, which is special software for Windows and Linux virtual machines that improves performance and makes integration much more seamless. The Guest Additions provide features such as mouse pointer integration and screen resizing.

Finally, you will configure your hard disks to be immutable, which means that you can repeat the lab activities because the changes will be discarded every time you start your virtual machines.

Perform the following steps to configure the Fedora 13 virtual machine, which ensures that your virtual environment corresponds to the environment used throughout the text.

1. If necessary, log on to your host PC with **Admin01** and a password of **P@ssw0rd**.

2. If necessary, double-click the **Oracle VM VirtualBox** icon on the desktop.

3. To attach the Fedora 13 NewHardDisk1 disk, click **Storage**, click **SATA Controller**, click the **+disk** icon, and verify that the **Fedora 13 NewHardDisk1.vdi** virtual drive was added. Click **Fedora 13 NewHardDisk1.vdi**. Click the **Hard Disk** arrow, click **SATA Port 1**, and then click **OK**.

4. To attach the Fedora 13 NewHardDisk2 disk, click **Storage**, click **SATA Controller**, click the **+disk** icon, and verify that the **Fedora 13 NewHardDisk2.vdi** virtual drive was added. Click **Fedora 13 NewHardDisk2.vdi**. Click the **Hard Disk** arrow, click **SATA Port 2**, and then click **OK**.

5. To start the Fedora 13 virtual machine, double-click the **Fedora 13 Virtual Machine** icon.

6. Log on to Fedora 13 as **Parallel OS Student** with a password of **Secret1**.

7. Click the **Network** icon on the menu bar, and click **System eth0**.

8. Wait for the connection to finish.

9. To open a Terminal session, click **Applications**, point to **System Tools**, and then click **Terminal**.

10. Type **su –** and press **Enter**.

11. Type **P@ssw0rd** and press **Enter**.

12. To obtain an IP address, type **dhclient –v eth0** and press **Enter**.

13. To start the search for the system configuration display, type **yum search system-config-display** and press **Enter**.

14. Wait for the search to finish.

15. To install the system configuration display, type **yum install system-config-display.i686** and press **Enter**.

16. When prompted to confirm that the changes are OK, press y and press **Enter**.

17. If you are prompted again, press y and press **Enter**.

18. To modify the monitor type, type **system-config-display** and press **Enter**, click the **Hardware** tab, click **Configure** for Monitor Type, and expand **Generic LCD Display**. Click **LCD Panel 1024x768**, click **OK**, click **Settings**, click the **Resolution** chevron, click **1024x768**, and then click **OK** twice.

19. Close the Terminal window.

20. To restart the system, click **System**, click **Shut Down**, and then click **Restart**.

21. Log on to Fedora 13 as **Parallel OS Student** with a password of **Secret1**.

22. To reset the resolution, click **System**, click **Preferences**, click **Monitors**, click the **Resolution** chevron, and click **1024 x 768**. Click **Apply**, click **Keep This configuration**, and then click **Close**.

23. To open the Ethernet Device dialog box, click **System**, point to **Administration**, click **Network**, type **P@ssw0rd**, click **OK**, and then click **Edit**.

24. To set the IP configuration, click **Activate device when computer starts**, and then click **Statically set IP addresses**. Type **192.168.0.11** in the Address text box, **255.255.255.0** in the Subnet mask text box, **192.168.0.1** in the Default gateway text box, and **192.168.0.1** in the Primary DNS text box. When you finish, click **OK**.

25. Close the configuration window.

26. To open a Terminal session, click **Applications**, point to **System Tools**, and then click **Terminal**.

27. Type **su –** and press **Enter**.

28. Type **P@ssw0rd** and press **Enter**.

29. Type **yum search hardinfo** and press **Enter**.

30. Wait for the search to finish.

31. Wait for the download to finish.

32. Type **yum install hardinfo.i686**, and press **Enter**.

33. When prompted to confirm that the changes are OK, press y and press **Enter**.

34. Repeat Steps 29 through 33 for **system-config-network**, **system-config-samba**, **system-config-printer**, and **system-config-lvm**.

35. To start partitioning the sdb disk, type **fdisk /dev/sdb** and press **Enter**.

36. Ignore the warning message.

37. To create the first primary partition on sdb, type **n** and press **Enter**, type **p** and press **Enter**, type **1** and press **Enter**, type **1** and press **Enter**, and then type **+1G** and press **Enter**.

38. To review the partition and write to the partition table, type **p** and press **Enter**, then type **w** and press **Enter**.

39. To format the partition as Ext2, type **mkfs /dev/sdb1** and press **Enter**.

40. To label the partition, type **e2label /dev/sdb1 Ext2** and press **Enter**.

41. To start partitioning the sdc disk, type **fdisk /dev/sdc** and press **Enter**.

42. Ignore the warning message.

43. To create the first primary partition on sdc, type **n** and press **Enter**, type **p** and press **Enter**, type **1** and press **Enter**, type **1** and press **Enter**, and then type **+1G** and press **Enter**.

44. To review the partition and write to the partition table, type **p** and press **Enter**, then type **w** and press **Enter**.

45. To format the partition, type **mkfs –t vfat /dev/sdc1** and press **Enter**.

46. To position to the /mnt directory, type **cd /mnt** and press **Enter**.

47. To make the directory for sdb1, type **mkdir sdb1** and press **Enter**.

48. To mount the sdb1 partition, type **mount ./dev/sdb1 –t ext2 /mnt/sdb1** and press **Enter**. (The command runs without the period.)

49. To make the directory for sdc1, type **mkdir sdc1** and press **Enter**.

50. To mount the sdc1 partition, type **mount ./dev/sdc1 –t vfat /mnt/sdc1** and press **Enter**. (The command runs without the period.)

51. To return to the root folder, type **cd ..** and press **Enter**.

52. To open the /etc/fstab file for editing, type **nano /etc/fstab** and press **Enter**.

53. Use the arrow key to move down to a new line.

54. To add the mount line for sdb1, type **/dev/sdb1 /mnt/sdb1 ext2 defaults 0 0** and press **Enter**.

55. To add the mount line for sdc1, type **/dev/sdc1 /mnt/sdc1 vfat defaults,dmask=000, fmask=111 0 0** and press **Enter**.

56. To write the file to disk, press **Ctrl+O** and then press **Enter**.

57. To exit nano, press **Ctrl+X**.

58. To remount the devices, type **mount –a** and press **Enter**.

59. To verify that the mount worked, double-click **Computer**, double-click **Filesystem**, double-click **mnt**, verify that the sdb1 and sdc1 folders appear, and then close the open windows.

60. To access this book's text on the Cengage Learning Web site, click the **Mozilla Firefox** icon on the taskbar, type **www.cengage.com** in the Address bar, and press **Enter**. Click the **Higher Education** link on the left, scroll down and click the **Course Technology** link under "Browse by Publisher," type **carswell** over "Enter author, title, ISBN, or keyword," and click **Search**.

61. To download the student data files, click **Guide to Parallel Operating Systems with Windows 7 and Linux, 2nd Edition**, click **Instructor Companion Site**, and click the **Data Files for Students (FedoraFiles)** link on the left. Choose the **Save File** option, and then click **OK**. When the download is complete, right-click the **tar.gz** file, click **Open Containing Folder**, and verify that the file was downloaded into the Downloads directory.

62. Open a terminal, type **cd Downloads**, and then press **Enter**. Type **su** and press **Enter**. Enter the **root** password and press **Enter**. To decompress the file to the /usr/local/bin/ directory, type **tar –zxvf makes.tar.gz –C /usr/local/bin/**.

63. Type **cd /usr/local/bin/** and press **Enter**. Type **chmod 555 [mM]ake[dAHQ]*** and press **Enter**.

64. To close the virtual machine, click **System**, click **Shut Down**, and then click **Shut Down**.

The following steps will set all of the virtual disks to discard any changes that students make. This will be helpful when multiple classes use the same computers. Steps 64 through 78 must be completed from the Host01 computer.

65. To open the Storage link and disconnect the virtual drives, click **Fedora 13 Virtual Machine.vdi**, click the **–disk** icon, click **Fedora 13 NewHardDisk1.vdi**, click the **–disk** icon, click **Fedora 13 NewHardDisk2.vdi**, click the **–disk** icon, and then click **OK**.

66. Close the Oracle VM VirtualBox window.

67. To open a Command Prompt window, click **Start**, point to **All Programs**, click **Accessories**, and then click **Command Prompt**.

68. To change to the VirtualBox folder, type **cd ** and press **Enter**, type **cd program files** and press **Enter**, type **cd Oracle** and press **Enter**, then type **cd Virtualbox** and press **Enter**.

69. Type **vboxmanage modifyhd "Fedora 13 Virtual Machine.vdi" -type immutable**, and then press **Enter**.

70. Type **vboxmanage modifyhd "Fedora 13 NewHardDisk1.vdi" -type immutable**, and then press **Enter**.

71. Type **vboxmanage modifyhd "Fedora 13 NewHardDisk2.vdi" -type immutable**, and then press **Enter**.

72. Type **exit** and then press **Enter**.

73. To start the VirtualBox console, double-click the **Oracle VM VirtualBox** icon on the desktop.

74. To reconnect the Fedora 13 NewHardDisk1.vdi file, click the **Storage** link, click **SATA Controller**, and click the **+disk** icon. Click **Fedora 13 NewHardDisk1.vdi**. Click the **Slot** arrow, click **SATA Port 1**, and then click **OK**.

75. To reconnect the Fedora 13 NewHardDisk2.vdi file, click the **Storage** link, click **SATA Controller**, and click the **+disk** icon. Click **Fedora 13 NewHardDisk2.vdi**. Click the **Slot** arrow, click **SATA Port 2**, and then click **OK**.

If an entry appears more than once, right-click one of the duplicate entries and click Remove Attachment.

76. To reconnect the Fedora 13 Virtual Machine.vdi file, click the **Storage** link, click **SATA Controller,** and click the **+disk** icon. Click the **Slot** arrow and click **SATA Port 0.** Click the **Hard Disk** arrow and click **Fedora 13 Virtual Machine.vdi.** Click **OK.**

77. Verify that the disks are in the following order: Fedora 13 Virtual Machine.vdi, Fedora 13 NewHardDisk1.vdi, and Fedora 13 NewHardDisk2. Then click **OK.**

78. To start the Fedora 13 virtual machine, click the green **Start** arrow.

79. To show the Fedora 13 virtual machine, click the green **Show** arrow.

All previous changes to the virtual hard drives will be discarded when you start the Fedora 13 virtual machine.

80. Log on to the Fedora 13 virtual machine with a password of **Secret1.**

81. Continue with the lab activities in the text.

Working with VMware

Getting Started with VMware

VMware is a company that provides x86 virtualization software. VMware Inc. is a subsidiary of EMC Corporation, and has its headquarters in Palo Alto, California. VMware Workstation, a virtual machine software suite for x86 and x86-64 computers, is made by VMware Inc. It is installed on an existing host operating system and allows the physical machine to run multiple operating systems simultaneously.

Note the following points about VMware:

- You need to have a license to use a VMware product. VMware offers full working versions of its software for evaluation purposes.
- You can load several guest operating systems. Each can be started, paused, and stopped independently. The host operating system and guest operating systems can communicate with each other through a common clipboard or using the network facility provided, as can guest operating systems if more than one is running.
- VMware virtual machines do not directly support FireWire.
- The Virtual Machine Disk (VMDK) file format, a type of virtual appliance, is used in VMware Workstation.
- You can mount both ISO images and host-connected physical devices as CD/DVD drives. For example, the DVD image of a Linux distribution can be downloaded and used directly by VMware.

Configuring the Host Computer

To enable the two virtual machines to communicate with the Internet and with each other, you will install Internet Connection Sharing (ICS). First, you connect the existing network adapter in your Host01 computer to the Internet. Next, you install a second network adapter—the Microsoft Loopback adapter—which has a separate connection to the virtual machines. You will enable ICS on the Internet connection to share the Internet with the Microsoft Loopback adapter.

To enable future activities, you will share and populate the TextShare folder with files from the Cengage Learning Web site. In addition, you will set up a shared generic printer.

Complete the following steps to prepare the Windows 7 host computer to support the virtual environment.

1. Log on to your host PC with **Admin01** and a password of **P@ssw0rd.**

2. To open the Add Hardware dialog box, click **Start,** click **Control Panel,** click the **View by** chevron, click **Small icons,** and then click **Device Manager.**

3. Right-click **Host01** and click **Add legacy hardware.**

4. Click **Next,** click **Install the hardware that I manually select from a list (Advanced),** and then click **Next.**

5. Scroll through the common hardware types, click **Network adapters,** and then click **Next.**

6. Click **Microsoft** under Manufacturer, scroll the Network Adapter list and click **Microsoft Loopback Adapter,** and then click **Next.**

7. To install the Microsoft Loopback adapter, click **Next.**

8. Wait for the installation to complete, and then click **Finish.**

9. To display the Network and Sharing Center, go back to the Control Panel and then click **Network and Sharing Center.**

10. To display the Local Area Connection Properties dialog box, click **Change adapter settings,** right-click the **Local Area Connection** entry (do not use Local Area Connection 2), and then click **Properties.**

11. To enable Internet Connection Sharing (ICS), click the **Sharing** tab, click **Allow other network users to connect through this computer's Internet Connection,** click **OK,** and then close the Network Connections window.

12. If asked about the connection type, click **Work,** click **Next,** and then click **Close.**

13. Close all open windows.

14. To share a printer on the Host01 computer, click **Start,** click **Control Panel,** click the **View by** chevron, and click **Small icons.** Click **Devices and Printers,** click **Add a printer,** and click **Add a local printer.** Select **Use an existing port** in the Choose a printer port window, click **Next,** scroll the Manufacturer list and click **Generic,** click **Generic/Text Only,** and click **Next** twice. Type **SharedPrinter** in the Printer name text box, click **Next** twice, uncheck **Set as default printer,** and then click **Finish.**

15. To create the TextShare folder on the Host computer, click **Start,** click **Computer,** and double-click **Local Disk (C:).** Note that your operating system drive might have a different name. Right-click the white space in the right pane, point to **New,** click **Folder,** type **TextShare,** and press **Enter.** Right-click **TextShare,** click **Properties,** click the **Sharing** tab, click **Share,** type **Everyone,** and click **Add.** Click **Share,** click **Yes, turn on network discovery and file sharing for all public networks** in the Network discovery and file sharing window, click **Done,** and then click **Close.**

16. To access this book's text on the Cengage Learning Web site, click the **Internet Explorer** icon on the taskbar, type **www.cengage.com** in the Address bar, and press **Enter.** Click the **Higher Education** link on the left, scroll down and click the **Course Technology** link under "Browse by Publisher," type **carswell** over "Enter author, title, ISBN, or keyword," and click **Search.**

17. To download the student data files, click **Guide to Parallel Operating Systems with Windows 7 and Linux, 2nd Edition**, click **Instructor Companion Site**, click the **Data Files for Students (TextShareFiles)** link on the left, click the entry after Download Now, and click **Run** twice. Click **Browse**, click **Local Disk (C:)**, double-click **TextShare**, click **OK**, click **Unzip**, click **OK**, and then click **Close**.

Downloading VMWare

Obtain a copy of VMware Workstation 7.1 with the appropriate license number.

Installing VMware

The installation of VMware uses the VMware Workstation Installer. Complete the following steps to install VMware.

1. To start the VMware Workstation Setup wizard, double-click **VMware-workstation-full-*x.x.x***. (The value *x.x.x* is the product version number.)

2. Click **Run**, click **Next**, click **Typical**, click **Next** four times to move through the windows, click **Continue**, enter the **License Key**, click **Enter**, and then click **Restart Now**.

3. After restarting the system, double-click the **VMware Workstation** icon on the desktop. Click **Yes, I accept the terms in the license agreement**, and then click **OK**.

 Steps 4 and 5 are needed only for a VMware software update. Skip these steps if no update is involved.

4. If the Software Updates window appears, click **Download and Install**, click **Continue**, click **Uninstall** to remove the current VMware Workstation, and click **Restart Now**.

5. After restarting the system, click **Next** in the VMware Workstation Setup window, click **Typical**, click **Next** twice, click **Continue**, and click **Restart Now**. Repeat Step 3.

6. In the VMware Workstation Activation window, click **Enter License Key**, enter the license key, click **OK**, and then click **Close**.

Installing Operating Systems in VMware

In the following sections, you will create virtual machines and virtual hard disks, and you will configure network adapters. When you finish, you will be ready to install a guest operating system. Recall that the virtual machines look like physical machines to the operating system installers.

Creating the First Virtual Machine for Windows 7

Here is a brief overview of the tasks required to create a virtual machine for Windows 7:

1. Start VMware.
2. Create the Windows 7 virtual machine, which will use Disk0.

3. Create two virtual disks (Disk1 and Disk2) and attach them to the virtual machine for future activities.

4. Connect the network adapter to the virtual machine.

 Prior to installing Windows 7, obtain the Windows 7 product key from your instructor.

Because each chapter in the text starts with Windows 7 activities first, you will create a virtual machine for Windows 7 first. Complete the following steps to create the first virtual machine.

1. If necessary, log on to your host PC with **Admin01** and a password of **P@ssw0rd**.

2. Insert the Windows 7 (32 bit) Installer disc image file in the CD/DVD drive.

 Do not install the 64-bit version of Windows 7; it does not have the DOS Edit text editor that is required for various activities in Chapter 8.

3. If necessary, double-click the **VMware** icon on the desktop.

4. Click **File**, click **New**, and then click **Virtual Machine**.

5. Select **Typical**, click **Next**, select **Installer disc image file (iso)**, and click **Next**.

6. Enter the Windows product key, and click **Next**.

7. Type **Windows 7 Virtual Machine** as the Virtual machine name, and click **Next**.

8. Enter **20** for the Maximum disk size (GB), click **Next**, and then click **Finish**.

9. Wait for the Windows installation to complete.

10. Wait for the VMware tools to be installed.

11. To create an admin user, click **Start**, click **Control Panel**, and then click **Add or Remove user accounts** under User Accounts and Family Safety.

12. To create a user account, click the **Create a new account** link, type **Admin01** over "New account name," select the **Administrator** option, and then click the **Create Account** button.

13. To set the password, click **Admin01**, click the **Create a password** link, type **P@ssw0rd** over "New password," and press **Tab**. Type **P@ssw0rd** over "Confirm new password," type **It's a Microsoft password** over "Type a password hint," and then click **Create password**.

14. Close the User accounts window. Click **Start** on the virtual machine. Click **Shut down**.

15. Click **VM**, click **Settings**, click **Add**, and select **Hard Disk**. Click **Next** twice. Check **Independent** and click **Next**. Type **2** as the Maximum disk size (GB), and then click **Next**. Type **Windows 7 NewHardDisk1.vmdk** as the Disk file, and then click **Finish**.

16. Click **Add**, select **Hard Disk**, and then click **Next** twice. Check **Independent** and click **Next**. Type **2** as the Maximum disk size (GB), and then click **Next**. Type **Windows 7 NewHardDisk2.vmdk** as the Disk file, and then click **Finish**.

17. Close the Virtual Machine settings window.

Completing Configuration

In this section, you will prepare the two hard disks (Disk1 and Disk2) for use in the text activities by partitioning and formatting them. As part of disk creation, you will download a set of script files to Disk1.

Next, you will go to *www.textpad.com* and download a trial version of the TextPad text editor, which you will use in Chapter 8.

Next, you will create the User01 Standard user account, which is used by some activities in the text. It is not a good practice to use the Administrator accounts for day-to-day computer activities.

Finally, you will configure your hard disks to be nonpersistent, which means that you can repeat the lab activities because the changes will be discarded every time you start your virtual machines.

Perform the following steps to configure the Windows 7 virtual machine, which ensures that your virtual environment corresponds to the environment used throughout the text.

1. To start the Windows 7 virtual machine, double-click the **Windows 7 Virtual Machine** icon.

2. Log on with the **Admin01** account and a password of **P@ssw0rd**.

3. To start Disk Management, click **Start**, click **Control Panel**, click the **System and Security** link, and then click the **Create and format hard disk partitions** link under Administrative Tools.

4. When the Initialize Disk dialog box appears, review the settings and then click **OK**.

 In Steps 5 through 8, you will create disk volumes for future activities. For other future activities, you will need unallocated space on these two disks. It is important that you do not create the volume over the entire disk.

5. To create and format an NTFS volume, scroll the bottom pane until Disk 1 appears, right-click in the **2.00 GB Unallocated** box, click **New Simple Volume**, and click **Next**. Type **1024** over the 2045 in the "Simple volume size MB" spinner box, and click **Next** twice. Type **NTFS** over the volume label, click **Next**, and then click **Finish**.

6. Close the **AutoPlay** window. Click **Format disk**, click **Start**, click **OK** twice, and click **Close**.

7. Go back to the Disk Management window. To create and format a FAT32 volume, scroll the bottom pane until Disk 2 appears, right-click in the **2.00 GB Unallocated** box, click **New Simple Volume**, and click **Next**. Type **1024** over the 2045 in the "Simple volume size MB" spinner box, and click **Next** twice. Click the **Format the volume with the following settings** arrow, click **FAT32**, type **FAT32** over the Volume label, click **Next**, and then click **Finish**.

8. Close the AutoPlay window. Click **Format disk**, click **Start**, click **OK** twice, and click **Close**.

9. Close all open windows in the Windows 7 virtual machine.

10. To configure the Internet Protocol, click **Start,** click **Control Panel,** click **Network and Internet,** and click **View network status and tasks.** Click **Change Adapter Settings,** right-click **Local Area Connection,** and click **Properties.** Clear the **Internet Protocol Version 6 (TCP/IPv6)** check box, click **OK,** and then close the Network Connections window.

11. To open User accounts management, click **Start,** click **Control Panel,** and then click **Add or Remove user accounts** under User Accounts and Family Safety.

12. To create a user account, click the **Create a new account** link, type **User01** over "New account name," retain the **Standard user** option, and then click the **Create Account** button.

13. To set the password, click **User01,** click the **Create a password** link, type **Secret1** over "New password," and press **Tab.** Type **Secret1** over "Confirm new password," type **It's one Secret** over "Type a password hint," and then click **Create password.**

14. Close the User accounts window.

If Internet Explorer cannot display the Web page, click Diagnose Connection Problems and click through to fix the problems.

15. To access this book's text on the Cengage Learning Web site, click the **Internet Explorer** icon on the taskbar, type **www.cengage.com** in the Address bar, and press **Enter.** Click the **Higher Education** link on the left, scroll down and click the **Course Technology** link under "Browse by Publisher," type **carswell** over "Enter author, title, ISBN, or keyword," and click **Search.**

16. To download the student data files, click **Guide to Parallel Operating Systems with Windows 7 and Linux, 2nd Edition,** click **Instructor Companion Site,** click the **Data Files for Students (Windows)** link on the left, click the entry after Download Now, and click **Run** twice. Click **Browse,** click **NTFS (E:),** click **OK,** click **Unzip,** click **OK,** and then click **Close.**

17. To move the files to a folder in the path of executables, double-click **NTFS (E:),** click **MakeABC,** hold down the **Shift** key, and click **MakeQUOTE.** Right-click in the highlighted area, click **Cut,** expand **Computer,** and double-click **Local Disk (C:).** Right-click **Windows,** click **Paste,** click **Continue,** type **P@ssw0rd,** and then click **Yes.**

18. To access the TextPad text editor, click the **Internet Explorer** icon on the taskbar, type **www.textpad.com** in the Address bar, and press **Enter.**

19. To start the download, click the **Download** button, click the **TextPad Downloads** link, and then click the **FTP (USA)** link.

20. When the File Download – Security Warning appears, click **Save.**

21. When the Save As dialog box appears, click **Save.**

22. Wait for the download to complete, and then click **Run.**

23. When the Internet Explorer – Security Warning appears, click **Run.**

24. Wait for the installation to start and then click **Next.**

25. Click **I accept the terms in the license agreement,** and then click **Next.** Click **Next** in the next two windows, and then click **Install.**

26. When the User Account Control dialog box appears, click **Yes.**

27. Wait for the installation to complete and then click **Finish.**

28. Close any open windows.

29. To open TextPad, click **Start,** point to **All Programs,** and then click **TextPad.**

30. To close the Tip of the Day, click Close.

31. To close the clip library, click the **X** on the Clip Library pane.

32. To close the search results, click the **X** on the Search Results pane.

33. To force updates to be installed, click **Start,** click **Control Panel,** click **Review your computer's status** under System and Security, click **Windows Update,** and then click **Check for updates.**

34. Wait for a response from Windows Update, and then click **Install updates.**

35. Click the **I accept the license terms** option button, and then click **Finish.**

36. Wait for the updates to install and then click the **Restart** button.

37. Click **Start** and then click **Shut down.**

38. Wait for any updates to be installed and then click **Restart now.**

39. Wait for the remaining updates to be installed.

40. Log on with the **User01** account and a password of **Secret1.**

41. Wait for the desktop to be prepared.

After these steps are completed, all changes to the Windows 7 operating environment will be discarded each time Windows 7 starts. This includes all virtual disks (Disk 0, Disk 1, and Disk 2).

42. Shut down the Windows 7 virtual machine.

43. Highlight **Windows 7 Virtual Machine** in the left panel. Click **VM,** click **Settings,** click **Hard Disk (SCSI)** in the Hardware tab, and then click **Advanced.** Check **Independent** mode and then click the **Nonpersistent** radio button. Click **OK.**

44. Repeat the preceding step for Hard Disk 2 (NewHardDisk1.vmdk) and Hard Disk 3 (NewHardDisk2.vmdk).

45. Click **OK** to exit the virtual machine settings and save the changes.

All changes made to the virtual hard drives will be discarded when you start the Windows 7 virtual machine.

46. To start the Windows 7 virtual machine, double-click the **Windows 7 Virtual Machine** icon.

47. Log on with the **User01** account and a password of **Secret1.**

48. Continue with the lab activities in the text.

Creating a Second Virtual Machine for Fedora 13

Here is a brief overview of the tasks required to create a virtual machine for Fedora 13:

1. Start VMware Workstation.

2. Create the Fedora 13 virtual machine, which will use sda. Install the Fedora 13 operating system with the disk image file (iso).

3. Create two virtual disks (sdb and sdc) and attach them to the virtual machine for future activities.

Installing Fedora 13

Complete the following steps to create the second virtual machine and install Fedora 13. Also, you will install the VMware tools, which is special software for Windows and Linux virtual machines that improves performance and makes integration much more seamless. The VMware tools provide features such as mouse pointer integration and screen resizing. (Skip this step if the VMware tools are installed with Fedora 13.)

1. If necessary, log on to your host PC with **Admin01** and a password of **P@ssw0rd**.

2. Insert the Fedora 13 Installer disc image file in the CD/DVD drive. If necessary, double-click the **VMware** icon on the desktop.

 You can also choose to install the Fedora 13 operating system on the virtual machine, which is not fundamentally different from installing on a physical machine. Pay careful attention to the following steps to install the Fedora 13 machine, which ensures that your virtual environment corresponds to the environment used throughout the text.

3. Click **File**, click **New**, and then click **Virtual Machine**.

4. Select **Typical**, click **Next**, select **Installer disc image file (iso)**, and click **Next**. Enter **Fedora13** as the Full name, enter **admin01** as the User name, and enter **P@ssw0rd** as the Password. Enter **P@ssw0rd** again to confirm, and click **Next**. Enter **Fedora 13 Virtual Machine** as the Virtual machine name, and click **Next**. Enter **10** for the Maximum disk size (GB), and click **Next**. Click **Finish**. Wait for the Fedora 13 installation to complete. Wait for the VMware tools to be installed.

5. Log in to Fedora 13 by typing **P@ssw0rd**.

6. To create a user, click **System**, point to **Administration**, and click **Users and Groups**. Type **P@ssw0rd** as the root password, and then click **OK**.

7. Click the **Add User** button, type **User01** in the Username text box, type **Parallel OS Student** in the Full Name text box, type **Secret1** in the Password text box, type **Secret1** in the Confirm Password text box, and click **OK**. Click **Yes** to create the user anyway.

8. To shut down Fedora 13, click **System**, and then click **Shut Down** twice.

Configuring Fedora 13

You will prepare the two hard disks (sdb and sdc) for use in the text activities by partitioning and formatting them. You will also configure your hard disks to be nonpersistent, which means that you can repeat the lab activities because the changes will be discarded every time you start your virtual machines.

Perform the following steps to configure the Fedora 13 virtual machine, which ensures that your virtual environment corresponds to the environment used throughout the text.

1. If necessary, log on to your host PC with **Admin01** and a password of **P@ssw0rd**.

2. If necessary, double-click the **VMware** icon on the desktop. Highlight **Fedora 13 Virtual Machine** under Favorites.

3. To attach Fedora 13 NewHardDisk1, click **VM**, click **Settings**, and click **Add**. Select **Hard Disk** and then click **Next** three times. Type **2** for the Maximum disk size (GB), and click **Next**. Enter **Fedora 13 NewHardDisk1.vmdk** for the Disk file, and then click **Finish**.

4. To attach Fedora 13 NewHardDisk2, click **Add**, select **Hard Disk**, and then click **Next** three times. Enter **2** for the Maximum disk size (GB), and click **Next**. Enter **Fedora 13 NewHardDisk2.vmdk** for the Disk file, click **Finish**, and then click **OK**.

5. To start the Fedora 13 virtual machine, click **Power on this virtual machine**.

6. Log on to Fedora 13 as **Parallel OS Student** with a password of **Secret1**.

7. Click the **Network** icon on the menu bar, and then click **System eth0**.

8. Wait for the connection to finish.

9. To open a Terminal session, click **Applications**, point to **System Tools**, and then click **Terminal**.

10. Type **su –** and press **Enter**.

11. Type **P@ssw0rd** and press **Enter**.

12. To obtain an IP address, type **dhclient –v eth0** and press **Enter**.

13. To start the search for the system configuration display, type **yum search system-config-display** and press **Enter**.

14. Wait for the search to finish.

15. To install the system configuration display, type **yum install system-config-display.i686** and press **Enter**.

16. When prompted to confirm that the changes are OK, press y and press **Enter**.

17. If you are prompted again, press y and press **Enter**.

18. To modify the monitor type, type **system-config-display** and press **Enter**. Click the **Hardware** tab, click **Configure** for Monitor Type, expand **Generic LCD Display**, click **LCD Panel 1024x768**, and click **OK**. Click **Settings**, click the **Resolution** chevron, click **1024x768**, and then click **OK** twice.

19. Close the Terminal window.

20. To restart the system, click **System**, click **Shut Down**, and then click **Restart**.

21. Log on to Fedora 13 as **Parallel OS Student** with a password of **Secret1**. To reset the resolution, click **System**, click **Preferences**, and click **Monitors**. Click the **Resolution** chevron, click **1024 x 768**, click **Apply**, click **Keep This configuration**, and then click **Close**.

22. To open a Terminal session, click **Applications**, point to **System Tools**, and then click **Terminal**.

23. Type **su –** and press **Enter**.

24. Type **P@ssw0rd** and press **Enter**.

25. Type **yum search hardinfo** and press **Enter**.

26. Wait for the search to finish.

27. Wait for the download to finish.

28. Type **yum install hardinfo.i686**, and press **Enter**.

29. When prompted to confirm that the changes are OK, press **y** and press **Enter**.

30. Repeat Steps 25 through 29 for **system-config-network, system-config-samba, system-config-printer**, and **system-config-lvm**.

31. To start partitioning the sdb disk, type **fdisk /dev/sdb** and press **Enter**.

32. Ignore the warning message.

33. To create the first primary partition on sdb, type **n** and press **Enter**, type **p** and press **Enter**, type **1** and press **Enter**, type **1** and press **Enter**, and then type **+1G** and press **Enter**.

34. To review the partition and write to the partition table, type **p** and press **Enter**, then type **w** and press **Enter**.

35. To format the partition as Ext2, type **mkfs /dev/sdb1** and press **Enter**.

36. To label the partition, type **e2label /dev/sdb1 Ext2** and press **Enter**.

37. To start partitioning the sdc disk, type **fdisk /dev/sdc** and press **Enter**.

38. Ignore the warning message.

39. To create the first primary partition on sdc, type **n** and press **Enter**, type **p** and press **Enter**, type **1** and press **Enter**, type **1** and press **Enter**, and then type **+1G** and press **Enter**.

40. To review the partition and write to the partition table, type **p** and press **Enter**, then type **w** and press **Enter**.

41. To format the partition, type **mkfs –t vfat /dev/sdc1** and press **Enter**.

42. To position to the /mnt directory, type **cd /mnt** and press **Enter**.

43. To make the directory for sdb1, type **mkdir sdb1** and press **Enter**.

44. To mount the sdb1 partition, type **mount /dev/sdb1 –t ext2 /mnt/sdb1** and press **Enter**.

45. To make the directory for sdc1, type **mkdir sdc1** and press **Enter**.

46. To mount the sdc1 partition, type **mount /dev/sdc1 –t vfat /mnt/sdc1** and press **Enter**.

47. To return to the root folder, type **cd ..** and press **Enter**.

48. To open the /etc/fstab file for editing, type **nano /etc/fstab** and press **Enter**.

49. Use the arrow key to move down to a new line.

50. To add the mount line for sdb1, type **/dev/sdb1 /mnt/sdb1 ext2 defaults 0 0** and press **Enter**.

51. To add the mount line for sdc1, type **/dev/sdc1 /mnt/sdc1 vfat defaults,dmask=000, fmask=111 0 0** and press **Enter**.

52. To write the file to disk, press **Ctrl+O** and then press **Enter**.

53. To exit nano, press **Ctrl+X**.

54. To remount the devices, type **mount –a** and press **Enter**.

55. To verify that the mount worked, double-click **Computer**, double-click **Filesystem**, double-click **mnt**, verify that the sdb1 and sdc1 folders appear, and then close the open windows.

56. To access this book's text on the Cengage Learning Web site, click the **Mozilla Firefox** icon on the taskbar, type **www.cengage.com** in the Address bar, and press **Enter**. Click the **Higher Education** link on the left, scroll down and click the **Course Technology** link under "Browse by Publisher," type **carswell** over "Enter author, title, ISBN, or keyword," and click **Search**.

57. To download the student data files, click **Guide to Parallel Operating Systems with Windows 7 and Linux, 2nd Edition**, click **Instructor Companion Site**, and click the **Data Files for Students (FedoraFiles)** link on the left. Choose the **Save File** option, and then click **OK**. When the download is complete, right-click the **tar.gz** file, click **Open Containing Folder**, and verify that the file was downloaded into the Downloads directory.

58. Open a terminal, type **cd Downloads**, and then press **Enter**. Type **su** and press **Enter**. Enter the **root** password and press **Enter**. To decompress the file to the /usr/local/bin/ directory, type **tar –zxvf makcs.tar.gz –C /usr/local/bin/**.

59. Type **cd /usr/local/bin/** and press **Enter**. Type **chmod 555 [mM]ake[dAHQ]*** and press **Enter**.

60. To close the virtual machine, type **poweroff** and then press **Enter**.

The following steps will set all of the virtual disks to discard any changes that students make. This will be helpful when multiple classes use the same computers. Steps 61 through 64 must be completed from the Host01 computer.

61. Highlight **Fedora 13 Virtual Machine** in the left panel. Click **VM**, click **Settings**, click **Hard Disk (SCSI)** in the Hardware tab, and then click **Advanced**. Check **Independent** mode, and then click the **Nonpersistent** radio button. Click **OK**.

62. Repeat the preceding step for Hard Disk 2 (NewHardDisk1.vmdk) and Hard Disk 3 (NewHardDisk2.vmdk).

63. Click **OK** to exit the virtual machine settings and save the changes.

64. To start the Fedora 13 virtual machine, double-click the **Fedora 13 Virtual Machine** icon.

65. Log on to the Fedora 13 virtual machine with a password of **Secret1**.

66. Continue with the lab activities in the text.

Index